WITHDRAWN

RENAISSANCE DRAMA

RENAISSANCE DRAMA

Renaissance Drama

Renaissance Drama as
Cultural History:
Essays from
Renaissance Drama
1977–1987

Edited by Mary Beth Rose

Northwestern University Press and

The Newberry Library Center for Renaissance Studies

EVANSTON 1990

Northwestern University Press
Evanston, Illinois 60201

Copyright © 1978, 1980, 1983, 1984, 1985, 1987, 1988, 1990 by
Northwestern University Press. All rights reserved.

ISBN 0–8101–0683–3 (cloth)
0–8101–0682–5 (paper)

Printed in the United States of America

Library of Congress Cataloging-in-Publication Data

Renaissance drama as cultural history : essays from Renaissance drama,
    1977–1987 / edited by Mary Beth Rose.
        p.   cm.
    ISBN 0-8101-0683-3. — ISBN 0-8101-0682-5 (pbk.)
        1. European Drama—Renaissance, 1450-1600—History and criticism.
2. Drama—17th century—History and criticism.   I. Rose, Mary Beth.
II. Renaissance drama (Evanston, Ill. : 1964)
PN1785.R46 1989   89-23129
809.2′0094—dc20   CIP

Foreword

*R*ENAISSANCE DRAMA AS CULTURAL HISTORY includes essays from previous volumes of *Renaissance Drama*. From over thirty years'
worth of distinguished contributions, many of which have become classics in the field, I have chosen eighteen that focus on the relationship of
the drama to cultural change. The essays include treatments of English,
Spanish, French, and Italian drama and articulate a wide variety of perspectives on their material. But each of these diverse approaches
embraces some form of historicism; and all the essays share a concern
with the effect that conflict in the social, sexual, political, theatrical, and
religious environments had on the drama. They also explore the contribution of theatrical forms to the ways in which Renaissance culture was
being shaped and changed.

The contributions are organized into groups centering on four topics:
revising authority and the politics of intertextuality and influence; ideologies and aesthetics of gender; transgression and rebellion; and class
conflict and social mobility. The essays appear here in their original form,
with the date of initial publication following the title in the Table of
Contents. Each of the essays serves to highlight important directions in
scholarship about Renaissance drama; and all continue to be significant
articulations of the perspectives and approaches they exemplify.

Since *Renaissance Drama* originated in 1956 under the founding editorship of S. Schoenbaum, subsequent editors have built on the tradition of publishing annually a group of essays that focus on a specified topic concerning the dramatic literature of England and the Continent from the fifteenth through the seventeenth centuries. Topics are selected in response to existing research that greatly interests both writers and readers; and, in some instances, the choice of topic plays a role in spotting issues and defining a direction of current research on Renaissance drama. Toward these ends topics have ranged from "Essays Principally on Dramatic Theory and Form" (1969), "Essays Principally on the Playhouse and Staging" (1971), and "Drama and the Other Arts" (1976) to "The Celebratory Mode" (1977), "Drama and Society" (1982), "Modes, Motifs, and Genres" (1984), "Essays on Texts of Renaissance Plays" (1988), and "Disorder and the Drama" (1990).

Published each year as a hard-cover collection of essays, *Renaissance Drama* became in 1986 a cooperative project involving the Newberry Library Center for Renaissance Studies, the English department at Northwestern University, and Northwestern University Press. Like my predecessors, I have continued to publish essays that examine the relationship of Renaissance dramatic traditions to their precursors and successors; have an interdisciplinary orientation; explore the relationship of drama to society and history; examine the impact of new forms of interpretation on Renaissance drama; and raise fresh questions about the texts and performances of Renaissance plays.

I am grateful to Catherine Belsey for coming up with the title for the present volume. Assistant Editor Frances Dolan helped to select many of the essays when they appeared originally and to arrange them in the form presented here. Susan Harris of Northwestern University Press offered many useful suggestions with unfailing patience and tact. Most of all I wish to thank Leonard Barkan, whose inspired editorship of *Renaissance Drama* (1974–85) produced half of the contributions to this book.

Mary Beth Rose
Editor

Contents

vii

Revising Authority:
The Politics of Intertextuality
and Influence

Drama and Society in the Age of Jonson: Shifting Grounds of Authority and Judgment in Three Major Comedies

DON E. WAYNE

M Y TITLE REFERS, of course, to L. C. Knights's book, first published in 1937.[1] It is hardly possible to diverge from Knights's views without acknowledging the extent to which one depends on them. His book remains one of a small handful of significant works in English concerned with the sociology of literature. It is regarded, rightfully, as a classic, and its approach to the social aspects of Jacobean drama has become canonical. But this approach must also be recognized as the product of an earlier moment in the history of thought dealing with the relationship between culture and society. Given recent developments in social theory, in the study of ideology, and in the sociology of knowledge, we need to revaluate the central thesis of Knights's book and the kind of criticism practiced there. The essay that follows is partly concerned with such a reassessment. In the main, however, it is an attempt to redefine the relationship between Jonsonian drama and its sociohistorical context.

Knights acknowledges only one way in which drama and society are related in the age of Jonson; that is, the drama is said to call upon religious

1. L. C. Knights, *Drama and Society in the Age of Jonson* (London, 1937).

and popular tradition to criticize bourgeois acquisitiveness and individualism. Indicative of this basic strategy are the titles of his focal chapters on
Jonson's plays: "Tradition and Ben Jonson," and "Jonson and the Anti-
Acquisitive Attitude." In this conception, the Jacobean theater is represented as a place where author and audience are joined in the communal
celebration of a traditional code of behavior and in the censure of those who
violate the code. The formula works well enough in the case of Jonson's
best-known play, *Volpone*. But elsewhere, the relationship between author
and audience is more problematic.

It is significant that the only major play of Jonson's omitted from
Knights's discussion is *Bartholomew Fair*, presumably because of its more
ambiguous treatment of the attitudes and behavior satirized in *Volpone* and
other plays. In a later essay, Knights relegates *Bartholomew Fair* to "the
category of stage entertainments: in them the fun is divorced from any rich
significance . . ." [2] Such a judgment is difficult to comprehend in the
light of more recent studies which have shown this to be among the most
intricate and ironic of Jonson's plays. [3] The moral and aesthetic criteria
that govern Knights's criticism prevent him from perceiving this irony,
and, consequently, from acknowledging the dramatic richness and power
of *Bartholomew Fair*. What makes this lapse all the more serious in my
view is that the source of irony in the play is fundamentally social and
ideological. I shall consider the ideological ambiguity of the play in some
detail later. For the moment, it is sufficient to say that in *Bartholomew Fair*
there is an unmistakable tension between, on the one hand, the traditional
moral doctrine of social obligation according to status, and, on the other,
the more modern principles of rational self-interest and voluntary contractual obligation. [4] The fact that Knights did not recognize such conflict in

2. "Ben Jonson, Dramatist," in *The Age of Shakespeare*, Vol. 2 of *The Pelican Guide to
English Literature*, ed. Boris Ford, rev. ed. (Hardmondsworth, Eng., 1969), p. 314.

3. See, e.g., Jonas A. Barish, *Ben Jonson and the Language of Prose Comedy* (Cambridge,
Mass., 1960), pp. 187–239; Jackson I. Cope, "*Bartholomew Fair* as Blasphemy," *RenD*,
VIII (1965), 127–152; Ian Donaldson, *The World Upside-Down* (Oxford, 1970), pp. 46–77;
Alvin B. Kernan, "Alchemy and Acting: The Major Plays of Ben Jonson," and George A.
E. Parfitt, "Virtue and Pessimism in Three Plays by Ben Jonson," both in *SLitI*, VI, no. 1
(1973), 1–22, 23–40.

4. The distinction between *status* and *contract* societies is generally attributed to the
nineteenth-century legal historian Sir Henry Sumner Maine; see his *Ancient Law*, 8th ed.
(London, 1880), pp. 168–170. While Maine's usage has been effectively repudiated

the play is symptomatic of the limitations of the social theory on which his criticism was founded.

It would be difficult to argue with Knights's central tenet that Jonson's plays exhibit an unremitting critique of acquisitiveness. The deformities of personality that drive Jonson's characters to seek power and self-aggrandizement in one form or another are ultimately linked to the lust for gold, a disease that is seen to threaten the entire body politic. The "humors" doctrine of characterization is rooted in a tradition of moral philosophy and in Galen's physiology. But it also amounts to a rudimentary social psychology, a technical apparatus for diagnosing the changes that affected English society in the Renaissance; and as such it involves an anticipatory awareness of the phenomenon of alienation in both the Marxian and existentialist senses of the term. Already at a very early stage of capitalist development in England, Jonson recognizes intuitively that the dislocation and division of the human subject (the necessary condition of subjectivity in the modern sense) are functionally related to historical disjunctions in the social organization of reality. Nor is he alone in this. The literature of the age is filled with a sense of the relationship between social fragmentation and psychological disorder. *King Lear* is the great mythopoeic embodiment of this principle. But in the case of other writers, who lack Shakespeare's "negative capability," the problem is articulated with a deep sense of irony born of the writers' self-conscious anxiety concerning their own place in society. Even the most outspoken critics of the age, who decry the breakdown of hierarchy, who moan the loss of an organic sense of unity and coherence, and who rail against individualism, subjectivism, and acquisitiveness, seem, as Paul Delany puts it, "to oppose in others tendencies which they sensed in themselves." [5]

One reason for this ironic self-awareness is that there is a definite relationship between what these writers criticize and the power they possess to make such criticism. This is an aspect of the literature of the age

---

because of its normative and evolutionist assumptions, the terms continue to be used descriptively in the field of jurisprudence and by social and intellectual historians. See, e.g., Christopher Hill, *Society and Puritanism in Pre-Revolutionary England* (London, 1964), p. 491; the distinction is also implicit in the models of society employed by C. B. Macpherson, *The Political Theory of Possessive Individualism, Hobbes to Locke* (Oxford, 1964), pp. 46–70.

5. Paul Delany, *British Autobiography in the Seventeenth Century* (London, 1969), p. 15.

that Knights tends to ignore. So, while he views Jonson as a social critic, he overlooks the ways in which Jonson is himself implicated in what he criticizes. My point is that the "attitude" of the Jacobean playwrights, Jonson pre-eminently, is far more complex than the phrase "anti-acquisitive" would suggest. While they may be satirizing the acquisitiveness associated with an incipient mercantile capitalism, the dramatists are themselves caught in something of a double bind concerning the place of their own work in this new economic, political, and social context.

The drama of the early seventeenth century does indeed reflect a prevailing sense of social and psychological disorder. These concerns can be related to socioeconomic developments that were transforming England into what C. B. Macpherson calls a "possessive market society," [6] and to the undermining in the Reformation of a universal doctrinal basis for moral judgment and behavior. But the literature of the period also reveals another aspect of the breakdown of feudalism and of the traditional doctrines and behavior patterns associated with the old order. Literature is now becoming a vehicle of the historical individuation of perception and experience that enabled the independence of mind we identify as a characteristic of the modern. At this time we see the first extensive evidence of a pluralization of roles and ideologies in developing Western European societies. In fiction, this tendency is manifested by the emergence of individualized characterization, by a corresponding plurality of authorial voices, personae, and styles, and by an increasing diversification of the social function of literature. Writers and their audiences may still be constrained by institutionalized relationships, but they are also beginning to play a relatively more active and independent role in the historical processes through which social institutions are both sustained and transformed.

Or, at least, they are beginning to imagine themselves as having a more independent and important role. In English literature we see this perhaps as early as Chaucer's *Canterbury Tales* where, for example, in the sequences concerning the Wife of Bath, the Pardoner, and Chaucer himself, the power of storytelling and the power of judgment vested in the audience of pilgrims, and, implicitly, in the reader, are thematized in a way that

6. Macpherson, *Political Theory of Possessive Individualism*, pp. 48, 61–62, 301 n.

makes this collection of tales more complex than its predecessors in the literary tradition. But it is in the Renaissance that this tendency toward individuation, self-assertion, and, at the same time, what has been described as a historical "splitting of the subject" [7] becomes more pronounced. The increasing complexity of social relations in the sixteenth and seventeenth centuries contributed to the developing complexity and diversity of literary discourse, first in the poetry written by Elizabeth's courtiers and, eventually, in the drama produced for a larger, more heterogeneous audience. What follows is an attempt to outline the particular form that such development takes in the work of Ben Jonson. I claim that after his early theatrical triumphs, culminating in *Volpone* (1606), Jonson begins to show signs of a disturbed awareness that his own identity as poet and playwright—and therefore his personal transcendence of the still rigid social hierarchy in which he lived and wrote—depended on the same emerging structure of social relationships that he satirized in his plays.

There is an interesting tension in Jonson's work between, on the one hand, the designation of rampant individualism as the origin of social disorder in Jacobean England, and, on the other, the poet's constant

---

7. I have deliberately avoided the more familiar phrase "dissociation of sensibility," coined by T. S. Eliot in his widely reprinted "The Metaphysical Poets" (1921) and employed by Knights in "Bacon and the Seventeenth-Century Dissociation of Sensibility," in *Explorations* (1943; rpt. New York, 1964), pp. 108–128, because Eliot's usage is too restrictive historically and is associated with doctrines concerning poetry that are notoriously problematic. The phrase "splitting of the subject," derived from Lacan's interpretation of Freud, occurs in a discussion of the multiple "voices" of the literary text by Guy Rosolato, "The Voice and the Literary Myth," in *The Languages of Criticism and the Sciences of Man*, ed. Richard Macksey and Eugenio Donato (Baltimore, 1970), p. 202. Rosolato's essay has a double impact that is typically Lacanian, i.e., striking speculative insight and maddeningly elliptical argumentation. There is, however, a historical component to his idea that makes it particularly relevant here (pp. 207–208). Another model of such a split in the subject of discourse during the later Middle Ages and the Renaissance—one that is both empirically and dialectically grounded in the idea of language as mediated by social *praxis*—is the "dialogic" or "polyphonic" conception that underlies Mikhail Bakhtin's *Rabelais and His World*, trans. Hélène Iswolsky (Cambridge, Mass., 1968). Bakhtin's study, with its emphasis on the pluralistic discourse of marketplace and carnival in opposition to an official language and culture, is of considerable relevance for an understanding of Jonson's comedies, especially *Bartholomew Fair*.

assertion of his own individuality and independence. One of the more disturbing and strikingly modern aspects of Jonson's plays is the way they point up the dilemma of attempting to distinguish between independence and fragmentation, between freedom and license. This tension is manifested in at least two ways. It appears, first, as an ambiguity in the playwright's relation to the individuals and the society he portrays. As Jonas A. Barish has noted, Jonson seems uncomfortably aware at times of a parallel between the social climbing of the satirized characters in his plays and his own aspirations to a position of status. [8] But there is yet another level at which such tension is evident; this concerns the poet's relation to his audience.

The audacious publication, in 1616, of a volume of poems and plays entitled *The Works of Benjamin Jonson* is generally regarded as a historical index of the literary artist's developing sense of self-importance. At the same time, Jonson's constant fretting about his readers' competency and his intermittent troubles with theater audiences indicate the growing importance of reader and audience response that occurred with the professionalization of literature and its expansion to a widening segment of society. The tension between these two loci of self-assertion and their respective demands for recognition, the one situated in the place of the author, the other in the place of the audience, is constantly present in Jonson's dramatic works. Often, he will incorporate into his texts (usually in a prologue, induction, or epilogue) a representation of the relationship between his own assertion of the place, the authority, the power of the poet and his audience's assertion of its own power to pass judgment. I want to focus now on the implications of such framing devices in Jonson's major comedies, and particularly, in *Bartholomew Fair*.

The pre-eminence of the poet's authority is stated unequivocally in the Epistle to *Volpone*: [9]

8. Barish, *Ben Jonson and the Language of Prose Comedy*, pp. 88–89.

9. Stephen J. Greenblatt, "The False Ending in *Volpone*," *JEGP*, LXXV, nos. 1–2 (1976), 103–104, offers an ironic reading of the Epistle in relation to other framing devices of the play. My emphasis in the present context is somewhat different, though not antithetical. Citations from the plays are to the modernized texts of the Yale editions: *Volpone*, ed. Alvin B. Kernan (New Haven, Conn., 1962); *The Alchemist*, ed. Kernan (1974); *Bartholomew Fair*, ed. Eugene M. Waith (1963). Citations from Jonson's nondramatic works are to *Ben Jonson*, ed. C. H. Herford and Percy and Evelyn Simpson, 11 vols. (Oxford, 1925–1952), with spelling modernized.

For, if men will impartially, and not asquint, look toward the offices and function of a poet, they will easily conclude to themselves the impossibility of any
man's being the good poet without first being a good man. . . . [The poet is he]
that comes forth the interpreter and arbiter of nature, a teacher of things divine
no less than human, a master in manners; and can alone, or with few, effect the
business of mankind . . .

Jonson's confidence here depends in part on the reputation he had already
succeeded in establishing for himself. But it also reflects the special status
of *Volpone* among his plays. For it is the tightest of Jonson's dramatic
works, with the possible exception of *The Alchemist* to which I shall turn in
a moment. Unlike most of the plays that precede or follow it, *Volpone*
shows little authorial intrusion in the action itself. Here the moral is
carried without the intervention of a character like Asper, Crites, Truewit,
or Manly to make sure that the audience grasps what the author would
have it understand. *The Alchemist* and *Bartholomew Fair* are also notably free
of such Jonsonian spokesmen, but neither of these plays has the confident
moral authority or the severity of *Volpone*. Jonson had discovered a formula
whereby he could unite the diverse elements of his audience in judging and
censuring the action on stage. This unity of judgment served to corroborate the author's claim to being the "arbiter of nature," hence of truth and
of public morals. At the same time, the social value of consensus in the
theater was that it provided a plausible sense that there existed a coherent
and absolute moral foundation in English society for grounding such
judgment.

Of course, the thematic and structural unity of *Volpone* and its apparent
ethical consistency depended on something of a red herring, that is, the
displacement of all vice and corruption to an Italian setting. The unity of
judgment on the parts of author and audience, and the credibility of an
absolute moral standard rendered possible by the play, depended on the
scapegoating of the Italians. Thus, writes William Empson:

London was jealous of Venice, as an aggressive leader of international maritime
trade, because London wanted to do that on a bigger scale. "Terrible pigs, that
tyrannous Council of Ten; they never think of anything but money." Jonson
could rely upon getting this reaction even from business men in his audience,
while most of the audience were enjoying the play as a satire upon business
men. [10]

10. William Empson, "Volpone," *HudR*, XXI, no. 4 (1968–1969), 654.

This is, however, a pretty tenuous basis for a reciprocity of judgments in the theater or for the moral sanctioning of a sense of community. As a theatrical event and experience, *Volpone* did not enable an affirmative mode of identification between the author and his audience. At the most, it permitted a sense of common purpose and of social order based on a strictly negative appraisal of a certain kind of acquisitive behavior that was conveniently displaced elsewhere.

Jonson could not have been satisfied by such a formula no matter how sublime his handling of it, and no matter how successful it may have been in the theater. He was far too concerned to expose folly and corruption in his own society, and to instruct his own countrymen "in the best reason of living" (another phrase from the Epistle to *Volpone*) to be content with a form of dramatic satire that depended on characters who were stereotypical Italian thieves and mountebanks. The plays that follow are located in a domestic setting. But, curiously, they lack the moral certitude that informs the theme and structure of *Volpone*. Whether or not Jonson consciously recognized a flaw in the ethical foundation on which he claimed to rest the "offices and function of a poet" is by no means clear. Certainly he continued to proclaim the high moral purpose of playing in the theater, and the absolute Truth on which the good was founded. In the *Discoveries* he could declaim grandly, citing the appropriate *locus classicus*, "*Veritas proprium hominis*":

> Truth is man's proper good; and the only immortal thing, was given to our mortality to use. . . . For without truth all the Actions of mankind, are craft, malice, or what you will, rather than Wisdom. Homer says, he hates him worse than hell-mouth, that utters one thing with his tongue, and keeps another in his breast. Which high expression was grounded on divine Reason. For a lying mouth is a stinking pit, and murders with the contagion it venteth. Beside, nothing is lasting that is feigned; it will have another face than it had, ere long . . .
>
> (ll. 531–542)

The word "feigned" refers to dissimulation or dissembling here. Poetry is, of course, another kind of feigning altogether, one carried out in the service of Truth and goodness. In the *Discoveries* Jonson managed to keep the distinction clear:

I could never think the study of Wisdom confined only to the Philosopher: or of Piety to the Divine: or of State to the Politicke. But that he which can feign a Commonwealth (which is the Poet) can govern it with Counsels, strengthen it with Laws, correct it with Judgments, inform it with Religion, and Morals, is all these.

(ll. 1032–1038)

But the pragmatics of the actual social context in which Ben Jonson had assumed the offices and function of a poet made it increasingly difficult for him to maintain such a neat distinction between poetic feigning and dissembling in the theater.

The Alchemist (1610) is in certain respects even more closed in structure than *Volpone*. Its action, as Ian Donaldson has observed, takes place almost entirely in a single interior setting, a house in London, the restrictiveness of which "has an unsettling effect upon the characters of the play, and, in turn, upon the audience itself." [11] The conclusion in which Lovewit, the returned master of the house, dispenses a mild and sympathetic justice, releases much of the tension and anxiety that has accumulated in the earlier scenes. I want to suggest, however, that this apparent relaxation only masks a deeper underlying tension in the play and in the relationships it sets going in the theater.

At the end of *The Alchemist*, Lovewit and his butler Jeremy, who has disguised himself throughout most of the action as Face, remain alone on stage. Lovewit has taken possession of the treasure which was accumulated in his absence by Face and his accomplices. He has also acquired, thanks to Face's devices, a rich widow, Dame Pliant. Lovewit recognizes Face's hand in his good fortune, and he acknowledges this by the offer of an exchange in kind:

LOVEWIT
. . . That master
That had received such happiness by a servant,
In such a widow, and with so much wealth,
Were very ungrateful if he would not be

---

11. Ian Donaldson, "Ben Jonson," in *English Drama to 1710*, ed. Christopher Ricks (London, 1971), p. 299.

A little indulgent to that servant's wit,
And help his fortune, though with some small strain
Of his own candor.

(V.v. 146–152)

What is thus legitimated here at the play's conclusion is not a judgment
and an action founded on an ethical absolute, but one founded on the
exigencies of power, self-interest, and reciprocal exchange.

Having announced his intention to reward Face, Lovewit gives his man
another order: "Speak for thyself, knave." The injunction is paradoxical;
Face is still a "knave," and he is still subject to a master's order. Yet he is
enjoined to speak for himself. And, to a degree, his new fortune is indeed
an expansion of his freedom. But that freedom depends on his ability to be
other than what he might be if he did not have to serve masters; he must
dissemble, and continue to dissemble in order to maintain his new-won
freedom. Thus though he is permitted to speak for himself, he must
continue to speak for others, to imitate others, to be a player and wear another's face. Now, he comes forward to speak the epilogue. He stands at
the edge of the stage where the narrow line between play and audience has
marked, up until now, the possibility of there being a limit to excess, a
limit to all the dissembling that has gone on in the play. It is a boundary
that has served to this point as the index of a norm for real *being* instead of
mere playing at being, a norm upon which judgment in the theater can be
shared by the author and his audience. Face's words are like nothing that
we have heard in *Volpone*:

LOVEWIT
    Speak for thyself, knave.

FACE
[Advancing] So I will, sir.

Gentlemen,

My part a little fell in this last scene,
Yet 'twas decorum. And though I am clean
Got off from Subtle, Surly, Mammon, Dol,
Hot Ananias, Dapper, Drugger, all
With whom I traded; yet I put myself
On you, that are my country; and this pelf
Which I have got, if you do quit me, rests,
To feast you often, and invite new guests.

(V.v. 157–165)

Implicit here is the drafting of a new contract to replace the "indenture tripartite / 'Twixt Subtle, Dol, and Face" (V.iv.131–132). Face refers to the feigning and the trading that have gone on in the previous scenes. But the speech refers as well to what goes on in society, and this includes relationships in the theater. The tone here is festive, light, even frivolous. Yet behind the frivolity lies a message that is disturbingly serious. Face has "traded" not only with all the gulls whom he mentions; he has also "traded" with his master Lovewit, and now he is trading with the audience. His speech implies that all is only dissembling and trading, and that this being the case it is perfect decorum for the one who trades best to be "clean / Got off . . ." Now he works a deal with his audience and his "country" that would require them to become accomplices in his future confidence games. The device may be viewed simply as a clever joke, and a good-natured manipulation of the audience's identification with the place of Lovewit in the play.

But we must remember that Face performs the role of an Epilogue here; clearly he speaks for the playwright and for future plays by his hand. The narrow line between the play and the audience seems suddenly, in these final words, to have dissolved. Jonson is standing before us as much as Face, and he is speaking not about relations among characters in a play but about his own relation to his audience, a relationship that has a social function not only in the theater but in the world at large. There is a confession implied here, a suggestion that we too have been traded with; but there is also an indication that there is only the possibility of trading between us. Unlike the closure maintained in *Volpone*, where we are able to join complacently in the final act of moral censure, the last scenes of *The Alchemist* leave us in an ambiguous position. It will not suffice to explain this ambiguity away, as one critic has recently done in a passing reference to *The Alchemist*, by asserting that the comic genre "seeks something that might be called 'emotional closure' rather than a strict psychological or moral justice . . ." [12] Descriptively the statement may be valid, but it does not explain the inconsistency between Jonson's theory and his practice as a comic dramatist after *Volpone*.

---

12. Nancy Lindheim, review of *Sir Philip Sidney: Rebellion in Arcadia*, by Richard C. McCoy, *Seventeenth-Century News*, XXXIX, no. 1 (1981), 6.

The opening up of the closed play-world at the end of *The Alchemist* is a momentary vision of the possible truth behind the "Truth" that Jonson so confidently espoused elsewhere. We may recall here the passage quoted earlier from the *Discoveries*, to the effect that "Truth is man's proper good . . ." and that "a lying mouth is a stinking pit . . .," and consider now with some irony the last words of that passage: ". . . nothing is lasting that is feigned; it will have another *face* than it had, ere long . . ." At the end of *The Alchemist* there is at least a momentary speculation that truth can only be "feigned," that there is only feigning, and that the "good man" can only be another Face. This admission threatens to undermine the poet's assumption of moral authority. However, Jonson keeps his footing, as did Face himself, by making us acknowledge our complicity in the assertion that comes in the epilogue. This time, the judgment which we corroborate and share with the author is a judgment of him and of ourselves; and since we are not likely to be too harsh on ourselves we allow him to get off as well, to return "to feast [us] often, and invite new guests." Face's epilogue to the play is as much a straight business deal between the dramatist and his audience, the negotiation or renegotiation of a contract.

The implied metaphor is literalized at the beginning of Jonson's next great comedy, *Bartholomew Fair* (1614).[13] In the Induction a "scrivener" comes onstage to read certain "Articles of Agreement indented between the spectators or hearers at the Hope on the Bankside, in the county of Surrey, on the one party, and the author of *Barthol'mew Fair* in the said place and county, on the other party . . ." The agreement stipulates "that every man here exercise his own judgement, and not censure by contagion, or upon trust, from another's voice or face that sits by him, be he never so first in the commission of wit . . ." The device is a cranky bit of satire; but it also constitutes an acknowledgment, however grudgingly, of the growing power of audiences in the public theaters, and an appeal

13. The importance of legal imagery in this play is emphasized by Ray L. Heffner, Jr., "Unifying Symbols in the Comedy of Ben Jonson," in *English Stage Comedy: English Institute Essays, 1954*, ed. W. K. Wimsatt, Jr. (New York, 1955), pp. 74–97, rpt. in *Ben Jonson: A Collection of Critical Essays*, ed. Jonas A. Barish (Englewood Cliffs, N.J., 1963), pp. 141–146; Jackson I. Cope, in the essay cited previously, discusses the theme of litigiousness and relates it to the traditional iconography of *Ate* or *Discordia* (pp. 144–146).

that they judge the scene with the same independence of mind the author imagines himself to have used in creating it.

In *Bartholomew Fair*, as Barish has suggested, a certain solidarity is struck between the author and his audience, motivated in part by the attacks of Puritans and civic leaders on the fleshly temptations of fairs and theaters. But it is a tenuous solidarity at best. The legalistic device of the "Articles of Agreement" reflects the weakening in the early seventeenth century of a reliable order of shared assumptions, embodied in popular tradition, religious ritual, and dogma, upon which to base moral and aesthetic judgment in the public playhouse. The feigned necessity of a contract mediating the relationship between independent parties to a literary or theatrical communication focuses, at the plane of the aesthetic, what is becoming a fundamental problem in all aspects of social life. With individuals acquiring a relatively greater sense of personal independence, and with the breakdown of a universal, authoritative belief system, it now becomes difficult—especially for those who eschew the too stringent spiritual community of the Saints—to sustain a sense of collective identity. The implication, not very hidden in *Bartholomew Fair*, is that patterns of spiritual and moral conduct have become blurred. In the Induction Jonson repeatedly puns satirically on the "*grounded* judgments and *understandings*" of the groundlings in the pit at the Hope. Yet despite the intended irony, *Bartholomew Fair* acknowledges that a regrounding of the social order is indeed under way in England, and the play offers an account of the principles upon which the new system of social organization will be constituted.

While the action of the play deals with this state of affairs in a more tolerant and open manner than is customary for Jonson, the contract read at the outset is typically severe. It includes an ironic deflation of the doctrine of "free-will" and a parody of what is viewed as the arbitrary rationality and the strictly quantitative equity of commercial law:

It is further agreed that every person here have his or their free-will of censure, to like or dislike at their own charge, the author having now departed with his right: it shall be lawful for any man to judge his six pen'orth, his twelve pen'orth, so to his eighteen pence, two shillings, half a crown, to the value of his place; provided always his place get not above his wit . . . . marry, if he drop but sixpence at the door, and will censure a crown's worth, it is thought there is no conscience or justice in that.

Once again, as in Volpone's hymn to his gold, Jonson rails against the symptoms of incipient capitalism, representing as a perverse confusion of categories the reduction of all value to a universal equivalent in money.

And, as in *Volpone*, this madness is represented as a debasement of human into animal nature. Beginning with his earliest "humors" comedies, Jonson had sought to comprehend contemporary social problems in psychological terms. In *Bartholomew Fair* the related, though somewhat different concept of "vapors" is introduced. The psychology is still primitive. "*Bartholomew Fair*," writes Barish, "reduces all human activity to the gross level of an organic disturbance." [14] To a degree, this reduction occurs in the framing device of the contract as well as in the main body of the play. The effect of the Induction is to extend the old doctrine of "humors" to the audience at the Hope. Among the multiple connotations of the word "grounded" in the jokes concerning the spectators of the pit is its association with the physiological origin of the humors and vapors in the lower regions of the body. The irony of the pun is thus enhanced by the juxtaposition of "grounded" with "judgments," ordinarily identified with human reason. In the text of the contract itself the image we get of the spectators is that they are obsessed by a dominant passion for the power of passing judgment, a passion that obstructs the functioning of the rational faculty upon which true judgment depends. The author continues to assume the magisterial persona of an arbiter, not only of good taste but of public morality as well. Yet now, frustrated in the performance of his rightful social office and function by the incompetence of a debased public, he is forced into a humiliating compromise, a contract that will limit his liability, guarantee his audience's attention for the space of about two and a half hours, and place a curb on the tendency of money to usurp the place of wit in validating judgment. The power of the audience is acknowledged. But the poet, forced to endure such frustration and humiliation, gains his revenge in the contempt with which the audience is treated in the last clauses of the contract:

In witness whereof, as you have preposterously put to your seals already (which is your money), you will now add the other part of suffrage, your hands. The play shall presently begin. And though the Fair be not kept in the same region that

14. Barish, *Ben Jonson and the Language of Prose Comedy*, p. 219.

some here, perhaps, would have it, yet think that therein the author hath observed a special decorum, the place being as dirty as Smithfield [the place near London where the actual Bartholomew Fair was held annually], and as stinking every whit.

The immediate reference for this "special decorum" is the fact that the Hope Theater was also used for bear-baiting contests and may well have stunk from the constant presence of animals within its confines. But another implication of these lines is that the public theater is a place where animals (i.e., members of the audience who have fallen below their human natures) are as readily found as at the fair.

The self-conscious metadrama of the Induction and the disdain for the audience implied there are compounded further by the fact that for another performance of this play Jonson wrote a separate Prologue and an Epilogue. These were addressed to James I before whom *Bartholomew Fair* was acted on the day following its first performance at the Hope (31 October 1614). The Epilogue is especially interesting in comparison with the contract of the Induction:

> Your Majesty hath seen the play, and you
>> Can best allow it from your ear and view.
> You know the scope of writers, and what store
>> Of leave is given them, if they take not more,
> And turn it into license.
> . . . .
> This is your power to judge, great sir, and not
>> The envy of a few. Which if we have got,
> We value less what their dislike can bring,
>> If it so happy be, t'have pleased the King.
>
> (ll. 1–5, 9–12)

In contrast to the parodic treatment of the theater audience's desire to judge and to censure in the Induction, and to the milder comedy with which Justice Adam Overdo's "warrant" is treated in the body of the play, here in the Epilogue the final "power to judge" is treated seriously and is vested in the king. The identification of that power with the monarch is not especially significant in itself. It is conventional for a play presented at court. It is also typical of Jonson to claim "the scope of writers" who have the judgment not to "turn it into license," and to identify that authorial capacity for aesthetic and moral judgment with the king's juridical power in relation to his subjects.

But what is especially interesting here is that in connection with the same play we have two very different kinds of framing devices, addressed to different audiences and different social classes. And in each case there is exhibited a deep preoccupation with the author-audience relationship. The address to the king and to the court mediates and helps to sustain the self-image Jonson puts forth in relation to the audience of the playhouse. The place of the author is finally privileged in opposition to that of the theater audience by an identification of his own judgment with the "power to judge" of the king. In this way, the place of the king, the highest earthly place, functions as more than just that of another audience of the play; it is the place of final authority, and as such it is the locus of the voice of the Father, the voice that *author-izes* (if I may be allowed the pun) the writer's voice even as it limits its scope.

Yet despite these efforts to sustain the authority of the poet in the speeches which frame *Bartholomew Fair*, the moral force that animates the "anti-acquisitive attitude" here is far less stable and consistent than it was in *Volpone*. This difference cannot be explained as a response to different audiences since *Volpone* was first played by Shakespeare's company at the Globe, where the social composition of the audience was probably not too different from that at the Hope.[15] Jonson's satiric treatment of the play-goers in the opening of *Bartholomew Fair* is complicated by the main action which follows, and the attitude that drives this play is in the end more ambiguous than the phrase "anti-acquisitive" would allow.

Underlying the bitterness of the contract as a satiric device is a deeper acknowledgment of the general shift that was under way at this time from an idea of community founded on doctrinal tradition to one based on market relations and contract law. It is significant, for example, that at roughly the same time that the Elizabethan and Jacobean drama reaches its apogee, contract law is established on a firmer footing in England. In 1602, a momentous decision in *Slade's Case* brought to culmination a gradual process whereby the mercantile notion of contract had been encroaching on the common law through the evolution of the action of

15. Alfred Harbage, *Shakespeare and the Rival Traditions* (1952; rpt. New York, 1968), p. 27.

assumpsit. The case brought with it, too, a considerable degree of confusion; for the distinction between debt and deceit, between contract and tort, was now, and for some time thereafter, obscured if not obliterated. [16] We can detect a similar type of confusion in the dramatists' representation of moral and contractual obligation. In *Bartholomew Fair* the "Articles of Agreement" point ironically to the increasing reliance on arbitrary regulation (contract law), in the absence of the more spontaneously recognized mechanisms of social control provided by a coherent and viable system of belief. Contractual obligation, enforced by an arbitrary, impartial, and impersonal authority, is satirically acknowledged as the way of containing the threat of anarchy in a society where the only consistent value appears to be that of the marketplace. But despite the fact that the "Articles of

16. The issues in *Slade's Case* are too complex to rehearse in detail. I have relied principally on the following: Theodore F. T. Plucknett, *A Concise History of the Common Law*, 5th ed. (Boston, 1956), pp. 637–651; H. K. Lücke, "Slade's Case and the Origin of the Common Counts," *Law Quarterly Review* (1965), pp. 422–445, 539–561, and (1966), pp. 81–96; S.F.C. Milsom, *Historical Foundations of the Common Law* (London, 1969), chap. 12; J. H. Baker, "New Light on Slade's Case," *Cambridge Law Journal*, XXIX (1971), 51–67, 213–236; and A.W.B. Simpson, *A History of the Common Law of Contract* (Oxford, 1975), pp. 281–315. The case brought to a head a controversy between the courts of Common Pleas and King's Bench concerning the respective boundaries of the actions of debt and of *assumpsit*, an action on the case associated with trespass and deceit. The intensity of the Common Pleas judges' opposition to any blurring of these judicial boundaries can be heard in the following pronouncement (quoted in Baker, p. 231) from another case in the same year: "Cleerly the action will not lye, for the debt is hereby not changed and these new devises of accions of the case cannot be mainteined. For there ought to be no accions of the case but grounded upon some fraud, for so are the words of the writt, *'machinans [defraudare] etc.'* What fraud is here committed?" While there has been a recent difference of opinion among legal historians as to whether the conflict between the courts was motivated primarily by economic self-interest or by intellectual concerns (see Baker, "New Light on Slade's Case," pp. 215–216; Simpson, *A History of the Common Law of Contract*, pp. 293–294), there is less disagreement concerning the effects of the decision in *Slade's Case*. These included the culmination of a process whereby *assumpsit* was extended into the area of law served by the action of debt. To my knowledge, Plucknett's assessment of the confusion created by this decision remains unchallenged in the recent debate: "two generations later we still find the learned Vaughan, C. J., lamenting that *Slade's Case* was 'a false gloss' designed to substitute *assumpsit* for debt. So it was; on principle, the decision is indefensible, for it obliterates the distinction between debt and deceit, between contract and tort" (*A Concise History of the Common Law*, p. 647; cf. Milsom, *Historical Foundations of the Common Law*, p. 304, and Baker, "New Light on Slade's Case," p. 227).

Agreement" are satiric in intent, the author reveals himself to be implicated in his own satire and in the new contractual basis of social obligation.

In contrast to its frame, the play itself sheds a very different light on the
contemporary preoccupation with authority, hierarchy, freedom, and
license. But it also tends to reinforce the idea of a contractual basis to
society. Where the attitude in the Induction is ironic, even caustic, in the
play's conclusion we detect a more conciliatory tone. A sense of community is restored not by means of a coherent theological, moral, or legal
code of behavior, but rather through the recognition that the desire for
pleasure and the consequent "frailty" of the flesh are universal conditions
among the descendants of Adam. In this respect, *Bartholomew Fair* is
"more radical than its author." [17] Where Jonson ordinarily distances himself from his audience, resting his claim to special status on his superior
learning, and representing the poet as combining the social functions of
priest and judge, in this play such roles are satirized and the satire inevitably touches the satirist himself.

Compared to most of Jonson's earlier plays, *Bartholomew Fair* has no
clear ethical foundation; it is more open, more inclusive, more ambiguous;
its action is sprawling, its cast of characters enormous, its overall effect
more fragmented and confusing. Jonson halfheartedly continues to support
the social and ethical norms espoused in the earlier plays. But the absurdity of Troubleall's insistence on having Justice Adam Overdo's "warrant"
before he will perform even the most basic functions such as eating has a
rippling effect that touches every aspect of the play. At the most, what
Bartholomew Fair urges is tolerance where all is vanity, even the vigilant
enforcement of law and order and of public morals. If couched in serious
terms this would have been a dangerous message to place on the stage; but
the confusion and the light-hearted humor of the play most likely tended
to distract attention away from its lack of moral certainty and from its
potentially subversive content.

This is about as close as Jonson ever gets to anything like an egalitarian
conception. Yet despite his retention of hierarchy as a necessary principle
of social order, there is in the conclusion of *Bartholomew Fair*, as Barish
maintains, a striking sense of solidarity in the theater: "One might sug-

17. Barish, *Ben Jonson and the Language of Prose Comedy*, p. 235.

gest, finally, that with this play, in which the reformers are reformed by the fools, Jonson confesses his own frailty and his own flesh and blood. Though he continues to satirize popular taste, he now—momentarily at least—identifies his own interests with it." [18] Barish's statement explicates a logic that underlies the relationship between the author, his characters, and his audience in the denouement of the play. But once this logic has emerged dramatically, it is contagious, affecting (or infecting) relationships within the larger framework of the Induction, and of the Prologue and Epilogue addressed to the king.

In the Epilogue, Jonson may indeed be seeking legitimation of his own authority through an identification with the king's "power to judge." But this authorization is more or less tainted by the play's satirical undermining of Justice Overdo's warrant and of the tutor Wasp's authority: "Nay, then the date of my *Authority* is out; I must think no longer to reign, my government is at an end. He that will correct another must want fault in himself" (V.iv.97–99). This is not to say that Jonson intentionally subverts the authority of majesty here, but only that his attempt to locate himself in a direct line of descent from that absolute locus of power is vitiated by the play's message that all human beings, regardless of their place in society, are flesh and blood and therefore subject to frailty. The Epilogue shows Jonson still claiming, as he did in the Epistle to *Volpone*, "the impossibility of any man's being the good poet without first being a good man." But as Barish suggests, the logic of the comic resolution in *Bartholomew Fair* conveys a sense of authorial self-irony that is lacking in the earlier plays.

Perhaps more than any other play of Jonson's, *Bartholomew Fair* lends itself to modern pragmatic, existential, or even absurdist interpretations. This is not necessarily anachronistic, for the play contains within its theme and structure the rudiments of such modern conceptual paradigms. Alvin B. Kernan writes in a brief but probing study that "Jonson's only answer to the vision of ultimate emptiness is the provisional one of accepting your own limitations and realizing that no warrant confers very much authority. Perhaps, in the long run, good sense and natural instinct are the surest and only warrants the world provides. . . . Even in the theater life gets its

---

18. *Ibid.*, p. 238.

business done and satisfies its needs by a reasonable adjustment of interests." [19] The statement is fine as a description of the relativistic ethic that seems to govern this play, but it needs to be put in historical perspective. For behind all the apparent uncertainty and the "vision of ultimate emptiness" of *Bartholomew Fair* is the model of a new ideology. It is not an ideology that Jonson necessarily espoused in theory, but it does appear in his text. Instead of a social order based on fixed, hierarchical ranks and relations determined by the warrant of authority (whether terrestrial or divine), the play depicts a world in which, as Kernan suggests, men are urged to rely for the ordering of their affairs on "good sense and natural instinct" in arriving at a "reasonable adjustment of interests." But what does it mean to state the play's ethic in these terms? Such phrases are not anachronisms when applied to *Bartholomew Fair*; but neither do they come to us already full of an inherent meaning that is timeless and universal. They refer to concepts with a history that is rooted ideologically in doctrines which Jonson's own drama and poetry helped to promulgate.

It is probably not just coincidence that some of the most perceptive readings of *Bartholomew Fair* point to the emergence of the idea of rational self-interest in the denouement as a key to the meaning of the entire play. Kernan refers to a "reasonable adjustment of interests" among the characters. Barish implicates the author and the audience as well when he writes that Jonson "now—momentarily at least—identifies his own interests with" popular taste. Such assertions have a historical basis to them. As Albert O. Hirschman has recently demonstrated, the term "interest" underwent important changes in meaning in sixteenth- and seventeenth-century writings that provided what Hirschman calls "political arguments for capitalism before its triumph." In place of the old connotation of avarice, a new conception arose of *interest* as the one human passion that had positive social value. It was argued that given the impossibility of effectively repressing the passions through reason, a relatively harmless passion had to be pitted against the more unruly ones in order to contain their destructive effects. The traditional dichotomy between reason and the passions was thus attenuated by the introduction of a third term, the "countervailing passion" of *interest*. This countervailing strategy

19. Kernan, "Alchemy and Acting," p. 22.

became, in turn, the foundation of the social-contract doctrine.[20] Jonson does not contribute directly to this semantic and ideological redefinition; but the comic resolution of *Bartholomew Fair* is a dramatization of the same basic principle.

What is perhaps most remarkable about *Bartholomew Fair* is that some of the very ideas that we take to be self-evident, immutable truths concerning society and human nature, truths which we assume to be pragmatic rather than doctrinaire, were first encoded as part of our own governing ideology in this play and in contemporary works like it. Despite the satire on contracts in the Induction to *Bartholomew Fair*, it is finally the idea of contract that emerges as a solution to the problem of maintaining order in society. By replacing the warrant of authority with a new basis of social order that amounted to a rational compromise, in Kernan's words "a reasonable adjustment of interests," Jonson's play contributed to the contemporary redefinition of the notion of interest and, consequently, to the idea of a social contract.

At the same time, in this early dramatization of the concept that the only effective social control is that of rational self-interest, we can see the emergence of another modern phenomenon, the problem of alienation. In *Bartholomew Fair* the cry of the vendors, "What do you lack? What do you lack?" becomes a refrain that has ontological as well as economic connotations. But unlike *Volpone*, which moralizes on the alienated condition of human beings driven by the pursuit of money and power, *Bartholomew Fair* attempts to provide an alternative to that condition within the limits of the new contractual system of social organization acknowledged in its conclusion.

For there is another side to the ideology of rational self-interest as it is dramatized in this play. It is evident in the conviviality with which the complex and tumultuous action is resolved. Jonson avoids a thoroughly cynical reduction of human relations to market relations and of ethical principles to the impersonal mechanisms of contract law. Justice Overdo's genial invitation, "home with me to my house, to supper," is a gesture

---

20. Albert O. Hirschman, *The Passions and the Interests: Political Arguments for Capitalism Before Its Triumph* (Princeton, N.J., 1978), pp. 14–42. See also Felix Raab, *The English Face of Machiavelli: A Changing Interpretation 1500–1700* (London, 1964), pp. 157–158, 233.

that bespeaks the happier side of the emerging middle-class ideology, the side Dekker had celebrated fifteen years earlier in the more grandiose bourgeois hospitality of Simon Eyre. But where the homely virtues of the middle classes are extolled with unambiguous mirth in *The Shoemakers' Holiday*, Jonson can manage only a resigned acceptance of the new order and of his own complicity in it. The Saturnalian conclusion of *Bartholomew Fair* compensates for the felt loss of a coherent moral code based on traditional, feudal conceptions of hierarchy, status, and *noblesse oblige* by offering a momentary vision that is as close as Jonson ever comes in his satires to an image of utopia, a vision of society in which mutual respect and tolerance are fundamental to the "interests" of all members.

To the extent that this is something of a utopian image, it is conveyed poetically by the reference to "home" which occurs twice in the closing few lines of the play, first in Overdo's invitation to supper, then in Cokes's response: "Yes, and bring the actors along, we'll ha' the rest o' the play at home." Cokes is referring to the puppets whose play has been disrupted by the Puritan, Zeal-Of-The-Land Busy. But his words have broader implications. As Barish points out, in the mouth of Cokes, "the archetypal puppet" among men, these final words "carry the human comedy indefinitely forward into the future."[21] Though Cokes is a satirized character, the context of his line does not allow for a satiric reading. If Jonson is being ironic, it is an irony of pathos rather than one of mockery and censure. In fact, Jonson shows uncharacteristic sympathy and a capacity for tolerance in his benign treatment of human folly here. Of course, a certain amount of self-interest may be involved, since the play is a comic defense of plays and playwrights. But there is also a deeper sense to the repetition of the word "home" and to its prominence as the final word spoken in the play. Jonson employs the same phrase "at home" in other, more solemn contexts in his writing. It is a figure that connotes the *integer vitae* as in:

> Nor for my peace will I go far,
>   As wanderers do, that still do roam,
> But make my strengths, such as they are,
>   Here in my bosom, and at home.
>   (*The Forest*, IV, 65–68)

21. Barish, *Ben Jonson and the Language of Prose Comedy*, p. 238.

The phrase, or an equivalent such as the verb "dwells," which concludes one of Jonson's best-known poems, "To Penshurst," occurs as a *leitmotif* in his poetry. [22] The frequency of such imagery suggests a habitual association of integrity and plenitude with the idea of home. With this in mind we can look back at Bartholomew Cokes's call for the relocation of the pleasures of the stage to the home and realize that it is more than just a continuation of Cokes's exuberant but mindless pursuit of pleasure. It is a recognition and an assertion of the mitigating, compensatory function of aesthetic play in a world in which Jonson and his contemporaries had begun to find it increasingly difficult to feel "at home."

A psychoanalytic study might have much to say about Jonson's dwelling on such domestic imagery; but in the present context, it makes more sense to view this preoccupation in the work of a major writer of the period as indicative of a sociocultural and historical problem rather than a personal one. This problem and the centrality of the figure of "home" in the contemporary orientation to its solution is admirably summed up by Christopher Hill:

> The forces of distruption had gone too far. Economic processes were atomizing society, converting it from a hierarchy of communities to the agglomeration of equal competing individuals depicted in *Leviathan*. . . .
> The economic tension of the community in process of breaking up is focused on the household, in transition from a patriarchal unit of communal production to a capitalist firm. . . . Neither a peasant hut nor the travelling household of the great noble nor the celibate community of the monastery was favourable to home life: that was developed by the middle class in town and country, whose houses began to replace churches as the centres of social life. . . . So, especially in towns, new, voluntary communities arose, independent of the parish. These new select groups were united by community of interest rather than by geographical propinquity or corporate worship. For a short time men could even envisage bringing about fundamental reform in the State via reform in the household. [23]

But household reform, the conviviality of the "new, voluntary communities," and the spirituality of the new sects built on the principle of

22. Other poems in which these terms figure in this way include: "To Sir Robert Wroth," *The Forest*, III, 13, 94; "An Epistle to Master John Selden," *Underwood*, XIV, 30; "An Epigram to My Muse, the Lady Digby, on her Husband, Sir Kenelm Digby," *Underwood*, LXXVIII, 8.

23. Hill, *Society and Puritanism*, pp. 487–488.

the covenant were bound up inextricably with the same economic "forces of disruption" to which Hill refers at the beginning of the above quotation. To the extent that institutions were sought to contain the atomizing effects of capitalist development, which meant containing voluntarism itself, the solutions arrived at tended to be based on the notion of contract. Thus, Hill writes of "contract communities" replacing "status communities." The household became the fundamental social unit of the "contract community," as is evident from the frequent parallels drawn in the sixteenth century between the patriarchal family and the state, and in the seventeenth, between the marriage contract and the social contract. Patriarchy in the family was the common basis of argumentation in conflicting doctrines concerning the foundations of state and society.[24] This being the case, it is not surprising to find Jonson employing the image of "home" in such different contexts as "To Penshurst," where social order is conceived in terms of degree and obligation according to prescribed doctrine,[25] and at the end of *Bartholomew Fair*, a comedy focused on the middle classes, where society is viewed as the product of a compromise, "a reasonable adjustment of interests," a social contract.

While it may be true that this shift from "status" to "contract" was grounded in a tradition—the Old Testament doctrine of the covenant between God and Israel—it is important that we not confuse contemporary rationales of observable transformations in seventeenth-century English society with the actual phenomena of social and political change.[26] When Knights writes of the dramatists working in an "anti-

24. See Hill, chap. 13; and Keith Thomas, "Women and the Civil War Sects," *Past and Present*, no. 13 (1958), rpt. in *Crisis in Europe 1560–1660*, ed. Trevor Aston (Garden City, N.Y., 1967), p. 332.

25. There are, in fact, contractual elements in poems of praise like "To Penshurst," especially where the relationship between poet and patron is concerned. I have discussed this question from a related perspective in "Poetry and Power in Ben Jonson's *Epigrammes*: The Naming of 'Facts' or the Figuring of Social Relations?" *RMS*, XXIII (1979), 79–103.

26. Hobbes buttresses the "Principles of Reason" on which he would ground his contractual model of society by the "Authority of Scripture," which provides the precedent of "the Kingdome of God, administered by Moses, over the Jews, his peculiar people by Covenant" (*Leviathan* [1651], ed. C. B. Macpherson [Harmondsworth, Eng., 1968)], chap. 30, p. 378; cf. chaps. 35 and 40). J.G.A. Pocock, "Post-Puritan England and the Problem of the Enlightenment," in *Culture and Politics from Puritanism to the Enlightenment*, ed. Perez Zagorin (Berkeley, Calif., 1980), pp. 97–99, argues that a common ground of the political theories of Hobbes and of Harrington was their interpretation of Israel as a theocracy—"a republic to Harrington, a monarchy to Hobbes"—founded by covenant.

acquisitive tradition inherited from the Middle Ages" he adopts the moralistic and conservative rationale of the playwrights themselves. In so doing, he neglects to distinguish between an ideological "conservatism" that appears to connect the morality of these plays to a medieval popular tradition and contrary indications which, if not always manifested overtly in the plays, are, nonetheless, embodied in the professional and commercial form of the new theaters.

Curiously, Knights does acknowledge such tensions in the work of lesser, more naïve playwrights like Dekker and Heywood. [27] But his treatment of Jonson is less dialectical. No doubt, that is partly because the tensions or contradictions between traditional morality and the emergent ideologies associated with capitalist development in England are not as obvious in Jonsonian drama. But Knights is too observant a critic in other respects to have missed this facet of Jonson's plays were it not for his deeply held conviction that the great drama of the period has an uncompromising moral unity and coherence which draws on and elaborates a solid and stable "sense of community." As Francis Mulhern has recently shown, the theme of "community" was a central and constant concern of *Scrutiny*, the journal with which Knights was closely associated and where portions of *Drama and Society in the Age of Jonson* first appeared. [28] In one sense, the moral conviction that drives Knights's reading of Jonson is a replica of the nostalgia and the longing that we find, at times, in Jonson's own works. Knights employs words like "tradition," "community," and "neighborliness" throughout his book in a way that is virtually the equivalent of Jonson's "at home." Indeed, the association is given by Knights himself in one characteristic sentence: "His [Jonson's] classicism is an equanimity and assurance that springs—'here at home'—from the strength of a native tradition." [29] The phrase in single quotation marks alludes to the same poem I have cited above. But where Knights shares Jonson's nostalgia, he lacks the seventeenth-century poet's capacity for self-irony.

The difference here is itself susceptible to historical and sociological analysis. Knights, F. R. Leavis, and the other Cambridge intellectuals who founded *Scrutiny* in the 1930s could imagine themselves as part of an independent "critical minority," whose task it was to oppose the alienation

27. Knights, *Drama and Society*, chap. 8.
28. Francis Mulhern, *The Moment of "Scrutiny"* (London, 1979), pp. 58–63.
29. Knights, *Drama and Society*, pp. 187–188.

of life and of language in modern commercial and industrial society by bearing witness to the moral, "organic community" of the past. [30] Ben Jonson was understandably attractive as a literary exemplar of the "culture" Knights and his colleagues sought to defend and as a precursor of their high-minded purpose. But Jonson could not have imagined himself to be engaged in such an enterprise with the same compelling belief in his own detachment from society's economic infrastructure. He might try to do so in the *Volpone* Epistle which, significantly, was written for a university performance. But he was not a university man. As an intellectual and a social critic, his situation was an ironic one. The "anti-acquisitive" culture to which he contributed was intimately bound up with the emerging commercial society of Jacobean England.

Capitalism was indeed on the rise, as it had been for some time. But it had not yet triumphed to the point where a sufficient surplus capital existed to sustain a large-scale educational apparatus, one that could produce not only a technically trained managerial elite but a cultural elite as well who could imagine themselves to be morally superior to and independent of the new economic order. Despite his constant efforts to represent himself as an intellectual rather than a mere playwright, as a poet in the most dignified sense of the term rather than one writing under a system of patronage in which flattery was obligatory, Jonson could not easily blind himself to the manner in which his claim to special status was dependent on the emerging commodity system of economic and social exchange. Acquisitiveness was only one aspect of the new system, an aspect that the moralist could confidently look upon with disdain; but contract was another, and the kind of social relationship it legitimated entailed a form of alienation from which it was more difficult to stand aloof.

The development of Jonsonian drama from *Volpone* to *Bartholomew Fair* is an index of Jonson's increasing awareness of this dilemma. Knights's focus on only the one side of capitalist development—accumulation, or in his more ethically loaded term, "acquisitiveness"—coupled with his need to view Jonson as an unwavering traditionalist, prevented him from recognizing the deeper significance of *Bartholomew Fair*. He was undoubtedly right in pointing out that earlier critics had overestimated the importance

30. Mulhern, *The Moment of "Scrutiny,"* pp. 33, 76–78.

of Jonson's classical erudition in evaluating his plays. But the alternative view of tradition which he proposed was, in its own way, limited. It was an oversimplification to represent Jonson as merely drawing on a traditional sense of community in order to construct a bulwark against the growing tendency of commodity exchange and the contractual regulation of such exchange to encroach upon fundamentally human relationships. Such a view depended on an eclipsing of the ambiguity and tension that provide the rich intellectual and psychological texture of Jonsonian drama. Indeed, it led to the dubious exclusion of *Bartholomew Fair* from among the more important of Jonson's plays.

Though *Drama and Society in the Age of Jonson* remains a landmark in the sociology of literature, its governing conception of the relations among the categories alluded to in its title—drama, society, history, and the psychology of the author-audience relationship—is too narrowly drawn. Knights's demand for a consistent moral "attitude" as the criterion of Jonson's greatness as a dramatist resulted in a flattening of the social and ideological terrain mapped in the plays. Conservative as he may have been in principle, Jonson demanded a status that was unacknowledged in the traditional social and cultural system from which England was then emerging. In using the theater as a space for negotiating that demand he provided his audiences with a model of the society which they themselves were already in the process of creating. Thus, despite his classicism and his traditionalism, Jonson looked ahead as much as he did backward in time. His work, together with that of other Elizabethan and Jacobean dramatists, marks a significant change in the sense that playwrights and their audiences had of their relation to history and to their society. [31]

31. I am grateful to colleagues at the University of California, San Diego, and particularly to Page Du Bois, Louis Montrose, and Michael Parrish for suggestions and criticisms that were helpful to me in the writing of this essay.

The Pharmacy of Machiavelli:
Roman Lucretia in Mandragola

RONALD L. MARTINEZ

I N A RECENT STUDY, Franco Fido treats critical views of Machiavelli's
Mandragola under three implicit headings: (1) meritorious accounts
that combine an awareness of the generic constraints on the play with a
sense for specifically Machiavellian—hence political—concerns;
(2) debatable interpretations that emphasize the resonances within the
play of the author's personal difficulties after the Medici restoration in
1512; and (3) speculative readings that attempt to associate the events of
the play with specific political agendas or with historical events contemporary with the play.[1] Fido concludes his survey by arguing for an understanding of *Mandragola* both as ironic valedictory, signaling the retreat

---

1. See Franco Fido, "Politica e teatro nel badalucco de Meser Nicia," now in *Le
metamorfosi del centauro: Studi e letture da Boccaccio a Pirandello* (Rome, 1977), pp. 91–108.
Giorgio Cavallini, *Interpretazione della Mandragola* (Milan, 1973), pp. 7–22, also gives a
summary of critical thought on the play. For some accounts in English, see Marvin T.
Herrick, *Italian Comedy in the Renaissance* (Urbana and London, 1960), pp. 80–85; Douglas
Radcliffe-Umstead, *The Birth of Modern Comedy in Renaissance Italy* (Chicago and London,
1969), pp. 116–134; Leo Salingar, *Shakespeare and the Traditions of Comedy* (Cambridge,
Eng., 1974), pp. 196–197, 199–200.

of political virtue from the *polis* to the bedroom, and as a plaything, "un badalucco," that serves to absorb the interest of an unemployed political genius.[2]

Fido's succinct study aims at imposing a measure of order on the disorderly house of *Mandragola* commentary: his lapidary summation argues the complete absorption of the play's complex tensions in the brilliant realization of the comic plot: "the imbalance between the end and the means is resolved, without apparent effort and without any residue, in the comic form."[3] In some respects, however, Fido may have done his work too well. A different approach to the play is that of Ezio Raimondi, who in a series of essays has taken soundings of the play's striking heterogeneity of inspiration and tonal register.[4] Raimondi's findings pose

2. Fido, pp. 107–108. For the convenience of the reader, Marvin T. Herrick's synopsis of the play follows:

Callimaco, a young Florentine who has been living in Paris for some years, has returned to his native city to see for himself a celebrated beauty, Madonna Lucrezia, wife of Messer Nicia Calfucci. The young woman has proved to be even more beautiful than reported, and he has fallen desperately in love with her. But what can he do? Lucrezia is as chaste as she is beautiful. Callimaco, who is no callow youth, perceives three weaknesses in the defense: the simplicity of the husband Nicia, the desire of the couple to have children, and the easygoing mother of the wife. Callimaco has reasoned soundly, and his campaign is successful, but not until he has engaged the help of the parasite Ligurio, who in turn has to call on a friar to win over the two women. It is Ligurio who devises the fraud that insures success: Callimaco poses as a learned physician from Paris who concocts a draught of mandragola guaranteed to make any woman conceive. There are complications, however, for it seems that the first man to cohabit with a patient who had drunk this potion will die within a week. Therefore it is necessary to kidnap some homeless young man to serve as the agent. This waif, of course, is Callimaco disguised as a strolling musician. Owing to the ready co-operation of the husband and mother-in-law, the arguments of the friar, and the expert timing of the parasite, everything runs like clockwork; the young man wins a beautiful mistress, the husband and his mother-in-law rejoice in the prospect of an heir, the parasite is sure of three meals a day for some time to come, and the father confessor is richer by 300 ducats [pp. 80-81].

3. Raimondi's important essays on Machiavelli are collected in *Politica e commedia dal Beroaldo al Machiavelli* (Bologna, 1972), pp. 141-286.

4. T. H. Sumberg, "*La mandragola*, An Interpretation," in *Journal of Politics*, XXIII (1961), 320-348; A. Parronchi, "La prima rappresentazione della *Mandragola*: Il modello per l'apparato. L'allegoria." in *La bibliofila*, LXIV (1962), 37-89. For Sumberg, Callimaco is generically the Prince, specifically a representation of the Medici, "patres patriae," who

the question of where we are to place *Mandragola* on a line that stretches from the Boccaccian *beffa* (trick) that inspires its comic situations to the learned context of Aristophanic satire to the political allegory that critics such as Sumberg, Parronchi, and Ridolfi claim to detect in the play.[5] If we are to see the play whole, we must be able to account both for the play's mocking tone—stridently in evidence from the acerbic prologue to the triumph of cuckoldry at play's end—and for its repeated invitations to judge the action in the context of Machiavelli's political thought. Once we have fully weighed both the play's levity and its gravity, we must come to terms with the undertone of pessimism and bitterness that many critics claim to detect in the apparently jocular events. The opinion of Nino Borsellino might be considered representative:[6]

The world of *Mandragola* is fervently anarchic, deprived of ideals, where the natural order of the instincts may be restored only through moral disorder. Machiavelli acknowledges this world with that sharp and lucid realism that does not conceal its bitterness: as if the "odd and spiteful bauble" of the comedy permitted him to relieve the oppressive malignity of fate [my translation].

---

will return to refertilize Florence, represented by Lucrezia, hitherto in the grasp of Nicia, who stands for political impotence. Ligurio might be Machiavelli himself. For Parronchi, the alignment of characters and historical personages is more exact: because, in his view, the first performance of *Mandragola* took place in September of 1518 as part of the celebrations commemorating the marriage of Lorenzo de Pierfrancesco de Medici to Marguerite de la Tour Angoulême, Callimaco must be Lorenzo returning "victorious" from France; Nicia is the ineffectual Piero Soderini, *gonfaloniere* for life of the Florentine republic (and whose wife was indeed sterile). Roberto Ridolfi, in his *Life of Niccolò Machiavelli,* 2d ed., trans. Cecil Grayson (Chicago, 1963), accepts the identification of Nicia with Soderini.

5. In *Commedie del Cinquecento,* ed. Nino Borsellino (Milan, 1962), I, xxvi. For substantially similar views, see G. D. Bonino, ed., *Il teatro Italiano,* II: *La commedia del 1500* (Turin, 1977), I, xliii–lii; and L. Russo, *Machiavelli* (Bari, 1957), p. 93. Raimondi, *Politica e commedia,* p. 162, merits citation: "Alla fine della commedia non si avverte liberazione alcuna, la parodia che si aggiunge al rito canonico della festa è come un veleno, un sospetto che non si placa nel trionfo gioioso e previsto della natura." The "dark" view of the play goes back at least to F. de Sanctis, *Storia della letteratura italiana,* ed. B. Croce (Bari, 1912), II, 94-102.

6. For the observation, see de Sanctis, *Storia,* p. 94. In many respects, my study vindicates de Sanctis's view of the play, if not his moral outrage and his anachronistic view that the play is superannuated.

With the intention of shedding some additional light on the problems raised by Machiavelli's play, I am proposing a detailed reconsideration of the textual relationship between *Mandragola* and Livy's account of Lucretia's suicide (*ab urbe condita,* I.57-59). Although the irony implicit in naming the (finally) pliable Florentine Lucrezia with the name of a Roman exemplar of chastity has been remarked, it has not served as a primary datum that might lead to a systematic view of the play.[7] Moreover, the consideration of Livy's text in conjunction with Machiavelli's addresses the principal critical problems outlined above; for the political result of the suicide in Livy's history plants for the critic the question of the political domain of Machiavelli's own text, while the somber events of Lucretia's death extend a dark background for the ribaldry and humor of Machiavelli's play. Let me first consider a few methodological questions.

Though topical allegories such as those of Sumberg and Parronchi have been attacked as unconvincing, it cannot be doubted that *Mandragola* invites some form of programmatic decoding. Felix Gilbert has defined Machiavelli's own brand of allegory as the discovery of general rules of political behavior in the events of classical antiquity.[8] Indeed, Machiavelli's argument that human nature is essentially invariable, and that states follow regular cycles of development (the Polybian thesis of *anakyklosis*) permits the construction of a transhistorical frame of interpretation within which the events of the present may be measured against those of antiquity.[9] The history of Rome and the history of contemporary Italy con-

---

7. One can do no better than quote de Sanctis: "La tragedia romana si trasforma nelle commedia fiorentina," *Storia,* p. 94. The idea that the play is at bottom tragic in mood is advanced by Benedetto Croce in "La commedia del rinascimento," reprinted in *Poesia popolare e poesia d'arte* (Bari, 1932), p. 247; the notion is developed by Russo, *Machiavelli,* p. 143. It has been restated recently by Ridolfi, *Studi sulla commedia del Machiavelli* (Pisa, 1968), pp. 65-66. Ian Donaldson's *The Rapes of Lucretia: A Myth and Its Transformations* (Oxford, 1982), appeared too late for me to exploit its rich inventory of literary and artistic treatments of Lucretia in the formulation of my own arguments. Donaldson addresses many of the issues I have considered in my own approach—the relation of political and sexual tyranny (p. 8) and the symbolism of Tarquin's knife (pp. 16-17), for example—but his own views of *Mandragola* are disappointingly conventional. His conclusion, that Machiavelli is *demythologizing* Lucretia (p. 93), could not be further from my own.

8. Felix Gilbert, *Machiavelli and Guicciardini* (Princeton, N.J., 1965), pp. 168-169.

9. For unchanging human nature, cf. Niccolò Machiavelli, *Discorsi sopra la prima deca di Tito Livio,* III, 43, in *Il principe e le opere politiche,* ed. Delio Cantimori (Milan, 1976), p. 451. English translations of the *Discorsi* are from *The Prince* and the *Discourses,* introd. Max

stitute two discourses that can be read in terms of one another—one way of defining allegory. The evidence for such an interpretive context may be found readily in *Mandragola,* from the references in the author's prologue to the corruption of the present age ("che per tutto traligna dall'antica virtù . . . il secolo presente") to the use of specifically Roman names (Lucrezia, Ligurio, Camillo) beyond the requirements of Plautine and Terentian example.[10] The comedy thus shares that comparative spirit that makes the juxtaposition of Roman and Italian events a reflex—indeed, a method—of the *Prince* and the *Discourses on the First Decade of Titus Livius.*[11] Nor is the play's political context merely general: readers have noted that Machíavelli situates Callimaco's departure from his native city in 1494, when the first French invasions of Italy, in Callimaco's words, destroyed the province of Italy (" ruinorno quella provincia").[12] As Luigi Russo observes, reflections on the effects of 1494 are uncharacteristic of the blandly apolitical Callimaco but typical of his author; Callimaco's

---

Lerner (New York, 1950) (translator of the *Discorsi* is Christine E. Detmold). Machiavelli's examples are the Gauls against the Romans and the hosts of Charles VIII against the Italians. For the "Polybian" thesis of cyclical history, see the *Discorsi,* I. For Machiavelli's use of Polybius, now generally accepted, see G. Sasso, *Niccolò Machiavelli, storia del suo pensiero politico* (Naples, 1958), pp. 308-315 (on the *anakyklosis*). As Sasso concludes, "La storia romana diviene dunque l'ideale criterio con cui il Machiavelli cerca di penetrare e di comprendere lo svolgimento della storia di Firenze." See also J.G.A. Pocock, *The Machiavellian Moment: Florentine Political Thought and the Atlantic Republican Tradition* (Princeton, N.J., 1975), pp. 186-194.

10. *Mandragola, prologo,* vv. 59-60. All citations to the play are to the edition of Franco Gaeta, in *Niccolò Machiavelli, Il teatro e tutti gli scritti letterari* (Milan, 1965), pp. 55-112; translations are mine. The language of the *prologo* also echoes the preface to Livy's *Ab urbe condita* (ed. R. S. Conway and C. F. Walters [Oxford, 1914]): "labente deinde paulatim disciplina velut desidentes primo mores sequatur animo, deinde ut magis magisque lapsi sint," etc., and Machiavelli's own adaptation of these ideas in the *Discorsi,* I, *proemio.* Hereafter *Ab urbe condita* is cited as *AUC.*

11. Gilbert, pp. 168-169; Sasso, p. 315. As in the prologue to the *Clizia* (Gaeta, p. 116), where Machiavelli explicitly describes the "translatio studii" from Greece to Rome to Italy, the names of the characters in *Mandragola* are both Greek (Sostrata, Timoteo, Siro, Callimaco, Nicia) and Roman (Lucrezia, Camillo, Ligurio).

12. Russo, p. 17. Machiavelli's idiom is a reference to the traditional designation of Italy as the "domina provinciarum." In *Discorsi* III.7 the revolt that expelled the Tarquins is compared with the expulsion of the Medici in 1494. See also I.48.

words in fact reiterate a phrase from the *Discourses*. [13] And the date does not simply dangle freely; Callimaco's opening soliloquy dates the action of the play to 1504, ten years after the first of the French invasions, establishing a mensuration by decades that recurs in the play and that corresponds to Machiavelli's division of political epochs in the allegorical *Decennali*, which begin in 1494. [14] In the context of Machiavelli's use of Livy both in *Mandragola* and in his commentary on the first *decade* of Livy's history, the ten-year segments in the play are linked to Livy's division of the books of his history into pentads and decades, which reflects the Roman practice of measuring years by *lustra*. [15] Though not necessarily coextensive, the measurement of time and of the articulations of narrative share common principles. Finally, as stated in the author's *prologo*, the *apparato* or stage set for *Mandragola* represents Florence, though the illusionism of the theater will permit, another day, the representation of Rome or Pisa. [16] For Parronchi, mention of Rome and Pisa helps to corroborate his view that the play celebrated the union of Lorenzo de Medici and his French bride. [17] But whether his hypothesis is proven or falsified, it remains suggestive that Machiavelli has chosen to mention both the illustrious model and parent of Florence—Rome—and Pisa, the city that was the most recalcitrant object of Florentine imperialism and

13. Russo, p. 17. For a parallel to "ruinorno quella provincia," see *Discorsi*, I.37. The political significance of *Mandragola* is acknowledged by Croce, p. 5, and L. Russo, *Commedie Fiorentine del '500* (Florence, 1939), pp. 15-16.

14. "Decennale primo," vv. 10-12 (ed. Gaeta, p. 236). For the importance of the ten-year interval in *Mandragola*, cf. Sumberg's list, pp. 40-41. Machiavelli's prefatory letter to the *Decennali*, addressed to Alamanno Salviato, refers to "transacti decenni labores Italicos" (Gaeta, p. 235). Verse 2 of the poem refers to the "duo passati lustri" and continues with "aveva il sol veloce sopra'l dorso / del nostro mondo ben termini mille / e quattrocento novanta quattro corso" (vv. 10-12).

15. For the division of the first 45 books of Livy's history, see T. R. Luce, *Livy: The Composition of His History* (Princeton, N.J., 1977), pp. 3-32, especially the last sentence on p. 32: "Scholars are agreed that in the extant books, including the missing decade 11-20, Livy blocked out his material according to pentads and decades." At Rome the closing of a *lustrum* entailed an official ceremony and included the taking of a census; cf. *AUC*, 47.1-7.

16. "Vedete l'apparato / quale or vi si dimostra: / questa è Firenze vostra; / un'altra volta sarà Roma o Pisa" (vv. 7-10).

17. Parronchi, pp. 71-79.

whose name dots the *Discourses* and the *Prince*.[18] Rome and Pisa frame Florentine ambitions much as the French and the Turks (both also mentioned in *Mandragola*) mark the outer sphere of Italian influence in Europe and the Mediterranean.[19] Thus the play's imagined spaces, as well as its imagined setting in time, are set in terms of the structure of Machiavelli's political vision.

My own argument, then, goes further than that of those who admit a general relationship of *Mandragola* to the major political statements, but remains distinct from the approaches of topical allegorists who discern a specific, historical *dramatis personae* in the characters of the play. More than a play with historical overtones, *Mandragola* is itself a form of theorizing about, and interpreting, history and politics. Moreover, with respect to the story of Lucretia in particular, Machiavelli is in an established Florentine humanist tradition, for it has been shown that for early humanists and republicans alike, the iconography of the rape of Lucretia was associated with anti-tyrannical and pro-republican views. At the same time, the story of Lucretia appears in panels that mark the progress of scientific perspective in the *scenografia* of the early Renaissance, such that Machiavelli's choice of Lucretia as part of his subject occurs in a context where a specific link between the Roman episode and the public spectacle of the *commedia* had already been established. Some elaboration of these points may be helpful.

Already in the late *trecento* the rape of Lucretia was the subject of a pro-republican *declamatio* by Coluccio Salutati, and thus figures in the complex debate, analyzed in detail by Hans Baron, over the relative merits of tyrannies or republics that agitated humanists of the early Renaissance.[20] To confirm the persistence of the Lucretia theme in the

18. For Pisa as the stumbling block of Florentine expansionist ambitions, see the *Discorsi*, I, 38; I, 53; II, 1; III, 16; III, 43; III, 48; and *Il principe* (ed. Cantimori,) v, xx, where the Pisans' tenacious love of their own freedoms is remarked.

19. For the Turkish threat in the Mediterranean, see the *Discorsi*, II, 1, where the Turks are among the heirs of military empire; see also the "Decennale primo," vv. 205-207, and Machiavelli's letter of 18 May 1521 to Guicciardini (*Lettere*, ed. F. Gaeta [Milan, 1961], p. 409). For Turks and the French compared, cf. *Il principe*, iv.

20. Hans Baron, *The Crisis of the Early Italian Renaissance* (Princeton, N.J., 1955). The entire study is relevant to the question of Machiavelli's pro-republican attitudes, tracing the progress and regress of republican enthusiasm in the early Humanist tradition. Co-

terms of the same debate, Guy Walton has shown that the Baltimore Lucretia panel, dated to 1504 or slightly after, caps a discernible tradition of representations of the rape of Lucretia and Brutus's subsequent oration over her body.[21] As Walton points out, the presence in the Baltimore Lucretia of the statues of David and Goliath and Judith and Holofernes make the anti-tyrannical polemic of the panel unmistakable, as these figures, once totems of Florentine resistance to Visconti tyranny, had come to signify the hostility of the Florentine republic to the continued dynastic pretensions of the Medici after their expulsion in 1494. The subject of Lucretia and Brutus (paired with the related episode of Appius and Virginia) is thus inscribed in a political iconography at the heart of Florentine civic concerns. In addition, as both Walton and Richard Krautheimer have shown, the Lucretia and Virginia panels, in their use of noble, classicizing architecture and their adoption of rigorous scientific perspective, are textbook examples of the so-called tragic scene. Krautheimer notes that the "tragic scene," whether devised for real or imaginary performances, evolves in close synchronization with the evolution of scientific perspective itself; its depiction of classical temples, arches, and plazas conform to canonical distinction, descending from Vitruvius through Alberti, between the archetypal "tragic" and "comic" scenes.[22] It is just such a "perspective," the famous Urbino panel, that

luccio Salutati refers to his declamation on Lucretia in a letter (*Epistolario di Coluccio Salutati*, ed. F. Novati, v. 4, [Rome, 1905] [Fonti per la storia d'Italia, v. 18], pp. 253-254); Novati gives in his note the passage to which Salutati refers, from Lucretia's answer to her father's and husband's pleas that she not commit suicide: "Nichil muliere mobilius: egritudinem animique motus nedum mollit sed extinguit tempus. si distulero, forsan incipient michi flagitiosa placere," etc. The passage is striking because it makes Lucretia's justification for suicide her fear of her own nature as a woman, "semper varium et mutabile."

21. Guy Walton, "The Lucretia Panel in the Isabella Stuart Gardner Museum in Boston," *Essays in Honor of Walter Freidlaender*, ed. by Marsyas, *Studies in the History of Art*, supplement II: a special volume, Institute of Fine Arts, New York University (1965), pp. 177-186. See figure I. The subject of Lucretia's rape and suicide is a popular subject of *cassoni* illustration throughout the quattrocento and cinquecento; Paul Schubring, *Cassoni*, (Leipzig, 1915) gives nineteen entries, of which eleven are illustrated. Of special interest are Sodoma's 1505 panels juxtaposing Lucretia with Judith; cf. *Textband*, p. 164, illustration in *Tafelband*, 1. 157, n. 735.

22. Walton, pp. 183-184; Richard Krautheimer, "The Tragic and Comic Scene in the Renaissance: The Baltimore and Urbino Panels," *Gazette des Beaux-Arts*, VI, XXIII (June 1948), 327-346. See also Parronchi, pp. 37-45.

Parronchi has identified as the backdrop for the first performance of *Mandragola,* placed by Parronchi in September 1518.[23] Whether the Urbino panel was, in fact, the scene for *Mandragola,* it is likely that the *apparato* for Machiavelli's play resembled it, for a description of the stage set of Bibbiena's *La Calandria,* one of Machiavelli's immediate dramatic models, has survived, often attributed to Baldessar Castiglione. The description is of a classicizing scene, with friezes and reliefs depicting Roman heroes, including the Horatii.[24] In the context of Machiavelli's own literary practice and political interests, it is hardly speculative to assert that a conspicuously classicizing backdrop for the bourgeois comedy of *Mandragola* would provide an ironic visual "perspective" on the action of the play just as the evocation of Roman Lucretia in the name of Nicia's wife Lucrezia provides *verbal* irony. An idealized antiquity represented both by allusion to Livy and the visual allusions of architecture frames the action of *Mandragola* and imposes a perspective from which the audience views and judges the events of the plot.

My exposition of Lucrezia's fall will be in three parts, with a prologue. After consideration of some general aspects of Machiavelli's use of Livy's text, the first part will consist of a description of the principal parallels between Livy's history and *Mandragola.* A calculation of the differences between the Roman and Florentine Lucretias yields an inventory of the differences for Machiavelli between the heroic civic virtue of the Romans and the corruption of the civic body in early cinquecento Florence. The second part of the study examines the function of ritual action in the two texts. In Livy's narrative, the episode of Lucretia and Brutus functions as an etiological fable: Lucretia's suicide makes her the sacrificial victim, the *pharmakos* whose destruction is instrumental in precipitating the expulsion of the tyrants and establishing the Roman republic. As such, Lucretia's tragedy is one of a series of episodes in the first decade that exemplify Aristotle's view in the *Politics* that offenses to women may serve as

23. Parronchi, pp. 54-56.

24. For the description, see Walton, p. 183; Bonino, pp. 445-448, reprints an even lengthier extract.

25. See the *Politics,* V. 10-15, 1311a34-1311b22. For examples from Machiavelli's text, cf. *Discorsi,* I.2, I.40, II.16, III.6, 26—whose rubric is: "Come per ragioni de femine se rovina uno stato."

catalysts precipitating revolutions in the state.[26] Machiavelli's interest in
Lucretia's story—as in the first decade of Livy in general—springs largely
from his concern for the problems of political innovation, whether during
the original foundation of a city or as a part of constitutional reform or
violent revolution. Thus *Mandragola,* too, as some readers have observed,
is itself an etiology of a new community, albeit one founded not on heroic
sacrifice but on the rational calculation of private advantage, on
acquisitiveness or *guadagno.* Third and finally—in the wake of studies
showing how the lore of the mandrake root penetrates the language and
action of the play—I turn to a discussion of the potent, ambiguous
medicine *mandragola* from the perspective of Lucretia herself as the *pharmakon* that purges Rome from the disease of tyranny.[26] The ambiguous
function of *mandragola* is the play's principal link to the sacrificial economy operating in Livy's account of Lucretia's suicide and its aftermath;
and it is only after an elucidation of the full semantic domain of *mandragola* in the play that we can begin to unravel the play's teasing final
ironies—foremost of which is the magnificent rejuvenescence of Lucrezia
herself. Because Lucrezia is the cynosure, the uniquely virtuous element in
the generally corrupt world of the play, both her submission and her final
transformation are central to our understanding of the play's meaning.

The specific parallels between Livy's text and Machiavelli's play are
framed by Machiavelli's use of several important Livian themes in *Mandragola.* First, Machiavelli's notorious remarks in the verse prologue,
referring to the corruption of the present age, repeat the fundamental
premise of Livy's vast history, which would, in the historian's words,

trace the progress of our moral decline . . . the sinking of the foundation of
morality as the old teaching was allowed to lapse, then the rapidly increasing
disintegration, then the final collapse of the whole edifice, and the dark dawning
of our modern day when we can neither endure our vices nor face the remedies
needed to cure them. The study of history is the best medicine for a sick mind; for
in history you have a record of the infinite variety of human experience plainly set

26. See Giovanni Aquilecchia, "Mandragola la favola si chiama," in *Collected Essays in
Italian Language and Literature Presented to Kathleen Speight,* (Manchester, 1971), pp. 74-
100; Ezio Raimondi, "Il veleno della *Mandragola,*" in *Politica e Commedia,* pp. 253-264;
Hugo Rahner, "Moly and Mandragora in Pagan and Christian Symbolism," in *Greek Myths
and Christian Mystery,* (London 1963), pp. 224-277.

out for all to see; and in that record you can find for yourself and your country both examples and warnings . . .[27]

Machiavelli, who identified profoundly with Livy's role as *laudator temporis acti,* adopts both in the *Discourses* and the prologue to *Mandragola* not only the idea of the monitory value of history but also the Livian metaphor of the state as a diseased body—a metaphor that will return in the medical-pharmaceutical register of *Mandragola.*[28] Second, Livy's treatment of the story of Brutus and Lucretia, condensing and focusing the prolix account of Dionysus of Halicarnassus, presents the events in strikingly *dramatic* terms.[29] Indeed, Livy explicitly compares the indigenous Roman tragedy of Lucretia to the Hellenic flavor of the parricidal Tarquins:

In ancient Greece more than one royal house was guilty of crime which became the stuff of tragedy; now Rome was to follow the same path, but not in vain, for that very guilt was to hasten the coming of liberty and the hatred of kings . . .[30]

One consequence of Livy's conspicuously dramatic treatment is that his episode follows the tragic unities: the rape and suicide of Lucretia, and Brutus's speech over her body, are narrated as if occurring without interruption; they all occur in Collatia, where Lucretia, the wife of Collatinus, resides; and the sequence of events presents a closely articulated plot, a rigorous sequence of cause and effect that culminates with the flight of Tarquin.[31] The fact that the sequence of events continues

27. *AUC praefatio* 6-9, trans. Aubrey de Selincourt, *The Early History of Rome* (London, 1960), p. 34.

28. Cf. *Discorsi,* I, *proemio;* "Nè ancora la medicina è altro che esperienza fatta dagli antiqui medici, sopra la quale fondano e medici presenti e loro iudizii. Nondimanco, nello ordinare le republiche . . . non si trova principe nè republica che agli esempi delli antiqui ricorra; II, *proemio:* "Laudano sempre gli uomini, ma non sempre ragionevolmente, gli antichi tempi, e gli presenti accusano"; III, i: "Egli è cosa verissima come tutte le cose del mondo hanno il termine della vita loro . . . E perchi'io parlo de' corpi misti, come sono le republiche e le sette, dico che quelle alterazioni sono a salute che le riducano inverso i principii loro."

29. Dionysus of Halicarnassus, *Roman Antiquities,* trans. E. Cary, Loeb Classics (Cambridge and London, 1952), II, 473-577.

30. Livy, *Early History,* p. 42.

31. For the dramatic thrust of Livy's account, see the remarks of R. L. Ogilvy, *A Commentary on Livy, Books I-V,* (Oxford, 1964), pp. 218-219.

through the night is made explicit in Ovid's version of the Lucretia-
Brutus story in the *Fasti,* which follows Livy closely.[32] Whichever the
textual stimulus for Machiavelli, in *Mandragola* the play's observation of
the unity of time is ostentatiously proclaimed by the corrupt priest
Timoteo at the beginning of the fifth act.[33] In the context of Livy's
theatrical treatment of the Lucretia story, Machiavelli's religious observ-
ance of the unity of time is both vestige and elaboration of the dramatic
tendencies in the historical text.

Finally, the Livian account of Sextus's violence against Lucretia is
framed in terms of his father Tarquinius Superbus's siege of Rutulian
Ardea; it is because the siege is stalled that Sextus and the other officers,
including Collatinus, fall to boasting of their wives' virtue, that "muliebris certamen" that leads directly to Sextus's fatal infatuation with
Lucretia.[34] The original context of the siege continues *as metaphor* through
Sextus's attack and defeat of Lucretia's virtue, justifying Livy's reference to
her loss of chastity with the formulaic term for the reduction of a city or
fortress: "expugnatum decus."[35] Livy's metaphor is hardly lost on
Machiavelli the student of military strategy and the psychologist of
human competition, and thus the action of *Mandragola* is more than once
conceived in the terms of a siege operation: the protagonists Callimaco
and Nicia bear the names of generals, one imaginary, one real; and the
terminology of assault and resistance appears in Callimaco's calculation of
Lucrezia's virtuous opposition to his desire ("mi fa la guerra la natura di lei

32. P. Ovidius Naso, *Die Fasten,* ed. Franz Böhmer (Heidelberg, 1957), vol. I, *Fasti*
II. 685-856. Ovid's emphasis on the nocturnal hour is noted by A. G. Lee, "Ovid's
Lucretia," in *Greece and Rome* (1953), pp. 115-117.

33. For discussion, see E. J. Webber, "The Dramatic Unities in the *Mandragola,*"
Italica, XXXIII, no. 1 (March 1956), 20-21, and C. S. Singleton, "Machiavelli and the
Spirit of Comedy," *MLN,* LVII (November 1942), 585-592.

34. *AUC,* I.57.3-6.

35. Compare "expugnato decus" of Lucretia's chastity with Livy's expression for the
expulsion of the Tarquins, I.59.2: "Ut praeceptum erat iurant; totique ab luctu versi in
iram, Brutum tam inde *ad expugnandum regnum* vocantem sequuntur ducem." Livy also
establishes a relation between the initial attempt of Tarquin's forces to seize Ardea by
storm—"temptata res est, si primo impetu *capi* Ardea posset" (I.57.3)—and Sextus's own
capture by the desire to rape Lucretia; "Ibi Sex. Tarquinium mala libido Lucretiae per vim
stuprandae *capit*" (I.57.20).

che è onestissima . . ." I.i., p. 62).[36] In the play's penultimate operation, the metaphor of siege is made comically explicit as Callimaco, disguised as the surrogate *garzonaccio,* is caught in the grip of a two-horned phalanx rallied to the cry of "San Cucù"—Saint Cuckoo. The disguised Callimaco, inserted into Lucrezia's bedroom, might be viewed as a sapper, a mine designed to "blow up" Lucrezia, the object of the play-as-siege.[37]

Machiavelli's borrowings from Livy the moralist, Livy the dramaturge, and Livy the poet and mythographer—drawing parallels between the chastity of a Roman matron and the integrity of the city—would give *Mandragola* a Livian cast even in the absence of more specific parallels with Livy's history. But specific parallels there are. Those that I will discuss immediately following are, with one major exception, known, though their implications for the interpretation of Machiavelli's text have remained largely unexplored. They are drawn from crucial junctures in Livy's episode and play correspondingly important roles in Machiavelli's comedy.

I

The first major parallel serves to link Sextus Tarquinius's mimetic desire for Roman Lucretia with Callimaco's for Lucrezia. The terminology of René Girard is strikingly appropriate to the triangle of Collatinus, Sextus, and Lucretia as Livy presents it.[38] Sextus conceives his desire for Lucretia *because* of her husband's ostentatious demonstration of her superior beauty and virtue. Because he desires to be the victor in the competi-

---

36. Callimaco's terms here for Lucrezia's chaste *natura* echo Machiavelli's twenty-fifth chapter of the *Principe*: "Io iudico bene questo, che sia meglio essere impetuoso che respettivo, perché la Fortuna è donna, et è necessario volendola tenere sotto, batterla e urtarla . . ."

37. The metaphor of Lucretia's virtue as a citadel is worked exhaustively in Shakespeare's *Rape of Lucrece,* vv. 221, 441, 465, 485-487, 723, 1172-1173.

38. For the mechanisms of mimetic desire and its role in ordering rivalry, cf. René Girard, *Violence and the Sacred,* trans. Patrick Gregory (Baltimore and London, 1975), esp. pp. 145, 169, 174-175. Girard gives a succinct definition on p. 145: "Rivalry does not arise because of the fortuitous convergence of two desires on a single object; rather, the subject desires the object because the rival desires it. In desiring an object the rival alerts the subject to the desirability of the object."

tion to decide whose is the most exemplary wife, Collatinus excites a rivalry that is only satisfied with Sextus's triumph over Collatinus's dearest possession, his wife:

Collatinus, pleased with his success, invited his friends to sup with him. It was at that fatal supper that Lucretia's beauty, and proven chastity, kindled in Sextus Tarquinius the flame of lust, and determined him to debauch her.

Thus Sextus desires Lucretia *because* she is chaste, *because* she belongs to another. And not merely any other. For Collatinus and Sextus are relatives; their rivalry echoes the archetypal fraternal rivalry stretching back in Roman history to the twins Romulus and Remus.[39] The web of consanguineous rivalry extends even to Brutus, himself related to both Collatinus and Sextus, though Brutus's response to Lucretia, though passionate, is more filial in its sexuality.

In *Mandragola,* Callimaco's desire for Lucrezia is instigated by the praises of another as well. And even more indirectly: Callimaco falls in love with a verbal report of Lucrezia's beauty given by Cammillo Calfucci, a relative of Nicia, Lucrezia's husband. That Callimaco has not yet seen Lucrezia when he falls in love with her is a result of literary history, which interposes between the model of Livy's history and *Mandragola* the rich medieval and Boccaccian examples of desire instigated by verbal report.[40] But these distinctions should not cloud the significance for Machiavelli's play of the fact that the desire of the seducer is stimulated in a context that is, immediately, that of masculine rivalry. As Callimaco notes in his opening soliloquy, the news of Lucrezia's beauty comes to him at the

---

39. The genealogical relationships of the Tarquins to Collatinus and Brutus are explained in detail in *Roman Antiquities,* vol. II, IV.64.1–4 and IV.68, 1-2 (pp. 473, 481). Boccaccio, in his *Commento alla divina commedia,* ed. D. Guerri (Bari, 1913) I, 54, recalls his lineage: "Bruto fu per legnaggio nobile uomo di Roma, perciochè egli fu d'una famiglia chiamata i Giuni, ed il suo nome fu Caio Giunio Bruto, e la madre di lui fu la sorella di Tarquino Superbo, re de' romani." Though Boccaccio's genealogy differs from Dionysus's (in fact makes much better sense), the point is maintained that Brutus is kin to the Tarquins.

40. The *vida* of the troubadour Jaufré Rudel, who falls in love with the countess of Tripoli by hearing reports of her beauty and grace, is the most famous example. (Cf. J. Boutière and A. H. Schutz, *Les biographies des troubadours* [Paris, 1964], pp. 16-17.) But Machiavelli's immediate examples are those of the *Decameron,* I,5; IV.4; VII.7.

instance of *Fortuna,* who thus disturbs an existence chiefly remarkable for its freedom from rivalries:

. . .I lived quietly pleasing everyone and taking pains to offend no one, so that I was accepted by the townspeople, by the gentlemen, by strangers, by the poor, by the rich . . . But when Fortune decided that I was having too easy a time of it, she ordered that one Cammillo Calfucci should arrive at Paris . . .

(I.1.61)

The excitement of sexual desire for Lucrezia deprives Callimaco of this tranquility and initiates him into the *certamen,* the competition of insatiable masculine desire, immediately provoked by the vehemence of Calfucci's praise, just as Collatinus's praise of Lucretia has excited Sextus:[41]

. . . he named madonna Lucrezia, wife of messer Nicia Calfucci, whose beauty and manners he praised so lavishly as to leave all astonished, and awakening in me such a desire to behold her that without further deliberation, and setting aside any consideration of war and peace in Italy, I set on coming here . . .

(I.1.61)

There are close incidental parallels to Livy in the above passage: Cammillo's excitement ("quasi che irato") recalls Collatinus's ardor in proclaiming his wife's virtue "certamine accenso";[42] Callimaco's indifference to the military situation between France and Italy echoes the abandonment of the stalled siege of Ardea by the soldiers and their transfer of interest to the "muliebris certamen." These minor parallels are significant especially in terms of the long-range effects of new passion on Callimaco. In a Machiavellian context, erotic passion, no less than political ambition, subjects its victim to the whims of Fortune—as Callimaco acknowledges—and plunges him into an uncertain world of risk. Though it is true that in the course of the play's action Callimaco, with considerable help from others, reaches his goal, there is more than one hint that

41. Machiavelli offers a pessimistic theory of competition in the *Discorsi,* I.37: "La cagione è, perchè la natura ha creato gli uomini in modo che possono desiderare ogni cosa e non possono conseguire ogni cosa: talchè essendo sempre maggiore il desiderio che la potenza dello acquistare, ne risulta la mala contentezza de quello che si possiede, e la poca sodisfazione d'esso."

42. *AUC,* I.57.7.

points to Callimaco as the plaything of Fortune. Callimaco's tedious
posturing, his Petrarchan protests of suicidal despair, mark him as a
victim of erotic furor, of the *aegritudo amoris* recognized as a disease since
the time of Hippocrates.[43] Moreover, if we look closely at the text, it is
apparent that Ligurio's objection, early in the play, to pursuing the
corruption of Lucrezia at the public baths because of the presence of other
suitors permits Machiavelli a sly acknowledgment of Callimaco's personal
mediocrity as well as a glance at the intrinsic instability of the enterprise
on which Callimaco has embarked.[44] As we shall see, these disturbing
possibilities implicit in Callimaco's project are realized at the play's conclusion. For the present, it may be recorded that the first principal parallel
with Livy's episode, describing the moment of the origin of desire and
thus the mainspring of the action, establishes the grounds for the ironic
subversion of Callimaco's erotic triumph, even as it provides the occasion
of tragedy in the Roman text. In the ferocious world of rivalry that
Machiavelli envisions as the stage of all public and private ambitions,
Callimaco's entry into the *certamen* for the favors of Lucrezia engages him
in a gamble which he cannot win, for in the slippery world of *Fortuna*,
triumph is the prologue of defeat. In Ovid's words: "Quid victor gaudes?
haec te victoria perdet."

By way of a corollary to the first major parallel to Livy, Machiavelli has
veined his text with unmistakable allusion to the Roman historian by
using the name of Cammillo Calfucci. Camillus, who saves Rome from
the Gauls, is the hero of Livy's first decade if there is one; Machiavelli

43. Radcliff-Umstead's strongly positive view of Callimaco (*The Birth of Modern Comedy in Renaissance Italy*, pp. 124-125) is, to this reader at least, exaggerated; Callimaco's
behavior and his dependence on Ligurio are reminiscent of Roderigo's simpering dependence on Iago in *Othello*.

44. Act I, scene 3 (p. 66): ". . . e potrebbe venirvi uomo a chi madonna Lucrezia
piacesse come a te, che fussi più ricco di te, che avesse più grazia di te; in modo che si porta
pericolo di non durare questa fatica per altri, e che intervenga che la copia dei concorrenti
la facciono più dura, o che dimesticandosi la si volga ad un altro e non a te." Callimaco's
willingness to seize any expedient ("per pigliare qualche partito bestiale, crudo, nefando,"
I.3 p. 67) is probably also an allusion to the resolution of Sextus—not Livy's Sextus, but
Ovid's in the *Fasti*, II.781 ff.: " 'exitus in dubio est, audebimus ultima!' dixit, / 'viderit!
audentes sorsque deusque iuvat.' "

remembers him generously and often in the *Discourses*.[45] It is Camillus who spends his exile from Rome precisely at Rutulian Ardea, the city besieged by Sextus and Collatinus—providing a topographic link between the story of Lucretia and the illustrious career of the savior of Rome.[46] Thus Cammillo Calfucci, Fortune's *agent provocateur* in Machiavelli's play, evokes a standard of political high seriousness against which the characters of the play, and their narrower concerns, will finally be judged.

To my knowledge, the second of the principal parallels I will discuss has not been noted in the literature on Machiavelli's *Mandragola*, though an ancillary source in a *novella* of Boccaccio has long been recognized.[47] The parallel is spread over two distinct episodes in the play. Preparing Callimaco for his placement inside Lucrezia's bedroom, Ligurio suggests that the lover persuade the wife to accept his suit by threatening to damage her reputation if she refuses: "dicale el bene le vuoi; e come sanza sua infamia la può essere tua amica, e con sua grande infamia tua nimica" (IV.iii.p.96). Ligurio's threat is a glancing but unmistakable echo of Livy's text, where it is Sextus's offer to destroy Lucretia's reputation that breaks her resistance to his lust:

But all in vain; not even the fear of death could bend her will. "If death will not move you," Sextus cried, "dishonor shall. I will kill you first, then cut the throat of a slave and lay his naked body by your side. Will they not believe that you have been caught in adultery with a servant—and paid the price?" Even the most resolute chastity could not have stood against this dreadful threat. Lucretia yielded. Sextus enjoyed her [*expugnato decore*], and rode away, proud of his success.[48]

---

45. For Camillus in the *Discorsi*: I.29, where he is juxtaposed to Consalvo Ferrante, the great Spanish soldier; II.23, where he is praised as an example of the rejection of the halfway measures in military and political decisions; II.2, cited in the text, where his exile to Ardea is an example of Fortune's manipulation of human events; III.23, on the reasons of Camillus's exile from Rome; III.30, where Camillus is remembered for his effective measures in the protection of Rome, and juxtaposed to the imprudence of both Savanarola and Soderini, who did not know how to manage the envy of their rivals.

46. *AUC*, V.44.

47. For the parallel with Boccaccio's story of Catella and Ricciardo Minutolo, *Decameron*, III.6, cf. Raimondi, pp. 180-181.

48. *AUC*, I.57.3-4.

Sextus shatters Lucretia's resistance by making of her greatest strength, her commitment to her reputation, a fatal weakness. It is the dilemma into which Sextus's threat forces her that necessitates her subsequent suicide, which, she maintains, can alone convincingly witness her innocence of any complicity with Sextus. Sextus's threat is thus the precise weapon that batters down the fortress of Lucretia's chastity and prepares the tragedy that ensues.

The echo of Sextus's proposal in Ligurio's coaching of Callimaco disappears from the report that Callimaco gives in the last act, after his success with Lucrezia. But Callimaco does relate Lucrezia's own testimony as to the accumulation of causes that forced her to yield to her lover. The passage is therefore functionally parallel to the moment where Roman Lucretia realizes that she must succumb to Sextus if she is to preserve her reputation:

Given that your cleverness, the stupidity of my husband, the simple-mindedness of my mother, and the unscrupulousness of my confessor have led me to do what I should never have done on my own, I judge [*voglio iudicare*] that all this results from a heavenly command that has so wished it . . .

(V.iv.109)

Lucrezia's enumeration and evaluation of causes here is important for several reasons: it reiterates a pattern often used in the play (indeed a pattern favored by Machiavelli in his analytical works), from the *dramatis personae* in the authorial *canzone* ("uno amante meschino / un dottor poco astuto, / un frate mal vissuto," etc., vv. 40-43, p. 57) to the rhetorical schemes adopted during the course of the play by Callimaco, Liurio, and Timoteo. Ligurio's version is the most succinct, as he argues regarding the possibility of corrupting the priest Timoteo:

CALLIMACO
Who will persuade the confessor?
LIGURIO
You, me, and money; our wickedness—and theirs.

(II.vi.77)

In effect, Lucrezia's list retrospectively reflects the plot of the play, which, under Ligurio's direction, has pitted the combined efforts of parasite, lover, husband, mother, and confessor against the resistance of Lucrezia's chastity. Significantly, however, the forces Lucrezia enumerates as acting upon her are not so much powers as defects—with the exception of *astuzia*, which is not Callimaco's in this case but Ligurio's. Where, in Livy's account, Lucretia is broken by the terror of infamy and Sextus's *victrix libido*, Florentine Lucrezia is constrained by *simplicità, tristizia*, and *sciochezza*. There is a calculated degradation in the nature of the forces that impinge on the chastity of Lucrezia, the cynosure; she succumbs not to violence but to cumulative, circumambient corruption.

Lucrezia's decision to accept Callimaco's offer entails her will alone, for her body has by then been conceded to the supposed *garzonaccio*, the surrogate who is to absorb the toxic properties of the *mandragola*. The distinction of mind and body is pertinent to the third of the principal parallels, noted recently by Ezio Raimondi.[49] In Livy's text, Lucretia's husband and father remind her that since she has not consented to Tarquin's violence willingly her mind remains free of guilt. This Lucretia concedes, without however exempting herself from punishment: "ego me etsi peccare absolvo . . . supplicio non libero" (I.57.9-10).[50] In *Mandragola* it is frate Timoteo who attempts to persuade Lucrezia that

Now that the act is a sin is nonsense, because it is the will that sins and not the body. And the cause of sin lies in displeasing the husband, but you please him; in enjoying pleasure, but you are displeased.

(IV.ii.89)

The distinction drawn here focuses its irony on the passage discussed in the previous major parallel. Callimaco's proposal of love requires not the physical submission of Lucrezia, but the full complicity of her will. On the face of it, this consent is fully granted to the lover. Lucrezia, continuing her account of why she surrenders to Callimaco's offer, appears to place herself entirely in Callimaco's hands:

49. See Raimondi, *Politica e Commedia*, pp. 202-203.
50. Boccaccio's version of the tragedy in his *De claris mulieribus* emphasizes Lucretia's motive in preserving her life so as to proclaim her innocence, "Fearing that if she died there would be no one to avenge her innocence, she unwillingly gave her body to the adulterer," trans. in Guido Guarino, *Concerning Famous Women* (New Brunswick, N.J., 1964), p. 102.

. . . I am not strong enough to refuse what heaven wishes me to accept. Therefore I take you as lord, master, guide: I wish that you be my father, my defender,
and my entire good: and what my husband has wanted for a single evening, I
wish him to possess forever. You will become his godfellow; you will come to
church, and from there you will come to breakfast with us . . .

(IV.iv.109)

Whether we choose to interpret Lucrezia's surrender to Callimaco's offer as
the fabliau-inspired victory of a *mal mariée,* or as the index of the corruption of the Florentine civic body, there can be no doubt that Lucrezia here
submits to Callimaco and comes to will what he wills. But the imperious
tone of the future tenses at the conclusion of the passage above also
suggests that Lucrezia's will, though placed under Callimaco's rule, has
taken on a very lively willfulness of its own—a crucial point to which I
shall return at the conclusion of my argument.

The three Livian parallels with *Mandragola* outlined above are central to
the development of Machiavelli's plot: one concerns the moment of Callimaco's embarcation on the slippery paths of desire and *Fortuna;* one the
etiology of Lucrezia's fateful submission to her seducer; one the ironically
pregnant fullness of her sudden complicity with Callimaco's desires.
Taken together, these three junctures profile Machiavelli's transformation
of Livy's episode of ritual, cathartic violence into a sly and cynical fable of
bourgeois accommodation and civic corruption. The defection of
Florentine Lucrezia from the example of heroic resistance and self-sacrifice
established by Roman Lucretia is the more striking because it had been
the explicit *purpose* of the Roman heroine to set an example of severity and
self-discipline for the benefit of future generations of free Romans: "nec
ulla deinde impudica Lucretiae exemplo vivet" (I.57.10). The seduction
of Florentine Lucrezia therefore marks a failure of the "antica virtù" to
maintain itself in the Florence of *Mandragola.* With the fall of Lucrezia,
cynosure of the play's intrigue and last surviving spark of ancient virtue,
the corruption of the present age advertised in the play's prologue appears
fully demonstrated.[51]

___

51. Consider a passage like *Discorsi* II, *proemio,* referring to the current conditions of
Italy: "perchè in questi (tempi) non è cosa alcuna che gli ricomperi da ogni estrema
miseria, infamia e vituperio, dove non è osservanza di religione, non di leggi, non di
milizia, ma sono maculati d'ogni ragione bruttura . . ."

II

Yet the most significant parallels between the text of Livy and that of Machiavelli remain to be discussed. These concern the *results* of Lucretia's suicide at Rome and of Lucrezia's submission at Florence. The last act of Machiavelli's comedy is by common consent a tour de force of comic harmony; the ambitions, however questionable, of all the principal characters are stunningly reconciled. Nicia anticipates an heir; Callimaco possesses his Lucrezia, Timoteo may look forward to alms, "grascia" for good works, Sostrata will be cared for in her dotage, while Ligurio, the chief architect of the successful conspiracy, earns his *pappo,* his free meals at Nicia's expense. The felicitous cooperation of flagrant self-interest diagrams a proleptic Hobbesian utopia, and few critics have resisted applauding the compelling, amoral joy that Machiavelli's sleight-of-hand provides.[52] Moreover, as Raimondi has noted, the final scene of the play is rich in references to both carnival festivity and Christian ritual, to the fulfillment of cyclical patterns of rebirth that Northrop Frye has termed the fundamental argument of comedy.[53]

Some form of rejuvenation is attributed to most of the characters: Nicia is to be reborn through his "figlio maschio," his male offspring ("Tu mi ricrei tutto quanto. Fia egli maschio?" III.8.p.86) though he starts to swell and blossom with self-regard well beforehand: "io paro maggiore, più giovane, più scarzo . . ." (IV.viii.p.101). Callimaco, in turn, must repeatedly be pulled back from the brink of suicide by Ligurio's stratagems, termed *rimedi* ("tu mi risusciti," I.iii.p.68), though such expressions often go no further than the stock gestures of Latin comedy.[54] More significant language is found in the play's final scene, as Timoteo observes to Sostrata that, in becoming a grandmother, she has "sprouted a

52. Leo Strauss, *Thoughts on Machiavelli* (Glencoe, Ill., 1958), pp. 284-286.

53. Raimondi, *Politica e Commedia,* pp. 214-216, 264; Aquilecchia, p. 99, n. 43. Lucrezia's remark (III.10, p. 88) "io sudo per la passione" and the chalicelike "bicchiere d'argento" (IV.3, p. 96) in which the potion of *mandragola* is administered infuse the lady's sacrifice of her body (as well as the "ordeal" of the *garzonaccio*) with parodic allusion to the Passion.

54. See, for example, Machiavelli's translation of Terence's *Andria,* II.i (ed. Gaeta, p. 16): "Tu mi hai risuscitato . . ."

new shoot on the old stock" ("messo un tallo in sul vecchio,"
V.vi.p.112).[55] In context, the remark works as a sly reference to the
insertion of a vigorous young breeding male in the household of the sterile
Nicia, a graft that promises to rejuvenate the declining house of
Calfucci.[56]

But the one rejuvenescence that makes all the others possible is, of
course, that of Lucrezia, who is marvelously refreshed, indeed transformed, by her night with Callimaco. "Gli è proprio, stamane, come se tu
rinascessi," Nicia announces with delight, marveling at Lucrezia's vivac-
ity ("tu sei molto ardita") where previous to her night with the *garzonaccio*
she had seemed half dead, "mezza morta." Most telling of all, Nicia
invokes one of the notoriously phallic totems of carnival to describe his
re-energized wife: "La pare un gallo."[57] In terms of the carnival humor
that pervades the last act of the play, the immediate reasons for Lucrezia's
revival are clear. The same *materia medica* that teaches Callimaco, disguised as a Parisian doctor, to analyze Lucrezia's *segno* (urine sample) as
cruda for lack of proper covering ("mal coperta")—technically speaking,
for lack of the proper decoction of the menses by the heat of male seed—
would reveal that a night of normal, healthy intercourse has purged
Lucrezia of the noxious humors accumulated due to Nicia's neglect of his
marital duties.[58] Lucrezia, with Callimaco's aid, has literally undergone a
healthful purge—a *catharsis*.[59]

55. The expression "un bel tallo" refers to the phallus in the fifteenth century "canto
carnascialesco" known as the "canzona degli ortolani." See C. S. Singleton, ed., *Canti
carnascialeschi del rinascimento* (Bari, 1936), p. 5.

56. The idea of the rejuvenation of the house of Calfucci should be viewed against the
background of Dante's remark, through Cacciaguida, that the Calfucci had become extinct
by Dante's day (*Paradiso*, 16.106). An undercurrent of futility, as well as folly, veins
Nicia's ambitions.

57. For the rooster as a symbol of fertility associated with carnival, see Emmanuel le
Roy Ladurie, *Carnival in Romans*, trans. Mary Feeney (New York, 1980), p. 323. See also
Paolo Toschi, *Le origini del teatro italiano* (Turin, 1955), p. 139.

58. For the ultimate authority on the operation of the semen on the female blood in
the *matrix*, cf. Aristotle's *Generation of Animals*, I.xx (729a10); II.iv (739b20); IV.iv.
(772a20).

59. On female purgations analogous to pollution among men, see the remarks of
Trotula of Salerno, *The Diseases of Women*, trans. Elizabeth Mason-Hohl (Los Angeles,
1940), pp. 1-3. Machiavelli uses the idea of a purge in *Discorsi*, II.v, for the historical
upheavals that obliterate civilizations: ". . . conviene di necessità che il mondo si purghi
per uno de' tre mod. . ."

Despite the rich Saturnalian flavor of the final act, it is important to emphasize that the play's festive rejuvenescence, as well as the sexual themes that pervade the action, are linked to the political outcome of Lucrezia's rape and suicide in Livy's history.[60] Livy's episode has a ritual function in Roman history as the first great conjuncture of the Roman constitution, a climacteric in the maturation of the Roman citizenry.[61] Placed strategically at the end of the first book of the *ab urbe condita,* Lucretia's suicide precipitates a chain of events that leads to the expulsion of the kings and the establishment of a republic; indeed, Livy, and the writers that follow him—including Boccaccio and Petrarch—are explicit in noting that it is precisely because of Lucretia's tragedy that Rome is re-founded as a republic.[62] The crucial turn of events begins when Lucius Junius Tarquinius Brutus, disguised as a simpleton in order to survive the tyranny of Tarquinius Superbus, jumps forward as Lucretia falls and draws the knife from her body. Since the passage is central to my argument, I quote at some length:

Her father and husband were overwhelmed with grief. While they stood weeping helplessly, Brutus drew the bloody knife from Lucretia's body, and holding it before him cried: "By this girl's blood—none more chaste till a tyrant wronged her—and by the gods, I swear that with sword and fire, and whatever else can lend strength to my arm, I will pursue Lucius Tarquinius the Proud, his wicked wife, and all his children, and never again will I let them or any other man be King in Rome."[63]

60. The carnival aspect of the play must not be underestimated. In addition to those carnival elements underlined by Raimondi (p. 215) and Toschi (pp. 12, 306-307) the *Mandragola* is set—if Ridolfi's deductions are correct—in late January or February, which is carnival time. In Machiavelli's day plays like *Mandragola* were conventionally staged during carnival festivities, whether their subject had any explicit link with carnival or not (Machiavelli's *Clizia,* for example, is set during carnival: "Ed è pur carnesciale," II.3., ed. Gaeta, p. 129).

61. Livy's description explicitly identifies the event with the pubescence, so to speak, of Rome as a political entity: "Dissipatae res nondum adultae discordia forent, quas fovit tranquilla moderatio imperii eoque nutriendo perduxit ut bonam frugem libertatis maturis iam viribus ferre possent" (*AUC,* II.i.6).

62. See note 21 above and the text, pp. 000-000. In the *Africa* (ed. N. Festa, [Florence, 1926]), III.651-802, Petrarch relates the story of Lucretia's suicide as the occasion that sparked the expulsion of the kings ("causa novande," 1.651); cf. also Cicero, *De finibus bonorum et malorum,* II.66: "Stuprata per vim Lucretia a regis filio testata cives se ipsa interemit. Hic dolor populi Romani, duce et autore Bruto, causa civitati libertatis fuit, ob eiusque mulieris memoriam primo anno et vir et pater eius consul est factus."

63. *AUC,* I.58.12-59.2.

The vehemence of Brutus's oath, and the miracle of his sudden, albeit artificial, transformation ignite the others, who follow their new leader in swearing an oath; led by Brutus, they raise a tumult that frightens Tarquin from Rome. These results have been predisposed by Lucretia herself, who before her suicide challenges the men of her household to avenge her if they are men enough, "si vos viri estis." Her challenge, and Brutus's response, have the effect of galvanizing the passive, grief-stricken men (cf. "luctu occupatis") into citizens worthy of political independence.[64] Lucretia provides Brutus not merely with the perfect opportunity for his sudden and dramatic self-manifestation as *liberator*;[65] she also provides the *culter*, the knife symbolic of the *virga* of power, flowing ("manatem cruore") with her generous blood, which Brutus seizes and passes to the others, joining them in a fraternal conspiracy of *liberi*.[66] Armed with her strength, they expunge the tyranny in retaliation for the expunction of her chastity. Lucretia's role is that of scapegoat, the *pharmakos* who assumes the virulence and opprobrium of the tyrant in her own person by literally incorporating his seed. Killing herself, she expiates her defilement and becomes (as in the later practice of *devotio*) an instrument for the renewal of Rome.[67] In addition, if she is herself the sacrificial victim, her blood—whose defilement by the "regia iniuria" is punctiliously mentioned by Brutus—is a *pharmakon*, a remedy both virulent with the tyrant's seed and virtuous because of Lucretia's sacrifice.[68] Touching it as it flows from the

64. As Ogilvy notes (p. 228), the fact that the Romans are described in Livy's text as "opifices ac lapicidas" (*AUC*, I.59.9) means that they were like slaves. That Spurius Lucretius, Lucretia's father, and Collatinus are overcome with grief implies that they have been unmanned; the effect is made more strongly in Ovid, *Fasti*, II.835-836: "ecce, super corpus communia damna gementes / obliti decoris virque paterque iacent."

65. For Machiavelli's concern with the importance of correct timing, "occasione," see *Il principe*, vi. See also *Discorsi*, II.29; for discussion, Gilbert, p. 159.

66. Cf. Ovid, *Fasti*, II.839: "stillanteque tenens generoso sanguine cultrum"; Petrarch, *Africa*, III.740-741: "Ille cruentum / Fervidus educens spumanti vulnere ferrum."

67. Ogilvy notes that the story of Lucretia is based on Greek stories including accounts of the expulsion of the Peisistratids. Recently, the function of the *pharmakos* in *Oedipus Rex* has been studied with brilliant results by J. P. Vernant, "Ambiguité e renversement; sur la structure enigmatique de "*Oedipe-Roi*," in *Echanges et communications: Mélanges offertes à Claude Lévi-Strauss* (Mouton, 1970); see also Girard, *Violence*, pp. 108-109.

68. Both the nourishing and medicinal or lustral aspects of Lucretia's blood (and its pollution by the seducer) are strongly implicit in the accounts; Ovid's "generoso sanguine"

phallic *culter,* the conspirators, wailing with effeminate grief, regain the masculine *virtù* that tyranny had stripped from them.

That Lucretia's power is, at the moment of her death, that of the phallus is unmistakable if Livy's passage is scrutinized.[69] Subsequent versions of the story, modeled on Livy's render more nearly explicit the sense in which Lucretia, through her heroic act, becomes masculine. Thus Ovid, in the *Fasti,* refers to her as "matrona virilis animo," a phrase echoed by Valerius Maximus, who makes Lucretia the chief (*dux*) of Roman chastity and ventures that her soul, truly virile, was misplaced in a woman's body by an error of Fortune: "Dux Romanae pudicitiae Lucretia, cuius virilis animus maligno errore fortunae muliebre corpus sortitus est . . ."[70] Ovid, too (though not Livy), gives to Lucretia the gesture of modesty at the moment of death attributed to the murdered Caesar, who fell so as to prevent any possibility of exposing himself.[71] And Livy's own description of Lucretia's fall—"prolapsa in vulnus moribunda cecidit"— echoes the fall of male heroes on the epic battlefield.[72] More significant still is the fact that Lucretia's insistence on exacting the full penalty for her minimal complicity with Sextus provides an example of that unyielding respect for the law that Machiavelli—among others—admired among

---

(*Fasti,* II.839) and "fortem castumque cruorem" are expressive of the enhancement of Lucretia's virility precisely because of her rape by the virulent Sextus. The idea is taken to its extreme form in Shakespeare's *Lucrece,* where Lucretia's blood separates: "Some of the blood still pure and red remained / And some looked black, and that false Tarquin stained" (vv. 1742-1743). For a brilliant dissection of *pharmakon* as a radically ambiguous term in Plato's language, see J. Derrida, "La pharmacie de Platon," in *La dissémination* (Paris, 1972), pp. 69-197.

69. The spotlight on the *culter* as phallic is in evidence from the point where Sextus enters armed into Lucretia's room ("stricto gladio," I.58.2; "ferrum in manu est," I.58.2) and continues when Lucretia draws her knife from beneath her garments ("Cultrum, quem sub veste abditum habebat . . . " I.58.11). Again, it is in Shakespeare's *Lucrece* that the phallic imagery becomes pervasive; cf. vv. 359, 364, 505, 1843 (364: ". . . at the mercy of his mortal sting").

70. Valerius Maximus, *Dicta et facta memorabilia,* ed. C. Kempf (Leipzig, 1888), VI.1 (p. 271).

71. *Fasti,* II. 830-831. See also Ogilvy's note to I.59.1, p. 226.

72. For example, the death of Pallas in the *Aeneid* (itself imitating Homer) X.486-489.

the Romans of the republican period.[73] Lucretia's act establishes the rigor of the law as above any and all circumstantial mitigation. It is thus no accident that Brutus, who is in a sense both Lucretia's final lover and her true spiritual offspring, is remembered by Machiavelli for his willingness to sacrifice his own sons to the rigor of the law when they conspire to return kings to Rome.[74] Because she establishes the primacy of law, because she reinvests Roman manhood with their lost phallic virtue, Lucretia is a true founder of the city, *urbis conditrix*, justly ranked in that small class of lawgivers and city-founders Machiavelli admired above all other persons.[75] *Contra* Augustine, who chops logic in dismissing the virtue of Lucretia's act in the *City of God*, Lucretia's exemplary demonstration of inflexible adherence to a draconian law for the sake of the future republic is not a private act of escape from shame but a public ritual, a sacrifice.

Another, related dimension of Lucretia's suicide must be mentioned at this point. I suggested earlier that Sextus's threat to dishonor Lucretia's memory—and Lucretia's submission to that threat—necessitate her suicide. Her death both punishes her justifiable moment of weakness in yielding physically to Sextus at all and frees her memory from any taint of blame in so doing. As the early Christian fathers (and, much later, Boccaccio), recall the event, Lucretia's suicide is lustral, washing her soul clean of Tarquin's lust and of any doubts regarding her own complicity.[76] Because Lucrezia's resolution and courage are described by Roman writers as virile, her suicide appears as a victory not only over her shame, but over her female nature. Thus, Livy's account of Tarquin's entrance into Lucretia's chamber stresses her physical vulnerability before the rapist:

Lucretia opened her eyes in terror; death was imminent, no help at hand. Sextus

73. Passages include *Discorsi*, I.1; I.11; I.18; I.23, III.22.

74. *Discorsi*, III.3.

75. "Discourse on reforming the government of Florence," in *The Prince and Other Works*, trans. Allan Gilbert (New York, 1941), p. 91: "In addition to this, no man is so much raised on high by any of his acts as are those who have reformed republics and kingdoms with new laws and institutions."

76. Jerome, *Adversus Jovinianum* I.46 (PL 23.287). See also Boccaccio, *Concerning Famous Women*, p. 103: "she cleansed her shame harshly."

urged his love, begged her to submit, pleaded, threatened, used every weapon that might conquer a woman's heart [*versare in omnes partes muliebrem animum*].[77]

The fear of loss of reputation vanquishes her resistance, and Tarquin's lust, significantly a feminine noun, emerges the victor (*victrix*):

Quo terrore cum vicisset obstinatum pudicitiam velut victrix libido . . .

The subsequent heroic, virile behavior of Lucretia marks the transformation that has taken place since the rape—indeed, because of the rape, for Lucretia's body transforms the virulent seed of the Tarquins into the force that restores the Romans—and the sense in which Lucretia's suicide, a typically masculine gesture in Roman culture, signifies her triumph over the feminine debility that necessitated her physical submission to Sextus.

The episode of Lucretia's suicide and its effect on Lucius Brutus and Rome is often alluded to in Machiavelli's *Discourses*.[78] It is discussed most extensively at the beginning of the third book, where Brutus's opportunism in seizing the moment offered by Lucretia's suicide is singled out for special praise:

. . . when on the occasion of the death of Lucretia, in the midst of the father, husband, and other relatives, he was the first to pluck the dagger from her breast and to make all present swear henceforth to suffer no king to reign in Rome.

(III.2)

In the following chapter, Brutus's severity in condemning his own sons for conspiring against the republic is also praised. The discussion of Brutus's merits takes place in the context of the thesis that opens the third

77. Ovid's version links Lucretia's physical vulnerability to Sextus with psychological vulnerability stemming from fear of dishonor: "quid faciat? pugnet? vincentur femina pugnans" (*Fasti*, II.801); "succumbit famae victa puella metu" (II.810). In *Discorsi*, I.19 Machiavelli points to the need for the successive kings of Rome to return periodically to the Romulean virtue of the city's foundation in order to prevent the onset of "effeminacy": "era bene poi necessario che gli altri re ripigliassero la virtù di Romolo, altrimenti quella città sarebbe diventata effeminata."

78. See I.3; I.9; I.16; I.17; I.25; I.28; I.58. The examples of the expulsion of Tarquin and the life of Camillus are in fact among the most frequently cited in the *Discorsi*.

book of the *Discourses*. The principle is elaborated in the medical terminology that Machiavelli uses following Livy's diagnoses in the histories:[79]

. . . and the means of renewing them is to bring them back to their original principles. For, as all religious republics and monarchies must have within themselves some goodness, by means of which they obtain their first growth and reputation, and as in the process of time this goodness becomes corrupted, it will of necessity destroy the body unless something intervenes to bring it back to its normal condition. Thus, the doctors of medicine say, in speaking of the human body, that "every day some ill humors gather which must be cured."

(III. 1)

In the context of the pathology of the civic body as Machiavelli presents it in the third book of the *Discourses*, the analysis of Lucretia's suicide as a remedy, a *pharmakon* that buys the health of the state and returns Rome to the pristine, virile origins of Romulus and Numa appears consistent with both the political and metaphoric dimensions of Machiavelli's thought.[80] But even after putting the suicide of Lucretia in the context of the political pharmacopoeia of the *Discourses*, and noting the continuity of medical terminology uniting the *Discourses* and *Mandragola*, we may well ask how the episode of Lucretia as an etiology of the republic can be translated into the narrower, bourgeois world of Machiavelli's comedy.

First, the function in Machiavelli's political typology of Lucretia's suicide as the opportunity for Brutus to return Rome to its principles informs Machiavelli's insertion of political details in *Mandragola*. As noted before, the date of action is placed in 1504, ten years after the invasion by Charles VIII that initiated the ruin of Italy but also provoked the restoration of republican rule to Florence. Thus, by the end of the date of the play's action, Florence had been a republic for a decade, exactly one

79. References to the sickness and health of the body politic are abundant in Machiavelli's text; cf. *Discorsi*, I.4: "e sono in ogni republica due umori diversi"; I.7; I.17: "e che quella corruzione che era in loro si fosse cominciata ad istendere per le membra, come le membra fossero state corrote era impossibile mai più riformarla"; II.1; II.5; II.30; III.49.

80. For the process of corruption in the civic body, see J.A.G. Pocock, *Machiavellian Moment* pp. 203-211. On the intrinsic difficulties of restoring a corrupted city, see *Discorsi*, I.17-18. See also Raimondi, p. 153.

of the intervals Machiavelli, in the *Discourses,* recommends might separate attempts to return the state to its principles after inevitable corruption:

> It would be desirable therefore that not more than ten years should elapse between such executions, for in the long course of time men begin to change their customs, and to transgress the laws; and unless some case occurs that recalls the punishment to their memory and revives the fear in their hearts, the delinquents will soon become so numerous that they cannot be punished without danger.
>
> (III. 1)

Lest the common interval of ten years appear too general to establish the parallel between *Mandragola* and the *Discourses,* it may also be noted that the relation between the invasions of the French armies and the invasion of the Gauls in early Roman history (like Lucretia's suicide, the event shocked the Romans into undertaking constitutional reforms) is made explicitly by Machiavelli, again in the *Discourses.* In Machiavelli's own terms, then, historical Florence, ruled by the complacent Pier Soderini and the *Otto di balia* is, or rather might have been, ripe for a constitutional crisis that would benefit the health of the republic.[81] That no such crisis is precipitated—that, in fact, the parallel of Roman and Florentine history invoked by Lucrezia's name is defective—is precisely the point: the intrigue of Callimaco and Lucrezia occurs not in a heroic political context uniting ancient Rome and modern Florence, but rather in the indigenously Florentine world of the Boccaccian bourgeois *novella,* the world of the ingenious trick, the *beffa.*[82] As Machiavelli argues in the *Discourses,* if the corruption of the citizenry proceeds too far the opportunity to "riprendere lo stato" and return it to its principles is irretriev-

---

81. *Discorsi,* III.43 and I.56. In Machiavelli's view Florence was faced with a historical obstacle to maintaining its freedoms because of its former servitude to Rome; see *Discorsi,* I.49 and II.1, for the harm to citizenship caused by servitude.

82. Machiavelli's debts to the *novelle* of Boccaccio are well established; for some inventories see Russo, *La commedia,* pp. 26-39, and Raimondi, pp. 180-181. For Machiavelli, Boccaccio's masterpiece suggests a world of bourgeois mercantilism which the "antica virtù" of the Romans—who played off private interest against public need—cannot penetrate. The political tragedy of Renaissance Florence, incapable of regaining the virtue of a true republic, is played out in the struggle between the Livian *fabula* of Lucretia and the Boccaccian register of the *beffa.*

ably lost.[83] The very transformation of literary genre from Livy's narrative tragedy to Lucretia to Machiavelli's *beffa*-inspired comedy is eloquent testimony of Machiavelli's typology of historical cycles at work: in *Mandragola*, an economy of seduction and accommodation replaces the catharsis of heroic violence in ancient Rome; the *virtù* that stood in Lucretia's suicide falls with Lucrezia's submission to the suffocating alliance of *astuzia, sciochezza, semplicità,* and *tristizia.*[84]

Second, just as Lucretia's suicide and its effects stage the foundation of a new community bound by her virile blood, Ligurio's plot in the comedy binds Timoteo, Nicia, Callimaco, Sostrata—and finally Lucrezia herself—in a new community based not on the austere rigor of the law but, rather, on the programmatic corruption of the civic role of each member. Early in the play we see Ligurio the parasite, Timoteo the corruptible priest, and Callimaco, the comically ruinous lover, conspicuously pledging their questionable faith to one another.[85] The allegiance is not merely the routine complicity of Latin comedy. In a unique moment of professed emotion, Ligurio, the social parasite, acknowledges an intimate fraternal kinship with his client, Callimaco: "il tuo sangue si affà col mio" (I.ii.p.67). The utterance has sinister portent if we compare the words of Ligurio's other chief conspirator, Timoteo, reflecting on his own seduction by the parasite: "This devil of Ligurio presented himself to me, and made me dip (*intignere*) my finger into a fault, where I've since place my arm and my whole body" (IV.vi.99). No reader of the Latin Bible can fail to hear the priest's allusion here to the possession of Judas by the demon and to Christ's pronouncement that one who dipped his bread in the dish with him would betray him: "Qui intingit mecum manum in paropside" (Matt. 26:23). Ligurio's elegant plot to seduce Lucrezia, which depends on the corruption of each conspirator for its success, is the model of a community where the characteristic act is betrayal.

The socially microcosmic nature of the community of conspirators has often been remarked; Sumberg in particular has noted the constitutive

83. Cf. *Discorsi,* I.17-18, and Pocock, pp. 203-211.

84. For Machiavelli's view of the usefulness of state violence in restraining the corruption of the populace, cf. *Discorsi,* II.2. On the function of decimations of the army, cf. *Discorsi,* III.49; see also Raimondi, p. 156.

85. I.3 (p.67): "non dubitar della fede mia" (Ligurio); III.6 (p. 85): "parmi avere contratta tele dimestichezza che non è cosa che io non facessi" (Timoteo).

role of the pseudo-betrothal—the *parentado,* as Timoteo jokes—that will unite Callimaco and Lucrezia in holy adultery.[86] The play's final procession to the church of the Servi, the sacred space embracing the typical collectivity of Christian Europe, on a day that, given the reference to Lucrezia's *puerpere* or purification, may well be the Feast of the Purification of the Virgin (Feb. 2), strongly reinforces the notion that the six characters, destined to collaborate in the formation of a most unusual household, are also the nucleus of a new community: *Mandragola,* like Livy's story of Lucretia, is an etiological fable.[87]

The new community, by Machiavelli's standards in the *Discourses,* is utterly corrupt. The behavior of the principal characters systematically displays an inventory of violations of civil and canon law and traditional piety. Nicia, the *paterfamilias* (!), accepts the certainty that a fellow citizen will die on his behalf, though he has qualms about the possibility of getting caught;[88] he stands just at the point where the threat of punishment provided by the laws no longer represses criminal behavior.[89] As far as Timoteo is concerned, even in Machiavelli's supposedly skeptical terms the pliable priest undermines the legitimate social authority of the

---

86. The idea of the play as descriptive of the establishment of a community is suggested as well by allusions to the epoch of the biblical patriarchs: Timoteo's reference to the daughters of Lot (III. 11, p. 89) and to the sterility of Rachel (who therefore requested mandrakes, cf. Gen: 30, 1-16) supplement Machiavelli's references to the antiquities of Rome. Compare for example Callimaco's mention of Nicia's desire for children (I.l, p. 63: "hanno un desiderio che muoiono") with Rachel's plea in Gen. 30:1: "Da mihi liberos, alioquin moriar."

87. V.2. The "washing" of Lucrezia and her reconsecration are usually the consequences of an actual parturition, not of a night of love. Nicia's anticipation of the ceremony continues the theme of Lucrezia's (and his) delivery from the toxic *mandragola.*

88. Cf. Nicia's extreme fear of the "Otto di balia" (II.6 p. 77-78). In Machiavelli's terms Nicia's corruption resides not so much in his callousness as in his willingness to let another engage in a dangerous enterprise in his stead and on his behalf; cf. Pocock, p. 204, where it is pointed out that for Machiavelli the model of public irresponsibility is the hiring of mercenaries.

89. *Discorsi,* I. 11-14. "Perchè dove manca *il timore di Dio,* conviene o che quel regno rovini o che sia sostenuto dal timore d'uno principe che sopperisca a' difetti della religione" (I.11). It is precisely such a "mancanza di divozione" that Timoteo (whose name recalls "timore di Dio) laments in the fifth act (p. 105). As Pocock notes (p. 192) "a substructure of religion is a prerequisite of civic virtue."

church—affirmed unambiguously in the first book of the *Discourses*—by violating the privileges of the confessional: "E si maravigliano poi se la divozione manca." Both Sostrata and Nicia cheerfully prostitute a virtuous wife in order to guarantee the legal and economic security that follows from having male heirs.

The principle in the name of which the characters engage in fundamentally antisocial acts is stridently inscribed in the *cognome* of Callimaco himself: *Guadagni*. Machiavelli, who draws from Dante's *Commedia* the family name of Nicia and Cammillo Calfucci (cf. *Paradiso* 16.106) has also remembered the poet's excoriation of the Florentine *nouveau riche* in the *Inferno*:

> La gente nova e i subiti guadagni
> orgoglio e dismisura han generate
> Fiorenza, in te . . .[90]

As Machiavelli writes in the *Discourses,* the pursuit of private gain at the expense of public good is one of the maladies that can afflict and destroy a republic.[91] So noxious is wealth to civic virtue, he argues, that it were better that the citizenry of a republic were kept poor so as to corrupt neither others nor themselves:

The cause of this is manifest, for it is not individual prosperity, but the general good, that makes cities great . . .

(II.2)

We have argued elsewhere that it is of the greatest advantage in a republic to have laws that keep her citizens poor.

(III.25)

By contrast, the characters of *Mandragola*—Nicia, Callimaco, even Sostrata—are explicitly prosperous. It is Nicia's great private wealth, and his desire to maintain it as such, that spurs him to desire the personal inconvenience of children:

90. Note Ligurio's instruction of Callimaco at IV.2 (p.96): "tu te la guadagni."
91. For Machiavelli's analysis of the effects of *acquistare* and *guadagno* on the political virtue of citizens, cf. *Discorsi,* I.5; II.i; II.30. For discussion, cf. Gilbert, pp. 175-176, 189.

. . . for having been married six years and not having had any children, the desire that both he and she have of having some—since they're very rich—is practically killing them.

(I.1.63)

Finally, as I have already suggested above, Machiavelli's metaphor for the health and corruption of the political bodies is a traditional one: that of the human body.[92] In this respect—whatever other models he may have consulted—one principal source is Livy's history, where the preface draws on the metaphor and whose first pentad includes the most important Roman instance of the metaphor, the speech of Menenius Agrippa familiar to all students of Shakespeare's *Coriolanus*.[93] In different ways, Machiavelli's echoes Livy's poem and its metaphor of the body in the prefatory chapters to all three books of the *Discourses*.[94] The importance of the metaphor of the body for *Mandragola,* whose title describes a remedy for sterility, can hardly be overstated. In addition to what is explicitly medical in the play—Callimaco's disguise as a Parisian physician and the gynecological and pharmaceutical lore that he spouts—the medical lexicon that operates in the play is directly linked to the relationship between Roman Lucretia as *pharmakos/pharmakon* for the Roman state and the rejuvenation of the characters in the comedy, especially Madonna Lucrezia herself. In Livy, the passage of the bloody knife, the *virga* of power, to Brutus and the other conspirators initiates the resurgence of Rome; in *Mandragola,* Lucrezia's restoration is attributed to the superior sexual potency ("iacitura") of Callimaco. At the same time, however, the collapse of ancient virtue begins with the fateful transmission of Callimaco's phallus to Lucrezia. To illuminate this important nexus linking Livy and Machiavelli's comedy, the meaning of the play's title—and thus the lore of the *mandragola*—must first be briefly considered.

92. For the conception of the state as a human body in antiquity and the Renaissance, see Leonard Barkan, *Nature's Work of Art* (New Haven, Conn., 1974), esp. pp. 97, 100, 115, 119, 151, 158-159.
93. *AUC,* II.32-33.
94. Texts in note 28, above.

III

The importance of traditional lore on the *mandragola* for the plot of Machiavelli's play has been illuminated by several recent studies.[95] Intrinsically, however, *mandragola* serves as the comprehensive rubric for sexual meaning in the play. As Callimaco describes it, *mandragola* can be made into a *pozione* that promotes not only fertility, but impregnation itself: "non è cosa più certa a ingravidare la donna che darli bere una pozione fatta di *mandragola*" (II.vi.p.75). Callimaco is presumably leaving out an important step when he suggests that the potion will cause pregnancy without futher interventions of the male. But the omission is significant because it suggests a metaphorical equation between the natural cause of Lucrezia's pregnancy—Callimaco's seed—and the fabulous *mandragola*. Consequently the numerous terms in the play that refer to the remedy—*pozione, rimedio,* Nicia's colloquial *suzzacchera, hypocràs*—may also be taken to refer to the seminal efficacy of the male.[96] It is thus no accident that, given the rhizomatic analogy between the mandrake root and the male *radice,* the play abounds in double entendres for the phallus, woven deftly into the play's richly idiomatic texture of language such that the comedy becomes a sustained carnival song, a canto carnascialesco with all of its ingeniously veiled obscenity.[97] Expressions like Nicia's "zugo a piuolo" (III.vii.p.86), and references to the "tallo in sul vecchio" for which Sostrata hopes, to the *spadaccino* or bodkin worn by Nicia at the capture of the potent *garzonaccio,* to the bladder and bauble (*vesciche, badalucco*), to the white-headed leek (in sodomizing position, "porro di dietro") are all circumlocutions for the sex of the male. Nicia, anticipating the events to take place in his own bedroom, expresses confidence that

95. See note 26, above, for citations.

96. The analogy between the mandrake root and the phallus is suggested when Timoteo observes the removal of Callimaco from Lucrezia's room: "e' cavano fuora el prigione," where *cavare* (extract, dig out) recalls one of the common terms for digging up the mandrake root; cf. Raimondi, p. 257, who cites a commentary to Dioscorides (1518): "iactantque tanto periculo *effodi* humana forma."

97. Machiavelli wrote several obscene carnival-songs, including "di uomini che vendone le pine" (Gaeta, p. 337), where the pine cone is an image for the penis: "e che direte voi che dal pin cola / un licor ch'ugne poi tute quei nocchi . . ." For similar examples, see also Singleton, *Canti, passim.*

"Pasquina enterrà in Arezzo"—that is, that the phallus will enter the "dark place" (a rezzo) successfully.[98]

The most important reference to the male sex from the perspective of the links between Livy and Machiavelli's comedy is brilliantly indirect. It comes during the hilarious scene of Nicia's examination of the *garzonaccio*—Callimaco in disguise—to determine if there any signs (*bolle*, sores) of syphillis or other venereal disease. Nicia's role of health inspector is transparently a ruse: what he really wants to do is touch and see, "toccare e vedere," Callimaco's body and its splendid endowment. As he puts it, he wants to get to the bottom of the matter, "toccare a fondo." He goes so far as to make sure that the mystery to be consummated between Lucrezia and the *garzonaccio* is already well underway before he leaves the room: "e innanzi volli toccare con mano come la cosa andava" (V.ii.p.107). Now, Nicia's expression "toccare e vedere" reflects a formula of Latin comedy, adopted in its turn by the *novella*, usually appearing in the mouth of a clever servant promising to show his master the facts of a given matter.[99] But Machiavelli's little scene in the fourth act also has more proximate literary antecedents in several tales of Boccaccio and in the *Calandria* of Bernardo Dovizi, where touching the facts of the matter has the same meaning: the phallus is the truth, the *fondo* of things.[100] For

---

98. "Tallo sul vecchio" as a circumlocution for the penis appears also in Singleton, *Canti*, p. 5. The phallic suggestiveness of the *spadaccino* or *stocco* is illuminated by Machiavelli's use of a similar double entendre in his *Clizia*, where Nicomacho—in bed with the servant Siro disguised as Clizia—is repeatedly poked by what Nicomacho takes to be a dagger ("mi sento stoccheggiare un fianco e darmi qua sotto el codrione cinque o sei colpi de' maladetti!" (V.3, p. 160). "Pasquina enterrà in Arezzo" (Pasquina will enter in Arezzo [the town] [in the dark place]) is for Nicia a fairly transparent circumlocution of the event that he anticipates in his bedchamber; cf. Boccaccio, *Decameron*, VI, *introduzione*, where Licisca refers to "Ser Mazza" (Sir club, staff) entering *Montenero* ("black mountain"). In addition to terms specific of the penis, Nicia is also fond of colloquial references to the backside, "Cacastecchi," "Cacasangue," "Scingasi!" ("stickshitter," "bloodshitter," "let him drop his pants," etc.).

99. For some examples, cf. *Decameron* III.6.19; IV.4.9; VII.7.34—significantly, the last two tales include the love-by-report device adopted in *Mandragola*.

100. See *Decameron*, II.3.30; III.10.17-18; Bibbiena's *Calandria* is one of Machiavelli's richer veins of suggestion for the language of his own play (I count some 28 parallels), especially phallic imagery, which is central in the *Calandria* because of the hero's disguise as a woman. The play's resolution thus requires some positive identifications: "Tutto l'ho

our play, Nicia's handling of his rival is not only the grotesque nadir of his cuckoldry and a strong suggestion of why he has failed to produce children, but also a parody of the ritual transmission of phallic virtue depicted in Livy's episode of Lucretia and Brutus: in other terms, it is a *translatio stultitiae* rather than, as in Livy's history, a *translatio legis* and *imperii*. I will return to this point in a moment.

Mandragola is not to be decoded as seminal virtue only; it is also to be interpreted as a figure for the scheme of sexual differentiation itself, for sexedness as the master *segno* at stake in the play. Alongside the ingenious references to the phallus there are marked references to the female sex: Nicia's exclamation ("potta di San Puccio") and the profoundly obscene reference by Timoteo to the *sgocciolatura,* the "draining" of the surrogate from Lucrezia's bedroom (V.i.p.105), are examples. Nicia's joke about how much the *garzonaccio* has enjoyed the *unto* (grease, chrism, oil) provides an ambiguous term whose meaning ranges from sexual lubricants to the *mandragola* itself. There is good reason for the sexual ambivalence of terms associated with *mandragola.* In the traditional lore regarding the plant, the mandrake is always described as both anthropomorphic and sexed, having the shape of a human body and displaying the marks of sexual differentiation.[101] It is thus the symbol of the scheme spelled out explicitly by Callimaco disguised as physician when he explains, in simple

---

maneggiato e tocco . . ."; "Fulvia l'ha tocco tutto, e trovatolo femina . . ." (Bernardo Dovizi da Bibbiena, *Calandria,* in *Il Teatro italiano,* ed. Bonino, pp. 67, 72; see also pp. 68, 73).

101. For contemporary medical information regarding the mandrake, cf. Raimondi, pp. 257-258, where Beroaldo's commentary to Apuleius's *Asinus aureus* is cited: "duo sunt genera mandragorae, mas et femina." The Renaissance authorities are largely dependent on the medieval encyclopedias like those of Isidore and Bartholomaeus Anglicus (who gives generous excerpts from Dioscorides); Isidore's account is relatively complete and succinct: "Hanc poetae *anthropomorphon* appellant, quod habeat radicem forma hominis simulantem. . .huius species duae: femina, follis lactucae similibus mala generans in similitudinem prunorum. Masculus vero, foliis betae similibus . . ." (*Etymol.,* XVII.9.30, PL 82.627). Reference to the power of mandrakes to cure sterility is also a feature of carnival songs, e.g., Singleton, *Canti,* p. 17 ("per chi vuole ingravidare, che mandragola si chiama").

but conspicuous medical Latin, the possible reasons for the couple's failure to procreate. [102]

Nam causae sterilitatis sunt: aut in semine aut in matrice, aut in strumentis seminariis, aut in virga, aut in causa extrinseca. [103]

It is as a model of sexual differentiation that the traditional account of the *mandragola* is both remedy and poison is most telling for the meaning of the play. As Callimaco-physician describes the drug, it will impregnate Lucrezia but also kill the first male that lies with her: its effect on the female is vital and benign; on the male, mortal. [104] As Aquilecchia has demonstrated, the folklore motif of the poisoned lady, who annihilates her consorts, has been grafted by Machiavelli to the conventional lore of the mandrake found in the encyclopedias and medical texts of the Latin West. But the additional inclusion by Machiavelli of reference to the ordeal of Tobit's bride, Sarah, who must be detoxified for several days before Tobit can expect to survive a night with her, [105] points the way to the naturalistic referent behind the fabulous lore in the presumed toxicity of the female sex itself—marked most sensationally by the medical myth that the *menses* have virulent properties. [106] Thus *mandragola,* in its widest sense,

102. For "scientific" explanation of how the mandrake can aid fertility, we have the account of Bartholomaeus Anglicus, *De rerum proprietatibus* (1601; repr. Frankfurt, 1964) XVII.104: "quod mandragora sumpta modo debito matrice disponit ad conceptionem quando primitus calor nimis et siccus conceptionibus materiam impedivit. Mulieres calidas et humidas disponit ad conceptionem, cum sit frigida et sicca." Medically, then, the mandrake aids conception only in the special case of a woman who is excessively humid and hot (in traditional medicine women are normally humid and cold); otherwise, like most substances that are cold and dry, the mandrake is toxic and inimical to life.

103. Callimaco's scholastic form of reasoning here parodies Machiavelli's own technique of dividing one question in the first chapter of *Il principe.* For the consequences of Machiavelli's reliance on these patterns of thought, cf. Pocock, pp. 158-159.

104. For the motif of the poisoned lady ("concubitus velenatus"), cf. Aquilecchia. pp. 88-89, and Raimondi, p. 257-258.

105. For the reference to Tobit, see Raimondi, p. 257. The text (in the Vulgate) is Tobit 6:1-22.

106. See Isidore, *Etymologiae,* XI.141, translated in "Isidore of Seville: The Medical Writings," trans. with intro. and comm. by W. D. Sharpe, in *Transactions of the American Philosophical Society,* N.S., LIV, part 2 (1964), pp. 46-49: "On contact with this gore,

embraces the full gamut of oppositions active in the play: both the opposition of male and female sexual power and the ambivalent power of the
drug, the *pharmakon*, the "remedy" that is both toxic and tonic, potion
and poison, *virtus* and *virus*. Nicia's outburst when Callimaco-physician
informs him as to the hitch in using the potent medicine describes the
mandragola exactly, for he calls it a *"suzzacchera,"* the name of a medicinal
drink composed of vinegar and sugar, both sweet and sour. From this
perspective, *mandragola*, the play's title, is the term that funnels into
Machiavelli's text the coexistence of medicinal and toxic properties, of
masculine and feminine aspects, in the defiled but virtuous blood of
Roman Lucretia.

But there is one more decisive feature of *mandragola*. Also termed *rimedi*
everywhere in the play are Ligurio's ingenious expedients for overcoming
the obstacles to the execution of the plot, which has as its object the
fertilization of Lucrezia. [107] Since Ligurio's need for constant resourceful-
ness enacts the Machiavellian commonplace that only a superior *virtù* can
repeatedly overcome the obstacles of *Fortuna*, his *rimedi* also take their
place under the rubric of *mandragola*, which thus sexualizes every device of
the plot. It is perhaps this sexualization of Ligurio's *rimedi* that accounts
for the alliance of Callimaco and Ligurio, for only Ligurio's skill makes
Callimaco's sexual energy efficacious. [108] Both Ligurio and Callimaco are
finally provided with keys to the "camera terrena" of Nicia's house, for
both brains and brawn are needed to complete the execution of the brilliant *beffa*. If, in the *Prince*, Machiavelli compares the successful man of
action to a centaur, because he can enlist both intelligence and feral
violence for his designs, in *Mandragola* no single character embodies that
ideal.

---

crops do not germinate, wine goes sour, grasses die, trees lose their fruit, iron is corrupted
by rust, copper is blackened. Should dogs eat of it, they go mad."

107. For Ligurio's many *rimedi*, cf. pp. 67, 71 (3 times), 75, 76, 77 (3 times), 79, 83,
91, 94, 95. The three uses on p. 77 (II.6) show Ligurio inventing new *rimedi* to overcome
fresh obstacles, fulfilling the Machiavellian notion that new and innovative solutions are
constantly required for the challenges of Fortune.

108. The sexual dimension of male *virtù* is rendered most brutally explicit in
Machiavelli's notorious reference, in the 25th chapter of the *Prince*, to Fortune as a woman
who must be treated roughly by the man who would master her.

The richness of Machiavelli's title, which should be rendered without the article ("la favola *Mandragola* si chiama") so as to preserve its comprehensiveness, should be evident: *mandragola* covers nearly everything in the play and, reflexively, the function of the play itself as an ambiguous *rimedio* administered to its audience. It is both full of the bitterness of the satirist who confesses in the prologue that he, too, knows how to speak ill of others—"sa dir male anch'egli"—and potentially a *rimedio* offering relief to its author and illumination to its audience, if not the definitive healthy purge that would restore the vigor of the Florentine civic body.

The function of *mandragola* in embracing both the sexual dyad and the ambivalent efficacy of the *pharmakon* is important for understanding the meaning of the transformation of Lucrezia at the conclusion of the play. As noted above, Lucrezia's reported words when presented with Callimaco's proposal display a strikingly healthy faculty of willing.[109] By submitting to Callimaco and the "miraculous" power of his sex, she has become a powerful, even commanding figure. Much is at stake here. Nicia's admiring comparison of his wife to the rooster, the phallic totem of carnival virility, testifies to Lucrezia's assumption, through submission, of a masterful power that parallels Roman Lucretia's assumption of heroic virtue through her suicide. In terms of the lore of *mandragola*, Callimaco's night with Lucrezia has drawn the imaginary toxicity from her body into himself; she, in return, has retained his seed and, in effect, his masculine potency. Translated back into the realistic psychology of the play, Lucrezia enters into the possession of a new and subtle mastery over those who appear to have triumphed over her virtue, just as Lucretia triumphs over her seducer through the effects of her sacrifice. Lucrezia is transformed from the single remaining spark of ancient virtue to the absolute mistress of the corrupt world of the play; as Ligurio puts it early in the play, Lucrezia is "atta a governare un regno," and it is that realm that she inherits at the play's end.

Cured of her resemblance to Roman Lucretia, Lucrezia comes to stand

---

109. V.6, p. 111: "Io l'ho molto caro, e vuolsi che sia nostro compare"; p. 112: "Dategliene dieci," Lucrezia's last words in the play, order her husband to give ten *grossi* to Timoteo, echo the circumstances at the conclusion of *Decameron* VII.7.36 ("datigli sette gigliati"): a suggestive parallel, as Peronella, too, has just finished cuckolding her husband in his presence.

for an ambiguous female power that thwarts the ideal political agendas of
the male *virtù* that, in Machiavelli's typology, strives to conquer history
and fortune.[110] Indeed, Lucrezia finally represents the female per-
sonifications Fortuna and Natura themselves, the traditional adversaries of
the designs of masculine desire.[111] In this respect the contrast with Roman Lucretia is again telling. In Livy's episode, Lucretia is powerful
because she becomes like a man, she triumphs over a timorous female
nature, she becomes "matrona animi virilis." Through her, the Roman
virtue triumphs over nature and natural corruption, restoring the state to
its pristine strength. In *Mandragola*, Lucrezia's submission to Callimaco
marks the final defection of ancient *virtù*; her alteration ("'ell' e stamane up
po' alterata," Nicia remarks) is itself a change of nature, as Callimaco had
hoped at the play's outset, that makes her a representative of changeable
nature herself, "semper varium et mutabile."[112] In her defection, the
corruption of nature triumphs over obstinate virtue.

The triumph of nature in Lucrezia's ascendancy requires a re-evaluation
of the apparent success of Nicia and Callimaco in the play. For the
consummation of Ligurio's ingenious plot marks the defeat not only of
ancient virtue but also of the illusion of Callimaco's (and Nicia's)
triumph. It is clear, in retrospect, that Nicia and Callimaco have been
driven by Nature and Fortune throughout the play: Nicia because he
wishes to preserve his fortune by propagating himself—the work of
Natura—and Callimaco because it was Dame Fortune herself who in-
flamed his desire with the verbal images of Lucrezia's beauty.[113] Indeed,

110. For this view of male *virtù* in Machiavelli's works, see Gilbert, pp. 192-198; and
Pocock, pp. 156-182, esp. p. 167, for an acute analysis of *virtù* as finally self-destructive.

111. For Machiavelli's view of *virtù* besieged by fortune—which it can surmount—and
by nature, which it cannot, see his letter 119 (ed. Gaeta, 1961, pp. 230-231); also *Il
principe* xxv (ed. Cantimori, pp. 92-94); *Discorsi*, III.9; "capitolo di fortuna," vv. 108-114
(ed. Gaeta, *Il teatro* . . . , p. 315). For discussion, cf. Pocock, p. 180.

112. For the problem of mutability, cf. *Discorsi*, I.42. For an analysis of corruption as
an irreversible change of nature, see Pocock, pp. 207-208.

113. That Nicia is victimized by his desire for offspring is clear from the play; but
Callimaco, too, is shown driven by a *libido* beyond his control: he threatens repeatedly to
adopt violent remedies or destroy himself; e.g., I.3 (p. 67); IV.4 (p. 97): "io mi gitterò in
Arno o io mi appiccherò o io mi gitterò da quella finestra o io mi darò d'un coltello in sullo
uscio suo." In Act IV.1 (p. 92) Callimaco gives a description of his condition ("le gambe

as the play progresses Callimaco and Nicia, whose relationship is established with exchanges of university Latin, become increasingly similar. Not only are they to be god-fellows, *compari,* because Lucrezia wills it, but their names, already linked by common recourse to military etyma, are doubly related: as echoes of Machiavelli's reliance on Boccaccio's character Calandrino (*Dec.* 8.3, 6; 9.3, 5) and on Bibbiena's related Calandro (from the *Calandria*) as models for Nicia; and as dispersed homophonies of Machiavelli's own full name.[114] Thus Calandro/Calandrino's prefix disappears from Nicia's first name and reappears in front of his last (*Cal*fucci) and in *Call*imaco's name, while Ni*cc*olò Ma*c*hiavelli yields the elements of Nicia and Callimaco. The point, I believe, is that Nicia becomes Callimaco's true father, which means that Callimaco is destined to become, in his turn, another Nicia. If Lucretia's suicide provides the perfect opportunity for the "stupefied" Brutus to become miraculously wise and purposeful, the *translatio stultitiae* conducted by Nicia in Lucrezia's bedroom marks the initiation of Callimaco into a household ruled and represented by the idiotic Nicia.[115]

As a figure of Nature and Fortune, Lucrezia is, at the conclusion of the play, the mistress of a world wholly in the grip of those two powers because of the loss of the ancient resolve to stand at any cost against the

---

triemono, le viscere si commuovono, il core mi si sbarba del petto . . .") that, as Raimondi notes (p. 202) is taken from Lucretius's sharply satirical view of erotic passion in the *De rerum natura* III. 152-158.

114. Machiavelli's flair for playing with names is beyond doubt. The protagonist of the *Clizia,* Nicomacho, is a collapsed version of *Niccolò Machiavelli* (cf. Ridolfi, p. 247). For the meanings of the names Nicia (= victorious) and Callimaco (= beautiful in battle) cf. R. Sereno, "A Note on the Names of the Personages of Machiavelli's *Mandragola,*" *Italica,* XXVI (1949), 56. Machiavelli's own nickname, *Machia* (cf. Ridolfi, p. 210), represents an operation on *Machiavelli* similar to that of *Nicia* on *Niccolò.* Machiavelli was, of course, well aware from Thucydides and Plutarch that *Nikia* was the name of the Athenian general who led the disastrous Sicilian expedition during the Peloponnesian War; cf. *Discorsi,* I.53; III.16.

115. As Hugo Rahner points out, Dioscorides gives as one of the names of *mandragola* the term *morion,* because the drug made from the plant is narcotic. In the context of our play, however, it might be suggested that the effect of *mandragora* in the broadest sense is *stupidity.* Cf. Rahner, p. 224, citing *De materia medica,* IV, 75, 7.

entropy of history.[116] A remarkable episode placed at the very heart of the play suggests, in an oblique but highly suggestive way, the depth of Machiavelli's melancholy understanding of the failure of the Florentine republic. In the third act (scenes iv, v, vi of twelve) Ligurio tests Timoteo's willingness to cooperate with the plan against Lucrezia by first suggesting an even more scandalous scheme: Timoteo is to persuade the abbess of a nunnery to administer a *pozione* to the pregnant daughter of Cammillo Calfucci so that she will miscarry. Citing the advantages to all concerned, and garnishing his reasoning with hints of subsequent contributions to the Church, Ligurio overcomes the pliant scruples of Timoteo, who agrees to attempt the service. The episode is striking for being an inverse parallel to the principal action of the play. Both of Ligurio's schemes are *rimedi* that entail administering a *pozione*. In one case, however, the object is impregnation; in the other, abortion. Both schemes call out the formulaic Machiavellian skill in assessing the pros and cons of a plan. In one case that skill is applied by Ligurio:

Observe how much good results from the course of action: you maintain the honor of the monastery, the girl's reputation and that of her family . . . and on the other hand you offend nothing more than an insensible unborn piece of flesh, which can be lost in a thousand ways [*che in mille modi si può sperdere*]

(III.v.84)

in the other case, by the newly converted Timoteo, who persuades Madonna Lucrezia with the same kind of argument: "el fine si ha a riguardare in tutte le cose: el fine vostro si è riempire una sedia in paradiso, contentare il marito vostro."

Another, deeper similarity also links the two schemes: the economy of sacrifice. In the scheme that Nicia accepts, adopting the treatment of *mandragola* for Lucrezia, a provision is made for the sacrifice of the surrogate who is to absorb the toxic properties of the drug. The life of the *garzonaccio,* whose ugliness and social marginality mark him as a traditional scapegoat, a *pharmakos,* is to be the price of the rejuvenescence of

---

116. For the destructive forces of the historical process, cf. *Discorsi* II.5; Gilbert, p. 198; Pocock, pp. 216–218. As Pocock points out, the republican system of Rome was also intrinsically unstable, though a virtuous republic can concentrate its energies and succeed politically for a long time.

Lucrezia and the household of Calfucci. By contrast, in Ligurio's test scheme for Timoteo the sacrificial victim is the imaginary unborn infant of Calfucci's imaginary daughter. That an infant, the desired object of the major plot, is the sacrificial victim of the imaginary microplot is not merely an exposure of the moral flexibility of the principal conspirators. The point of the episode is to place at the play's center a symbol of that which, in the full Machiavellian sense, is sacrificed by all the characters in the play: the "antica virtù" itself, precisely that which, in the Roman tragedy of Lucretia, is born. Ligurio argues to Timoteo that the abortion of the fetus is trivial because it tends to be lost in so many ways, "in mille modi si può sperdere." His idiom is hauntingly reminiscent of a passage in the *Discourses* where Machiavelli points to the multiple ways in which a republic may be betrayed:

. . . no adequate remedies existing for similar disorders arising in republics, it follows that it is impossible to establish a perpetual republic, because in a thousand unforeseen ways its ruin may be accomplished [*per mille inopinate vie si causa la sua rovina*].

(III.17)

One of the funniest plays ever written, *Mandragola* holds at its heart an etiological fable of the defection of ancient virtue and the failure of a free republic. The tale of Lucretia, for Machiavelli the inception of a utopian ideal of civic virtue, gives the measure that permits *Mandragola* to be grasped as the etiology of dystopia.

"Steale from the deade?":
The Presence of Marlowe in
Jonson's Early Plays

JAMES SHAPIRO

> Jonson is the legitimate heir of Marlowe.
> —T. S. Eliot (1919)

ELIOT'S OBSERVATION has proved a critical dead-end. The twentieth century has resisted the view that Marlowe and Jonson are related, let alone that Marlowe is Jonson's poetic precursor. Instead, critics have viewed Jonson's and Marlowe's poetics as fundamentally opposed: where Marlowe is father of blank verse tragedy, Jonson is master of prose comedy. Where Marlowe is heir to a native dramatic tradition, Jonson is imitator of the classics. And where Marlowe (and his works) are iconoclastic, subversive, and morally unstable, Jonson (and his works) are conservative, satiric, and corrective. The source of this polarity can partially be traced back to Jonson himself: it was he who derided the "scenicall strutting, and furious vociferation" (Herford and Simpson, hereafter H&S, 8:587) of plays like *Tamburlaine,* and he who "was often heard to say" that the "mighty lines" of "Mr. Marlow" were "examples fitter for admiration than for parallel" (H&S 11:145).

The current generation of Jonson scholars has focused with increasing intensity on Jonson's classicism, especially in regard to his conception of imitation. While recent studies by Richard S. Peterson, Thomas M. Greene, Katherine Maus, Douglas Duncan, and others have en-

75

larged our understanding of Jonson's dramatic (and especially nondramatic) works, they have inevitably read back into Jonson's plays a classicism Jonson only later came to advocate. Concomitantly, this critical emphasis has shifted attention away from Jonson's formative involvement in the popular drama of the 1590s.[1] The result is a figure who would have been unrecognizable to Philip Henslowe when he hired Jonson in 1602 to write additions to *The Spanish Tragedy,* or to London audiences that had seen Jonson act the part of Zulziman at that converted bear-baiting pit, the Paris Garden.

I offer a revisionist reading of Jonson in response to (and in way of explanation of) Jonson's own revisionist account of his artistic development.[2] The irony, of course, is that Jonson's self-fashioning has, in Eliot's words, led to a reputation "of the most deadly kind that can be compelled upon the memory of a great poet. To be universally accepted; to be damned by the praise that quenches all desire to read the book . . . and to be read only by historians and antiquaries" (Eliot 147). What needs to be addressed is what compelled Jonson to refashion his identity as a playwright, what led him to suppress (and in his collected "*Works*" efface) evidence of his extensive participation in the popular dramatic tradition.

Extending Eliot's observations, I argue that a major reason for this suppression is the pressure Jonson experienced as a popular dramatist confronted with Marlowe's legacy. This is not to say that Jonson's engagement with Marlowe excluded other poetic encounters. It did not. Kyd, we know, figured largely in Jonson's development. And we also know from his *Conversations with Drummond* and *Discoveries* that he was widely and deeply read in classical, Continental, and especially English authors, and had a vigorously emulative response to many of them. Marlowe's influence was formative, however, in a way that Dekker's, Marston's, Shakespeare's, or Kyd's was not; it would redirect the nature of Jonson's development as a popular playwright[3] and would generate the unusual constellation of imitative strategies Jonson employed in his early dramatic output.[4]

I have spoken of Jonson's relationship to Marlowe in terms of filial succession (as Eliot does in describing him as Marlowe's "legitimate heir") in part because Jonson understood and experienced literary succession in these patriarchal terms.[5] For Jonson, literary and filial succession follow remarkably similar patterns. In his plays and criticism they are often conflated or confused, something that should come as no surprise given Jonson's obsession with creating not just sons of Ben, but a veritable "Tribe" of male successors (Davis; Summers and Pebworth). The need to designate literary heirs in terms of patrilinear descent was coupled with a desire to choose a (literary) progenitor (though we cannot choose our fathers, nor, as Harold Bloom puts it, can poets choose their precursors) and to reject one whose influence was inhibiting. Tellingly, when we turn to Jonson's formative drama—especially plays like *Every Man in His Humour* and *Poetaster*—Jonson's exploration of poetic succession becomes thematically intertwined with the Oedipal struggle of young men (who are poets) attempting to escape repressive fathers (who are blocking figures not to young love but to the heir's poetic development). Jonson's concern with poetic succession calls to mind Freud's remark in "A Disturbance of Memory on the Acropolis" that it "seems as though the essence of success were to have gotten farther than one's father, and as though to excel one's father were forbidden" (11:247).

Jonson's response to Marlowe's influence often resembles that of a son to his father: first emulating, then rejecting, then coming to terms with and succeeding the paternal figure. Jonson was sensitive to patrilinear tensions and dangers to succession; he writes in his *Discoveries* that "[g]reatnesse of name, in the Father, oft-times helpes not forth, but o'rewhelmes the Sonne: they stand too neere one another." He recognizes that the "shadow kils the growth; so much, that wee see the Grand-child come more, and oftener to be the heire of the first, then doth the second." The immediate heir, overwhelmed by this influence, "dies betweene," while "the Possession is the third[']s" (H&S 8:576). Jonson's remarks help explain his evasive maneuver of skipping a generation in tracing his artistic lineage: we need to exercise some care in taking him at face value when he tells us that Horace and Martial are his progenitors rather than Kyd and Marlowe. In this regard Jonson's strategy resembles a general Renaissance tendency to downplay connections between itself and its medieval antecedents, preferring instead to trace its lineage to classical models; in both cases self-definition is contingent upon an assertion of independence (and difference) from immediate forebears.

Jonson's conception of the filial basis of poetic imitation is elaborated in an illuminating passage in his *Discoveries,* where he defines imitation as being able "to convert the substance or Riches of an other Poet" to one's own use by making "choice of one excellent man above the rest," whom one must follow until one grows a "very Hee: or, so stile him, as the Copie may be mistaken for the Principall" (H&S 8:638). Like a son growing in the image—and shadow—of his father, the poet grows into this "very Hee" before, ideally, transcending his progenitor. It may be that the hint of Oedipal tension in Jonson's relationship to Marlowe gave rise to the fantastic claim—reported and subsequently dismissed by John Aubrey—that it was Ben Jonson who "killed Mʳ Marlow yᵉ poet on Bunhill, comeing from the Green-curtain playhouse" (H&S 1:178). For Jonson, overcoming Marlowe would not be this easy.

To maintain that Jonson is Marlowe's legitimate heir, that his work reflects a strong anxiety about Marlowe's influence, necessarily calls for a reappraisal of Jonson's ideas of imitation and of his evolution as a poet and playwright. It has implications as well for the recurrence of parody and poetasters in Jonson's early drama, for his unusual thematic attention to the struggle between fathers and sons in these early plays, and for the ways in which his mature comedies, notably *Volpone,* are informed by a more improvisational engagement with and appropriation of the Marlovian model. It may also clarify the extent to which the process of canon formation is contingent upon the dynamics of literary influence,[6] and may help explain why Marlowe's reputation declined so precipitously by the mid-seventeenth century.

I

Had Jonson not escaped hanging in 1598 (after killing the actor Gabriel Spencer) he would most likely be remembered as one of Henslowe's journeymen, the author of a half dozen or so lost Elizabethan plays, mostly tragedies, along with the unusual humours play that had been staged the month of his arrest. Francis Meres, in his *Palladia Tamis,* would have offered the finest praise during the playwright's life, ranking Jonson along with Marlowe, Kyd, and Shakespeare in his list of English tragedians. Only fragments of Jonson's output would have survived: those passages (apparently from tragedies or tragical histories) anthologized in Robert Allott's *Englands Parnassus* (1600). Other sources concur in depicting Jonson as a maker of popular tragedies. For John Weever, in his *Epigrammes in the Oldest Cut and Newest Fashion* (1599), he is "embuskin'd Jonson" (Bradley 6). And Henslowe's *Diary* records payments in 1598 for the "tragedie of bengemens plotte" and in 1599 for the collaborative "tragedie" *Robert II, King of Scots.* Jonson was also paid for a tragical history, *Richard Crookback* (1602), and collaborated with Thomas Dekker on a domestic tragedy called *The Page of Plymouth* (1599), with Henry Chettle and Henry Porter on *Hot Anger Soon Cooled* (1599), and with Thomas Nashe on *The Isle of Dogs* (1597); all of these plays (and perhaps others) that Jonson wrote for Henslowe's companies are either lost or suppressed (H&S 11:307–08). Henslowe also paid him for additions to Kyd's *Spanish Tragedy,* evidently confident of Jonson's ability to write in a style compatible with Kyd's outmoded vein. Dekker tells us elsewhere that Jonson had spent some time playing Hieronimo in provincial performances, as well as performing the title role in *Zulziman,* a lost play that might have capitalized on the success of exotic eastern tragedies generated by Marlowe's *Tamburlaine* (H&S 1:13–14). Jonson's apprenticeship in popular tragedy was apparently extensive. As for Jonson's early comedies, the only record we have is his comment to Sir William Drummond that half his comedies were not in print; it may be, as Jonson's Oxford editors suggest, that he was using the term "comedy" loosely to signify plays in general (H&S 1:283). At any rate, even this fragmentary list is enough to suggest that we need to be wary when Jonson speaks of *Every Man in His Humour* as his first fruits. He apparently labored long and hard first to master Elizabethan tragedy, then equally hard to efface any record of this enterprise.

The fragments of Jonson's verse contained in Allott's anthology offer a brief and suggestive glimpse of his dramatic style in the mid- to late-1590s. Two are rhymed couplets:

> Those that in blood such violent pleasures have,
> Seldome descend but bleeding to their grave.

and

> Warres grea < t > est woes, and miseries increase,
> Flowes from the surfets which we take in peace.
>
> (H&S 3:363)

For some, the formal, sententious couplets are the stuff of Elizabethan
revenge tragedy (Barton 18), though such lines would be equally at
home in a history play. In either case they sound like the pronouncements of an authoritative figure in a homiletic drama; there is little
sense of irony or of the playful undercutting that characterized Jonson's subsequent treatment of such "fustian."

The longest excerpt quoted by Allott is more helpful:

> Gold is a sutor, never took repulse
> It carries Palme with it, (where e're it goes)
> Respect, and observation; it uncovers
> The knottie heads of the most surly Groomes,
> Enforcing yron doores to yeeld it way,
> Were it as strong ram'd up as Aetna gates.
> It bends the hams of Gossip Vigilance,
> And makes her supple feete, as swifte and winde.
> It thawes the frostiest, and most stiffe disdaine:
> Muffles the clearnesse of Election,
> Straines fancie unto foule Apostacie,
> And strikes the quickest-sighted Judgement blinde.
> Then why should we dispaire? Dispaire, away:
> Where Gold's the Motive, women have no Nay.
>
> (H&S 3:363)

The speech appears to be a fairly conventional soliloquy, spoken by a
scheming and villainous protagonist who brushes aside misgivings
about his plotting, confident in his misogynistic conviction that women
are ultimately swayed by gold. Stylistically, the speech resembles the
generalized blank verse characteristic of much of the drama of the
mid- to late-1590s, a style indebted to Marlovian tragedy: strongly
end-stopped lines, joined by syntactic suspension through iteration
and conjunctive clauses into a swelling verse paragraph, here capped
by a syntactically strained couplet. Instead of classical allusions, Jonson invokes the emblematic figures of the homiletic tradition: "Election," "Judgement," "Vigilance," and "Apostacie."

Jonson's finest re-creation of an earlier Elizabethan mode is to be
found in his additions to *The Spanish Tragedy*. Anne Barton has argued compellingly that the additions in the 1602 quarto are by Jonson
and that they are characteristic of thematic concerns—especially the

relationship of father and son—that recur in his plays. Yet even in re-creating Kyd's style Jonson turns to Marlowe, according to Barton, as "a way of keeping himself in touch with other manifestations of the popular idiom he needed to invoke in writing his additions" (18–28). Thus, in the fifth addition, Jonson echoes a pair of famous lines from *Doctor Faustus* ("Had I as many soules, as there be Starres, / I'de give them all for Mephostophilis" [Bowers 2:171]) in a passage that could easily have come from *Tamburlaine:*

> I tell thee, Vice-roy, this day I have seene revenge,
> And in that sight am growne a prowder Monarch
> Than ever sate under the Crowne of Spaine.
> Had I as many lives as there be Starres,
> As many Heavens to go to, as those lives,
> Ide give them all, I, and my soul to boote,
> But I would see thee ride in this red poole.
>
> (Boas 95–96)

The infinite comparisons (as many lives as stars, as many heavens as those lives), the overwhelming pride, the disdain for life when weighed against revenge, and the swelling and suspended verse paragraph all hark back to the bragging blank verse of Marlowe's Scythian shepherd. Moreover, the triumph described here is visualized in characteristically Marlovian terms—another's humiliation—worth attaining even at the Faustian price of one's soul.

If Jonson indirectly recalls Marlowe in these additions, he takes him on directly in a dramatic fragment—probably written a few years before *Sejanus His Fall* (1603)—called *Mortimer His Fall.* Little is known about this work, other than the brief editorial note appended to it in the 1640 Folio that states the obvious: "Left unfinished."[7] It reflects a Jonson that antedates his defensive inclusion of parody and poetasters, one that indicates an urge to move beyond the derivative tragedies of his early engagements in Henslowe's service. It also antedates the repertory of features that would soon be associated with Jonson: colloquial prose, contemporary settings, admonitory satire, and rambling plots and subplots filled with gulls and humours.

The surviving outline indicates that Jonson planned a play modeled on Marlowe's *Edward II,* which was still being staged by the Admiral's

Men as late as 1602.[8] We have here the stuff of Marlowe's tumultuous denouement: the haling away of Kent, the humiliation and torture of the king, and the hired assassins and torturers (H&S 7:58). Jonson appears to have sought to go beyond Marlowe with a radically new type of tragedy, replete with choruses of "Ladyes," "Courtiers," and "Countrey Justices, and their Wives." What is so striking in this case is the discrepancy between Jonson's theoretical plans and pronouncements and the survivng fragment of the first hundred or so lines from the play. If the outline of the plot did not signify his intention to include these various choruses, we would never guess it from the opening soliloquy of the play, which begins in the traditional vein of the overreacher soliloquizing on his triumph over rivals and over Fate.

Mortimer His Fall is a *de casibus* play in the popular tradition, mingling English history and revenge drama, and as such comes closest to the traditions Jonson repudiates elsewhere in his plays and criticism. Its opening scenes are in blank verse (with a few rhymed couplets). Internal evidence suggests that the scenes were written before the end of the century.[9] There are few feminine endings, the syntax is fairly stilted, and Jonson does not enjamb over phrase boundaries, as Jacobean and Caroline dramatists regularly did. The dialogue is awkward and unnatural. Consider, for example, Mortimer's first encounter with the queen:

> ISABEL
> My Lord! sweet Mortimer!
> MOR.
>   My Q. my Mistresse!
> My Soveraigne! nay, my Goddesse! and my Juno!
> What name, or title, as a marke of Power
> Upon me, should I give you?
> ISABEL
> Isabel,
> Your Isabel, and you my Mortimer:
> Which are the markes of Paritie, not power,
> And these are titles, best become our love.
> MOR.
> Can you fall under those?
> ISABEL
> Yes, and be happie.
>   (H&S 7:61–62)

If we encountered such wooden dialogue in a mature Jonson play we might suspect that he was engaged in burlesque: it is but a stone's throw from here to the lovers' exchange in Littlewit's puppet show in *Bartholomew Fair* ("O Leander, Leander, my deare, my deare Leander, / I'le for ever be thy goose, so thou'lt be my gander" [H&S 6:130]).

The opening soliloquy, however, is a tour de force, and stands in a tradition reaching back to morality Vice figures, through Marlowe's soliloquizing overreachers—Faustus, Barabas, the Guise, and Mortimer. The speech also looks forward to Jonson's more complex handling of the overreacher in his depiction of Volpone and Sir Epicure Mammon. The style of the passage also bears a strong resemblance to Jonson's efforts in this vein excerpted in Allott's anthology.

It is worth juxtaposing the speech with its parallel in *Edward II*, a gloating tirade which Marlowe places immediately before the play's reversal. In both passages a Machiavellian Mortimer has just overthrown the king and his brother, and, having eliminated all rivals and won the love of Isabel, exults:

> This Rise is made, yet! and we now stand, ranck'd,
> To view about us, all that were above us!
> Nought hinders now our prospect, all are even,
> We walk upon a Levell. Mortimer
> Is a great Lord of late, and a new thing!—
> A Prince, an Earle, and Cosin to the King
> At what a divers price, doe divers men
> Act the same things! Another might have had
> Perhaps the Hurdle, or at least the Axe,
> For what I have, this Crownet, Robes, and Waxe.
> There is a Fate, that flies with towring spirits
> Home to the marke, and never checks at conscience.
> Poore plodding Priests, and preaching Friars may make
> Their hollow Pulpits, and the empty Iles
> Of Churches ring with that round word: But wee
> That draw the subtile, and more piercing ayre,
> In that sublimed region of Court,
> Know all is good, we make so, and goe on,
> Secur'd by the prosperity of our crimes.
> To day, is Mortimer made Earle of March. . . .

(H&S 7:60)

And now Marlowe's:

> The prince I rule, the queene do I command,
> And with a lowly conge to the ground,

> The proudest lords salute me as I passe,
> I seale, I cancell, I do what I will,
> Feard am I more than lov'd, let me be feard,
> And when I frowne, make all the court looke pale,
> I view the prince with Aristarchus eyes,
> Whose lookes were as a breeching to a boye.
> They thrust upon me the Protectorship,
> And sue to me for that that I desire,
> While at the councell table, grave enough,
> And not unlike a bashfull puretaine,
> First I complain of imbecilitie,
> Saying it is, *onus quam gravissimum,*
> Till being interrupted by my friends,
> *Suscepi* that *provinciam* as they terme it,
> And to conclude I am protector now,
> Now all is sure, the Queene and Mortimer
> Shall rule the realme, the king, and none rule us. . . .
>   (Bowers 2:87–88)

Jonson here challenges Marlowe at his strength: the Machiavellian overreacher assured of his control over fate and fortune, enthralled with his own villainy, disdainful of rivals or threats, proud especially of his skill in duplicity. The passage surely refutes the claims of those who glibly assert that Jonson could not write tragedy. Apparently, he could pen tragedies too easily, though he could not yet discover his own, original voice in this genre.

Yet Jonson must have also realized that something was missing: Marlowe's handling of history must have struck him as more slippery, more subversive, than a cursory experience of *Edward II* would suggest. While a providential history is consistently recalled (one thinks here of Mortimer's speech on cruel Fortune's wheel), it is simultaneously exposed as a construct no less fictional than the other generic constructs Marlowe resurrects and undermines in his plays. I'm suggesting here that Jonson, in the act of imitating *Edward II,* became aware of this tension or subversion underlying his model—and broke off his attempt, unwilling or unable to appropriate or work around this Marlovian characteristic. To imitate the surface stylistic features was not to capture the essence of what made Marlowe's art so compelling and disturbing. Jonson may well have sensed that Marlowe's more complex and cynical handling of historical process offered a powerful critique of his own, and revealed it as inadequate if not anachronistic. If so, he recognized more than Marlowe's more derivative heirs, like Robert Greene and George Peele, who, while appropriating Marlowe's visual and verbal style in works like *Selimus* and *The Battle of Alcazar,* often appear oblivious to the subversive features of Marlowe's plays (Berek). Possibly, in response to this tension with his precursor, Jonson saw the implications of the historical relativism underlying his Marlovian model, and tried to wrest the story into a more providential historical model by introducing such moral signposts as the classical choruses and the Nuncius. In any event, the attempt failed, but it pointed the way for Jonson's movement past stylistic imitation toward a fuller engagement with the Marlovian sensibility.

When Jonson returned to tragedy in *Sejanus His Fall* and *Catiline,* the incipient classicism found in *Mortimer* would predominate and perhaps enable him to break from an inhibiting style, a confusing voice that drowned out his own. I suspect, however, that *Sejanus*'s classicism masks a more fundamental debt to the providential model of historical process that Marlowe had employed (and subverted); if so, *Sejanus*'s failure on the London stage may be attributed more to what was perceived in 1603 as an inadequate and anachronistic vision of historical process than to its classical trappings. In his emerging preference for comedy over tragedy Jonson would come to acknowledge that poets' "eminence appeares but in their owne way. Virgils felicity left him in prose, as Tullies forsooke him in verse." "Each," Jonson acknowledged, "hath his way of strength" (H&S 8:589).

II

In his efforts at writing a new kind of drama—the humours plays and comical satires of 1598 through 1602, including *Every Man In, Every Man Out,* and *Poetaster*—Jonson would find newer and more successful strategies for confronting Marlowe. We should remember that in these years Marlowe was still a vital literary force: Henslowe's companies alone record a hundred performances of his plays in the closing years of the decade, while three posthumous editions of *Hero and Leander,* the third edition of the Ovidian *Elegies,* and a translation of Lucan's *Pharsalia* were published between 1598 and 1600. Though buried, Marlowe was not yet dead, as his publisher, Thomas Thorpe, reminded Londoners in 1600: Marlowe's "ghoast or Genius is to be seene" still, walking in "the Churchyard in (at the least) three of four sheets" (Bowers 2:279).

The problem Jonson experienced in emulating Marlowe surfaces early in *Every Man In,* when his poetaster Matheo gets caught passing off a version of Marlowe's famous lines as his own:

> Rare creature, let me speake without offence,
> Would god my rude woords had the influence
> To rule thy thoughts, as thy fayre lookes do mine,
> Then shouldst thou be his prisoner, who is thine.
> .   .   .   .
> Be not unkinde and fayre, mishapen stuffe
> Is of behaviour boysterous and rough:
> .   .   .   .
> And I in dutie will exceede all other,
> As you in bewtie do excell loves mother.
>
> (H&S 3:249)

Lorenzo Junior identifies the passage—"S'hart, this is in Hero and Leander"—and when Prospero asks him not to interrupt, he responds in frustration that Matheo "utters no thing but stolne remnants," and is unforgiving: "A pox on him, hang him filching rogue, steale from the deade? its worse then sacriledge" (H&S 3:249). In appropriating Marlowe's verse, Matheo has crossed the line separating creative emulation from literary theft. The mention of sacrilege suggests that Jonson was sensitive about his own emulative encounter with this now dead but still popular and influential poet. By exaggerating the imitative encounter until it is simply outright theft, and by placing between himself and Marlowe a poetaster as intermediary, Jonson avoids acknowledging the extent of his own debt, and more broadly, dodges the question of how a poet comes to terms with the burden of the recent past—a task of a different order than the classical emulation Jonson comfortably espoused. This Jonsonian response would become a familiar one in the plays of this period.

It is no accident that the Folio version of Jonson's *Every Man in His Humour* contains what is probably the first occurrence of the word "parody" in English literature, in the final act, when the much abused poetaster (his name now anglicized to Matthew) is caught with his pockets and hose stuffed with the bombast of stolen verse. When Justice Clemen confiscates one of the offending scraps and reads the scrambled opening lines of Samuel Daniel's *Delia*—"Unto the boundlesse Ocean of thy face, / Runnes this poor river, charg'd with streames of eyes" (H&S 3:400)[10] —Ed Knowell delightedly exclaims: "A Parodie! a parodie! with a kind of miraculous gift, to make it absurder then it was" (H&S 3:400). Jonson, too, was possessed of this miraculous gift, and central to his emergent relationship with Marlowe, to his stealing from the dead, is his recourse to parody. In his response to Marlowe, Jonson exemplifies Harold Bloom's definition of the poet who "is not so much a man speaking to men as a man rebelling against being spoken to by a dead man (the precursor) outrageously more alive than himself" (*Misreading* 19). For Jonson, this rebellion took the form of parody.

At the heart of Jonson's parodic act is ambivalence, an ambivalence signaled in the prefix "para," meaning both nearness and opposition, "beside" and "against" (Hutcheon 30–49).[11] The parodic quotation of a precursor is necessarily an act of homage and canonization. For if the quoted (even ridiculed) text is not readily recognized by the audience, the parody is ineffective and perhaps unintelligible. Parody, however grudgingly, acknowledges a precursor. At the same time, it "critically attacks established, popular literary works and brings into question their very relevance to present literary and social conditions" (Rose 45).

Marlowe's premature death exacerbated the problem of his influence for many, and for Jonson, eight years his junior, in particular. Throughout his life Jonson's rivalries were characterized by direct, unmediated confrontation: his man-to-man combat in the Dutch wars— in which he slew his rival before both camps and took "opima spolia from him" (H&S 1:139)—is representative of this attitude. A similar impulse can be detected in his role in the so-called War of the Theaters, his fatal encounter with Gabriel Spencer, and his struggles with Marston, Dekker, Daniel, Inigo Jones, and others. But Marlowe's death made this kind of aggressive, unmediated confrontation impossible.[12] One way of understanding Jonson's recourse to parody, then, is to see his parodic quotations as acts of exorcism—in this case exorcising the anxiety of stealing from the dead; the German word for quoting (*zi-*

tieren) conveys just this in its secondary meaning as "the calling up of ghosts" (Rose 17). Jonson, through imitative quotation, can simultaneously evoke and set to rest, exorcise and thereby come to terms with the troubling (not least because dead) precursor.

Great parody—like great forgery—depends upon an artist's absolute mastery of a predecessor's style. One of Jonson's finest attributes, exemplified in his drama between 1598 and 1602, and apparent throughout his career, is his superb skill at imitating the verse styles of his predecessors. Critical interest in Jonson as master of prose comedy has obscured this. We should wonder instead why a metrist with such a fine ear for distinctive verse rhythms should relinquish the medium in favor of prose. It may well be that Jonson mastered this skill in his early collaborative years in the theater. He subsequently showed delight in displaying this mimetic capacity: in the self-consciously anachronistic but delicious Poulter's measure of the Vice Iniquity in *The Devil Is an Ass;* the Skeltonics of *The Fortunate Isles;* the Kyddian rhetoric of his additions to *The Spanish Tragedy;* the highly wrought Elizabethan love poetry of *A Tale of a Tub;* and the jingling rhymes of the puppet show in *Bartholomew Fair,* which grafts Marlowe's rhymed couplets to the clumsier rhythm of Richard Edward's *Damon and Pithias.* The list—and with it Jonson's range—could easily be extended: despite Jonson's harsh judgments of Donne's metrical style, his facility at imitating Donne's elegies (elegies themselves indebted to Marlowe's earlier translations) was such that critics still dispute which one of them wrote the "The Expostulation." When Jonson wanted to approximate—or parody—the stylistic features of rivals and predecessors he could do so masterfully. Father to prose comedy, he was heir to the great experimental age of Elizabethan versification.

His urge to display this talent borders on the compulsive in some of the plays of the late 1590s. He seems to need to pause to reassert for himself, and for his audience, his ability to mimic, to display his control over, the style of precursors which he feels he has fully digested. Consider the wonderfully irrelevant battle of bombastic blank verse in *Every Man In,* where Jonson, through Justice Clemen, displays his technical virtuosity at reproducing the modulations of Elizabethan end-stopped pentameter, quite close to what he was the first to describe as "Marlowe's mighty line." Clemen, in what Prospero refers to as the "height of stile," recites,

> Mount the <e> my Phlegon Muse, and testifie,
> How Saturne sitting in an Ebon cloud,
> Disrobd his podex, white as ivorie,
> And through the welkin thundred all aloud.
>
> (H&S 3:283)

Jonson, while demonstrating his mastery of iambic pentameter (here emphasizing the lines' artificiality through rhyme), also suggests that—despite classical allusions, ornate vocabulary, suspended and elaborate syntax, metrical regularity, and high astounding terms characteristic of Marlovian verse—the style is as obnoxious and as windy as what Clemen actually describes: a flatulent father of the gods, or rather, tellingly, son to the father of the gods, Ops, overthrown by his aspiring son.

Jonson cannot seem to resist showing (with an almost childlike delight and crudity) his expertise in imitating this style. He next takes it "a step or two lower" with a triple rhyme that accentuates the unnaturalness of the verse even further:

> From Catadupa and the bankes of Nile,
> Where onely breedes your monstrous Crocodile:
> Now are we purposd for to fetch our stile,
>
> (H&S 3:284)

here recalling antecedents like Tamburlaine's exotic peregrinations through Africa:

> From thence to Nubia neere Borno Lake,
> And so along the Ethiopian sea,
> Cutting the Tropicke line of Capricorne,
> I conquered all as far as Zansibar.
>
> (Bowers 1:217)

When revising the play for the Folio edition Jonson omitted this poetic exchange, perhaps recognizing in retrospect how revealing this was of his emulative anxiety. Even Wellbred found the last example "too far fetcht." For Jonson, the style remained not only flatulent and monstrous, but also foreign, a claim which accords with his later criticism that Marlowe's language fled "from all humanity" (H&S 8:587).

The unmasking that is central to these plays works on several levels: just as the Buffones, Matthews, and Littlewits are unmasked, so too are the outmoded, artificial, and unnatural styles of Jonson's predecessors. For Jonson, the process of revision is a gauge of self-correction (which is, I suppose, why he could not fathom a Shakespeare who never blotted a line). Jonson is obsessed with revision, with identifying and unmasking the vestigial elements of his native progenitors, then parodying, demystifying, and casting them out. Freud's comment on this process in his *Jokes and Their Relation to the Unconscious* offers an explanation for this behavior: "*Parody* and *travesty* achieve the degradation of something exalted in another way: by destroying the unity that exists between people's characters as we know them and their speeches and actions, by replacing either the exalted figures or their utterances by inferior ones. . . . The same mechanism is also used for *unmasking,* which only applies where someone has seized dignity and authority by a deception and these have to be taken from him in reality" (8:201). The deceiver here is Marlowe, whose style, for Jonson, had "nothing in [it] but the scenicall strutting, and furious vociferation, to warrant [it] to the ignorant gapers" (H&S 8:587).

Jonson's meticulous revision of *Every Man In* for inclusion in the Folio (Jackson 221–39) provides a striking example of the process of unmasking and casting out, here directed at his own earlier dramatic output, his first acknowledged and legitimate offspring. Jonson thus effectively buries remaining traces of tension; as Jonas Barish puts it, the "presence of tension in Jonson reveals itself most obviously in his insistent claim to be without tension" (87). Far more than "[d]ramatic probability and stylistic consistency" (H&S 1:366), as Herford and Simpson would have it, account for Jonson's revisions of *Every Man In.* A comparison of the Quarto and Folio texts suggests the intentions underlying Jonson's revision and testifies to his ongoing struggle to efface the influence of native progenitors. The allusion to Tamburlaine in the 1601 Quarto, subsequently deleted along with the contest over bombastic blank verse, provides a case in point. In the earlier version

Knowell speaks of his servant Musco disguising himself "with so spe-ciall and exquisite a grace," as a strutting, swaggering soldier, "that (hadst thou seene him) thou wouldst have sworne he might have beene the Tamberlaine, or the Agamemenon of the rout" (H&S 3:239). In the revised version of the play the servant is demoted to one of the "decay'd, ruinous, worme-eaten gentlemen of the round": a "Serjeant-Major, if not a Lieutenant-Coronell," but assuredly not a Tamburlaine (H&S 3:353).

A more significant and far-reaching revision is the deletion of Knowell Junior's rejoinder to his father, an impassioned defense of orginality in poetry:

> Opinion, O God let grosse opinion
> Sinck & be damnd as deepe as Barathrum.
> If it may stand with your most wisht content,
> I can refell opinion, and approve
> The state of poesie, such as it is,
> Blessed, aeternal, and most true devine:
> Indeede if you will looke on Poesie,
> As she appeares in many, poore and lame,
> Patcht up in remnants and olde worne ragges,
> Halfe starvd for want of her peculiar foode,
> Sacred invention, then I must conferme,
> Both your conceite and censure of her merrite. . . .

> (H&S 3:285)

The speech, which continues for another twenty lines, rehearses by now familiar arguments: the weak poet is "halfe starvd for want of her peculiar foode / Sacred invention," terms recalling those used earlier in describing Matheo's theft from Marlowe. Jonson also attacks "braine-lesse guls" who "utter their stolne wares / With such aplauses in our vulgar eares" and an audience that sets "no difference twixt these empty spirits, / And a true Poet." Jonson here invokes the New Comic situation so familiar to Shakespearean comedy and gives it a twist: the source of tension between father and son is not a woman but Poetry it-self, described by the young male lover in terms usually reserved for his beloved. But the unification toward which the play drives is not the creation of a new family structure through the marriage of man and woman, but a new poetic order that follows a true poet's union with Poetry herself. As Jonson himself struggled to overcome and circumvent forbidding poetic models like Marlowe during the years in which he forged his style, his plays often appropriate this intergenerational conflict inherent in New Comedy and reformulate this strife as an interpoetic one. That the speech is directed at a father figure most likely played by Shakespeare (in the Chamberlain's Men's production of 1598) adds another dimension to the complexities of interpoetic relations. In the revised version this confrontation between aspiring son and repressive father (who admits to having once dreamt "on naught but idle Poetrie" [H&S 3:197]) is omitted, replaced by Justice Clemen's cheery observation that poets "are not borne everie yeere, as an Alderman." Knowell Junior's reply is now brief: "Sir, you have sav'd me the labour of a defence" (H&S 3:400). Herford and Simpson's claim that "[f]ew Elizabethan plays owe less, in fact, to the stimulus or guidance of previous literature than *Every Man in his Humour*" (1:345) needs to be reversed: few Elizabethan plays evince so earnest and desperate a struggle to repudiate the stimulus of poetic precursors.[13]

Jonson, through the juxtaposition of poetaster and true poet, reiterates the belief, repeated in his critical writings, that imitation which never goes beyond mere mimicry is fatal to all but the strongest of poets. He writes in *Discoveries* that "wee so insist in imitating others, as wee cannot (when it is necessary) returne to our selves" (H&S 8:597). The feared loss of poetic identity, the possibility of being consumed (rather than having a "Stomacke to concoct, divide, and turne all into nourishment" [H&S 8:638], that is, consume another's poetic authority) dogged Jonson. He returned to it in his next play, *Every Man out of His Humour,* where weak poets become fixed at the level of mimicry. The play is about literary indigestion: the play's many imitators, lacking the necessary "stomach to concoct, divide, and turn all to nourishment," swallow what they take in "crude, raw, or indigested" (H&S 8:638). In the end either they are purged or their lips are sealed; the result is essentially the same. The imitators who fill the play take on the characteristics Jonson ascribes in *Discoveries* to derivative poets who are "like Children, that imitate the vice of Stammerers so long, till at last they become such; and make the habit to another nature, as it is never forgotten" (H&S 8:597). *Every Man Out,* which has the notoriety of being the longest extant English Renaissance play, is almost unactable in the form that has come down to us (and it has not been acted professionally since the Restoration [H&S 9:185–88]), since Jonson chose to add material for the printed version, the first of his works that he saw into print. The result, as one critic puts it, is "a book about a play about literature" (Dunford 147). The unusual features of the play can partly be accounted for in terms of Jonson's confrontation with and exploration of his relationship to native predecessors, his increasing conviction of independence from them, and his use of parody and poetasters in triumphing over them. It also suggests the extent to which Jonson was nervously aware of the dangers that awaited those who imitated too servilely for too long. Characteristically, in asserting (with no irony) that "he follows in no poet's footsteps," Jonson quotes from Horace on the title pages of the Quarto and Folio: *"Non aliena meo pressi pede"* (H&S 3:419).

Each of Jonson's humorous characters in *Every Man Out* chooses a literary style (and the attendant world implied by this style) and attempts both to inhabit that world entirely and to impose that world upon others. In Anne Barton's terms, the output of Jonson's contemporaries and forebears becomes "a kind of barometer to the folly of those characters who read and quote from it" (73). Terrance Dunford takes this argument a step further in his "Consumption of the World: Reading, Eating, and Imitation in *Every Man out of His Humour*," where he argues that the inhabitants of the play " 'read' their world and consume it in their readings by attempting to project them upon reality." Ultimately, each character "claims that his book (and its literary form) is the only true articulation of reality," while "all other texts are relegated to the category of 'art'" (133). It is but a short step from here to the larger submerged claim that Jonson, casting out and exposing these gulls, effectively undermines the mimetic claims of the Elizabethan models consumed by these humours and thereby claims greater fidelity to reality and life for his own art. Saviolina peppers her discourse with phrases borrowed from Sidney and Greene ("from whence she may steal with more security"). Fungoso lounges about, reading from Sidney's *Arcadia,* while his sister Fallace prefers Lyly's Euphuistic prose. Puntavolo is enamored of the conventions of romance, Brisk of Daniel, Clove of Marston. While there is no imitator of Marlowe, Clove urges Orange to "talke fustian a little," and Buffone tosses out

odd bits of hyperbolic blank verse reminiscent of Tamburlaine's histrionic gestures:

> With that, the moody squire thumpt his brest,
> And rear'd his eyen to heaven, for revenge.
>
> (H&S 3:508)

One gull can praise another for the manner in which he "doth so
peerelesly imitate any manner of person for gesture, action, passion,
or whatever," while another acknowledges that only by consuming
others can growth occur: "if we fed upon another, we should shoot up
a greate deale faster, and thrive much better" (H&S 3:581). All are punished, in a play that "is a parody of literature and the ease with which
literary forms are imitated" (Dunford 147), and whose structure provides an ideal medium for Jonson to repudiate poetic precursors, asserting his emergent originality and independence, and measure the
distance that separates the true poet, who can properly digest and absorb a (by now outmoded) poetic tradition, and those amateurish imitators who merely choke on it.

As the above examples show, central to the *Every Man* plays (and to
Poetaster) is Jonson's imposition of a poetaster between himself and
the object of parody. Poetasters are useful, perhaps necessary intermediaries for Jonson, through which he can confront precursors. In their
faithful and woefully unoriginal mimicry they resemble the children
who cannot shake the habit of imitating the stutterer. Transferring his
criticism to the mimic and not the object of imitation, Jonson can
mock the weak while indirectly confronting the strong, simultaneously
admiring and rejecting poetic models. The poetasters are thus scape-
goats, bearing Jonson's anxiety more justifiably directed at the authority of poetic precursors. By heaping scorn upon their ignorant delight
in the very models he wants to repress and reject, and by inviting and
exhorting us to scorn these characters, their values, and their poetic
preferences, Jonson indirectly corrects and revises the work of his
predecessors.

Intrinsic to Jonson's inclusion of parody and poetasters is his juxtaposition of styles. We might think here of Shakespeare's response to
Marlowe in his *Merchant of Venice* (not just in relation to *The Jew of*

Malta but in its depiction of the Prince of Morocco as a debased Tamburlaine whose hyperbolic and bombastic blank verse is set off against the conversational stage prose spoken by other characters) (Bradbrook 191–93). It is a technique especially attractive to writers of comedy, more so for writers of realistic social comedy, whose aim is the representation of love and life and the problems of social relation. For such authors, parodic juxtaposition becomes a useful device for foregrounding an unrealistic—Jonson might say untruthful—mode of life and love and language. If the aim of the comic dramatist is the creation of a meaningful comic world, then one of his first tasks is to challenge (by juxtaposition or by parodic subversion) the inadequate dramatic worlds offered by previous artists. Untimely ripped from their world by poetasters, the conventionality of older comic worlds cannot help but reinforce for audiences the illusion (and thereby the inadequacy) of older poetic visions, while presumably recommending the comic world, in Jonson's case the prose world, in which they are embedded.

Jonson foregrounds filial strife, parody, poetasters, plagiarism, and especially revision yet again in *Poetaster,* the last of his "comical satyres" and a play which marks a "turne" in his engagement with Marlowe. In *Poetaster* the problem of Marlowe's influence surfaces in act 1, scene 1, when a poet-dramatist (and, confusingly, *not* the poetaster of the title) enters reciting the closing lines of "the hastie errours of our morning muse":

> Then, when this bodie falls in funerall fire,
> My name shall live, and my best part aspire.
>
> (H&S 4:206)

The poet is Ovid, the poem the fifteenth elegy of book 1 of his *Amores.* And in the ensuing scene he must confront a repressive father, Ovid Senior, intent on blocking his poetic career. The elegy he recites is about envy—which pains the living poet, not the dead one. Significantly, it is also about canonization and the making of a masculine literary-historical tradition. After a brief digression, Ovid proceeds to read the forty-four-line elegy in its entirety, an unusual dramatic strategy for Jonson, especially so early on in a play. The first eight lines read:

> Envie, why twitst thou me, my time's spent ill?
> And call'st my verse, fruit of an idle quill?
> Or that (unlike the line from whence I sprung)
> Wars dustie honours I pursue not young?
> Or that I studie not the tedious lawes;
> And prostitute my voyce in everie cause?
> Thy scope is mortall; mine, eternall fame:
> Which through the world shall ever chaunt my name. . . .
>
> (H&S 4:207)

By the third or fourth couplet attentive listeners might have remembered where they had heard those lines before: Marlowe's notorious and recently banned (and burned) translations of Ovid's *Elegies:*

> Envie, why carpest thou my time is spent so ill,
> And termes our works fruits of an idle quill?
> Or that unlike the line from whence I sprong,
> Wars dustie honors are refused being yong?
> Nor that I studie not the brawling lawes,
> Nor set my voyce to sale in everie cause?
> Thy scope is mortall, mine eternall fame,
> That all the world might ever chaunt my name. . . .
>
> (Bowers 2:338)

There is no Lorenzo here to cry foul, no critic exclaiming "steale from the deade? its worse than sacriledge." In light of the subject of the poem—the paradox that only in death the poet most triumphs and most lives—it is hard to believe that Jonson could have included this Marlovian imitation with no sense of the irony involved. Yet, despite the similarities between the passages, Jonson no doubt saw his version as a substantial revision of Marlowe, and made no objection when his translation was included in editions of Marlowe's elegies after 1602, with the words "The same by B.J."

The alterations range from factual to stylistic. Jonson, for instance, corrects Marlowe's mistaken rendering of Accius (Lucius Accius) as Plautus (a fine point of classical scholarship that had only recently been set right), no doubt experiencing the kind of self-satisfaction evident in the marginal notes to his copy of Chapman's *Homer* (e.g., *"O quam inepte haec omnia, et sequentia!"* (H&S 11:594) [Oh, how inept is all this and that which follows!]). J. B. Steane, comparing the two versions, stresses Jonson's regularization, his smoothing out of Marlowe's rougher edges (280–301). Marlowe's "brawling" laws become Jonson's "tedious" ones; "bond-men cheat" is changed to "slaves be false." More tellingly, Marlowe's

> Therefore when flint and yron weare away,
> Verse is immortal, and shall nere decay,

is bled dry in Jonson's

> The suffering Plough-share or the flint may weare:
> But heavenlie Poesie no death can fear.

Jonson, however, more closely approximates Marlowe's vein when he alters

> Let base conceited wits admire vilde things,
> Faire Phoebus leade me to the Muses springs

to a vivid and forceful

> Kneele hindes to trash: me let bright Phoebus swell,
> With cups fill flowing from the Muses well.

As Steane observes, the greatest difference in their sensibilities is apparent in their translations of Ovid's final couplet (282). Jonson writes,

> Then when this body falls in funeral fire,
> My name shall live, and my best part aspire,

a couplet whose balance and closure differ sharply from Marlowe's—

> Then though death rackes my bones in funerall fier
> Ile live, and as he puls me downe, mount higher

—lines that neatly encapsulate Marlovian violence, paradoxical and continuous struggle, and defiant assertion of autonomy. In his precise, sure-handed revisions of Marlowe's translation we can locate Jonson's parting of ways. His revision reflects an increasing self-confidence in his poetic choices, one that acknowledges (and literally copies) Marlowe's strengths while with equal ease departs freely from what it finds remiss or defective in this precursor's style. For it is to Marlowe's verse style, above all, that the early Jonson responded most powerfully, a style that could charm not only the "innocent gapers" in the theater but aspiring poets, too. Henry Petowe, one such poet, speaks to this power, and to the challenge of Marlowe's style to those who would "contend" with it, in his continuation, "The Second Part of 'Hero and Leander,' Containing Their Further Fortunes" (1598):

> What mortal soul with Marlowe might contend,
> That could 'gainst reason force him stoop or bend?
> Whose silver charming tongue moved such delight
> That men would shun their sleep in still dark night
> To meditate upon his golden lines,
> His rare conceits and sweet according rhymes.
>
> (Orgel 95)

There are not many descriptions in Tudor and Stuart literature of how poets actually respond to each other's work,[14] and Petowe's imaginative re-creation of what it meant to confront Marlowe's legacy is instructive: the poetic encounter is violent and competitive; the task of the enthralled poetic heir is to force his precursor to "stoop or bend." Petowe—whom even the *Dictionary of National Biography* calls a "poetaster"—completed Marlowe's *Hero and Leander* feebly. He failed to grasp, as Jonson would, the precarious balance between imitation and admiration. In Jonson's brief poetic encounter with Marlowe in *Poetaster* we witness a poet whose response to Marlowe was extending well beyond stylistic imitation toward a fuller contention with and appropriation of Marlowe's art.

III

Jonson's mature comedies, especially *Volpone,* mark a "counter-turne" in his development as dramatist. Critics like Barton have attributed this to his construction of a drama built upon the principles of

Aristophanic Old Comedy, with its limited interest in love and romance, its political topicality, its satiric bite and harsh, often violent
humor, and its exposure of vice and unregenerate behavior (113ff.).
But for Jonson "Comedia Vetus" was not Aristophanic but the native
homiletic tradition of the Vice play,[15] a dramatic form, as David Bevington and Bernard Spivack have shown, that powerfully informed
Marlowe's drama (especially *The Jew of Malta* and *Doctor Faustus*) and
that provided a model much closer at hand than Aristophanes for the
savage farce, ambivalent closure, structural repetition, and sympathetic villains that recur in Jonson's mature comedies.

In *Volpone,* then, Jonson moves full circle: Marlowe's influence,
once threatening, proves beneficent, as Jonson returns to *The Jew of
Malta* in creating his most powerful and memorable play. With this re-
ceptive imitative response Jonson's absorption of Marlowe is nearly
total, any anxiety of influence replaced by a mimesis that *completes*
and ultimately *exhausts* Marlowe's art. Jonson is able here to contain
and control the Marlovian tone and the Marlovian overreacher within
the confines of his own comic design. Critical attempts to label *Volpone* as a corrective, Aristophanic, or satiric comedy undervalue the
extent to which the work is informed by Jonson's appropriation and
transformation of Marlowe's dramatic form. In terms of Thomas M.
Greene's taxonomy of imitation, Jonson here exhibits the most sophisticated kind of imitation—"dialectical" or "improvisational"—in
which the artist moves through imitation to originality (43–48).[16]

In *Volpone,* Jonson responds to what was proleptically Jacobean in
Marlowe's play: the radical skepticism, slippery moral center, Machi-
avellianism, and Italianate intrigue anticipate the spirit and concerns
that would inform so many Jacobean tragedies. When revived at the
court of Charles I by Heywood forty years after its inception, *The Jew
of Malta* must have seemed remarkably modern in its cynical social and
political vision. Jonson recognized and exploited this quality: he
found in Marlowe's play a world in which money's corruptive power
could sever master from servant, husband from wife, and perhaps
most disturbingly, parent from child (though Jonson characteristically
replaces father/daughter with father/son). Marlowe's *The Jew of Malta*
also served as a paradigm for a world of repeated playacting and dissembling, one irremediably corrupt politically and judicially, and

where the execution of authority remains problematic. In this respect, yet another effect of Marlowe's play is felt in the troubling conclusion of Jonson's comedy, a feature found as well in the unsettling closure of Shakespeare's earlier emulative encounter with *The Jew of Malta* in *The Merchant of Venice* (Shapiro).

From the outset, as T. S. Eliot first observed, *Volpone* immerses us in a Marlovian universe—stylistically, visually, and thematically:

> Good morning to the day; and, next, my gold:
> Open the shrine, that I may see my saint.
> Haile the worlds soule, and mine. More glad then is
> The teeming earth, to see the long'd-for sunne
> Peepe through the hornes of the celestiall ram,
> Am I, to view thy splendor, darkening his:
> That, lying here, amongst my other hoords,
> Shew'st like a flame, by night; or like the day
> Strooke out of chaos, when all darkenesse fled
> Unto the center.
>
> (H&S 5:24–25)

The speech—for Eliot "in the manner of Marlowe, more deliberate, more mature, but without Marlowe's inspiration" (154)—conflates Faustus's aspiring soliloquy with Barabas's opening speech. Recalling Faustus in his study and Barabas in his countinghouse, the play opens with the overreacher, isolated, declaring his devotion to his object of desire. At the same time, as with Faustus and Barabas, we sense in Volpone's chambers a stifling feeling of enclosure heightened by the protagonist's restlessness, his desire for play, and his desire, simply, for more. Volpone's opening speech also invokes a Marlovian restructuring of values and the playful undermining of theological and ethical claims.

Structurally, too, *Volpone* owes much to Marlowe's work, most notably in Jonson's creation of a plot based on repeated, virtually identical scenes. Thus, Volpone's gulling of Voltore, Corbaccio, and Corvino in the second, third, and fourth scenes of act 1 follow a dramatic pattern Marlowe had employed in representing Tamburlaine's successive and ultimately numbing conquests of Mycetes, Cosroe, Bajazeth, and Calapine; in Faustus's repeated and eventually demeaning demonstration of his powers with Benvolio, Frederick, Martino, the Carter, the

Horse-courser, and the Hostess; and in Barabas's murderous schemes against Lodowick, Mathias, Jacomo, Barnadino, and Calymath. We have here a dramatic unfolding radically different from the kind developed by Shakespeare. Intrinsic to this almost compulsive repetition are the protagonist's reiterated assertions of self, paradoxically coupled with his insistence on role-playing, masking, and self-fashioning, as that self is shown to be a fictional, pliable construct (Greenblatt). Volpone's disguise as a mountebank likewise harks back to Barabas's playing the part of another professional entertainer, a French musician.

In comparing *Volpone* with *The Jew of Malta* Eliot justly argues that Jonson, like Marlowe, should be considered as a master of farce and caricature, a creator of a drama of great and terrifying directness, a creator, too, of a drama that intentionally lacks the third dimension, depth, that we have come to associate with Shakespeare and Shakespearean drama. Eliot is instructive in setting Marlowe and Jonson together against Shakespeare: the feature "which distinguishes Barabas from Shylock, Epicure Mammon from Falstaff, Faustus from . . . Macbeth" is an animating power, an artistic wholeness and dramatic universe (157). Jonson, like Marlowe—and to a great extent through Marlowe—discovered the possibilities generated by what Eliot describes as two-dimensionality, or alternatively, of caricature. Put another way, where language is subordinated to character in Shakespeare's play, character is virtually an extension, a creation of language in the works of Marlowe and Jonson. The search for depth or coherence of character in Jonson (as in Marlowe) is a search for identity, and that identity is attained when a voice or language is found. Marlowe's drama can thus be seen as helping to liberate Jonson from the dominant Elizabethan comic form—Shakespearean New Comedy—allowing for a remarkable release of creativity and originality in the mature comedies that followed.

Jonson's imitative encounter presents us, then, with a double completion, a double act of caricature: the first kind in the caricatured types in the *Every Man* plays (characters who become associated not only with various humours but with various literary styles); the second kind in their successors, the full-blown caricatures in *Volpone* and *The Alchemist*. Volpone and Sir Epicure Mammon are not marginalized poetasters, constantly scrutinized and criticized by onstage critics, but grand overreaching caricatures, infused with an animating spirit, holding forth unabashedly and bombastically.

When Jonson stopped putting Marlovian characters in their place, when he was no longer preoccupied with overcoming his Elizabethan precursors, he let his characters acquire sufficient enormity—of vitality and vice—and thereby allowed for what Eliot, I think rightly, finds a beautiful, serious, and somber poetic vision. It is a richly imaginative and exuberant world, one that insists that we not approach Jonson as archeologists, mining his works for lodes of classical authority, but consider him through what Eliot calls a "knowledge of Jonson," which I understand to mean a knowledge of how he came to be what he is remembered for, and the relationship of his talent to a native tradition, a tradition he reshaped by translating the Marlovian overreacher to a new, comic, and unflinchingly severe universe. This Jonsonian strategy led Eliot to conclude (in terms critics have usually reserved for Marlowe) that we find in Jonson "a brutality, a lack of sentiment, a polished surface, a handling of large bold designs in brilliant colours" (159). Jonson, having fully digested his poetic forebear, plays out the dramatic possibilities cut short by Ingram Friser's fatal blow at the Inn at Deptford.

When Jonson was to turn again, nostalgically, to Elizabethan models in his late years—in plays like *A Tale of a Tub, The Sad Shepherd,* and *The Magnetic Lady*—he would turn to the Shakespearean world of pastoral and romance he had rejected in favor of the Marlovian (Barton). Barton, in her excellent account of Jonson's nostalgia for Elizabethan dramatic forms he had once repudiated, makes too little of the distinction (emphasized by Eliot) between the Marlovian and Shakespearean impulses in Elizabethan drama. Jonson had mostly followed the Marlovian one and had exhausted it; in turning back he would explore a path not taken. In his late years, even as *Doctor Faustus* and *The Jew of Malta* were staged at court and at the public theaters, Jonson shows little interest in responding anew to their challenge. He had already transformed the tradition that he had inherited, bequeathing to his followers a dramatic tradition that, along with its major rival, Shakespeare's, left little room for what had been the infinite riches of Marlowe's style—a style that, as a result, appeared too raw, undigested, and crude for the sensibilities of subsequent generations of theatergoers, though, in fact, it had simply been a patrimony too carefully and too thoroughly consumed by Marlowe's heirs.[17]

Notes

1. Important exceptions, emphasizing Jonson's development in relation to native dramatic traditions, are offered by Alvin Kernan, Robert Watson, and especially Anne Barton, whose illuminating chapter on "Jonson and the Elizabethans" proved an important point of departure for this study, in part because Barton *does not* explore Marlowe's influence on Jonson. Kernan's foreword to *Two Renaissance Mythmakers,* in which he alludes to Marlowe and Jonson in terms of the succession of "a great tragic mythmaker" by "a great comic mythmaker," offers a suggestive link between Marlowe and Jonson studies. Finally, Robert Watson's book (which was published only after this essay was completed) provides a valuable account of Jonson's parodic response to the styles of his Elizabethan predecessors in his comedies.

2. For alternative and cogent readings of Jonson's development as a dramatist (but which often follow Jonson's own revisionist procedure) see the work of W. David Kay and Richard Helgerson.

3. Nor was Jonson alone in facing the problem of Marlowe's influence: Shakespeare, Chapman, Greene, Peele, Petowe, Raleigh, Donne, and others also sought to complete or compete with Marlowe's work.

4. Harold Bloom's theory of the "anxiety of influence" offers an obvious and valuable point of departure for describing Jonson's response to Marlowe's legacy, though Bloom chooses to describe Jonson as a poet who "has no anxiety as to imitation, for to him (refreshingly) art is *hard work*" (*Influence* 27). I stress "point of departure" because in crucial ways Bloom's model does not quite contain (or explain) Jonson's filial response, especially Jonson's movement through imitation to originality, nor is it sufficiently sensitive to complexities of imitation that arise in a commercial, competitive, and collaborative popular theater. It is valuable, though, in championing individual consciousness as the locus of a dynamic process of artistic and psychological interaction, in a critical age where author-centered criticism has become increasingly marginalized. My understanding of Jonsonian imitation in this essay is located between Bloom's suggestive patriarchal model and Thomas M. Greene's theory in *The Light in Troy.* While Greene focuses exclusively on Renaissance appropriations of classical texts (and is also weak on imitation in the drama), his emphasis upon the tension between reverence and rebelliousness that characterizes imitation in the Renaissance, and his typology of imitation that moves from "sacramental" and "eclectic" to more complex "heuristic" and "dialectical" imitative strategies, offers a model of literary influence that also clarifies literary relations between native predecessors and their heirs. The consciousness of anachronism that

Greene sees as a defining feature of Renaissance imitation of classical texts was also characteristic of the response of Renaissance authors to their native forebears: Michael Drayton, for example, speaks of Marlowe as having "in him those brave translunary things, / That the first Poets had" (in "To My Most Dearely-Loved Friend Henry Renolds, Esquire, of Poets and Poesie" [1627], qtd. in MacLure 47), while Jonson alludes to "the *Tamerlanes* and *Tamer-Chams* of the late Age" (H&S 8:587).

5. So much so, that, for instance, when Jonson mentions a woman writer he does so to deny her authorship. Thus: "Sir P. Sidney had translated some of the Psalmes, which went abroad under the name of ye Countesse of Pembrock" (H&S 1:138).

6. One result of the recent trend in Renaissance studies toward new historicism and cultural poetics has been that comparatively less attention is now being paid to the profound effect on canon formation of author-centered features such as literary influence and the kind of patrilinear model to which Jonson was committed (as opposed to other ideological, social, or cultural influences recently explored by such Jonson critics as Richard Helgerson, Don E. Wayne, and Joseph Loewenstein). Concomitantly, discussions of that essentialized term "patriarchy" are losing an important specificity when the kind of tensions and contradictions embedded in patriarchal processes (like the male intergenerational strife at the heart of Jonson's conception of influence) are overlooked.

7. Subsequently expanded to "Hee dy'd, and left it unfinished." See the H&S discussion (7:53–54).

8. See *Henslowe's Diary* (Foakes and Rickert 205) where Henslowe lists payment for two "sewtes a licke for the playe of mortymore" (i.e., *Edward II*).

9. A dissenting view is offered by Barton (338–40), who dismisses the Oxford editors' assertion that "it is clearly early work" (7:53) and follows an earlier tradition that considered it "the last draught of Jonson's quill."

10. In the 1601 Quarto version Jonson quotes from Daniel correctly: "Unto the boundlesse ocean of thy bewtie, / Runnes this poor river, chargd with streames of zeale" (H&S 3:284). Matheo here admits to having "translated" the lines "out of a booke, called *Delia.*"

11. I am indebted in the following discussion to Margaret A. Rose, *Parody//Meta-Fiction,* and Linda Hutcheon, *A Theory of Parody.*

12. Though a number of important poets and dramatists died in the early 1590s, it is curious that only Marlowe is consistently remembered as a *dead* poet. See, for example: Shakespeare's allusion in *As You Like It* to Marlowe as "dead shepherd"; Peele's reference to Marlowe's "writing passions for the soules below"; and the reminder by the author of the Parnassus plays, in reference to Marlowe, that what "Our theater hath lost, Pluto hath got."

13. The problem of Jonson as Marlowe's poetic heir cannot be separated from Jonson's general ambivalence to paternal authority. Psychological speculation may perhaps cast some light on the case of Jonson's difficulties with authority—political, poetic, and paternal (see, in this regard, Donaldson; Rollin; and Pearlman). E. Pearlman's illuminating essay shows how Jonson, in his life and work, reiterated a concern with (and a struggle against) authority. In seeking to fill the void created by the death of a natural father

he never knew, Jonson repeatedly sought his replacement—in the Scottish grandfather mentioned in *Discoveries,* his schoolmaster Cambden, the priest who converted this son of a Protestant clergyman to Catholicism, and his bricklayer stepfather. Pearlman concludes that all "that can be said with certainty is that Jonson wants and needs to acknowledge parental figures," that "again and again he returns in his work to just such a theme," and that a "common subject in his plays is the relation of father to son" (371).

14. Thomas Carew's "To Ben Jonson uppon occasion of his Ode to Himself" is another, and germane to my argument. Carew describes poetic emulation as a process of "overcoming" one's rival; imitation is defined not as theft but as the "opima spolia" of a victorious encounter:

> & if thou owercome
> A knottie writer, bring the bootie home.
> Nor think it theft, if the rich spoyles so torne
> From conquerd Authors, be as Trophies worne.
>
> (H&S 11:335–36)

15. See *Conversations,* 1.410 (H&S 1:143–44). He uses the term in another (perhaps Aristophanic) sense in the Induction to *Every Man Out* where Cordatus speaks of Asper's "strange" play as "somewhat like *Vetus Comoedia*" (H&S 3:436). Jonson was not unique in calling the native interlude tradition Old Comedy: see, for instance, *The Returne of Pasquill* by Thomas Nashe (Marlowe and Jonson's collaborator), where Nashe speaks of *"Vetus Comaedia* [that] began to prick him at London in the right vaine, when she brought forth Divinitie wyth a scratcht face . . ." (McKerrow 1:92).

16. This originality is no less apparent in Jonson's subsequent "mature" comedies, *The Alchemist* and *Bartholomew Fair* and *The Devil Is an Ass.* That Marlowe was still a "provocative agent" in these plays is apparent, for example, from Jonson's great Marlovian overreacher, Sir Epicure Mammon, and from Littlewit's stage version of *Hero and Leander* at the puppet show. I hope to expand upon these and other concerns in a book-length study of the literary interrelations of Marlowe, Jonson, and Shakespeare.

17. This essay, in an earlier and abbreviated form, was read at the Marlowe Society session of the 1984 MLA Convention. The expanded version has profited from the criticism of David Scott Kastan, Stuart Kurland, Claire McEachern, Peter L. Rudnytsky, Michael Shapiro, Alvin Snider, and Edward W. Tayler. I am also grateful for an NEH summer stipend that allowed me time to work on this.

Works Cited

Allott, Robert. *Englands Parnassus: Or, The Choysest Flowers of Our Moderne Poets.* London, 1600.

Barish, Jonas A. *Ben Jonson and the Language of Prose Comedy.* Cambridge: Harvard UP, 1960.

Barton, Anne. *Ben Jonson, Dramatist.* Cambridge: Cambridge UP, 1984.

Berek, Peter. "Tamburlaine's Weak Sons: Imitation as Interpretation Before 1593." *Renaissance Drama* ns 13 (1982): 55–82.

Bevington, David M. *From "Mankind" to Marlowe.* Cambridge: Harvard UP, 1962.

Bloom, Harold. *The Anxiety of Influence: A Theory of Poetry.* New York: Oxford UP, 1973.

_____. *A Map of Misreading.* New York: Oxford UP, 1975.

Boas, Frederick S., ed. *The Works of Thomas Kyd.* Oxford: Clarendon, 1901.

Bowers, Fredson, ed. *The Complete Works of Christopher Marlowe.* 2 vols. Cambridge: Cambridge UP, 1973.

Bradbrook, M. C. "Shakespeare's Recollections of Marlowe." *Shakespeare's Styles.* Ed. Philip Edwards, Inga-Stina Ewbank, G. K. Hunter. Cambridge: Cambridge UP, 1980. 191–204.

Bradley, Jesse Franklin, and Joseph Quincey Adams. *The Jonson Allusion Book.* New Haven: Yale UP, 1922.

Davis, Joe Lee. *The Sons of Ben: Jonsonian Comedy in Caroline England.* Detroit: Wayne State UP, 1967.

Donaldson, Ian. "Jonson and Anger." *Yearbook of English Studies* 14 (1984): 56–71.

Duncan, Douglas. *Ben Jonson and the Lucianic Tradition.* Cambridge: Cambridge UP, 1979.

Dunford, Terrance. "Consumption of the World: Reading, Eating, and Imitation in *Every Man out of His Humour.*" *English Literary Renaissance* 14 (1984): 131–47.

Eliot, T. S. "Ben Jonson." 1919. *Selected Essays.* London: Faber, 1932.

Foakes, R. A., and R. T. Rickert, eds. *Henslowe's Diary.* Cambridge: Cambridge UP, 1961.

Freud, Sigmund. *The Standard Edition of the Complete Psychological Works of Sigmund Freud.* Trans. James Strachey et al. 24 vols. London: Hogarth, 1953–74.

Greenblatt, Stephen. *Renaissance Self-Fashioning: From More to Shakespeare.* Chicago: U of Chicago P, 1980.

Greene, Thomas M. *The Light in Troy: Imitation and Discovery in Renaissance Poetry.* New Haven: Yale UP, 1982.

Helgerson, Richard. *Self-Crowned Laureates.* Berkeley: U of California P, 1983.

Herford, C. H., and Percy and Evelyn Simpson. *Ben Jonson.* 11 vols. Oxford: Oxford UP, 1925–52.

Hutcheon, Linda. *A Theory of Parody: The Teaching of Twentieth-Century Art Forms.* New York: Methuen, 1985.

Jackson, Gabriele Bernhard, ed. *Every Man in His Humor.* By Ben Jonson. New Haven: Yale UP, 1969.

Kay, W. David. "The Shaping of Ben Jonson's Career." *Modern Philology* 67 (1970): 224–37.

Kernan, Alvin, ed. *Two Renaissance Mythmakers: Christopher Marlowe and Ben Jonson.* Selected Papers from the English Institute, 1975–76, ns 1. Baltimore: Johns Hopkins UP, 1977.

Loewenstein, Joseph. "The Script in the Marketplace." *Representations* 12 (1985): 101–14.

McKerrow, Ronald B., and F. P. Wilson, eds. *The Works of Thomas Nashe.* 5 vols. Oxford: Blackwell, 1958.

MacLure, Millar. *Marlowe: The Critical Heritage, 1588–1896.* London: Routledge, 1979.

Maus, Katherine Eisamen. *Ben Jonson and the Roman Frame of Mind.* Princeton: Princeton UP, 1984.

Orgel, Stephen, ed. *The Complete Poems and Translations.* By Christopher Marlowe. Baltimore: Penguin, 1971.

Pearlman, E. "Ben Jonson: An Anatomy." *English Literary Renaissance* 9 (1979): 363–94.

Peterson, Richard S. *Imitation and Praise in the Poetry of Ben Jonson.* New Haven: Yale UP, 1981.

"Petowe, Henry." *Dictionary of National Biography.* Ed. Leslie Stephen and Sidney Lee. 66 vols. London: Oxford UP, 1885–1901.

Rollin, Roger B. "The Anxiety of Identification: Jonson and the Rival Poets." *Classic and Cavalier: Essays on Jonson and the Sons of Ben.* Ed. Claude J. Summers and Ted-Larry Pebworth. Pittsburgh: U of Pittsburgh P, 1982. 139–56.

Rose, Margaret A. *Parody//Meta-Fiction.* London: Croom Helm, 1979.

Shapiro, James. "'Which Is *The Merchant* Here, and Which *The Jew?*': Shakespeare and the Economics of Influence." *Shakespeare Studies* (forthcoming).

Spivack, Bernard. *Shakespeare and the Allegory of Evil.* New York: Columbia UP, 1958.

Steane, J. B. *Marlowe: A Critical Study.* Cambridge: Cambridge UP, 1964.

Summers, Claude J., and Ted-Larry Pebworth. *Classic and Cavalier: Essays on Jonson and the Sons of Ben.* Pittsburgh: U of Pittsburgh P, 1982.

Watson, Robert. *Jonson's Parodic Strategy: Literary Imperialism in the Comedies.* Cambridge: Harvard UP, 1987.

Wayne, Don E. "Drama and Society in the Age of Jonson: An Alternative View." *Renaissance Drama* ns 13 (1982): 103–29.

Way Stations in the Errancy of the Word: A Study of Calderón's La vida es sueño

RUTH EL SAFFAR

I N ANSWER to Derrida's assessment of the written word's nature as "coupée de toute responsabilité absolue, de la *conscience* comme autorité de dernière instance, orphaline et separée dès sa naissance de l'assistance de son père" (Derrida's emphasis), Thomas Greene in *The Light in Troy* restores meaning to the word by anchoring it—albeit temporarily—in a series of more or less nurturing contexts.[1] For Greene *écriture* is not so much a "Dickensian child-hero" as an entity acquiring "a kind of ubiquitous foster parent in the presence of the maternal culture that has adopted it" (16). Though neither Greene nor Derrida underscores it—in fact, *because* neither underscores it—their respective metaphors regarding the written word's fate provide interesting commentary on the unconscious ground out of which their speculations arise. Derrida's written word is severed from any absolute responsibility, and from consciousness as ultimate authority, because of its condition as "separée dès sa naissance de l'assistance de son *père*." Its hope for stability, for a responsible communal contribution, however, according to Greene, comes from the "*maternal* culture that has adopted it" (emphasis added).

The paternal and maternal metaphors—their unconscious association with authority and errancy on the one hand, and with nurture and stability on the other—plunge us into what Greene calls a "communal intuition" (23) as long-standing as it has been, until very recently, inexpressible. Indeed, it is the nature of metaphor, as Greene later points out so insightfully, to allude to the "intuitions of relationship conceivable within a given culture" (22). Only now, with the perspective provided by recent efforts to understand the social and psychological effects of almost exclusively female parenting in early childhood are we in a position to bring to consciousness some part of the nexus of associations that allows a writer to envision an ungrounded word as both without consciousness and without paternity.[2] The unspoken metaphor in this case yokes responsibility and consciousness with the presence of the father.[3] A less radical view of the nature of the word, on the other hand, one that gives it temporary shelter against the winds of chance and change, restores, through the maternal metaphor, the possibility of communication that Derrida's orphaned word has lost. Greene's "maternal culture" links the notion of exchange and interaction with the idea of mother.

Taken together, the two metaphors evoke primordial images of the post-edenic nuclear family: the child (word) is abandoned by its father (intention, consciousness), yet it is given by the mother (context) a place in which, temporarily, to experience interaction. Derrida's challenge to the Western philosophical, logocentric tradition, which Greene modifies but does not ultimately refuse, depends precisely on the radical absence of the father. That absence, as we shall see in the analysis of Calderón's *La vida es sueño* that follows here, opens up language and culture, indeed, the whole notion of identity, to confrontation with the abyss. The acquisition of literacy brings alterity with it, as Derrida so powerfully intuits (179–80). The sense of separation, absence, and fatherlessness that literacy brings as its necessary complement, however, is exactly what it needs most to hide. Out of the paternal void it will create, therefore, its own spectral authority, an authority grounded, as Calderón saw only too clearly, on fear and illusion, and having ultimately no referent beyond itself.

With the mass interiorization of the notion of language as *écriture*, as that which is *written*, not spoken, Western culture in the sixteenth century turned to the image not only of the word, but of the self as an entity separate from its environment.[4] The itinerary of the written word, whose description Derrida so persuasively offers, mirrors curiously that of Western culture, tracing out the solitary, fatherless wanderer in a culture given over since the Renaissance to the collective errancies of massive migrations—from farm to town, from native country to colonies. The written word, which allows for the first time—enforces, in fact—a separation between speaker and audience, between knower and known, spawned the fictions of the rogue and adventurer in a world that was throwing its sons and fathers in successive waves across oceans, into battle, and to universities away from home.

The condition of a written culture is that it identifies the self with the faculty of intellect, and must take toward the emotions and senses an attitude of distrust if not of outright hostility and rejection. The Cartesian *cogito* is a perfect philosophical representation of consciousness from the standpoint of written culture, just as *Lazarillo de Tormes* or *Robinson Crusoe* captures that culture in literature. What has tended to get lost, in this process of upheaval that the apotheosis of the intellect both fosters and reflects, is the sense of rootedness and culture that would ground either the flesh-and-blood wanderer or the errancies of the written word. It is with that issue that Greene and Derrida, using parental metaphors, continue to struggle.

In the *mundus* fomented in the Renaissance out of the collective phenomena of empire, conquest, large-scale education, and a print culture, the image of "father" elides with that of vagrant, abandoner, while "mother" becomes associated with charity, the foster home, the roadside inn. It should not come as a surprise that Spain would lead Western Europe in drawing out from the explosions of print, gunpowder, empire, and money in the sixteenth century the literary ramifications. *Lazarillo de Tormes* (1554) and *Don Quixote* Part I (1605) break, ahead of the rest of Western Europe, with the traditional literary forms to present characters, like their writers, at odds with their contexts, isolated, abandoned and abandoning, outside the order of patriarchy, and homeless. The novel, which so accurately images the effects of *écriture* on consciousness, develops first in that country in which separation, social upheaval, conquest, migration, and emigration are most deeply experienced by the populace. Both *Lazarillo de Tormes* and *Don Quixote*, while reflecting on the surface the crises of characters torn from the stabilities of home and an agriculturally based economy, also explore the limits of language: its distortions, its failures, and its capacity to confuse, mislead, and openly deceive. As will Derrida four centuries later, these texts reveal the written word's identity with rupture, absence, and instability.

The literary reaction to the slippage and rootlessness so accurately revealed in *Lazarillo de Tormes* and *Don Quixote* can be found in the scripts prepared—sometimes in as little as twenty-four hours—for the theaters that began as popular street performances in the 1580s and had moved, by the 1630s also into the sumptuous surroundings of the court. Both in its orientation toward the masses of citydwellers—often poor and illiterate—who flooded the urban centers from the countryside in the second half of the sixteenth century, and in its later turn toward the more refined audience of the court, the Spanish national theater affirmed the patriarchal order rendered so suspect in novels produced in the same period.

Walter Ong has noted that drama is—despite its oral delivery—the genre most thoroughly assimilated into the written culture.[5] As such, it is the genre most likely to affirm—in compensation—the paternity and maternity that the print culture tends by its very nature to destroy. In the Spanish *comedia* from the beginning the norms of father, king, and church are reinforced within a context premised on their erosion. The honoring of the rural, oral culture that Lope de Vega (1565–1635) evokes in so many of his early plays appeals to the nostalgia of an audience uprooted from an agriculturally based economy. In this sense his plays do cater, as Lope himself declared they ought in his *Arte nuevo de hacer comedias*, to the desires of the audience.[6] They speak to the pain and anger of a displaced urban community no longer supported by the values the plays enshrine, allowing them to channel their resentment against the "bad guys" who represent book learning and the destruction of the popular culture.

In Lope's *Fuenteovejuna* the rustic simplicities of plain language, communal feelings, simple foods, loyalty to the king, and marital fidelity are set off against the decadence of the excessive schooling, hedonism, and individualism of the noblemen of town and court. Lope's plays tend to associate loyalty to the king and marital fidelity with characters of old-Christian origin and peasant stock, while the villains are from the nobility. The nobles flaunt their education and power, threatening in the process to destroy not only the community, but the country as a whole.

In the theater of Calderón—a theater no less conservative than Lope's but aimed now not so much at the newly urbanized peasantry as at the nobility for whom court theaters were built during the reign of Philip IV (1621–65)—the easy distribution along class lines of good and evil characters so prevalent in the plays of Lope is no longer possible. While honor to king and father and marital fidelity remain central to the value system propagated in Calderón, the challenges to the institutions of patriarchy have moved in-house. Since both the upholder and the devaluer of the vaunted social norms can be found within the same social class, indeed, within the same family, class issues no longer claim center stage in the plays. What does persist, however, is the sense of danger facing the community from that which lies outside of it. The community—whether rural or urban, peasant or noble—is one held together by patriarchal values. It is menaced—whether by noblemen or by servants, rebels, and women—by those characters who have no place within its structure.[7]

What Calderón shows so strikingly—as we shall see in the particular case of *La vida es sueño*—is that it doesn't matter whether the outsider is a villain or a victim. His or her very presence as an entity unnamed or unaccounted for by the system requires that he or she be eliminated. The drama in the hands of Calderón is clearly the consummate instrument of literacy, the genre most thoroughly implicated in the written word's pretense to substance, and therefore the genre most deeply committed to preserving its fictions of presence and authority against the ever-present undertow of absence and meaninglessness.

When, as with *Lazarillo de Tormes* and *Don Quixote* before Calderón's time, and with Derrida in our own, the fact of the abandoning father and the wayside (and wayward) mother is directly confronted, the result is a text in which meaning and determinacy are radically called into question, in which all notions of hierarchy—conceptual as well as social—are relativized. In Calderón, writing for an entrenched and embattled nobility in a medium by its very nature oriented toward the tastes and values of the dominant social group, the drama revolves around the problem of upholding patriarchal structures in the face of a consistently debased image of father, king, and husband.[8]

Calderón's characters struggle, not surprisingly, for definition—to recover for themselves, out of the ever-impending threat of erasure, a solid sense of place and of meaning. Psychologically or otherwise, the issue in play after play revolves around a father who has abandoned his son, a husband who kills his wife, or a nobleman who abuses his privilege. And the point will be, in play after play, that however unjust their actions are, the figures who embody the patriarchy—father, husband, potentate—must prevail. Their presence is the determinant of order and context, and it falls inevitably on the characters who remain outside that order either to find a place within it, or to accept their death or expulsion.

To fail to see that it doesn't really matter whether the rejected characters are reconciled with the social order or not is to misread these plays. The given, in every case, is that the individual is subordinate to the structure.[9] And so we find, in Calderón, a forced reinstallation of the "nuclear family" that the written culture has in fact destroyed. The new identity—mother/culture, father/authority—is one now removed from the passions, the flesh, and the oral culture that literacy has supplanted. The new matrix in which the word finds meaning is the social structure, a structure removed from the hurly-burly of desire, and independent of reference to the material world. And the new authority is the word of the king. The king's consort is no fleshly, birth-giving, passion-centered woman, but the social order, fixed, unchanging. The character who would join this new family cannot attain a place within it simply by being of woman born. He must be born again into it, and born again by rejecting the ties of flesh and passion which threaten the order.

La vida es sueño (1635) is one of Calderón's best-known, and yet most puzzling plays. Successive generations have wondered over its many seeming anomalies, asking, for example, how it is that Calderón's perfect prince—the figure Segismundo comes to embody at the end of the play—could incarcerate the very soldier who supported his right to the throne.[10] Critics also continue to wrestle with the question of Rosaura's role in the play. Although her struggle for identity parallels that of Segismundo, and although her presence in his life has a powerful catalytic effect, the perfect prince that Segismundo becomes is called upon to renounce his love for her.[11] Critical readings of the play also tend to grapple with the confused process of transformation undergone by Segismundo: why is it particularly logical to conclude, because "life is a dream," that one must therefore strive to "obrar bien," to "do good works"? The question becomes even more vexing when we realize that Segismundo must finally know that he was tricked—that the experience in the palace that he was told was only a dream was not in fact a dream at all.[12]

The complications that have inhibited understanding of *La vida es sueño* dissolve when we recognize at the outset that the play is dealing not so much with a crisis in the life of Segismundo as with the survival of the social structure when that which guarantees it—the figure of the king—loses its pretense to invulnerability. *La vida es sueño* focuses on the question of succession in a system built on the illusion of permanence. It throws into conflict, in other words, the mutually exclusive notions of synchrony and diachrony, and with it, the equally incompatible claims of nature and culture. It asks, as it probes the difficulties of replacing the father with the son, the more general question of how any system can incorporate within it those terms that challenge its all-sufficiency.

The play locates itself at the fulcrum point where failed words and ineffective images require the ingestion of new information in order to restore their lost grounding in experience. At that fulcrum point are centered the very issues the system is otherwise occupied in keeping veiled: the issues of birth and death, of procreation and succession. These are the places of horror and fascination at which the system, otherwise self-enclosed, self-sufficient, and nonreferential—is forced to ingest elements foreign to itself, to expose itself to the truth of its alienation and meaninglessness.

By drawing attention to the moment when the failures in the system are beginning to show, Calderón invites his audience to experience the vertigo of a world without system, only to end by shutting the doors tight once again, returning us once again to the safety of enclosure. The king, Basilio, is old as the play begins. He is yielding, as his nephew Astolfo says, "to time's familiar disdain" ("al común desdén del tiempo," 1.5.534–35).[13] Since he is widowed and apparently without a natural heir, the pretenders to the throne have materialized in the form of his niece Estrella and his nephew Astolfo—offspring of his two younger sisters. The two aspirants to the throne plan, in Act 1, a political marriage so as peacefully to succeed their uncle as rulers of Poland.

What the audience already knows and the aspiring cousins are soon to find out, however, is that the peaceful succession they imagine is threatened on two counts. Out in the fierce countryside, in that no-man's-land where outsiders arrive within the borders of the established order—here represented by Poland—we have already encountered, beastly and raving, the king's dark secret. He has in fact had a son, and therefore, by rights, there exists a legal heir to the throne. That son, however, was born in most inauspicious circumstances, as the king finally confesses to his niece and nephew toward the end of Act 1. Out of fear of his infant son's destructive potential, he tells them, he decided to announce that the child had died, and to have him guarded in a tower in the wild terrain near the border.

What could easily be missed in Basilio's impassioned account of the many signs the heavens gave of Segismundo's violent nature is that birth itself introduces chaos into the serene order that he has established. To die and to be born, Basilio points out, are similar ("el nacer y morir son parecidos," 1.6.666–67). The theme is echoed by Segismundo, who has already cried out that man's greatest sin is to be born ("pues el delito meyor del hombre es haber nacido," 1.2.111–12), and is a leitmotif in the theater of Calderón. One's salvation consists in dying to the flesh of that original birth. Basilio's manner of establishing such a salvation is to retreat from the world. His success as a king is not unrelated to his image as a man "more given to study than to women" ("más inclinado a los estudios que dado a mujeres," 1.5.535–37), a "Wise Thales" who rules "against time and oblivion" ("contra el tiempo y olvido," 1.6.579,607). Anyone who aspires to a place within this kingdom will also be expected to sever his connection with woman, desire, the instincts, the flesh.

The denial of the flesh, of course, is provisional, and ultimately time-bound. The king does age, the rejected son does grow up to make his blood claim, the passions do insist. It is simply that the preservers of the order must deny as long as possible these intrusions. Basilio, as it turns out, is only one of a foursome of male characters all of whom will be called upon, in the name of the system, to refuse the flesh. All will do so as a matter of course, and all will be honored for their actions.

The opening scenes of Act 1 provide the spectacle of not one, but two characters living in no-man's-land. Both have been rejected by their fathers, and both struggle for self-definition in a labyrinthine world which offers no lexicon for their predicament. Besides Segismundo, whose speech is filled with oxymorons which declare their incapacity to provide him definition (he calls himself a "living skeleton" ["esqueleto vivo"] and an "a living dead man" ["animado muerto"] (1.2.201,202), we meet Rosaura, a woman dressed as a man, a Muscovite just entering Poland, a stranger, like Segismundo, without country or father.[14]

Rosaura's triple onus is to be from Moscow when the center of rule is Poland, to be illegitimate when paternal recognition establishes identity, and to be nonvirginal and unmarried, when being married requires virginity as a precondition. Only in the "manly" act of coming to Poland can she reclaim the identity the conditions of her birth have denied her. Her effort throughout the play will be to reclaim the recognition that both father and lover have heretofore refused her and to lose, thereby, her indeterminacy.

Rosaura, on threat of death for having inadvertently discovered Segismundo, tells her story to Clotaldo, the king's trusted tutor who has been given the task of guarding Segismundo and keeping secret his identity. Clotaldo quickly realizes, without so confessing, that the figure before him is his own child, and is horrified further to learn that she comes to Poland not so much to seek him out as to regain the honor she lost by becoming the lover of none other than the king's nephew and pretender to the throne, Astolfo.

By the end of Act 1 the story of courtly treachery has been fully exposed: Basilio, his wife Clorilene having died in childbirth, has rejected his son, banishing him to the life of a beast in the mountains at the kingdom's border; Clotaldo, having seduced Violante, the Muscovite mother of Rosaura, has abandoned both woman and child to find power in Poland; and Astolfo, having seduced and abandoned Rosaura in Moscow, has also come to Poland, hoping to become king by marrying his cousin Estrella. All of the men, having experienced the attractions of the flesh, have left women and children out of their lives in favor of a place of rule at court.[15]

Act 1 divides the two worlds represented in the play into two equal parts: on the one hand, in scenes 1 through 4, the violent countryside, inhabited by monstrous creatures, neither male nor female, neither beast nor man, neither living nor dead; on the other, in scenes 5 through 8, the court—serene, urbane, bloodless, peopled with characters fully identified with their position and role. The first scenes reveal the lies on which the social order that dominates the last scenes in the act depends.

In Act 2, the two opposing worlds that are so radically separated in Act 1 are brought together. Rosaura comes to court, now in woman's dress, under the name of Astrea. Segismundo, in a trial prepared by his father to test the stars ("I want to find out if the heavens, though it is not possible that they lie . . . might temper or lessen their decree"; "Quiero examinar si el cielo que no es posible que mienta . . . o se mitiga o se templa," 2.1.1102–03, 1106) also comes to court. The new amalgam of court and country proves disastrous. Segismundo, infuriated by the realization of his father's rejection, plays havoc with the conventions of court, killing a servant, attempting rape, and seeking revenge on Clotaldo and Basilio. Rosaura at court proves only slightly less embarrassing to the powers that be. She threatens to expose Astolfo's infidelity, thus ruining his chances to marry Estrella, and also puts at risk her father's honor, since if he were to acknowledge her as his daughter he would be obliged to kill Astolfo.

Only in Act 3, when the rejected figures return to their place of indefinition—Segismundo to his skins and imprisonment, Rosaura to her masculine attire—can the miracle of resolution take place. It takes place not by violent overthrow, however, though by now, word of Segismundo's existence having spread, the kingdom is divided and civil war threatens. The resolution takes place through the transformation of Segismundo. Deciding that there is no way to distinguish the lived experience of his life of imprisonment from the supposedly dreamed experience of life at court, he realizes that the choice of how to live is finally his. In a crucial confrontation between duty and desire—established when Rosaura, who has gotten nowhere with either Astolfo or Clotaldo, comes to the country to beg his support—Segismundo lays aside his own desire for Rosaura and opts instead to help her win back her rightful husband Astolfo. Segismundo choses the side of honor over that of passion because he associates the former with "the eternal" ("lo eterno," 3.10.2982), while the latter is "a beautiful flame that is turned to ash by any passing wind" ("llama hermosa que la convierte en cenizas cualquier viento que sopla," 3.10.2979–81). Segismundo, marshaling all of his willpower, goes against his passionate nature, resisting Rosaura's attractiveness, forgiving Clotaldo and Basilio, and, in the last scene, calling upon Astolfo to marry and Clotaldo to recognize Rosaura. In the end, honor is restored, and the successor to Basilio has peacefully ascended to the throne. The kingdom is intact.

By acting as he has acted, Segismundo completes the portrait of ruling male figures in the play, refusing, like Astolfo, Basilio, and Clotaldo, the seductions of feminine beauty. Segismundo wins his right to the throne, in fact, on that basis, for it was desire for Rosaura that colored all his actions up until 3.10, and refusal of that desire that made his decision of clemency toward Clotaldo and Basilio possible.

The crisis of succession is resolved in a relatively orderly fashion. It is ultimately orderly, however difficult the transition, because it preserves difference and hierarchy. No two people can ever occupy the same position at the same time within the system. Sexual encounter, on the other hand, represents a radical threat to difference and hierarchy and thus can never find a place within the social order. Segismundo's glorious resolution to the problem of succession is rarely understood to be intimately linked with, dependent on, in fact, the negation of sexual union. Procreation must always take place outside the bounds of the structure.

Segismundo's renunciation of desire for Rosaura affirms the very essence of the world Calderón depicts in *La vida es sueño*. Rosaura, as inspirer, as bringer of life, as a signifier of passion, is associated with the maternal world—with the emotions, the unconscious, the mother tongue, the oral culture—which must be kept out of a world whose order is defined by the law of the word of the father. The issues of the play are only finally resolved when each father confers identity on the offspring he has engendered. In so doing, he confers life, an identity, upon a being otherwise lost in the labyrinth. The fathers do not, however, reintegrate the mothers. Clorilene and Violante, the mothers of Segismundo and Rosaura, have no place in the final resolution.

What Calderón makes clear is that the ultimate scapegoat is not the male rival but the woman. Until Segismundo mandated it in the last lines of the last scene in Act 3, neither Astolfo nor Clotaldo was willing to accept responsibility for Rosaura. Both feared entanglement with the other in the form of violent confrontation if either accepted her in her "dishonored" state, and preferred instead to sacrifice her.[16] Woman comes into the structure only when her place is one agreed upon by all the men involved, and when that place fits into the already established order. Her presence as wife, therefore, is acceptable, but her presence as lover or mother triggers passions and emotions that destabilize the order. Thus the deep love that Segismundo has felt for Rosaura in all three acts of the play must be sacrificed if he is to take an exemplary place in his culture.

As René Girard has pointed out in numerous places, culture requires for its stability the rigorous maintenance of hierarchy and difference.[17] Its task is to expel ritually the threats to difference that simultaneity and identity present, and therefore, to expel that which suggests passion and desire. The expression of horror that simultaneity and identity evoke is represented in Calderón in the frequent elision in his works of sexual desire and incest.[18] Fear of history, of time, is but an aspect of an all-pervasive fear, throughout Calderón's works, of generativity, of breaking out of self-enclosed systems, of merging with something other.

The overcoming of the passions for which Segismundo is regularly applauded is intimately linked with the wife murders critics have scrambled to justify or explain in Calderón's honor plays. It all has to do with that heroic effort of intellect, alluded to at the beginning of this paper, to master the senses and the emotions, or, if not to master them, at least to keep them at bay. When the intellect is not in charge, in this view, chaos reigns. Basilio's description of Segismundo's birth perfectly captures the fear that the presence of birth and death inspire. On the day Segismundo was born, he says, "the two celestial lights entered into battle" ("los dos faroles divinos a luz entera luchaban," 1.6), and

The heavens darkened,	Los cielos se oscurecieron,
the buildings shook,	temblaron los edificios,
the clouds rained stones,	llovieron piedras las nubes,
the rivers ran blood.	corrieron sangre los ríos.

(1.6.696–99)

The constant linking of birth with death in the play, and of both with sin reveals a world in which terror is the psychic dominant. Anything, rather than open up again that fearful, bloody reminder of our contingency. Better the study of the stars, the refusal of the passions, the books, the tower.

We can now see, from the other side, the new linking of marriage and succession. Succession is simply the temporal expression of the marriage. It is the suppression of union in favor of conjunction. Succession is stalled marriage, the recognition of the need for the other, but the postponement of it out of fear. Succession grants a space of time during which one experiences peace, stability. It then requires, in payment, a sudden withdrawal of all that is peaceful, a fall into violence and confusion, which will then be followed, once again, by peace and stability. If we apply that model not only to the succession of kings, but to all moments of exchange, we see that what Calderón addresses in *La vida es sueño* is also the difficulty of allowing cultural and linguistic systems to acknowledge their connection to any reality outside themselves. Through the metaphors of violence, passion, and chaos Calderón reveals the degree to which the written culture has separated itself from the oral culture—the world of the mother—from which it arose. In place of the rejecting father it creates a spectral version of paternity and authority whose fallibility is only exposed at moments of crisis.

The problem confronted in *La vida es sueño* of opening the reigning order to change—of naming a new king and establishing the marriage partners for the next generation—comes ultimately to be a problem not only of succession and procreation but of referentiality, and, more specifically, a problem of acknowledging the otherwise suppressed existence of the other—the mother, the child, the countryside, life, death, desire, and the unconscious. The movement that takes place in Western Europe in the Renaissance from a primarily oral to a primarily literate culture provokes a whole series of rifts in consciousness, rifts reflected in the relation between word and thing, between author and audience, and—metaphorically at least—between parent and child. Both *Lazarillo de Tormes* and *Don Quixote* expose the emptiness, madness, and lawlessness that such rifts foster, revealing, at the same time, a nostalgia for the oral culture that has been left behind.

By the time Calderón writes *La vida es sueño* the print culture has become so entrenched in the consciousness of the elite that the mother and the unconscious are perceived no longer as objects of longing, but of threat and fear. Confronted with the seemingly uncontrollable realities of the world of life and blood and passion, the typical Calderonian hero recoils in fear and loathing. His task, if he is to become part of the "happy ending" that is the return of a threatened kingdom to order, is to abandon his investment in desire and the mother, and cling to the foster parent of the "maternal culture" whose father presides, like Basilio in his tower, over the system of differences which will temporarily house him.

In the world Calderón creates, the world of the immured written culture, the father has already abandoned the child, and the mother is already debased. That is the starting point, as it is in the life of Segismundo. Given that situation of orphanhood, the hero has only two choices: to give himself up to the situation Derrida described as the condition of the written word, to wander, without responsibility or consciousness, or to accept the temporary shelter of the foster home, as Greene has suggested that words do. When Segismundo takes up his place at the end as his father's successor, he does so knowing that the place he has won is temporary: that in the tower a rebel soldier rages, that in the court Rosaura continues to attract with a desire that cannot be permitted to find expression, that despite all astrological and mathematical formulas, time will finally have its way. But for the moment, there is meaning.

Notes

[1]Greene's effort to reserve a place for meaning in the light of Derrida's discussions on the nature of language occupies the bulk of his chapter 1. The quote from Derrida comes from "Signature Event Context," and is cited in Greene's book on 11. The citation appears in the English translation on 181.

[2]The bibliography on the subject has become rich in the last decade. Among the most influential American studies are Dinnerstein, Rich, Miller, and Chodorow.

[3]The metaphor also validates the presupposition of modern psychology from Freud through Lacan that culture, and, more basically, the resolution of the child's frustrated

desire to remain one with the mother, is structured around the assimilation of the word of the father.

[4]Havelock makes clear the intimate connection between a sense of the self as autonomous and the development of a written culture, studying the emergence of that process in Greek culture from Homer to Plato. In the *Republic* Plato exhorts a rejection of poetry as a model for learning because of its association with the identifactory processes through which knowledge is transmitted in an oral culture. As Havelock puts it, "The doctrine of the autonomous psyche is the counterpart of the rejection of the oral culture" (200). The process was reactivated on a mass scale in the Renaissance when the invention of the printing press created the conditions for the education of young boys on a scale never before known. For more on this see Walter J. Ong, "Latin Language Study as a Renaissance Puberty Rite," in *Rhetoric, Romance and Technology,* and "Transformations of the Word and Alienation" in *Interfaces of the Word.*

[5]See Ong's "Media Transformation: The Talked Book," in *Interfaces of the Word,* and also "From Epithet to Logic: Miltonic Epic and the Closure of Existence" in the same volume. In the latter article he says " . . . the epic, even when written, remains in some way essentially oral and . . . the drama, despite its oral presentation, is essentially a written genre, the genre first (from Greek antiquity) completely controlled by writing. . . . A dramatic hero is not entirely commensurate with an epic hero. . . . The drama, more perhaps than other genres, abetted the development of chirographic noetic structures and states of consciousness" (212 n. 32).

[6]Lope defends his practice of giving the audience what it wants in his long poem *Arte nuevo de hacer comedias en este tiempo* (1609).

[7]No one better than Edwin Honig has seen how women and nonaristocratic characters stand in Calderón's plays as figures of threat: "In the autocratic society of Calderón's plays, every family seems to be a miniature Spain seeking to preserve itself against the real or imagined, but always chronic, invasions of lawless forces from outside" (61).

[8]A. A. Parker, in "Santos y bandoleros en el teatro español del siglo de oro," notes how central to Calderón's dramaturgy is the problem of the father as flawed patriarch: "He [Calderón] saw that the question of paternal authority had complicated shades of meaning, and in his theater the moral upheaval that the abuse of that authority could cause a son came to be a fundamental problem that greatly preoccupied him" (402–03; translation mine). See also Parker's "The Father-Son Conflict in the Drama of Calderón."

[9]This subordination of individual to society is a characteristic of Calderonian theater that has allowed critics to insist on the nontragic essence of the theater of the Christian baroque that Calderón so well represents. A. A. Parker has pointed out in "Towards a Definition of Calderonian Tragedy" that the "self-assertive construction of a private world of one's own is, for Calderón, the root of moral evil" (223). Henry W. Sullivan and Ellie Ragland-Sullivan update the notion of Christian tragedy, giving it a Lacanian twist, but maintaining, essentially like Parker, that success—a happy ending—is one in which the individual submits to the "law of the name-of-the-father."

[10]The debate on the justification of imprisoning the rebel solider has engaged the passions of a great many critics. Some of the best-known articles on the subject are: Parker, "Calderón's Rebel Soldier and Poetic Justice"; May; Halkhoree; Connolly; and Heiple. See also Cesáreo Bandera.

¹¹See, for example, Sloman, Whitby, Wilson, and de Armas.

¹²Lipmann takes up insightfully the relationship between epistemological and moral problems at the end of the play. Among other commentators who have discussed the relationship between the intuition that life is a dream and Segismundo's conversion are Sloman, Pring-Mill, and Hesse.

¹³All citations will give act and scene and line number. The translations into English are my own.

¹⁴Echevarría also addresses, through the image of the monster, the question of expression as experienced through Calderón's plays. He says: "'The monstrosity of differing species,' then, turns out to be two things: on the one hand a logical or discursive impossibility, since it deals with simultaneously contradictory predicates; on the other, an impossible vision, ambiguous, difficult to interpret, made up of appearances in conflict. . . . the essence of the monstrosity of differing species is its changing nature, which cannot be captured in language" (translation mine).

¹⁵The generality of this decision in Calderón's plays is pointed out by Honig when he says, "there is an underlying assumption [in Calderonian drama] that women, like poets, madmen, and devils, are as fascinating as they are dangerous and disruptive. . . . Women subsist on the margins of the serious life; they have nothing to do with the business of living in a world charged with purpose, patrimony, and passionate missions" (22).

¹⁶Borinsky points out the timelessness of the male bonding system, built on the elimination of an otherwise conflict-producing woman, by showing its presence in Calderón's *A secreto agravio secreta venganza*, and Borges's short story, "La intrusa."

¹⁷The question is most vigorously probed in *Violence and the Sacred*, though references to issues of difference and hierarchy recur throughout Girard's work. For other clear statements regarding "degree," or difference, see "Myth and Ritual" and "The Plague."

¹⁸The topic is taken up, with special reference to *La vida es sueño*, in Gisele Feal and Carlos Feal-Deibe's "Calderón's *Life Is a Dream*: From Psychology to Myth." The incest motif is more overt, however, in other plays by Calderón, most notably *La hija del aire, Los cabellos de Absolón,* and *La devoción de la cruz*. Commenting on the last play Honig says, "In effect the Genesis story demonstrates an archetypal incest situation inherent in man's disobedience, his fall from God's grace, and his knowledge of good and evil. Taken as a paradigm for man's earthly condition, the sexual crime called original sin derives from a transgression against divine command, a transgression that brings with it the knowledge of guilt."

Works Cited

BANDERA, CESÁREO. *Mimesis conflictiva*. Madrid: Gredos, 1975. 253–60.

BORINSKY, ALICIA. "Benefits of Anachronism: A Disorder in Calderón Papers." *The Rhetoric of Feminist Writing*. Ed. Diana Wilson. *Denver Quarterly* 18 (1984): 84–93.

CHODOROW, NANCY. *The Reproduction of Mothering: Psychoanalysis and the Sociology of Gender*. Berkeley: U of California P, 1979.

CONNOLLY, EILEEN M. "Further Testimony on the Rebel Soldier Case." *BCom* 24 (1972): 11–15.

DE ARMAS, FREDERICK. "The Return of Astraea." *Calderón de la Barca At the Tercentenary: Comparative Views*. Lubbock: Texas Tech P, 1982. 135–59.

DERRIDA, JACQUES, "Signature Event Context." *Glyph I*. Baltimore and London: Johns Hopkins UP, 1977. 172–97.

DINNERSTEIN, DOROTHY. *The Mermaid and the Minotaur: Sexual Arrangements and Human Malaise*. New York: Harper, 1976.

ECHEVARRÍA, ROBERTO GONZÁLEZ. "El 'monstruo de una especie y otra'." *Calderón: Códigos, monstruos, Icones*. Centre d'Etudes et Recherches Sociocritiques, 1982. 27–58.

FEAL, GISÈLE, and CARLOS FEAL-DEIBE. "Calderon's *Life Is a Dream*: From Psychology to Myth." *Hartford Studies in Literature* 6 (1974): 1–28.

GIRARD, RENÉ. "Myth and Ritual in Shakespeare." *Textual Strategies: Perspectives in Post-Structuralist Criticism*. Ed. Josué V. Harari. Ithaca: Cornell UP, 1979.

———. "The Plague in Literature and Myth." *To Double Business Bound*. Baltimore: Johns Hopkins UP, 1978.

———. *Violence and the Sacred*. Trans. Patrick Gregory. Baltimore: Johns Hopkins UP, 1972.

GREENE, THOMAS. *The Light in Troy: Imitation and Discovery in Renaissance Poetry*. New Haven and London: Yale UP, 1982.

HALKHOREE, P. "A Note on the Ending of Calderón's *La vida es sueño*." *BCOM* 24 (1972): 8–11.

HAVELOCK, ERIC A. *Preface to Plato*. Cambridge: Harvard UP, 1963.

HEIPLE, DANIEL L. "The Tradition Behind the Punishment of the Rebel Soldier in *La vida es sueño*." *BHS* 50 (1973): 1–17.

HESSE, EVERETT. "El motivo del sueño en *La vida es sueño*." *Segismundo* 3 (1967): 55–67.

HONIG, EDWIN. *Calderón and the Seizures of Honor*. Cambridge: Harvard UP, 1972.

LIPMANN, STEPHEN. "Segismundo's Fear at the End of *La Vida es sueño*."
    MLN 97 (1982): 380–90.
MAY, T. E. "Segismundo y el soldado rebelde." *Hacia Calderon*. Ed. H.
    Flasche. Berlin: Walter de Gruyter, 1970. 71–75.
MILLER, JEAN BAKER. *Toward a New Psychology of Women*. Boston:
    Beacon, 1976.
ONG, WALTER J. *Interfaces of the Word*. Ithaca and London: Cornell UP,
    1977.
_____. *Rhetoric, Romance and Technology*. Ithaca and London: Cor-
    nell UP, 1971.
PARKER, A. A. "Calderón's Rebel Soldier and Poetic Justice." *BHS* 46
    (1969): 120–27.
_____. "The Father-Son Conflict in the Drama of Calderón." *Forum
    for Modern Language Studies* 2 (1966): 99–113.
_____. "Santos y bandoleros en el teatro español del siglo de oro." *Ar-
    bor* 43–44 (1949): 395–416.
_____. "Towards a Definition of Calderonian Tragedy." *BHS* 39
    (1962): 222–37.
PRING-MILL, R.D.F. "La victoria del hado en *La vida es sueño*." *Hacia
    Calderón*. Ed. H. Flasche. Berlin: Walter de Gruyter, 1970. 53–70.
RICH, ADRIENNE. *Of Woman Born: Motherhood as Experience and Insti-
    tution*. New York: Harper, 1976.
SLOMAN, A. E. "The Structure of Calderón's *La vida es sueño*." *MLR* 48
    (1953): 293–300.
SULLIVAN, HENRY W., and ELLIE RAGLAND-SULLIVAN. "*Las tres justicias en
    una* of Calderón and the Question of Christian Catharsis." *Critical
    Perspectives on Calderon de la Barca*. Eds. José A. Madrigal, David
    Gitlitz, et al. Lincoln, NE: Society for Spanish and Spanish-American
    Studies, 1981. 119–190.
VEGA CARPIO, LOPE FÉLIX DE. "Arte nuevo de hacer comedias en este
    tiempo." 1609. *Dramatic Theory in Spain*. Ed. H. J. Chaytor. Cam-
    bridge: Clarendon, 1925, 14–29.
WHITBY, WILLIAM M. "Rosaura's Role in the Structure of *La vida es
    sueño*." *HR* 27 (1960): 16–27.
WILSON, E. M. "On *La vida es sueño*." *Critical Essays on the Theater of
    Calderón*. Ed. Bruce W. Wardropper. New York: New York UP,
    1965.

Arcadia Lost: Politics and Revision in the Restoration Tempest

KATHARINE EISAMAN MAUS

I

THE MOST POPULAR PLAY on the Restoration stage was *The Tempest*, as revised by John Dryden and William D'Avenant in 1667. Pepys thought it was "good, above ordinary plays" when he saw it on its opening night; he was to attend eight performances in the next two years. "After dinner, to the Duke of York's house to see the play, *The Tempest*, which we have often seen; but yet I am pleased again, and shall be again to see it."[1] In 1674 the revised *Tempest* was staged for the first time as an "opera," with elaborate scenery and several new songs. According to John Downes, "All things were perform'd in it so exceedingly well, that not any succeeding Opera got more money."[2] The play was more often revived than any other between 1660 and 1700; innumerable contemporary allusions indicate that virtually everyone was familiar with it. It continued to be

1. *The Diary of Samuel Pepys*, ed. R. Latham and W. Matthews (London, 1970), IX, 48 (3 February 1668).

2. John Downes, *Roscius Anglicanus* (London, 1708), p. 34. A Restoration "opera" was not entirely sung; it was usually a lavishly staged production involving vocal and instrumental music, and spoken dialogue as well. In its proportion of speech to song it was more like a modern musical than like a modern opera.

127

received favorably through the eighteenth century, and into the nineteenth.

Modern critics, however, have not shared the enthusiasm of the Restoration audience. "To appraise this wretched stuff in the light of critical
rules would be absurd," Hazelton Spencer fumes, calling the play "the
worst, as it was the most successful, of the Restoration adaptations prior to
1700."[3] Allardyce Nicoll complains that it panders to "the immoral,
degenerate qualities of the age."[4] The Dryden-D'Avenant *Tempest* has
received more sympathetic, or at least more tactful, attention from a few
critics who see the revision as an attempt to render Shakespeare's dense
language more immediately comprehensible in performance, to reshape
the play according to neoclassic norms, to make Shakespeare's improbable
fictions more acceptable to a scientifically minded audience, or to exploit
the new scenic resources of the Restoration stage.[5] I will argue, however,
that the revised *Tempest* is best understood in terms of sociopolitical issues
which were of primary practical importance in the latter half of the seventeenth century. The new play redefines the limits and uses of sovereignty.

II

It certainly seems plausible enough to assume that the collaborators
undertook the revision with more-or-less coherent goals in mind. Dryden
and D'Avenant alter *The Tempest* far more than *Troilus and Cressida* or

3. *Shakespeare Improved* (Cambridge, Mass., 1927), pp. 201, 203.

4. *Dryden as an Adapter of Shakespeare* (London, 1922), p. 17.

5. The best discussion is in the introduction to the 1667 *Tempest* in Maximilian Novak
and George Guffey, eds., *The Works of John Dryden* (Berkeley, Calif., 1970), X, 319–343.
All line references to the D'Avenant-Dryden *Tempest* are to this edition. Montague
Summers, in *Shakespeare Adaptations* (London, 1922), p. cvii, describes the way the revised
Tempest makes use of the Restoration stage. While helpful, some of the claims these critics
make raise new questions. If D'Avenant and Dryden are writing neoclassic comedy, why do
they observe the unities of time and action so much more loosely than Shakespeare does in
his very tightly constructed play? If their audience is too sophisticated to accept
Shakespeare's implausibilities, why does it applaud the far greater offense to reason represented by Ariel's magical cure of a mortally wounded boy, or the devils impersonating
Fraud, Pride, Rapine, and Murther who dance before the guilty courtiers? If the collaborators wish to take advantage of the new scenic resources of the Restoration stage, why do
they omit Shakespeare's masque of Ceres, a fine opportunity for the display of theatrical
magnificence?

Macbeth—they take only about a third of their material from the original play, displacing and rearranging the Shakespearean material to serve the demands of a substantially new plot.[6] A brief summary will suggest the extent of the alteration.

Like Shakespeare, Dryden and D'Avenant begin their play with a storm and a shipwreck. Shortly thereafter, however, the adaptation diverges from the original. As the revised *Tempest* begins, Prospero has managed to raise his two daughters, Miranda and Dorinda, to adolescence in ignorance of his foster-child Hippolito, whom he also brought as an infant to the island. Hippolito is the rightful Duke of Mantua, disinherited in the same coup that overthrew Prospero himself. Hippolito is doomed, according to his horoscope, if he ever beholds a woman; Prospero therefore keeps the young people apart by threats. The girls, however, finally disobey their father's injunctions. Dorinda begins a conversation with Hippolito; infatuation ensues. When Prospero chides his daughters for their insubordination he quickly discovers Dorinda's passion, and wonders why Hippolito remains unharmed.

Meanwhile, Prospero sends Ariel to bring Ferdinand to Miranda. They fall in love but, as in the Shakespearean version, Prospero refuses to allow an unimpeded courtship. He sends Ferdinand to a cave in which he has sequestered Hippolito. From Ferdinand, Hippolito learns that there is more than one woman in the world, and inductively reasons that if one is good, more are better. The four young people assiduously pursue their courtships—but inevitably, given the inexperience and guileless volubility of the participants, misunderstandings arise on all sides. Eventually a jealous Ferdinand challenges Hippolito to a duel. Hippolito, ignorant of the martial arts, is badly wounded and falls unconscious. Furious, Prospero dismisses Ariel to find Gonzalo, Alonzo, and Antonio, whom he has been tormenting with ingenious apparitions. When the shipwrecked

6. Roughly, the Shakespearean material is disposed as follows: the second half of Shakespeare's I.ii becomes II.ii and III.v in the Dryden-D'Avenant version; Shakespearean material from II.ii and V.i is incorporated with considerable variation into II.iii, III.i, and V.ii of the adapted play. Four scenes (I.i, I.ii, II.i, and II.ii) begin in the same way as their Shakespearean counterparts, but diverge from the earlier play as they proceed. Acts II and IV of the Shakespearean *Tempest* have no equivalent in the Dryden-D'Avenant version. II.iv, II.v, III.iii, III.iv, III.vi, V.i, most of V.ii, and all of Act IV in the revision have no equivalent in Shakespeare.

courtiers arrive, Prospero declares his intention to execute Ferdinand at daybreak for Hippolito's murder.

The next day, Prospero rejects Miranda's last-minute efforts to save her lover's life. Ariel, however, announces that he has revived Hippolito by a combination of medicine and magic. The still-groggy Hippolito claims that he is no longer promiscuously inclined—but more misunderstandings among the lovers nearly lead to another fight at the bedside. All difficulties, though, soon resolve themselves. Alonzo, Antonio, and Prospero are already reconciled by the happy circumstances of Hippolito's recovery and Ferdinand's pardon. The couples prepare to be wed, though Hippolito, Miranda, and Dorinda are still ignorant of their marital responsibilities.

In the revised *Tempest* the low characters—Stephano, Mustacho, Ventoso, and Trincalo—are all sailors, and like their Shakespearean counterparts they quickly find each other once ashore. Stephano proclaims himself duke, Mustacho and Ventoso viceroys. Trincalo rejects their pretensions, and attempts to gain a title himself by marrying Caliban's sister Sycorax. Stephano arrives on an ambassadorial mission, ostensibly to make peace with Trincalo, but actually to seduce Sycorax. The scene ends in uproar. The low characters do not reappear until the end of the final scene, when they and the rest of the company watch Ariel and his lover Milcha perform a saraband.

The script of the operatic *Tempest* differs little from the Dryden-D'Avenant play. Scenes are sometimes rearranged and speeches cut to allow room for new songs and special stage effects; the text includes elaborate descriptions of scenery and other mechanical devices. The initial storm scene features witches who fly about on wires, as does Ariel, throughout the play, at every opportunity. Tables vanish, and holes open onstage to give the guilty courtiers a view of the hell that awaits them. The fifth act includes a nuptial masque, and ends with a choral version of "Where the bee sucks, there suck I." Although D'Avenant had died in 1668, and Dryden did not help with the operatic version, the Restoration *Tempest* was understandably still considered their play. The text of the 1674 opera continued to be ascribed to them on the title pages of subsequent editions.

III

What are we to make of all this? The plot alterations inaugurated by Dryden and D'Avenant react in very significant ways upon the character of Prospero. Shakespeare's Prospero is, by his own account at least, an educator, a dealer in revelatory illusion, who would prefer not to acknowledge the coercive implications of his power. In Milan he puts "the manage of his state," the sordid business of day-to-day politics, in the hands of his practical, opportunistic brother; though he fiercely resents his overthrow, his forced isolation on the island really only completes his retirement, and gives him an opportunity to construct his own Arcadia.[7] In the masque he has performed for Miranda and Ferdinand at the end of Act IV, his imagination need not be constrained by the imperfections of reality. He is free to recreate the golden world:

> Earth's increase, foison plenty,
> Barns and garners never empty.

7. The importance of pastoral to *The Tempest* has received considerable attention. The major treatments are: Frank Kermode, Introduction to *The Tempest*, Arden Shakespeare (London, 1964), xiv–lxiii. This introduction was first published in 1954. Stephen Orgel, "New Uses of Adversity: Tragic Experience in *The Tempest*," *In Defense of Reading*, ed. R. Poirier and R. Brower (New York, 1962), pp. 110–132. Northrop Frye, *A Natural Perspective* (New York, 1965), pp. 149–159. Frye also expounds his views on pastoral in *The Tempest* in his introduction to the play in *The Pelican Shakespeare*, ed. Alfred Harbage (London, 1969), pp. 1369–1372. Harry Berger, "Miraculous Harp: A Reading of Shakespeare's *Tempest*," *ShStud*, V (1969), 253–283. David Young, *The Heart's Forest: A Study of Shakespeare's Pastoral Plays* (New Haven, Conn., 1972), pp. 148–191. Thomas McFarland, *Shakespeare's Pastoral Comedy* (Chapel Hill, N.C., 1972), pp. 146–175. Kermode, Frye, and McFarland emphasize the positive aspects of the pastoral vision and are extremely sympathetic to Prospero. Berger, who stresses the neurotic element in Prospero's constitution, makes a good case for a "darker" reading of *The Tempest*, but I think he misreads the final act. Orgel perceptively distinguishes between Prospero's experience and the experience of the other characters in *The Tempest*, and shows how Prospero's perspective differs from the perspective of the audience. Young is more interested in the theatrical self-consciousness of *The Tempest* than in the issues that directly concern me here, but he agrees that the play moves toward a recognition that "apparently unalterable opposites . . . are mutually complementary, aspects of the same thing" (p. 170).

> Vines with clust'ring branches growing,
> Plants with goodly burden bowing;
> Spring come to you at the farthest
> In the very end of harvest.
>
> (ll. 110–116)[8]

Gonzalo, Prospero's good-hearted, foolish old supporter, is intuitively sensitive to his lord's version of the marvelous island—he is the only one to notice the miraculous freshness of his salt-drenched clothes—and in his plans for the island he effectively articulates Prospero's ideal:

> All things in common nature should produce
> Without sweat or endeavor. Treason, felony,
> Sword, pike, knife, gun, or need of any engine
> Would I not have; but nature should bring forth,
> Of its own kind, all foison, all abundance
> To feed my innocent people.
>
> (II.i.155–160)

Gonzalo would "with such perfection govern, sir / T'excel the golden age." His fellows ridicule his guileless refusal to recognize the necessity of labor or the demands of sexuality. "The latter end of his commonwealth forgets the beginning," exclaims the worldly wise Antonio, who understands the contradiction implicit in the idea of a governing power which never asserts itself against the subject's will.

Not surprisingly, the pastoral ambitions of Shakespeare's Prospero render him profoundly suspicious of anything unteachable or unassimilable—anything which, by demanding to be repressed, sets limits upon his power or calls his benevolence into question. He must resort to force or threats of force with Caliban, who rejects his tutelage; with Ariel, who forgets his debt of gratitude; with Alonso and Antonio before they repent of their usurpation; with Trinculo and Stephano when they attempt to overthrow him. Prospero never really need fear that these intransigent elements will successfully displace him from his position of power on the island. He resents them so violently because they force him to realize that

---

8. All line references to the Shakespeare play are to *The Pelican Shakespeare*, ed. Alfred Harbage (London, 1969).

his pastoral vision is anomalously managerial and competitive, that it can be enacted only at the expense of Caliban's or Ariel's version of Arcadia.

Miranda, the apt student, presents no problem until the arrival of Ferdinand divides her loyalties; when she protests against Prospero's treatment of her beloved, she elicits a violent outburst of rage. "What, my foot my tutor? . . . One word more shall make me chide thee, if not hate thee" (I.ii.467–476). Shakespeare's Prospero is anxious about sexuality, particularly female sexuality. The only mother on the island has been a witch whose pregnancy changed her sentence from death to exile, rendered her indestructible. For Prospero the mother is necessary but also stubbornly unassimilable, a potential competitor, and so he fears that Sycorax might be typical. When Miranda asks innocently, "Are you not my father?," he answers with peculiar insistence upon his wife's chastity.

Early in Shakespeare's play, Prospero reacts to all these "things of darkness" by repressing them—enslaving Caliban, subduing Ferdinand, threatening to peg a sullen Ariel in the entrails of an oak. In the Shakespearean version, though, Prospero's repressive impulses are eventually modified and overcome; thus many critics see him as a white magician, or even as a version of the author himself. For Prospero's power is essentially transformational; he aims to alter reality rather than fix it in some eternal shape. He must therefore be acutely conscious of time, of the need to seize the appropriate day. "I find my zenith doth attend upon / A most auspicious star" (I.ii.181–182). He accepts the limits set upon him by fate and by his contract with Ariel, and begins to interpret his own activity in terms of timely revelation, of fruition, rather than as the maintenance of a static order. He supervises the courtship of Miranda and Ferdinand by both encouraging and restraining it, forbidding premature indulgence in the interests of a decorous and fertile consummation. Eventually Prospero's acceptance of the relation between change and creativity modifies his vision of a timeless Arcadia, and leads him to a reconciliation with the un-Arcadian elements he initially finds most threatening. He forgives the courtiers, blesses the daughter he has lost, and acknowledges Caliban as his own.

The Dryden-D'Avenant Prospero begins with the same obsessions and anxieties; the second scene of the play, in which Prospero talks to Miranda, Ariel, and Caliban, is reproduced almost word for word. But Prospero's repressive tendencies are here exaggerated. He is kin to the neurotic and domineering father of a farce. While Shakespeare's Prospero selectively represses the intransigent elements of his world, the Dryden-D'Avenant Prospero makes no such discrimination. Hippolito, Dorinda, and Miranda, who "murmur not . . . but wonder" are kept in caves like Caliban, their freedom of movement severely restricted. Furthermore, the sexual aspects of Prospero's anxiety are developed at much greater length. Instead of dealing frankly with Hippolito or his daughters, he misrepresents vital information; the extreme sexual naïveté of the young people in the revised *Tempest* is the source of much of its comic humor as well as its near-tragedy. Knowing that the children will take metaphor for literal fact, this Prospero employs satiric tropes which betray his own state of mind. He tells his daughters that men are "all that you can imagine ill," more dreadful than "the curled Lion or the rugged Bear."

> DORINDA
> Do they run wild about the Woods?
> PROSPERO
> No, they are wild within Doors, in Chambers
> And in Closets.
>
> (II.iv.106–108)

To Hippolito, the new Prospero describes women as "the dangerous enemies of man":

> Their voices charm beyond the Nightingales;
> They are all enchantment, those who once behold 'em
> Are made their slaves forever.
>
> (II.iv.47–49)

The magic of sexual attraction competes with Prospero's art, and (like his own "enchantment") it seems to his mind a negative process, enslavement rather than liberation.

Dorinda, Miranda, and Hippolito discover their sexuality despite Prospero's injunctions: "I find it in my Nature," says Dorinda, "because my father has forbidden me" (II.iv.132–133). The new Prospero deals not in revelation, but in concealment; the progress of the plot toward marriage and forgiveness represents a violation rather than an expression of his will.

D'Avenant and Dryden part company more and more drastically with the Shakespearean text, as they delimit a fundamentally static and beseiged character, without the means to cope with or reconcile himself to the manifold threats he perceives in his world. Their Prospero can never acknowledge his relationship to Caliban; at the end of the new play he merely orders the savage back into the cave.

In the fifth act of the original *Tempest*, Shakespeare's Prospero struggles to overcome his resentment against his brother and his brother's accomplices.

> Though with their high wrongs I am struck to th' quick,
> Yet with my nobler reason 'gainst my fury
> Do I take part. The rarer action is
> In virtue than in vengeance. They being penitent,
> The sole drift of my purpose doth extend
> Not a frown further.
>
> (V.i.25–30)

Conversion, not persecution, is now his aim. In the revised *Tempest*, on the other hand, the D'Avenant-Dryden Prospero struggles not to outgrow his anxieties and obsessions, but rather to reify them—to impose them on the people he controls. This Prospero torments people who are conscious of their sin from the outset. "Alas, I suffer justly for my crimes," Alonzo exclaims in the first scene, when he believes the ship will sink. Antonio ascribes the shipwreck to divine justice:

> Indeed we first broke truce with Heav'n;
> You to the waves an Infant Prince expos'd,
> And on the waves have lost an only Son;
> I did usurp my Brother's fertile lands, and now
> Am cast upon this desert Isle.
>
> (II.i.21–25)

The new Prospero's persecution of the sinners—much more relentless than in the Shakespearean *Tempest*—thus has no particular moral or educational purpose. His power is essentially sinister, as he admits when he calls upon his spirits in a crisis. "I thought no more to use their aids; (I'm curs'd because I us'd it)" (IV.iii.159–160). He is not inclined to forgiveness even

as the play begins to close; after Ferdinand has wounded Hippolito he tells
Alonzo:

> Blood calls for blood; your Ferdinand shall dye,
> And I in bitterness have sent for you,
> To have the sudden joy of seeing him alive,
> And then the greater grief to see him die.
>
> (IV.iii.150–153)

Not Prospero's will, but the "blessed day," the miraculous and unantici-
pated circumstance of Hippolito's recovery, transforms the Restoration
Tempest from revenge tragedy to comic romance.

It is possible to imagine a play in which the new Prospero's primitive
and unself-conscious moral nature would become the occasion for satire,
but this does not seem to be the point of the Dryden-D'Avenant *Tempest*.
In Shakespeare's version Prospero's Arcadian ideal is not idiosyncratic;
Ariel, Gonzalo, Caliban, Miranda, and Ferdinand all articulate some version of it. In the D'Avenant-Dryden adaptation, though, the pastoral no
longer constitutes a shared ideal—indeed, it does not seem available as an
ideal at all. Gonzalo's speeches are cut, Ariel's songs deleted or shortened.
Caliban is no longer mysteriously susceptible to beauty, but prefers his
sister Sycorax because she is bigger than Prospero's daughters. Lacking the
Arcadian vision, which calls into question the competitive, coercive, and
manipulative aspects of power, the ruler has no impulse to reconcile his
activity with factors that limit and define it.

In the Shakespearean *Tempest* the courtiers are returning from the marriage of Alonso's daughter, Claribel, and the king of Tunis. Gonzalo,
spokesman for Arcadia, identifies Tunis with ancient Carthage, and compares Claribel with "the widow Dido." The Virgilian reference is important, because Aeneas's conquest in Italy depends upon his rejection of the
distraction Dido represents. He must repress the demands of his sexuality
in order to found his city—a city which, in later years, will come into its
own as it once again resists the Punic threat. Against such a background,
the marriage of Claribel represents a new sort of foreign relations—a
political strategy no longer repressive or competitive. Tunis-Carthage is
now accepted rather than resisted; it is the solution of romantic comedy
rather than of tragedy or epic. It is not surprising that the shallow cynics
Antonio and Sebastian, who mock Gonzalo's naïve pastoral vision, reject

also his identification of Tunis with Carthage, and all the consequences implicit in that identification. And it is not surprising that in the D'Avenant-Dryden *Tempest*, the goal of the sea voyage has changed. These courtiers, "in defense of Christianity," have been fighting to drive the Moors out of Portugal—not to wed but to war with Africans upon the competitive Virgilian principle.

In other words, the revised *Tempest* contains no model for the Shakespearean Prospero's ultimate gesture of acceptance and reconcilation. There is no process by which love might be related to death, or poetry to passion; all change is thus of necessity revolutionary or destructive. The Shakespearean Ariel sings "Full fathom five thy father lies" to Ferdinand as he leads him to Miranda, so that the prince decides that she must be "the goddess / On whom these airs attend." In the revised version the funeral song no longer leads to Miranda, and the new Ferdinand unlike the earlier one finds the song simply "mournful." The link between death and sexuality is severed, and Ferdinand cannot now find the rich and strange metamorphoses of his father's drowned body either wonderful or reassuring.

It is, therefore, highly significant that Dryden and D'Avenant omit in their revision the masque of Ceres with which Shakespeare's Prospero celebrates his daughter's betrothal. In the original *Tempest*, Prospero attempts to supply a heretofore missing maternal principle, which in the first act he had been prone to regard as competitive with his own creative and procreative power. The heroine of the masque is the fertile grain goddess, the original patroness of the unproblematic golden world over which Prospero wishes he could preside. Ceres' productivity, though, is dependent upon her daughter, Persephone, and limited by her daughter's affiliation with the king of the underworld, the principle of death. Early in the masque, Juno and Ceres banish Venus and Cupid, the rival mother and child, who represent the darker, uncontrolled aspects of sexuality; and Ceres excludes winter and death from the blessing she gives Miranda and Ferdinand: "Spring come to you at the farthest / In the very end of harvest" (IV.i. 115–116). Ceres does not mention her absence. But the proximity of love and death, creation and destruction, is reasserted in the harvest dance which follows.

The nymphs who were cold and chaste at the beginning of the masque are made "fresh" by their encounter with the phallic sicklemen, whose death-dealing "grim reaper" aspect is inseparable from their virile and life-giving sexuality. The sweaty reapers represent all the "things of darkness" which threaten Prospero's Arcadian vision—the necessity of labor, the necessity of death, the necessity of passion—and also the ultimate inseparability of the things of darkness from the things of light. In this scene the proximity of nymphs and reapers reminds Prospero of Caliban's proximity, and of the plot to usurp his kingly power. The same proximity of idealism and necessity, creativity and destructiveness, will also lead Prospero, finally, to acknowledge Caliban as his own.

The Shakespearean Prospero thus uses pastoral to transcend pastoral—or at least to achieve a more mature and comprehensive vision than Gonzalo's naïve utopianism will permit. But while the original Prospero dreams of a world in which repression is unnecessary, the Restoration Prospero, entirely devoid of the Arcadian impulse, dreams instead of a world in which repression is merely unproblematic. In the 1674 operatic *Tempest* he, too, stages a masque—the festivities upon which the play ends.[9] Not surprisingly, its symbolism differs markedly from Shakespeare's. The new masque begins as Amphitrite asks her husband Neptune for calm seas. Good weather is described entirely in negative terms: "Tethys no furrows now shall wear, / Oceanus no wrinkles on his brow." Neptune's control over the elements clearly depends upon sheer power—"You I'll obey," sings Aeolus, "Who at one stroke can make / With your dread trident, the whole earth to shake." Authority here takes the same form as Prospero's did in the first act. All the obstreperous winds are "boistrous prisoners" safe in their "dark caverns," just as Miranda, Dorinda, Hippolito, and Caliban were once sequestered. "To your prisons below / Down, down you must go," Aeolus commands; "We / Will soon obey you cheerfully," reply the tritons and nereids, acquiescing with a thoroughness that Dorinda, Hippolito, Miranda, Caliban, and even Ariel have been unable to match. The Dryden-D'Avenant Prospero learns nothing in the course of the play; in the operatic version, the masque at the end of the fifth act only emphasizes his intransigence.

9. The masque of Amphitrite and Neptune is printed in all seventeenth-century editions of the revised *Tempest* after 1674. It is most easily available to the modern scholar in *The Complete Works of Thomas Shadwell*, ed. Montague Summers (London, 1927), II, 265–267. Shadwell was probably responsible for the additions to the D'Avenant-Dryden script made for the operatic production.

IV

The Restoration audience could not have preferred the revised version of *The Tempest* because it was more poetic, complex, or imaginative than the original. It is tempting to think, in light of the foregoing analysis, that they did find it more plausible. The D'Avenant-Dryden adaptation is much more explicitly and exclusively political than the Shakespeare play. The puns on "art" in I.ii. are cut, and so are the two speeches in Shakespeare's *Tempest* most obviously concerned with artistry—the address to Ferdinand after the masque ("we are such things as dreams are made on"), and Prospero's renunciation speech, his promise to break his rod and drown his book. In the Restoration adaptation, however, Prospero's expanded political role compensates somewhat for his lack of artistic self-consciousness. As he tells Alonzo when he resolves to execute Ferdinand:

> Here I am plac'd by Heav'n, here I am Prince,
> Though you have dispossessed me of my *Millain*.
> (IV.iii.148–149)

He has seven subjects to the Shakespearean Prospero's three—seven subjects whose interaction constantly threatens to overwhelm his authority. In the Restoration *Tempest*, though a political role is no longer synonymous with an artistic or priestly role, politics alone is enough to keep one busy.

Since the revised play is so determinedly a play about government, current political theory might help illuminate reasons for the differences between the two Prospero's, and for the appeal of the later conception to Restoration audiences. In 1612, when Shakespeare's *Tempest* was first performed, James I's earliest theoretical tracts on kingship were little more than a decade old. In *Basilikon Doron* and *The Trew Law of Free Monarchy*, both published at the end of the sixteenth century, James had maintained that he held his royal position by divine right. He used as a supplementary argument a patriarchal theory of kingship which derived the state from the family, and conceived of kingly authority as an extension of fatherly power. Patriarchalists take a limited view of the subject's freedom, maintaining that he has no more right to choose his ruler than children have to choose their fathers. This restriction need not be irksome, however, since the king's fatherly care is originally and ideally loving, and only incidentally coercive. Thus Shakespeare's Prospero, with his vision of an unoppressive golden age, resents Caliban's refusal to accept the role of adoptive child.

The idea that the origin of states is familial was in fact a very old one.[10] But in this particular form it became an important polemical weapon in the seventeenth century, when the Stuarts and their supporters found patriarchalism an attractive basis for their absolutist claims. The theory retained adherents until the end of the century, when the Whiggish John Locke dealt it a death blow,[11] but it had met with fierce opposition even before the Civil War. Populists like Winstanley, and even some absolutists like Hobbes and Digges, wanted to replace the patriarchalist doctrine with a theory of a conventional state—a government based upon a contract among free individuals, rather than one based upon naturally occurring hierarchical relationships.[12] The notion of the father-king came increasingly under attack in the war years and after, and patriarchal theorists became increasingly defensive in their pronouncements. As the century wore on, patriarchalism seemed increasingly nostalgic—an attempt to recover the lost monarchical privilege enjoyed by the early Stuarts.

Clearly, when a theory like this one is current and controversial, a political reading of *The Tempest* would make Prospero a version of the patriarchalist father-king. But in the 1660s, when Dryden and D'Avenant are collaborating on their revision of *The Tempest*, the figure of the father-king—at least in its more extravagant or extreme forms—is already becoming anachronistic. It is not surprising that the D'Avenant-Dryden Prospero seems so threatened by change, so willing to employ repressive tactics in order to maintain his shaky authority.

10. See, for example, Aristotle, who begins his *Politics* with a discussion of the household, arguing that the "elementary relationships" of husband and wife, parent and child, master and servant precede both logically and temporally the more complicated relations among the citizens of the *polis*. But Aristotle considers patriarchal kingship only one of several kinds (see III.xiv. 14). For an account of the fortunes of patriarchalism during the Civil War, Commonwealth, and Restoration, see Gordon Schochet, *Patriarchalism in Political Thought* (New York, 1975), pp. 159–224.

11. John Locke, *The First Treatise of Government* (London, 1690).

12. Thomas Hobbes, *Leviathan, or the Matter, Form, and Power of a Commonwealth, ecclesiastical and civil* (London, 1651), pts. I and II. Dudley Digges, *The Unlawfulnesse of subjects taking up armes against their soveraigne* . . . (Oxford, 1643).

Shakespeare's Prospero learns to allow for and accept unassimilable and potentially competitive elements—the maternal principle, for example, omitted by patriarchal theorists like James Maxwell, who render the fifth commandment as "Honora patrem etc."[13] But he can afford to be generous. Trinculo and Stephano, or villains like Sebastian, think in terms of usurpation; they implicitly accept a monarchical system of government even while they attempt to subvert the individual in charge. Kingship as an institution is taken for granted.

The low characters in the Dryden-D'Avenant *Tempest* are not even aware of Prospero's existence until the end of the fifth act. Instead, they make their own arrangements among thesmelves:

MUSTACHO

Our ship is sunk, and we can never get home agen: We must e'en turn Salvages, and the next that catches his Fellow may eat him.

VENTOSO

No, no, let us have a Government.

(II.iii.48–51)

Stephano appoints himself duke, and makes Mustacho and Ventoso his viceroys. "Agreed, agreed!" they shout together. Although their pregovernmental state of nature is a sham, since their relations on the island are based on prior relations aboard ship, the low characters obviously believe they are constituting a state on contractual grounds.[14] They immediately and hilariously encounter the difficulties contractual theorists always take pains to treat: the problem of who could "speak for the people" in the absence of any constituted authority or procedures, and the problem of a person who refuses to accept the contract. "I'll have no laws," Trincalo declares, and goes off to form his own government with Caliban as his subject and Caliban's sister as his queen. Main plot and subplot in the Restoration *Tempest* seem curiously exclusive, at least when compared with

13. *Sacro Sancta Regem Majestas, or, the Sacred and Royal Prerogative of Christian Kings* (Oxford, 1644), p. 161.

14. For more information on Dryden and Hobbes, see Louis Teeter, "The Dramatic Use of Hobbes' Political Ideas," pp. 341–373, and John A. Winterbottom, "The Place of Hobbesian Ideas in Dryden's Tragedies," pp. 374–396, in *Essential Articles for the Study of John Dryden*, ed. H. T. Swedenberg (Hamden, Conn., 1966).

the tightly constructed Shakespearean model. In fact, though, the very detachment of the low characters constitutes a threat more subtle, but also more dangerous, than the threat of usurpation in the Shakespeare play. The Dryden-D'Avenant Prospero is besieged, not in his person, as is the Shakespearean Prospero, but in his role. The ideological basis of his authority is subverted by the possibility that the patriarchal conception of monarchy is bankrupt.

The utter failure of the sailors' attempts at self-government is important, though, because it helps define sources for the conservatism of postwar monarchists like Dryden and D'Avenant. The revised *Tempest* is not in the least subversive of the monarchical principle; it merely refuses to grant to the king and father special prerogatives in other kinds of endeavor. Prospero with all his faults is a just and orderly ruler, and the postwar royalists consider justice and order the primary virtues of the good sovereign. The conception of a Prospero who is limited but nonetheless efficient is typical of Dryden's pessimistic conservatism. [15] In *Absalom and Achitophel* and *The Hind and the Panther* he argues for traditional forms not because he has illusions about their transcendent goodness, but because he

---

15. I will concentrate on Dryden in the following few pages, partly because his work is more familiar to the general reader, and also because, according to his introduction to the revised *Tempest*, D'Avenant was concerned less with adapting the main plot than with devising scenes for the low characters. The prologue on Shakespeare is entirely Dryden's work. However, the ideas that I attribute to Dryden here are commonplace enough in the later seventeenth century; they are shared not only by D'Avenant but by many Restoration conservatives—including, most likely, the majority of playgoers in the 1660s and '70s. For D'Avenant's simultaneous loyalty to, and disenchantment with, Charles II, see Alfred Harbage, *Sir William D'Avenant: Poet Venturer 1606–1668* (Philadelphia, 1935), pp. 135–141. David Ogg, in *England in the Reign of Charles II* (Oxford, 1934), gives a thorough and entertaining account of the way political and theoretical issues intersect during the later part of the seventeenth century. See particularly I.139–141, and II.450–523. The importance of Dryden's politics for his literary practice has received a great deal of attention. See, e.g., Bernard Schilling, *Dryden and the Conservative Myth: A Reading of Absalom and Achitophel* (New Haven, Conn., 1961), pp. 1–95; Alan Roper, *Dryden's Poetic Kingdom* (London, 1965), pp. 50–103; Ann T. Barbeau, *The Intellectual Design of John Dryden's Heroic Plays* (New Haven, Conn., 1970), pp. 3–54; Stephen N. Zwicker, *Dryden's Political Poetry* (Providence, R.I., 1972); Isabel Rivers, *The Poetry of Conservatism 1600–1745* (Cambridge, Eng., 1973), pp. 127–174; Sanford Budick, *The Poetry of Civilization* (New Haven, Conn., 1974), pp. 81–110.

believes that radical change necessarily brings about worse evils. Any tradition, any constituted authority, is better than none. Like his Prospero, he has a lively suspicion of lurking chaos; the source of satiric vigor in poems like *MacFlecknoe* and *The Medall* lies largely in the tension between immoral disorder and a justly repressive authority.

Dryden sides with the forces of order, but he defines that order carefully; Charles II is no omnipotent Shakespearean Prospero, but "a king, who is just and moderate in his nature, and who rules according to the laws, whom God has made happy by joining the temper of his soul to the Constitution of his government."[16] Charles's virtue, for Dryden, lies not in his extravagant assertions of power, but in his willingness to limit that assertion. Shakespeare throughout his long career is fascinated by the managerial personality, whether good or evil; in Dryden's plays absolutist aspirations are inevitably and unmistakably foul both in their sources and their effects.

This is not to say that Dryden is insensitive to a conception of authority which is both more ambitious and less coercive. His prologue begins with a recognition, somewhat like the Shakespearean Prospero's, that creative and destructive potentials are inseparable.

> As when a Tree's cut down, the secret root
> Lives under ground, and thence new branches shoot,
> So, from old *Shakespeare's* honoured dust, this day
> Springs up and buds a new reviving Play.
>
> (ll. 1–4)

Shakespeare, not Prospero, is the ultimate patriarchalist authority figure, embodying the monarch, the father, the artist, and the magician all at once:

> *Shakespeare*, who (taught by none) did first impart
> To Fletcher wit, to labouring Jonson art,
> He, Monarch-like, gave those his subjects law,
> And is the nature which they paint and draw.

---

16. Dedication to *All For Love*, a play not yet available in the California Dryden. It is reproduced in *Dryden: The Dramatic Works*, ed. Montague Summers (London, 1932), IV, 177.

> But *Shakespeare's* Magick could not copy'd be,
> Within that Circle none durst walk but he.
>
> (ll. 6–9, 19–20)

This kind of omnipotence, however, is both unique—an attribute of the creatively heroic ancestor—and archaic, inimitable in a self-conscious modern world.

> I must confess t'was bold nor would you now
> That liberty to vulgar wits allow
> Which works by Magick supernatural things:
> But *Shakespeare's* pow'r is sacred as a Kings.
> Those legends from old Priesthood were received,
> And he then writ, as people then believed.
>
> (ll. 21–26)

Modern artist and audience lack the confident vision conferred by the old unquestioning belief—they can recapture it, if at all, only in a prologue's moment of sentimental nostalgia. Perhaps a sense of loss always accompanies the evocation of traditional simplicity, but here that loss seems so absolute and irrevocable that the naïve golden world of fifty years ago lacks any contemporary urgency at all. However regretfully, the adapters find that they must shoulder aside Shakespeare's central concerns, or at best grant them a marginal status. The fundamental problems are different now, and demand a new, if in some ways inferior, treatment.

In fact, though, when D'Avenant and Dryden separate Prospero's kingly authority from any special innovative genius, they do not so much repudiate the possibility of political creativity as relocate it. The real hero of the Dryden-D'Avenant *Tempest* is Ariel, who believes that Prospero's power over him is unjust. "Why should a mortal by Enchantments hold / In chains a spirit of aetherial mold?" (IV.iii.274–275). Nevertheless, he obeys Prospero in very trying circumstances. Finally, when Prospero assumes that Hippolito is dead, and resolves to execute Ferdinand, Ariel on his own initiative succeeds in resurrecting the wounded boy. Ariel, not Prospero, is responsible for the happy denouement; Ariel, not Prospero, learns to exploit repressive circumstances in productive ways. The potential for a creative political order resides not with the benevolent monarch, but with the loyal, resourceful subject.

Like the treatment of Prospero, the new emphasis on Ariel in the revised *Tempest* has parallels in Dryden's other work. In the Shakespearean *Tempest*, Prospero's sense of his imaginative resources is bound up with his sense of control over other people. Dryden, however, characteristically makes a sharp distinction between political power and creative potency, and locates the latter not with the monarch but with the subject. In *Astraea Redux, Annus Mirabilis, Absalom and Achitophel*, and *Britannia Redivivia*, poetic vocation finds its best and fullest employment in the celebration of the sovereign. The panegyric in *Annus Mirabilis* becomes an alternative to "serving King and Country" in the wars;[17] it is the literary version of a service required of all loyal and capable subjects. Poets are not kings, nor kings poets; Flecknoe's pretenses to sovereignty only emphasize his creative bankruptcy, and in the preface to *All For Love* Dionysius and Nero (bad kings both) render themselves ridiculous by aspiring to poetic laurels.[18] Ariel, whose creative initiative preserves the comic ending to the revised *Tempest*, is a type of the imaginatively loyal subject so crucial to Dryden's sense of himself as a citizen and, eventually, as laureate.

The revised *Tempest*, in other words, is the product of a staunch but distinctively Restoration brand of conservatism. Politicized by the traumatic events of the mid-seventeenth century, D'Avenant and Dryden believe that between Shakespeare and themselves, 1612 and 1667, there is a great gulf set. They find themselves forced to reconceive Prospero and his subjects, in order to bring them into line with their version of a well-run state. This kind of preoccupation cannot have seemed anomalous or unintelligible to contemporaries. Certainly the published script of the operatic version indicates that the set designer, at least, was fully aware of the play's political implications. The published text of the opera lovingly describes the new scenery:

the Curtain rises, and discovers a new Frontispiece, join'd to the great Pilasters, on each side of the Stage. This frontispiece is a noble Arch, supported by large wreathed Columns of the Corinthian order; the wreathings of the Columns are beautifi'd with Roses wound round them, and several Cupids flying about them. On the Cornice, just over the Capitals, sits a Figure with a Trumpet in one hand,

17. *The Works of John Dryden*, I, 50.
18. Preface to *All for Love, Dryden: The Dramatic Works*, IV, 185.

and a Palm in the other, representing *Fame*. A little further on the same Cornice, on each side of the Compass-pediment, lie a Lion and a Unicorn, the supporters of the Royal Arms of *England*. In the middle of the arch are several Angels, holding the King's Arms, as if they were placing them in the midst of that Compass-pediment. Behind this is the Scene, which represents a thick Cloudy Sky, a very Rocky Coast, and a Tempestuous Sea in perpetual Agitation. [19]

This explicit reference to England's real king must be intended as a sort of defense, as a way of pointing out the differences where art and life might otherwise seem uncomfortably close. Charles II is *not* Prospero, the frontispiece claims. Its tranquil, symmetrical design flatly contradicts the scene behind it, which depicts nature confused, dangerous, "in perpetual Agitation." The frontispiece makes traditional claims for the king's stable, central position in the natural and divine order of things. Its iconology recalls precisely those myths of royal omnipotence central to the prewar court masque—the myths so conscientiously purged from the revised *Tempest*.

As the description indicates, this frontispiece acts as a sort of visual frame for the dramatic action. It is, on one hand, a way of containing and limiting the significance of the play—a warning to the audience not to confuse the impotent, repressive Restoration Prospero with the real powers that be. Mediating between the play and the audience, it emphasizes the unreality of the dramatic spectacle, and thus keeps the potentially frightening implications of the fiction within reassuring bounds. However, the frontispiece is also (like the prologue celebrating Shakespeare) a marginal, nostalgic element, subverted by the action at center stage. The frame can seem not more true or reliable than the dramatic fiction, but less—a sort of *de post facto* window dressing which unfortunately stresses just those analogies it was apparently designed to defeat.

One suspects, in fact, that the ambivalence of this new scenery, which denied and at the same time emphasized the contemporary relevance of the Restoration *Tempest*, constituted part of its appeal. In an era when the Stuart mythology seemed increasingly inappropriate, as well as indispensable, the average Restoration playgoer must have been keenly—even painfully—sensitive to the various claims of competing ideologies. A play

19. *The Complete Works of Thomas Shadwell*, ed. Montague Summers, II, 199.

which acknowledged such difficulties, but which also transmuted them into gorgeous and apparently escapist spectacle, must have been extraordinarily compelling. If the Restoration audience greeted the revised *Tempest* with unparalleled enthusiasm, it is probably because Dryden and D'Avenant, and the operatic producers after them, managed to address the hopes and fears of large numbers of their contemporaries.

Triumphal Drama: Form in English Civic Pageantry

GORDON KIPLING

IN LONDON during the sixteenth century, the art of the civic triumph enjoyed a popularity unparalleled elsewhere in England.[1] In its early history, the development of the triumph in London had closely paralleled the development of the great Corpus Christi cycles in the provinces; while the citizens of York, Chester, and Coventry continued to expand and perfect their traditional religious pageants, London concentrated upon civic triumphs, devising increasingly elaborate pageants to honor their sovereigns, welcome foreign princes, and celebrate military victories.

1. In the Renaissance the art of the triumph was a European—not just a London —phenomenon. Thus, much of what I shall have to say here is applicable to Paris, Bruges, or even Rome, and I shall use examples from outside London where necessary to illuminate my argument. Nevertheless, there are some different approaches: in Italy and throughout Southern Europe, the procession tended to be more important than the pageant structures, and the dramatists' efforts were spent more in devising emblematic chariots and floats than in the arches. In Northern Europe, however, the pageant arches became more important, and the dramatist spent most of his effort in devising them. In London, we see both types at the same time: "Royal Entries" tended to emphasize stationary pageant structures; "Lord Mayors' Shows" tended to emphasize chariots and floats.

But with the suppression of the Corpus Christi cycles in the provinces during the sixteenth century, the civic triumph enjoyed an efflorescence in the capital. From mid-century on, in addition to frequent pageant shows to celebrate a coronation or royal marriage, Londoners staged annual triumphs to mark the inauguration each 29 October of the Lord Mayor of London. By the end of the century, these shows had become so popular and influential that the most illustrious of Shakespeare's fellow dramatists eagerly sought commissions to devise them: Jonson, Peele, Middleton, Marston, Dekker, Heywood, Webster, and Munday either designed civic triumphs in their entirety or at least wrote speeches for the actors in these shows. Nor did the poets regard such efforts as mere hackwork; most published accounts of their pageantry, counting these effusions among their best works. Undoubtedly, most would have agreed with Dekker that

Tryumphes, are the most choice and daintiest fruit that spring from *Peace* and *Abundance;* Loue begets them; and Much Cost brings them forth. *Expectation* feeds upon them but seldome to a surfeite, for when she is most full, her longing wants something to be satisfied. So inticing a shape they carry, that *Princes* themselves take pleasure to behold them; they with delight; common people with admiration.

Compared to the honor of designing a London triumph, the fame of a common playwright must have seemed paltry indeed.[2]

As Dekker's language makes clear, Renaissance poets thought of these shows primarily as "triumphs"; our modern terms—"royal entries," "*tableaux vivants,*" or even "Lord Mayors' Shows"—decidedly miss the point. When kings, visiting princes, or mayors entered the city and traveled through streets decorated with tapestries and punctuated by elaborate pageant structures, Londoners saw these shows as continuing a

2. *The Dramatic Works of Thomas Dekker,* ed. Fredson Bowers (Cambridge, 1953–1961), III, 230. Since neither Shakespeare nor any of his successors as "ordinary poet" to the King's Company (Fletcher, Massinger, Shirley) devised triumphs during their tenure of office, we may suspect that contractual obligations to the playhouse may have prohibited any such activities. For this, see G. E. Bentley, *The Profession of Dramatist in Shakespeare's Time, 1590–1642* (Princeton, N.J. 1971), pp. 111–144. Shakespeare, however, as one of the King's Servants, apparently marched in James I's coronation procession. E. K. Chambers, *William Shakespeare* (Oxford, 1930), II, 73.

form of celebration begun by the Caesars. William Lilly's comparison between Charles V's triumphant entry into London (1522) and the triumphs of Pompey and Scipio is merely typical:

> What ioye eke was / the tryumphe of Scipion
> And of hym Pompey / to the romayns echone
> Lyke ioye to vs Charles / prince of Clemency
> Is at thy comyng / with pusaunt kyng Henry.[3]

The conscious classical parallel becomes even more obvious when we consider the structure of the English royal triumph. Just as the Roman procession moved from the Campus Martius, outside the walls of the city, to the Capitol, where an offering of thanksgiving was made in the Temple of Jupiter, so the London procession followed one of two similar routes. Foreign princes and native kings returning from abroad usually began their triumphs in Southwark and proceeded over the Bridge and through the streets to St. Paul's, where a *Te Deum* service of thanksgiving was held. Most coronation processions, however, conventionally entered the City from the Tower, proceeded through the City to Westminster, and often celebrated a *Te Deum* in the Abbey. In Roman and English processions alike, crowds lined the streets, and triumphal arches or similar structures appeared at various stations along the route.[4] Even the elaborate triumphal chariots of the Roman celebration found their English counterparts in the "Chares" routinely provided for the noble visitor and his retinue. "Diversly appareilled" to "accorde wyth thestatis of them that shalbe in them," the most "richely garnysshed" was reserved for the *triumphator,* and it might be emblematically decorated. In 1588, for example, Queen Elizabeth triumphantly rode through London in a symbolic "chariot-throne made with foure pillars behind to have a

3. *Of the tryūphe / . . . that Charles themperour / & the most myghty redouted kyng of England . . . were saluted with / passyng through London* (London, 1522), fol. a iv[r].

4. For recent books on the London triumph, see Sydney Anglo, *Spectacle, Pageantry, and Early Tudor Policy* (Oxford, 1969); David M. Bergeron, *English Civic Pageantry, 1558–1642* (Columbia, S.C., 1971); Glynne Wickham, *Early English Stages, 1300–1660,* 2 vols. (London, 1959–1972). For the Roman triumph, see Robert Payne, *The Roman Triumph* (London, 1962); H. Versnel, *Triumphus; an Inquiry into the Origin, Development and Meaning of the Roman Triumph* (Leiden, 1970).

canopie, on the toppe whereof was made a crowne imperiall, and two lower pillars before, whereon stood a lyon and a dragon, supporters of the armes of England, drawne by two white horses."[5] Similar chariots, such as the *"Chariot Triumphant"* drawn by two "luzernes" and containing "a *Russian Prince* and *Princesse*," were common sights in seventeenth-century Lord Mayors' triumphs.[6]

Throughout the history of the form, civic triumphs in London were almost always accompanied by allusions to their Roman originals, whether in speech, dramatic action, or pageant structures. Upon the occasion of important military victories, for example, English sovereigns riding through London tended to repeat the Roman pattern with literal fidelity. After his victory at Agincourt, Henry V led his prisoners through London in a triumph worthy of a Caesar.[7] In a similar fashion, Henry VII's triumph after Bosworth Field included a display of the spoils of the vanquished and an offering of his victorious battle standards in St. Paul's, just as Roman *triumphators* had dedicated theirs in the Temple of Jupiter.[8] To commemorate her victory over the Spanish Armada, Queen Elizabeth, "imitating the ancient Romans, rode into London in triumph":

She was carried thorow her sayd City of London in a tryumphant chariot, and in robes of triumph, from her Palace unto the Cathedrall Church of Saint Paul, out of the which the ensignes and colours of the vanquished Spaniards hung displayed.[9]

Celebrations of political and social occasions—the arrival of a foreign prince, a coronation, or a Lord Mayor's installation—were similarly

5. *The traduction & mariage of the princesse* (London, 1500), fol. 3ᵛ; John Nichols, *The Progresses and Public Processions of Queen Elizabeth* (London, 1823), II, 538–539.

6. Dekker, "Britannia's Honor," *Dramatic Works*, IV, 89.

7. James Hamilton Wylie, *The Reign of Henry the Fifth* (Cambridge, 1919), II, 257–269.

8. *The Great Chronicle of London*, ed. A. H. Thomas and I. D. Thornley (London, 1938), pp. 238–239; *The Anglica Historia of Polydore Vergil, 1485–1537*, ed. Denys Hay, Camden Soc., 3d. Ser. (London, 1950), LXXIV, 4–5.

9. Richard Hakluyt, *The Principal Navigations, Voyages, Traffiques & Discoveries of the English Nation* (London, 1907), II, 400.

triumphal.[10] We have already seen how Charles V, entering the city upon a state visit in 1522, seemed as orthodox a *triumphator* as Caesar to the Londoners. So Henry VI's entry into London in 1432 was said to surpass the triumphs of Julius Caesar and Scipio; King James passed to his coronation in 1603 beneath Stephen Harrison's "Arches of Triumph"; and even the mayors of London found themselves transformed into Roman *triumphators,* for "The *Praetorian* Dignity is therefore come from the ancient Roman, to inuest with Robes of Honor, our *Lord Maior* of *London:* Their *Consuls* are our *Sheriefes:* their *Senators* our *Aldermen.*" [11]

Because Renaissance Englishmen thought that "the triumphs of the Romans excelled all their other shews," [12] they tended to regard their own triumphs as one of the most important forms of their national drama, "the most choice and daintiest fruit that spring from Peace and Abundance." Because we see them as a succession of *tableaux vivants,* however, we tend to regard them as mere nondramatic spectacles. Thus, modern criticism often robs the civic triumph of any sense of dramatic coherence by equating the separate pageant structures with theaters and reducing the *triumphators* to a moving audience of one:

Normally, in northern countries, the processional element was incidental. The one audience was the noble visitor—a moving audience that advanced from outer gate to city hall or palace. . . . As he approached each new place, music from a special gallery or scenic device, or perhaps hidden, must welcome him. Addresses and allegorical shows must impress on him the loyalty of the subjects, their special compliments, and at times their needs. Hence both the dramatic conventions and the scenic forms of the *tableaux vivants* were determined by their origin as street decoration; they were never drama.

10. As Sir William Segar, a learned participant in many of these spectacles, points out: "Triumphs haue bene commonly vsed at the Inauguration and Coronation of Emperors, Kings, and Princes: at their Mariages, Entry of cities, Enterviewes, Progresses and Funerals. Those pompous shewes, were first inuented and practised by the Romanes whom diuers other Princes haue imitated" (*Honor military, and ciuill, contained in foure bookes* [London, 1602], p. 138).

11. Dekker, IV, 82; *Great Chronicle,* pp. 169–170 (verses by Lydgate); Stephen Harrison, *Arches of Triumph* (London, 1604).

12. Raphael Holinshed, *Chronicles* (London, 1808), IV, 466.

They were showpieces, looking like picture or architectural structure or heraldic device—showpieces that by means of living actors were able to move, to speak, or to sing; showpieces that took their places beside the tapestries, the painted "histories," and the ornamented gates and fountains as part of the decorations for a festival.[13]

To an age familiar with the proscenium theater, this may well make a lot of sense. The noble visitor, the "one audience," watches passively "down here" while the actors—if they can be called that—perform "up there" in the pageant. But because the shows in each "theater" are brief, and because the noble visitor moves on to a new show, the sense of drama remains very limited. Speeches are usually monologues; only tenuous thematic comparisons link the pageants to one another. There is no conflict, no action, merely a series of three-dimensional pictures fleshed out with live performers.

But to a Tudor spectator, this description would seem very strange, for his eyes were trained upon the *triumphator's* splendid procession while it encountered the city's pageants. As a Londoner watched this spectacle of procession and pageantry from his "standing" along the street, who could blame him for thinking himself the true audience for whom this show was designed? As Dekker complains, "the multitude" —that is, the humble Londoners who line the streets—are "our Audience, whose heads would miserably runne a wooll-gathering, if we doo but offer to breake them with hard words."[14] For such an audience, the *triumphator,* far from a passive viewer of a series of playlets, would seem the protagonist of a drama which takes all London as its stage. In fact, Richard Mulcaster makes this very point about Elizabeth I's coronation triumph: "If a man shoulde say well," he writes, "he could not better tearme the citie of London that time, than a stage wherein was shewed the wonderfull spectacle, of a noble hearted princesse toward her most louing people."[15]

13. George R. Kernodle, *From Art to Theatre: Form and Convention in the Renaissance* (Chicago, 1944), p. 62. But on the same page Kernodle also observes, "in Northern Europe the royal procession kept some aspects of the triumphal parade."

14. Dekker, II, 255.

15. *The Passage of our most drad Soueraigne Lady Quene Elyzabeth through the citie of London to westminster the daye before her coronacion* (London, 1558), fol. Aii[v].

Such theatrical characterizations of London triumphs are far from idle metaphors. By carefully exploiting the dramatic possibilities inherent in the encounter of *triumphator* and pageant, the designers of these "wonderfull spectacles" obliged their "noble hearted" protagonists to play roles, not merely attend performances. Thus, the approach of Katharine of Aragon in 1501 miraculously causes the gates of the Castle of Policy to swing open. "Who openyd these gatis?" inquires the captain of the castle, "what, opened they alone?" Then, searching the skies as the triumphant princess approaches, he discovers the reason:

> The bright sterre of Spayne, Hesperus, on them shone,
> Whoes goodly beames hath persid mightily
> Through this castell, to bring this good lady,
> Whoes prosperous comyng shall right joyefull be.[16]

Not all such encounters produced such spectacular results, of course, but the "miracle" wrought by an approaching *triumphator* did become one of the most popular scenes in the history of these shows. The Blessed Virgin might descend from a cloud to bless the king, the illustrious dead might awaken to greet their successors, or the approach of the prince might breathe life into mere pageantry:

Also att the Stockys ther dyd stand a pageaunte off an ylonde betokenyng the Ile off englonde compassede all abowte with water made in silver and byce lyke to waves off the see and rockys ionyng therto. . . . And att the comyng off the emprowr the bestys dyd move and goo, the fisshes dyd sprynge, the byrdes dyd synge reioysing the comyng off the ij princes the emprowr and the kynges grace.[17]

Even if the *triumphator* were determined to do no more than watch the show, such carefully contrived incidents as these would have made him appear to interact with the pageant actors. But many did willingly perform roles in these triumphal dramas, and particularly skillful performers—Elizabeth I for example—greatly impressed their subjects with an astonishingly varied performance, sober and humble at one pageant,

16. London, College of Arms, MS. 1st M. 13, fol. 35ᵛ.

17. Anglo, p. 197. We still find the "miracle" wrought by the approaching *triumphator* the central device in Anthony Munday's Lord Mayors' Shows in the early seventeenth century. In 1611 and again in 1616, the approach of the newly installed Lord Mayor had power to resurrect his revered predecessors from their tombs (Bergeron, pp. 149–151, 156–157).

extravagantly rhetorical at the next. Thus, early in her 1559 coronation triumph, Elizabeth paused before a pageant representing "The vniting of the two howses of Lancastre and Yorke," and listened with care as the child actor advised her to seek concord among the contending factions in her realm as her grandparents had. Then, "after that her grace had vnderstode ye meaning thereof, she thanked the citie, praised ye fairenes of the worke, and promised that she woulde doe her whole endeuour for the continuall preseruacion of concorde, as the pageant did emport." At another station, however, this solemn and respectful demeanor explodes into a histrionic display that might have done credit to the Globe. As she pauses before a pageant which contrasts a "decayed commonweale" with a "florishyng commonweale," an expositor explains to the queen that the cause of the decay of the first commonwealth is the neglect of the book which one of the pageant characters, Truth, holds in her hand. The book, he declares, is an English Bible, and only by embracing it can Elizabeth show that she "vnderstandste the good estate and nought" necessary to plant Wealth in her kingdom "and barrennes displace." At this point, Elizabeth's performance becomes politically as well as dramatically crucial; acceptance or rejection of the book which Truth now offers the queen becomes a test of the *triumphator's* intentions with respect to the Protestant faith. Melodramatically, Elizabeth not only accepts the *Verbum veritatis,* but

when her grace had learned that the Byble in Englishe should there be offered, she thanked the citie therefore, promysed the reading therof most diligentlye, and incontinent commaunded, that it should be brought. At the receit wherof, how reuerently did she with both her handes take it, kisse it, & lay it vpon her breast to the great comfort of the lookers on.

Certainly her performance delighted a staunch Protestant like Richard Mulcaster, who concluded upon seeing it that "God will undoubtedly preserue so worthy a prince, which at his honor so reuerently taketh her beginning." [18]

Even the henchmen marching with the *triumphator* in procession often donned costumes and performed crucial mimetic actions. In most coronation triumphs, for example, actors representing the king's illustrious ancestors, the dukes of Normandy and Aquitaine, would walk just before

18. *The Passage of our most drad Soueraigne,* fols. Bi^r-Bi^v, Ciiii^v, Eiiii^v.

the chariot costumed in "old fashioned hats, powdered on their heads, disguised."[19] Whifflers, usually dressed as "devells and wyldmen," were conventionally pressed into service as actors. Thus, in the 1617 mayoral triumph, the crowd was kept back by "men masked as wild giants who by means of fireballs and wheels hurled sparks in the faces of the mob and over their persons." [20] And certainly "those twelve that rode armed" in Sir John Swinnerton's mayoral procession came prepared to play their scene in Dekker's *Troia-Nova Triumphans,* for just at the climactic moment they fired their pistols in volley, frightening away Envy and assuring Sir John's achievement of Honor.[21]

Such encounters as these provided the pageant artist with the raw materials for a fully developed dramatic plot. As the *triumphator* moves from pageant to pageant through the streets of London, he can be made to perform a mimetic action predetermined by the dramatic craft of the civic dramatist. The anonymous dramatist who designed Katharine of Aragon's triumph, for example, cast her as the heroine of a medieval dream vision. By carefully structuring the princess's pageant encounters, he makes Katharine travel from earth, through the spheres of the cosmos, to an apotheosis upon the Throne of Honor above the firmament. At the first pageant, on London Bridge, Saints Katharine and Ursula descend from the "Court Celestial" to announce that the princess will be "conveyed . . . to honor" in the heavens, where she will become the star Hesperus set among the "stars bright." Thereafter, Katharine begins her ascension, climbing from the earthly Castle Policy (pageant two), to the

19. The appearance of these traditional figures was already "an old custom" when they marched in the coronation procession of Anne Boleyn (*Tudor Tracts, 1532–1588,* introduction by A. F. Pollard [Westminster, 1903], p. 14). Cf. Edward VI's coronation procession in John Leland, *Collectanea,* 2d ed. (London, 1774), IV, 311. They were still marching in coronation processions during the Restoration; see John Ogilby, *The King's Coronation* (London, 1685), p. 1.

20. "But all proved unavailing to make a free and ample thoroughfare" (*Calendar of State Papers, Venetian, 1617–1619* [London, 1909], XV, 61). "Devells and wyldmen" were traditional by 1575 (E. K. Chambers, *The Elizabethan Stage* [London, 1923], I, 136). Cf. the young men of Edinburgh, who would traditionally dress as Moors to serve as whifflers in the "convoy before the cairt triumphant" (Anna Jean Mill, *Mediaeval Plays in Scotland* [Edinburgh, 1927], pp. 188–191, 202–203).

21. Dekker, III, 245. See discussion of this triumph below.

sphere of the moon (pageant three), to the sphere of the sun (pageant four), to the throne of God the Father (pageant five). At each station she acquires the virtues she will need for the next stage in her ascent. Finally, she is invited to take a throne beside Honor himself, a throne fixed upon the eternal foundation of the seven virtues and set above the cosmos (pageant six).[22] By the time she reaches St. Paul's, Katharine has performed in the same sort of narrative plot that might characterize a more conventional drama.

By means of a similar structuring of pageant encounters, Thomas Dekker's *Troia-Nova Triumphans* (1612) contrives to make Sir John Swinnerton serve as the hero of a morality plot in which the new Lord Mayor acquires the virtues he will need to conquer Envy. In this case, Dekker skillfully employs mobile pageants to represent Sir John's successive mastery of the necessary virtues.[23] Thus, as the mayor rides in triumph, he first encounters the triumphal chariot of Neptune, who proclaims that he has come "thus farre-vp into th'Land . . . Beyond his Bownds" that he might "with his Sea-troops wait" his "wish't arriuall to congratulate." By having Neptune join Sir John's triumphal procession, Dekker thus represents London's mastery of the seas in dramatic action: the *triumphator* of the seas yields to triumphant London and becomes a mere henchman in the Lord Mayor's procession. In this same pattern, the mayor next encounters the triumphal chariot of Virtue, who likewise yields to join his lordship's more triumphal procession, for London's success is based upon virtue, not just merchant seamanship. Now armed with Neptune's strength and the assurance of Virtue, Sir John is prepared to encounter the Castle of Envy, which blocks his passage to Guildhall. Because Envy cannot stand up to Virtue, the *triumphator* passes safely on to the Temple of Fame, where the goddess assures the mayor that he and London are enrolled in her eternal book. Having achieved fame, Sir John now adds the goddess's temple to his procession and turns about for a final attack upon Envy. This time, Envy is not merely avoided, but defeated. "On, on," shouts Virtue from Sir John's

22. College of Arms, MS. 1st M. 13, fols. 33ᵛ–43ᵛ.

23. In London Lord Mayors' triumphs, the civic pageants were designed to be carried in procession. As soon as the mayor had encountered a pageant in the streets and heard the explanatory speeches, it joined his procession and traveled immediately before him.

procession, "The beames of *Virtue* are so bright, / They dazzle *Enuy:* On, the *Hag's* put to flight." On this cue, "those twelue that ride armed" in the mayor's procession "discharge their *Pistols,* at which *Enuy,* and the rest, vanish, and are seene no more." Finally, the new Lord Mayor and his by-now splendid procession arrive before Justice, who welcomes him and explains his duties.[24]

Not all triumph plots are narratively structured of course; some may more properly be described as conceptual or typological expositions. Thus, barely a year after Henry VII overthrew the House of York upon Bosworth Field, he was literally crowned—pageant by pageant—in the streets of York. The plot is a clearly defined one, but it is based upon the coronation ceremony instead of a narrative fable. At the first station, Ebraucus gives Henry the keys to the city and a crown descends from heaven to cover a Union Rose. In the next, a council of past English kings awards him with the Scepter of Wisdom, while at a third station, a pageant-David invests the king with the Sword of Victory. Now that Henry has received all of the coronation regalia, the Virgin Mary descends from Heaven in a final pageant to present him with God's blessings.[25] By contrast, Anne Boleyn's triumphal plot is typological in structure. In pageant after pageant, she receives a series of golden gifts— gold coins, Paris's golden apple, a gift of "golden" verses, the golden crown of a queen. As the pageant speakers make clear, these are all emblems of the golden age that can be renewed upon her coronation. But the Golden Age requires its Saturn, and in return for these gifts, London asks a golden gift from Anne: a new son of the king's blood who shall bring that golden world to his people.[26]

The decided homiletic emphasis in most of these plots may tempt us to draw parallels between the art of the triumph and the art of the morality play. In fact, however, this didactic function of the civic triumph derives more directly from medieval and Renaissance conceptions of the Roman triumph. Petrarch's *Trionfi,* for example, exemplifies one of the chief

24. Dekker, III, 231–247.

25. H. A. Smith, "A York Pageant, 1486," *London Mediaeval Studies* (1939), 382–398; John C. Meagher, The First Progress of Henry VII," *RenD*, N.S. I (1968), 49–59.

26. *Tudor Tracts,* pp. 12–19.

organizing principles in the plot of a civic triumph, a principle which
demands that the *triumphator* must acquire certain virtues at one station
before he may pass on to the next. Thus the *Trionfi* takes the form of a
series of six pageantlike allegorical triumphs arranged in a homiletic
series. As Petrarch describes these triumphs, each allegorical *triumphator*
conquers his predecessor and falls victim to his successor; beginning with
the Triumph of Love, Chastity overthrows Love, Death overthrows
Chastity, Fame overthrows Death, Time overthrows Fame, and Eternity
overthrows Time. In England, the illustrations for this poem—tapestries,
pictures, and manuscript illuminations—far outstripped the influence of
the poem itself. In one illustration, for example, Death would be riding
her ox-drawn triumphal chariot with Chastity bound and lying at her
feet. In the next, the Lady Fame would triumphantly ride her triumphal
chariot, drawn by four winged horses, while Death lay chained and
helpless at her feet.[27] At times, the *Trionfi* were even translated from
illustrations to pageantry. In 1579, for example, Queen Elizabeth witnessed a pageant performance based upon Petrarch's Triumph of Chastity. First, Cupid entered the queen's presence in his triumphal chariot.
Next, Dame Chastity with her four maids—Modesty, Temperance, Good
Exercise, and Shamefastness—entered, threw Cupid from his chariot,
despoiled him of his cloak, and took away his bow and arrows. Chastity
then mounted the chariot, rode to the queen, and presented her with
the spoils of conquest: the cloak, bow, and arrows.[28]

As they traveled through the streets of the city, many a London
triumphator also found himself obeying the familiar homiletic logic of
this Petrarchan classic. Katharine of Aragon was obliged to understand
Noblesse and Virtue before she might ascend to the sphere of the moon.
She then gained philosophical wisdom upon the moon before she could
ascend further to the sun, and so on. In similar fashion, Mulcaster takes

27. Cf. Sir Thomas More's "Tapestry Poem," *The English Works of Sir Thomas
More,* ed. W. E. Campbell and A. W. Reed (London, 1927), I, 332–335. See also
D. D. Carnicelli's introduction to his edition of Lord Morley's *"Tryumphes of
Fraunces Petrarcke"*: *The First English Translation of the "Trionfi"* (Oxford,
1972).

28. Edwin Greenlaw, Charles Grosvenor Osgood, Frederick M. Padelford, eds.,
The Works of Edmund Spenser: A Various Edition (Baltimore, Md., 1934), III,
355. See also III, 301, 354–355, 359, 398.

particular care to point out the dependence of each new pageant upon its successor during Queen Elizabeth's coronation triumph:

The mater of this pageāt depēdeth of them yt went before. For as the first declared her grace to cōe out of ye house of vnitie, ye second yt she is placed in ye seat of gouernement staied with vertue to the suppressiō of vice, and therefore in the third the eight blessinges of almighty god might well be applyed vnto her: so this fourth now is, to put her grace in remembrāce of the state of the common weale, which Time with Truth his doughter dooth reuele, which Truth also her grace hath receiued, and therfore cannot but be mercifull and carefull for ye good gouernemēt therof.[29]

Perhaps Dekker's 1612 triumph for Sir John Swinnerton even more clearly approximates Petrarch's idea. When Sir John encounters Neptune in his triumphal chariot, Neptune yields and becomes a henchman to Sir John's triumph. Next come encounters with Virtue (who also rides a triumphal chariot) and Fame, each repeating this initial pattern. In a variation upon the Petrarchan pattern, the triumph of Virtue succeeds the triumph of Neptune; the triumph of Fame succeeds that of Virtue. Together, these three moral triumphs now make possible Sir John's destruction of Envy. Significantly, each of the pageants which Sir John conquers takes a place in the mayor's procession just proceeding him; in both the Roman procession and the *Trionfi* illustrations, that position is reserved for the conquered.

In addition to the Petrarchan Trionfi, pageant designers also drew from another traditional formula in designing their plots. According to an extremely popular description of the Roman triumph that appears in many moral and allegorical works of the late Middle Ages, the victorious *triumphator* was paid a triple honor.[30] First, all people, whether of high or low estate, should meet him "with grete Ioye & reuerence, in þer beste and richeste aray." Second, all his captives, "fetrid and manaclid," should "rownde abowte environ his chare" and go through the streets with him in procession. Third, the *triumphator* should ride in a chariot like a god, wearing the mantle of Jupiter and crowned with laurel. But along with

---

29. *The Passage of our most drad Soueraigne,* fol. Di^v.
30. Bromyard, *Summa Praedicantium,* T.v.36; *Gesta Romanorum,* chap. xxx; John Gower, *Confessio Amantis,* VI.2328–2490; John Lydgate, *The Serpent of Division,* ed. H. N. MacCracken (London, 1911), pp. 53–54.

this "triple honor" goes a dose of humility. In order "to schewe clerely þat all worldely glorie is transitori and not abidynge and evidently to declare þat in hiȝe estate is none assurance," a "Ribald" sat uppermost in the triumphal chariot, where he might "smyte þe conqverroure euer in þe necke and uppon þe hed." "Know thyself," he would shout at the *triumphator,* reminding him that despite the purple cloak of Jupiter he was merely mortal.[31] Furthermore, upon the day of a triumph any man might heap what scorn he would upon the conqueror, without fear of punishment. Where honor is freely given, vanity must be sternly suppressed.

The widespread popularity of this moral emblem undoubtedly explains why the plots of so many English triumphs describe the protagonist's achievement of fame or his discovery of a true honor based upon virtue instead of lineage. Thus Katharine of Aragon travels through the streets of London in search of the Throne of Honor, only to find that

> Honour, ye wott well, the rewarde of vertue is,
> And thoughe that vertuelesse many a man or this
> Hath semyd honourable, yet was he not so;
> Such honour is counterfaite and is lightly goo.

Over a century later, Sir John Swinnerton must similarly go to the House of Fame and learn that *"in this* Court *of* Fame / *None else but* Vertue *can enrole thy* Name" before he can defeat Envy.[32] Indeed, the achievement of Honor became the single most important theme of the London mayoral triumph as the titles of so many of them suggest: *The Triumphs of Honor and Industry, The Triumphs of Honor and Virtue, Monuments of Honor, Britannia's Honor,* and even *The Triumphs of Fame and Honor.*[33] Very few London *triumphators* took the stage without encountering some representative of Honor—whether a temple, a chariot, a globe, or even a character named Honor. In each case, the purpose of the *triumphator's* encounter with these structures and characters is the

31. Lydgate, *Serpent of Division,* pp. 53–54.

32. College of Arms, MS. 1st M. 13, fol. 43ᵛ; Dekker, III, 240.

33. Devisers and dates as follows: Thomas Middleton, *Triumphs of Honor and Industry* (1617) and *Triumphs of Honor and Virtue* (1622); John Webster, *Monuments of Honor* (1624); Thomas Dekker, *Britannia's Honor* (1628); John Taylor, *Triumphs of Fame and Honor* (1634).

same: he must learn that however great the glory of his name and office, true honor depends upon his selfless service to the commonwealth.

In order to enforce this distinction between mundane glory and honorable duty, some dramatists provide their *triumphators* with uncomfortable "Ribalds," even while setting them in chariots and surrounding them with obsequious nobles. The entry of Mary Queen of Scots into Edinburgh in 1561 shows how far the dramatist's license to humble his protagonist might extend. At the first pageant station, an angel presents Mary with the keys to the city, an English Bible, and a Protestant Psalm book—pointed enough gifts, perhaps, for a Catholic queen. Next, she witnesses a scene designed to show her what papist idolators like herself might expect if they cling to their Catholic ways. In the "Venegance of God upon Idolatry," she sees the fire of the Lord consume Korah, Dathan, and Abiram because of their rebellion against the congregation of Moses. Perhaps she does not need to be told that Moses in Scotland is John Knox, but lest she miss the point, a priest is also burned in the very act of elevating the Host at the altar. In John Knox's Scotland, the idolatry of the Host will not be tolerated. But Mary is still not through with witnessing the fiery vengeance of the Lord: at a final pageant, the Beast of the Apocalypse burns before her eyes. If Moses had represented John Knox in the previous pageant, there can be little doubt whom the Beast of the Apocalypse is meant to figure in this one.[34]

In London triumphs, the admonition of the "Ribald" is usually not this bold, but it does occur—occasionally with devasting results. The creator of Katharine of Aragon's triumph of 1501, for example, is particularly adept at administering the licensed dose of humility. As the princess ascends the heavens where she will become the star Hesperus, she pauses upon the sphere of the sun where she sees an image of her husband, represented as King Arthur riding a stellar chariot. The stellar chariot is her husband's seven-starred constellation, Arcturus, which Englishmen then knew as "Arthur's constellation." Thus, as the princess rides the streets of London in her own triumph, she suddenly confronts her own husband riding through the heavens in a magnificent star-chariot. While she pauses before this vision, she becomes a part of the grand design to

34. Mill, 188–191; in the context of the antipapal imagery, I assume that the reference to "the dragon" must mean the Beast of the Apocalypse.

the London audience. No longer a *triumphator* riding in her own earthly triumph, she now takes her place as a henchman in Arthur's grander celestial one. The Petrarchan logic of the pageant diminishes her while exalting Arthur; just as the Chariot of Fame replaces the Chariot of Death in successive illustrations to the *Trionfi*, so Arthur's stellar chariot supercedes Katharine's earthly one. In the pageant as in life, forces beyond her control doom her to ride as a mere henchman in the triumphal procession of the Tudor dynasty. Only after she learns her subordinate place in this English dynasty can she complete her journey to the Throne of Honor. A place has been made ready for her there, she discovers, not because of her own intrinsic worth, but because she is the wife of a Tudor prince.

In most cases, however, triumph dramatists admonished their protagonists to "know themselves" in a less devastating way. Typically, a triumph plot equips the *triumphator* with the virtues and knowledge that he will need to succeed as king or mayor, thus winning glory for himself, his city, and his country. The particular virtues necessary to his success will, of course, depend upon the occasion, Thus, when Henry VI entered London in 1432, the pageant designer understandably focused upon the boy-king's necessary education. First, Nature, Grace, and Fortune shower him with their gifts: strength and fairness of body, the seven Gifts of the Holy Ghost and the seven matching Gifts of Grace, and Prosperity and Wealth. These are the gifts that are his by right of birth into the royal house of England. But to be successful as a king, Henry discovers at the next pageant, he must improve these gifts by means of Dame Sapience and the Seven Liberal Arts; he must, in short, go to school. In the two succeeding pageants, he finds that his throne depends upon law and that he must become a Well of Mercy to his subjects; presumably his scholastic education will prepare him to distinguish between Justice and Mercy in ruling his subjects. If he succeeds in ruling properly, as the final two pageants make clear, he will be worthy of the two crowns of England and France that he has inherited, and the Heavenly Trinity will keep him from "all damage" during his reign.[36]

    35. See my book, *The Triumph of Honor* (Leiden, 1977), chap. IV, for a complete discussion of this triumph.

    36. *Great Chronicle*, pp. 156–170.

When Elizabeth I performed her coronation triumph over a century and a quarter later, however, the pageant designer emphasized the virtues of concord and adherence to religious truth that the queen would find necessary in an England divided by the Reformation. Thus, in order that she might know her duties more clearly, the dramatist posted a summary statement of all that she had learned in her triumphal passage through the city:

> The first arch as true heyre vnto thy father deere,
> Did set thee in the throne where thy graund father satte,
> The second did confirme thy seat as princesse here,
> Vertues now bearing swaye, and vyces bet down flatte.
>
> The third, if that thou wouldst goe on as thou began,
> Declared thee to be blessed on euery syde,
> The fourth did open Trueth, and also taught thee whan
> The commōweale stoode well, & when it did thence slide.
>
> The fifth, as Debora declared thee to be sent
> From heauen, a long comfort to vs thy subiects all,
> Therefore goe on, O Queene, on whom our hope is bent,
> And take with thee this wishe of thy towne as finall.[37]

Although hereditary right and personal virtue qualify her to occupy the English throne, Elizabeth discovers, they will not in themselves guarantee the successful continuance of her reign. If she hopes to "go on as she began," she must play the role of a Deborah, delivering her nation from the oppression of its Jabin (Philip of Spain), thereby upholding true religion and restoring the commonwealth to its previous flourishing estate. By enthusiastically clasping the English Bible to her breast, she signifies her willingness to perform this difficult role that her subjects have thrust upon her.

Mayors' triumphs are particularly characterized by such dramatic revelations of the *triumphator*'s future duties. In 1585, just before the Armada, Peele saw Wolstan Dixi's chief duty as the defense of queen and country. Only in this way might he "adde to Londons dignity, / And Londons dignity . . . adde" to his.[38] Thirty-two years later, however, Thomas

---

37. *The Passage of our most drad Soueraigne*, fol. Ej^v.
38. *The Life and Minor Works of George Peele*, ed. David H. Horne (New Haven, Conn., 1952), p. 210.

Middleton was preparing his mayor to enter the "Castle of Fame or Honour" by schooling him in the arts of peace. Accordingly, at the beginning of his triumph, Dame Industry reminds him that she is "the life-blood of praise: / To rise without me, is to steal to glory." As one of Industry's "sons," a place is reserved for him in the Castle of Honor, but in order to claim that place

> Great works of grace must be requir'd and done
> Before the honour of this seat be won.
> A whole year's reverend care in righting wrongs,
> And guarding innocence from malicious tongues,
> Must be employ'd in virtue's sacred right
> Before this place be fill'd.[39]

Just as the "Ribald" warns the *triumphator* not to "wex prowde" in the "worldly glorie" of his triumph, so the Lord Mayor finds that the glory and adulation of his fine triumph have only brought him "a whole year's reverend care." His lesson parallels the one that Henry V learns on the eve of Agincourt: "What infinite heart's-ease must kings neglect that private men enjoy."

The protagonists of these triumphal dramas, of course, might react to these moral exhortations and doses of humility in different ways. As we have seen, Elizabeth I was able to transform Lady Truth's gift of a Bible into a melodramatic statement of support for the Protestant faith, a performance that evidently won her great favor in the eyes of her subjects. Two years later, however, Mary Queen of Scots found herself performing the same scene, but with quite the opposite results. As she approached one of the triumphal arches in her coronation procession, a "cloude opynnit" and a child "discendit doun as it had bene ane angell, and deliuerit to hir hienes . . . ane bybill and ane psalme buik." The angel declared these gifts "to be emblems of her defending the Reformed religion." But instead of kissing the Bible and clasping it to her breast, as Elizabeth had done, Mary "began to frown. For schame sche could not refuise it, but she did no better, for immediatelie sche gave it to the most pestilent Papist within the Realme." Such a refusal to "play the role" assigned to her could not be expected to win her any support among the

---

39. *The Works of Thomas Middleton,* ed. A. H. Bullen (London, 1886), VII, 303.

followers of Knox.[40] A few other similar instances suggest that *triumphators* did not always play their roles gladly,[41] but Henry VII's reaction to the role he assumed during his triumphal entry into Bristol in 1486 more nearly illustrates the ideal. Saluted in pageant after pageant as a king sent by God "to reforme thyngs that be contrarious / Unto the Comen Wele," Henry responds by seeking to restore Bristol's shipbuilding and clothmaking industries, which had lately fallen into decay:

After Evensonge the Kinge sent for the Mayre and Shrife, and Parte of the best Burges of the Towne, and demaunded theym of the Cause of ther Povertie; and they shewde his grace for the great Losse of Shippes and Goodes that they had loost within 5 yeres. The King comforted theym, that they shulde sett on and make new Shippes, and to exercise ther Marchandise as they wer wonte for to doon. And his Grace shulde so helpe theym by dyvers Means like as he shewde unto theym, that the Meyre of the Towne towlde me they harde not this hundred Yeres of noo King so good a Comfort.[42]

Such a response is dramatically as well as politically appropriate. It shows that the king is willing to perform in earnest the role that his subjects have thrust upon him in the triumphal drama.

For Londoners in the Renaissance, the Roman celebration of military victory had been transformed into a civic drama of moral triumph. The king or mayor who rode through the streets of London did not merely witness a series of pageant shows; he also played the lead in the "wonderfull spectacle" that the London multitude witnessed. The plots for these triumphal dramas were based upon the *triumphator*'s encounters with the series of pageants that awaited him in the streets. By cleverly defining and arranging the pageant encounters, the dramatist made his protagonist perform any number of actions: ascend the heavens, fulfill a knightly quest, conquer envy, travel to the House of Fame, become a

40. Mill, p. 190; Knox's report here is probably extremely prejudiced.

41. Compare Anne Boleyn's supposed anger at the Easterlings, who "set the Imperial eagle over the royal arms and her own" upon one of her coronation pageants, and the Bishop of Winchester's intimidation of a painter who had dared to portray Henry VIII holding "a booke, whereon was wrytten *Verbum Dei*" during Philip of Spain's London triumph (Anglo, pp. 250 n. 2, 329).

42. Leland, IV, 202; Meagher, p. 72.

king, or—more simply—accept a series of symbolic gifts and give one in return. The possibilities are as endless as the dramatist's imagination. But because the Roman triumph had itself become a moral emblem to Renaissance Londoners, these encounters became moral as well. As the Petrarchan moral pattern would have it, the *triumphator* often accomplishes a series of moral triumphs in his passage through London, each one dependent upon its predecessor. The dramatist, of course, arranges these moral encounters because he finds them significant; the virtues that the protagonist masters in his drama are the virtues that the dramatist and his audience hope their governors will master in performing the duties of their offices. The "general end" of this drama, as Spenser might have explained it, is "to fashion a magistrate." But where the writer of an epic hopes to teach by example rather than rule, the deviser of a triumph teaches by mimesis. After performing his role in the triumphal drama, perhaps the magistrate is now fit to perform it again in "real life."

Ideologies and Aesthetics
of Gender

Corneille and Cornelia: Reason, Violence, and the Cultural Status of the Feminine. Or, How a Dominant Discourse Recuperated and Subverted the Advance of Women

TIMOTHY J. REISS

THE YEARS between 1540 and 1650 in Europe were years of disaster, dissolution, and war.[1] We are by now familiar with the debate over human reason and the increasingly felt need for some new "instauration" that accompanied it during this same century. Less common is the awareness that these matters are part of the *same* sociocultural transformation, and that to understand fully the passage to the modern era we must try to fit the issues essential to that passage into these apparently different historical events. To cultural historians, Erasmus and Machiavelli, More and Guicciardini, Budé, Vives, Calvin, Ramus, Bodin, Scaliger, Heinsius, Grotius, and Descartes are usually far more familiar than the Schmalkaldic wars of central Europe, the details of the religious wars in France, the revolt against the Spanish Hapsburg crown in the Netherlands, Italy, Portugal, and Catalonia, the facts of the Thirty Years War, of the English civil wars, of the Frondes in France, and indeed the knowledge that at some time during these hundred years almost every European power was at war with every other.

171

The following argument concerns the debate about the relation between gender and reason during these years—most particularly as it appears in the work of Pierre Corneille. I will show how that debate was entirely caught up on the one hand in the general debate over human reason, and on the other with the urgent discussions about the confused and unstable condition of the political and social order, everywhere subverted by uncertainty and violence. One need scarcely add that the debate ultimately concerned the cultural status of women. It passed, I wish to show, through three principal moments:

1. The argument that there was only one kind of human reason, that it was quite unconnected with sexuality, and therefore equally powerful in both men and women, grew ever stronger. The high points in this aspect of the debate may be situated in the mid-sixteenth century, in the 1630s (Descartes, du Bosc, Corneille), and at the very end of the seventeenth century: with the Cartesians, François Poulain de la Barre in France (1670s) and Mary Astell in England (1690s).[2]

2. In the mid-seventeenth century, some sort of almost subterranean feeling seems to have grown that because of the specific way in which men had participated in the historical development of societies, *their* reason was inseparable from violence. On the other hand, however, because women had been historically excluded from the making of society and culture, reason in them (not *female* reason, but simply Reason as acting within women) was free of that violence, and could thus offer a solution to the dangerous decay of political and civil order. The future might perhaps lie with women, even though the arguments and hints remain ambiguous and unclear. They are made the more problematic because of political philosophy's theoretical *exclusion* of women from active participation in political order (as we will see). In France, the major proponents of the idea that women might rationally resolve the problem of the violent decay of societies, besides the implications of the *salon* movement and the preciosity accompanying it, were Pierre Corneille and Poulain de la Barre.[3]

3. At the end of the seventeenth century, that distinction between men's and women's reason was asserted more "violently." The hopes for political salvation through nonviolent reason in women were abandoned.[4] The idea that women's reason was of a different order was again reaffirmed: tranquil passion, calm emotion, depth of senti-

ment, nurturing instinct, and the rest now defined such nonviolent reason, in a return to a belief in traditionally asserted female attributes. But they had acquired a positive, rather than a negative, value. By such means women, possessing no responsibility at all for cultural or political production (indeed, long since theoretically excluded from them), could nonetheless be included at least in the first—as consumers, of course, or producers of a subordinate culture. The turning point in the debate was marked by the *Querelle des femmes* at the end of the century in France, most especially by writings of Boileau, Perrault, La Bruyère, Fénelon, and Mme de Maintenon. The issue arose afresh at this time almost as a side effect of the *Querelle des anciens et des modernes*.[5] The dominant culture thus found the means to *coopt* the strong arguments about women's reason, leaving it as a "positive" characteristic, but making it gender specific and thus able to be subordinated to what was then given as men's more powerful reason. This reason has to do, then, first with what was said about women and women's status, and second with what that *saying* established as a consequence. I wish to show that Corneille's plays of the late 1630s and early 1640s were particularly important texts in this process, both for articulating the political optimism about women's rationality and for representing the contours of its failure.

I. The Birth of a Reason Common to All Humans

The treatment of women's status by the dominant Judeo-Christian tradition is largely familiar: woman was responsible for the Fall, she was lubricious, in thrall to sexual passion, instinct, animality, and so on. Her virtues were the corresponding ones of passivity, modesty, chastity, temperance, silence, and obedience: virtues for which women had not infrequently been idealized in some quarters. Some early writers had implied that women were fully as rational as men: writings by Hildegard of Bingen, Hroswitha, and Julian of Norwich were exemplary (though no one ever took them up), while Marie de France urged such a claim in the prologue of her *Lais*. But as the examples suggest, as Marie indeed said, and as was frequently asserted well into the seventeenth century and even later, such reason came from God, whose handmaiden woman was.[6] The view did parallel certain arguments

about reason as manifest in man as well, but in either case it was entirely
different from asserting that women share with men a human and self-
responsible rationality. Despite ambiguities and equivocations, writers
mostly agreed on the inferiority, danger, and irrationality of women.

Before the mid-sixteenth century, the only real proponent of an unambiguous view that women, like men, possess and can use an entirely
human reason was Christine de Pisan at the beginning of the previous
century. And hers remained a lone voice.[7] Only at the end of the fifteenth century, with Cornelius Agrippa, and then half a century later
still, did a new note begin to be sustained, echoing the growing debate
on the nature of reason in general.

In 1545 Sir Thomas Elyot's fictional debate between a traditional
misogynist, Caninius, and a supporter of women, Candidus, clearly
gave the advantage to the latter. It did so, revealingly, by enabling Candidus to argue that women's reason was better than men's because it
was ineluctably tied up with virtues of tranquillity and guardianship.
Reason as it functioned in women was thus in direct opposition to
what could be seen in men, where reason was inseparable from the activities characteristic of the hunter. "And so ye conclude," Candidus
exults,

that the power of reason is more in the prudente and diligent kepynge, than in
the valiaunt or politike geating: And that Discrecion, Election [Judgment], and
Prudence, whiche is all and in everye part reason, doo excell strengthe, wytte,
and hardinesse: And consequentely they, in whome be those vertues, in that
that they have them, do excell in iuste estimacion them that be stronge, hardy,
or politike in geattynge of any thynge. . . .

We have agreed, adds Candidus, that prudence ("which in effect is
nothing but reason") is thus better conceived as belonging to women
more than men, and especially that prudence "in kepyng" is more useful
than "valiauntnesse in geattyng." Further, because prudence is better
than courage, and because prudence *is* reason, so women are "more excellent than men in reason," and, generally speaking, "woman . . . as it
seemeth is more perfit than manne" (Elyot Ciii.v–Cv.r).

Because "naturall reason is in women as well as in men," Elyot concluded that women could hold the highest political and social positions with entire propriety: "then have women also Discrecion, Elec-

tion, & Prudence, which do make that wisedome, which perteineth to governaunce. And perdy [he finally concludes this exchange], many artes and necessarie occupacions have ben inuented by women. . . ." This claim was identical to that made by François de Billon just ten years later, who attempted to list all the inventions in question (22v–32v). He also based his argument on the claim that God had given men and women "an identical and unique form of soul, such that between these souls there is no sexual difference." Women, he added, "share the same understanding as men, the same reason, identical speech. . . ." Everything men can create, he remarks a little later, women can also, and "where the intellect of the one can penetrate, so too can penetrate the other's intellect" (1v, 7r).

That the matter was nevertheless not entirely free from ambiguity was indicated by Billon's remark, as he urged identity of soul, reason, and speech, that "the wise woman edifies and ornaments a household." He congratulated certain Italian cities (particularly Naples), for being less concerned with "interior decoration" than with "striving to keep the Women quite orderly [*bien en ordre*] and brilliantly lovely [*clairement luysantes*]—and rightly so: since wherever a beautiful Woman appears, everything is brightened [*clarifié*] by her presence" (1v). To speak of this as ambiguous is an understatement: for Billon as for so many others, however "equal" women's reason might be, it was to be used in a masculine world. Whatever the claims made by men for women and reason, "the lady, shall we venture to say, turns out to be merely a wife." As Ruth Kelso went on later: "The assignment of woman to the domestic end [was thought] perfectly natural and necessary because of her function in bearing and nourishing children. Her more delicate frame and more gentle disposition specially fit her for this, as they unfit her to endure the strenuous exercises and turmoil of public life."[8] Women may have been blessed with the same reason as men, we conclude from this, but it was to be put to use in the private, not public, sphere.[9]

Elyot, Billon, and others were walking a fine but quite visible line. They viewed men's reason as tainted by the addition of a negative value: that of violence. Rather than simply remove that value, in favor of some kind of *morally* "neutral" reason (i.e., a reason that is not internally predetermined but may be freely used to achieve certain *human* goals), they chose to *add* a set of values seen as positive. But those positive values came perilously close to those now-familiar ones of nurturing warmth, instinctual and childlike appreciation of the good and the beautiful, and some sort of boundless protective and passive absorption of the potentially harmful. They were unable to elaborate a concept of neutral and purely *human* reason. Such a failure, the inability of all these writers (with the possible exception of Elyot) to succeed in freeing reason from sexual bonds, prefigured the more drastic and permanent failure of the late seventeenth century.[10]

II. Man's Power and the Theoretical Exclusion of Women from State Authority

The positive value attributed to reason in women was perhaps only the more sympathetic side of a coin of which Machiavelli, for example, showed the less attractive obverse. This was important, because along with the difficulties and equivocations involved in the argument from reason itself (where it concerned women), the very political thinking which sought generally to respond to the apparent dissolution of the European polity during this period seemed actually to exclude women from participating in the organization of that polity— Elyot's assertions to the contrary notwithstanding. This *theoretical* exclusion from the political arena was an important factor in the conceptual failure to assert women's equality and freedoms. We will also see how that exclusion eventually helped reconfirm the claim that women's reason was particular to their sex (whereas men's will be "neutral").

Machiavelli's *Prince* had long since written male/female violence into reason of State itself, describing how the masculine *virtù* essential to the efficient ruler of a new state must learn to take female *Fortuna* by force: just as, he wrote, a spirited violent young man had to learn to take a woman.[11] Such metaphors were far from innocent, and it is therefore hardly coincidental that a century later Machiavelli's view was taken up, metaphorically and literally, by a man who was not simply a theorist (as the Florentine was by the time he wrote) but who had the power to make his word law: I mean Armand-Jean du Plessis, Cardinal-Duc de Richelieu. In the *Political Testament* that he wrote for Louis XIII in case of his own prior death, the minister constantly referred to the need for princes to enjoy a "*mâle vertu.*" The phrase is no more than indicative of a general subordination of women to men's power as it was expressed throughout this text written between 1632 and 1638.

For my present purpose the matter and dates are important, for it often appears, we will see, as though Corneille were responding directly to Richelieu on this issue.

However, I would first like to take a look at a text of possibly even greater significance: Cardin Le Bret's *De la souveraineté du Roy* of 1632. By the time he published this volume, Le Bret was already an old man. Trained in law, he had started his public career more or less at the beginning of Henri IV's reign. By 1632, a recognized expert in the monarchical constitution, he had for years been a member (with Richelieu) of the Royal Council, the king's principal and immediate advisory body. While he was obviously without the enormous power of Richelieu, it seems clear enough that Le Bret's position and reputation meant his voice would be heard. More than that, however, with his *Souveraineté du Roy* Le Bret had written what became the "textbook" of the monarchy under Louis XIV. That his arguments coincide with the far briefer ones set out by Richelieu should hardly surprise us. Nonethelesss, the violence of his discussion where it concerned women might appear somewhat gratuitous, linking reason of State, human reason, and men's aggressivity.

Since Le Bret's book was presented as a discussion of French constitutional law, he began by running through the legal foundations of the monarchy itself. He quickly got to the question of the Salic Law (whose application to the crown he explicitly recognized as an interpretation of the law governing the inheritance of fiefs), writing that "women are unable to mount the throne" ("incapables de parvenir à la Couronne"). Such a maxim, he then continued,

conforms to the law of nature, which, because it created woman imperfect, weak, and feeble, as much in body as in mind, placed her under man's power. To that end, nature enriched him with stronger judgment, firmer courage, and more robust physical strength. We can thus see that divine law wills woman to recognize and render obedience to her husband, as to her head [*chef*] and to her King. And not only does such law not give woman any authority in Empires and Kingdoms, but on the contrary we see in Isaiah chap. 3 that God threatens to give his enemies women as mistresses, as an insupportable curse.

That, he continues immediately, "is why the whole of Antiquity greatly disparaged the Lacedemonians for letting themselves be ruled by their women" (Le Bret 31–32).

It was not, I think, mere chance that led Descartes (after others) to choose precisely this example of Sparta as the epitome of the well-ordered State. He argued the case in the second part of the *Discours de la méthode,* where he asserted that the best and most stable polity was founded upon a coherent set of laws promulgated by a single author, as Sparta's were by Lycurgus.[12] Unlike Le Bret and Richelieu, Descartes implicitly included women in all human rational organization, as he did in the entire argument about reason itself. For if rational mind is of a different order from body, and if sexuality is attached only to the latter, then clearly reason is not male or female but simply human. The singular rational authority lawfully ordering Lacedemonia, Descartes proposed, was exactly analogous to reason's authority over body and the emotions (as he was to write in the 1649 *Passions de l'âme,* following Richelieu's similar statements in the *Testament*).[13]

Descartes's argument made women epistemologically and politically the equal of men. His logic was adopted not only by Poulain de la Barre in 1673 but already by Corneille from the 1637 *Le Cid* on: what role was played by the Infante, Doña Urraque, if not the demonstration of nonviolent reason taming passion? (The only character in the play to do so, male or female.) The point was also recognized by means of the very same Spartan metaphor by one of Katherine Philips's friends, precisely with respect to her translations from Corneille. In a liminary poem prefixed to "the divine Orinda" 's 1667 *Works,* praising her translation of Corneille's *Pompée,* this woman poet ("Philo-Philippa") wrote: "Train'd up to Arms, we Amazons have been, / And Spartan virgins strong as Spartan Men: / Breed Women but as Men, and they are these; / While Sybarit Men are Women by their ease."[14] (The continued use of this comparison, as we will see, offers something of a benchmark with regard to attitudes toward the status of women.)

Women, wrote Le Bret, however, had to be excluded from the throne because monarchs needed to be "warlike and belligerent" (*guerriers et belliqueux*). Those reasons, like women's feebleness, divine law, and tradition's condemnation of the Spartans, were added to the Salic exclusion, just because that law itself did not nominally reject women from accession to the crown, but simply from "succession to fiefs," an objection, be it noted, that Le Bret rejects as "specious" (33). Because it helps embed Corneille further in this debate, I will also note here a metaphorical use of the Salic Law entirely parallel to Le Bret's argument: a use I have not elsewhere come across. It occurs once again in a liminary poem to the Philips collection just mentioned. The author of this poem was the Royalist Abraham Cowley, and his reference was wholly demeaning of women. He wrote that Orinda had canceled "great Apollo's Salick Law . . . / Man may be Head, but Woman's now the Brain."[15]

Cowley and Le Bret differed scarcely at all from Richelieu, writing (at least in the second case) virtually at the same moment. The Prince's reason (of State), we saw, was presented as a "masculine virtue" that overcomes "Passion," enabling clear and distinct human "Reason" to function (Richelieu 276, 327, 329). Since passion, Richelieu asseverated, was the proper characteristic of women, it followed that even if *some* women rulers had been more or less temperate (was this "moderation" in deference to Marie de' Medici, whose son was Louis XIII?), the fact remained that

few are of this nature, and one must confess that just as a woman undid the world, so nothing [!] is more capable of ruining States than this sex, when, setting its foot firmly upon those who govern them, it moves them at will and, as a result, badly. For the best thoughts of women are almost always bad, given that they are led by their passions, which normally take the place of reason in their minds. But reason is the one and only true moving force that must kindle and stimulate those to action who are in the Service of public affairs. (31)

Such views simply echoed general opinion, and the kinds of tales that circulated about women rulers testify to such repressive attitudes.[16]

Spurious testimony of the sort certainly facilitated (for example) Richelieu's condemnation of women as hypocrites, incapable of keeping

secrets, and generally irrational. Like Le Bret's his vocabulary was
quite violent, and indeed justified the criticism made of men by Marie
de Gournay in 1622 and 1625, in two short but important texts (notably the first): *De l'égalité des hommes et des femmes* and *Grief des
dames.* Like Elyot and Billon, she urged that women possessed the
same rational minds as men, and were just as capable of occupying all
public office, except that they had been placed in a subordinate position by male violence, and were currently kept there by an oppression
no less real for being more subtle in its application of force: techniques
of mockery, arrogance, condescension, disdain, and general dismissal
of women's views and interruption of their arguments.[17] Her plea was
a strong one, but had no long-term effects. Gournay herself indeed suffered the familiar fate of Renaissance women writers in a masculine
culture: scornful and often scurrilous mockery in her lifetime, silence
and total neglect after her death. Her kind of argument was repeated in
1643 in an anonymous text, *La femme généreuse:* "Having made
women slaves and prisoners, men have deprived them of knowledge,
as the sole weapon and tool available to make war on men and elaborate their deliverance."[18]

However ineffective such assertions may have been in the long term,
for the present they reinforced the arguments of such as Descartes and
Corneille, against writers like Richelieu or Le Bret. Over these years
writers had developed a strong argument in favor of a single *human*
rationality, which, however, had never been able to reach full fruition
in women because of men's original violence and continuing oppression.

One of its strongest versions is to be found in a text published by
Pierre Corneille's Norman compatriot Jacques Du Bosc, just three
years after *Cinna,* the principal of the four plays I will be looking at
here. The Franciscan Du Bosc had already published two fairly standard treatises on woman's place as a good wife, but in his 1645 *Femme
héroïque,* he applied to women a quite different set of qualities: "The
principle of heroic virtue is not reason alone, but something better and
stronger." It is, he wrote, "a divine instinct or motion [that] it is better
to follow than reason itself." The Cornelian overtones are quite apparent, and so too is the assertion of equality between women and men:
whatever diversity there may be, wrote Du Bosc, "it is small and does
not justify teaching different ethical standards and expectations to the
two sexes."[19]

The question now to be posed was *how* could that fruition be realized, and to *what end?* The answer would be found in the general condition of violence and political decay that appeared endemic in Europe at this time, and in the search for a solution to it.

III. Corneille's Solution to Violence through Reason in Women

In the major plays of the period between 1637 and the mid-1640s, I would suggest that Corneille undertook an examination of certain political solutions to precisely that question. In *Le Cid,* for instance, the question takes the following form: supposing we wish to establish a strong, stable State, under conditions where it is violently threatened from outside its borders (France's situation in 1637, fighting against Spain and the Empire, eventually to establish both its frontiers and its European-wide power), then what must be the relation between the subject and political authority? What will be the obligations of the one toward the other? What will be the rights and duties of each? What consequences flow from that relation? In a period when the upper aristocracy was still demanding a real share in political power, and when these claims were seriously undermining the unity of a State only just being created as a "Nation," such questions were most urgent.

A gulf lies between the claims of Don Diègue and Don Gomès and the attitude of Rodrigue. The former put the satisfaction of personal quarrels and private concerns before all else. Rodrigue recognizes a duty to place the public interest first.[20] The question is one of a complete transformation in aristocratic attitudes and behavior. Rodrigue's final submission to the King and to state authority marks the recognition of a political and social necessity clearly and closely bound to demands proceeding from the contemporary situation of France. Dramatic changes were in progress: the slow creation of a "Nation," the centralization of political power, the "defeudalization" of the nobility, the attempt to unify the internal forces of the State (industrial, social, economic), the invention of a national culture, the development of France as a European power.

In *Horace* (1640) the same kind of experiment is taken rather further: if the individual owes everything to the State (as Rodrigue seems to accept at the end of *Le Cid*), what would that mean in respect to personal and private relationshps? How could interhuman relationships persist that did not depend upon the State? And how could civil society remain stable and secure without such personal and private relationships? It is worthwhile considering how very many times words like "inhuman," "brutal," and their derivations occur in this play (as well as others by Corneille at this period). Very often they do so in terms of an opposition between men and women:

> Mais quand on peut sans honte être sans fermeté,
> L'affecter au dehors c'est une lâcheté:
> L'usage d'un tel art nous le laissons aux hommes,
> Et ne voulons passer que pour ce que nous sommes.[21]

Many other exchanges suggest a similar opposition, but this rejoinder, fairly typical of the resolute and determined Sabine, asserts a viewpoint toward which Corneille himself seems sympathetic: "Loin de blâmer les pleurs que je vous vois répandre, / Je crois faire beaucoup de m'en pouvoir défendre," responds old Horace, whose patriotic virtue is never in doubt, and with whose views tradition tends to ally Corneille himself.[22]

And what results from an argument according to which the individual (here, Horace) owes everything to the State? According to *Horace*—however it may be justified, regardless of its ambiguities, and whatever attitude one may take with respect to it—the consequence is entirely clear: *violence*. Indeed, it permeates *all* levels and kinds of human relationships: violence toward the "enemy" (who is scarcely such, we may recall), toward one's friends, toward one's closest relations, toward oneself, and even (at least potentially) toward the very political authority which demanded this duty. Valère (who aspired to Camille's love) may indeed be biased when he argues that Horace should be punished for having placed himself above the law and for threatening, therefore, society and political authority. But Tulle is not, when he asserts essentially the same thing: that he owes to Horace his scepter and his throne; and when he then, by his pardon, places Horace above the law (saying the State has a need of protection greater than its need to punish its putative protector). And where will this violence lead? That is exactly what cannot be answered: for the State can no longer control it. In fact *Horace* shows how this particular political path tends toward the destruction of the very order it sought to maintain.

The question *Horace* raises—as "brutally" and uncompromisingly as possible—concerns, then, the matter of violence, its consequences, its term, the possibility of controlling it, and its inevitable querying of the very power in whose service it is supposed to be. Hannah Arendt has written in this regard:

The chief reason warfare is still with us is neither a secret death wish of the human species, nor an irrepressible instinct of aggression, nor, finally and more plausibly, the serious economic and social dangers inherent in disarmament, but the simple fact that no substitute for this final arbiter in international affairs has yet appeared on the political scene. Was not Hobbes right when he said: "Covenants, without the sword, are but words"? (5)

In its conclusion, *Horace* sinks into an entirely pessimistic view of the inevitability of such violence. It is a violence setting Horace himself, as the King repeats, "au-dessus des lois" ("above the laws," 5.3.1754), simply because the King owes to Horace not only his continued rule in Rome, but indeed his "mastery" of two States ("Qui me fait aujourd'hui maître de deux Etats," line 1742). In such a case, the bearer of violence threatens the very existence of political authority and therefore of the State itself. The spectator may finally agree with Valère's assertion:

> Faisant triompher Rome il se l'est asservie,
> Il a sur nous un droit, et de mort, et de vie,
> Et nos jours criminels ne pourront plus durer
> Qu'autant qu'à sa clémence il plaira l'endurer.[23]

This potential menace of violence will in fact become the basic justification of Horace's existence: "Vis pour servir l'Etat," says the King ("Live to serve the State," 5.3.1764). The balance forged in *Le Cid* has been lost. Violence now reigns as the necessary sign of an absolute duty toward the State: witness, for example, the otherwise absurdly inexplicable quarrel between Camille and Sabine, over which one of them is the more harmed by war between Rome and Alba (3.4). Violence is thus established, without exception, within all human relations. At the same time, such violence could only be, in some sense, *impossible,* for it inevitably tends toward the overthrow of the very political authority it is supposed to uphold.

Cinna (1642) proposes a quite different response and a kind of solution to the difficulty. The play begins just where *Horace* concludes: in a permanently violent situation. That violence is not only generally political (Emilie is determined to keep alive the memory of the bloody civil wars—whose events weigh no less heavily upon Auguste, until his final decision), but is also personal. At that level it is expressed as an opposition between Emilie's blind and confused passion, and the reason *eventually* embodied by the emperor.[24] Emilie expresses her situation in the first scene of the play, as she explains the wish to avenge herself: "impatients désirs" ("passionate desires"), "Enfants impétueux de mon ressentiment / Que ma douleur séduite embrasse aveuglément," which, she exclaims, inflict themselves upon her in spite of herself. "Haine" ("hatred"), "rage" ("fury," "madness"), her "abandon" to "ardents transports" ("self-abandonment" to "burning paroxysms"), her "fureur" ("rage"), and so forth. Such words are important signs.[25]

Indeed, no less than Le Bret in his *Souveraineté,* Richelieu, as we have seen implied, spoke constantly, both in his *Mémoires* and in the *Testament,* of the absolute need for anyone ruling over a State to submerge everything beneath Reason. In the minister's view, knowledge, power, will, and political action (*savoir, pouvoir, vouloir, faire*) together compose a set. "Passion," lack of control, puts an end to that political Reason and leads necessarily to ruin. Emilie herself is not unaware of it, and hesitates before the decision that tempts her. Will she be drawn on by passion, or return to reason? "Je sens refroidir ce bouillant mouvement" ("I feel this furious outburst grow cold," 1.1.270). Or, again: "Mon esprit en désordre à soi-même s'oppose; / Je veux, et ne veux pas, je m'emporte, et je n'ose, / Et mon devoir confus. . . ."[26] Cinna, too, is drawn between reason and passion, between Auguste's strong State and the total disorder that would follow their conspiracy's success. Violence has indeed focused itself in the protagonists' very minds and spirits.

The two events used by Corneille to elaborate the play, Augustus's accession to the Empire and Cinna's conspiracy, were in actuality separated by twenty-five years. Bringing them together enables him to put the reason of State/passion contradiction in the form of two opposing "voices."[27] One of these seeks to maintain violence (marked in the play by terms of confusion, darkness, blindness, anger, and so on), while the other wants peace and tranquillity (indicated by clarity of sight, brightness, visible display, reason). Violence and State dissolution are thus not given as part of a historical process, but as simultaneous with the possibility of "redemption," and a concrete solution to the permanent threat of violence is implied by the imposition of one of those "voices" upon the other: which is *then* presented as a dismissal of the past by the establishment of a particular form of sovereignty.

In *Cinna* the question thus becomes one of words, embodied by particular *speakers,* and it can then be resolved not through physical conflict, but by the imposition of one form of discourse (Auguste's). The question may, then, be one of conflict and clemency, but it is above all one of the relation between language, power, and a certain conception of reason (reason of State as well as rationality in general): together these compose a network of relations potentially able to resolve the problem of violence performed in *Horace,* and everywhere urgent in the contemporary political reality of France and of Europe as a whole. That in Corneille the matter should take the form of verbal conflict may seem obvious, since we are speaking of the theater. But it has a specific importance in the present context: the most important speaker will be a woman. She intervenes at the very moment when Auguste himself, having discovered the conspiracy and treachery of Emilie and Cinna, cannot imagine any alternative to continuing the violence that has racked Rome for decades. He recalls the details of the ghastly civil wars (4.2.1130–41), and then wonders:

> Mais quoi! toujours du sang, et toujours des supplices!
> Ma cruauté se lasse, et ne peut s'arrêter,
> Je veux me faire craindre, et ne fais qu'irriter;
> Rome a pour ma ruine une Hydre trop fertile.
> Une tête coupée en faite renaître mille,
> Et le sang répandu de mille conjurés
> Rend mes jours plus maudits, et non plus assurés.[28]

Auguste finds himself confronting a situation he cannot resolve in any way. At this point, Livie comes to his help, offering him what she calls "les conseils d'une femme" ("a woman's advice," 4.3.1197). She requests that he moderate his male "séverité" ("harshness"), which has so far made "beaucoup de bruit" ("a lot of commotion"), but "sans produire aucun fruit" ("without any result"). He should learn to show clemency.

Georges Couton tells us the formula was already used both in Dion Cassius's and in Seneca's history (1:1616). Indeed, Le Bret had himself referred to Livia and Augustus when speaking of princely clemency in general, remarking that she "often" told the emperor how "the monarch's true clemency was to punish public injuries and forgive those committed against himself" (583 [mispaginated for 563]). These matters seem to me less important than that Sabine had played a similar role throughout *Horace,* that the Infante in *Le Cid* had demonstrated like concerns, and that Pauline will perform such a part in *Polyeucte.* More significant still may be the tradition intimated earlier, and emphasized by Ian Maclean. He has argued that the "role of advocacy ascribed to women" in the drama of this period (citing Boyer's *Porcie romaine,* Mairet's *Marc-Antoine* and Corneille's *Polyeucte*), reflects "the commonplace about female clemency and *misericordia*" and the belief in "the physical inferiority of women, who, unable to act, are reduced to pleading" (180). Clearly, the use of the word "reduced" prejudges the case—as though the nonviolence of speech were automatically inferior to the violence of action: one might think of it as the "Rambo syndrome." But that issue was central to the seventeenth-century dispute as it should be in our own critical debate. The point, surely (there can be no other of much importance), is that it *worked.*

Auguste may well respond to Livie: "Vous m'aviez bien promis des conseils de femme: / Vous me tenez parole, et s'en sont là, Madame."[29] He nonetheless follows the advice she has given: her woman's language, as he puts it, the speech she has made available to him ("vous me tenez parole"). The several possible meanings of his phrase are not unimportant either (whether or not "intended" by Corneille): not only "keep a promise," but "tenir parole" perhaps as in "tenir un discours" ("to hold forth [in speech]," "to speak publicly"), "tenir" as in "hold out" or "offer," but also as in "hold on to." Livie's speech translates into immediate action on the part of Auguste and provokes an immediate change in Emilie's language as well.

Not only does Emilie speak in the following scene (with Livie) of her "joy" (4.4.1267), but above all she exults in her *désaveuglement* ("unblinding"), her lack of confusion, her clarity of vision: "Mon noble désespoir ne m'a point aveuglée, / Ma vertu tout entière agit sans s'émouvoir, / Et je vois malgré moi plus que je ne veux voir."[30] Livie has made possible the imposition of the emperor's voice: as much hers as his. And that it is an achievement of her speech, rather than of his physical violence, is emphasized right away by the demand that the opposition remain *silent*. The emperor demands of Cinna:

> Observe exactement la loi que je t'impose,
> Prête sans me troubler l'oreille à mes discours,
> D'aucun mot, d'aucun cri n'en interromps le cours,
> Tiens ta langue captive, et si ce grand silence. . . .[31]

Indeed, Cinna gives something like a promise (itself a verbal performance of acceptance)—"I will obey you, my lord"—which, even if occasionally hard to keep, nonetheless implies that a complete change has taken place.

Once again, it is the women who announce this transformation. Not only was Livie wholly responsible for the act of clemency, but it will be the empress who first of all reminds everyone of what makes sovereignty inviolable, and who secondly relates the fruitful consequences in the peace and tranquillity these two will create. The importance of the act of mercy to this end is already apparent. The inviolability of sovereignty would mean (in this case) an end to civil war. What Livie observes is the unbridgeable distance lying between the Prince and any private being (including the Prince's own). This distance was at the time, both in theory and practice, something of a cliché—provided, of course, the right to sole sovereignty was recognized in the person occupying it.

Speaking of the death of Emilie's father, Livie asserts:

> Sa mort, dont la mémoire allume ta fureur
> Fut un crime d'Octave, et non de l'Empereur.

> Tous ces crimes d'Etat qu'on fait pour la Couronne,
> Le Ciel nous en absout, alors qu'il nous la donne. . . .[32]

Emilie herself confirms this aspect of Auguste's victory, emphasizing that "le Ciel a résolu votre grandeur" ("the Heavens have determined upon your glory"), as she simultaneously notes that her own change of "heart" but reflects the transformation of State (5.3.1720–24). What has occurred is more than an imposition of attitude or even of a particular State power. They are, as it were, "absorbed" by a State the form of whose power is expressed through Livie. That State will become divinized, and its glory will be "ratified," so to speak, by Auguste's apotheosis. So, after her call to clemency (making present stability possible in erasure of the past), her reminder of sovereignty's inviolability (making stability possible by present political conditions), it is Livie, once again, who expresses the future fruits of tranquillity:

> Oyez ce que les Dieux vous font savoir par moi,
> De votre heureux Destin c'est l'immuable loi.
> Après cette action vous n'avez rien à craindre,
> On portera le joug désormais sans se plaindre,
> Et les plus indomptés renversant leurs projets,
> Mettront toute leur gloire à mourir vos Sujets.[33]

Auguste accepts the "augury," emphasizing, once again, how the imposition is one of *speech:* the act of clemency and its results, he concludes, must now be "published" abroad (the verb is *publier:* here, "to announce publicly by word of mouth or written broadsheet or poster"; 5.3.1779–80).

To be sure, as this transformation is announced, we must note not only how profoundly it is marked by what has been presented throughout as the voice of a Reason specifically manifest in Livie (Emilie's lust for violence being essentially "manly," or, as it is often referred to, "brutish"), but also how gradually a hint of something "other" has become present. To assert the possibility of a stable State, Corneille appeared obliged to refer increasingly to divine warranty: as though human powers and politics had no hold upon themselves. Cinna and Emilie's failure is ultimately not only theirs but that of Corneille's own solution: in a kind of impossible utopia—confirmed subsequently, perhaps, by *Polyeucte* (1643), whose hero's apotheosis implies his abandonment of all real political action, while the distant emperor's intentions seem to promise the continued violence of Christian persecution. Violence and the permanence of war may well have been gathered up into some higher stability and calm, but at the price, it would appear, of an abdication of the human (not, now, in favor of the brutish, but in that of the divine). In Corneille's own theater, that development may be followed, after *Polyeucte,* through *La mort de Pompée* (1643–44), the absence of whose eponymous protagonist, however glorious his death, only underlines the ultimate failure of violence, and then to the divine story of *Théodore* (1645–46). This exploration ends in the utterly abandoned violence of the plays written during the Frondes (1648–53).

In this failure, one may perhaps see prefigured a more general one of the future French polity itself, where, under Louis XIV and between Colbert and Le Tellier, was played out this opposition between a (relatively) pacific policy and an entirely aggressive, militaristic one. The culmination of the latter in the Revocation of the Edict of Nantes, the wars of the Augsburg League and those of the Spanish Succession, led directly to the catastrophic last years of the Sun King's reign. We may also see in it the future failure to achieve any change in the *view* of women or their real status. Through *Polyeucte,* where Pauline plays the strongest role, Corneille had gradually come to an understanding of Reason in women as able to bring about stability and nonviolence, but it was becoming progressively less political in its action, and ever more marginal with respect to political authority.

The sequence culminated in *La mort de Pompée* (1643); and it was doubtless not chance that inspired Katherine Philips to translate that very play.[34] Two women, one the embodiment of romantic love, the other the representative of moral virtue and courage, Cléopâtre and Cornélie, strive through the play to maintain a middle way between the violence of Ptolemaic Egypt and the ruin of Republican Rome. Photin, Ptolémée's amoral counsellor, is characterized by Cléopâtre as wholly given up to "violence" (2.3.602), Ptolémée himself constantly yields to "transports violents" (2.4.711), while César, if he does not actually cede to such a "transport violent," resists it only because he smolders with a slower and deeper anger (4.1.1080–82). For her part,

Cléopâtre, hating her brother's advisers and scorning his lack of moral courage, nonetheless tries to save him and bring about peace between Egypt and Rome. Her failure is signaled by the praise she receives from Antoine (3.3.946–52), and her accession to the throne at the play's end. Both foretell future wars.

Cornélie is at once more complicated and more indicative of Corneille's failure. She it was whom "Philo-Philippa"'s liminary verse to Philips's collection of poetry picked out especially for praise: "In the French Rock Cornelia first did shine, / But shin'd not like her self till she was thine. . . ." The particular praise was apposite because, alone of all those in the play, her role was invented by Corneille. In his 1660 "Examen," the dramatist noted that he had followed Lucan closely, save in this one detail: "I have added only what concerns Cornelia, who appeared to offer herself automatically, since according to historical truth she was in the same ship as her husband, when he landed in Egypt. That is what caused me to pretend she was captured, and brought before Caesar, even though history does not mention it" (1:1075).

It would appear she is introduced to play a rather special part: a reasoned middle path between Rome and its destruction, between Caesar and her debt to and love for Pompey, and all the time under the tension of the desire for vengeance. From the first, she plays the role of the "femme forte." When she is brought before César, her initial speech is one of defiance:

> César, car le Destin que dans tes fers je brave
> Me fait ta prisonnière, et non pas ton esclave,
> Et tu ne prétends pas qu'il m'abatte le coeur
> Jusqu'à te rendre hommage et te nommer seigneur.[35]

But the defiance simply provides the setting to reveal her moral rectitude, as she later warns César of Ptolémée's plot against his life (4.4). When César praises her virtue, she responds simply that the reason for the warning is that she wants vengeance for herself, however much she may regret it (as she had earlier exclaimed: "O Ciel! que de vertus vous me faites hair" ["O Gods! how many Virtues must I hate!"], 3.4.1072). Once he releases her, as he has promised, "je te chercherai partout des ennemis" ("I shall make new business for thy Sword," 4.4.1379).

Finding herself caught between Pompée's death and César's virtues, between the destruction of Republican Rome and the possible creation of some new order, between her duty toward Rome (the need to punish Ptolémée) and her desire to avenge her loss, she strives to reason her way toward balancing them, as she says to César:

> Je t'avouerai pourtant, comme vraiment Romaine,
> Que pour toi mon estime est égale à ma haine,
> Que l'une et l'autre est juste, et montre le pouvoir,
> L'une de ta vertu, l'autre de mon devoir:
> Que l'une est généreuse, et l'autre intéressée,
> Et que dans mon esprit l'une et l'autre est forcée.[36]

The equilibrium breaks down, however. She foretells a conflict that will last through three generations (4.4.1387: indeed, Gnaius and Sextus Pompey were to fight on against Caesar's Rome, while Cinna was the great Pompey's grandson). She foretells how Roman youth will rise against Caesar himself, since he will have flouted their will by marrying Cleopatra (5.4.1750–52). Unable to maintain the balance of reason, maintained by Livie at the end of *Cinna,* Cornélie foresees a future of ongoing war and violence. The voice of mediating Reason has collapsed. In real life the way was prepared for the Frondes.[37]

The final failure of this sequence of plays implied that for Corneille, indeed, violence—the specific violence of Reason in men—was no solution to any political difficulty at all. At the same time, however, he now no longer had any solution to offer. He had started, like Gournay, to find some sort of response in Reason in women: that of Doña Urraque, the Infante; that of Sabine; that of Livie. Such a view (like Descartes's and Du Bosc's) was directly opposed to Richelieu's idea of woman (the singular general term is deliberate) as just "what" was most "capable de nuire aux Etats" ("able to destroy States").[38] Richelieu exacerbated metaphorical arguments advanced by Machiavelli, translating them into literal requirements. The theoretical exclusion of women from political authority will eventually have its counterpart in their exclusion (as producers) from the dominant culture and a renewed emphasis on a specifically "female reason." But that is to get slightly ahead of my argument.

Not only Richelieu, but Cardin Le Bret explicitly asserted women's exclusion from political authority. And in this case, it was almost as though Corneille had the author of *De la souveraineté du Roy* (a lawyer like the dramatist himself) textually in mind. On one occasion, rejecting any idea that queens might share in their husbands' power, and adopting like Richelieu the pejorative dominant Judeo-Christian tradition that women were irrational and passionate, Le Bret wrote:

It would be most dangerous if women of this rank had power equal to their husbands; the more so as their ambitious nature never allows them to rest until they have usurped the benefits of sovereign authority, and finally subdued their husbands beneath their sway. . . . (43)

Perhaps Le Bret was thinking of Catherine and Marie de' Medici, but Corneille does not hesitate to turn this claim about women's "naturel ambitieux" against him. In *Le Cid,* speaking about Don Diègue and Don Gomès, Chimène exclaims: "Maudite ambition, détestable manie, / Dont les plus généreux souffrent la tyrannie!"[39] Her and Rodrigue's fathers are, after all, both men. For Chimène, ambition (as it was for Gournay and others) is another form of male violence. But Le Bret then went on to provide some examples of such behavior. Here is one of his most important, with his subsequent comments:

Roman history says the same about Livia, who wishing to share equal authority with her husband, tore from the Senate's hands, Virgulania and Plancina, accused of capital crimes. . . .

Assuredly, their weak spiritedness does not let them remain within the bounds of moderation, once they see themselves raised to this high degree of honor. They immediately give way to insolence and vanity, and that gives them such presumption as to feel wounded unless they rule absolutely. . . . (43–44)

It is hard not to see Corneille as making a deliberate attempt to answer specific charges against women, brought by such as Richelieu and Le Bret. In that regard, one cannot justifiably dismiss the significance of these female protagonists of Cornelian tragedy, these

"femmes fortes," as the century referred to them (*"femmes héroï-
ques,"* in Du Bosc's phrase), on the grounds they were distinguished
from the multitude of women, and therefore a source for no generally
applicable characterization or argument. So, Ian Maclean, acknowledging the "importance of feminism and feminist thought to [tragedy]
and the intimate connection between the portrayal of the dramatic
heroine and that of the *femme forte,"* concludes with precisely that
dismissal: "In both cases, these figures are contrasted with the mass of
their own sex, and associated with male attributes and roles" (193).
Quite obviously, male protagonists of tragedy were also to be distinguished from "the mass of their own sex."

Both were figures expressing idealized qualities, rarified beyond the
everyday. They may be taken as expressing an ideal both in respect to
human qualities and in respect to human relationships. And here, what
is important—enormously so, it seems to me—is the very specific contrast created between *certain* female protagonists and *all* male ones.
Women in all the plays are indeed associated with male attributes and
roles: Chimène, Camille, Emilie. . . . We may add Médée, Cléopâtre (in
Rodogune), and, of course, to some extent, Cornélie—hence the failure, there, of Reason in women. All the men participate in these attributes. The important point surely is that some women play a very different role: that of reason in the service of nonviolence and a peaceful
solution to all political conflict and the inevitable tendency of society
toward dissolution.

Reason in women, that is to say, has been clearly distinguished from
Reason in men. But it has certainly *not* been made into some qualitatively *different* "reason" (as it had been and will be again), specifically
apt for "domestic" or "nurturing" circumstances. Reason in women is
no different from that in men (as Gournay, Descartes, Du Bosc, and
others had said): the essential variant is its freedom from other, external constraints. The development of society in history has ineluctably
made men dependent on violence. This is clear in the historically descriptive parts of political writings by Machiavelli, Le Bret, and Richelieu (to take only those I have mentioned), and it is evident, too, in the
political situations forming both the fictive and the real background to
Corneille's theater. Those historical constraints have borne upon
women externally as part of that violence, and inevitably, too, in the

way they have themselves, like men, internalized it (as victims rather than oppressors, as sufferers rather than agents). Because such violence was not a basic element in their *use* of reason, however, women could show that Reason itself was not *essentially* violent, and so hope to create a society free of it. Such would be the culmination of the debate, before it collapsed in the 1670s.[40]

IV. Corneille and the Times

The question of women's place in culture, as I have just been suggesting its presence in Corneille, seemed to parallel the more general form it took in the French and English seventeenth centuries. Carolyn Lougee comments that from about 1620 on, "feminist" thinking in France, very soon supported in some manner by the *salons* of Rambouillet and (a little later) Lambert, by writings like Gournay's *Egalité des hommes et des femmes,* François de Soucy's *Triomphe des dames* (1646), and such others as we have glanced at here, questioned certain traditional ethical presuppositions: "Alterations in social values," she writes, "made weak woman into the representative of delicacy." Further, such changes became a fundamental attack against "the heroic ethic of masculinity" and devalued mere "physical force." She argues that masculine encomia of brute strength and violence began to give way before a new vision describing "the social mission of women in public positions as pacification" (Lougee 31–33).

I do not think that claim can be sustained. Such an argument was certainly being made, as we have seen at some length, and a masculine ethic of reason-in-violence was indeed being challenged. With equal certainty it did not cede its place and was to return in force and with cultural effects due to last into the twentieth century.

Nonetheless, the dispute *was* put in these terms in the 1630s and 1640s, and I have tried to show how importantly Corneille participated in it. In this regard, the choice of Livie was a significant one. We have just seen how Le Bret used her to make the pejorative argument (we saw earlier how he was to use her name—once—more generously). It is of course the case that this personage was wholly given both by Seneca (*Moral Essays, De clementia,* 1.9) and by Dion Cassius (*History of Rome,* bk. 55, pars. 14–22), that the first supplied a good part of Auguste's discourse to Cinna (*Cinna* 5.1: including the order that he not speak), while Dion recounted the conspiracy right through. Both wrote directly and in so many words of the "woman's advice" Livia gave, and both quoted it. The fact remains that Corneille *chose* to emphasize that aspect of the story, that it *does* stand as a reply to Le Bret, and that Livia will become one of the major illustrations of female ability and power. In 1668 Marguerite Buffet was to write: "Livia, Augustus's wife who ruled with him. This great Emperor consulted her in all the most important business of the Empire. Tiberius her/his son [*son fils*] valued her counsel so highly that he preferred it to [that of] his closest associates in regard to the public business of his State" (327). No doubt Buffet might have been thinking of Corneille's play, and that itself would be of some interest for the study of "feminism" in this period. So far as I know, any such connection has passed unnoticed.

With respect to the wider questions raised by Corneille's plays (and others), it is scarcely unimportant that in 1673, in his *Egalité des deux sexes,* Poulain de la Barre was to maintain that violent male reason was only necessary at a certain stage in the evolution of societies. Poulain provided an entirely Hobbesian story about the formation of civil society ("Freudian," too, in that it recounted a seizure of power by younger brothers from fathers or older brothers), in which male violence was inscribed from the start: a violence, injustice, and tyranny that excluded women from all types of power, education, and freedom. Women were characterized from the start by "gentleness and humanity," and naturally abhorred "carnage and war." Reason played but a small part in this social formation, being essentially submissive to authoritarian violence. At a later stage, however, a more civilized moment, "the precision, discernment, and culture" of women will have to come to dominate, if society is to survive.[41]

The attempt and the need to pass from violence to tranquillity, and its specific connection with an opposition between male and female, had been elaborated clearly in Corneille's theater between *Le Cid* and *La mort de Pompée* prior to the equally clear failure of the plays written during the Frondes.[42] By this time, indeed, the opposition between an essentially masculine violence and the feminine as pacific reason had become something of a commonplace. The 1670 free translation of Agrippa's celebrated text may provide a last exemplary indication:

So had Women but the power of *making Laws,* and *writing Histories,* what Tragedies might they not justly have published of Mens unparalleled villany? Amongst whom are daily found so many *Murderers, Theeves, Ravishers, Forgers, Fierers of Cities,* and *Traytors,* who in the time of *Joshua* and King *David,* [we may well recall here the association forged between Charles II and David by this date] *robb'd* in such vast multitudes, that they *march'd* in a posture of War, and made them Captains of their *padding Bands,* (a trick they have scarce forgot at this very day) whence so many *Prisons* became crowded, and so many *Gibbets* loaded with their Carkasses. Whereas on the contrary, to Women we owe the *invention* of all things usefull or beneficial to Mankind [!], which may either adorn and enlighten our dark *Minds,* or relieve and accomodate the necessities of our frail *bodies.* (Agrippa 51)

We need not, then, be very surprised to find a dramatic discussion echoing that of the *salons,* and even of the later thought of someone like Poulain: opposing masculine violence to a new feminine voice of reason, of a reason that was, besides, fundamentally social and collective, rather than individualist. At the same time, it was profoundly political. In Corneille, for example, Doña Urraque, Sabine, Livie, and Cornélie are all preoccupied not just with personal concerns (though that, too), but with a legitimate order of society and the State. Such reason was publicly manifested among the *précieuses* of the *salons* by a kind of physically ascetic worldly freedom that contrasted visibly with the traditional ideal of women's virtue as a "chastely" repressive behavior, itself supposedly needed to counter irrational female sensuality.

Lougee spoke, we saw, of women coming to represent a sort of delicate, pacific reason. At a first stage (and still, but with finality, in Poulain) this was clearly not particular to women, but was a common *human* reason typified by Descartes's arguments—whether or not his writings were the direct or immediate source. People asserted such universal reason was quite separate from a violence that resulted from specific historical conditions, and which therefore was not at all some essential or inevitable element attached to reason. They further argued that those same *historical* conditions meant that such untrammeled and pure reason was found only in (some) women, in no men. A subsequent stage was very soon reached, however, where that delicate but powerful reason became once again the old emotional instinctivism, now given a positive rather than a negative evaluation.

V. Women's Reason Subdued

From the early 1670s on, Nicolas Boileau had been working on his
tenth Satire. It was published twenty years later, in 1694. This violently
misogynist diatribe quickly became an element in the *Querelle des anciens et des modernes*. Charles Perrault swiftly responded with his
Apologie des femmes. Regnard entered the lists with his *Satire contre
les maris*. The dramatist Pradon and some tens of others threw themselves into the fray. As in the case of the *Querelle* itself, we are not
dealing here with fundamental differences of opinion or argument—
all were agreed on the terms—but rather with a question of who will
have power over the actual production of culture. Similarly, though
there may have been some disagreement as to attitudes, all were pretty
much agreed as to what role women were to be allowed to play (and
those have indeed become the operative terms).

In these texts, therefore, women may be helpful or harmful, condemned or praised, but they are always subordinate and secondary to
men. La Bruyère's view of women as *children* or appreciated *objects*
was quite typical. Women fail to achieve knowledge, he wrote in
1692, either because their intellectual makeup is simply insufficient,
or because they are lazy-minded, because they are too concerned with
their appearance, because their concentration span is too short, because their talent is for manual work, because they prefer to pay attention to their household, because they cannot concentrate on serious
matters, because their curiosity is for nonintellectual affairs, or because
their tastes run to matters other than mental ones. Women, that is to say,
are fundamentally childlike. Or they are ornamental *things:* "we look
upon an educated woman as upon a beautiful weapon: it [*elle* = "she" as
well as "it"] is artistically engraved, admirably polished, and exqui-
sitely worked; it is a museum piece, to be shown to the curious but not
for use; it can be utilized neither in war nor in hunting, no more than
can be a show horse, however well trained." With equal animosity, he
had written in an earlier section of his *Caractères:* "You must judge
women exclusively from shoe to hair style, more or less as you measure a fish from head to tail" (pars. 6, 49).

Those who believed they were defending women, while less abu-
sive, certainly did not assume their status was equal to that of men. Re-
plying to Boileau, who had run through all the old familiar "argu-

ments" against women, Perrault in his *Apologie* had not so much defended women as their chastity and purity as wives and mothers, their ability to run a household, look after husbands, and bring up children suitably. In his preface, he spoke of the poem as a defense of "l'amitié conjugale," asserting that such friendship accorded with the "first laws of Nature and of Reason, which require a perfect union between those who marry: wise, useful, and entirely honest laws." Some, he admitted, might find such ideas "bien bourgeoises," but they outdo those recommending laziness and idleness (*Apologie* 35). In England, even Mary Astell wrote that women's education would enable them better to fulfill their maternal tasks (38, 129): though it is not always easy to tell when Astell is being sarcastic, her dismissal of husbands as by and large worthless and an unnecessary weight upon the backs of wives accompanied the dismissal of the public world in favor of the private. As in the case of Perrault, that tended toward a positive evaluation of women's familial role.

Just as women were set to play a secondary, more private, role in the marital and domestic arrangement (reason as the instrument for the proper education of [male] children), so, too, they could find a similar role in the cultural world. Once again, it was Perrault who put the case with most clarity: "We know the exactness of their discernment for things that are fine and delicate. The sensitivity they have for what is clear, lively, natural, and commonsensical; and the abrupt distaste they reveal toward everything obscure, dull, constrained and awkward." Women are among those who are "naturally" endowed with "good taste and good sense" (*Parallèle* 37–38). Men, Perrault argues, are endowed with an ordered, lawful, regular reason. It works as one with the laws of nature and the laws of correct, transparent, limpid language—such as should be found in fine literature. Women have a more *immediate* access to such letters. Unblocked by concern for rules, endowed with those same fine and delicate qualities of judgment and discernment so useful in the domestic sphere, with gentler sentiments, a natural sense of taste, a sure instinct for the beautiful, women have a prompter correct response to works of art. They can therefore be finer critics. Consumers and presenters of culture, they should not be its producers.

Those apologetics were entirely typical. The grand project of human Reason had been defeated. There was now a man's and a woman's reason, qualitatively different. It was, to be sure, a reason rather than an unreason, but that simply made it the more invidious: for it meant that women were included, but as second-class citizens. Consumers of the dominant masculine culture, they could nonetheless have their little corner to themselves. When women started to produce massive quantities of writing after the repeal of the Licensing Act in 1695 (in England at least), it was of chapbooks and diaries, letters, novels aimed specifically at women—a whole subculture of literary production. Women were not therefore entirely excluded from culture (a dangerous proposition). When Mary Wollstonecraft dared argue a century later that women do share the same rationality as men, that therefore she should have equal rights of productive access to the dominant culture (up to a point, at least), she swiftly drew down upon herself the wrath of such as Horace Walpole, Hannah More, and Richard Polwhele. She was not entirely a lone voice (Mary Anne Radcliffe was a particularly strong one), but she herself was caught in many of the difficulties caused by an internalization of this perfidious "separate but equal" doctrine.

The difference between male and female reason given credence in the late seventeenth century, by such as Boileau and Perrault, La Bruyère and Addison, was swiftly and entirely consecrated. The novel dealt especially with the sentiments and affections because such affairs were supposed to be particularly suited to female instinctual rationality (May 204–45). *That* was in fact a way of recuperating and subduing Reason in women by making it qualitatively different from, and inferior to, Reason in men. Indeed, we now have men's and women's reasons. By means of novels, diaries, chapbooks, and especially literary journals there was throughout the eighteenth century an "increased female participation in literary culture," but the ideology clearly held that participation to be subordinate and secondary. Throughout these years we find indeed an ever increasing "use of literature to maintain a restrictive status quo."[43]

At the outset, I mentioned how the example of Sparta became something of a motif with regard to the equality of men and women. We may therefore with some interest see how that case is turned toward the subordination I have been tracing:

Bodily strength [wrote Catharine Macaulay in 1790] was the chief object of Spartan discipline. Their cares on this subject began with the birth of their offspring; and instead of entailing the curse of feebleness on their women for the sake of augmenting their personal beauty, they endeavoured to improve their natural strength, in order to render them proper nurses for a race of heroes. (24–25)

From a training to entire equality to one of ideal maternity, it would clearly be but a short step to complete futility. In 1868, and thus considerably later than the texts we have been considering, the Belgian doctor Hyack Kuborn wrote in a report on women miners commissioned by his government (telling us a lot about the possible practical results of the developments explored here): "however it may be, the andromaniacal daughters of Lacedemonia wrestling on Mount Taygite [sic], never achieved the equanimity, robustness and powerful energy of the Spartan men."[44]

Obviously, here, women have finally been reduced to complete subordination. Indeed, this final patronizing placement of women in an entirely subsidiary position that ostensibly "gave" them duties of equal importance to those of men, while carefully defining them in terms of men or of children, was perfectly summed up in the writings of that late eighteenth-century Schafly, Hannah More. At one point in her work on education she took note of the special nature of the early seventeenth-century arguments, so as to belittle and demean them—in favor, naturally, of a modern subordination:

At the revival of letters in the sixteenth and the following century, the controversy about this equality was agitated with more warmth than wisdom; and the process was instituted and carried on, on the part of the female complainant, with that sort of acrimony which always raises a suspicion of the justice of any cause; for violence commonly implies doubt, and invective indicates weakness rather than strength. The novelty of that knowledge which was bursting out from the dawn of a long, dark night, kindled all the ardors of the female mind, and the ladies fought zealously for a portion of that renown which the reputation of learning was beginning to bestow.[45]

While after that original moment the warmth and pretensions had died away, and "perished with" the "names of the flattered" and the "works of the flatterers," the contest has, she laments, "been revived with added fury" in her own day. And rightly she suspects that the issues upon which it touches are potentially more far-reaching, because the growth in social consciousness and the effects of two revolutions have meant these debates can envisage actual social equality, political rights, and concrete freedoms: "whereas the ancient demand was merely a kind of imaginary prerogative, a speculative importance, a mere titular right, a shadowy claim to a few unreal acres of Parnassian territory, the revived contention has taken a more serious turn, and brings forward political as well as intellectual pretensions." The "imposing term of *rights*" has been advanced, she angrily objects, with a view not only of lighting female vanity, but of exciting "in their hearts an impious discontent with the post which God has assigned them in his world" (144).

Of that sort of thing, Erna Reiss has remarked with some justice that such as Hannah More and Anna Barbauld "accepted the old conventional ideal of womanhood," and accordingly "were quite content to sink the personality of woman entirely in that of man, to accept it as her mission in life that she should be not complementary but ancillary to him" (3–4). The identity of all these later arguments to what Perrault and Boileau, Pradon and Addison, Regnard, La Bruyère and Chesterfield *all* argued hardly needs observing, and certainly not emphasizing.

We should therefore be very careful of any assessment according to which "it was not until the late seventeenth century, however, that women began to express publicly sentiments that might be labelled feminist, recognizing that women as a group suffered discrimination and should be given rights and privileges because of, not despite, their femaleness."[46] Any "recognition" relying upon assumptions that femaleness is characterized by a different *quality* of reason from the masculine, upon an idea that female action is ancillary to the male, and upon a proposition that women's cultural, social, and political rights are subordinate and secondary to those of men, requires a rather peculiar definition of "feminist." Merry E. Wiesner's own phrase in the sentence I just quoted perhaps reflects her unconscious but unerring awareness of this: women "should be *given* [?!] rights."

Such, then, was the outcome of the dispute over reason, gender, violence, social order, and the status of women, that was an integral part of the intellectual history of the first three quarters of the seventeenth century in France (and England)—working out of a general "crisis of Instauration," and into the eventual consolidation of a new dominant sociocultural environment. Pierre Corneille's role in that elaboration was important, and, I think, unrecognized. That he, like Gournay, Poulain, Madeleine de Scudéry, the Cartesian poet Anne de La Vigne, and the Cartesian feminist Mary Astell, like the learned women Marie-Catherine Desjardins (Mme de Villedieu), Ann Lefèvre (Mme Dacier), Elizabeth Elstob, and so many others, were the losers is a historical fact, some of whose elements I have sought to trace. To understand how that failure and loss occurred is important, lest perhaps they be repeated.

Notes

1. I thank Mary Beth Rose for her attentive reading of this essay, and Patricia J. Hilden for discussion of all these matters.

2. Such an assumption clearly lay behind Descartes's close intellectual relations with Princess Elisabeth of Bohemia (1640–50) and Henry More's with Anne [Finch], Viscountess Conway (1651–79).

3. An opposition between men and women in terms of their relative violence had already been tied to discussions of reason in the sixteenth century, and was clearly connected at one level with arguments about the virtues of women's passivity.

4. The arguments had indeed been political: both the general recovery of society and the particular improvement of women's status by equal education, participation in government, equality under the law (especially in marriage), and so forth. Both in England and France the debate did "suggest broad political goals," Hilda Smith's contrary claim notwithstanding (201). She asserts that the "lack" of such goals explained the failure of the arguments. I will argue that the dominant culture found a way to negate the complex debate and recuperate the liberating arguments for the purpose of asserting a subordinate status for women.

5. For further discussion of these issues, see Reiss, "Revolution." See also, in general, Rose.

6. See Wiesner 17–21. As exemplars of the later views, she names Rachel Speght and Anne Wheathill, both early seventeenth-century figures.

7. For a fine recent discussion of Christine de Pisan's achievement, see Schibanoff.

8. Kelso 1: 31. However much she may argue that *some* women succeeded in escaping the constraints imposed in Tudor times, Pearl Hogrefe essentially confirms this view.

9. The view remained constant in many writers throughout the seventeenth century (see, e.g., the texts in Henderson and McManus), and indeed at the end of the eighteenth century Wollstonecraft began her publishing career with just such an argument, while Anna Barbauld and Hannah More never desisted from it.

10. Tilde Sankovitch has argued that some women did attempt to ally a claim to equality of reason with a rejection of masculine violence in this period. She takes the example of Madeleine (1520–87) and Catherine (1542–87) Desroches. See "Inventing Authority of Origin: The Difficult Enterprise," in Rose 227–43. Sankovitch views this effort as a failure. One may say the same of the so-called "Swetnam" controversy in England between 1615 and the 1620s.

11. Pitkin has explored this question. The debates about women rulers were evidently extensive in the age of Mary Tudor, Mary Queen of Scots, Catherine de' Medici, and above all of course, Elizabeth. Constance Jordan has recently published an important essay on this matter.

12. The *Discours de la méthode* was published in 1636, but it had been written over the preceding ten years, almost exactly contemporaneously therefore with Richelieu's *Testament* (this last being known, but not actually published until 1688).

13. Unlike either Le Bret or Richelieu, Descartes was of course a powerless exile in Holland—as was the Palatine royal family, with whose daughter Elisabeth he was to become such a close intellectual friend.

14. Philips [liminaries]. This posthumous edition (Philips died of smallpox in 1664) was edited by a man addressed in a letter from Philips as "Poliarche." Emory University's copy has a marginal notation in a seventeenth-century hand, indicating that Poliarche was Sir Charles Cotterel.

15. Such attitudes on the part of the men presenting Philips's poems posthumously were entirely common—and encouraged perhaps by the poet herself, who remarked in a letter prefixed to the collection that writing poetry was "unfit for my Sex," and who translated Sabine's "pour le sexe" (in the first speech of *Horace*) as "our weak Sex." In that light, it was hardly surprising that her editor, Cotterel, echoed Cowley in his sentiments: "some of [her poems] would be no disgrace to the name of any Man that amongst us is most esteemed for his excellency in this kind, and there are none that may not pass with favour, when it is remembred that they fell hastily from the pen but of a Woman."

16. I cannot forbear telling one such story, partly because it concerns Marie de' Medici's aunt, Catherine, partly because it occurs in the correspondence of one of the most learned women of her time, Anne Conway. In a letter of November 1651 her brother related a visit to Rouen cathedral. There, wrote John Finch, he saw the rich vestments belonging to the Chapter: "There was in one of them a Diamond in the Centre of a Circle of Pearle, the Diamond was valued at 200,000 li [pounds] but as the Keeper told me it was stolne by Queen Katherine Medicis when the Archbishop of Rouen married her, she then cutt that Diamond off from the Archbishop's back and putt a Topaz in the Roome of it." Finch himself treats the tale with appropriate skepticism: "How it could be done in the

face of the Congregation I know not" (Conway 56–57). I add that the Medici princesses were also the butt of criticism stemming from the popular accusation that they had introduced Machiavelli-style politics into France—further ammunition for anti-women arguments and cries about hypocrisy.

17. These texts are available in a volume whose editorial material did nothing to dispel the slurs on Gournay (Schiff 55–97). De Gournay's writings are not easy to come by. Apart from the above, her writings on poetry, language, and Montaigne's *Essays* have been published by Uildriks. Her "novel" has recently been republished (Gournay). Proposals to produce a modern edition have yet to bear fruit.

18. *La femme généreuse qui monstre que son sexe est plus noble, meilleur politique, plus vaillant, plus sçavant, plus vertueux, et plus oeconome que celuy des hommes* (Paris: François Piot, 1643), 97–98. Quoted in Maclean 54. These terms of 1643 were, not altogether surprisingly, recalled with luminous similarity in 1928 by Virginia Woolf, whose Orlando expresses exactly that aspect of men's oppression, "armoured with every weapon as they are, while they debar us even from a knowledge of the alphabet!" (100).

19. Jacques Du Bosc, *La femme héroïque* (Paris, 1645), 7, 74. Quoted in Stegmann 2: 271. A recent short writing has sought to explore Corneille's "feminist" treatment of women (Venesoen). These 84 pages try to show how the young Corneille, struggling with the essentially erotic impulses of his very youth, created strong and independent women—worthy of their creator's genius. This is a rather idiosyncratic work, and does not really add much either to our knowledge of real male/female relations in the seventeenth century, or to their conceptualization, or to what we know of the social, political and cultural status of women, or to the history of their oppression. All depends on the poet's preoccupations.

20. Rodrigue and Chimène love one another and are expected to wed. Don Diègue, Rodrigue's father, quarrels with Don Gomès, Chimène's father, over their respective abilities to protect the kingdom of Castille. The latter strikes the former, who, too old to defend himself, exhorts his son to uphold family honor. Gomès is killed in the resulting duel. His daughter wants vengeance. In the meantime, Rodrigue beats off a Moorish invasion and saves the kingdom, receiving the honorary title of "Le Cid" from the Moors' leader. Don Sanche, a pretender to Chimène's hand, challenges Rodrigue and is defeated. After more vengeance seeking, the King, persuaded by his daughter, the Infante (who has herself been in love with Rodrigue and fought off temptation to take advantage of the situation), orders all to desist, and marriage is projected for Rodrigue and Chimène sometime in the future. Rodrigue replaces his father and Gomès as principal defender of the kingdom.

21. "But when you can be weak without shame, / To affect resolve outwardly is mere cowardice: / We leave to men the use of such tricks, / And wish to appear only as what we are" (*Horace* 3.5.941–44; ed. Couton). All references are to this edition, by act, scene, and line. Because Philips's translation of *Horace* is incomplete, these are my own, and stay as close to the original as possible. All translations above a line in length are in the notes, others are in the text. The play was Corneille's version of the fight between the Horatii and the Curiatii to decide whether Rome or Alba would be dominant. He in-

vented family ties between the two by making Sabine, Horace's wife, Curiace's sister, and Camille, Horace's sister, Curiace's fiancée. The play starts before the decision to resolve the conflict by using champions, and we hear the events leading up to it. After Horace has returned victorious, Camille excoriates him for killing Curiace. Outraged, and accusing her of treason, Horace stabs her to death. Brought before the king, Tulle, Horace is defended by Sabine and his father, and prosecuted by Valère, who loved Camille. Tulle decrees that Horace should live, but only as Rome's defender.

22. *Horace* 3.5.951–52: "Far from dispraising the tears I see you weep, / I think I do very well to be able to restrain myself from doing likewise."

23. *Horace* 5.2.1507–10: "In winning victory for Rome he has made it his slave, / He has right of life and death over us, / And our criminal lives can last / Only as long as he is pleased to extend his clemency."

24. This opposition is dealt with in more detail and with emphasis on the political/personal relation and the general situation in France in Reiss, "Voix." Some parts of the present essay come from that text. In this play, Emilie and Cinna (at her urging) plot to kill Auguste, who has recently become emperor, after the civil wars and myriad conspiracies. Cinna hesitates; Auguste considers abdicating, but is persuaded by Cinna to remain (since he has otherwise no excuse to assassinate him); Emilie exhorts Cinna to hold strong and avenge her father's death. The plot is revealed to Auguste. Persuaded by Livie, his wife, he pardons the conspirators.

25. "Impetuous offspring of my bitter animosity / That my spellbound grief embraces blindly." All these references are from *Cinna* 1.1.

26. *Cinna* 1.1.121–24: "My disordered spirit contradicts itself, / I want, and I don't want, I am carried away, I dare not, and my confused duty. . . ."

27. Although Auguste says later on (4.2.1248) that he has ruled for twenty years already, this nowhere affects the play's action or debate.

28. *Cinna* 4.3.1162–68: "But what! always blood, and always torture! / My cruelty grows exhausted, and cannot cease, / I want to make myself feared, I only succeed in aggravating matters; / Rome contains, for my ruin, too fertile a Hydra. / One head cut off gives birth to a thousand more, / And the spilled blood of a thousand conspirators / Makes my life more accursèd, and not more secure."

29. *Cinna* 4.3.1245–46: "You did indeed promise me a woman's advice: / You keep your word, and those are such, Madame."

30. *Cinna* 4.5.1374–76: "My noble despair has not blinded me, / My entire *vertu* [here, something like: "magnanimous, energetic positive faculties"] quickens without being transported by self-interest, / And in spite of myself I see more than I want to see."

31. *Cinna* 5.1.1426–29: "Follow exactly the rule I am imposing upon you / Without interrupting me, lend your ear to what I will say to you, / Do not interrupt with a word or a cry, / Hold your tongue prisoner, and if this utter silence. . . ."

32. *Cinna* 5.1.1607–10: "His death, whose memory sets alight your rage / Was Octave's crime, not the Emperor's. / All crimes of State committed for the Crown, / The Heavens forgive them us, once they have granted it. . . ."

33. *Cinna* 5.3.1755–60: "Listen to what the Gods tell you through me, / And what is the immutable law of your destiny. / After this action you have nothing to fear, / The

yoke will henceforth be borne without complaint, / And the least subdued will abandon their plans, / And consider all their glory lies in dying your subjects."

34. The translation was, it would seem, performed. In his notice to the reader, the printer says the translator added various songs "to lengthen the Play, and make it fitter for the Stage, when those that could not be resisted were resolved to have it acted" (*Pompey* [v], in Philips). According to Sir Edward Dering's epilogue to the play, the performance occurred in Ireland (65), presumably at the behest of the Countess of Cork, to whom it is dedicated ([iii–iv]). All translations of *Pompée* are Katherine Philips's.

35. *Pompée* 3.4.985–88: "Caesar, that envious Fate which I can brave, / Makes me thy Prisoner, but not thy Slave, / Expect not then my Heart should ere afford / To pay thee Homage, or to call thee Lord."

36. *Pompée* 5.4.1725–30: "But as a Roman, though my Hate be such, / I must confess, I thee esteem as much. / Both these extreams Justice can well allow: / This does my [your] Virtue, that my Duty show. / My sense of Honour does the first command; / Concern, the last, and they are both constrain'd."

37. In Katherine Philips's case, it may be that the choice of this play reflected her own commentary on Charles II's vengeance over the regicides (paralleling Caesar's over Ptolemy). There, too, the future would confirm that violence only begets violence: not this time in Charles II's death, but in James II's exile and the 1688 Glorious Revolution.

38. Richelieu 301. Cf. 324, 370–71, but especially 328–29.

39. *Le Cid* 2.3.457–58: "Cursèd ambition, frightful madness, / Under whose tyranny the most magnanimous suffer."

40. It is worth observing here that exactly this argument was made in a time of violence much closer to us. During the First World War, many argued that masculine violence led inevitably to women's subordination, and could be stopped only by using the reason and experience of women, themselves untainted by a history of militaristic violence (Marshall). The same point was made of course in Virginia Woolf's later *Three Guineas*.

41. Poulain 22–26, 37. The Cartesian and Hobbesian aspects of Poulain's work have yet to be studied, as too its relation with the later work of Mary Astell, whose arguments (in *Proposal*, 1694, 1697) reveal many similarities (verbal as well as conceptual).

42. On these plays, see Couton's interesting study.

43. Shevelow 121–22. Cf. Hunter. The latter suggests that great "sympathy" was shown to women in the *Gentleman's Magazine,* but that, of course, is precisely how the repression succeeds!

44. Nyack Kuborn, report to the Belgian government, 1868, 8–9. Kuborn's chief source was the ideologue Pierre-Jean-Georges Cabanis. My information is from Hilden (31). This lecture is an offshoot of her important work on women workers and the industrial revolution in Belgium.

45. More 6.142–43. Macaulay adopted a similar tack (49).

46. Wiesner 15. She is referring here to Smith, passim.

Works Cited

Agrippa, Henry Cornelius. *Female Pre-Eminence: Or, The Dignity and Excellency of That Sex, above the Male.* An Ingenious Discourse: Written originally in Latine, by Henry Cornelius Agrippa. . . . Done into English, with Additional Advantages, by H[enry] C[lare]. London, 1670. *The Feminist Controversy of the Renaissance.* Intro. Diane Bornstein. Delmar, N.Y.: Scholars' Facsimiles & Reprints, 1980.

Arendt, Hannah. *On Violence.* 1969. New York: Harcourt, 1970.

Astell, Mary. *A Serious Proposal to the Ladies for the Advancement of Their True and Greatest Interest.* . . . 4th ed. London, 1701. New York: Source Book, 1970.

Billon, François de. *Le fort inexpugnable de l'honneur du sexe femenin.* Paris, 1555. Intro. M. A. Screech. Wakefield: S. R. Publishers. New York: Johnson Rpt. The Hague: Mouton, 1970.

Buffet, Marguerite. "Traitté sur les eloges des illustres sçavantes, anciennes et modernes." *Les nouvelles observations sur la langue françoise.* . . . Paris: Cusson, 1668.

Conway Letters: The Correspondence of Anne, Viscountess Conway, Henry More, and Their Friends, 1642–1684. Ed. Marjorie Hope Nicolson. New Haven: Yale UP. London: Humphrey Milford, OUP, 1930.

Corneille, Pierre. *Oeuvres complêtes.* Ed. Georges Couton. 3 vols. Paris: Gallimard-"Pléiade," 1980–87.

Couton, Georges. *Corneille et la Fronde.* Clermont-Ferrand: Publications de la Faculté des Lettres, 1951.

Elyot, Sir Thomas. *The Defence of Good Women.* . . . 1545. *The Feminist Controversy of the Renaissance.* Intro. Diane Bornstein. Delmar, N.Y.: Scholars' Facsimiles & Reprints, 1980.

Gournay, Marie Le Jars de. *Le Proumenoir de Monsieur de Montaigne.* 1594. Intro. Patricia Francis Cholakian. Delmar, N.Y.: Scholars' Facsimiles & Reprints, 1985.

Henderson, Katherine Usher, and Barbara F. McManus, eds. *Half-Humankind: Contexts and Texts of the Controversy about Women in England, 1540–1640.* Urbana: U of Illinois P, 1985.

Hilden, Patricia J. "Women in Coal Mines: Belgium's *biercheuses,* 1890–1914," unpublished lecture, 1986–87.

Hogrefe, Pearl. *Tudor Women: Commoners and Queens.* Ames: Iowa State UP, 1975.

Hunter, Jean E. "The Eighteenth-Century Englishwoman: According to the Gentleman's Magazine." *Women in the Eighteenth Century and Other Essays.* Ed. Paul Fritz and Richard Morton. Toronto: Hakkert, 1976. 73–88.

Jordan, Constance. "Woman's Rule in Sixteenth-Century British Political Thought." *Renaissance Quarterly* 40 (1987): 421-51.

Kelso, Ruth. *Doctrine for the Lady of the Renaissance.* Urbana: U of Illinois P, 1956.

La Bruyère, Jean de. *Les caractères.* Paris: Michallet, 1692.

Le Bret, Cardin. *De la souveraineté du Roy.* Paris: Toussaincts du Bray, 1632.

Lougee, Carolyn C. *"Le paradis de femmes": Women, Salons, and Social Stratification in Seventeenth-Century France*. Princeton: Princeton UP, 1976.

Macaulay, Catharine [Sawbridge]. *Letters on Education, with Observations on Religious and Metaphysical Subjects*. 1790. Intro. Gina Luria. New York: Garland, 1974.

Maclean, Ian. *Woman Triumphant: Feminism in French Literature, 1610–1652*. Oxford: Clarendon, 1977.

Marshall, Catherine, C. K. Ogden, and Mary Sargant Florence. *Militarism versus Feminism: Writings on Women and War*. Ed. Margaret Kamester and Jo Vellacott. London: Virago, 1987.

May, Georges. *Le dilemme du roman au xviiie siècle: Étude sur les rapports du roman et de la critique (1715–1761)*. New Haven: Yale UP, 1963.

More, Hannah. *Strictures on the Modern System of Female Education; with a View of the Principles and Conduct Prevalent among Women of Rank and Fortune*. Vol. 6 of *The Works*. 7 vols. New York: Harper, 1847.

Perrault, Charles. *L'apologie des femmes*. Amsterdam: Braakman, [1694].

_____. *Parallèle des anciens et des modernes en ce qui regarde les arts et les sciences. Dialogues. Avec le poème du Siecle de Louis le Grand, et une epistre en vers sur le genie*. 2nd ed. 4 vols. in 1. 1692–97. Geneva: Slatkine, 1971.

Philips, Katherine [Fowler]. *Poems by the Most Deservedly Admired Mrs Katherine Philips, the Matchless Orinda*. To which is added, Monsieur Corneille's *Pompey* and *Horace*, tragedies. With several other translations out of the French. London: J. M. for H. Herringman, 1667.

Pitkin, Hannah Fenichel. *Fortune Is a Woman: Gender and Politics in the Thought of Niccolò Machiavelli*. Berkeley: U of California P, 1984.

Poulain de la Barre, François. *De l'égalité des deux sexes*. Paris: Fayard, 1984.

Reiss, Erna. *Rights and Duties of Englishwomen: A Study in Law and Public Opinion*. Manchester, Eng.: Sherratt & Hughes, 1934.

Reiss, Timothy J. "Revolution in Bounds: Wollstonecraft, Women, and Reason." *Gendered Subjects: Theoretical Dialogues on Sex, Race, Class, and Culture*. Ed. Linda Kauffman. Oxford: Blackwell, 1988.

_____. "La voix royale: De la violence étatique ou, du privé à la souveraineté." *Pierre Corneille: Ambiguités*. Ed. Michel Bareau. Edmonton: Alta, 1988.

Richelieu, Armand-Jean du Plessis, Cardinal-Duc de. *Testament politique*. Ed. Louis André. Paris: Laffont, 1947.

Rose, Mary Beth, ed. *Women in the Middle Ages and the Renaissance: Literary and Historical Perspectives*. Syracuse: Syracuse UP, 1986.

Schibanoff, Susan. "Taking the Gold out of Egypt: The Art of Reading as a Woman." *Gender and Reading: Essays on Readers, Texts, and Contexts*. Ed. Elizabeth A. Flynn and Patrocinio P. Schweickart. Baltimore: Johns Hopkins UP, 1986. 83–106.

Schiff, Mario L. *La fille d'alliance de Montaigne: Marie de Gournay*. Essai suivi de "L'égalité des hommes et des femmes" et du "Grief des dames." Paris: Champion, 1910.

Shevelow, Kathryn. "Fathers and Daughters: Women as Readers of *The Tatler*." *Gender and Reading: Essays on Readers, Texts, and Contexts*. Ed. Elizabeth A. Flynn and Patrocinio P. Schweickart. Baltimore: Johns Hopkins UP, 1986. 107–23.

Smith, Hilda. *Reason's Disciples: Seventeenth-Century English Feminists.* Urbana: U of Illinois P, 1982.

Stegmann, André. *L'héroïsme cornélien: Genèse et signification.* 2 vols. Paris: Colin, 1968.

Uildriks, Anne. *Les idées littéraires de Mlle de Gournay.* Gröningen: Rijksuniversiteit, 1962.

Venesoen, Constant. *Corneille apprenti féministe, de "Mélite" au "Cid."* Paris: Lettres Modernes, 1986.

Wiesner, Merry E. "Women's Defense of Their Public Roles." Rose 1–27.

Woolf, Virginia. *Orlando: A Biography.* 1928. New York: Penguin, 1946.

———. *Three Guineas.* 1938. New York: Harcourt, 1966.

Leaky Vessels: The Incontinent Women of City Comedy

GAIL KERN PASTER

T HE INCONTINENCE on which this essay will focus is not the relatively comfortable subject of sexual incontinence in women but its much less comfortable analogue—bladder incontinence. In venturing upon a topic still somewhat protected by the taboo of silence, one risks evoking critical embarrassment or distaste. Even now, when so much critical attention is directed on the social formation of the body and its literary representations in early modern Europe, the cultural inhibitions which are part of my subject make what goes on in the bedroom easier for us to discuss than what goes on in the bathroom or—to be less anachronistic—on the chamberpot or in the privy. However, I am encouraged to do so by the intensity of current theoretical efforts to disentangle nature and culture, to see how the ideological constructions of culture masquerade as "the natural." It is just such criticism which must be particularly wary of marginalizing the literary reproduction of any behavior, and especially an everyday behavior so rarely mentioned in literary discourse let alone represented onstage.[1]

There are two dramatic occasions in city comedy which represent women needing to relieve themselves—in *Bartholomew Fair* when

the need for a chamberpot brings Win Littlewit and Mrs. Overdo to Ursula's booth and in *A Chaste Maid in Cheapside* when the gossips at the
Allwit christening wet the floor beneath their stools. I will argue that
these representations are not beneath our critical notice, but rather
constitute important instances of city comedy's complex articulation
of gender—the weaker vessel as leaky vessel. At these moments onstage two affective formations are at work: one involves that signifying practice we call "manners"; the other employs a more or less familiar discourse about the female body—an anxious symptomological
discourse to be found in Renaissance medical texts, in iconography,
and in the proverbs of oral culture. This discourse, as we shall see, in-
scribes women as leaky vessels by isolating one element of the female
body's material expressiveness—its production of fluids—as excessive, hence either disturbing or shameful. It also characteristically
links this liquid expressiveness to excessive verbal fluency. In both formations, the question is one of women's bodily self-control or, more
precisely, the representation of a particular kind of uncontrol as a
function of gender.

As Mikhail Bakhtin and others have argued, this question of bodily
control took on a new interest and urgency in early modern European
culture. In particular, as Norbert Elias makes clear in *The History of
Manners,* standards of "outward bodily propriety" in early modern Europe were undergoing a gradual but decisive transformation which he
links to the formation of the state (55). Although the educational treatises and etiquette manuals which provide most of Elias's evidence emphasize new restrictions and requirements in table manners, this transformation affected all forms of social behavior including the
expression of those "natural" functions which most concern me here.
Elias attributes the structural changes, at least in part, to interlocking
desires within the ruling class to control the impulses of their social inferiors (137) and, as far as their own behavior was concerned, to dif-
ferentiate themselves socially from those below them (100). This last
desire, of course, is self-perpetuating because the standard-setters are
continually required to produce new social refinements as their
modes of behavior gradually diffuse downward in the social formation
and thereby blur the boundaries of class. The psychic mechanism for
this mode of production is shame, and Elias argues that new feelings of

delicacy and repugnance about behaviors acceptable to medieval society indicate a progressive lowering of the shame threshold discernible from at least 1530, when Erasmus's treatise "De ciuilitate morum puerilium" appeared (53, 71, 101). Despite the implication in the treatise's English title—"A lytell booke of good maners for chyldren"—that Erasmus addresses children of both sexes, his intended audience is, in fact, aristocratic boys—the primary standard-setters of the future. But Elias, like Erasmus, largely ignores gender as a variable in his analysis of social change. Yet the process of differentiation through manners which forms class boundaries also functions in the construction of gender. Thus the injunctions against urinating or defecating in public, for example, though frequently ignored in practice even among upper-class males, begin to inscribe what Jacques Lacan calls "the laws of urinary segregation" (151)—laws which employ gender norms in order to compel restraint and, more important, to distinguish between the norms of restraint for men and women. The modesty which is an ethical norm for women governs not only their own expression of excretory functions but also what men may or may not do in the presence of women. Elias quotes from German court regulations of 1570 which label those who would relieve themselves in front of ladies as "rustics who have not been to court or lived among refined and honorable people" (131).

This lowering of the shame threshold affects discourse no less than behavior. One proof of Erasmus's success in inscribing greater shame in the boys he addresses is that, unlike later writers on manners, he does not seem reluctant to mention the behavior he is trying to refashion (Elias 58). But it is just this growing delicacy, especially as displayed by those imitating without sufficient warrant the more refined behavior of their social superiors, which makes possible the famous joke in *Twelfth Night* against Malvolio when the upstart steward spells out an unmentionable word and commits a verbal trespass against Olivia by seeming to possess forbidden, shameful knowledge of her: "and thus makes she her great P's" (2.5.89).[2] Euphemisms—the discursive formations of shame—have emerged. Indeed, the habit of euphemism (here both employed and breached unconsciously by Malvolio) is even displayed by the much less delicate Autolycus, who excuses himself from the company of Perdita's shepherd family by pretending urinary need: "Walk before toward the sea-side . . . I will but look upon the hedge and follow you" (*Winter's Tale* 4.4.826–28). The business— which the Arden editor dismisses as "merely a dramatic device (chiefly for the groundlings)" (133n)—produces more verbal refinement from Autolycus than we might expect, perhaps because he uses excretory manners to mark the social differences between himself and his companions—persuading the two rustics that he is "courtier *cap-a-pe*" (4.4.736).

These two Shakespearean examples seen in the sociogenetic context provided by Elias imply the social expressiveness of my theme and its relevance to larger questions of class and gender in city comedy. The taboo of silence, for example, which still exists to some degree for us, does not exist for Erasmus primarily because his treatise appears early in the formation of discursive norms for bodily behavior (74). But Elias's argument also implies that euphemisms like those employed and breached by Malvolio and Autolycus assume a greater instrumentality for people in more vulnerable or ambiguous social positions—for people, that is, like women. In *Bartholomew Fair,* both Win Littlewit and Mrs. Overdo display much greater reluctance than Autolycus did to acknowledge their urgent bladders. Finding herself among a group of strangers at Ursula's booth, Dame Overdo must "entreat a courtesy" of Captain Whit (4.4.183), but she cannot reply to his expansive offer to "shpeak out" and "entreat a hundred" (4.4.184) because—"with modesty" (185)—the courtesy she requires can only be unspoken. Win's reluctance is even more noticeable. Leaving Ursula's booth with her husband, she holds back from his entreaty to see more of the fair together, saying, "I know not what to do. . . . For a thing I am ashamed to tell you, i'faith, and 'tis too far to go home" (3.6.110, 112–13). But she reacts indignantly to the assumption that her embarrassment is caused by the presence onstage of Leatherhead, the puppet-seller: "Hang him, base bobchin, I scorn him" (117). The sensation of shame is a function of social structure; in hierarchical societies, Elias argues, one does not feel the same bodily shame before inferiors as before equals or superiors (138). By such logic, Win has no reason to feel ashamed, no social cause for verbal squeamishness if she, like Autolycus, feels superior or at least equal to her companions onstage. But the violence of her response may tell us more than her word. Poor Win is experiencing a redundancy of shame, which is here the social shame of *feeling ashamed* to acknowledge urgent bodily need not to, but merely in the presence of, an inferior like the hobbyhorse-seller. Or, if we accept what she says, then her husband's presence or even the otherwise unacknowledged presence of an audience has molded Win's confusion, has called forth a redundancy of euphemism: "I have very great what sha'call'um, John" (3.6.117–18).

If Win's problem is more cultural than physical, so too is its solution. Ursula's booth—the fair's central locus—is usually associated with the body as part of the play's apparent celebration of Carnival. Thus, in Jonathan Haynes's recent Bakhtinian representation of the booth's symbolic functions, "the material bodily principle is magnificently embodied in the enormous flesh of the pig-woman Ursula and in her booth, which caters to all the body's needs (eating, drinking, defecating, fornicating)" (647). Here, as so often, the call of culture is mistaken for the call of nature, and a generic "body" which, like Leatherhead's puppets, lacks sex or gender stands in for concealed cultural norms which distinguish sharply between the bodily "needs" of men and women. No character in *Bartholomew Fair* is known to defecate in Ursula's booth. And only female characters are shown to need her chamberpot—in actuality "the bottom of an old bottle" (4.4.199–200)—because, unlike Autolycus or any other male character in this period who needs to urinate, they cannot merely "look upon" the nearest stage property hedge but are tied by the invisible leading-strings of culture to a concealed receptacle. Thus is Malvolio's verbal trespass constituted; "thus makes she her great P's."

As Haynes suggests, Jonson may well intend Ursula's booth to situate his festive advocacy of "the material bodily principle" and Ursula, by virtue of her office, may represent at one level a de-idealized version of the goddess Nature. Such a symbolic placement is itself fully conventional in binary Renaissance constructions of gender whereby man is associated with culture and woman with nature (Maclean 2–4, passim). We ought to notice that Ursula describes herself as an archetypal representation of woman because, in standing over the hot fire, she becomes a vessel leaking and melting, to be known by her loss of being—loss of content, form, and integral identity—and marked,

like Olivia, by the liquid letters she makes: "I shall e'en melt away to
the first woman, a rib again, I am afraid. I do water the ground in knots
as I go, like a great garden-pot; you may follow me by the S's I make"
(2.2.48–51). She and her booth are mutually identifying—in Overdo's
words, "the very womb and bed of enormity, gross as herself"
(2.2.101–02). Yet, as proprietor of the booth and supplier of the
chamberpot, Ursula crosses over the boundaries of gender to become
the agent of culture, the instrument of patriarchy, for the cultural
norms which constrain Win Littlewit and Mrs. Overdo to seek out the
booth as privy function to keep them there as prostitutes. That is, because the booth is the central locus of desire in the fair, it serves prevailing cultural requirements in transforming the women from subjects to objects. The chamberpot has become a bawd, the "jordan" a
seller of flesh literalized in Jordan Knockem, the horse-courser. Perhaps Ursula herself senses some of the ideological contradictions in
her function, because she objects to helping Mrs. Overdo to a jordan
and tells Whit to find Captain Jordan instead: "I bring her! Hang her,"
she tells Whit furiously, "Heart, must I find a common pot for every
punk i'your purlieus? . . . Let her sell her hood and buy a sponge"
(4.4.195–98).

There is a wonderful irony here, at least as far as Win Littlewit's putative transformation is concerned. In persuading the pregnant Win to
pretend a "longing" to eat Bartholomew pig, John Littlewit had
caused his wife to manifest one of the conventional weaknesses of
women—the bizarrely irrational longings of pregnancy which must be
satisfied in order to prevent harm to mother and unborn baby (Eccles
64). If visiting the Fair is an act of irrational appetite, the proctor will
sanction and justify his weakness by displacing it on to his wife and
through her to women at large:

You may long to see as well as to taste, Win. How did the 'pothecary's wife,
Win, that longed to see the anatomy, Win? Or the lady, Win, that desired to
spit i'the great lawyer's mouth after an eloquent pleading? I assure you they
longed, Win; good Win, go in, and long. (3.6.12–16)

Similarly, it is Win who publicly confesses having "very great what
sha'call'um" but later the proctor seems to have it too. Ursula tells

Whit that "an honest proctor and his wife are *at it*, within" (4.4.200, emphasis added), thus forcing poor Mrs. Overdo to wait to use the bottle. But, given the multiple functions of Ursula's booth, we should also notice here the multiple significations of her discourse—the sexually suggestive ambiguity of "at it." It can hardly be coincidental, then, that once Littlewit has abandoned his wife at Ursula's booth in order to see how his puppet show is going forward, other conventional uses of her and Mrs. Overdo can also be culturally sanctioned. As Ursula tells Knockem, "Persuade this between you two to become a bird o'the game, while I work the velvet woman within (as you call her)" (4.5.16–18).

How and why these two women find themselves at Ursula's booth, therefore, is just as revealing of gender norms as what happens to them afterwards; the chamberpot is bawd indeed. It is not that Ursula confuses the two city wives with Ramping Alice or any of the other Bartholomew birds, but rather that she and Knockem merely act upon the implication of the wives' presence, without male escort, at her booth. Here, unlawful access to the otherwise inaccessible woman is made possible by the odd but crucial mediation of the chamberpot: it discloses their vulnerability, announces an occasion of physical and social permeability.[3] But I want to go on to argue that there are even deeper issues in contemporary constructions of woman than merely the linkage which Jonson's play establishes between the whore and the city wife who thus makes "her great P's." This issue—most fully expressed, as we shall see, in *A Chaste Maid in Cheapside*—uses the familiar Renaissance association of women and water not only to insinuate womanly unreliability but also to define the female body even when it is chaste as a crucial problematic in the social formations of capitalism. If, as Natalie Zemon Davis has argued, the deepening subjection of women in the early modern period can be understood as a "streamlining" in the patriarchal family for the economic efficiency required by emerging capitalist modes of production (126), then representations of the female body as a leaking vessel display that body as beyond the control of the female subject, and thus as threatening the acquisitive norms of the family and its maintenance of status and power.

That women's bodies were moister than men's and controlled cyclically by that watery planet, the moon, was a given of contemporary

scientific theory; that their bodies were also notable for the production of all sorts of liquids—breast milk, menstrual blood, tears, and
"great P's"—was in part a predictable construct of humoral theory and
in part the inevitable result of primitive obstetrical techniques and the
reproductive practices of the upper class (and whoever wanted to imitate them). Dorothy McLaren has persuasively demonstrated the cor-
relation between the extremely high fertility rates among rich women
and their abandonment of breastfeeding, arguing that "the choice for
wives during their teeming years in pre-industrial England was an infant in the womb or at the breast" (46). But while this choice may have
been dictated largely by class norms, that fact is less important to my
argument than the possibility that women, whether suckling infants or
suppressing the flow of milk after annual childbirth, must often have
seemed ready to overflow at the breast. Indeed, early gynecologists
even believed that women who had never been pregnant could have
milk in their breasts, that "marriageable virgins . . . full of juice and
seed" could have as much breast milk as wet nurses (Eccles 53).

   Both popular and medical discourse, moreover, conceptualized all
these fluids as related forms of the same essential substance. Breast
milk was the purified form of menstrual blood, "none other thing than
blood made white" (Crawford 51). It changed color according to function by means of a process that occurred in two veins—"occult passages"—which carried the fluid back and forth between the breast and
the womb (Eccles 52). And to judge from the discursive evidence of
one proverb—"Let her cry, she'll piss the less" (Tilley G443)—tears
and urine also may have seemed interrelated in nature and function,
flow from one orifice draining or even stopping flow in another.

   This cultural association of women and liquids was so deeply inscribed that it required little empirical support, as we have seen in the
case of the milk-laden virgins.[4] Given the intractability of gynecological disease in the period and the incessant childbearing of an important female minority, evidence for an iconology of women as leaky
vessels must have seemed undeniable. Obstetrical instruments did in
fact leave women mangled after difficult or protracted labors, threatening them with urinary incontinence (MacDonald 273). And even
among women who gave birth more easily, the frequency of childbearing must have severely weakened control of the lower musculature.

Or, as another of Tilley's proverbs puts it, "like an old woman's breech, at no certainty" (W667).

But here, predictably, the neutrality of gynecological facts breaks down before the insinuations of popular discourse. Uncertainty in the lower parts bespeaks unreliability in the constructed woman; overproduction at one orifice bespeaks overproduction at the rest. The demonized womb, for example—fully animate, capable of movement, sensitive to smells—was "so greedy and likerish" for male seed, according to one midwifery manual, "that it doth euen come down to meet nature, sucking, and (as it were) snatching the same" (*Complete Midwife's Practice Enlarged* [1659], qtd. in Eccles 29). "A likerish tongue a likerish tail," says the proverb (Tilley T395). More important, in its likerous behavior the greedy womb bears a metonymic resemblance to women at the gossips' meeting, a comic subgenre which Linda Woodbridge has linked to prevalent anxieties about gender boundaries in early seventeenth-century England (224–39). In the most striking example of the genre, John Skelton's "The Tunning of Elynor Rumming" (written around 1517 but reprinted in 1609), gossips with naked paps and untrussed hair rush into the alewife's house to taste her latest brew, bringing their household goods to barter if they have no money. One of them gets so horribly drunk that "she pyst where she stood" (373); then, having overflowed at one end, she proceeds to flow at the other: "Then began she to wepe" (374). Another woman, whose paunch "was so puffed / And so with ale stuffed," barely escapes the same embarrassment: "Had she not hyed apace, / She had defoyled the place" (570–73). That such drinking women are also typically garrulous is obviously very much to the point: Skelton's Latin colophon invites women "marked with the dirty stain of filth" or "who have the sordid blemish of squalor" or "who are marked out by garrulous loquacity" to listen to his record of their deeds (452).

The action in Skelton's poem is a particularly coarse example of a portentous metonymic chain: a woman who leaves her house is a woman who talks is a woman who drinks is a woman who leaks. Any point in the linkage may imply or abridge the rest. Thus, going abroad is itself a leak, even potentially a flood, as in John Northbrooke's argument against allowing city wives and widows to go to the theater: "They wander abroade . . . and runne from house to house, and at the

last go after Satan. Give the water no passage, no not a little (sayth Syr-
ach) neyther giue a wanton woman libertie to go out abroade" (68).
Talking is also leaking, of course, especially in the emblem literature:
for Geoffrey Whitney, a leaky barrel emblematizes "the blab," a figure
unidentified by gender. But, in the fable portion of the emblem, the
barrel itself—with water pouring from its many holes—is the one
filled by the daughters of Danaus as a punishment for killing their husbands (12; see the accompanying illustration). That these daughters
are visually absent from the emblem may imply the conventional force
of their association with the barrel or perhaps the suppressed patriarchal anxieties to which gossiping women give rise. Pour as they will,
the daughters of Danaus cannot fill their barrel or stop it from leaking:
"No paine will serue, to fill it to the toppe, / For, still at holes the same
doth runne, and droppe" (5–6). On the facing leaf (B3r; see illustration) is Whitney's emblem of the proud Niobe, "Which, yet with
teares, dothe seeme to waile, and mone" (6). In both emblems, the iconography is only partially present; in the second emblem, like the first,
the offending woman is visually absent. What seems to link them thematically for Whitney is the question of female insubordination and its
patriarchal punishment—perpetual leaking.

What is all too obvious in the coarse physical detail of Skelton's
poem is also present by implication in Whitney's emblems: the threat
of female independence has been renegotiated as an issue of female
self-control in a form—a leaky form—obviously related to talkative-
ness, but far more shameful. It is the potential shamefulness of the association of women and water which I want to emphasize, a shamefulness present even when the trope is apparently reversed or subverted.
When it is reversed, the dangerous unreliability of women can be used
to establish the dangerous changeability of water, especially the waters of the body. Thus one John Fletcher, writing a 1623 treatise on
urine, that most fetishized of bodily liquids, admits the difficulty of diagnostic practices based upon a bodily liquid likely to change in appearance from day to day, "so that here especially the infame, that
vrine is a lying strumpet, hath some appearance of truth" (110). (He
goes on, of course, to try to save urine from its metaphoric contamina-
tion by woman by arguing that, despite its apparent changeability,
urine remains a valuable and truthful diagnostic tool.)

THE Poëtes faine, that DANAVS daughters deare,
I ioyned are to fill the fatall tonne:
Where, thoughe they toile, yet are they not the neare,
But as they powre, the water forthe dothe runne:
No paine will serue, to fill it to the toppe,
For, still at holes the same doth runne, and droppe.

Which reprehendes, three sortes of wretches vaine,
The blabbe, th'ingrate, and those that court fill,
As first, the blabbe, no secrets can retaine.
Th'ingrate, not knowes to vse his frendes good will.
The couetous man, thoughe he abounde with store
Is not suffisde, but couets more and more.

Superbia

OF NIOBE, beholde the rufefull plighte,
Bicause shee did dispise the powers deuine:
Her children all, weare slaine within her sighte,
And, while her selfe with wringinge teares did pine,
Shee was transfornde, into a marble stone,
Which, yet with teares, dothe seeme to waile, and mone.

This tragedie, thoughe Poëtes firste did frame,
Yet maie it bee, to euerie one applide:
That mortall men, shoulde thinke from whence they came,
And not presume, nor puffe them vp with pride,
Leste that the Lorde, whoe haughtie hartes doth hate, [state,
Doth throwe them downe, when sure they thinke theyr

Fabula Niobe Ouid. 6. Meta. examp.

De numero filiorum, vide Aul. Gellium lib. 20. cap. 6.

Effe procul læti, cernam ne funera vultu,
Nec fueila tota mærore in orbe facta.
Hei spretis natis repeti, ita figurata superis:
Me miseram? Deum spisso ita nisi.

Dura gens deorum lacrymis, & marmore mutatæ.
Sic mihi mori dolor est, sit nulli vita, dolor.
Dispice, mortales, quid sit superos contra fallere,
Et quid sit magnum respondisse Deos.

B 3   In vir

The trope comparing women and water appears in a subverted form in the famous iconographic depiction of female virginity as a sieve that does not leak, an allusion to the Vestal Virgin Tuccia who carried water in a sieve from the Tiber to the Temple of Vesta in order to prove her virginity. Roy Strong has catalogued numerous examples of the motif in portraits of Queen Elizabeth, who carries a sieve to symbolize not only her physical virginity but also the connection between that virginity and her ability to rule (68). Yet, clearly, the association of Elizabeth with Tuccia's sieve, even though it links the queen to another, ostensibly historical woman, serves to separate her strongly from womankind as a whole—and thus from the contradictions of a woman ruler. For women less politically motivated to maintain the virgin state, the iconographic representation of Elizabeth's self-command produces an unflattering implication: if not-leaking becomes something of a mythological miracle reserved for a long-gone Roman lady and the occasional virgin queen, then leaking remains the normal punitive condition for women, and melting mother Ursula remains their representational archetype: "you may follow me by the S's I make."

But far more even than the leaking women of *Bartholomew Fair,* the female characters of *A Chaste Maid in Cheapside* reproduce a virtual symptomology of woman that insists on the female body's moistures, secretions, and productions as a shameful token of uncontrol. Although this symptomology is most striking in the christening scene in act 3, it is present from the very beginning of the play, when Mrs. Yellowhammer diagnoses her weeping daughter's languor as greensickness and prescribes a husband as the appropriate therapy:

> You had need to have somewhat to quicken
> Your green sickness—do you weep?—a husband!
> Had not such a piece of flesh been ordained,
> What had us wives been good for?—to make salads,
> Or else cry'd up and down for samphire.
>
> (1.1.4–8)

As R. B. Parker has pointed out in his fine edition of the play, Mrs. Yellowhammer here associates sexually provocative foods like highly seasoned salads with urinary function: samphire was considered to be both an appetite stimulant and a diuretic, provoking urine and an appetite for meat (7n). This early connection between sex and urination is repeated elsewhere in the play as part of a larger discursive link between urine and sexual incontinence (lv). But, like Elias discussing the history of manners, Parker fails to see how deeply implicated this linkage may be with contemporary constructions of gender and anxieties about its boundaries.

In fact, though Parker is perhaps the play's most astute and sympathetic reader, he finds the urinary aspect of its discursive exploration of sexuality distasteful: it is "a criticism of eroticism pushed too far" (lv). His discomfort is not surprising, since—if Elias is correct about the progressive lowering of the shame threshold—we are far less able even than Middleton's contemporaries to speak easily about excretory functions except in medical or scientific discourses. And we tend to segregate excretory discourse from erotic contexts as ferociously as we prosecute the laws of urinary segregation. Who can forget how central this very issue of "unisex" public restrooms was in the ERA debate, particularly among its female opponents. A provocative counterassertion of feminist demands was evident in a widely circulated poster showing the back view of two men in what is obviously a public restroom. But in between them, with her legs in a wide straddle parodying the male posture at urinals, stands a booted blonde in a fringed miniskirt. Contemporary contestants for power—in Lacanian terms, for possession of the phallus which is concealed in this poster but which we are supposed to imagine this tall female invader now possesses— have met and mingled in the toilet. The urinal has become an object of desire, a symbol of contested privilege. We, who have seen how the privy in *Bartholomew Fair* functions to subordinate women as sexual objects, may want to call this poster "Ursula's revenge."

But I also want to argue that what links this poster to representations of woman in *A Chaste Maid in Cheapside* is the symbolic use of the urinary function in contemporary discourses of power. In the early seventeenth century this representation, rather than implying contests for control of public territory—such as the restroom—implies instead contests for control of the central domestic territory of the patriarchal family—the female body itself. In *A Chaste Maid* this contest occurs most frequently as a function of competing explanations of behavior, as characters propose interpretations of motive and act which seem to be irreconcilable. These discursive collisions are most evident where the behavior of women is concerned. Thus, because Cheapside takes the physical frailty of women for granted, symptomological explanations for female behavior—such as Mrs. Yellowhammer's response to Moll's tears—are readily available to articulate gender difference. But such conventions are radically destabilized by Cheapside's equally widespread acceptance of an economic determinism that opens the categories of class and gender to structural redefinition.

In the play, not surprisingly, bladder incontinence in particular is presented as an attribute of women of all ages, from the new Allwit baby who is taken offstage in act 2 to get her bum wiped to the drunken gossips who wet the floor in act 3 and discuss, among other things, a nineteen-year-old daughter who cannot be married because of "a secret fault"—that she too freely wets her bed (3.2.93). Her mother's willingness to reveal the shameful attribute at all, of course, is presented as a function of drink; as one gossip remarks cynically, wine can do what friendship cannot—cause women to talk freely as it causes women to leak.

The play's symptomological discourse of women is perhaps most striking in the christening scene. There the gossips' enthusiastic eating and drinking finally chases their host from the room as their wet kisses chase Tim Yellowhammer, though not before one of the drunken gossips actually falls on him and requires a hoist up. The scene as a whole bears a strong resemblance in tone and action to Skelton's "Tunning of Elynor Rumming," except that instead of celebrating an alewife's latest brew the gossips celebrate the safe delivery of the fecund Mrs. Allwit and christen a brand-new arrival to the sisterhood of woman. "A large child," say the gossips, "she's but a little woman!" (3.2.14). The baby is, in fact, presented as a miniature woman rather than a baby girl, and Middleton's broad comic play throughout the christening on the extraordinary facts of the baby's parentage serve to underscore the asymmetry of gender and generation in a particularly striking way. Though the gossips claim to see a resemblance between the baby and Allwit, their inspection of the baby's features effects a metonymic redistribution similar to what we observed in the subtext of the sieve portrait. The gossips do not know what we do: that because the baby has not been fathered by Allwit, only her resemblance to her mother has a foundation in nature. And it is a resemblance which the gossips link specifically to the two interchangeable thresholds of female appetite and vulnerability: the baby has her "mother's mouth up and down, up and down!" (3.2.13). In this context the question of family resemblance is thoroughly effaced by the constitutive force of gender. The gossips really see in the baby a small version of themselves:

> A very spiny creature, but all heart;
> Well mettled, like the faithful, to endure
> Her tribulation here and raise up seed.
>
> (3.2.16–18)

The celebratory momentum of the christening itself produces an even deeper sense of gender identity, because the gossips regress into an infantile gluttony and incontinence which brings them into the tight circle of mother-daughter resemblance.

The christening, in early modern Europe, was an occasion that typically called for much eating and drinking, even when celebrated in Lent, as this one is (Burke 191–99). The signal feature of this christening, however, is less the communal carnivalism than a demarcation of gender even sharper than what we have seen in *Bartholomew Fair,* as the men band together in vocal disgust at the women's gluttony, drunkenness, reeking wet kisses, and finally incontinence: "They have drunk so hard in plate," comments Allwit to his manservant, "that some of them / Had need of other vessels" (3.2.171–72).

Allwit's male anxiety at the christening scene could not be clearer or more representative of patriarchal feelings, even though they issue from a man whose apparent desire to give over his rights to his wife's body to the man who can keep them both in material comfort seems at first glance to invert the patriarchal ethos. He stands apart as choric commentator while the nurse passes around comfits and wine. In his account of their gluttony, the women become sexually overpowering, grabbing at phallic sweetmeats with "long fingers that are wash'd / Some thrice a day in urine" (3.2.52–53), culling all the "long plums" and leaving nothing but "short wriggle-tail comfits, not worth mouthing" (3.2.63–64). The greedy mouth, furthermore, merges with the greedy womb, as the women stuff their pockets as they stuff their mouths: "Now we shall have such pocketing: see how / They lurch at the lower end!" (3.2.54–55). Allwit seems to see them in a sisterly collusion with his prolific wife, threatening to deprive him of a substance which he defines as both material and sexual:

> No mar'l I heard a citizen complain once
> That his wife's belly only broke his back;
> Mine had been all in fitters seven years since,
> But for this worthy knight,
> That with a prop upholds my wife and me,
> And all my estate buried in Bucklersbury.
>
> (3.2.65–70)

For Allwit, the threat posed by a collective, hence Amazonian female appetite and female fertility is so catastrophic that it supplants the male rivalry which is virtually normative in plays of the period and which Middleton's city comedies, with their obsessive feuding of merchant and gallant, usually lay bare. Indeed, what mitigates our sense of Allwit's sexual anomalousness in giving up his wife's sexual services is that he so clearly defines them rather as sexual demands—and costly sexual demands at that. Her latest pregnancy, for example, is marked by a longing for "pickled cucumbers"—a sexually suggestive longing far more anxiety-provoking than anything Win Littlewit or even the Duchess of Malfi manifests, since Allwit hopes the cucumbers will "hold [his] wife in pleasure / Till the knight come himself" (1.2.9–10). Mrs. Allwit's appetites, it would seem, can be satisfied only by dint of a sexual, financial, and psychological effort and expense which Allwit has craftily transferred to Sir Walter. It is Allwit who congratulates himself on his escape from the alienated labor of sexual performance and the attendant anxieties of sexual possession:

> These torments stand I free of; I am as clear
> From jealousy of a wife as from the charge:
> O, two miraculous blessings! 'Tis the knight
> Hath took that labour all out of my hands:
> I may sit still and play; he's jealous for me,
> Watches her steps, sets spies; I live at ease,
> He has both the cost and torment.
>
> (1.2.48–54)

Here the enemy of middle-class conservation of wealth is woman: "They never think of payment," complains Allwit (3.2.79) to the man who does offer payment for sexual privileges in the house, as they flee the room together. Here then, uniquely, cuckoldry becomes wittoldry. Erstwhile male rivals become partners in arms banding together to conserve for themselves, and for the variously fathered offspring whom they feel obliged to support, an economic and sexual substance which the appetite of woman and her conspicuous lack of self-control threaten to destroy.

In *A Chaste Maid in Cheapside,* however, the thematizing of female uncontrol through the discursive association of women and water, though even more striking than it is in *Bartholomew Fair,* is also more complicated because water symbolism and urinary references, while largely identified with women, are not exclusively so. The play's two most potent males, Sir Walter Whorehound and Touchwood Senior, especially, are linked with water symbolism in its male form—as semen. Thus in the play's dramatic economy, Sir Walter (pronounced "water") opposes his cousin Sir Oliver Kix, whose name means "dry stalk" (lv) and who will lose an inheritance to the watery Walter if his marriage remains infertile—or, in the terms of this dramatic idiom, dry. We cannot be surprised, therefore, that water—when it is male water—has changed, now representing power, not leaking or loss of control. Male water—unlike female leaking—has economic value and under the right circumstances can even be shared in order to preserve or enlarge dynastic claims. Thus Sir Oliver seeks to cure his own dryness by ingesting medicinal water from Touchwood Senior, who promises that he "has got / Nine children by one water that he useth" (2.1.174–75). Of course he administers his "water" to the two Kixes separately—sending Sir Oliver off on a five-hour horseback ride after he has drunk the milky liquid and taking Lady Kix off to receive his more potent brand of liquid medicine in bed. The Kixes are so pleased with the effects of Touchwood's water—though presumably for different reasons—that, at the end of the play after Lady Kix has conceived, a delighted Sir Oliver exults in his new-found potency and in the victory of his "water"—conveniently hybridized—over that of his cousin: "The child is coming and the land comes after; / The news of this will make a poor Sir Walter" (5.3.14–15). And he, rather than Mas-

ter Allwit, becomes the play's contented cuckold, inviting the Touchwoods to join their household.

This identification of water with male potency rather than simply
with female leaking would appear to redefine the thesis with which
this essay began, especially since Middleton seems interested in presenting male potency in so exaggerated a form that it starts to resemble
the loss of self-control I have been associating with leaking women.
The Touchwoods, for example, have impoverished themselves
through overproduction:

> Life, every year a child, and some years two;
> Besides drinkings abroad, that's never reckon'd;
> This gear will not hold out.
>
> (2.1.15–17)

A virtual Priapus with an unquenchable thirst for such nondomestic
"drinkings," Touchwood himself admits to having imperiled the har-
vests in nearby villages by taking so many girls out of service at hay-
making time. For his part, Sir Walter worries that his unacknowledged
offspring will marry, incestuously, the children of a future marriage.
But Middleton creates a wonderfully comic context for his male fertility gods by linking the biological fact of male potency to the far more
remarkable social facts of the play—that is, to the ingenious social and
discursive arrangements by which male authority in Cheapside masks
and serves its sexual drive and social ambitions. In these arrangements, of course, since they focus so closely on strategic containments
of female appetite and reproduction and on the strategic promotion of
male potency, we return full circle to the social construction of wom-
en as shamefully leaky vessels with which we began.

From a feminist perspective, the extent to which this construction
helps to maintain an existing structure of gender differentiation is
clearly visible. So too are the ideological contradictions which any
systematic articulation of gender must seek to efface and which here
become particularly evident in Middleton's characterization of Moll
Yellowhammer and Lady Kix. Of the women in Cheapside, Moll and
Lady Kix are the most labile emotionally, hence—according to the
play's normative symptomology—sexually the most deprived. Full

consideration of their circumstances, however, exposes the discursive tyranny and incompleteness of any merely gynecological interpretation of their behavior. Thus the "naturalness" of Lady Kix's grief and frustration at her seven years of childlessness is deconstructed by the presence of a strong economic incentive for reproduction: "Think but upon the goodly lands and livings / That's kept back through want on't," she tells her husband (2.1.150–51)—"it" being, of course, Sir Oliver's "brevity," his phallic insufficiency. Her tears, then, are causally linked to her husband's dryness. But here the authority of gender to classify behavior—which is so compelling in the christening scene—is undercut by powerful, competing economic and class determinants which bind the Kixes to each other and finally to a mutual reliance upon the potency of the Touchwood "water."

In the case of Moll Yellowhammer, Middleton is primarily interested in showing how social authority—here represented by the older generation—uses the discourse of nature oppressively to serve its own selfish ends. Thus the weeping Moll's emotional lability in the opening scene is immediately rationalized by her parents symptomologically— as the telltale sign of maidenly greensickness. But their strong desire to supply the conventional remedy—a husband of their choice—only calls the interpretive completeness and objectivity of their diagnosis into question: Moll weeps not from greensickness, or at least not only from greensickness; she weeps more obviously from the effects of her mother's scolding and her parents' tyranny in the question of marital choice. By this logic, more tyranny will produce more water, more "leaking," and the constraints of culture will continue to be defined as inherent biological flaws in the nature of woman.

The exchange between the Yellowhammers about their daughter's behavior, furthermore, is also particularly revealing of the ideological tensions and contradictions which the asymmetry of gender occasions. Mr. Yellowhammer scolds his wife for using socially pretentious diction to describe Moll's behavior just as she scolds their daughter for the ideologically aberrant behavior itself. "Errors?" he repeats. "Nay, the city cannot hold you, wife, / But you must needs fetch words from Westminster" (1.1.26–27). He identifies her language as the diction of a gadabout, a gossip; of a woman who cannot be contained at home. His instruction in diction, intended to establish his authority and re-

assert the discursive boundaries of class, insists upon a patriarchal nomenclature for the faults of women and the presence of universal truth
in the particular case:

> . . . cracks in duty and obedience?
> Term'em e'en so, sweet wife.
> As there is no woman made without a flaw,
> Your purest lawns have frays and cambrics bracks.
>
> (1.1.33–36)

The Yellowhammers would proceed from symptom to cause, from
the leak to the "crack," thence to the effective social remedy: "'tis a
husband solders up all cracks" (36). (The process may be particularly
effective for a daughter whose dancing her mother has likened to that
of "a plumber's daughter" [21].) But while the Yellowhammers clearly
envision the therapeutic process as mechanical—plugging the hole,
mending the leaky pipe-joint with the husbandly tool—we are bound
to regard it as ideological. And the seemingly gratuitous authority lesson which Yellowhammer has provided his wife reinforces the point:
in this play, men discharge virtually all the responsibilities of culture,
including the primary one—the containment of women.

In act 5, after trying unsuccessfully to elope by boat with Touchwood Junior, Moll pretends to sicken and die. Once again, her parents
offer the diagnosis of nature to mask the constrictions of parental authority: "she has," her father asserts, "catch'd her bane o'th'water"
(5.2.7). We supply the contextually subversive pun on the knight's
name. The counterfeit illness itself complete with a climactic swoon is
never offered up to diagnosis in the play; but it was fully diagnosable
by current medical and popular thinking as suffocation of the mother,
that is a literal rising up of the cold, sexually deprived uterus toward
the hotter organs; the sufferer fainted from the compression of heart
and lungs (Eccles 77). Perhaps Middleton's audience recognized in
Moll's counterfeit swoon not only a literary allusion but a gynecological symptom—the simulated fulfillment of her mother's diagnosis at
the beginning of the play—since the swoon, like the tears, was symptomatic of hysterical sexual frustration. Only by imitating Juliet and
undergoing a false funeral does Moll escape her parents' discursive tyranny in a marriage to Touchwood Junior.

Yet Moll is a more obedient member of her culture, a more easily contained vessel, than her parents are able to recognize. Unlike Juliet, she has never initiated any part of her secret courtship, elopement, death, and resurrection but has taken direction from her resourceful lover and his powerful brother. In the discourse of this play, she merely makes a choice between kinds of male potency—refusing Sir Walter, her "bane o'th'water," for the more vital fluid of her lover. Hers is a resurrection from drowning in the wrong water, but it is a resurrection ritualized and sanctioned by communal waters—the tears of the mostly female mourners. The reported deaths of the lovers "makes a hundred weeping eyes, sweet gossip," Lady Kix tells a companion at the funeral (5.4.22). The communal overflow, releasing the lovers from the Yellowhammers' restrictive containment, becomes the signal for the lovers to arise. Moll's tears have been transferred to the community and her sexual deprivation has been remedied by her husband's controlling potency. While he says he has been momentarily rendered speechless by joy—"My joy wants utterance" (5.4.45)—his return to self-command is defined as ejaculation—sex becoming discourse—and thus as sexual command. "Utter all"—that is, speak and ejaculate—"at night," his brother tells him (5.4.46). Just as Lady Kix's weeping has been controlled by Touchwood Senior's sexual power, so Moll's has been suppressed by the junior brother's.

Like the daughters of Danaus in Whitney's emblem, the leaky women of Middleton's Cheapside cannot by themselves keep their barrels full or their holes plugged. Attempting such impossible tasks becomes the self-imposed responsibility of the patriarchal order. In this play, moreover, the tasks themselves offer patriarchy the distinct advantage of promoting unusually stable male alliances—between Master Allwit and Sir Walter; between Touchwood Senior and the Kixes; between the Touchwood brothers themselves—to get the job done. But, while the play seems to suggest that these male alliances are forged by necessity—a necessity occasioned by female unreliability and appetite—we can perceive in the construction of women as leaky vessels the powerful interests of patriarchal ideology. At the end, the leaky vessels of Cheapside have been contained, perhaps because they, unlike Win Littlewit or Mrs. Overdo, have not ventured into the free space of a fairground to follow mother Ursula and find the public chamberpot, Ursula's revenge.

Notes

1. The fine essay by Peter Stallybrass, "Patriarchal Territories: The Body Enclosed," was published too late in 1986 for me to incorporate its argument into mine, except for two citations below, but the reader of both essays will note how closely Stallybrass's opposition between the closed and open female bodies provides strong contextual corroboration for my analysis of the leaking body. I would also like to thank Boyd Berry, to whom I owe the reference to John Northbrooke, and Theodore Leinwand, who reminded me of Linda Woodbridge's work on the gossips' meeting.

2. Jonathan Goldberg offers an analogous reading of these letters from a somewhat different perspective, arguing that if Malvolio "is the scapegoat for anxieties about class and social hierarchies, he is also the locus for the unstable social constructions of sexuality" (217). The logic which I have educed from Elias's argument about manners suggests that Malvolio is disgraced not only by extracting a shameful alphabet from the counterfeit letter but by appearing not to know the transgressive limits of a behavior becoming increasingly forbidden and shameful.

3. See Stallybrass on the contrasting signs of the chaste women—silence, the closed mouth—and the signs of the whore—"her linguistic 'fullness'" and her open mouth (126–27).

4. It is important to note, however, that other symbolic and iconographic uses of bodily fluids were both positive in connotation and complexly linked to gender difference. Caroline Walker Bynum has argued that—at least in the late medieval period—"theologians and natural philosophers assumed considerable mixing of the genders" (435) not only with respect to physical attributes but specifically in the symbolic depiction of a nurturant Christ, whose bleeding wound becomes identified with Mary's lactating breast (427–30).

Works Cited

Bakhtin, Mikhail. *Rabelais and His World.* Trans. Hélène Iswolsky. Bloomington: Indiana UP, 1984.

Burke, Peter. *Popular Culture in Early Modern Europe.* London: Temple Smith, 1978.

Bynum, Caroline Walker. "The Body of Christ in the Later Middle Ages: A Reply to Leo Steinberg." *Renaissance Quarterly* 39 (1986): 399–439.

Crawford, Patricia. "Attitudes to Menstruation in Seventeenth-Century England." *Past and Present* 91 (1981): 47–73.

Davis, Natalie Zemon. *Society and Culture in Early Modern France: Eight Essays.* Stanford: Stanford UP, 1975.

Eccles, Audrey. *Obstetrics and Gynaecology in Tudor and Stuart England.* Kent: Kent State UP, 1982.

Elias, Norbert. *The Civilizing Process.* Vol. 1 of *The History of Manners.* 1939. Trans. Edmund Jephcott. New York: Pantheon, 1978.

Fletcher, J. *The Differences, Causes, and Judgments of Urine.* London, 1623. STC 11063.

Goldberg, Jonathan. "Textual Properties." *Shakespeare Quarterly* 37 (1986): 213–17.

Haynes, Jonathan. "Festivity and the Dramatic Economy of Jonson's *Bartholomew Fair.*" *ELH* 51 (1984): 645–68.

Jonson, Ben. *Bartholomew Fair.* Ed. Eugene M. Waith. The Yale Ben Jonson. New Haven: Yale UP, 1963.

Lacan, Jacques. *Ecrits: A Selection.* Trans. Alan Sheridan. New York: Norton, 1977.

MacDonald, Michael. *Mystical Bedlam: Madness, Anxiety, and Healing in Seventeenth-Century England.* Cambridge: Cambridge UP, 1981.

McLaren, Dorothy. "Marital Fertility and Lactation, 1570–1720." *Women in English Society, 1500–1800.* Ed. Mary Prior. London: Methuen, 1985. 22–46.

Maclean, Ian. *The Renaissance Notion of Woman: A Study in the Fortunes of Scholasticism and Medical Science in European Intellectual Life.* Cambridge: Cambridge UP, 1980.

Middleton, Thomas. *A Chaste Maid in Cheapside.* Ed. R. B. Parker. The Revels Plays. London: Methuen, 1969.

Northbrooke, John. *A Treatise.* London, ?1577. STC 18670. Ed. Arthur Freeman. New York: Garland, 1974.

Shakespeare, William. *Twelfth Night.* Ed. J. M. Lothian and T. W. Craik. The Arden Shakespeare. London: Methuen, 1975.

_____. *The Winter's Tale.* Ed. J. H. Pafford. The Arden Shakespeare. London: Methuen, 1966.

Skelton, John. *The Complete English Poems.* Ed. John Scattergood. New Haven: Yale UP, 1983.

Stallybrass, Peter. "Patriarchal Territories: The Body Enclosed." *Rewriting the Renaissance: The Discourses of Sexual Difference in Early Modern Europe.* Ed. Margaret W. Ferguson, Maureen Quilligan, and Nancy J. Vickers. Chicago: U of Chicago P, 1986. 123–42.

Strong, Roy C. *Portraits of Queen Elizabeth.* Oxford: Clarendon, 1963.

Tilley, Morris Palmer. *A Dictionary of Proverbs in Seventeenth Century England.* Ann Arbor: U of Michigan P, 1950.

Whitney, Ge[o]ffrey. *A Choice of Emblemes.* 1586. STC 25438. Facsimile rpt. The English Experience, 161. Amsterdam: Da Capo, 1969.

Woodbridge, Linda. *Women and the English Renaissance: Literature and the Nature of Womankind, 1540–1620.* Chicago: U of Illinois P, 1984.

Moral Conceptions of Sexual Love in Elizabethan Comedy

MARY BETH ROSE

I

CRITICS HAVE NOTED OFTEN that Elizabethan romantic comedy is a dramatic form which can be distinguished as a generic celebration of marriage. Contrasting the erotic teleology of romantic comedy (which she calls "pure comedy") with the moral corrective of satire and the tragicomic emphasis on plot, Helen Gardner has written that

> The great symbol of pure comedy is marriage, by which the world is renewed, and its endings are always instinct with a sense of fresh beginnings. Its rhythm is the rhythm of the life of mankind, which goes on and renews itself as the life of nature does. . . . The young wed, so that they may become in turn the older generation, whose children will wed, and so on, as long as the world lasts. The end of comedy declares that life goes on.[1]

I would like to acknowledge my gratitude to the Monticello College Foundation and the Newberry Library, whose generous support made possible the research for this essay.

1. Helen Gardner, *"As You Like It,"* in *Modern Shakespearean Criticism,* ed. Alvin B. Kernan (New York, 1970), pp. 193–194.

In romantic comedy, then, the sexual love that leads to marriage sym-
bolizes the ongoing life of society, which, in Elizabethan terms, in turn
suggests a spiritually integrated cosmos. But this configuration, which
Shakespeare discerned and exploited until it had been thoroughly
imagined and expressed, was by no means always developed or even
implicit in earlier Elizabethan comedies. John Lyly was the first Elizabethan playwright to clarify the aesthetic realization that the theme of
erotic love could be used to organize the disparate materials of early
romantic comedy into a coherent design; yet, unlike the comedies of
Shakespeare, Lyly's plays never acclaim sexual love and rarely end in a
festive celebration of marriage. This essay seeks to trace the ways in
which Elizabethan comic form developed in plays by Lyly, Robert
Greene, and Shakespeare in accordance with the precise erotic teleology
Gardner describes by relating changes in the dramatic representation
of love and marriage to similar patterns of change in conceptualiza-
tions of love and marriage in the nondramatic literature, particularly
in Elizabethan courtesy and conduct books.

Two salient modes of conceptualizing erotic love and marriage
emerge from the complex controversy over changing sexual values articulated in Elizabethan conduct literature: a dualistic sensibility, in
which sexual love is idealized beyond physical existence on the one
hand or derided as lust on the other, and which views marriage as a
necessary evil; and a more realistic, multifaceted sensibility, which,
while retaining much of the skepticism about erotic love contained in
the first view, nevertheless begins to conceive of affectionate marriage
with great respect as the basis of an ordered society. Taking into account the inevitable overlapping and intermingling of shifting values
and attitudes, historians have shown that in late-sixteenth- and early-
seventeenth-century England, the second sensibility was gaining
ground over the first.[2] What I would like to suggest is a parallel development between this shift in *mentalité* and the changing representations of sexual love and marriage that characterize the growth of Elizabethan comedy: Lyly, whose comic structures embody the dualistic

2. This change in sensibility is particularly apparent in the upper and middle classes,
to whom my remarks are limited. The most comprehensive treatment of this subject is
Lawrence Stone, *The Family, Sex, and Marriage in England 1500–1800* (New York,
1977).

sensibility, was unable to develop romantic comedy beyond a certain point; while Greene developed the form to a limited extent and Shakespeare brought it to fruition with *As You Like It* and *Twelfth Night* by representing a more complex vision, in which sexual love and marriage have increased significantly in moral stature and prestige.

My purpose in comparing changing moral and sexual attitudes to altering dramatic representations of sexual love is not, therefore, to demonstrate causal connections between them, but to show that the same concepts and values which inform the one can be seen as informing the other; and that the shifts discernible in one form are similarly discernible in the other. As a result my method involves suggesting reciprocal influences among kinds of evidence often thought to have a different value: the imagination of the individual artist, the aesthetic requirements of the comic form, and contemporary moral and religious writings about love and marriage. By synthesizing some familiar interpretations of the plays with the richly suggestive discoveries of historians, the following essay attempts to formulate a new perspective on the cultural context and development of Elizabethan comedy.

II

Lawrence Stone and other historians of the relations between the sexes have demonstrated convincingly that the institution of marriage enjoyed a considerable rise in prestige in post-Reformation England.[3] The precise origins and chronology of this change in sensibility are as difficult to determine as is the actual sexual conduct of medieval and Renaissance men and women. In terms not of actual behavior, but of the moral prestige granted to sexual love and marriage, it is clear, however, that those medieval values governing sexual relations which were officially articulated by homilists, theologians, and poets were predominantly ascetic. Although H. A. Kelly argues in his book *Love and Marriage in the Age of Chaucer* that a commonsensical, concrete

---

3. See, for example, Stone, pp. 135–138. Also see Christopher Hill, "The Spiritualization of the Household," in *Society and Puritanism in Pre-Revolutionary England* (London, 1964), pp. 443–481, and C. L. Powell, *English Domestic Relations 1487–1653* (New York, 1917).

counterideal of married love existed among ordinary people in the
Middle Ages, he concedes that homilists praised only the abstract aspects of love and marriage and actively discouraged the as-yet unmarried from ever marrying at all. Sexual love was, needless to say, considered out of the question as a basis for marriage, which was regarded by
the upper classes as an alliance for the enhancement of family property and as an outlet for the avoidance of fornication. Indeed sexual love
was virtually out of the question, period. It is true that St. Jerome, who
felt that love between men and women was at best "to be endured, not
enjoyed," and preferably "to be avoided if at all possible," represents
the extreme of medieval opinion; nevertheless carnal love, even for
purposes of procreation, was usually conceptualized as tainted with
some odor of sin and was, at best, conceived of as morally neutral.[4]
Celibacy was upheld as the ideal behavior to be emulated, not only by
priests and nuns, but by the whole community.[5] Even St. Paul, cited so
often later by sixteenth- and seventeenth-century Protestant preachers as the main scriptural authority in their vehement defenses of marriage, could be seen to consider marriage as merely a necessary evil:
"For I would that all men were even as I myself am . . . [i.e., celi-
bate]," he writes in 1 Corinthians, "It is good for them if they abide
even as I doe. But if they cannot absteine, let them marrie: for it is better to marrie then to burne" (vii.7–9).

During the Renaissance, conjugal loyalty and affection replaced
celibacy as the officially idealized pattern of sexual conduct.[6] Yet like
other forms of medieval thought, much of the consciousness of love,
marriage, and sexuality persisted into the Renaissance.[7] Stone reports
that "marriage among the property-owning classes in sixteenth-century England was . . . a collective decision of family and kin, not an in-

4. Henry Ansgar Kelly, *Love and Marriage in the Age of Chaucer* (Ithaca, N.Y.: 1975), pp. 247, 284–285, 300, 315.

5. Kelly, p. 315, and Stone, p. 135.

6. Stone, pp. 135–138, and Hill, pp. 443–481. Also see Louis B. Wright, *Middle-Class Culture in Elizabethan England* (Chapel Hill, N.C., 1935), pp. 201–227; Ian Ma-clean, *The Renaissance Notion of Woman* (Cambridge, Eng., 1980), p. 59; and Carroll Camden, *The Elizabethan Woman* (New York, 1952), pp. 109–148.

7. Linda T. Fitz, "What Says the Married Woman: Marriage Theory and Feminism in the English Renaissance," *Mosaic,* XIII (Winter 1980), 1–22; and Peter Laslett, *The World We Have Lost* (New York, 1965), pp. 130–131.

dividual one . . . Property and power were the predominant issues which governed negotiations for marriage."[8] Individual, rather than parental choice of a spouse, let alone prior affection between potential mates, seemed foolish, undesirable. The eminent sixteenth-century humanist Vives, whose works were accessible in English, observes, for example, that "they that marry for love shall lead their life in sorrow."[9] Montaigne, whose translated essays were also available after 1603, is less hostile to erotic love than Vives; nevertheless he affirms what he construes to be the essential incompatibility of erotic love and marriage:

Love disdaineth a man should holde of other then himselfe, and dealeth but faintly with acquaintances begun and entertained under another title; as mariage is. Alliances, respects and meanes, by all reason, waigh as much or more, as the graces and beautie. A man doth not marie for himselfe, whatsoever he alledgeth; but as much or more for his posterity and familie. The use and interest of mariage concerneth our off-spring, a great way beyond us. Therefore doth this fashion please me, to guide it rather by a third hand, and by anothers sence, then our owne: All which, how much doth it dissent from amorous conventions? . . . *I see no mariages faile sooner, or more troubled, then such as are hudled up for amorous desires.* There are required more solide foundations, and more constant grounds . . . this earnest youthly heate serveth no purpose.[10]

Furthermore, while priestly celibacy no longer flourished as an idealized model of behavior after the Reformation, the distrust of sexual desire and the ideals of maidenly virtue—virginity—and wifely chastity continued to preoccupy the Renaissance imagination of the moral and spiritual life well into the seventeenth century.

It is worth dwelling briefly on the tremendous spiritual weight put on sexuality in the Renaissance. A good example is the emphasis placed on premarital female virginity. Many have argued that the perceived necessity for premarital female chastity, as well as the double standard of sexual morality, arose originally from the economic need

8. Stone, p. 87.
9. John Louis Vives, "Howe the mayde shall seeke an husbande," in *Instruction of a Christian Woman,* trans. Richard Hyrde (London, 1557), book I, chap. xvi.
10. Michel de Montaigne, *The Essayes,* trans. John Florio (London, 1603), p. 510.

to legitimize property for the purposes of inheritance;[11] however this
may be, the ideal of virginity accrued moral and theological overtones
and became for poets a useful means of dramatizing female social and
spiritual life. One need only think of Britomart, Spenser's embattled
knight of chastity, dueling her way through a world full of erotic peril.
In a courtesy book entitled *Instruction of a Christian Woman* (1523)
and dedicated to Catherine of Aragon, Vives elaborates powerfully the
consequences that loss of virginity entails for a young woman:

Turn her which way she will, she shall find all things sorrowful and heavy,
wailing and mourning, and angry and displeasureful. What sorrow will her
kinfolks make, when every one shall think themselves dishonored by the
shame of that maid? What mourning, what tears, what weeping of the father
and mother and bringers up. Dost thou quite them with this pleasure for so
much care and labor? Is this the reward of thy bringing up? What cursing will
there be of her acquaintance. What mocking and babbling of those maids, that
envied her before. What a loathing and abhorring of those that loved her.
What flying of her company when every mother will keep not only their
daughters but also their sons from the infection of such an unthrifty maid. And
wooers also, if she had any, all flee away from her. . . . I rehearse the hate and
anger of folks for I know that many fathers have cut the throats of their daughters, brethren of their sisters, and kinsmen of their kinswomen.[12]

Could any young woman possibly have endured such an onslaught of
threatened damnation, social ostracism, personal guilt and despair,
open ridicule, and family catastrophe? In a chapter about when a maid
should leave the house (to which his answer is never, unless absolutely
necessary and, in that case, certainly never alone), Vives evokes a
world of sexual desire which, like the world of Spenser's Britomart, is
fraught with spiritual dangers. "Howsoever she turneth herself from
God unto men, whether she like or be liked of them, she forsaketh
Christ, and of Christe's spouse suddenly becometh an adulterer."[13]
This statement, striking in its lucidity, starkly conveys the perils of sexuality, the evils of it, and the human responsibility for it; Vives has here
clarified the association of sexuality with sin. Female entrance into the

11. Stone, p. 637, and Keith Thomas, "The Double Standard," *Journal of the History
of Ideas,* XX (1959), 195–216.
12. Vives, "Of the Kepying of virginitee and chastitee," book I, chap. xii.
13. Vives, "How the mayde shall behave hyr self forth abode," book I, chap. xii.

sexual world, whether through body or mind, by choice or unwittingly, whether by reciprocating male affections or merely remaining the passive object of them, is equivalent to sin, *is* sin. Even when sexual love is viewed with a less holy and foreboding gloom, it is often regarded instead as bitterly degrading, bestial, and absurd. Once again we can turn to Montaigne for the liveliest and most direct articulation of this attitude:

> When all is done, I finde that *love is nothing els but an insatiate thirst of enjoying a greedily desired subject* . . . which becometh faulty by immoderation and defective by indiscretion. . . . Now considering oftentimes the ridiculous tickling, or titilation of this pleasure, the absurd, giddie and harebrained motions wherewith it . . . agitates . . . that unadvised rage, that furious and with cruelty enflamed visage in loves lustfull and sweetest effects: and then a grave, sterne, severe surly countenance in so fond-fond an action . . . I beleeve that which *Plato* sayes to be true, that *man was made by the Gods for them to toy and play withall.* . . . And that nature in mockery leaft us the most troublesome of our actions the most common: thereby to equal us, and without distinction to set the foolish and the wise, us and the beasts. . . . In all other things you may observe decorum, and maintaine some decencie: . . . this cannot only be imagined, but vicious or ridiculous.[14]

Moral bankruptcy and degeneracy, fear, humiliation, and a kind of ridiculous madness: what fools these mortals be! Such distressing associations are made over and over again in Renaissance discussions of the place of sexuality in social and moral life. But were there not more positive conceptions of erotic love, beyond, that is, such occasional, begrudging tributes as Robert Burton's parenthetical concession that love "by a perpetual generation makes and preserves mankind, propagates the Church"?[15] One answer, of course, is that just as classical writers had treated love both philosophically and sensually, so Christian writers recognized both a sacred and a profane love.[16] This dualistic, idealizing cast of thought granted love the highest respect and prestige when it was conceived of either as separate from, or having transcended, sexual desire. I cannot do justice here to the profound

14. Montaigne, p. 527.
15. Robert Burton, *The Anatomy of Melancholy,* in *Seventeenth-Century Prose and Poetry,* ed. Alexander M. Witherspoon and Frank J. Warnke (New York, 1963), p. 192.
16. John Charles Nelson, *The Renaissance Theory of Love* (New York, 1958), p. 67.

and complex legacy that the Renaissance inherited from this mode of conceptualizing love, which had been articulated systematically in Christian orthodoxy.[17] But of the many literary variations on the theme of this tradition which are of immediate relevance to English Renaissance drama, Neoplatonism and the related phenomenon of Petrarchism are salient.

The ideas of the Florentine Neoplatonist Marsilio Ficino are expanded and popularized in Castiglione's *The Courtier,* which was translated by Thomas Hoby in 1561. In the fourth book of *The Courtier* the favored figure of the ladder of love, inherited from Plato's *Symposium,* is set forth in eloquent detail. In this image the beauty of the female beloved inspires the male lover to ascend by stages a metaphorical ladder which will lead him to the beauty that "shall make a universal conceite, and bring the multitude of them to the unitie of one alone, that is generally spred over all the nature of man." Now able to ascend by contemplating its own beauty, the soul of the lover then transcends this stage, along with all earthly things, to gaze on "the maine sea of the pure heavenly beautie." Castiglione allows for the appropriateness of sensual love in the young; but the mature, civilized society has transcended sexuality. While the female beloved serves the crucial but limited function of original inspiration, the true Neoplatonic lover will keep "alwaies fast in minde, that the bodie is a most diverse thing from beautie, and not onely not encreaseth, but diminisheth the perfection of it." The speech in which the ladder of love is described includes many of the characteristically idealistic love themes: sacrifice (in this case of the soul to God through burning or consuming of the body); liberation from the self; transcendence; transformation; the ideals of contemplation and union with God.[18]

Sears Jayne points out that Platonism became permanently associated in the English mind with Petrarchism.[19] The Neoplatonic ideas of love both as "a cosmic phenomenon informing the universe and ap-

17. See, for example, Irving Singer, *The Nature of Love* (New York, 1965); Maurice Valency, *In Praise of Love* (New York, 1975); and Denis de Rougemont, *Love in the Western World,* trans. Montgomery Belgion (New York, 1956).

18. Baldesar Castiglione, *The Courtier,* trans. Thomas Hoby (London, 1588). See book 4, which Hoby describes as telling "of honest love."

19. Cited in Neal L. Goldstein, "*Love's Labor's Lost* and the Renaissance Vision of Love," *SQ,* XXV (Summer 1974), 339.

parent in nature," and as an independent force transcending nature and creating its own world directly influenced the Petrarchan tradition through Castiglione and Pietro Bembo.[20] As in Castiglione, the beloved in Petrarch's poetry remains an idealized, unattainable icon. Although in Petrarch the lover oscillates "between restrained wooing and distant adoration," actual union is nevertheless envisaged only in dreams. Leonard Forster stresses the central importance of the lover's experience of love as dual, as "interpenetration of pleasure and pain. . . . The elaboration and exploitation of antitheses is the essence of Petrarchism."[21] The Petrarchan style and diction, which reached England via Wyatt and Surrey in the first half of the sixteenth century, was most notably exploited in the latter half by Sidney, Spenser, and Shakespeare and their followers in the numerous, fashionable sonnet sequences of that period, sequences which created an image of a courtly, melancholy, obsessive lover, doomed to frustration and rejection, a little foolish for putting so much hope and faith in the desire of a woman.

According to the mentality being described, sexual desire, even when conceived as leading to a consciousness of the divine, was never considered beneficial or good in itself. Loved women were better left exalted, remote, and untouched. It is therefore not surprising to discover that where idealization of women occurred, misogyny was rarely far behind. With significant exceptions, English Petrarchism and its corollary, anti-Petrarchism, tend to articulate that consciousness which simultaneously exalts and idealizes the image of Woman while regarding actual women with neglect or contempt.[22] Notwithstanding the persistence of this mode of thought in our culture, what is both new and significant in the English Renaissance is that this dualizing, polarizing consciousness begins to break down, to lose its authority as the predominant, or at least as the only, articulated view of women and sexuality. A burgeoning awareness of a more complex, problematic moral and emotional reality ensues; and it is in this changing moral

---

20. Leonard Forster, *The Icy Fire: Five Studies in European Petrarchism* (Cambridge, Eng., 1969), p. 21.

21. *Ibid.,* pp. 1–60.

22. Regarding exceptions, see, for example, C. S. Lewis's discussion of Spenser as the poet of married love in *The Allegory of Love* (Oxford, 1958), pp. 297–360.

atmosphere that romantic comedy, with its celebration of married love, comes into its own as a dramatic form.

In the development under discussion, the work of John Lyly represents an encounter between the dualistic, idealizing Petrarchan sensibility to which he was heir and the more realistic, multifaceted view of married love which was beginning to announce its presence both in the drama and in the moral and religious outpourings of the surrounding society.[23] Lyly was the first great Elizabethan playwright to recognize the importance of the erotic love theme to the coherence and design of his plays; consequently he was the first to organize early romantic comedy by subordinating the disruptive medley of spectacle, song, ritual, pageant, magic, folklore, slapstick, and farce which comprised it to a central love story. Lyly emerged from the tradition of aristocratic early-sixteenth-century humanism in which literature existed in service to the prince and the state, not as an independent profession. As G. K. Hunter has demonstrated, Lyly's values and beliefs, his apparent disdain of writing for the increasingly powerful, popular public theater, doomed him to outlive his early success and to die in disappointed poverty, having hopelessly depended on favors from Queen Elizabeth that never were forthcoming.[24] But the anachronistic humanist idealism which tied Lyly to an outmoded literary tradition caused him to conceive of his plays as select entertainments, dramatizations of the elegant, refined manners of a stately court; as a result, while Lyly retained many of the native traditions that gave Elizabethan comedies their vitality, he also imposed on them a new sense of integration, balance, and grace. Nevertheless, the lack of flexibility in his conception of sexual love prevented Lyly from developing romantic comedy in accordance with the changing sensibility around him.

23. Cf. Robert Weimann, *Shakespeare and the Popular Tradition in the Theater,* ed. Robert Schwartz (Baltimore, 1978), p. 197: "It is a new sense of the interdependence of character and society, and a fully responsive interplay between dramatic speech and dramatic action in the process of reproducing the cause and effect of human behavior that defines 'realism' in the Renaissance theater." Weimann also makes the point (p. 173) that Lyly stood "at the very threshold" of such a complex apprehension, remaining "too bewildered to realize that the contradictions (which he points out) are about to yield a new and superior unity."

24. G. K. Hunter, *John Lyly: The Humanist as Courtier* (London, 1962).

In his early success, *Euphues* (1578), and its successor, *Euphues and his England* (1580), Lyly creates an image of love and sexuality which he develops throughout his plays, and which is recognizable as emanating from that polarizing consciousness which posits idealization of women or misogyny, chaste worship or lust, as the only possibilities for love. In these two tracts, Lyly establishes a prose style which, with its witty similitudes, puns, antitheses, and parallelisms, mirrors his ideal of a learned, courtly, graceful, and sophisticated society. As a means of recommending manners and morals to their readers, both of these courtesy books wittily relate the adventures of two elegant young men, Euphues and Philautus, whose coming of age Lyly depicts as an ongoing encounter with temptation in the form of love and desire. In the indiscriminate, capricious fickleness of most of the female characters and the continually wrongheaded, hopelessly infatuated state of Philautus, Lyly depicts sexual desire as a compulsive, impersonal, and ridiculous passion, which can be understood only in direct contrast to reason and wisdom. "What new skirmishes dost thou now feele between reason and appetite, love and wisdom, danger and desire?" Philautus asks, rhetorically echoing conventional Petrarchan sentiments and antitheses.[25] All in all we are expected to perceive that "the disease of love . . . is impatient, the desire extreame, whose assaultes neyther the wise can resist by pollicie nor the valiant by strength."[26] One wants to protest that the sensible could ignore this self-indulgence by intelligence, so utterly self-centered, obsessive, and infantile an experience does love become when Lyly presents it. As might be expected, Euphues' heroism consists in his transcending sexual desire, his realization that "the effect of love is faith, not lust, delightful conference, not detestable concupiscence, which beginneth with folly and endeth with repentance."[27] At the end of *Euphues and his England* we find this polarized perspective figured forth concretely. In a concluding diatribe Euphues, who has returned to Italy from a visit to England determined to devote the remainder of his life to soli-

25. John Lyly, *Euphues and his England,* in *The Complete Works of John Lyly* (Oxford, 1902), II, 89.
26. *Ibid.,* p. 112.
27. *Ibid.,* p. 158.

tary idealization of the Virgin Queen, exhorts the Italian women, whom he misogynistically maligns, to be like the English women, whom he sentimentally idealizes. Philautus ends up in a second-best, rebound marriage that pointedly does not ensue from any of his perpetual courtships.

This configuration, in which love remains a marginal experience, finding fulfillment either in the dream life or in an unsatisfactory lowering of expectations, becomes a structural principle in Lyly's plays. *Sapho and Phao* (1584) concludes with the image of an idolized female monarch, victorious over desire and remaining an object of the chaste, constant adoration of a solitary admirer and subject. Although *Endymion* (1588) ends with several happy couplings, the hero of the play conceives an impossible, idealizing love for the Moon who, descending to the action in the form of a chaste and benevolent queen, rewards the hero for his solitary devotion by restoring his youth and granting him permission to worship her from afar for the rest of his life with celibate, contemplative, Neoplatonic joy.

Lyly's preference, clearly, is for sublimation; and his habitual tendency is to dissociate sexual love, which he distrusts, from social order, which he idealizes. In Lyly's earliest play, *Campaspe* (1584), a distracted Alexander the Great at last magnanimously transcends his love for a lower-class woman who does not return it. The potential threat to the orderly, efficient running of society implicit in Alexander's sexual desire is domesticated to a harmless, frivolous interlude, a digression in the career of his greatness. Lyly replicates this situation in *Sapho and Phao*: the virtuous monarch, Sapho, overcomes her unseemly attraction for a lower-class boatman, Phao, and usurps the capricious authority of Venus by capturing Cupid, in an elegant victory over desire.

In Lyly, then, sexual desire, while powerful and unavoidable, cannot be incorporated in a civil, humane society. Instead it must be conquered, overcome. Lyly accounts mythically for the inevitable association of chaos and sexuality in one of his most absurd, charming, and misogynistic plays, *The Woman in the Moon* (1593). Here his conception of female weakness and duplicity is allegorized in Pandora, a drastic parody of the remote, idealized Petrarchan lady. Pandora, a sort of ur-woman, is created by Nature and then abandoned to the whimsical mercy of the envious planets. In a mad, obsessive, and uncivil chase, several shepherds pursue the helplessly victimized, indiscriminate, perpetually inconstant and deceptive Pandora through a series of comically futile attempts to possess her. In one of Lyly's repeated images of sexual desire, Pandora, like the heroine of *Euphues,* ends by being attracted to a clown.

In spite of Pandora's outrageous behavior, the real cause of these ridiculous effects is actually desire itself. The play begins with an image of the longing shepherds kneeling to Nature, begging and praying for the creation of a female. The three reasons which the shepherds give for desiring a woman turn out to be the very reasons cited in the Elizabethan *Book of Common Prayer* as the justifications for marriage: the procreation of children; the avoidance of fornication; and the need for companionship.[28] Nevertheless, marriage, if and when it enters the scene at all, is not granted much prestige in a Lyly play. The shepherds in *The Woman in the Moon* end by praising a single life, while Pandora is assigned to permanent residence in the moon—remote and heavenly, but also wayward, fickle, and false.

It should be emphasized that, although erotic love which, with one exception, is always Lyly's subject, is continually presented by him as a threat to the brilliant, graceful society patterned in Euphuistic prose, the tone of his comedies is invariably delicate, witty, and light. This refinement of mood is partially achieved by the ordered introduction of that mixture of musical, magical, folkloric, allegorical, and mythological material which Elizabethan comic playwrights loved: singing and dancing; magic fountains and wells; Ovidian transformations; gods and goddesses; fairies and monsters; ugly, wise old hags who speak with the cynical clairvoyance of desire. All of these characters and motifs, woven together with witty repartee, constitute not a narrative of rising intensity with which we are asked to identify, but a series of static tableaux, balanced against one another, which we are asked to admire.[29]

Lyly's allegorical characters and static, balanced scenes serve as emotional distancing devices. M. C. Bradbrook has noted aptly that in

28. *The First and Second Prayer Books of Edward VI* (1549; rpt. London, 1949), pp. 252–258.

29. Cf. Hunter, p. 103.

Lyly's comedies passion is merely a postulate;[30] the evocation of felt
emotion is not part of the playwright's courtly representation of love
as a wooing game, a witty lark which provides an amusing, if occasionally dangerous, diversion from the serious activities of society. When
erotic love is first appropriated from the Petrarchan lyric and begins to
be dramatized, it is seen as abstract, magical, playful.

Along with the fact that erotic love is dramatized abstractly as a
frivolous game, I believe there is also another reason that Lyly's basically negative and skeptical portrayal of love and sexuality never violates the brittle gaiety of his comedies. Although sexual desire, whether or not it leads to marriage, is viewed by Lyly and many others as
dangerous, humiliating, anarchic, and absurd, still the consequences
of indulging it appear determined beforehand. There is no need to
take a complicated, certainly not a suspenseful view of the matter; the
moral position of sexuality is fixed and predictable: "All this the world
knows . . . well." What I am suggesting is that the consciousness that
polarizes love is inherently undramatic.[31] As has been noted, this di-
chotomizing perspective, in which love becomes either degrading lust
or spiritual idealization, traditionally took poetic form in the lyric, a
genre designed to explore individual emotion, not to represent situ-
ational conflicts that drive toward resolution among various characters. Lyly's sense of dramatic conflict is epitomized in *Campaspe,* in
which, in a story of unrequited love, there is never once dramatized a
scene alone between the frustrated, powerful lover Alexander the
Great and his unresponsive, captive beloved Campaspe. As a result
love is depicted as an isolating, self-absorbed experience; the meaningful conflict is clarified not as an emotional struggle between Alexander and Campaspe, but as an abstract debate taking place in Alexander's mind, an intellectual exercise. Furthermore, in an imaginative
vision that, like Lyly's, idealizes the superiority of the elegant, contem-

30. M. C. Bradbrook, *The Growth and Structure of Elizabethan Comedy* (Cambridge, Eng., 1979), p. 65.

31. Cf. Robert J. Meyer, "'Pleasure Reconciled to Virtue': The Mystery of Love in Lyly's *Gallathea,*" *SEL,* XXI (1981), 193–208, in which the author correctly warns us not
to assess Lyly's "masque-like" and "non-developing" drama in terms other than its own.
My purpose is not to judge Lyly's dramaturgy as inferior, but to point out why, given his
moral perspective on sexual love and his structural techniques, Lyly could develop romantic comedy only to a limited extent.

plative soul, which has managed to remove itself from the muddy contingencies of physical existence, we must recognize a level of perception that is profoundly anticomic, particularly insofar as comedy is associated morally, emotionally, psychologically, and symbolically with birth, rebirth, the cycle of the seasons, with ongoing, natural life.[32]

Northrop Frye has clarified the necessary structural relationship between fulfilled sexual love and the form of romantic comedy as Shakespeare discerned and perfected it. Frye shows that the sense of vitality underlying comedy often takes the form of a drive toward identity which, in romantic comedy, is always erotic. The harsh and irrational laws which impede the fulfillment of the sexual drive of the hero and heroine must be overcome in order to bring about the freedom and self-knowledge which will form the basis of the new society symbolized in the festive conclusion. Romantic comedy, then, dramatizes that longing for a happy ending which is a wish-fulfillment fantasy of attaining all of one's desires with neither social, emotional, nor moral cost: "Jack shall have Jill / Nought shall go ill." It should be mentioned that by wish-fulfillment Frye does not mean escapism, although romantic comedy can serve that purpose. But Frye stresses instead what he calls "an imaginative model of desire." In his comedies Shakespeare pits the world of individual imagination and sexual desire against the more tangible world of social and historical fact, causing the spectator to question the reality of both worlds and then reconciling the claims of both in a final, inclusive vision of the social and spiritual harmony symbolized in marriage.[33]

Interestingly, in a later play, *Mother Bombie* (1589), Lyly moves toward a comic plot in which wit and vitality *are* joined to sexual desire. But the emphasis in this play remains with the servants' intriguing, not with the inherent drama of erotic love that gives shape to romantic comedy. Love still is not represented as a felt emotion. Lyly consequently fails to unite love with marriage. G. K. Hunter believes, not

---

32. See Susanne K. Langer, *Feeling and Form* (New York, 1953), pp. 326–350.

33. Northrop Frye, "The Argument of Comedy," in *Modern Shakespearean Criticism,* ed. Kernan, pp. 165–173; *A Natural Perspective* (New York, 1965), pp. 118–126; and *Anatomy of Criticism* (Princeton, N.J., 1957), p. 184.

without justice, that what Lyly gains in narrative and integrative power in this play, he sacrifices in delicacy and grace.[34]

Yet the fact that Lyly moves in *Mother Bombie* toward an uncharac-
teristically festive conclusion celebrating marriage, no matter how unsuccessful the attempt, indicates that he is beginning to detect a more
profound pattern at the heart of the comic form. Although Lyly could
discern this possibility, though, his polarized conception of love and
sexuality prevents him from either fully imagining its ramifications or
realizing them artistically. These achievements instead can be found to
coexist in the drama with a different set of articulated beliefs which,
while retaining much of the Renaissance sense of the wicked bestiality
and folly of sexual desire, nevertheless included these skeptical elements in a larger configuration that unites love with marriage and conceives of the combination as the foundation of an ordered society. I am
not, of course, arguing that polarized conceptions of love and sexuality expressed in Neoplatonic and Petrarchan patterns and images disappeared from post-Lylyan Elizabethan comedy, but that these conceptions became part of an expanded vision that incorporates the
dualistic sensibility but is not limited to it. The fact that romantic comedy, a dramatic form which celebrates erotic love and marriage, flourished in the environment of a new sensibility which embraced marriage both as the spiritual foundation of society and as the repository
of hope for personal happiness strongly suggests a parallel development between the increasingly complex, optimistic comic representations of eros that followed Lyly's plays and the more positive moral
conceptions of sexual love and marriage that were beginning to be articulated in Protestant conduct literature.

III

Whether or not it originated with the Protestant theologians of the
sixteenth and early seventeenth centuries, this optimistic vision of
marriage was articulated explicitly by them. As Lawrence Stone points
out, "sanctification of marriage—'holy matrimony'—was a constant
theme of Protestant sermons . . . which were directed to all classes in

---

34. Hunter, pp. 227–228, 243.

British society."[35] Forty years ago, in a seminal article entitled "The Puritan Art of Love," William and Malleville Haller showed how "it was the Puritan preachers who set forth an ideal pattern of love and marriage based upon traditional Christian morality, vitalized for the popular imagination in terms of the English Bible, and adapted to the new conditions in which men were having to live."[36]

Reiterating the holiness of the married state, the Puritan preachers went about idealizing marriage and the family with all the fervid determination that their Catholic forefathers had lavished upon celibacy and virginity. The Puritans no longer felt the need to attack the prestige of celibacy: "There is no man now so dull as to think it is a sin to marry," Heinrich Bullinger announces confidently in the important *Golden Book of Christian Matrimony,* translated by Miles Coverdale in 1543.[37] In the Puritan outpourings of sermons, conduct books, and spiritual autobiographies, marriage becomes "the type and source of all human relations, the seminary and model of all polities, the church and the state in little, the image and reflection of Christ's union with his elect."[38] John Dod and Robert Cleaver's influential courtesy book, *A Godlie Form of Household Government* (1598), makes it plain that the proper running of one's household has become, like the preservation of virginity, a matter of the greatest spiritual importance, of salvation and damnation.[39]

Several salient themes mark those Puritan tracts which idealize marriage as the basis of an ordered society. First, rather than stressing the avoidance of fornication or even the procreation of children, these documents instead emphasize a third motive for marriage, which was added by Archbishop Thomas Cranmer to the *Book of Common Pray-*

---

35. Stone, pp. 135–136.

36. William and Malleville Haller, "The Puritan Art of Love," *HLQ,* V (1941–1942), 242.

37. Heinrich Bullinger, *The Golden Book of Christian Matrimony,* trans. Miles Coverdale (London, 1543). Cf. William Perkins, *Christian Oeconomie or Houshold Government* (London, 1631), III, 683. Perkins sees celibacy as a kind of punishment for those isolated and marginal figures who are unable to participate in normal social life.

38. William and Malleville Haller, p. 270.

39. John Dod and Robert Cleaver, *A Godlie Forme of Householde Government* (London, 1598). See, for example, "Epistle Dedicatorie."

er in 1549:[40] namely, companionship, or the relief of what Milton was later to call "that . . . God forbidden loneliness."[41] This new emphasis on the spiritual, rather than the physical quality of the marriage relation, along with the Puritan stress on the unique relationship between each individual and God, accompanied a recognition of the value of individual, rather than parental, choice of a marriage partner; the importance of the woman as helpmate and companion; the need for love in marriage; and, finally, the desire for personal happiness.

The Puritans linked happiness inseparably by hope to their ideal of love and marriage. When the Hallers remark drily that "it was a nice and subtle happiness these men conceived for themselves when they abandoned celibacy and embraced matrimony," they are referring to the latent contradictions in Puritan thought on this subject.[42] While insisting on the obedience and subordination of women, for example, the Puritans simultaneously stressed woman's importance, both as a companion to her husband and as supervisor of the newly exalted household.[43] Furthermore, the fact that Puritan doctrine gives woman's soul full equality with man's in the sight of God grants woman an undeniable dignity. Similarly, the Puritans continue to express a wholehearted distrust of sexual desire, dwelling—often with obsessive relish—on "abominable adulterers, stinking whoremongers, unclean fornicators, and detestable sodomites";[44] yet their perception that sex in the context of marriage—when practiced with moderation, of course, and as a solemn religious duty—is a "holy and undefiled action"[45] does grant consummated erotic love a distinct prestige. Further, while the Puritans strongly emphasize the importance of individual choice of a mate, deriding "the buying and selling of children among parents and the forced marriages,"[46] they nevertheless insist

40. See Stone, p. 136.

41. John Milton, *The Doctrine and Discipline of Divorce,* in *John Milton: Complete Poems and Prose,* ed. Merritt Y. Hughes (Indianapolis, 1957), p. 707.

42. William and Malleville Haller, p. 250.

43. Hill, pp. 443–481.

44. Thomas Becon, "Preface," in Bullinger, *The Golden Book Of Christian Matrimony.*

45. Perkins, p. 689.

46. Samuel Hieron, "The Marriage Blessing," in *The Sermons of Master Samuel Hieron* (London, 1635), p. 405.

on parental consent to a match. Finally, while the preachers reiterate that adultery, which should be punished with death, is the only reason to dissolve a marriage, the logical extension of their arguments about the absolute necessity of companionship results eventually in Milton's divorce tracts where, in arguments that surely would have horrified the preachers, Milton declares that incompatibility alone is sufficient cause to declare a marriage void.

The Puritan tracts therefore comprise a complex expression of double-mindedness: women must be totally subordinate while also being fully capable and equal; freedom of choice in marriage must be pursued, while absolute obedience to parents is maintained; individual personality and desire must be asserted and fulfilled, but spiritual authority and social stability must never be violated. The preachers did not acknowledge these potential contradictions, however much their unforeseen consequences may have revealed the strains inherent in them. It is one of the striking features of post-Lylyan romantic comedy that a similarly complex, apparently inconsistent or paradoxical awareness of the moral ambivalence of sexual desire, freedom of choice in marriage, and the social and spiritual position of women is both evoked and resolved; and that the reconciliation of these erotic tensions itself becomes the subject of the drama.

Robert Greene's popular comedy, *Friar Bacon and Friar Bungay,* written in 1589–1590 for the public theater, provides an excellent example of the reciprocal relation between this complex moral and sexual awareness and the development of romantic comedy. *Friar Bacon* is a characteristically chaotic medley, but, as in a Lyly comedy, a dominant love story gives the play its shape. Unlike Lyly, however, Greene develops the love story as a conflict which first arises from the diverse social, emotional, and sexual needs of three individuals and then moves through a suspenseful confrontation to a resolution in which all protagonists are married and happy.[47] A brief review of the plot will recall how this works.

---

47. See Norman Sanders, "The Comedy of Greene and Shakespeare," in *Stratford-Upon-Avon Studies,* III (1961), 40. Sanders observes that Greene realized the dramatic possibilities of love, "the surprises, psychological quirks and inconsistencies of human love which constitute its logic in art as in life."

Edward, the Prince of Wales, amusing himself by hunting in the country, has become infatuated with Margaret, a farmer's daughter, whom he has been attempting to seduce while disguised as a farmer. But Margaret is not interested and, his ploy failing, Edward sends his friend Lord Lacy to plead his case for him. Lacy and Margaret fall genuinely in love. The germane point about this material is that Greene works through the ensuing erotic complications to a wish-fulfillment conclusion in which "nought shall go ill" by dramatizing love and sexuality as variable, complex components in the moral and social lives of his characters. Edward, the future king of England, cannot possibly marry a commoner and is merely trifling with Margaret; unlike Lyly's Alexander, who overcomes his inappropriate infatuation in isolation and goes off alone to heroic martial exploits, Edward relents in a fully dramatized confrontation with Margaret and Lacy, from which he exits happily and honorably to marry the princess of his father's choice. Lacy, an earl, in turn proves *his* worthiness by ignoring conventional class barriers and marrying the farmer's daughter, Margaret of Fressingfield, the woman of his own personal choice. Interestingly, all of Edward's wooing is rhetorical, allegorical, and cast in the conventional antitheses of the Petrarchan lover: "Her bashful white mixed with the morning's red / Luna doth boast upon her love cheeks" (i.56–57), he recites, recalling the Renaissance sense of the abstract impersonality of sexual desire.[48] In contrast Lacy speaks of his love with a straightforward passion full of concrete references to his immediate, individual situation: addressing Edward he says, "Love taught me that your honor did but jest / That princes were in fancy but as men, / How that the lovely maid of Fressingfield / Was fitter to be Lacy's wedded wife / Than concubine unto the Prince of Wales" (viii.19–23).

Finally, it is Margaret's character—her wit, vitality, gratitude, and chastity—which gives love its felicity and dignity, therefore making possible the harmonious and stable society of the conclusion, in which the two marriages simultaneously take place. At one juncture Margaret, wrongly thinking Lacy has betrayed her, decides to become a nun. "And now I hate myself for that I loved / And doted more on him than

48. All citations are from Robert Greene, *Friar Bacon and Friar Bungay, Drama of the English Renaissance,* ed. Russell A. Fraser and Norman Rabkin (New York, 1976), pp. 359–382.

on my God . . . / All love is but lust, but love of heavens" (xiv.13–14, 18), she says, despairingly polarizing the position of love in the moral life. But the point is that Margaret *is* in despair when she makes this speech. The scene in which Lacy confronts her in her nun's habit and persuades her to marry him reads like a final farewell to medieval ideals of love and sexuality: "Either a solemn nunnery or the court; / God or Lord Lacy. Which contents you best. / To be a nun, or else Lord Lacy's wife?" (xiv.82–84). She replies, "The flesh is frail . . . / Off goes the habit of a maiden's heart; / And, seeing Fortune will . . . / All the shroud of holy nuns, farewell. / Lacy for me, if he will be my Lord" (xiv.86, 89–92).

Thus does *Friar Bacon* provide a fledgling example of the way in which Elizabethan comedy, like the Puritan marriage tracts, manages to have things both ways. In the courtship of Lacy and Margaret, individual choice and healthy sexual desire leading to marriage are conjoined and affirmed. But Greene also suggests the anarchy and folly of sexual desire by having two of Margaret's suitors destroy each other, as well as having Edward change costumes for a time with the Fool. Similarly, the Margaret-Lacy union recommends the harmonious breakdown of traditional class and rank barriers. But Edward's happy acceptance of an arranged marriage assures us that the courtly, aristocratic hierarchy, despite the welcome intrusion of the pastoral world, has remained intact. And, while it is the heroine's sexual powers—both of resistance and surrender—that have brought about these congenial conditions, she nevertheless acknowledges her subordination at the end of the play in a speech of joyfully grateful obedience. The private claims of individual personality and desire have been asserted, recognized, and assimilated into a public vision of social harmony.

Northrop Frye has remarked that "The presiding genius of comedy is Eros, and Eros has to adapt to the moral facts of society."[49] As we have seen, Lyly's polarized attitude toward eros as either deviant or ideal makes such an adjustment impossible. Greene takes romantic comedy a step further by working both with Lyly's perspective and with a different set of moral terms, one in which sexual love gains legitimacy as the true source of a coherent society. Although many elements in *Friar Bacon* remain chaotic and virtually unassimilable, the

49. Frye, *Anatomy of Criticism*, p. 181.

love story does give the play a distinct shape; consequently it moves significantly toward the vision of inclusiveness symbolized in marriage that is the crowning achievement of Elizabethan comedy. The movement from Lyly to Greene therefore comprises a development from a view of sexual love as abstract and impersonal, polarized, static, emotionally simple, and morally predictable to another vision which, while retaining much of the skepticism of the first perspective, incorporates it into a view of eros as more concrete, individualized, dynamic and suspenseful, essentially creative, and morally and emotionally complex.

It was by his unique ability both to discern and express this movement that Shakespeare brought romantic comedy to fruition. The early comedy *Love's Labor's Lost* (1594–1595) can be read in this light as a self-conscious comment on what Shakespeare perceived to be the structurally inevitable relationship between sexual values and the comic form. *Love's Labor's Lost* begins with the youthful King of Navarre and three lords swearing to retire from social life for three years, declaring war against their "own affections / And the huge army of the world's desires" (I.i.9–10).[50] The absurdity of this oath, which is broken immediately when four eligible young ladies appear, is in part a revelation of the absurdity of sexual desire itself, with its imperious, mechanical urgency. But more important than the silliness of the vow of celibacy is its unnaturalness and futility. "The sea will ebb and flow, heaven show his face: / Young blood doth not obey an old decree" (IV.iii.211–212), states Berowne, the wittiest of the young lords, at the moment of the play when self-knowledge begins. The rejection of celibacy, however, is not enough; the King, Berowne, and company also must learn the meaning of eros as itself a civilizing force, as well as a force that must be civilized. Shakespeare conveys their sophomoric callowness as an infatuation with verbal wit, an enchantment with their own cleverness. Upon deciding to pursue his heart's desire, Berowne immediately begins to posture and attitudinize in the conventional courtly manner of a Petrarchan lover, the manner which Edward assumes in *Friar Bacon.* The wit and charm engendered by this pose recall Lyly; as in Lyly, these qualities make up the substance of the

50. All citations are from William Shakespeare, *Love's Labor's Lost,* ed. Alfred Harbage (Baltimore, 1973).

play. But *Love's Labor's Lost* eventually rejects the courtly-love syndrome as sterile, shallow, and static. Love conceived as a frivolous game is simply inadequate: when the men approach the women in ridiculous disguises, the women see through them at once. Sensing that the men are not quite ready for grown-up reality which, in Elizabethan comedy means married love, the women, true to romance tradition, demand a year of separation complete with appointed tasks for their lovers before marriage can take place. The play therefore ends with the promise of marriage and not the actuality; the exchange of overblown rhetoric and narcissistic posturing for a plain style and shared experience has not yet come to pass. Consequently, the profound emotional and psychological demands of the comic form have not been completely met, a fact which is acknowledged directly in a brief conversation between Berowne and the King. Berowne grumbles,

> Our wooing doth not end like an old play;
> Jack hath not Jill. These ladies' courtesy
> Might well have made our sport a comedy.
> > KING
> Come, sir, it wants a twelvemonth and a day
> And then 'twill end.
> > BEROWNE
> That's too long for a play.
>
> (V.ii.864–868)

Shakespeare is announcing clearly here the structural secret of romantic comedy. This clarification of the relationship between fulfilled sexual desire and the comic form releases his ability to represent love as the complex spiritual, emotional, and psychic force that guarantees the perpetuation of society. What is stated so boldly in *Love's Labor's Lost* is fully dramatized in the great comedies that follow: for example, *Love's Labor's Lost* concludes with a song celebrating summer and winter and suggesting the alliance among fruitful sexual love, the predictably recurring cycle of the seasons, and the ongoing life of society; in ensuing comedies like *A Midsummer Night's Dream* (1595) and *As You Like It* (1599), this seasonal imagery becomes fully integrated into the action and poetry, clarifying the inevitable association between human sexuality and great creating nature.

The King of Castile, a character in *Friar Bacon,* remarks at one point that "Men must have wives and women will be wed" (xiii.20). "The world must be peopled" (II.iii.237)," says Benedick in *Much Ado About Nothing* (1598),[51] and there are no facts of life to which romantic comedy assigns greater value than these. As we have seen, this dramatic celebration of generative sexuality would not have been possible without a significant increase in the prestige of marriage, which historians have shown took place in the Renaissance. The movement out of the forest and back into court that dramatizes the harmonious alliance between sexual and social life which characterizes Shakespeare's pastoral comedies and which is also evident in *Friar Bacon* is never completed in a Lyly play. Shakespeare manages to develop Greene's optimism about sexual love and social life while eliminating his crude awkwardness, just as he refines Lyly's skepticism while retaining his grace and sense of design.

When viewed in terms of chronological development, Shakespeare's romantic comedies, like the Puritan marriage tracts, reveal an increasing sense of confidence that sexuality as individual assertion can be organized for society's good. At the same time—and the difference from modern conceptions of romantic love is crucial—sexual desire is never idealized for its own sake, never seen as by itself leading to personal happiness, never conceived as a positive value—as love— apart from marriage or procreation. The sexual anxiety that haunts and humiliates the Renaissance mind is always present in Shakespearean comedy, mocking the hope of unique or ideal love with its distrustful sense of the mechanical impersonality of sex. It is the imperative, arbitrary quality of sexual desire that makes it seem bestial and foolish to the Elizabethans; but in Shakespearean comedy submission to this imperative also joins humanity to nature in fruitful union. Sexuality therefore presents itself as a paradox: the human need for sexual relationships could lead to the mindless disruption of society; but without fulfillment of this need, there would be no ordered society at all.

Shakespeare's rendering of Berowne in *Love's Labor's Lost* as commenting with freely conscious knowingness on the absurdity of his

51. All citations are from William Shakespeare, *Much Ado About Nothing,* ed. Louis B. Wright and Virginia A. La Mar (New York, 1968).

own desires reveals an early effort to encompass the paradoxes of sex; but the abstract choreography of the play makes full dramatization of this issue impossible. The dramatic conflict of *A Midsummer Night's Dream* is, of course, set in motion by the issue of individual choice of a mate versus forced marriage. Although the young lovers triumph over irrational parental opposition to their desires, their victory is suffused with irony. While the lovers imagine they are defiantly asserting their individuality, the lack of differentiation among them and the mix-up in the forest clarify both their lack of uniqueness and the arbitrary quality of their choices. Demetrius never does know what hit him when he returns to Helena, any more than he ever did when he loved and rejected her in the first place. The arrogance and complacence of both Theseus and the young lovers are further qualified by the final assertion of the irrational, imaginative authority of the fairies; and the absurd, arbitrary, and mysterious nature of sexual desire is distilled in the joyful parody of Bottom's dream. While the tensions inherent in achieving erotic identity are never resolved, the suggestion in *A Midsummer Night's Dream* is that harmony is attained by the intervention of a benevolent, reconciliatory providence, which manifests itself on the social level in the final wedding feast.

As Arthur Kirsch has shown in his masterful analysis of *Much Ado About Nothing,* the tensions between freedom of choice and submission to authority are not necessarily imposed from without, but are rooted psychologically in sexuality itself.[52] Claudio and Hero never acknowledge these internal tensions between the immediate demands of their appetites and their deeper fears of surrender and rejection in love. They become engaged thoughtlessly, following the conventional clichés of society while never imagining the complex, mixed nature of sexual love; as a result of their psychological and emotional oblivion, they remain completely vulnerable to doubt and fear. Claudio and Hero are contrasted to the witty Beatrice and Benedick who, more thoughtful and consequently more wary of love's complications and paradoxes, pride themselves on their independence. But this brilliant couple needs the manipulative, busybody society of *Much Ado* to liberate them from the lonely trap of their uniqueness. Released from their

52. Arthur Kirsch, *Shakespeare and the Experience of Love* (Cambridge, Eng., 1981), pp. 40–70.

fears, they are free to join society by loving one another. Benedick and Beatrice are one of the first outstanding pairs of lovers in Shakespeare, the first to command complete sympathy because of their individuality. "Man is a giddy thing and this is my conclusion" (V.iv.120–121), Benedick announces at the end of *Much Ado,* revealing that the paradoxical awareness of sexual desire, enjoyed by the audience of *A Midsummer Night's Dream* with a kind of superior irony, is appropriated in *Much Ado* by Benedick and Beatrice themselves, who are humbly aware that in seeming to lose their individuality, they have in fact gained self-knowledge. In the sense of gratitude for life which is consequently released in them, Shakespeare exhibits the same awareness of the joyful mysteries of sexual love that he has always portrayed. But I believe that in individualizing Benedick and Beatrice to the extent that he has and in allowing them to achieve self-knowledge, he reveals an enhanced respect for the human dignity of sexual life as well.[53]

As I have tried to show in discussing the Puritan marriage tracts, the increasing moral prestige of love and marriage in the Renaissance was accompanied by a wider acknowledgment of the social, emotional, and spiritual dignity of women, whose freedoms of action and influence were nevertheless explicitly and severely limited. Developing an insight latent in Greene, Shakespeare seems to have assimilated these paradoxical facts imaginatively by giving women the heroic roles in many of his major comedies; their heroism consists, however, in choosing to preserve the status quo by wisely and lovingly assimilating themselves to it. Rosalind in *As You Like It* is the supreme romantic comic heroine.[54] With her realism, openness, and depth, she seems blessed with self-knowledge from the beginning, superbly adapted to exploit successfully the ironies of experience and desire. The mastery of her erotic quest is epitomized in her education of Orlando, in whom she instills a knowledge of the demands of love for a real woman in ac-

53. Cf. R. A. Foakes, "The Owl and the Cuckoo: Voices of Maturity in Shakespeare's Comedies," *Stratford-Upon-Avon Studies,* XIV (1972), 132; and B. K. Lewalski, "Love, Appearance and Reality: Much Ado About Something," *SEL,* VIII (1968), 243. For an opposite view of Beatrice and Benedick, see A. P. Rossiter, *"Much Ado About Nothing,"* in *Shakespeare: The Comedies,* ed. Kenneth Muir (Englewood Cliffs, N.J., 1965), p. 51.

54. Cf. Clara Claiborne Park, "As We Like It: How a Girl Can Be Smart and Still Popular," in *The Woman's Part,* ed. Carolyn Ruth Swift Lenz, Gayle Greene, and Carol Thomas Neely (Champaign, Ill., 1980), pp. 100–116.

tual life that allows him to grow beyond the shallow, remote conventionalities of the Petrarchan lover.[55] The extent to which Rosalind's individuality remains in complete spiritual harmony with nature becomes apparent in the way she controls the timely release of erotic energy embodied in the array of marriages at the end of the play. Just as the negative components of sexual desire are largely displaced onto Claudio and Hero in *Much Ado,* so the other couples in the procession at the end of *As You Like It* suggest the less attractive aspects of sexuality, leaving the Rosalind-Orlando union relatively free of ironic qualification. The fact that Rosalind finds the freedom to accomplish all that she does while disguised as a boy and then sheds this disguise at the end of the play again brings to mind the insoluble contradictions of the female condition, much as these contradictions present themselves in the Puritan marriage tracts. But Shakespeare emphasizes reconciliation, not contradiction; nothing like the sentimental, didactic surrender of Margaret in *Friar Bacon* exists to mar the feeling of harmony at the end of *As You Like It.* If any paradox about the loving surrender of individual identity to society comes to mind, it is the Christian one of losing in order to gain, dying in order to live.

That the potentially contradictory functions of Rosalind's disguise should be reconciled symbolically in marriage clarifies the idea that the erotic teleology of Elizabethan comedy demands an "imaginative model of desire" which is based upon the harmonious resolution of sexual conflict. Given his skeptical, polarized view of sexual love, Lyly could not make the desired reconciliation demanded by the wish-fulfillment pattern at the heart of the comic form. Greene discerned the need to harmonize both the anarchic and the civilizing components of sexual desire into a vision of social and spiritual harmony. But it was Shakespeare who perfected this vision, drawing out all its implications with neither awkwardness nor sentimentality. I have implied that the witty vitality with which Shakespeare endows the lovers in *Much Ado* and *As You Like It* contributes to an enhanced sense of their individuality and self-knowledge; since the imperative, urgent impersonality of sexual desire was what made it seem both dangerous and ridiculous to the Elizabethans, these more individualized characterizations consequently suggest a greater respect for the human dignity of sexual ex-

55. Cf. Kent Talbot Van Den Berg, "Theatrical Fiction and the Reality of Love in *As You Like It,*" *PMLA* (October 1975), pp. 885–893.

perience. But comedy cannot accommodate too much individuality, any more than it can lose its sense of the ridiculous. As is well-known, comedy focuses not on the destiny of the individual, which ends in death, but on the destiny of human society as a whole, which is perpetual.[56] Interestingly, in his last romantic comedy, *Twelfth Night* (1600), the play in which Shakespeare completely masters and exhausts the possibilities of this form of drama, he focuses less on the self-knowledge of the characters and more on the intervention of a benevolent providence in sorting out human affairs satisfactorily.[57] On the one hand, the idea of a benevolent providence assisting human destiny illuminates all of his romantic comedies; and, on the other, the lovers in *Twelfth Night* are distinctly more individualized than those in *Love's Labor's Lost* or *A Midsummer Night's Dream*. But it is a question of emphasis and degree.

Elizabethan romantic comedy was able to achieve its aim—the representation of a harmonious, spiritually integrated society symbolized in marriage—in a cultural environment in which love and marriage were gaining moral prestige and, as a corollary, personal happiness and freedom began to be considered goals worth pursuing. Currently a debate has arisen about whether Puritan marriage ideology, which, like Rosalind's disguise in *As You Like It,* enhanced female dignity and autonomy while at the same time explicitly reinforcing the double standard, had positive or negative effects for women.[58] The important point here is that a clear correspondence exists between the potentially contradictory view of sexual values presented in the Puritan tracts and the representation of sexual tensions in Elizabethan comedy. In both forms we can see certain conceptual antitheses beginning to take

56. Gardner, p. 193.

57. Cf. Salingar, pp. 240–242. Salingar believes that "*Twelfth Night* is the summing-up of a major phase of Shakespeare's writing, the last romantic play at the end of a decade, because it deals with the psychological value of revelry and its limits as well; it is a comedy about comedy . . . As the play advances, psychological mistakes dissolve into 'errors' of identity; Time and Nature, assuming the guise of Fortune, are stronger than characters' 'reason,' their conscious will. Although the actors have been given some of the depth and self-awareness of individuals in real life, they are caught up in a situation that evidently belongs less and less to real life and increasingly to the stage."

58. See Fitz, "What Says the Married Woman," and Juliet Dusinberre, *Shakespeare and the Nature of Women* (London, 1975).

shape: personal freedom and social convention; happiness and stability; civilization and its discontents. But neither the theologians nor the
playwrights drew final attention to the conflicts implicit in their conceptions of erotic love and marriage. The Puritan preachers simply did
not perceive the inherent contradictions in their sexual values. Although the playwrights discerned the outlines of comic structure in
the drama of sexual desire seeking and finding satisfaction, they represented potentially conflicting erotic forces mainly in order to reconcile them. In Shakespearean comedy happiness and stability are the
same.

Keith Thomas has linked the preponderance of sexual humor in Tudor and Stuart England to a pervasive anxiety about changing sexual
relationships. As Thomas recognizes, among its many functions, comedy can perform the conservative one of introducing potentially disruptive elements only to represent them as harmoniously assimilated
within the existing social structure.[59] As the implications of the idealization of marriage and the claims of the individual self became more
pressing, conflicts which were evoked but contained in one form of
drama became grist for the mill of other forms. In Jacobean England
love and sexuality began to be subjected to the savage scrutiny of satire
and tragedy.

Tracing the growth of romantic comedy in Elizabethan England provides insight into the ways in which people conceived of their emotional experience and represented it not only to the world, but to
themselves. When the most intimate emotions are given popular, public expression in dramatic forms, we can perceive the paradoxes and
contradictions that comprised the mental formulations of sexual love
as England moved into the modern age. The drama not only illuminates the inner life of the surrounding culture, but plays a significant
part in creating it. An awareness of this reciprocal relation between
sexual values and their symbolic representation in dramatic forms
should become increasingly germane as scholars move more deeply
into unearthing the history of the private life.

59. Keith Thomas, "The Place of Laughter in Tudor and Stuart England," *TLS* (21 January 1977), pp. 77–81. Also see Mary Douglas, "The Social Control of Cognition: Some
Factors in Joke Perception," *Man,* III (September 1968), 361–376.

Alice Arden's Crime

CATHERINE BELSEY

I

O N SUNDAY 15 February 1551 Alice Arden of Faversham in Kent procured and witnessed the murder of her husband. She and most of her accomplices were arrested, tried, and executed. The goods of the murderers, worth a total of £184. 10s. 4½d., and certain jewels, were forfeit to the Faversham treasury. The city of Canterbury was paid 44 shillings for executing George Bradshaw, who was also present at the murder, and for burning Alice Arden alive. [1] At a time when all the evidence suggests that crimes of violence were by no means uncommon, Alice Arden's crime was cited, presented and re-presented, problematized and reproblematized, during a period of at least eighty years after it was committed. Holinshed, pausing in his account of the events which constitute the main material of the *Chronicles of England, Scotland and Ireland* to give a detailed analysis of the murder, explains that the case transgresses the normal boundaries between public and private:

1. J. W. Ebsworth, ed., *The Roxburghe Ballads*, Vol. VIII, pt. 1 (Hertford, Eng., 1895), p. 48.

for the horribleness thereof, although otherwise it may seeme to be but a private matter, and therefore as it were impertinent to this historie, I have thought good to set it foorth somewhat at large.[2]

This "horribleness," which identifies Alice Arden's domestic crime as belonging to the public arena of history, is not, I want to argue, a matter of the physical details of the murder, or even of the degree of premeditation involved. On the contrary, the scandal lies in Alice Arden's challenge to the institution of marriage, itself publicly in crisis in the period. Marriage becomes in the sixteenth and seventeenth centuries the site of a paradoxical struggle to create a private realm and to take control of it in the interests of the public good. The crime coincides with the beginning of this contest. *Arden of Faversham*, which can probably be dated about 1590,[3] coincides with a major intensification of the debate about marriage, and permits its audience glimpses of what is at stake in the struggle.

II

There are a great many extant allusions to Alice Arden's crime.[4] It was recorded in the *Breviat Chronicle* for 1551, in the diary of Henry Machyn, a London merchant-tailor, and in Stow's *Annals of England* (1592, 1631) as well as in Holinshed's *Chronicles* (1577, 1587). Thomas Heywood gives it two lines in his 17-canto poem on the history of the world, *Troia Britannica* (1609), and John Taylor in *The Unnaturall Father* (1621, 1630) invokes it as an instance of God's vengeance on murderers. In addition to the play, which ran to four editions between 1592 and 1633,[5] "[The] complaint and lamentation of Mistresse Arden" was printed in ballad form, probably in 1633.

The official record of the murder was given in the Wardmote Book of Faversham, reprinted in Wine's Revels edition of the play, together with

2. Printed in M. L. Wine, ed., *The Tragedy of Master Arden of Faversham*, The Revels Plays (London, 1973), p. 148. I have silently modernized all Renaissance typography. All references to the play are to this edition.

3. Wine argues for a date between 1588 and 1591, *ibid.*, p. xlv.

4. For details see Wine, *Tragedy of Master Arden*, pp. xxxvii-xxxviii.

5. *Ibid.*, p. xix-xxi.

Holinshed's account and the ballad. According to the Wardmote Book, Arden was "heynously" and "shamefully" murdered, and the motive was Alice's intention to marry Mosby, a tailor whom she carnally kept in her own house and fed with delicate meats, with the full knowledge of her husband.[6] The value judgment established here is constant in all the accounts, and the word "shameful" defines the crime in the *Breviat Chronicle*,[7] in Holinshed,[8] on the title page of the first edition of the play, and again in the ballad.[9] What is contested in these re-presentations is not, on the whole, the morality of the murder, but its explanation, its meaning. Specific areas of the story are foregrounded or reduced, with the effect of modifying the crime's significance. The low social status of Mosby, and Arden's complaisance, for instance, both intensify the disruption of matrimonial conventions, and these elements are variously either accounted for or played down. Arden's role in the story differs considerably from one narrative to another. My concern is not with the truth of the murder, not with an attempt to penetrate beyond the records to an inaccessible "real event," not to offer an "authoritative" interpretation of Alice Arden's crime. Rather, I want to examine the implications of the constant efforts at redefinition.

In Holinshed's analysis Arden was a gentleman, a tall and comely person, and Mosby "a blacke swart man." According to the marginal gloss in the second edition of the *Chronicles*, Alice's irrational preference is an instance of the radical difference between love and lust,[10] and her flagrant defiance of the marriage bond accountable in terms of human villainy: "Thus this wicked woman, with hir complices, most shamefullie murdered hir owne husband, who most entirelie loved hir all his life time."[11] But running through Holinshed's narrative is another account of the murder not wholly consistent with this view of Arden as innocent victim, which emphasizes God's vengeance on his greed for property. In this account Arden's avarice, repeatedly referred to in the story, is finally

6. *Ibid.*, pp. 160–161.
7. *Ibid.*, p. xxxvii.
8. *Ibid.*, p. 155.
9. *Ibid.*, p. 169.
10. *Ibid.*, p. 148.
11. *Ibid.*, p. 155.

his undoing. His complaisance is a consequence of his covetousness: "bicause he would not offend hir, and so loose the benefit which he hoped to gaine at some of hir freends hands in bearing with hir lewdnesse, which he might have lost if he should have fallen out with hir: he was contented to winke at hir filthie disorder . . . "[12] After Arden's death, the field where the conspirators had placed his corpse miraculously showed the imprint of his body for two years afterward. This field was Arden's property, and in 1551 he had insisted that the St. Valentine's fair be held there, "so reaping all the gaines to himselfe, and bereaving the towne of that portion which was woont to come to the inhabitants." For this he was bitterly cursed by the people of Faversham.[13] The field itself had been "cruellie" and illegally wrested from the wife of Richard Read, a sailor, and she too had cursed him, "wishing manie a vengeance to light upon him, and that all the world might woonder on him. Which was thought then to come to passe, when he was thus murdered, and laie in that field from midnight till the morning" on the day of the fair.[14] Again the marginal gloss spells out the moral implications: "God heareth the teares of the oppressed and taketh vengeance: note an example in Arden."[15] The murder is thus part of the providential scheme.

These two versions of Arden—as loving husband and as rapacious landlord—coexist equally uneasily in the play. Here the element of complaisance is much reduced: Arden has grounds for suspicion but not certainty. Mosby's baseness is a constant theme, and underlines Alice's irrationality. But what is new in the play is the parallel between Arden's dubious business deals and Alice's. A good part of the plot is taken up with Alice's negotiations with possible murderers. Michael is to carry out the crime in exchange for Susan Mosby. Clarke is to provide a poison, and subsequently a poisoned picture, in exchange for Susan Mosby. Greene gets £10 and a promise of £20 more, with land to follow, for his "plain dealing" in carrying out the murder (I, 517). Greene subcontracts the work to Black Will and Shakebag for £10. Finally, in desperation, Alice increases her offer to Black Will to £20, and £40 more when Arden is

12. *Ibid.*, p. 149.
13. *Ibid.*, p. 157.
14. *Ibid.*, p. 159.
15. *Ibid.*

dead. They leave triumphantly with their gold when the work is completed (XIV, 249). Mosby, too, is part of this world of economic individualism, and there are indications that his motive is not love of Alice so much as desire to come by Arden's money (e.g., VIII, 11–44). He quarrels with Alice in terms of "credit," "advantages," "Fortune," and "wealth" (VIII, 80–92). If the play has any explanation to offer of Alice Arden's crime it is social and economic rather than providential. The event is primarily an instance of the breakdown of order—the rape of women and property—which follows when the exchange of contracts in a market economy supplants old loyalties, old obligations, old hierarchies.

But there are elements of the play which this reading leaves out of account. Some of the dialogue between Alice and Mosby invites a response which contradicts the play's explicit project, defined on the title page, of showing "the great malice and dissimulation of a wicked woman, [and] the unsatiable desire of filthie lust." In these speeches it is marriage which is identified as an impediment to true love, and images familiar from the poetry of the period seem to offer the audience a position of some sympathy with Alice's repudiation of the marriage bond:

> ALICE
> Why should he thrust his sickle in our corn,
> Or what hath he to do with thee, my love,
> Or govern me that am to rule myself?
> Forsooth, for credit sake, I must leave thee!
> Nay, he must leave to live that we may love,
> May live, may love; for what is life but love?
> And love shall last as long as life remains,
> And life shall end before my love depart.
> MOSBY
> Why, what's love, without true constancy?
> Like to a pillar built of many stones,
> Yet neither with good mortar well compact
> Nor cement to fasten it in the joints
> But that it shakes with every blast of wind
> And, being touched, straight falls unto the earth
> And buries all his haughty pride in dust.
> No, let our love be rocks of adamant,
> Which time nor place nor tempest can asunder.
>
> (X.83–99)

The natural and elemental images and the biblical echoes momentarily ennoble Alice's defiance of patriarchy. Early in the play Clarke makes explicit this other face of the crime:

> Let it suffice I know you love him well
> And fain would have your husband made away,
> Wherein, trust me, you show a noble mind,
> That rather than you'll live with him you hate
> You'll venture life and die with him you love.
>
> (I.267–271)

In these instances the play presents Alice Arden's challenge to the institution of marriage as an act of heroism. Alice rejects the metaphysics of presence which guarantees the social enforcement of permanent monogamy, in favor of a free sexuality, unauthorized within the play as a whole, but glimpsed at isolated moments:

> Sweet Mosby is the man that hath my heart;
> And he usurps it, having nought but this,
> That I am tied to him by marriage.
> Love is a god, and marriage is but words;
> And therefore Mosby's title is the best.
> Tush! Whether it be or no, he shall be mine
> In spite of him, of Hymen, and of rites.
>
> (I.98–104)

The ballad, almost certainly derived from the play, redefines the problem yet again. For the first time the woman is the unequivocal subject of the narrative, in contrast to the play, where the title indicates that it is Arden's tragedy rather than Alice's. The ballad reduces the story to two main elements—Alice's love and the series of contracts for the murder. These negotiations are recounted in all their detail within a text of only 192 lines. Arden's rapacity is ignored, and Holinshed's "blacke swart" Mosby becomes a man of "sugred tongue, good shape, and lovely looke" (l. 11). The ballad is a record of contracts made and broken for love. There is no explicit doubt of Alice's wickedness: her "secret dealings" come to light and are duly punished by her death (l. 167). At the same time, a curious formulation, perhaps a slip of the pen, picks up something of the element of ambivalence in the play: "And then by Justice we were straight condemn'd, / Each of us came unto a shameless end . . . " (ll. 165–166).

"Shameless" here is unexpected—appropriate to their (impudent) behavior, perhaps, but not to their (disgraceful) execution. On a reading of the word in use during the fifteenth century, "shameless" could mean "free from disgrace" (OED, 3). Perhaps a parapraxis betrays the unconscious of the text, a world well lost for love, and Alice Arden heroic on the scaffold, exposing herself to death through death.

However that may be, these repeated reinterpretations of the events, reproblematizations of the murder, may be read as so many attempts to elicit a definitive meaning for Alice Arden's crime. In each case this definitive meaning remains elusive, in the sense that each text contains elements not accounted for in its over-all project. I want to argue that what is at stake in these contests for the meaning of the murder is marriage itself, but first I should like to draw attention to the prominence given to parallel cases in the period.

III

The existing historical evidence gives no reason to believe that there was a major outbreak of women murdering their husbands in the sixteenth century. [16] What it does suggest, however, is a widespread belief that they were likely to do so. The Essex county records for the Elizabethan period, for instance, reveal no convictions for this crime, but they list several cases of frightened husbands seeking the protection of the courts. In 1574 a Barnston man complained that his wife, "forgetting her duty and obedience as a wife, had sundry times maliciously attempted to bereave her husband of his life, so that he stand in great fear" both of her and of two men from Dunmow, her "adherents," who haunted his house at night. [17] In 1590 a man called Philpott complained that John Chandler, then living with his wife, had given his consent to Philpott's death, and Rowland

16. See, e.g., F. G. Emmison, *Elizabethan Life: Disorder* (Chelmsford, Eng., 1970); C. S. Weiner, "Sex Roles and Crime in Late Elizabethan Hertfordshire," *Journal of Social History*, VIII (1975), 38–60. Weiner gives no instances at all. Emmison lists 131 cases of murder brought before the Essex county courts in the Elizabethan period. In three of these (or possibly two, if the case of the Great Wakering woman mentioned on p. 149 is the same as the one listed on p. 150), women were charged with poisoning their husbands. In each case the woman was acquitted, which implies (since acquittals, except in cases of employers murdering their servants, are rare) that the evidence must have been very slender.

17. Emmison, *Elizabethan Life: Disorder*, p. 162.

Gryffyth deposed that he had been hired to carry out the murder. [18] The records of the ecclesiastical courts in the same county include two cases, both in 1597, of men who refused to live with their wives for fear that they would be murdered by them. [19]

When the crime was actually committed, it seems that notoriety instantly followed. In 1573 Anne Sanders (or Saunders) consented to the murder of her husband, a London merchant, by her lover, George Browne. The case rapidly became as widely known as the Arden murder. It was recorded by Arthur Golding in a pamphlet published in the same year and again in 1577; it was probably the subject of an anonymous pamphlet called "A Cruell murder donne in Kent" published in 1577; [20] the story was told by Holinshed and Stow again; and it was recounted by Antony Munday in *A View of Sundry Examples* (1580). Like the Arden case, the Sanders murder elicited a play, *A Warning for Fair Women* (probably ca. 1590) and a ballad, "The wofull lamentacion of mrs. Anne Saunders, which she wrote with her own hand, being prisoner in newgate, Justly condemned to death." [21] In the ballad Anne Sanders begs all women to be warned by her example; the play, unable to account in any other terms for so scandalous a crime, shows Anne, in an allegorical dumb show instigated by the Furies, suddenly torn between chastity and lust, then pledging herself to Browne in a ceremony which evokes the "sacrament prophane in mistery of wine" between Paridell and the adulterous Hellenore. [22]

In 1591 Mistress Page of Plymouth was executed with her lover and two other men for the murder of her husband. A ballad by Thomas Deloney

18. *Ibid.*, p. 199.

19. F. G. Emmison, *Elizabethan Life: Morals and the Church Courts* (Chelmsford, Eng., 1973), p. 162. Surprisingly, there were only two instances of women protesting that they were similarly frightened of their husbands, and one of these had already been subject to marital violence.

20. Joseph H. Marshburn, "*A Cruell Murder Done in Kent* and Its Literary Manifestations," *SP*, XLVI (1949), 131–140.

21. Hyder Rollins, ed., *Old English Ballands 1553–1625* (Cambridge, Eng., 1920), pp. 340–348.

22. Charles Dale Cannon, ed., *A Warning for Fair Women* (The Hague, 1975), ll. 803–815 s.d. Cf. *The Faerie Queene*, III.ix.30. It is worth noting that, according to Golding's account, Anne Drurie, Browne's accomplice, must have been suspected of poisoning her own husband, since she denied the allegation on the scaffold (see Cannon, p. 224).

appeared at once, recording "The Lamentation of Mr Pages Wife of Plimouth, who, being forc'd to wed him, consented to his Murder, for the love of G. Strangwidge." [23] Here the ambivalences implicit in the Arden narratives are foregrounded to produce a radical contradiction between sympathy and condemnation. The ballad gives a graphic account of the miseries of enforced marriage:

> My closen eies could not his sight abide;
> My tender youth did lothe his aged side:
> Scant could I taste the meate whereon he fed;
> My legges did lothe to lodge within his bed.
>
> (ll. 29–32)

At the same time,

> Methinkes the heavens crie vengeance for my fact,
> Methinkes the world condemns my monstrous act,
> Methinkes within my conscience tells me true,
> That for that deede hell fier is my due.
>
> (ll. 41–44)

In the circumstances it is particularly regrettable that *Page of Plymouth* by Jonson and Dekker, performed by the Admiral's Men in 1599, is now lost, as is *The History of Friar Francis*, produced, according to Henslowe's diary, in 1593/4, though not necessarily for the first time. [24] According to Heywood in 1612, when *The History of Friar Francis* was performed at King's Lynn it had the gratifying effect of inducing an apparently respectable woman in the audience to confess that seven years before she had poisoned her husband for love of a gentleman in precisely the same way as the protagonist of the play. Heywood is here writing in defense of the moral efficacy of stage plays, and it is worth noting that of the three instances he cites of the providential operation of the drama, two concern women murdering their husbands. In the second case it was the method of murder shown on the stage which caused "a woman of great gravity" to

23. F. O. Mann, ed., *The Works of Thomas Deloney* (Oxford, 1912), pp. 482–485. I am grateful to Margot Heinemann for drawing my attention to this ballad.

24. H. H. Adams, *English Domestic or Homiletic Tragedy, 1575–1642* (New York, 1943), pp. 193–194.

shriek loudly, and after several days of torment to confess that she had driven a nail into the temples of her husband twelve years before. She was duly tried, condemned, and burned. [25]

IV

According to John Taylor, writing in 1621, *"Arden of Feversham*, and *Page of Plimmouth*, both their Murders are fresh in memory, and the fearfull ends of their Wives and their Ayders in those bloudy actions will never be forgotten." [26] The prominence allotted to these cases, the suspicion which seems to have been prevalent in Essex in the period, and Heywood's instances of the salutory effects of stage plays in bringing such crimes to light, all point to a preoccupation with the possibility of women murdering their husbands which is not accounted for in any of the individual texts I have discussed. In *Arden of Faversham* Alice Arden defines her problem specifically in terms of the institutional regulation of sexuality by marriage:

> nothing could enforce me to the deed
> But Mosby's love. Might I without control
> Enjoy thee still, then Arden should not die;
> But, seeing I cannot, therefore let him die.
>
>   (I. 273–276)

It is a contest for the control of sexuality in the period which throws marriage into crisis and precipitates the instability of the institution which is evident in crimes like Alice Arden's.

The history of marriage in the Middle Ages is a history of an effort to regulate sexuality by confining it within a framework of permanent monogamy. From the twelfth century onward the Church gradually extended its control over marriage, making efforts to contain instances of divorce and bigamy by urging with increasing insistence the public solemnization of matrimony after due reading of the banns on consecutive Sundays. [27] Since at the same time private marriage in the presence of

25. Thomas Heywood, *An Apology for Actors* (London, 1612), sig. G 1^v–2^v.

26. John Taylor, *Works* (London, 1630), p. 140.

27. Michael M. Sheehan, "The Formation and Stability of Marriage in Fourteenth-Century England: Evidence of an Ely Register," *MS*, XXXIII (1971), 228–263; G. E. Howard, *A History of Matrimonial Institutions*, 3 vols. (Chicago, 1904), I, 361.

witnesses was held to be valid and binding,[28] it was easy enough to produce just cause or impediment after the event. However, the banns were no guarantee against bigamy, since they were easily evaded by those who had anything to fear. In consequence, the process of taking control was slow and laborious, so that in 1540 it was still the case that bigamy was widespread, and that "no mariage coulde be so surely knytt and bounden but it shulde lye in either of the parties power and arbitre . . . to prove a precontracte a kynnerede an alliance or a carnall knowledge to defeate the same . . . "[29] Many of the cases which came before the ecclesiastical courts depended on such ingenuities, but Michael M. Sheehan finds, after investigating the late fourteenth-century register of the consistory court of the Bishop of Ely, that there at least "the court was primarily a body for the proof and defence of marriage rather than an instrument of easy annulment."[30] The commitment of the court to the stability of marriage above all other considerations may be illustrated by one of the cases Sheehan cites. The marriage between John Poynant and Joan Swan was annulled on the grounds of the husband's impotence. Joan married again, and John took up with Isabel Pybbel. When Isabel became pregnant John prepared to marry her, but the court investigated the matter and found that, since John was apparently not impotent after all, his marriage to Joan Swan should be restored. John protested, claiming affinity within the forbidden degrees between Joan and Isabel, but the court was not impressed, and the original marriage was eventually reinstated.[31]

The Anglican church took over on behalf of the sovereign this effort to control the institution of marriage through the ecclesiastical courts, but not without a struggle which generated a high degree of uncertainty about the nature and permanence of marriage. The introduction of registers of births, marriages, and deaths in 1538 was a move toward population control, but at the same time the Reformation introduced a liberalization

28. Lawrence Stone, *The Family, Sex and Marriage in England, 1500–1800* (London, 1977), p. 31; Howard, *Matrimonial Institutions*, I, 336 ff. Sheehan, "Formation and Stability of Marriage," p. 253.

29. Preamble to 32 Hen. VIII, ca. 38, cited by C. L. Powell, *English Domestic Relations 1487–1653* (New York, 1917), p. 62.

30. Sheehan, "Formation and Stability of Marriage," p. 263.

31. *Ibid.*, p. 261.

of marriage which found a focus in a debate about divorce that remained legally unresolved, apart from a brief interlude during the Commonwealth, until the nineteenth century.[32]

The Catholic church had permitted separation *a mensa et thoro* (from bed and board) for adultery, cruelty, apostasy, or heresy, and divorce *a vinculo matrimonii* on the basis either of impotence or of a prior impediment to valid marriage on grounds of consanguinity, affinity, or precontract. The act of 1540 attempted to abolish precontract as grounds for divorce, but had no practical effect. Meanwhile, most of the newly Protestant states had introduced divorce with remarriage for the innocent party in cases of adultery and desertion. Similar legislation was urged in England, and was incorporated in the *Reformatio Legum Ecclesiasticarum* of 1552. This was defeated in the House of Commons, but the divorce provision had been sanctioned independently, when a commission under Cranmer had approved the remarriage of the divorced Northampton in 1548, a decision that was confirmed by Parliament in 1552. In practice, however, the ecclesiastical courts largely refused to put the law into operation, and in consequence the position of marriage remained extremely confused and controversial for the rest of the century. The divorce debate reached a high point in the 1590s, with the result that in the Canons of 1597 Convocation declared all remarriage after divorce illegal. These were not sanctioned by Elizabeth, but the principle was reiterated in the Canons of 1604 which were approved by James I, though without silencing the controversy.[33]

The importance of the divorce debate lies in its polarization of conflicting definitions of marriage. Broadly, the Anglican position was that marriage was indissoluble, that couples were joined by God for the avoidance of fornication and the procreation of children, and that there was no remedy but patience for marital disharmony and discontent. The position of the radical Protestants is familiar from Milton's divorce tracts, which carry the Puritan arguments to their logical climax. Equally

32. The Cromwellian Marriage Act of 1653 placed the whole matter in the hands of the civil magistrates but gave no indication of the possible grounds for divorce. This legislation was not re-enacted after the Restoration (Powell, *English Domestic Relations*, pp. 99–100).

33. For an account of the legal position see Howard, *History of Matrimonial Institutions*, II, 76–85; Stone, *Family, Sex and Marriage*, pp. 37–41; Powell, *English Domestic Relations*, pp. 61–100; Ernest Sirluck, ed., *The Complete Prose Works of John Milton* (London, 1959), II, 145–146.

broadly, the Puritans held that marriage was a civil covenant, a thing indifferent to salvation, that it depended on consent, and that where this was lacking the couple could not be said to be joined by God, and could therefore justly be put asunder. The Reformers varied in the causes of divorce they were prepared to admit. Only Milton gave real prominence to discord as a cause, while Henry Smith, at the other extreme though still within the pro-divorce lobby, recognized divorce for adultery but vigorously repudiated incompatibility as grounds:

If they might bee separated for discorde, some would make a commoditie of strife; but now they are not best to be contentious, for this law will hold their noses together, till wearines make them leave struggling, like two spaniels which are coupled in a chaine, at last they learne to goe together, because they may not goe asunder.[34]

Not all the Reformers were so optimistic about the couple learning to go together. According to Martin Bucer, whose *De Regno Christi* was addressed to Edward VI when the author was Professor of Divinity at Cambridge, the Church's refusal to permit divorce compelled it to tolerate "whordoms and adulteries, and worse things then these," "throwing men headlong into these evils."[35] "Neither," he argued, "can God approve that to the violation of this holy league (which is violated as soon as true affection ceases and is lost,) should be added murder . . . "[36] John Rainolds, writing in 1597, insists that if divorce is forbidden crimes like Alice Arden's are bound to follow: a husband may be forced to live in permanent suspicion, or worse—

And how can he choose but live still in feare & anguish of minde, least shee add drunckennesse to thirst, & murder to adultery: I meane least she serve him as *Clytemnestra* did *Agamemnon*, *Livia* did *Drusus* as *Mrs. Arden* did her husband?[37]

V

There is some evidence for the bitterness of the struggle. John Dove, who preached a sermon against divorce in 1601, records that many people found his view offensive, "as unseasonable for the time, and unpleasing to

34. Henry Smith, *A Preparative to Marriage* (London, 1591), p. 108.
35. Milton's translation, *Complete Prose Works*, ed. Sirluck, II, 447.
36. *Ibid.*, p. 470.
37. John Rainolds, *A Defence of the Judgment of the Reformed Churches* (London, 1609), p. 88.

the auditory."[38] Rainolds wrote his plea for divorce in 1597, but explains in a letter to Pye published in 1606 that the Archbishop of Canterbury at that time "thought it not meete to be printed: as containing dangerous doctrine." He urges Pye to cut out any references to him (Rainolds) in his own argument if he wants to get into print, especially since the Canons of 1604 have hardened the orthodox line.[39] Rainolds's own *Defence of the Judgment of the Reformed Churches* was published in 1609. The archbishop's censorship seems to have been evenhanded, since at about the same time he also discouraged Edmund Bunny from publishing his case against divorce—in order to avoid controversy, on the grounds that he had already "staied" one of the contrary persuasion.[40] Bunny's book appeared in 1610. Later William Whately argued for divorce on grounds of desertion as well as adultery in books published in 1617 and 1624. Whately was brought before the Court of High Commission, and promptly reverted to the Anglican doctrine of the indissolubility of marriage.[41]

Even between the radicals there was considerable sectarianism on this issue. Milton, of course, encountered a good deal of controversy, and was denounced by his fellow Puritans for his divorce pamphlets.[42] And at the very beginning of the debate an interesting piece of sleight of hand shows how delicate the whole issue must have been. In 1541 Miles Coverdale's translation of Bullinger's treatise on marriage was published as *The Christen State of Matrimonye*. Primarily a plea for marriage as a union of minds, and a corresponding repudiation of the Catholic doctrine of celibacy as a way of perfection, this included a chapter recommending divorce not only for adultery but also for "lyke and greater occasions."[43] *The Christen State of Matrimonye* was remarkably popular. Three new editions appeared within five years, and two more before the end of the century. Meanwhile, in 1542, there appeared *The Golden Boke of christen matrimonye* "newly set forth

38. John Dove, *Of Divorcement* (London, 1601), Preface.

39. Reproduced in John Howson, *Uxore dismissa propter Fornicationem aliam non licet superinducere* (Oxford, 1606).

40. Edmund Bunny, *Of Divorce for Adulterie and Marrying againe* (Oxford, 1610), Advertisement to the Reader.

41. William and Malleville Haller, "The Puritan Art of Love," *HLQ*, V (1941–1942), 235–272, 267–268.

42. Christopher Hill, *Milton and the English Revolution* (London, 1977), pp. 131–132.

43. H. Bullinger, *The Christen State of Matrimonye* (London, 1541), fol. lxxvii.

in English by Theodore Basille." "Theodore Basille" was Thomas Becon, and *The Golden Boke* was acutally Coverdale's translation of Bullinger again, with four chapters silently omitted, including the one on divorce.

The contest for the meaning of marriage cannot be isolated from the political struggles which characterize the century between the Reformation and the English revolution. Both sides make explicit the parallel between the family and the state, marriage and the monarchy. "A householde is as it were a little common-wealth;"[44] "A Familie, is a naturall and simple Society of certaine persons, having mutual relationship one to another, under the private government of one."[45] At one extreme Milton argues for liberty within marriage as directly analogous to liberty in the commonwealth:

He who marries, intends as little to conspire his own ruine, as he that swears Allegiance: and as a whole people is in proportion to an ill Government, so is one man to an ill mariage. If they against any authority, Covnant, or Statute, may by the soveraign edict of charity, save not only their lives, but honest liberties from unworthy bondage, as well may he against any private Covnant, which hee never enter'd to his mischief, redeem himself from unsupportable disturbances to honest peace, and just contentment.[46]

And if this position was not made explicit in the radical treatises before 1642, nonetheless it was identified by Anglican orthodoxy as implicit in the Puritan arguments. According to Bunny, divorce can lead only to "disorder."[47] Marriage cannot be dissolved at will any more than can the bond between master and servant, parent and child, "the Prince and the Subject." And for this reason, "the more heed should bee taken, that no such gap should be opened to any, as wherby the looser sort, when they should get their desire in this, should cast about to obtaine the like in

---

44. Robert Cleaver and John Dod, *A Godlie Forme of Householde Government* (London, 1612), p. 13. The first edition of this popular work appeared in 1598. Cf. William Gouge, *Of Domesticall Duties* (1622), pp. 16–17, cited by Haller, "Puritan Art of Love," p. 246.

45. William Perkins, *Christian Oeconomie, Works* (Cambridge, Eng., 1618), III, 669–700. *Christian Oeconomie* was written in Latin in 1590 and translated by Thomas Pickering in 1609.

46. Sirluck, *Complete Prose Works of Milton*, II, 229.

47. Bunny, *Of Divorce*, p. 161.

other things also of greater consequence."[48] Dove, whose name entirely
belies his political position, argues strenuously that,

As when a servant runneth from his M. the chaine of bondage doth pursue him,
and bring him back againe to his maister, so when a woman leaveth her husband,
the lawe of Matrimony is as a chaine to draw her back againe to her husband . . .[49]

The libertines who believe in divorce pervert the scriptures for their own
licentious ends, "Even as others will proove rebellion and high treason out
of the scriptures, that the people are above their King."[50] The parallel
between domestic patriarchy and authoritarian monarchy is a commonplace of the seventeenth century, and reaches its most notorious formulation, of course, in Robert Filmer's *Patriarcha*, written during the 1640s.[51]

Alice Arden, held in the chain of bondage which is marriage, in a period
when liberty is glimpsed but not authorized, is caught up in a struggle
larger than her chroniclers recognize. But it may be the political significance of Arden's assassination which causes Holinshed to identify Alice
Arden's crime as marking the border between private and public,
pamphlet and history.

VI

There is an indication in *Arden of Faversham* that in opting for Mosby in
place of Arden, a freely chosen sexuality based on concord in place of the
constraints of the institution of permanent marriage, Alice Arden may be
committing herself to a form of power more deadly still, and less visible.
Mosby's individualism is precisely that:

> Yet Mistress Arden lives; but she's myself,
> And holy church rites makes us two but one.
> But what for that I may not trust you, Alice?
> You have supplanted Arden for my sake
> And will extirpen me to plant another.

48. *Ibid.*, p. 52.
49. Dove, *Of Divorcement*, p. 33.
50. *Ibid.*, p. 51.
51. Gordon J. Schochet, *Patriarchalism in Political Thought* (New York, 1975).

> 'Tis fearful sleeping in a serpent's bed,
> And I will cleanly rid my hands of her.
> But here she comes, and I must flatter her . . .
>
> (VIII.37–44)

The episode could be read as an allegory of the transition to the affective nuclear family, itself a mechanism of regulation more far-reaching but less visible than the repressive ecclesiastical courts. Arden's absolute rights over Alice are clear, and his threats are directed not against his wife but against the man who means to rob him of her, for which he

> Shall on the bed which he thinks to defile
> See his dissevered joints and sinews torn
> Whilst on the planchers pants his weary body,
> Smeared in the channels of his lustful blood.
>
> (I. 40–43)

This overt power and violence give way in Mosby's version of marriage to distrust and surveillance veiled by flattery; in an individualist society of "equals" authoritarian modes of control are replaced by reciprocal fear between partners within the social body. Further, flattery and death are the metaphorical destiny of the wife in the new family. Her standing improves (though always in subjection to her husband) but at the cost of new and more insidious forms of control.

Puritan marriage, founded on consent, is "appointed by God himselfe, to be the fountaine and seminary of all other sorts and kinds of life, in the Common-wealth and in the Church." [52] To this end the family becomes quite explicitly an ideological apparatus, "a schoole wherein the first principles and grounds of government and subjection are learned: whereby men are fitted to greater matters in Church or Common-wealth." [53] In Puritan definitions of marriage and the family as "the Fountain and Seminary of good subjects," [54] it is made very clear that "the holy and righteous government thereof, is a direct meane for the good ordering both of Church and Commonwealth; yea that the Lawes thereof beeing

---

52. Perkins, *Christian Oeconomie*, p. 671.
53. Gouge, *Of Domesticall Duties;* Haller, "Puritan Art of Love," p. 246.
54. Sirluck, *Complete Prose Works of Milton*, II, 447.

rightly informed, and religiously observed, are availeable to prepare and dispose men to the keeping of order in other governments."[55] To ensure that the family becomes an adequate model and source of good government, the treatises recommend family prayers, grace before meals, keeping the sabbath, the education of the children and the servants, and the inculcation of the fundamental principles of law and order. The family, separated from the public realm of politics, nonetheless becomes a microcosm of it and, by practice and by precept, a training ground for the ready acceptance of the power relations established in the social body:

For this first Societie is as it were the Schoole, wherein are taught and learned the principles of authoritie and subjection. And looke as the superior that faileth in his charge, will proove uncapable of publike imployment, so the inferiour, who is not framed to a course of Oeconomicall subjection, wil hardly undergoe the yoake of Civill obedience.[56]

The "liberalism" of the Reformers implies a constant scrutiny of marriage for "fitnes of mind and disposition,"[57] since harmony and concord are the precondition of a realm of hearth and home regulated from within. Vigilantly protected from sedition, and isolated from public and political affairs, the family is held in place in the social body as a model of the proper distribution of authority and submission, and thus the fountain and seminary of good subjects.

Read as a political event, Alice Arden's crime was a defiance of absolutism and, in common with the constant reproblematization of such crimes in the period, as well as the great numbers of "divorces" established in the sixteenth century without recourse to the civil or ecclesiastical authorities,[58] it constitutes evidence of the instability of central control at the time. Within a century of Arden's death the absolute power was to have been supplanted and Charles I executed in the name of the liberty of the people of England. The concomitant of this liberty was the construction of the affective nuclear family as an invisible mechanism of correction and control. The chain of bondage had given way to a net of power.

55. Pickering, in Perkins, *Christian Oeconomie*, Epistle Dedicatory.
56. *Ibid.*
57. Sirluck, *Complete Prose Works of Milton*, II, 605.
58. Powell, *English Domestic Relations*, pp. 61–62, 69–70.

VII

The century following Alice Arden's crime was one of crisis—economic, ideological, and political. With hindsight it is possible to interpret many of the events of this period as elements in the social upheaval which found a focus in the civil war of the 1640s. On this reading of the period, the institution most evidently in crisis was the monarchy, but it is also apparent that challenges to authority and authoritarianism were delivered in a number of spheres, many of them more obviously remote from the institution of monarchy than the more explicitly analogous institution of the family. Clearly, such a reading of the history of this period, available to us retrospectively, was only partly accessible in the period itself, and it is this which accounts for the repeated attempts to define and redefine Alice Arden's crime, and which explains why it was so important and so impossible to furnish it with a final meaning. The assassination of Arden is never justified, but it is variously identified as a part of God's providential plan, as a tragedy, as the effect of social and economic change, or as an act of unauthorized heroism, a noble transgression of an absolute law. The re-presentations of the crime are (sometimes contradictory, never neutral) contributions to a discursive struggle for the meaning of resistance to absolutism. *Arden of Faversham* is one of the documents in this struggle, perhaps a relatively complex analysis, but by no means an isolated instance of the attempt to make sense of insurrection.

Meanwhile, the divorce debate, reaching a crisis in the decade which also produced three plays on the theme I have discussed, in the final years of Elizabeth's apparently successful efforts to hold at bay the pressures for social change, is the site of a discursive contest between distinct modes of social control. Its relevance to my argument is not simply that it provides a context for our understanding of the plays, but that it enables us to perceive more sharply what is at stake in this contest. Offering a promise of freedom from the "chain" (the recurring metaphor for authoritarianism) of marriage, the radical position on divorce leads in reality to a new mode of control, no longer centralized and overt, but internalized and invisible. The new family of the seventeenth century, still under "the government of one," remains a place in which power is exercised privately in the interests of public order. Alice Arden's bid for freedom, as the play implies, would have led, had it succeeded, to a new form of subjection, both for the woman within the family and for the family within the state. No text of the 1590s could formulate this point in these terms. Indeed, the explicit identification of the family as a mechanism of social control probably has its tentative beginnings in the nineteenth century. Nonetheless, Mosby's threat that he will subject Alice to surveillance, flattery, and death indicates a glimpse in this text of an issue which is more complex than the simple opposition between authority and freedom, control and consent.

Modern marriage, modern domestic patriarchy, and the modern family as an ideological apparatus were produced in the struggles, dispersed across a range of institutions and practices, of the sixteenth and seventeenth centuries. In this sense the discursive history of Alice Arden's crime is a significant part of the history of the present.

Transgression and Rebellion

The Beginnings of Elizabethan Drama: Revolution and Continuity

G. K. HUNTER

A STANDARD ASSUMPTION of literary history is that a group of young men, born of "middle-class" parentage in the 1550s and 1560s and graduating from Oxford or Cambridge between 1575 (Lyly) and 1588 (Nashe)[1] created between them the normal forms of Elizabethan Drama, casting behind them the primitive techniques and attitudes of preceding generations, designated "Tudor Drama," "Late Medieval Drama," or whatever other diminishing title distaste elects to supply. I call this assumption "standard" not because I seek to denigrate it (in the recurrent modern mode); there is much evidence that these young men perceived themselves, and were perceived by contemporaries, as constituting what would nowadays be called a radical movement and that the movement marked the beginning of something genuinely new. But the very obviousness of the general point leaves a number of supplementary questions unanswered because not asked. In particular I wish to ask the question *how* this group came to achieve their effect on drama.[2] The question is a purely instrumental one that does not seek to go beyond the evidence generally available in the words they wrote. This leaves, of course, the further issue of the status we give to these words. If we are to understand what the "University Wits" say as a simple description of the facts of the case, then we must suppose that it was expertise in classical culture that led to the creation of the new drama. But this connection seems to be part of the rhetoric of their social situation rather than expressive of any vital link that joins university culture to popular drama. I shall argue that the link can be seen more clearly in terms of the central issue of Elizabethan intellectual life—the theological debate about the relation of individual conscience to the established hierarchies of the world. I shall argue that it was the perception of the individual voice as justified (in all senses of that word), even when socially isolated, that released the more obvious formal and literary powers we easily recognize. That the University Wits despised the popular theater they found when they came to London can hardly be disputed. The university milieu which had given them their claim to importance had anchored their sense of identity in the Humanist learning they had acquired there, their fluent command of a battery of Greco-Roman names, historical and fictional stories, self-conscious logical and rhetorical devices, tags and quotations, which provided the lingua franca of Humanist-educated Europe. In social terms these were, of course, means of defining an elite status, and they seem at first to offer only resistance to a demeaning function in popular entertainment, where (as Shakespeare was to point out) "nature is subdued / To what it works in, like the dyer's hand." Robert Greene more than once tells us how he suffered a sad decline into playwriting; and even though his narrative is more interesting as myth than as history it is worth pausing on. In *Francesco's Fortunes* (1590) we hear that Francesco (the Greene alternate) "fell in amongst a company of players, who persuaded him to try his wit in writing of comedies, tragedies, or pastorals, and if he could perform anything worthy of the stage, then they would largely reward him for his pains." And so Francesco "writ a comedy which so generally pleased all the audience that happy were those actors in short time that could get any of his works, he grew so exquisite in that faculty." (Greene 8: 128) In Greene's *Groatsworth of Wit* (1592) the story has become even more slanted. Roberto (the same hero, with another name) has come to an impasse in the Bohemian life he had thought to lead. He has been outsmarted and made penniless by the prostitute he planned to control. He is thrust out of doors, and sitting against a hedge he vents his wrath in English and Latin verses. On the other side of the hedge there happens to be a player, who now approaches Roberto:

Gentleman, quoth he (for so you seem), I have by chance heard you discourse some part of your grief . . . if you vouchsafe such simple comfort as my ability will yield, assure yourself that I will endeavour to do the best that either may procure your profit or bring you pleasure; the rather for that I suppose you are a scholar, and pity it is men of learning should live in lack.

Roberto, wondering to hear such good words . . . uttered his present grief, beseeching his advice how he might be employed. Why easily, quoth he, and greatly to your benefit; for men of my profession get by scholars their whole living. What is your profession, said Roberto. Truly sir, said he, I am a player. A player, quoth Roberto, I took you rather for a gentleman of great living, for if by outward habit men should be censured, I tell you you would be taken for a substantial man. So am I where I dwell (quoth the player) reputed able at my proper cost to build a windmill.

(12: 130–31)

The player goes on to indicate that he has greatly prospered by penning and playing folktales and moralities. "But now my almanac is out of date." He now needs a graduate, like Roberto, to catch the more sophisticated tastes of the present "in making plays . . . for which you shall be well payed if you will take the pains."

Roberto, perceiving no remedy, thought best to respect of his present necessity to try his wit and went with him willingly; who lodged him at the town's end [in a brothel]. . . . Roberto, now famoused for an arch-playmaking poet, his purse like the sea sometime swelled, anon like the same sea fell to a low ebb; yet seldom he wanted, his labors were so well esteemed.

(12: 132, 134)

His new profession earns him the much-needed money, but money earned under these circumstances is seen to be incapable of securing moral stability. Roberto so despises those from whom he earns his money that he can only define his difference from them by cheating them: "It becomes me, saith he, to be contrary to the world, for commonly when vulgar men receive earnest they do perform; when I am paid anything aforehand I break my promise" (Greene 12: 134). His money is spent among criminals and debauchees to support a way of life which produces execution for some and repentance before death for Roberto. It is at this point that Greene can proceed to warn "those gentlemen his quondam acquaintance that spend their wits in making plays" (Marlowe, Peele, [?Lodge/Nashe] and "two more that both have writ against these buckram gentlemen") to "never more acquaint them [the players] with your admired inventions" (Greene 12: 141, 144).

The story as thus told is a powerful one. But as far as the history of Elizabethan drama is concerned, the details leave much to be desired.

There is no evidence that Greene's dramatic talents had the electrifying effect he describes. And we should note that he tells much the same story about his prose romances of love. In *The Repentance of Robert Greene* (1592) we hear not only that the "penning of plays" turned him into a swearer and a blasphemer, but that

These vanities [plays] and other trifling pamphlets I penned of love and vain fantasies were my chiefest stay of living, and for those my vain discourses I was beloved of the vainer sort of people who, being my continual companions, came still to my lodgings, and there would continue quaffing, carousing and surfeiting with me all the day long.

(12: 178)

Greene is much clearer about the status he is losing than about the skills he is acquiring. He implies that all he has to do to succeed is to turn his university-trained cleverness toward the writing of popular literature and lo! he will grow "exquisite in that faculty." The extant popular plays of Greene, Peele, and Lodge, however, do not at all support this idea; they are quite unlike any model the university could have provided from the works of Seneca, Plautus, or Terence. In their multitudes of characters, their wide range across space and time, their carelessness of plot consistency, their interest in romantic love, their reluctance to stay inside the boundaries of genre, their tendency to heavy moralizing, such plays fit almost exactly the terms of neoclassical scorn with which Sir Philip Sidney had greeted the English plays of the early 1580s. *James IV, Edward I, The Battle of Alcazar, Alphonsus of Aragon,* and *A Looking Glass for London and England* all fall easily under Sir Philip's rubric of "mongrel tragicomedy [with] some extreme show of doltishness" (Sidney 135–36) and are in fact much more like those warhorses of the popular stage, *Clyomon and Clamydes* or *The Famous Victories of Henry V,* than they are like anything in classical drama.

What, then, did the university contribute toward a new theatrical creation that was not provided by a professional knowledge of the stage? The evidence that contemporary comment provides is extraordinarily evasive. In the second part of the Cambridge play *The Return from Parnassus* (1601–03) the graduates Philomusus and Studioso seek to follow along the Greene path and try to secure employment as actors and scriptwriters from the leading actors of Shakespeare's company, Burbage and Kemp. The brush-off they receive indicates some of the impediments that still lay, even in the next decade, in the path of those who sought to travel from a Humanist education to a career in the popular theater. Kemp tells the graduates: "Few of the university men plays well; they smell too much of that writer Ovid and that writer Metamorphosis and talk too much of Proserpina and Jupiter." (4.3.1766–68)

Kemp's entirely plausible expression of what we can recognize as the recurrent tension between the stage and the academy seems to be confirmed on the other side of the same coin by the rhetoric of self-definition that the Wits themselves indulge in. Nashe, for example, relies entirely on attainments in the classical languages to make his distinction between authentic and merely imitative playwrights. In his preface to Greene's *Menaphon* (1589) entitled "To the gentlemen students of both universities" Nashe tries to draw an impassible line between authentically learned men and those hangers-on or pretenders that he refers to ironically as "deep read schoolmen or grammarians," students, that is, who have never passed from the grammar school to the university. These will, he assumes, display the superficialities of a classical education; but it will be easy to detect them as outsiders masquerading as insiders, for they are "at the mercy of their mother tongue, that feed on naught but the crumbs that fall from the translator's trencher." These are essentially lower-class persons whose incapacities betray them as existing only at the intellectual level of the "serving man" or of the dealer in "commodities" (that is, the merchant). (Nashe 3: 312)

Nashe's attack on lower-class pretenders to learning becomes more specific in the famous following passage in which he deals with the kinds of plays that such grammar-school authors are capable of writing. Again, the central issue is ignorance of Latin: such men can "scarcely Latinize their neck-verse if they should have need"; they are the "famished followers" of "English Seneca" (often thought to refer to Thomas Newton's 1581 collection of Seneca's plays), because they are incapable of reading the original; and yet they "busy themselves with the endeavors of art" (Nashe 3: 313)—where "art" has the sense of specialized knowledge that is found in such phrases as "Master of Arts." It looks, from much of the reference in this passage, as if Thomas Kyd is the playwright most particularly aimed at. And indeed if *The Spanish Tragedy* came out in 1588 (as is often supposed) then Kyd must have provided in 1588/89 an obvious example of a nonuniversity playwright with a great theatrical success on his hands. The obvious objection to such identification is that *The Spanish Tragedy* has few if any of the characteristics specified; indeed it is unusually full of Latin verse, some of it, apparently, of Kyd's own composition, and if the play within the play was actually performed in "sundry languages" then it also contained considerable dialogue in French, Italian, and Greek as well. Such evidence, however, tells us little about the intention that prompted Nashe's words. "Grub Street hacks," "outsiders" are clearly necessary to the self-definition of any group seeking to lay claim to the "inside" position, and Nashe is no more likely to have been in search of accuracy and justice, when he attached names to labels, than Pope was in *The Dunciad*. If a Kyd had not existed, Nashe would have had to invent him (as, in the passage in question he very nearly did).

If Thomas Kyd was in fact merely a famished follower of authentic graduate playwrights, then it is a great gap in nature that we do not know who these men were or what they wrote; there are not even plausible candidates. It seems more rational to suppose that there were no such model playwrights; and this probability is reinforced by the parallel case of Shakespeare. Greene's famous 1592 attack on Shakespeare (12: 144) as yet another despicable outsider, jumped-up actor, and jack-of-all-trades ("Johannes fac totum"), pranking himself in the "feathers" he has stolen from the graduates, has no more detail of evidence to support it than appears in the case of *The Spanish Tragedy*. *Titus Andronicus* and *Richard III* are indeed plays that draw on a considerable, even if only grammar-school, acquaintance with the classics. If this derived from new work in drama by the University Wits, then once again one must note that the lines of filiation have disappeared. But it is more probable that the whole issue of "authentic" and "imitative" dramaturgy is only the fantasy of a socially insecure group of graduates, anxious to destabilize the opposition.

To deny the accuracy of such polemical rhetoric is not, however, to deny altogether the creative importance of this generation of University Wits in the history of Elizabethan drama, though it is certainly to deny their claim to tell the whole story in their own terms. One fact remains, which must not be underplayed or denied: the success of Marlowe's First Part of *Tamburlaine* (usually dated 1587) completely fulfilled the self-confidence of the group of graduates to which he belonged. Here at last we have a work of popular entertainment which openly claims classic status, whose presence visibly altered the landscape in which it appeared and charged its environment with new meanings. Of course, given the general lack of information, it is impossible to say that there were no popular plays like *Tamburlaine* written before *Tamburlaine;*[3] but the self-consciousness of innovation which pervades its language, the comments of contemporaries, the immediate appearance of imitations, all combine to tell us that this was seen as an originating event, even if it was so only because it was so seen. The originality of *Tamburlaine* was not noted primarily, however, in terms of dramaturgy. His contemporaries spoke of Marlowe as above all a poet, and the Prologue to *Tamburlaine* shows that Marlowe agreed with them. But the point being made is not only about versification, narrowly conceived; it is rather a point about the spirit that speaks through a poetry which is (as Michael Drayton was later to remark) "all air and fire" (3: 229) or (to quote Marlowe himself) "Like his desire, lift upward and divine." And this is, it will be noticed, a return to dramaturgy by the back door. For the theatrical function of a poetry as distinctive and powerful as that of *Tamburlaine* is to require of the auditor that he follow the action inside a particular given focus. In crude terms one can say that in *Tamburlaine* Marlowe presented the history of the outsider, the man of talents rather than of background, not in the traditional terms of social marginality but locked into a system of values where energy and desire are everything and need the great outside only to secure the greatest resonance "like the fa-burden of Bow bell," as Greene remarked (7: 8). Set against the hero's unfettered expression of individual will, the "insiders" of *Tamburlaine* are seen as passive, conformist, hesitant, as if only waiting to be taken over or destroyed by the individual whose force comes from believing in himself more than in anything outside.

It is time to ask the question how far the Marlovian vision and the Marlovian verse that conveys it are the product of a particular kind of education or representative of what we understand to have been the aspirations of the group of University Wits. Certainly there is little, if anything, in it that can be charged against imitation of classical authors read at university. But it is a mistake (as I have suggested above) to think that the focus of university education in this period was literary. The excitement of intellectual life in the sixteenth century came less from classical poetry than from the controversies of theology and from the techniques by which these could be conducted (see Kearney). From today's point of view the whole interest of such activities looks merely technical; but if we are to understand the excitement roused in the spirit of the times we can hardly afford to stop there. Clearly in such matters as the acceptance or rejection of sacraments, the belief or disbelief in the efficacy of works, the view taken on the mediation of the saints, the status of Purgatory, the function of vestments, we are dealing with the interlocking parts of total systems, where one false move can betray a whole understanding of the life of man, not only in eternity but in the daily life of earth as well. If the excitement of *Tamburlaine* can be seen to grow out of the intellectual energies generated in such disputes, then it becomes possible to argue that the play reflects its graduate generation at a deeper level than those we have so far considered.

Writing in 1588, Robert Greene spoke of the self-confident energy of Marlowe's verse as the expression of atheism: "daring God out of his heaven with that atheist Tamburlaine" (7: 8). Perhaps it is improper to make too much of the vocabulary used here. The context of the comment (Greene's jealousy of Marlowe's success) is not one likely to guarantee accuracy in the critical remark made. And "atheist" was in this period only a term of general abuse, with little necessary connection to specific doctrine (Febvre, ch. 2, sec. 6). On the other hand Marlowe was soon to acquire, and perhaps already had acquired, a considerable reputation as a freethinker. The idea that the power of *Tamburlaine* is directly connected to "atheism" may indeed point us toward more complex issues than are usually attached to Greene's scandals, for there are a number of interesting connections, which are largely obscured by the archaic vocabulary.

The more modern image of Marlowe is often presented in terms of that largely fictional genus "the Renaissance man"—Burckhardt's creatively amoral egotist, whether seen as artist (Aretino, Michelangelo,

Cellini) or as prince (Cesare Borgia, Julius II, Bernabo Visconti). But "Renaissance individualism," at least as it reached England, had rather different sources. And these take us back to the question of atheism once again. The key figures in such general growth of individualism as one can observe in England are neither artists nor the sacred monsters of royalty (egotism in the powerful is a characteristic so constant that it is hard to imagine it as having a history); they are rather the purveyors of reformed theology, Luther and Zwingli and Calvin and their native disseminators. The "Renaissance man" type of egotist who defines his individuality *against* orthodoxy is necessarily limited in the range of imitation he can inspire, for it is integral to his stance that he remain exceptional. Luther, however, and the other reformers, embodied individualism not against but inside orthodoxy, and indeed declared the sense of self to be the necessary basis of "true" orthodoxy. In this form the sense of the unique centrality of individual consciousness could penetrate throughout the culture of Europe to a degree not possible for the tyrants and exploiters of an older mode. And this was, as I say, the form in which "the Renaissance" pervaded England, so that, in England at any rate, the New Learning or Humanism inevitably explored classical forms and attitudes inside a world filled with the noise of challenge to intellectual conformity. In his search for justification by faith alone the individual could no longer hope to discover his identity by finding his place in any external system, for faith can only be felt and known inwardly. The doctrine of the slavery of the will (the *servum arbitrium*) required, paradoxically, that the individual remain in continued personal contact with the sources of God's Grace if he was to hope for eventual escape from the chains of Satan's power (Luther 327–32). The Reformed individual was thus continually caught up as protagonist in the largest and most terrifying drama that can be imagined, required to struggle and ask and decide and achieve, in a Satanic world, and without any external mediation. It would be surprising if this raw demand for extraordinary human capacity, marking the eventual irrelevance of external restraint, could be kept out of other areas of life, most significantly those where individual destiny must mean something more like secular fulfillment than loss of self in the Grace of God.[4] Of course, even the states which endorsed the Reformation struggled continuously against its antinomian tendencies, especially as these manifested themselves in political contexts. In England the hundred years or so between the 1530s and the 1640s saw a continuous effort to maintain system, order, consensus, in loyalty to the nation, the sovereign, the church, the tradition (as reinterpreted). Not all the weapons available to the state were equally effective, however. Nationalist fervor, suspicion of and contempt for foreigners, was a powerful means of securing consensus against the Pope, the Spaniards, and the Jesuits, but these positions were most powerfully argued by radical believers in the unmediated presence of Christ in the individual life. The corrosive solution that dissolved the foreign threat also ate into the English hierarchy.

The political argument against individualism was weakened on yet another front. The language of intellectual argument for loyalty inherited, inevitably, the language of Erasmian Humanism, of persuasion to civil order by the civilized consent of an educated elite (such as is addressed in the ironic mode of More's *Utopia,* for example) of finely disputable interpretations of uncertain texts (as in Erasmus's New Testament), of specialized and technical knowledge allowed to develop its own pragmatic justification ("arts" of war, health, navigation, algebra were all published in English in the fifties and sixties).[5] The English "Renaissance" book with probably the widest influence, Foxe's *Acts and Monuments* ("Foxe's Book of Martyrs") of 1563, was not only an epic of nationalism but also an epic of humble individualism (of widows, cooks, fishermen, brewers, and bricklayers, as well as scholars and clergymen) divinely justified in their rejection of the institutions of social control. The conflict depicted is not in the high romantic mode of *The Golden Legend,* set in exotic regions and the remote past. Foxe presents his readers with the recent and the local, describing lives rooted in the commonplaces of the ordinary and inculcating truth more by the evidence of shared experience than by any doctrinal argument. In all these cases, I would argue, a sense of the potential power of the unmediated individual, though disseminated primarily in religious terms, is bound to have created, in imagination at least, an idea that every self is capable of fulfillment and definition by resistance to conformity or convention. This is certainly the note in Elizabethan drama that we hear sounded clearly, for the first time, in *Tamburlaine.* The energetic individualism that appears in *Tamburlaine* has little or nothing to do with the "Renaissance individualism" of the late Quattrocento princes. Tamburlaine starts from nowhere and his dizzying rise to power is entirely self-generated out of assumptions that have nothing to support them in the world outside. He is totally free of the complacency of power, turning his eyes, as soon as he has achieved any one thing, to further horizons where he can test himself still further. The attitude of mind that is depicted here seems to be one that it is not inappropriate to consider as an atheistic version of the Lutheran soul in its search for justification through faith—atheistic because in this case the believer has simply excluded God from the equation and concentrated his faith on himself, at once justifier and justified.

If this was, in fact, the source of Marlowe/Tamburlaine's access of dazzling theatrical energy, his hunger for justification by power, it cannot surprise us that it was a source from which the other University Wits shrank back. They rushed to imitate the style, yet were voluble in their abhorrence of the beliefs of the man; and they seem not to have been too troubled by the contradiction. Presumably they took it that *Tamburlaine*'s lofty rejection of theatrical as of other conformism, and the new possibilities that this opened up for dramatic poetry, need bring only the *style* of self-assertion into fashion in the theater; they hoped to be able to spend Marlowe's legacy without remembering the means by which he had acquired it.[6]

By and large they were justified in their hope (as we shall see below). The history of Elizabethan drama is a history of compromises rather than of revolutions. But the initial revolution represented by *Tamburlaine* probably had to occur before the compromising could begin. Compromise is only likely to occur when two different systems of roughly equal weight and value are close enough to make exchange of elements a natural process. Greene's fulminations at the self-esteem of the acting fraternity do not open any path toward compromise: the values espoused by the two sides are too different to permit exchange. But when *Tamburlaine* had taken the stage by storm the Wits at last had a counter they could lay on the table. Of course we have no way of knowing how the negotiations proceeded, or if anyone was conscious that there was a process that might be called "negotiation." The evidence we possess suggests that no clones of *Tamburlaine I* could be produced; even *Tamburlaine II* represents a change of focus and a retreat into compromise. I have suggested that the other Wits took fright at the intellectual radicalism of Marlowe's play. One may also suspect that the innate conservatism of the theatrical institutions also exerted pressure toward a drama that might offer Tamburlainean excitement inside more traditional forms. What forms were these? Marlowe refers to his immediate predecessors as "rhyming mother wits"; but we cannot tell who these men were. There are, however, a few plays surviving from the decade before *Tamburlaine* that outline theatrical conditions that Marlowe seems to be flouting, quite deliberately, even while they deal with issues that Marlowe picks up (and changes).

The *Conflict of Conscience,* by Nathaniel Woodes, "Minister, in Norwich," is dated 1579 in the Malone Society Reprint, but 1572 (1570–81) in Harbage/Schoenbaum. In terms of technique the work could have been written at any time in the preceding fifty years; but its subject has a density and detail that mark the onset of the drama of particular lives. The hero, usually referred to as *Philologus,* represents, in fact, a real person, one Francis Spira, an Italian lawyer of the earlier part of the century who was persuaded to abandon the truths of Protestant doctrine and to revert to the falsehood of Catholicism; then, faced by the horror of the offense he had given to God and his conscience, he fell into despair and killed himself. Throughout the play we are shown the tragic destiny of the individual conscience, pressed on by the loss of everything that is desirable in the world—"fair children . . . wife most amiable . . . delicate diet . . . life lascivious," and by the certainty of the dungeon and the stake, "dolorous death which would me betray / And my felicity from me take away" (1596–1600). After interminable argument and temptation Spira proves unable to resist the pressure all around him. Then, of course, he has to face the opposite torment from within, and the certainty of not a temporary but an eternal loss. The rigorous logic of Spira's story (as told by Calvin and associates in 1549) is not, however, a logic that the dramatic form Woodes is using can sustain. He calls his play a "comedy" *(An excellent new comedy entitled The Conflict of Conscience, containing the most lamentable history of the desperation of Francis Spera, who forsook the truth of God's gospel for fear of the loss of life and worldly goods).* But for all the elasticity of the term "comedy" in the period

Woodes seems to have decided, at an early stage, to revise his work and evade the inexorable logic of the individual career.

In the first version of the play Woodes showed in Spira's suicide the logical consequence of his status as a mere "Philologus," that is someone "that loves to talk, / And common of the word of God, but hath no further care/ According as it teacheth them, in God's fear for to walk" (43–45), so that "Here may worldlings have a glass, their states for to behold" (2392). But at some point after the printing Woodes seems to have reconsidered the generic truth of what he had said in the Prologue: that

> a comedy will hardly him permit
> The vices of one private man, to touch particularly
> . . . .
> For if that SPERA had been one, we would straight deem in mind,
> That all by SPERA spoken were, our selves we would not find.
>
> (38–42)

The concern for immediate effect on an audience thus drives Woodes to insert cancel pages at the beginning and the end of his text, so that he can not only omit Spira's name but also provide comfort, even to "worldlings," by demonstrating that God can forgive sinners, though they may seem to be beyond Grace. In the new version Spira no longer commits suicide, but dies in God's time not his own. The pursuit of Christian consensus and the mode of "comedy" thus conspire together, as traditionally, to distort "the facts of the case." It looks as if the tragic potential of Spira's story could not at this time find any corresponding support in aesthetic or theatrical understanding; it is not until we come to Marlowe's handling of the parallel story in *Doctor Faustus* that we meet a capacity to handle individual rejection of consensus as tragic heroism.[7]

Woodes's play is an interesting historical document of the conflict between individual character on the one hand and the poetic range and dramatic form that the pre-*Tamburlaine* theater allowed, on the other hand. The plays of Robert Wilson demonstrate the nature of these theatrical constraints more effectively in terms of the achievements they made possible. Wilson was a well-known actor, one of the "twelve of the best" chosen in 1583 to be players for the queen, and noted in the account of this formation in Stowe's *Annals* (1615 edition) "for a quick, delicate, refined, extemporal wit" (Chambers 2: 349). As an actor-writer he was, presumably, one of that group that Greene and Nashe thought of as desperately anxious to buy the superior talents of the university graduates. Little sign of this appears, however, in the extant work. His *The Three Ladies of London* (1581)— probably his best play—shows his remarkable skill as a manipulator of theatrical responses, a skill that comes to life with particular vividness if we think of this play as not only a vehicle for his company (whatever it was at this time) but more particularly as providing a vehicle for himself in the role of the clown-raisonneur Simplicity. Simplicity, we should notice, is another outsider figure. But he is an outsider who has neither desire nor talent to become an insider. He is the rude but innocent countryman who reaches London without having any grasp on the nature of its capitalist activities and who is continually exploited by the devotees of Lady Lucre, whose corruptions he can perceive but whose dominance he is powerless to affect. Alone among the twenty-three speaking characters in the play Simplicity is never absorbed into the system ruled by Lucre; but this intransigence does not give him the status of a hero. Wilson indicates how easy it is to read Simplicity's innocence as ignorance, his naïveté as simplemindedness, his failure as his own fault. We may accept the doctrinal truth of what Simplicity says about the world, but we cannot identify with him (any more than we can identify with the Fool in *King Lear*). Like the Fool's, his career is a record of failure.[8] We leave him, toward the end of the action, being whipped for crimes he did not commit, while the well-placed criminals he has sought to expose look on and urge the need for exemplary punishment so that society can be properly protected. The eventual rescue of society from the vices of capitalism cannot come, we learn, from any of the characters inside the play. In the last scene a characterless "Judge Nemo" descends from heaven (as it were) and condemns everyone in sight. Simplicity's point of view is justified, but Simplicity is not around any more to enjoy the justification. The importance for the audience of the fact that this is a secular variant of the story of Christ's career in the world is obvious enough; but the political consequence should also be mentioned: the rescue of society, it is implied, cannot derive from any effort by any individual but will emerge from the operation of larger forces far outside human reach. The author and the audience can end the play in moral unison, but this is a unison in submission which flattens all the individual characters in the action.

Robert Wilson's *The Cobbler's Prophecy* of 1590 was probably performed at court (Chambers 3: 516), but it has few characteristics that mark it as exclusively courtly; and we may assume, I think, that it was performed also in the public theater. It offers an interesting companion-piece to *The Three Ladies of London,* especially if we allow the figure of Raph Cobbler to be another persona designed by Wilson for himself and therefore strictly comparable to Simplicity in the earlier play. The Cobbler is another bewildered prole, this time caught up by fiat of the Olympian gods into a prophetic eloquence which he pours out on rulers and wrongdoers alike. But, like Simplicity, Raph Cobbler remains very much a marginal figure as far as effective action is concerned. The effective movement to rescue society from the dalliance of Venus and Contempt (two versions of effeminacy) is supplied by Sateros, the soldier, who drives the whole action toward a morally rejuvenating war. The Cobbler, it seems, is going to end up punished (like Simplicity) for his violent and opinionated opposition to his social superiors, but he is pardoned at the last minute, and the gods restore him to proper humility as a working cobbler. Once again the author identifies himself with a truth-teller; but a truth-teller (even one with supernatural eloquence) is necessarily a marginal figure in terms of social restoration, constantly liable to get above himself, constantly endangered, and protected only by the jokes and ambiguities he shares with the audience (again like the Fool in *Lear*). The vices of society may be exposed in such ways, but social reform must come about by other means. The community that Simplicity or Raph Cobbler establish with the audience in the playhouse is a community of powerlessness, cemented by their joking together while they wait for the powers out of reach to make their unforecastable appearance. Simplicity and Raph Cobbler secure their powerful bond of comic consensus between the stage and the auditorium only because they present social vice from the essentially ineffective viewpoint of its victims. They show clowns to be better moralists than lords, but such subversions are essentially comic and collusive, easily accommodated inside the existing social hierarchy.

There is nothing here that corresponds to the University Wit voice of such a character as Nashe's Jack Wilton, equally powerless in his social role, but offering his readers, as it were, a way out of their standard subjection, the way of self-sufficient skepticism, even cynicism.[9]

The clearly understood relation between actor and audience in the popular theater of the eighties is shown with great clarity in the Prologue that Wilson wrote for *The Three Ladies of London*. Humble and undogmatic, Wilson leaves the decision about the kind of play he has written to the judgment of his auditors. Like the later (and markedly different) Prologue to *Tamburlaine,* Wilson begins by running through a number of the things that do not appear in his play. This is not a mythological nor yet a militaristic play, not one dealing with gods and devils, not a love play, not a pastoral or countrified play. What then? He defines it, in fact, only as a commercial play, one designed to please and so to sell. Its power to please is like that of a stall set up in front of a shop: there is a variety of goods that might attract customers, some one way, some another. But the decision, the "lead," he is careful to say, will always come from the customer, not the author.

The Prologue

To sit on honour's seat it is a lofty reach:
To seek for praise by making brags ofttimes doth get a breach.
We list not ride the rolling racks that dim the crystal skies,
We mean to set no glimmering glance before your courteous eyes:
We search not Pluto's pensive pit, nor taste of Limbo lake;
We do not show of warlike fight, as sword and shield to shake:
We speak not of the powers divine, ne yet of furious sprites;
We do not seek high hills to climb, nor talk of love's delights.
We do not here present to you the thresher with his flail,
Ne do we here present to you the milkmaid with her pail:
We show not you of country toil, as hedger with his bill;
We do not bring the husbandman to lop and top with skill:
We play not here the gardener's part, to plant, to set and sow:
You marvel, then, what stuff we have to furnish out our show.
Your patience yet we crave a while, till we have trimm'd our stall;
Then, young and old, come and behold our wares, and buy them all.
Then, if our wares shall seem to you well-woven, good and fine,
We hope we shall your custom have again another time.

To turn straight from Wilson's Prologue to *The Three Ladies of London* to Marlowe's Prologue to *Tamburlaine* is to move straight from the deference of the actor to the arrogance of the author, from pleading to command, from "clownage" to the "tragic glass," from "jigging veins of rhyming mother wits" to "high astounding terms." If theatrical excitement can be assimilated to the excitement of participating in a revolution (even if only a revolution of sensibility) then here indeed we find the revolution the Wits had been hoping for:

> From jigging veins of rhyming mother wits,
> And such conceits as clownage keeps in pay,
> We'll lead you to the stately tent of war,
> Where you shall hear the Scythian Tamburlaine
> Threat'ning the world with high astounding terms
> And scourging kingdoms with his conquering sword.
> View but his picture in this tragic glass,
> And then applaud his fortunes as you please.

Marlowe is not asking his audience to see if they can find anything attractive on his sedulously trimmed "stall." He will "lead" them, and they have no alternative but to follow. In some of the terms he uses Marlowe is clearly at one with Greene and Nashe: his "rhyming mother wits" are placed in the same category as Nashe's "deep read grammarians . . . at the mercy of their mother tongue"; but Marlowe, unlike his fellow graduates, moves directly from his condemnation of others to his demonstration of himself, exemplifying in the play that follows the overwhelming alternative he has to offer. Clownage, commercialism, vernacular limitation, lower-class verse forms, have all been swept away; in their place the audience will now be shown a "scene . . . more stately furnished than ever it was in the time of Roscius . . . not consisting . . . of a Pantaloon, a Whore and a Zany, but of Emperors, Kings, and Princes, whose true tragedies (*Sophocleo cothurno*) they do vaunt"—as Nashe in his *Pierce Peniless* (1592) described the new English stage (Nashe 1: 215). Marlowe's appeal to the audience (without which the play could not have been a success) is directed not toward identification with a familiar world endorsing familiar values but toward astonishment at finding oneself in free flight into the dangerous unknown. The audience is not to be reassured, but everywhere terrified, horrified, stimulated, by the discovery that this is not a world in control but one in continual instability, one whose energies point not toward completion but only toward the further reaches of desire.

The creative daring of *Tamburlaine*'s author, his clear intention to defy theatrical orthodoxy, mirrors exactly the creative daring of his hero. The destruction of social hierarchy inside the action finds external correspondence in the conquering rhetoric of the new mode of theatrical projection. Author and hero may be "outsiders," but they are not content to be understood as provincials or "clowns," having to cling to the margins of "good society" for justification. The Reformation had given to every individual the possibility of a unique power as the echo-chamber of the voice of God, and Humanism had added to this the sense that the *novus homo* could become, by the transforming power of education, the agent of cultural *renovatio*. Marlowe drew on both these contemporary images by way of creative parody. Tamburlaine's declared confidence in himself as God's elected "scourge" reinterprets conscience as a directive toward conquest, so that absolute power becomes the evidence of righteousness and divine favor.[10]

The writing of *Tamburlaine* thus answers, it would seem, the question I posed at the beginning of this essay. The sense of liberated individuality that Tamburlaine projects, and the accompanying invitation to every individual in the audience to project his own fantasies of Tamburlainean behavior—undoubtedly this created a new sense of what the theater could do. The rash of conqueror plays that followed show contemporary response to the liberation thus provided. Of course there had been plays of tyrannic exorbitancy before this time. But the older mode of *Cambyses* or *Apius and Virginia* dealt primarily with the decline of kingship when power becomes its own justification; the wickedness of such tyrants was represented as a collapse of true humanity (under God) into an animal ferocity of desire. Following the lead of *Tamburlaine,* such plays as Greene's *Alphonsus, King of Aragon,* Shakespeare's *Richard III,* Peele's *Alcazar,* the anonymous plays *The True Tragedy of Richard III* and *Selimus,* deal with usurpation rather than tyrannic rule, with the rise rather than the fall of power. But in imitating *Tamburlaine* they change its mode. What they offer is the image of a world controlled by *Realpolitik,* through which the outsider must make his way by appropriate treachery and manipulation, using a series of plots and deceptions to open up the cracks and mistrusts between members of the ruling clique. In *Tamburlaine* itself only the opening moves of the hero conform to this pattern: he allies himself with Cosroe to defeat Mycetes, and then, in possession of the army, he decides to overthrow Cosroe as well. But even in this move Tamburlaine is presented as more a force of natural selection than a plotter; and thereafter his opponents are arranged in a paratactic sequence, so that the emphasis lies on "the long majestic march and energy divine" rather than on the political process by which the victories are achieved. But the heroic energy of Marlowe's verse seems to be the one fuel able to sustain such movement; and after *Tamburlaine* even Marlowe himself seems disinclined to sustain that note. The other conqueror plays I have mentioned keep it only as a special effect. The weblike structure of power in any polity realistically considered requires the outsider who wishes to become an insider to move by a series of indirections, "with windlasses and with assays of bias," as Polonius describes it (*Hamlet* 2.1.65–66). In such structures grand gestures are ruled out, almost of necessity. The edifice of resident power can only be brought down by concealment, cunning, and apparent humility. And so something of the pre-*Tamburlaine* dramaturgy comes to be reinstated. The spectacle of great criminal careers that derive from Marlowe continues to invite an appalled identification from the audience, but the method of identification has slipped a couple of notches. In Marlowe's Guise or Barabas, in Richard III or Selimus, we find our attention engaged once again with the wiles of the Tudor Vice figure, whose abstracted characteristics have now been integrated into the psychological processes of *Realpolitik* (see Spivack). Another aspect of this is the return to "clownage," to the "fond and frivolous gestures" that *Tamburlaine* (as printed, at least) was supposed to have sent into exile.[11]

As I have said, no doubt some of the pressure leading to this turn from revolution to compromise came from the institution of the theater itself, from the despised actors that Greene had represented as existing at an intellectual dead-end, and in desperate need of the new drama that only the graduate generation could supply. The generation of the University Wits certainly did have an effect on the history of the

Elizabethan drama: plays with an analytic and political view of the historical process achieved popularity (*The Massacre at Paris, The Battle of Alcazar,* for example), though without altogether displacing chivalric romance—remember that *Mucedorus* was the most reprinted play of the era. The hybrid Moralities largely withered away. The clumsily moving and heavily moralistic fourteener (whose predictable rhythms seem to have been specially designed to carry clichés) was abandoned in favor of the expressionistic power of speech-accented blank verse. In all these aspects the generation of the middle nineties inherited a remade medium. But in other ways, many of them central and inescapable, the revolution was only fulfilled to the degree that the French Revolution was fulfilled by the reign of Louis Philippe. A structure of highly various, loosely connected scenes, here Asia, there Africa, drawing on a wide range of characters and events, some high-class, some low, some comic, some tragic, continued to provide the staple fare. Shakespeare offers us *Realpolitik* but flanks it with clown comedy; and at the end of his career he is willing to return to the jigging veins of Gower and the humble self-exculpations of Time. Behind the changes a deep continuity continues to manifest itself.

If we are surprised at this development it is mainly because we bring an inappropriate focus to bear. The history of Elizabethan drama is normally written as part of the history of literature or else as an aspect of intellectual history; but it is less either of these than it is the history of specific institutions, of the theatrical companies, their economic practices, their buildings, their relationships to the centers of power and patronage. The University Wits sought to change the conditions of playwriting, for good authorial reasons; they sought to redefine it as an activity that would allow them to impose their literary values on the extant institutions. In such matters, however, individuals may propose, but institutions dispose. And institutions seldom accept change unless there are good institutional reasons for doing so (decline in profits, problems of public order, trouble with censorship). At a later point in the story it may well be that the literary taste of the court may have had an effect on such popular playwriting as might reach the court. But at the dates we are considering this does not seem to be an important factor. In the generation of the University Wits, if the graduates were to make any headway in the popular theater, they had to learn to live inside the requirements of its trade. The trade, no doubt, was content to accept the up-market elements that graduate writers could supply, so long as they stayed inside the traditional popular forms that actors knew how to manage and that the public was used to. The ambition to move outside these constraints required for its fulfillment nothing less than a new cultural milieu.

Notes

[1]The dates we know (or believe on the basis of good evidence) are as follows:

Lyly	born 1554	graduated 1575 M.A.
Peele	born 1557	graduated 1579 M.A.
Lodge	born 1557	graduated 1577 B.A. +
Greene	born 1558	graduated 1583 M.A.
Marlowe	born 1564	graduated 1587 M.A.
Nashe	born 1567	graduated 1586 B.A. +

The phrase "graduated B.A. + " is used to indicate that the student took the B.A. in that year and stayed on at the university, but did not graduate M.A.

[2]See, for example, Salingar, who describes how "actor's companies, employing the University wits, established the technical conventions of Elizabethan staging, which remained broadly similar from the building of the first playhouse in 1576 to the closing of the theatres in 1643" (2, 66). The nomenclature used to describe the periods is, of course, very mixed. In *English Drama,* ed. Wells, the period before Marlowe is called "Tudor and Early Elizabethan Drama" (no distinction between these two being observable inside the chapter). In vol. 5 of *The Cambridge History of English Literature* tragedy up to *Selimus* (1592) and *Locrine* (1591) is called "Early English Tragedy."

[3]The word "popular" must be stressed in this context. J. P. Brawner in his edition of the anonymous *The Wars of Cyrus* (1942) has argued that the Marlovian versification of this play should be dated some ten years before *Tamburlaine.* But *The Wars of Cyrus* is a courtly play designed for performance by singing boys. Academic tragedy in Latin (such as Richard Legge's *Richardus Tertius,* c. 1580, and the anonymous *Solymannidae* of 1582) offers precedents, but once again in a very different medium.

[4]The social liberation that Reformed doctrine could provide under certain circumstances has been discussed most commonly in terms of capitalist enterprise, as in Weber, and Tawney.

[5]Robert Recorde, *The Castle of Knowledge* (1556) and *The Whetstone of Wit* (1557)—the latter dealing with algebra; Thomas Tusser, *A Hundred Good Points of Husbandry* (1557); William Bullein, *The Government of Health* (1558); Peter Whitehorne [translating Machiavelli], *The Art of War* (1560); Richard Eden [translating Cortes], *The Art of*

Navigation (1561); William Bullein, *A Bulwark against All Sickness* (1562); Richard Rainolde [translating Aphthonius], *The Foundation of Rhetoric* (1563); William Bullein, *A Dialogue against the Fever Pestilence* (1564); Humphrey Baker, *The Wellspring of Sciences* (1568)—dealing with arithmetic.

⁶The style alone was sufficient to raise strong moral and social objections. The third satire of the first book of Joseph Hall's *Virgidemiarum* (1598) gives a full account. Hall charges that those whom Ben Jonson was later to describe as "the ignorant gapers" at *Tamburlaine* (Jonson, VIII, 587) will be morally damaged by identifying with the hero: "some upreared, high-aspiring swain . . . doth set his soaring thought / On crowned kings . . . As it might be the Turkish Tamburlaine. / Then weeneth he his base drink-drowned spright / Rapt to the three-fold loft of heaven's height, / When he conceives upon his feigned stage / The stalking steps of his great personage, / Graced with huff-cap terms and thundering threats / That his poor hearers' hair quite upright sets . . . Now swooping inside robes of royalty / That erst did scrub in lousy brokery."

⁷In "*Dr. Faustus:* A Case of Conscience," Lily B. Campbell conducts an extended comparison of these two plays.

⁸For an interesting and relevant comment on the social role of the Fool character see Weimann.

⁹I believe that there is no need to argue the inappropriateness of such a controlling cynicism in the theatrical context of that period.

¹⁰The role of Tamburlaine as the "scourge of God" has been most elaborately treated in Battenhouse, but in terms opposite to those proposed here.

¹¹See the preface to *Tamburlaine* by the printer (Richard Jones)—"To the gentlemen readers and others that take delight in reading histories: I have purposely omitted and left out some fond and frivolous gestures, digressing and, in my poor opinion, far unmeet for the matter, which I thought might seem more tedious unto the wise than any way to be regarded, though haply they may have been of some vain-conceited fondlings greatly gaped at what time they were showed upon the stage in their graced deformities."

Works Cited

BATTENHOUSE, ROY W. *Marlowe's "Tamburlaine": A Study in Renaissance Moral Philosophy.* Nashville: Vanderbilt UP, 1941.

BRAWNER, J. P., ed. *The Wars of Cyrus.* Illinois Studies in Language and Literature 28: 3–4. Urbana: U of Illinois P, 1942.

CAMPBELL, LILY B. "Dr. Faustus: A Case of Conscience." *PMLA* 67 (1952): 219–39.

CHAMBERS, E. K. *The Elizabethan Stage.* 4 vols. Oxford: Clarendon, 1923.

DRAYTON, MICHAEL. "To my most dearly loved friend, Henry Reynolds, Esquire." *The Works of Michael Drayton*. Ed. J. W. Hebel and K. Tillotson. 5 vols. Oxford: Blackwell, 1934–41.

FEBVRE, LUCIEN. *La probleme de l'incroyance au xvi^e siecle*. Paris: Michel, 1942.

GREENE, ROBERT. *The Life and Complete Works in Prose and Verse*. Ed. Alexander B. Grosart. 15 vols. Printed for private circulation only, 1881–86.

HALL, JOSEPH. *Poems*. Ed. Arnold Davenport. Liverpool: Liverpool UP, 1949.

JONSON, BEN. *Works*. Ed. C. H. Herford and Percy and Evelyn Simpson. 11 vols. Oxford: Clarendon, 1925–52.

KEARNEY, HUGH F. *Scholars and Gentlemen: Universities and Society in Pre-Industrial Britain 1500–1700*. London: Faber, 1970.

LUTHER, MARTIN. *On the Bondage of the Will. Luther and Erasmus: Free Will and Salvation*. Ed. Philip S. Watson and B. Drewery. Philadelphia: Westminster, 1969.

MARLOWE, CHRISTOPHER. *The Plays*. Ed. Roma Gill. London: Oxford UP, 1971.

NASHE, THOMAS. *The Works*. Ed. R. B. McKerrow. 5 vols. London: Sidgwick and Jackson, 1904–10.

The Three Parnassus Plays. Ed. J. B. Leishmann. London: Nicholson and Watson, 1949.

SALINGAR, LEO. "The Elizabethan Literary Renaissance." *A Guide to English Literature*. Ed. Boris Ford. Harmondsworth: Penguin, 1955.

SIDNEY, PHILIP. *An Apology for Poetry*. Ed. Geoffrey Shepherd. London: Nelson, 1965.

SPIVACK, BERNARD. *Shakespeare and the Allegory of Evil*. New York: Columbia UP, 1958.

TAWNEY, R. H. *Religion and the Rise of Capitalism*. London: Murray, 1926.

WARD, A. W. and A. R. WALLER, eds. *The Cambridge History of English Literature*. 15 vols. Cambridge: Cambridge UP, 1907–27.

WEBER, MAX. *The Protestant Ethic*. New York: Scribner, 1930.

WEIMANN, ROBERT. *Shakespeare and the Popular Tradition in the Theater*. Baltimore: Johns Hopkins UP, 1978.

WELLS, STANLEY, ed. *English Drama: Excluding Shakespeare*. London: Oxford UP, 1975.

WILSON, ROBERT. *The Cobbler's Prophecy,* 1594. Ed. A. C. Wood. Oxford: Malone Society Reprints, 1914.

_____. *The Three Ladies of London,* 1590. Vol. 6 of Dodsley's *Select Collection of Old English Plays.* Ed. W. C. Hazlitt. 15 vols. London: Reeves and Turner, 1874–76.

WOODES, NATHANIEL. *The Conflict of Conscience,* 1581. Ed. Herbert Davis and F. P. Wilson. Oxford: Malone Society Reprints, 1952.

The Crowd in Theater and the Crowd in History: Fuenteovejuna

ANGUS MacKAY AND GERALDINE McKENDRICK

LOPE DE VEGA'S play *Fuenteovejuna,* dating from the early seventeenth century and based on real events which took place in 1476, presents us with the image of a justified and exemplary rebellion by the oppressed against their tyrannical lord.[1] It is this image, coupled with other features of the drama, which no doubt accounts for the enduring attraction of the play over the years. Basically, the plot tells the story of a group hero, the decent people of Fuenteovejuna, who, goaded by the barbaric treatment inflicted on them by their lord, the *comendador mayor* of the military Order of Calatrava, Fernán Gómez de Guzmán, rose up in a "peasant fury" one April night, stormed the house of the *comendador,* and, after a fierce conflict, savaged him to death.

By almost all his actions the *comendador* reveals that he is a tyrant, disrupting the harmony which should characterize the relationship between lord and vassals, and continually abusing his authority by stepping beyond the bounds of what is legal. His main crime is that of arbitrary sexual enjoyment from which none of the women is safe, but in the course of attempting to fulfill his desires he also abuses the males

311

of the town and totally disregards those locals who, under him, constitute part of the urban authority or government. The rebellion,
therefore, is justified. It is a rebellion in which *all* the people of Fuenteovejuna participate. Naturally, Lope peopled his "crowd" with individuals, but these individuals are transcended, and the generic crowd
becomes the hero in a peculiarly convincing and dramatic way.[2] They
act as one and, after the deed, they continue to act as one. What they
have done is, of course, shocking, even if we, the audience, know that
it is justified. Inevitably, therefore, the Catholic kings send a judge to
Fuenteovejuna to determine who led the rising and who is responsible.
But when putting his questions, even under torture inflicted oñ women
and children, the only answer he gets is: "Fuenteovejuna did it."

JUDGE

That boy!
Tighter, dog, I know
that you know. Tell who it was!
Keeping quiet? Tighter, you drunk.

BOY

Fuenteovejuna, sir.[3]

The dramatic crowd not only acts as one but it provides its own justifications with the result that the "peasant fury" of the play is replete
with disciplined, structured actions. The cry of ";Fuenteovejuna!,"
for example, is accompanied by the fundamental justification of the
rebellion which consists of a combination of what may be termed "naïve monarchism" and the accusation of tyranny leveled against the *comendador* and his men.[4] This is a combination which is repeated
many times:

MENGO

Long live the kings, our
lords!

ALL

Long may they live!

MENGO

Death to tyrannical traitors!

ALL
Death to treacherous tyrants![5]

To this fundamental justification, however, two others of lesser importance should be added. In the first place, the "naïve monarchism" is to some extent linked to a wider "national" perspective, the actions taking place within a historical context in which the *comendador* is depicted as treacherously aiding the Portuguese enemy against the legitimate monarchs, Ferdinand and Isabella. Secondly, the *comendador* and his men are repeatedly depicted as "bad Christians" as well as tyrants, an accusation which, as will be seen, is not without its significance:

ALL
Fuenteovejuna! Long live King Ferdinand!
Death to bad Christians and traitors![6]

Of course it would be idle to pretend that a great deal of the play was not the product of Lope de Vega's dramatic imagination. His Fuenteovejuna is, as a place, characterized by an idealized and primitive arcadian harmony, and its honorable peasants are unconvincingly capable of debating learned and metaphysical problems in homely rustic speech.[7] This harmony/honor is violently overturned by the evil *comendador,* and it is only by the counterviolence of rebellion that harmony/honor is restored. It has been argued, and rightly so, that Lope de Vega marked each of these three stages with important ritualistic ceremonies. In Act 1, when the people of Fuenteovejuna welcome their *comendador* in a ritualistic manner on his entry into the town, the ceremony emphasizes the harmony that should prevail between a lord and his subjects. In Act 2 a wedding ceremony, once again ritualistically emphasizing the harmony that should prevail among the people of Fuenteovejuna, is violently interrupted by the *comendador* who puts an end to the festivities and carries off the wedding couple by force. Finally, in Act 3, the ritualistic acts of the crowd, terminating in the murder of the comendador, mark the transition to a situation of harmony/honor restored.[8]

The play, then, has a dramatic and group hero, the crowd, and this crowd acts in a structured and ordered way with justifications for resorting to what Natalie Davis would call "The Rites of Violence." But since

Lope de Vega based his play on a historical episode which took place in 1476, several intriguing questions arise. Did "the crowd in history" act in the same way as the ordered "crowd in the play"? Were the rituals of violence in 1476 as prevalent as in Lope's creation? In short, was the historical crowd as dramatic and ritualistic as the fictional crowd?

There are two important narrative accounts of the events which took place in Fuenteovejuna during the late night and early morning of the 22–23 of September 1476. In his *Crónica de las tres órdenes de Santiago, Calatrava y Alcántara* Rades y Andrada provided the material from which Lope de Vega drew the essential elements for his play. But, whereas for Rades the *comendador* was undoubtedly a tyrant, Alonso de Palencia in his *Crónica de Enrique IV* depicted him as a kind and generous lord who even visited the sick of Fuenteovejuna.[9] According to Palencia the only complaint that could be leveled against the *comendador* would seem to be one relating to an increase in taxes.[10] However, although diametrically opposed in their sympathies, both Rades and Palencia are in substantial agreement as to what happened during the uprising. In addition to these two narrative accounts it is of course necessary to bear in mind documentation which relates more or less indirectly to the events in question and to other episodes of a similar nature.

As for Fuenteovejuna itself it is difficult to categorize its inhabitants as either peasants or townsmen.[11] Certainly with its 985 *vasallos,* that is some 4,500 inhabitants, it could hardly be described as a village. On the other hand its extensive pastoral lands, its location astride the sheepwalks of the Mesta, and its production of wool and honey made it more markedly rural than most of the other agro-towns of the region. In what follows, therefore, it must be remembered that, quite apart from the fact that rural society had its own hierarchies, these "peasants" lived within a context of institutions which were urban in nature. More important still, the annual revenues of Fuenteovejuna, amounting to some 80,000 *mrs,* attracted the attention of the great lords of the region, including above all the city of Cordoba.[12] To whom did Fuenteovejuna belong? This was the problem which in a significant way lay behind the uprising of 1476.

The later medieval period in the kingdom of Castile witnessed a flood of royal privileges or *mercedes* in favor of the great nobility, and among these *mercedes* the alienation of towns, previously belonging to the lordships and jurisdictions of the larger royal cities, figured prominently. It was in this way that Cordoba, which was especially affected by these alienations, lost Fuenteovejuna. Already in the 1450s the city of Cordoba and the inhabitants of Fuenteovejuna had been involved, along with others, in resisting the depredations of the great lords, particularly the master of the Order of Alcántara. Then in 1460 Henry IV granted the towns of Fuenteovejuna and Bélmez to Pedro Girón, who also happened to be master of the Order of Calatrava. Girón, faced with the certainty of a tenacious opposition on the part of the Cordoban authorities, entered into a series of complicated transactions by means of which Fuenteovejuna and Bélmez, which had been granted to him as an individual, were eventually exchanged with Osuna and Cazalla, which belonged to the military order of which he was master. In this way the conflict with Cordoba over the jurisdiction and lordship of Fuenteovejuna and Bélmez was off-loaded four years later on to the Order of Calatrava. Despite the resistance of Cordoba, therefore, Fuenteovejuna had become an *encomienda mayor* of the Order by 1464, and by 1468–69 the *comendador mayor* of Calatrava, Fernán Gómez de Guzmán, had established his headquarters in the town.[13] The latter, of course, was the "tyrant" who was murdered in the "peasant fury" of 1476.

Like Lope de Vega's crowd, the rebels of 1476 thought that their actions were legitimate and, far from displaying guilt, they rejoiced at the outcome of their violence. Indeed they acted not only as if they were, in some sense, royal agents but as if as a collectivity they had the right, in these specific circumstances, of correcting defective government or, at the very least, of executing proper royal policies. But how could they justify themselves when, on the face of it, Fuenteovejuna had legally passed into the possession of the Order of Calatrava and its commander, Fernán Gómez de Guzmán? As we shall see, "the crowd" was not, as Palencia would have us believe, simply a base rabble or "furious multitude" (*furiosa multitud*). It included, or was influenced by, men of substance, both in Fuenteovejuna and Cordoba itself. Although not all the participants in the uprising would appreciate all the justifications for the violence and murder, all of them would be aware of at least some of the justifications. What were these?

At the most theoretical-practical level there was, astonishingly for the kingdom of Castile, the notion of a solemn pact or contract. The notion seems anachronistic because Castilian kings during the fifteenth century, and in particular John II (1406–54), had largely succeeded in establishing that they were above the law, held their power directly from God, and had at their disposal a form of "absolute royal power."[14] Yet this trend in the increase of the monarch's theoretical powers had not been without its setbacks. In particular the *cortes* of Valladolid of 1442 had grasped the opportunity presented to them when John II fell temporarily into the hands of his noble opponents. And in effect the very first petition of this *cortes* established a solemn pact (*pacto*), contract (*contracto*), and law (*ley*) between the king and his subjects concerning the very kind of royal privileges of alienation which had affected Cordoba and Fuenteovejuna.[15] The *procuradores* reminded the king that "during the last ten years your majesty has given away certain villages, towns, and places belonging to other cities and towns, and you have divided them off and separated them from [these cities and towns] in order to give them away, by means of which the said cities and towns have been greatly affronted and damaged."[16] By the solemn pact and contract (*pacçion e contracto*) such grants were, with very minor exceptions, to cease, and both John II and his successors were to be bound by the pact or contract, notwithstanding any future use of the Crown's absolute royal power to the contrary. If any kings should fail to observe the contract, then those subjects who were affected by any such royal privilege could "organise real or verbal resistance of any kind that can be envisaged, even if it is by an affray with armed men, and notwithstanding whether such a privilege or grant is carried into effect or not."[17] More specifically it was stated that "the inhabitants of such cities and towns and places and castles can, on their own authority and without any punishment, return to the lordship of the royal crown of your kingdoms at any time, and can resist by force of arms, or by any other means, the person to whom such a privilege might be granted."[18] Clearly, by the terms of this pact or contract, Henry IV's alienation of Fuenteovejuna had been illegal, and the rebels' right to organize an uprising against the *comendador mayor* was legally sanctioned.

All the circumstantial evidence suggests that some of the rebels of 1476 were probably aware of this right to resort to arms. At the very least two points are abundantly clear. Firstly, if during the night's events the crowd did not actually know that their actions could be interpreted as a legitimate attempt to restore Fuenteovejuna to the royal city of Cordoba, and thus to the Crown, then this legitimation was, as we shall see, immediately adopted in a ritualistic way on the morrow of the *comendador*'s murder. Secondly, the authorities of Cordoba, who were implicated in the revolt, had for long been aware of the right to use force and had in fact manipulated political events in order to have this right confirmed.[19] In the divisions resulting from the attempted deposition-in-effigy of Henry IV in 1465, for example, the Order of Calatrava had largely sided with the king's enemies, and the city of Cordoba had seized its chance to obtain royal approval to regain lost territory, including Fuenteovejuna, by force: "because we order all of you, and each and every one of you, to join together and go to the said places and their lands . . . and enter, take, and empower yourselves in them . . . for me and for the Crown of my kingdoms and for that said city of Cordoba."[20] Ten years later an even more wide-ranging confirmation was obtained from Queen Isabella, who not only promised both to restore to Cordoba all those lands and places which had been illegally alienated and to annul all future alienations, but also guaranteed the right of the inhabitants of these areas "to rise up and rebel on our behalf and on behalf of our royal Crown without receiving or incurring any pain or punishment as a result."[21]

The evidence relating to the events of the night of 22 September indicates that there were further grounds for the legitimation of violence. Although, unlike Lope, Rades does not actually use the word "tyrant," his description of the *comendador*'s actions makes it clear that they constituted tyrannical behavior which, by entailing *maltratamiento* and an arbitrary disregard for the persons and property of the people of Fuenteovejuna, legitimated rebellion. In addition the *comendador,* according to Rades, was providing military support for the king of Portugal against the Catholic kings, and thus the rebels' "monarchism" and their cry of "Death to the traitors!," far from being "naïve," constituted a political stance which justified their violence:

That knight had perpetrated *maltratamiento* on his vassals, having many soldiers in the town to support the king of Portugal, who claimed to be king of Castile. And he allowed these overbearing soldiers to commit serious outrages and affronts to the people of Fuenteovejuna, eating up their wealth. In addition to this, the *comendador mayor* himself had inflicted great outrages and infamies on those of the town, taking their daughters and wives by force, and robbing them off their wealth, in order to maintain those soldiers which he had . . . [22]

Finally, although Rades does not explain why, the rebels also considered the *comendador* and his men to be "bad Christians" (*malos Christianos*). Such a charge during this period immediately suggests hostility toward New Christians (*conversos*), but in fact there is no evidence that Fernán Gómez was a *converso,* and recent research has shown that the explanation is more straightforward. For some time Fernán Gómez had been at odds with the ecclesiastical authorities of Cordoba over revenues and properties in Fuenteovejuna and Bélmez. Not only had he usurped the tithes of these areas, but he had prevented the canons of Cordoba cathedral from taking possession of lands and properties which had been bequeathed to them by one of their recently deceased colleagues, Fernán Ruiz de Aguayo. The upshot was that not only were the *comendador* and his supporters excommunicated, but also both Fuenteovejuna and Bélmez were subjected to an interdict. Thus, shortly before the uprising, the actions of the "bad Christians," that is Fernán Gómez and his men, had affected all the people of Fuenteovejuna inasmuch as all church services, apart from the baptism of infants and penance for the dying, had been suspended.[23]

The existence of these sophisticated justifications for the use of legitimate violence makes it impossible to accept the view, implied by Palencia, that the actions of the rebel crowd were the irrational, almost meaningless, manifestations of a crazed and chaotic bunch of savages. It is true, as we shall see, that Palencia did credit the crowd with some planning and organization, and he does mention that an increase in taxes constituted a pretext for the violence, but essentially he saw the crowd as a "*furiosa multitud,*" made up of "ferocious peasants" (*feroces rústicos*) who lurked menacingly in the woodlands, and whose iniquitous actions were rendered all the more violent by the fact that hunting had endowed them with "savage habits" (*hábitos feroces*). And, inevitably, Palencia maintains that after the crazed bloodletting, the crowd turned to pillaging: "Afterwards they took the gold, silver, and other items of wealth, and they became enraged with the *comendador*'s servants, who had been their friends."[24]

In fact the crowd was highly organized. For a start the people of Fuenteovejuna had planned the uprising. Both Rades and Palencia are agreed on this point. According to Rades, "all of them with one will and accord decided to rise up against [the *comendador*] and kill him," while Palencia states that Fernán Gómez's fate was planned at "secret meetings" and "illegal reunions."[25] Further, both chroniclers are agreed that the people of Fuenteovejuna had formed themselves into a sworn association. Palencia merely refers to "the wicked sworn conspiracy of those of Fuenteovejuna," but Rades, when accounting for the subsequent failure of the royal judge to obtain information, asserts emphatically that "they were in a sworn association."[26] In fact by entering into such an association the people of Fuenteovejuna had resorted to a traditional form of organization which had characterized other similar episodes in medieval Castile, including the *hermandades,* and which would be highly influential in the Revolt of the Comuneros of 1520.[27] In 1296 in Cuenca, for example, all the town's inhabitants, like those of Fuenteovejuna, entered into a sworn association, "all as one," in order to remain a royal town, defend their laws (*fuero*), uphold justice, and prevent anyone powerful from "perpetrating wrong, force, dishonour, or arrogance."[28] Moreover, as Gutiérrez Nieto has pointed out with respect to the *comunidad* of Toledo in 1520, a sworn association had other distinct advantages apart from that of uniting opposition to a common enemy. In preparing for justified violence, leadership might well be provided by the town's council or *regimiento.* But however legitimate, violence was certain to be followed by reprisals, with the ringleaders receiving exemplary punishment. An alternative, therefore, was a sworn association which implicated all the inhabitants and made it clear that the town as a whole was resisting tyranny and injustice.[29] Indeed in the case of Fuenteovejuna, as we shall see, even the women and children participated in the rites of violence. The crowd, therefore, was Fuenteovejuna itself. It was this factor that led to the royal judge's failure to extract information, and it was also this factor which excited the admiration of both Rades and Lope de Vega. Rades makes his admiration manifest:

An examining judge came from the royal court to Fuenteovejuna, with a commission from the Catholic Kings, in order to find out the truth about the affair, and to punish the guilty. But even though he tortured many of those who had been present at the death of the *comendador mayor,* no one was ever willing to confess who were the captains and those responsible for that crime, nor would they give the names of those involved. The judge asked them: "Who killed the *comendador mayor?*" They replied: "Fuenteovejuna." He asked them: "Who is Fuenteovejuna?" They replied: "All the inhabitants of this town." In the end all the replies were the same, because they had sworn an oath that, even if he should torture them to death, they would give the same reply. And what is more to be admired is that the judge had torture applied to many women and very young youths, and they displayed the same constancy and spirit as the strongest of the men.[30]

The existence of a sworn association meant, of course, that the social composition of the crowd was not, as Palencia would have us believe, simply one of "*feroces rústicos.*" In fact, as Rades makes clear, everyone participated in one way or another in the violence that was perpetrated that night. To begin with, the initial attack involved the urban officers and oligarchs, as well as the *vecinos*: "the *alcaldes, regidores,* judicial officials and council joined together with the other inhabitants and, armed, they forced their way into the houses of the *encomienda mayor,* where the *comendador* was."[31] Then, after the *comendador* had been mortally wounded, but before he died, the women of Fuenteovejuna turned up with tambourines and rattles to celebrate the death of their lord. The children, too, turned up to solemnify the *comendador*'s murder. And all of them—men, women, and children—participated in the macabre rejoicings that subsequently took place in the square of Fuenteovejuna. Then, too, there were others who had participated indirectly. Historians have suspected, on the basis of convincing circumstantial evidence, that the oligarchs of Cordoba aided and abetted the preparations for the uprising.[32] Indeed Palencia alleges—and the allegation is by no means improbable—that Don Alonso de Aguilar, the greatest noble in the region and *alcalde mayor* of Cordoba, had sent messengers to Fuenteovejuna to incite rebellion.[33]

The existence of a sworn association and the assertions of those interrogated that the culprit was Fuenteovejuna as a united whole, however, did not imply that, for the occasion, the crowd had no structure or hierarchy. As has been seen, men, women, and children intervened in the violence at different times and in different ways. Moreover, we know from Rades that the children imitated their mothers: "The children also organised a company with its captain, in imitation of their mothers, and, arranged in the order that their age made possible, went to solemnify the said death." As for the women, "they had made . . . a flag, and had appointed a captain and lieutenant." Were the women, in turn, imitating the men? Rades, it will be remembered, described how those interrogated by the judge refused to confess who the "captains" were. In all probability, therefore, the rebels had their flag, their captains, and their lieutenants—a hierarchy and organization subsequently imitated by the women and children.[34] If this is the case, then the crowd was not dissimilar to an *hermandad* or *comunidad*—both of these organizations being characterized by, among other things, a sworn association, collective decision-making, and the existence of captains.[35] Thus in the *cortes* of Ocaña of 1422, for example, we find allegations of townspeople, led by *capitanes de comunidad,* rising up against the *alcaldes, regidores,* and other urban officials. Similarly, those participating in the *comunidad* of Baza of 1520 were accused of joining together in a sworn association in order to create a *comunidad,* with syndics and a captain, and to strip the *corregidor's* lieutenant of his staff of office.[36] In both the examples just cited the *común* was opposed to the urban authorities, and in such cases it was usual for the insurgents to elect alternative officials to replace them. The case of Fuenteovejuna was different: there was no *corregidor* and, as has been seen, the *regidores* and *alcaldes* participated in the sworn association. In other respects, however, there was little difference. Indeed, as will be seen, the people of Fuenteovejuna later performed the same rituals involving *varas* (staffs of office) and the reappointment of officials.

With a structured organization and justified objectives, the actions of the crowd of Fuenteovejuna during the night of violence made sense, despite the apparent chaos. This was made manifest by the *voz* or "cry." In late medieval Castile the *voz* was the oral equivalent of a flag or banner—that is, it subsumed, in highly "telegraphed" form, all those elements which signified what its supporters stood for. The *voz,* therefore, by implication revealed a policy or program, and as a matter of fact chroniclers often briefly explain the essential program signified by the *voz.* For example, Rades, while telling us that the *comendador* maintained the *voz* of the king of Portugal, immediately adds in explanation, "who claimed to be king of Castile."[37] Translated into direct speech, the *voz* of the people of Fuenteovejuna was: "Fuenteovejuna! Fuenteovejuna! Long live King Ferdinand and Queen Isabel! Death to the traitors and bad Christians!" ("¡Fuenteovejuna! ¡Fuenteovejuna! ¡Vivan los Reyes don Fernando y doña Isabel! ¡Mueran los traidores y malos cristianos!") This *voz* revealed their program. (a) *¡Fuente-ovejuna! ¡Fuenteovejuna!* The crowd, made up of the people of Fuen-teovejuna and organized as a sworn association, rose up collectively against the tyrannical *comendador.* Logically, when the roy⸱⸱ judge later asked that the guilty persons be named, the invariable answer was: "Fuenteovejuna did it." (b) *¡Vivan los Reyes don Fernando y doña Isabel!* The crowd was supporting the Catholic kings against the king of Portugal and against those who, like Fernán Gómez, main-tained the Portuguese king's *voz.* But in another sense the crowd was also acting as an extension of government, putting into effect what the monarchy should have done, indeed secretly wanted to do. Quite apart from the *comendador's* tyranny, Fuenteovejuna did not belong to him or to the Order of Calatrava—it belonged to the royal city of Cordoba and, hence, to the Crown. The subsequent actions of the rebels, as we shall see, revealed that they were conscious of this situation. Thus, during the crisis, they arrogated to themselves special powers in order to supplement royal authority and to act on behalf of the Crown. But, once the crisis was over, a whole new set of rituals would be put into oper-ation to restore a "proper" and "harmonious" political order. (c) *¡Mueran los traidores y malos cristianos!* The traitors were, of course, those who maintained the *voz* of the king of Portugal, and the bad Christians were Fern´an G´omez and his men who had been excommunicated and who had caused Fuenteovejuna to be placed under an interdict.

The *voz* of the crowd presaged the gruesome way in which Fernán Gómez was to be killed and his corpse desecrated amid scenes of jubi-lation. According to Rades, the rebels stormed the headquarters of the *encomienda mayor* and, after killing fourteen men, finally reached Fernán Gómez, dealing him mortal wounds which left him stretched out, unconscious, on the floor. Before he died, however, they threw his body out of a window, and those below in the street caught the fall-ing *comendador* on the points of their upturned lances and swords. These men then proceeded to tear out his beard and hair, and smash his teeth with the pummels of their swords. At this stage, and before Fernán Gómez finally expired, the women and children, with their captains, lieutenants, flags, and musical instruments, turned up to celebrate and "solemnify" the death of the *comendador.* Subsequently all the men, women, and children carried the body to the square of Fuenteovejuna amid great rejoicings, and "there all the men and women tore the corpse to pieces, dragging the body along the ground and perpetrating great cruelties and mocking insults to it."[38] Finally, as a culmination to these particular scenes, they refused to hand over the *comendador's* remains to his servants for burial. Palencia, with variations, tells a similar story. According to him the *comendador* was already dead, and the corpse already half destroyed, before the defenestration, the crowd below finishing off the process by ripping the body into pieces. Moreover he adds that an old woman who tried to collect the shapeless bits and pieces in a basket was whipped, while a Franciscan who wished to bury the remains was lucky to escape with his life.

Gruesome as these scenes were, they make sense. Obviously the *comendador's* house could not contain all the people of Fuenteovejuna, but the need for total participation was met by throwing Fernán Gómez to those who remained below in the street. Whether Rades is accurate about the precise moment of the *comendador's* death is not of vital importance. What was important was that all the people of Fuenteovejuna, including the women and children, should have been perceived as participating in some way in the ritual murder, and therefore before death occurred. Once again the actions transferred responsibility from individuals to the collectivity: "Fuenteovejuna did it."

But did the savage acts of violence inflicted on the body simply reflect a crazed fury or did they carry some symbolic or ritual meaning? It is difficult to ascribe any precise significance to the tearing out of the beard and hair, and the smashing of teeth, and the references to the "great cruelties" and "mocking insults" proferred to the corpse in the square are extremely vague. The beard and hair, of course, were symbolic of honor and virility, as is evidenced by the fact that the Cid prided himself that his beard had never been plucked, whereas that part of the beard which he had wrenched from the face of his enemy, García Ordoñez, had never grown properly again.[39] Given Fernán Gómez's sexual atrocities, therefore, the uprooting of his beard and hair could represent an attack on his virility, and it is by no means improbable that the "great cruelties" and "mocking insults" included the act of castration.

In more general terms, however, the torturing of the body, the desecration of the corpse, and the refusal to permit burial all point to the

conclusion that the crowd was behaving in a quasi-official manner—
that is, it was carrying out actions which properly belonged to the
realm of *official* punishments. The savagery inflicted on the body of
the traitor, Fernán Gómez, was no more appalling than that envisaged
and approved of by Alfonso X in the law code of the *Siete Partidas*.
The fate of the traitor, according to law, should be that "they kill him
cruelly for it, dragging his body along the ground, or dismembering it,
so that it be a warning to everyone not to do the same thing." Subjects,
in fact, should give traitors "the strangest manner of death possible."[40]
Alfonso X talked in terms of "dismembering" (*desmembrando*) and
"dragging" (*rastrando*); Rades says that "they cut him into pieces,
dragging him"(*le hizieron pedaços, arrastrandole*). Were the people of
Fuenteovejuna not in fact accurately enacting what was envisaged in
the *Siete Partidas?* What is more, the law fully backed up the crowd in
its refusal to allow burial. Firstly, traitors could not be buried in the
land of those whom they had betrayed: "For Holy Church did not
think it fit that they should be buried in hallowed ground. On the contrary they ordered that if it was discovered that they were buried
there, their bones should be taken out and scattered in the fields or
burned. . . ."[41] Secondly, being excommunicated, Fernán Gómez
could not be buried by the Church. Thirdly, because of the interdict no
one in Fuenteovejuna could be properly buried.[42] Was the crowd,
then, not acting on behalf of the lay and ecclesiastical authorities?

After the murder, the crowd continued to behave in an ordered and
ritualistic manner. Rades partly hints at this:

After they had killed the *comendador mayor* the people of Fuenteovejuna removed the staffs and offices of justice from those who had been appointed by
the Order, to whom the jurisdiction belonged, and gave them to whom they
wished. Then they turned to the city of Cordoba and commended themselves
to it, saying that they wanted to be in Cordoba's jurisdiction, as they had been
before the town fell into the hands of Pedro Girón.[43]

In fact part of what Rades is here describing was the traditional ritual
and symbolic behavior implicit in most such episodes, as is evidenced
by the numerous examples during the revolt of the *Comuneros*. The
removal of the *varas* or staffs of office by the people denoted that
whoever the office-conferring authority had been, this authority was

no longer recognized. Indeed, frequently these degradation ceremonies entailed no hostility to the persons of the officeholders, who would subsequently be reinstated.[44] Hence, since the officials in Fuenteovejuna had participated in the rising, it is highly likely that they had their staffs and offices restored to them by the people. Yet political order and harmony would not be fully reestablished until Cordoba's lordship had been visually, orally, and ritually restored.

In Lope de Vega's play, as has been noted, the transitions from harmony, to disharmony, and to harmony restored are marked by ritualistic episodes. In real life the restoration of harmony was accompanied by even more elaborate rituals. Fortunately these were considered to be so important that they were written down and described by notarial documents attested to by witnesses.[45]

At one level, of course, the people of Fuenteovejuna and the Cordoban authorities were anxious to confirm that they were simply obeying the commands of the Catholic kings, and to this end there was, naturally enough, much citing of royal letters. In addition, however, Fuenteovejuna was being restored to Cordoba, and the purpose of each ritual was to act as "a sign of the reintegration, restitution, and continuation" of Fuenteovejuna in the city's lordship. These rituals involved the symbolic appropriation of the urban space, rites of purification, and symbolic acts of jurisdiction. As in Lope's play, the theoretical objective was the restoration of harmony. Thus when Juan de Berrio, *alcalde mayor* of Cordoba, symbolically "began to hear and deal with legal cases" in Fuenteovejuna, "he gave it as his judgement that all should live in peace and concord."[46]

The Cordoban authorities were indeed remarkably quick to appear on the scene. By the morning of Monday 29 April their representatives, made up of two *alcaldes mayores,* three *regidores,* and one *procurador,* were already installed, along with the council and officials of Fuenteovejuna, in a monastery or hermitage near the town. Later the same day they moved to some taverns (*mesones*) just outside the town walls, and there then began the series of rituals which were to continue throughout the following day. As each episode took place, a public scribe (*escribano público*) was asked to produce testimonies for some or all of the leading participants. For the most part these were the Cordoban authorities, although those of Fuenteovejuna were not averse to asking for copies as well: "and each one of them in the name of the said lord council of the said city asked me, the said public scribe and notary, to give each one of them a public and written testimony, signed by me and bearing my sign."[47] Such documents, themselves the product of a form of ritual, also bore the names of witnesses to the events, and in some cases they reveal that the rites were performed to accompanying acclamations of confirmation by the people of Fuenteovejuna.

The rituals appropriating the urban space began on the Monday. The officials and people of Fuenteovejuna formally invited the Cordoban authorities to make an entry through the gate of the Cal Maestra. The doors of course had been shut on purpose, and the Cordoban officials ceremoniously opened them "as a sign of possession." They then entered to the enthusiastic rejoicings and shouts of the people of Fuenteovejuna: "Long live the king and queen, our lords, and lord Cordoba!"; "Cordoba! Cordoba! Cordoba!" Next day all the four town gates—those of the Corredera, San Sebastian, Cordoba, and the Cal Maestra—were, at different times, to be the *foci* of other rituals. Outside the San Sebastian gate, for example, the officials of Fuenteovejuna took the *procurador* of Cordoba, Pedro Rodríguez Cobo, by the hands, "and put him and placed him physically and on his feet inside the said town of Fuenteovejuna." In front of the assembled crowds Cobo then "walked physically and on foot within the said town along the street which is in front of the said San Sebastian gate, from some parts to others, and, being within, he locked the doors of the gate of the said town to the countryside, and then he opened them, being on the inside, all of which . . . he said . . . that he had done . . . as a sign of reintegration and restitution."[48] The ritual was similar with respect to all four gates, except that at the first one a key was ceremoniously handed over, and at the last gate *all* the Cordoban officials, and not just the *procurador,* carried out the ritual actions. Watched by the people, "Cordoba" had been placed bodily within the walls, "Cordoba" had walked in the streets of Fuenteovejuna, "Cordoba" had locked and opened the gates—the new lord was in town and Fuenteovejuna had been ritually invested.

Rituals of purification involved the removal of polluting elements associated with the recently murdered *comendador mayor.* Two of these elements, the pillory and the gallows, were the visible reminders of Fernán Gómez's exercise of lordship. When the crowd had celebrated their murder of the *comendador* by taking his body to the square and dismembering it, they had perhaps not acted unfortuitously, because it was in the square that the *comendador* had dispensed his form of justice and it was there, too, that the pillory was located. It was to this square that the officials from Cordoba and the crowds now repaired, and Pedro Rodríguez Cobo, on behalf of the city of Cordoba, symbolically removed some stones from the base of the pillory with his own hands, proclaiming that Cordoba ordered the pillory and its base to be removed and destroyed. And in effect the crowds returned at a later stage to watch another Cordoban official pull down the pillory, destroy it, and flatten the ground on which it had been erected. Meanwhile the gallows, which rested on three brick pillars outside the town walls, had been subjected to a similar ritual of destruction.[49] A third polluting element was more personal. Immediately after the final ritual at the gate of the Cal Maestra one of the Cordoban oligarchs "took a lance with his own hands and knocked down and destroyed the top of the inside wall, which is above the said gate of the Cal Maestra, where there were depicted some figures and arms, which are said to be the arms of the said *comendador mayor.* "[50]

Appropriating the urban space and destroying visual vestiges of the late *comendador's* person and his exercise of lordship, however, were not enough. Rituals were needed to establish that lord "Cordoba" now effectively administered judicial power in Fuenteovejuna. It was this need which explains the charming episodes involving fictitious lawsuits. In the square at Fuenteovejuna there was a stone bench or platform for the administration of justice. Inevitably, perhaps, the *procurador* of Cordoba sat on this bench in front of the crowds as "a sign of the reintegration and restitution" of Fuenteovejuna to the city's lordship. He was followed by Juan de Berrio, *alcalde mayor* of Cordoba, who "climbed up and sat himself on the said bench and tribunal and, as a sign of the said possession . . . and as *alcalde mayor* of the said city of Cordoba and its territory, and in the presence of the said people, began to hear and determine cases, and gave it as his verdict that everybody should be and live in peace and concord."[51] Visually, orally, and ritually, lord "Cordoba" had decided that harmony and law and order should be restored. Indeed so important was this rite that later, and once again in the presence of the crowds, it was repeated. After the privileges of Fuenteovejuna had been solemnly confirmed by the Cordoban officials in the church of Santa María, "then immediately on the said day, month, year, and hour, and in the presence of us, the said Gómez González and Gómez Fernández, public scribes and notaries, the said Juan de Berrio sat down on the said bench and tribunal as *alcalde mayor* in order to hear and determine cases, ratifying, using, and continuing the said possession. . . ."[52]

It is fortunate that descriptions of these rituals have survived. It is equally unfortunate that these written documents cannot properly convey the extent to which these rituals must have been extraordinarily rich in sensory references. When the *procurador* of Cordoba, representing the lord "Cordoba," walked up and down the streets of Fuenteovejuna, did he do this in a solemn and deliberate manner, amid silence, or did he walk gaily amid much rejoicing? What exactly were the mocking insults proferred to the corpse of Fernán Gómez in the square? We shall never know. But we can be certain that the persons, events, and rituals which have been considered constituted a vivid kind of language, the equivalent, perhaps, of Lévi-Strauss's *bonnes à penser*—that is, they were rituals with which to think. As for the events of the night of the uprising, they illustrated an even more important feature. To the questions put by a baffled judge, the reply had invariably been: "Fuenteovejuna did it." But in doing what they did the crowd demonstrated that the ritualistic and symbolic was not merely a reflection of political action—it constituted an essential part of it. In real life Fuenteovejuna had witnessed events and rituals which were every bit as dramatic and sophisticated as those which Lope de Vega subsequently presented on the stage.

Notes

[1] All citations from the play are from the edition by Francisco López Estrada. All translations from the play and from historical sources are our own.

[2] Larson 86: "For the first time in Lope, and for one of the first times in literature, we have in Fuenteovejuna a group hero."

3

JUEZ

¡Ese muchacho!
Aprieta, perro, yo sé
que lo sabes. ¡Di quién fue!
¿Callas? Aprieta, borracho.

NIÑO

Fuente Ovejuna, señor.

(2211–15)

⁴The expression "naïve monarchism" appears to have been first used by Blum 335. Its use here does not imply that the ideology, characterized by long-standing traditions and concepts of a proper social order, as well as appeals to the Crown, was necessarily a naïve phenomenon. Indeed Herrero has cogently argued that Lope's play is about the triumph of the monarchy and the people over the tyranny of feudalism.

5

MENGO

¡Los reyes, nuestros señores, vivan!

TODOS

¡Vivan muchos años!

MENGO

¡Mueran tiranos traidores!

TODOS

¡Traidores tiranos mueran!

(1811–14)

6

TODOS

¡Fuente Ovejuna! ¡Viva el rey Fernando!
¡Mueran malos cristianos, y traidores!

(1882–83)

⁷See Larson 95–100

⁸See Larson 109–12.

⁹For the chroniclers' accounts, see Rades 79^V–80^R; Palencia 286–87. Since all subsequent citations from these chroniclers will be to the pages indicated, no further page references will be given.

¹⁰Palencia: "La única queja del vecindario parecía ser el aumento de pechos por causa de las rentas anuales."

¹¹For what follows, see E. Cabrera et al. 122.

¹²On Cordoba during this period, see the excellent book by J. Edwards.

¹³For a more detailed discussion of all this process, see Cabrera et al. 113–17; Ramírez de Arellano 448–50.

[14]See MacKay 131–42

[15]See *Cortes,* 394–401

[16]" . . . vuestra sennoria ha dado çiertas aldeas e villas e logares de algunas çibdades e villas e las ha deuidido e apartado dellas para las dar desde diez annos a esta parte, enlo qual las dichas çibdades e villas han rresçebido grant agrauio e danno."

[17]" . . . fazer rresistençia actual o verbal de qual quier qualidad que sea o ser pueda, avn que sea con tumulto de gentes de armas e quier se cunpla o non cunpla la tal merçet o donaçion."

[18]" . . . los vezinos delas tales çibdades e villas e logares e castillos se puedan tornar e tornen ala vuestra corona rreal de vuestros rregnos por su propia actoridad en qual quier tienpo e rresistyr por fuerça de armas e en otra manera al tal aquien fuere fecha la dicha merçet syn pena alguna."

[19]For what follows, see Cabrera et al. 117–19; Ramírez de Arellano 452–57.

[20]" . . . porque vos mando a todos e a cada uno de vos que vos juntades e vades a los dichos logares e sus terminos . . . e los entredes e tomedes e vos apoderedes de ellos . . . para mi e para la mi corona de mis regnos e para esa dicha çibdad de Cordoba."

[21]" . . . de se alzar e rebelar para nos e para la nuestra corona real sin por ello caer ni incurrir en pena ni calunia alguna."

[22]"Auia hecho aquel Cauallero maltratamiento a sus vassallos, teniendo en la villa muchos soldados para sustentar en ella la voz del Rey de Portogal, que pretendia ser Rey de Castilla: y consentia que aquella descomedida gente hiziesse grandes agrauios y afrentas a los de Fuenteovejuna, sobre comerseles sus haziendas. Vltra desto, el mesmo Comendador mayor auia hecho grandes agrauios y deshonras a los de la villa, tomandoles por fuerça sus hijas y mugeres, y robandoles sus haziendas, para sustentar aquellos soldados que tenia . . ."

[23]For this new and important evidence, see Cabrera et al. 119. The interdict may also help to explain the absence of one feature, the ringing of bells to summon the populace, which was a traditional constituent element in Castilian urban unrest.

[24]Palencia: "Después se apoderaron del oro, plata y otras riquezas, y se ensañaron con los criados del Comendador, antes sus amigos."

[25]Rades: " . . . determinaron todos de vn consentimiento y voluntad alçarse contra el [*comendador*] y matarle." Palencia refers to "secretas reuniones celebradas en los escondrijos de los montes" and states: "En aquellos escondrijos tenían sus conciliábulos y allí maquinaba la multitud la desgracia del infeliz Comendador."

[26]Palencia: "la inicua conjuración de los de Fuenteovejuna"; Rades: "estauan conjurados."

[27]For an excellent analysis of these traditional forms of organization, see Gutíerrez Nieto 319–67.

[28]Gutíerrez Nieto 338: "Así, en 1296, en el concejo de Cuenca, todos los vecinos se juramentarán de 'ser todos unos' para la conservación de la ciudad en el realengo, defensa de su fuero, que se cumpla el recto ejercicio de la justicia y para que nadie 'no faga tuerto ni fuerza ni deshonra ni soberbia'."

[29]Gutíerrez Nieto 354.

[30]"Fue de la Corte vn Iuez Pesquisidor a Fuenteovejuna, con comision de los Reyes Catholicos, para aueriguar la verdad de este hecho, y castigar a los culpados: y avn que

dio tormento a muchos de los que se avian hallado en la muerte del Comendador mayor, nunca ninguno quiso confessar quales fueron los capitanes o primeros mouedores de aquel delicto, ni dixieron los nombres de los que en el se auian hallado. Preguntauales el Iuez, Quien mato al Comendador mayor? Respondian ellos, Fuenteovejuna. Preguntauales, Quien es Fuenteovejuna? Respondian, Todos los vezinos desta villa. Finalmente todas sus respuestas fueron a este tono, por que estauan conjurados, que avn que los matassen a tormentos no auian de responder otra cosa. Y lo que mas es de admirar, que el Iuez hizo dar tormento a muchas mugeres y mancebos de poca edad, y tuuieron la misma constancia y animo que los varones muy fuertes."

³¹Rades: " . . . se juntaron . . . los Alcaldes, Regidores, Iusticia y Regimiento con los otros vezinos, y con mano armado, entraron por fuerça en las casas de la Encomienda mayor, donde el dicho Comendador estaua."

³²See Cabrera et al. 119–21.

³³Palencia: "Mensajeros enviados por D. Rodrigo Girón y D. Alfonso de Aguilar para preparar sus dañados fines, les excitaron a dar muerte al Comendador . . . "

³⁴Rades: "Estando en esto, antes que acabasse de espirar, acudieron las mugeres de la villa, con Panderos y Sonages, a regozijar la muerte de su señor: y auian hecho para esto vna Vandera, y nombrado Capitana y Alferez. Tambien los mochachos a imitacion de sus madres hizieron su Capitania, y puestos en la orden que su edad permitia, fueron a solenizar la dicha muerte, tanta era la enemistad que todos tenian contra el Comendador mayor."

³⁵See Gutiérrez Nieto 341–42.

³⁶For these examples, Gutiérrez Nieto 342, 349–50.

³⁷Rades: " . . . la voz del Rey de Portogal, que pretendia ser Rey de Castilla."

³⁸Rades: " . . . y alli todos los hombres y mugeres le hizieron pedaços, arrastrandole, y haziendo en el grandes crueldades y escarnios."

³⁹See *Poema de mio Cid* 3283–90.

⁴⁰*Siete Partidas,* Part 2, Tit. 28, *Ley* 2: " . . . que lo matassen cruelmente por ello, rastrandolo, o desmembrandolo, en manera que todos tomassen escarmiento, para non fazer otro tal"; "la mas estraña muerte que pudiessen."

⁴¹*Siete Partidas,* Part 2, *Tit.* 28, *Ley* 2: "Ca non lo touo por bien Santa Eglesia, que fuessen soterrados en lugares sagrados. Ante mandaron, que si lo fallaron y metidos, que sacassen ende sus huesos, e los derramassen por los campos, o los quemassen . . ."

⁴²*Siete Partidas, Part* 1, *Tit.* 9, *Ley* 15; *Part* 1, *Tit.* 13, *Ley* 8.

⁴³"Los de Fuenteovejuna despues de auer muerto al Comendador mayor, quitaron las varas y cargos de justicia a los que estauan puestos por esta Orden, cuya era la jurisdicion: y dieron las a quien quisieron. Luego acudieron a la ciudad de Cordoua, y se encomendaron a ella, diziendo querian ser subjetos a su jurisdicion, como auian sido antes que la villa viniesse a poder de don Pedro Giron."

⁴⁴See Gutiérrez Nieto 356–57; McKendrick 250.

⁴⁵These have been published by Ramírez de Arellano 476–503.

⁴⁶Ramírez de Arellano 492: " . . . comenzó a oir e librar pleitos e dio por su sentencia que todos esten e vivan en paz e concordia . . . "

⁴⁷Ramírez de Arellano 488: " . . . e cada uno dellos en el dicho nombre de los uichos senores concejo de la dicha cibdad pidieron a mi el dicho escribano publico e notario que les diese a cada uno testimonio en publica forma firmado e signado . . . "

[48]Ramírez de Arellano 494: " . . . tomaron por las manos al dicho Pedro Rodriguez Cobo procurador de los dichos senores concejo de la dicha cibdad de Cordoba . . . e metieronle e pusieronle corporalmente de pies dentro de la dicha villa de Fuente Bexuna . . . e el dicho Pedro Rodriguez Cobo . . andovo corporalmente de pies dentro en la dicha villa por la calle que esta delante de la dicha puerta de Sant Sebastian de unas partes a otras e cerro sobre si las puertas de la dicha villa de la dicha portada contra el campo e luego abriolas lo qual . . . dijo . . . . lo habia fecho e facia e fizo en senal de reintegracion e restitucion."

[49]See Ramírez de Arellano 491, 497, 500–01.

[50]Ramírez de Arellano 502: " . . . tomo con sus manos una lanza e derribo e derroco la corteza de la pared de encima de la dicha puerta que dicen de la cal maestra de parte de dentro de la villa que estaban ende pintadas ciertas figuras e armas que diz eran las armas del dicho comendador mayor."

[51]Ramírez de Arellano 492: " . . . subio e se asento en el dicho poio e consistorio e en senal de la dicha posesion . . . e como alcalde mayor de la dicha cibdad de Cordoba e su tierra en presencia de la dicha gente comenzo a oir e librar pleitos e dio por su sentencia que todos esten e vivan en paz e concordia."

[52]Ramírez de Arellano 500: "E luego incontinente en el dicho dia e mes e ano e hora suso dichos en la dicha presencia de nos los dichos Gomez Gonzalez e Gomez Fernandez escribanos publicos e notarios el dicho Juan de Berrio se asento en el dicho poio e consistorio como alcalde mayor para oir e librar pleitos retificando usando e continuando la dicha posesion . . . "

Works Cited

ALFONSO X. *Siete Partidas. Los códigos españoles concordados y anotados*. 12 vols. Madrid: M. Rivadeneyra, 1872–73.

BLUM, JEROME. *The End of the Old Order in Rural Europe*. Princeton: Princeton UP, 1978.

CABRERA, EMILIO, et al. "La sublevación de Fuenteovejuna contemplada en su V centenario." *Actas del I Congreso de Historia de Andalucía: Andalucía Medieval*. Vol. 2. Córdoba: Publicaciones del Monte de Piedad y Caja de Ahorros de Córdoba, 1978. 113–22.

Cortes de los antiguos reinos de León y de Castilla. La Real Academia de la Historia. Vol. 3. Madrid: M. Rivadeneyra, 1866.

DAVIS, NATALIE ZEMON. "The Rites of Violence: Religious Riot in Sixteenth-Century France." *Past and Present* 59 (1973): 59–91.

EDWARDS, JOHN. *Christian Cordoba: The City and Its Region in the Late Middle Ages.* Cambridge: Cambridge UP, 1982.

GUTÍERREZ NIETO, JUAN IGNACIO: "Semántica del término Comunidad antes de 1520: Las asociaciones juramentadas de defensa." *Hispania* 136 (1977): 319–67.

HERRERO, JAVIER. "The New Monarchy: A Structural Reinterpretation of Fuenteovejuna." *Revista Hispánica Moderna* 36 (1970–71): 173–85.

LARSON, DONALD R. *The Honor Plays of Lope de Vega.* Cambridge: Harvard UP, 1977.

MACKAY, ANGUS. *Spain in the Middle Ages: From Frontier to Empire, 1000–1500.* London: Macmillan, 1977.

MCKENDRICK, GERALDINE. "The *Dança de la Muerte* of 1520 and Social Unrest in Seville." *Journal of Hispanic Philology* 3 (1979): 239–59.

PALENCIA, ALONSO DE. *Crónica de Enrique IV.* 3 vols. Ed. A. Paz y Mélia. Madrid: M. Rivadeneyra, 1973–75.

Poema de mio Cid. Ed. Colin Smith. Oxford: Clarendon, 1972.

RADES Y ANDRADA, FRANCISCO DE. *Crónica de las tres órdenes de Santiago, Calatrava y Alcántara.* Ed. D. Lomax. Barcelona: Ediciones El Albir, 1980.

RAMÍREZ DE ARELLANO, RAFAEL. "Rebelíon de Fuente Obejuna contra el comendador mayor de Calatrava Fernán Gómez de Guzmán." *Boletín de la Real Academia de la Historia* 39 (1901): 446–512.

SALOMON, NOËL, *Recherches sur le thème paysan dans la "comedia" au temps de Lope de Vega.* Bordeaux: Bordeaux UP, 1965.

VEGA CARPIO, LOPE DE, and CRISTOBAL DE MONROY. *Fuente Ovejuna (Dos Comedias).* Ed. Francisco López Estrada. Madrid: Castalia, 1969.

Subjectivity, Sexuality, and Transgression: The Jacobean Connection

JONATHAN DOLLIMORE

A NY STUDY of transgression finds itself, of necessity, and soon, asking some searching questions—e.g.: does transgression primarily refer to an action, a social practice, or even more generally still, the struggle to produce alternative cultures and knowledges? How do we assess its success or failure? And who is "we"? Who decides whether transgression is regressive or progressive, revolutionary, or reactionary—or neither? Such a study raises questions which invite—demand perhaps—a materialist analysis, by which I mean an analysis which seeks to be theoretically rigorous, historically aware, and politically involved.

Issues of transgression are inextricably bound up with those of subjectivity, and if poststructuralism enables us better to understand transgression in the Renaissance, this is perhaps because its conceptions of subjectivity are actually closer to those found in the Renaissance than is commonly reckoned. Often, essentialist conceptions of the self which only take effective hold in the Enlightenment and are then subsequently developed within Romanticism and Modernism, have been erroneously aligned with those in the Renaissance. Consider for example that great imperative of the Renaissance, *Nosce teip-*

335

sum, know thyself. Today, for poststructuralism, know thy discursive formations. But surely in the Renaissance also: terminology apart, did not *nosce teipsum* mean something like that? Though it has generally been appropriated by humanist criticism as a recognizable origin of itself, it may nevertheless have something crucial in common with the formulations of poststructuralism. Of the few central beliefs uniting the various poststructuralisms (and connecting them with postmodernism) this is one of the most important: human identity is more constituted than constitutive; constituted by, for example, the preexisting structures of language and ideology, and by the material conditions of human existence. Thus is the subject decentered, and subjectivity revealed as a kind of subjection—not the antithesis of social process but its focus.

In the Renaissance also the individual was seen as constituted by and in relation to—even the effect of—a preexisting order. To know oneself was to know that order. There is most obviously perhaps the tripartite division of the soul, a model inherited from classical culture and undergoing various further subdivisions in the intervening centuries. And as regards being an effect of a prior order we need only consider Richard Hooker's declaration: "God hath his influence into the very essence of all things, without which influence . . . their utter annihilation could not choose but follow" (2:26). Or the commonplace with which Sir John Davies begins his *Nosce Teipsum*: God wrote the law directly into the hearts of our first parents. Hooker concurs: the law of Reason, the universal law of mankind, is "imprinted" in men's souls and "written in their hearts" (1:166,228). And when Montaigne and Bacon stress the determining power of social custom, they are developing the same idea of an order prior to and determining of the individual, though now of course with the crucial difference that it is a nonteleological order, historical rather than divine, material rather than metaphysical.[1]

Obviously there are far-reaching differences between Renaissance metaphysics and poststructuralism. For one thing the Renaissance view of identity as constituted (metaphysically) was also and quite explicitly a powerful metaphysic of social integration. In other words, to be metaphysically identified was simultaneously to be socially positioned—the subject in relation to the Prince, the woman in relation to the man, and so on. Metaphysics here underpins a discursive formation of the subject, of subjection. This link between subjectivity and subjection, which for poststructuralism has to be disclosed before it can be resisted, is, by comparison, both made explicit and endorsed in the Renaissance. Another difference: within Renaissance metaphysics a constituted identity might nevertheless be essentially fixed (e.g., the soul as divine creation) in a way that poststructuralism would also reject (identity is not only constructed but contingently so). Despite these differences, however, poststructuralism is helping us to see again what the Renaissance already knew: identity is in-formed by what it is not. It also helps us to see that if (as was apparent in the early seventeenth century) identity is clearly constituted by the structures of power, of position, allegiance, and service, any disturbance within or of identity could be as dangerous to that order as to the individual subject. Hooker, in a now famous passage, asked: "see we not plainly that obedience of creatures unto the law of nature is the stay of the whole world?" (1:157). Equally plain of course is that in this view disobedience is literally world shattering. The metaphysical construction of subjectivity is also an admission—and production—of its disruptive potential, a disruption in and of the very terms of its construction. A conception of the self as socially and/or metaphysically constituted produces one idea of transgression while a conception of the self as essentially (if not socially) unified and autonomous, quite another. That difference is addressed in what follows.

II

Lillian Faderman, in her book *Surpassing the Love of Men* (ch. 4), records two separate cases of women in France who in the sixteenth century were punished for using transvestite disguise and deploying dildos in their lesbian relations.[2] From one modern point of view these women's transgression is deeply suspect. I'm not referring to the conservative perspective which condemns sexual deviance per se, but to another perspective, one which might actually endorse deviance in principle, at least if it were seen as a quest for authentic selfhood. But here, precisely, is the problem; even (or especially) from this radical perspective, the women's behavior was inauthentic, not truly transgressive: in their use of men's clothing and the dildo they were trying to imitate precisely that masculine order which they should have been transcending. This, then, was regressive, not progressive, false, not true consciousness. Compare the heroine of *Rubyfruit Jungle* (1973) who articulates the perspective in question when confronted with a butch/femme lesbian bar: "That's the craziest, dumbass thing I ever heard tell of. What's the point of being a lesbian if a woman is going to look and act like an imitation man? Hell, if I want a man, I'll get the real thing not one of these chippies" (Brown 47–48). Or again, the anonymous interviewee cited by Esther Newton: "I hate games! I hate role playing! It's so ludicrous that certain lesbians, who despise men, become the exact replicas of them!" (7).

But the question remains: why were those two French women in the sixteenth century found so threatening? One of them was sentenced to be burned and the other hanged, punishments dictated, apparently, not by their lesbianism per se but their transvestism and use of the dildo—*at once*, I want to suggest, appropriations of masculinity, inversions of it, and substitutions for it.

The kind of transgression whose test they retrospectively failed, namely, transgression as a quest for authenticity, has been a powerful idea from romanticism through modernism and into the sexual revolution. Underpinning and endorsing the philosophy of individualism, it suggests that in defying a repressive social order we can dis-cover (and so be *true* to) our *real* selves. Its view of human subjectivity is essentialist. Moreover it affirms that truth and reality are profoundly subjective, inextricably bound up with the essential self. For convenience and only provisionally I call this idea of transgression humanist. Clearly it is rooted in the essentialist humanism generated by the Enlightenment and undergoing various mutations ever since. And in our own century, it stems from what might fairly be called a radical humanism. Consider one of its classic expressions, André Gide's *The Immoralist* (1902). In that novel sexual transgression becomes a quest for the essential self. Its hero, Michel, throws off the culture and learning which up to that point have been his whole life, in order to find himself, "the authentic creature that had lain hidden beneath it . . . whom the Gospel had repudiated, whom everything about me—books, masters, parents, and I myself had begun by attempting to suppress. . . . Thenceforward I despised the secondary creature, the creature who was due to teaching, whom education had painted on the surface" (51). He composes a new series of lectures in which he shows "Culture, born of life, as the destroyer of life" (90). The true value of life is bound up with individual uniqueness: "the part in each of us that we feel is different from other people is just the part that is rare, the part that makes our special value" (100). Here, effectively, the self is understood in terms of a presocial, individuated essence, nature, and identity, and on that basis is invested with a quasi-spiritual autonomy. Culture has repressed this authentic self, and the individual embarks on a quest to recover it, a quest which is an escape from culture.

The significance for our culture of humanist transgression, this escape from repression into the affirmation of one's true self, can hardly be overestimated. Contrary to what has sometimes been implied, it didn't appear with existentialism; nor did it disappear when that movement ceased to be fashionable. And its prevalence has led us to misconceive both the significance and practice of transgression in earlier periods, especially the Renaissance, and even in some of our own contemporary subcultures. What intrigues me about that earlier period, especially its drama, is a mode of transgression which finds expression through the inversion[3] and perversion of just those preexisting categories and structures which humanist transgression seeks to transcend, to be liberated from; a mode of transgression which seeks not an escape from existing structures, but rather a subversive reinscription within them—and in the process a dis-location of them. I call this, again provisionally, transgressive reinscription. Examples preliminary to the main instances which follow might include the malcontent who haunts the very power structure which has alienated him, seeking reinscription within it but at the same time demystifying it, operating within and subverting it at the same time; the revengers whose actions constitute an even more violent bid for reinscription within the very society which has alienated and dispossessed them; the assertive woman, the woman on top,[4] who simultaneously appropriates, exploits, and undermines masculine discourse.

Humanist transgression in the name of authenticity has never been able to comprehend this other kind of transgression, that performed in the name of inversion, perversion, and reinscription. Moreover humanist transgression has proved wanting. Marked indelibly with the traces of idealist culture, it was perhaps inevitable that it should prove wanting. Inevitable, too, that in the wake of its failure we should become deeply skeptical about the very possibility of transgression. Because, in the words of Michel Foucault, "there is no single focus of great Refusal, no soul of revolt, source of all rebellions, or pure law of the revolutionary" (95–96)—because of that, there now seems to be only law itself, coercively or ideologically at work: coercively in the sense of being actively and increasingly repressive, ideologically in the sense of actively preempting resistance and subversion because somehow preceding and informing them. And so in recent years we have become preoccupied with the so-called containment of transgression—not merely its defeat by law, but its production and harnessing by law for law's own ends.

There is, for example, a functionalist argument to the effect that transgression may only be licensed, a kind of ritual safety valve which, far from undermining the existing order, actually reinforces it. Then there is the psychological version of this argument: paradoxically the sacred is most valued by the sacrilegious, and real faith lies in honest doubt. This argument includes Richard Sennett's notion of disobedient dependence, a defiance presupposing the very dependence it is trying to subvert, and in which "transgression is perhaps the most important element." This is a defiance based upon dependence, a rebellion not so much against authority as within it; the transgressor indeed disobeys but authority regulates the terms. As such this form of disobedience "has very little to do with genuine independence or autonomy . . . the world into which a person has entered through the desire to transgress is seldom however a real world of its own, a true alternative which blots out the past" (Sennett 33–34).[5] Sennett's argument might then be broadly supported by a structuralist or indeed poststructuralist argument to the effect that transgression, especially transgressive inversion, too often remains within—i.e., *merely* reverses—the binary opposition which structures both it and the law being contravened. (This would be the critique, in theoretical guise, of the "mannish" lesbian.) There are, then, at least three versions of this powerful argument whereby transgression is contained.

Stephen Greenblatt engages with such arguments in his seminal studies of authority and subversion. In *Renaissance Self-Fashioning*, a book which marks an immensely rewarding contribution to Renaissance studies, he argues that Marlowe's heroes remain embedded in what they oppose: "they simply reverse the paradigms and embrace what the society brands as evil. In so doing, they imagine themselves set in diametrical opposition to their society where in fact they have unwittingly accepted its crucial structural elements." In *Faustus* "the blasphemy pays homage to the power it insults" (209, 212). Greenblatt has in mind here that extraordinary moment when Faustus seals his pact with the devil by uttering Christ's dying words on the cross: "consummatum est." Faustus willfully ends himself; he sells his soul to the devil. Creation recoils; his blood congeals. Via the expression of a perverse masochism, with its disturbing mix of abjection and arrogance, this act, in one sense the supreme antithesis of everything Christ died for—he died after all to save us all—is identified with Christ. Is not this transgression contained, the unintended reverence paid by the sacrilegious to the sacred? Or is it rather a transgressive reinscription, a demonic perversion of the sacred? And what else (one might be led to wonder) was Christ in his death but the keenest image of abjection and arrogance, that transgressive masochism which has played such an important part in making and unmaking our culture, not least in the figure of the martyr, and which figures over and again in the cultural depictions of the crucifix? Faustus violates Christianity in the name and image of Christ; assimilating Christ to his opposite he thereby discloses the possibility that this opposite may be latent within Christ. Similarly, as I've argued elsewhere (Dollimore, *Radical Tragedy* ch. 6), this play associates God with his antithesis, with those secular tyrants who, in contemporary reality, were legitimating themselves in the name and image of God. What we witness here is something resembling the Freudian proposition that the repressed returns via the very images, structures, and mechanisms of repression itself: the words which consummate the renewal of man, his salvation, these words return to signify the opposite of salvation which is damnation, and they signify also the desire which only damnation can acknowledge and which salvation must repress. If it makes sense to think of evil as the repressed of Christianity, then this process also constitutes the return of the repressed in the supreme image of its repression: the dying Christ.[6]

I want to suggest that what is overlooked, both in humanist transgression and in some recent arguments for the inexorable containment
of transgression, is the part played by contradiction and dis-location
in the mutually reactive process of transgression and its control. I'm
using the term contradiction in its materialist sense to denote the way
social process develops according to an inner logic which simultaneously, or subsequently, effects its negation. Three paradigms of this
derive from Hegel, Marx, and Freud—Hegel's theory of the master/
slave dialectic, Marx's theory of the fundamental contradiction between the forces and relations of production, and the Freudian proposition just referred to, namely, the return of the repressed via the mode
of its repression. In a revolutionary conjuncture contradictions may
contribute to the disintegration of an existing order, though only (usually) through terrible suffering and struggle. That has to be said. In a
nonrevolutionary conjuncture contradictions render social process
the site of contest, struggle, and change. And, again, suffering. The
contradictions which surface in times of crisis are especially revealing:
they tell us that no matter how successful authority may be in its repressive strategies, there remains something potentially uncontrollable not only in authority's *objects* but in its *enterprise*, its rationale,
and even its origin.

Deviancy, whether of Faustus's kind or that of the transvestite, plays
a revealing part here, both as that which becomes especially visible in
times of crisis, and that which focuses the inherent contingency of,
and potential contradictions within, power. This is why we are mistaken if we think that deviancy exists outside of the dominant order.
Though socially marginal the deviant remains discursively central:
though an outcast of society s/he remains indispensable to it. For example: the process of identifying and demonizing deviance may be
"necessary" to maintaining social order, either in the sense that deviancy poses an actual threat, or that it is perceived as threatening, or
that a prevailing authority is able to relegitimate itself through that
process of identifying and demonizing deviance. In practice these
three responses to deviance are rarely separable.

Taking the example of deviancy, consider another but quite different instance of transgressive reinscription. The late Gāmini Salgādo
once described the vagabonds of the Elizabethan low-life pamphlets as
follows:

Seen through the disapproving eyes of respectable citizens they were nothing but a disorderly and disorganized rabble, dropouts from the social ladder. But seen from within, they appear to be like nothing so much as a mirror-image of the Elizabethan world picture: a little world, tightly organised into its own ranks and with its own rules, as rigid in its own way as the most elaborate protocol at court or ritual in church. (13)

From the respectable view, then, these rogues were merely the dregs of civilization—potentially dangerous, it's true, but in no way a part of the real social order. From another view they comprise a mirror-image of that order. But if the second view is accurate, do not the rogues become another clear instance of transgression contained, of a subculture which has internalized the structures and values of the dominant culture? Are they not paradoxically reproducing the laws which exclude and oppress them, even as they seem to be escaping and subverting those laws? Not exactly, because this very mimickry of the dominant involves a scandalous inversion. In the words of one contemporary observer: "these cheaters turned the cat in the pan, giving to diverse vile patching shifts an honest and godly title, calling it by the name of law . . . to the destruction of the good labouring people" (Salgādo 15). And feeding back through that inversion is an equally scandalous interrogation of the dominant order being mimicked; civil society is itself shown to be rooted in a like corruption. If this subculture imitates the dominant from below, it also employs a strategy whereby it undermines the dominant. Even as civil society endlessly displaces corruption from the social body as a whole onto its low-life (this in all likelihood corresponding to the first view above, that of the respectable citizens who see the low-life as society's waste product), the latter reveals both the original source and full extent of corruption within the dominant itself (Salgādo 16, 174). Inversion becomes a kind of transgressive mimesis: the subculture, even as it imitates, reproducing itself in terms of its exclusion, also demystifies, producing a knowledge of the dominant which excludes it, this being a knowledge which the dominant has to suppress in order to dominate.

In summary, then: change, contest, and struggle in part are made possible by contradiction and focused internally through deviancy. For all their differences both Foucault and Derrida lend support to this argument. Foucault, in the *History of Sexuality*, speaks of resistance not as outside power but inscribed within it as its irreducible opposite

(96). And Derrida has stressed in *Positions* the political effectiveness of inverting binary oppositions, of inversion as a stage in displacement.[7] The force of these arguments, both of which are complex and which I can only allude to here[8] but whose importance I want to stress, increases if we observe further the extent to which binarism produces an instability in the very process of categorically dividing the world. It both produces ambiguities which it can't contain and invites transgression in and of its own terms. Thus the opposition us/them produces the scandal of the internal dissident; the opposition masculine/feminine produces the scandal of the transvestite, not to mention the troubling ambiguity of the hermaphrodite.

For my purposes here, the most interesting and relevant senses of "inversion" and "perversion" are not primarily or specifically sexual. Traditionally inversion could mean reversal of position and reversal of direction, both being inimical to effective government and social stability. This sense of *active* alteration is there even more strikingly in perversion. Especially interesting is the slippage in an *OED* definition from divergence to evil: "turned away from the right way or from what is right or good; perverted, wicked"; similarly with another definition: "not in accordance with the accepted practice; incorrect, wrong." It is in this sense of actively altering—a divergence which is also a turning back upon—that the female transvestite of the early seventeenth century could be described as an "invert" and not at all in the sense of that word coined and popularized by the nineteenth-century sexologists (e.g., Krafft-Ebing and Havelock Ellis).

III

The female transvestite was indeed a deeply disturbing figure in the early seventeenth century.[9] As Lisa Jardine has recently reminded us, nowhere was the tension and struggle between classes, between residual and emergent cultures, between the mercantile order and what it was actually, or seemed to be, replacing, between rank and wealth, more apparent than in the obsession with dress and what it signified socially (141–42, 150).[10] Hence the attacks on the dress violations of the emergent (middle) class and the insubordinate (female) sex. The ideology of gender difference was just as fundamental as that of class in securing the social order. In fact patriarchy, class, and hierarchy all presupposed a law of gender difference which was at once divinely, naturally, and socially laid down, the law descending from the first through the second to the third.

It is *against and (again) in terms of* this metaphysic that dress violation occurred. A significant focus for the controversy was, of course, the theater, which, like the transvestite, was seen both to epitomize and promote contemporary forces of disruption. There was, for example, the general cultural disturbance generated by the theatrical emphasis on artifice, disguise, and role playing. Its significance can be gauged in part by looking at the range of objections to the theater as a place which subverted metaphysical fixity.

To begin with, the players were seen to undermine the idea that one's identity and place were a function of what one essentially was— what God had made one. The idea of a God-given nature and destiny had the corollary that nothing so essentially predetermined could or should ever change. In the words of one satirist, it was not so much that the player disguised his real self in playing; rather he had no self apart from that which he was playing: "The Statute hath done wisely to acknowledge him a Rogue and errant, for his chiefe essence is, *A daily Counterfeit* . . . His {profession} is compounded of all Natures, all humours, all professions."[11] The association here of the player and the rogue is significant. Both were itinerants and masterless men, sometimes both subjected to the same vagrancy laws (alternatively the player might be a royal servant—an interesting opposition in itself). They transgressed fixity not only because they were without fixed abode, but also because they lacked the identity which, in a hierarchical society, was essentially conferred by one's place in that society. But there was a further link among rogues, masterless men, and the players; according to some observers the theaters quite literally brought them into association, being the place "for vagrant persons, Masterless men, thieves, . . . contrivers of treason, and other idle and dangerous persons to meet together" (Chambers 4:122). Again we see the same anxiety: social stability depended crucially on people staying just as they were (identity), where they were (location), and doing what they always had done (calling). When the rogue meets the player two lawless identities converge.

This concern with unfixed identity was not unique to the theater; society and politics more generally contained a theatrical dimension,

what Greenblatt calls "the theatricalisation of culture." Renaissance
courts involved theatricality "in the sense of both disguise and histrionic self-presentation," while court manuals and rhetorical hand-
books offered "an integrated rhetoric of the self, a model for the formation of an artificial identity" (162). And dissimulation was of course
essential for the practice of realpolitik. The theater, then, provided a
model, indeed a sustained exploration, of the role playing which was
so important for social mobility, the appropriation and successful deployment of power. It follows that the recurring emphasis within
Elizabethan and Jacobean plays on life itself as a process of playing was
not merely theatrical projection; the world as a stage, life as artifice:
these were ideas which the theater derived from as well as conveyed
to its culture. As Louis Montrose has pointed out, this has a fascinating
consequence: "If the world is a theatre and the theatre is an image of
the world, then by reflecting upon its own artifice, the drama is holding the mirror up to nature" (57).

Another, related, charge against the players is that in their dress violations they—again like the "street" transvestites—transgressed the
natural and fixed order of things by willfully confusing categories
which it was thought imperative should be kept distinct, especially
within the categories of gender, rank, and class. Boys playing women,
menials playing those of a higher rank and breeding—to some these
actions seemed deep violations of the principle of fixed division on
which civilization rested. In Act 5, scene 5, of *Volpone* Mosca enters
dressed as a gentleman:

> MOSCA
> But what am I?
> VOLPONE
> 'Fore heav'n, a brave *clarissimo*; thou becomest it!
> Pity thou wert not born one.
> MOSCA
>   If I hold
> My made one, 'twill be well.
>
>   (5.5.2–5)

Mosca prevaricates beautifully. It's a reply which is at once deferential and contemptuous, self-effacing and arrogant. 'Twill be well because he is not the real thing, never could be, and isn't now even pre-

suming; but conversely, 'twill be well because the imitation, the travesty of the real thing can also usurp it and to all intents and purposes become it. What price, then, that metaphysical guarantee of social differentiation when it is so easily abolished in the confusion it was supposed to preempt and render impossible? It is a moment of concentrated ambiguity, of irony (irony and ambiguity tend to be intrinsic to transgressive reinscription and alien to humanist transgression). It is also a moment of appropriation in which there surfaces the play's underlying knowledge, at once (for Jonson) exhilarating, ambivalent, appalling, and violent; a knowledge which incites yet also fears that riot of the perverse, the antisocial, and the antinatural which are *Volpone*.

One further aspect of dress violation associated with the theater also contravened divine and natural law: the abomination of boys dressing as girls. For John Rainolds the boy transvestite destroyed the fragile moral restraint containing an anarchic male sexuality; the boy incited his male audience into every kind of perversion, mostly homosexual, but heterosexual too. Rainolds saw adult male sexuality not just as anarchic but as satanically polymorphous, seemingly capable of attaching to the forbidden with alarming ease.[12] Rainolds apart, the transgressions associated with the boy players, be they actual or imagined, rendered the theatrical self-consciousness surrounding transvestism complex and shifting; it provoked questions which were teasingly unanswerable: for example—and this is a question especially intriguing for us today—which, or how many, of the several gender identities embodied in any one figure are in play at any one time?

IV

In *The Roaring Girl* (1608–11), a play with a transvestite hero/ine and in the 1620 pamphlet controversy over cross-dressing, which treated issues similar to those in the play, the contemporary sexual metaphysic was turned inside out: gender division was recognized as central not to a divinely sanctioned natural order but to a contingent and oppressive social order. Correspondingly the representation of gender inversion generates an interrogation of both the sexual metaphysic and the social order. Moll Cutpurse, the transvestite hero/ine of

The Roaring Girl, is variously described as one who "strays so from her kind / Nature repents she made her" (1.2.211–20); who some say "is a man / And some both man and woman" (2.1.190–91), and yet others that she is "a codpiece-daughter" (2.2.89):

> a thing
> One knows not how to name: her birth began
> Ere she was all made: 'tis woman more than man,
> Man more than woman, and (*which to none can hap*)
> The sun gives her two shadows to one shape
> (1.2.128–32; italics added)

And yet this creature who so violates the natural order and traditional gender divisions by dressing as a man also does things better than a man: "I should draw first and prove the quicker man," she says (4.1.76)—and she does. In the process she attacks masculinity as a charade, asserting its failure *in its own sexual terms* (2.9.290 ff.), something which the language of the play echoes elsewhere, facetiously, but defensively, too (cf. 2.1.326 ff.; 2.2.75 ff.; 3.1.142 ff.). Moll also offers the truly exceptional view of prostitution as a sexual exploitation rooted in economic exploitation and patriarchal power:

> In thee I defy all men, their worst hates,
> And their best flatteries, all their golden witchcrafts,
> With which they entangle the poor spirits of fools.
> Distressed needlewomen and trade-fallen wives,
> Fish that must needs bite or themselves be bitten,
> Such hungry things as these may soon be took
> With a worm fastened on a golden hook:
> Those are the lecher's food, his prey, he watches
> For quarrelling wedlocks, and poor shifting sisters.
> (3.1.90–98)[13]

Recognizing all this, and being shown, too, where the power lies in this social order, the politics of inversion become persuasive, perhaps irresistible; this is Moll, about to thrash the predatory Laxton: "I scorn to prostitute myself to a man, / I that can prostitute a man to me" (3.1.109–10). Moll's denunciation of Laxton before she beats him up shows that the thrashing is partly in revenge for his not untypical masculine blend of misogyny and promiscuity (cf. 2.2.252–55), to which of course the prostitute can indeed testify (and perhaps also confirm): if these things appear incompatible—isn't misogyny a kind of hatred, and promiscuity a kind of love, albeit a debased one?—in reality they go hand in hand.

It's in these ways that *The Roaring Girl* begins to disclose how, because of the complex connections between sexuality, gender, and class, between sexual and economic exploitation, economic and political anxieties can be displaced into the domain of the sexual and, conversely, the sexual comes to possess enormous signifying power. Indeed, the king himself intervened in 1620 to try to eliminate female transvestitism.[14] He, like many others at that time, felt female transvestites were usurping male authority. This is indeed exactly what Moll does throughout the play, and especially when she beats up Laxton. But perhaps more importantly the transvestite was contributing to a knowledge and a culture which undermined the discursive formations of authority itself, through her perverse reinscription within those formations. This can be further illustrated, briefly, from the pamphlet controversy.

Hic Mulier, the voice of female transvestites in the most interesting pamphlet, *Haec Vir* (1620), insists that gender difference is an effect of custom only. Custom becomes the cause where once it was only the effect. Again, inversion. This is also an instance of what was to become the classic move in ideological demystification: the metaphysical is first displaced by, and then collapsed into, the social. Shorn of its metaphysical sanction, law, especially in the Renaissance, is in danger of losing its prescriptive power. Nothing is more absurd, nothing more foolish, says Hic Mulier, than custom. In fact, it is "an idiot" (Sig.B2; spelling modernized). The radical implications of this assertion can be seen from an observation of Montaigne's: "We may easily discern, that only custom makes that seem impossible unto us, which is not so" (1:39). Throughout the pamphlet Hic Mulier seems to be in sympathy with this remark of Montaigne's, but nowhere is her appropriation of the idea more challenging than in the way she dissolves both law and ideological fixity into a celebration of change and transformation and, by implication, a celebration of her potential rather than her fixed nature: "Nor do I in my delight of change otherwise than as the whole world does" (Sig.B). At a time when many thought of change as synonymous with evil, or at least decline and degeneracy, this was indeed provocative. Hic Mulier is not only shameless but, as Sandra Clark has recently pointed out, she suggests that shame itself "is a concept framed by men to subordinate women to the dictates of arbitrary custom" (175). Hic Mulier claims, too, that women are as reasonable as men. And then the crucial claim: "We are as free born as men, have as free election, and as free spirits; we are compounded of like parts, and may with like liberty make benefit of our creations" (Sig.B3). It's a claim whose force in *this* instance comes through a demystification generated across inversion.

But consider now a misgiving voiced by Linda Woodbridge and shared by many others: "To me the one unsatisfying feature of the otherwise stimulating transvestite movement is that it had to be transvestite: Renaissance women so far accepted the masculine rules of the game that they felt they had to look masculine to be free" (145). For understandable reasons Woodbridge seems to prefer the "hermaphroditic vision" (145 and cf.317). The transvestite and the hermaphrodite: both were disturbing images; perhaps they are less so now. Potentially the hermaphrodite dissolves gender difference and, at least in its associated idea of androgyny, has become acceptable. Even in the Renaissance the figure could "symbolise the essential oneness of the sexes" (Woodbridge 140), and, with reference back to Plato's *Symposium*, the recovery of an original lost unity (itself intrinsically sexual). The idea remains alive today, of course; Kaja Silverman reminds us that the notion of an original androgynous whole, similar to that projected by Aristophanes, is absolutely central to the psychoanalytic theories of Jacques Lacan, where the human subject is defined in terms of an essential, intrinsic lack, because it is believed to be a fragment of something larger and more primordial (152–53). But the transvestite? S/he is a strange and disturbing figure still, though for different reasons now than in the Renaissance. Isn't s/he a figure who has exchanged one kind of incompleteness for another? If misgivings persist they are not exactly moral; I mean we don't exactly or openly disapprove. Isn't it rather that, as Woodbridge implies, the transvestite seems to be a victim of false consciousness, and by switching gender roles rather than dissolving them, reinforces the very sexual division which s/he finds oppressive? In this view the transvestite fails the test of humanist transgression, a perspective which pervades literary criticism still. But if the hermaphrodite threatens the binarism of gender through ambiguous unity, the female transvestite of the early seventeenth century positively disrupts that same scheme by usurping the master side of the opposition. To invoke again the earlier distinction between different kinds of transgression, the transvestite represents a subversive reinscription within, rather than a transcendence of, an existing order, while the hermaphrodite is often appropriated as a symbol of just such a transcendence. Essentially the aggressive female cross-dresser inverted the metaphysics of difference: from being a divine law inscribed essentially in each of God's subjects, which knowledge of self would confirm, sexual identity (and difference) is shifted irretreivably into the domain of custom, of the social, of that which can be contested. Perhaps this is the mode of transgression denied to the hermaphrodite, at least when associated with the mythological, the presocial, the transcendent.

V

What I've just offered have been partial readings of the *Haec Vir* pamphlet and *The Roaring Girl*, partial not in the sense (at least this isn't what I'm confessing) of being distortions of the texts, but rather readings that focus upon textual elements which can be correlated with oppositional cultural elements within Jacobean society, and consequently possible audience positions and reading responses. But the representation of the transvestite in the pamphlet and the theater is part of a cultural process whose complexity is worth exploring further. The complexity I'm concerned with isn't that supposed intrinsic property of the text which politically motivated critics always distort (in biased readings) and impartial critics transparently represent (in long readings). It's the complexity which is first and foremost a social process, and within which the text was, and still is, implicated. Viewing the text as part of a social process raises, unavoidably, the question of the containment of transgression. Both play and pamphlet have been seen to move toward a closure which contains—even eradicates—their challenging elements.

The *Haec-Vir* pamphlet ends, notoriously, with Hic Mulier declaring that women like her have only become masculine because men have become effeminate. They have taken up men's cast-off garments in order to "support a difference"(Sig. C2V)—in effect to maintain a sexual difference being abandoned by men. And if men revert to being masculine, the Hic Mulier figure continues, women will once again become feminine *and* subordinate. Actually this conclusion barely constitutes containment. To see this argument as somehow cancelling what went before is probably to interpret the pamphlet according to inappropriate notions of authorial intention, character utterance, and textual unity (all three notions privileging what is said finally as being more truthful than what went before). The Hic Mulier figure (an abstraction) is a vehicle for a variety of defenses of the transvestite, radical *and* conservative, and there is no good reason, given the genre, to privilege the one over the others as more truthful, more sincere, more representative, or to be dismayed that some of these arguments are incompatible with each other. Presumably, if the different defenses had been split between several Hic Mulier figures the problem (for us) would disappear—again alerting us to certain, not necessarily appropriate, interpretative assumptions. But it is also true that this culminating defense, conservative as it is, still partakes of the same fundamental challenge to gender division as the other defenses: to suggest that gender difference can be maintained through cross-dressing and inversion is still to maintain or imply the crucial claim: it is difference working in terms of custom and culture (and so contestable) rather than nature and divine law (and so immutable). Even with this conservative (ironic?) defense, then, sexual difference is sustained by the very inversion which divine law forbids, and the fact that it can be so sustained is simultaneously a repudiation of the claim that sexual difference is itself dictated by divine or natural law.

The Roaring Girl is a much more interesting instance of containment. Right at the outset we're alerted to the fact that Mary Frith, the real-life cross-dresser on whom the play is based, is being given a more virtuous image than she in fact possessed (Dedication 19 ff.; Prologue 26–27). The play plays down Frith's criminality. She seems to have been several times arrested and variously recorded as being a bawd, thief, receiver, gang leader, and whore, all of which, as Andor Gomme remarks, the character Moll Cutpurse definitely is not, and is only falsely accused of being in the play.[15] Whereas the deviance of Mary Frith remained in certain respects implacably immoral and antisocial, in the figure of Moll Cutpurse she is remade as the moral conscience of the selfsame society whose gender categories she transgresses. More specifically, Frith/Moll is appropriated for a partial critique of patriarchal law, sexual exploitation, and aristocratic culture. At the same time she remains "isolated from the very social structure which her courage and vitality have done so much to enliven and renew" (Rose 389–90). In this respect Frith/Moll is represented in the tradition of the warrior woman and the folk figure of Long Meg of Westminster, both of whom distinguish true morality from false, the proper man from the braggart, and finally submit to the former (see Shepherd esp. 70–72). At the same time, Moll, a figure who epitomizes the abnormal and the degenerate, and who also apparently incites lewdness in others, paradoxically helps regenerate a degenerate society and especially its ailing patriarchal basis: "Moll: Father and son, I ha' done you simple service here" (5.2.206). Thus the relationship between the dominant and the deviant is nothing if not complex: if the demonizing of the deviant other leads to suppression and even extermination, the colonizing of the (internal) deviant involves an assimilation which re-forms, ethically and literally, even as it re-presents. The play reconstitutes Mary Frith as Moll Cutpurse, who in turn is used to reconstitute a social order while remaining on its margins—reformed and reforming but not finally incorporated; hence Moll's parting injunction to the assembled "gentlemen" of the final scene, "I pursue no pity: / Follow the law" (252–55).

In this case containment isn't the reaction of power after, and in response to, the event of subversion. It's intrinsic to the process of literary representation, social contest, and social change. Perhaps, then, containment is best seen as always already in play, even before we can identify a dominant-subversive opposition, or indeed anything like a subversive event. But by the same token, containment can effect rather than defeat change (and this doesn't presuppose the desirability or otherwise of that change; it might be reaction or progress or, as in this play, complex elements of both with each differently appropriated for different audience positions). Rather than seeing containment as that which preempts and defeats transgression we need to see both as potentially productive processes. *The Roaring Girl* presents a process in which containment of the deviant forms the basis of one social faction offering a critique of, and taking power from, another. In a more radical dynamic, containment, in the very process of repressing one kind of subversive knowledge, actually produces another. It is to the latter process that I now turn.

VI

Perhaps the most interesting theatrical containment of the transvestite challenge occurs in Fletcher's *Love's Cure* (1624?).[16] Indeed, one wonders if the play was written as a conservative response to the controversy, since it directly addresses the most challenging claim or implication of the radical transvestite, namely, that gender division and inequality are a consequence not of divine or natural law but of social custom. The play centers on the severe cultural disturbance generated by the fact that Clara, a girl, has been brought up as a boy and wants to remain one, while her brother, Lucio, has been brought up as a girl, which he wants to remain, despite the fact that society is now demanding that both return to their normal gender ascriptions. It's a humorous situation and one played up as such. But the play also acknowledges that what is at stake is nothing less than the legitimacy of the whole social order, hinging as it does on a "naturally" sanctioned law of sexual difference. This is a play about the perversion of nature by culture (or "custom"—1.2.47, 2.2.95–97) with the eventual triumph of nature: "Nature (though long kept back) wil have her owne" (4.4.61–62; cf.2.2.248–59, 4.2.187–90, 5.3.90–94).

The cultural conditioning of both Lucio and Clara seems to go deep. Parents and others try yet fail to restore the children to their natural selves; the father, Alvarez, cries angrily:

> Can strong habituall custome
> Work with such Magick on the mind, and manners
> In spight of sex and nature?
>
> (2.2.140–42)

The answer is, apparently, yes. But then nature succeeds where authority has failed; attraction to the opposite sex awakens the siblings' own "true" natural instincts, and gender incongruities are resolved.

Clara switches from being aggressive to being acquiescent, and Lucio does the reverse. Right order prevails.

We might say that *Love's Cure* produces transgression precisely in order to contain it, and in the most insidiously ideological way: desire which initially appeared to contradict nature is reconstituted by nature in accord with her (?) order. Reconstituted, not repressed: desire itself is transformed, not coerced, back from the perverse to the natural. But in the process the very masculine code of honor which is affronted by Lucio's perverse failure of masculinity is shown to border on a perversity even more excessive than his. It is as if containment, in reinstating nature over culture—that most fundamental and violent of binary oppositions—protests too much about both. Thus the strategy of containment resembles the unintended power of the subordinates who execute the commands of the powerful and of whom the Governor complains:

> How men in high place, and authority
> Are in their lives and estimation wrong'd
> By their subordinate Ministers? *yet such*
> *They cannot but imploy.*

> (4.3.119–22; emphasis added)

Masculine sexuality is shown to be complex and unstably implicated within the whole social domain. Either nature doesn't contain it or nature contains too much to be conceived any longer as natural. What is especially fascinating about this text is that a relegitimation of masculinity coexists with an ironic critique of it, and a representation of masculinity's cultural unconscious. An urbane text, it nevertheless discloses a violent scenario—social, psychic, and sexual (what has sometimes been mistaken for decadence).

Most obviously and consciously there is the fact that Lucio's effeminacy, construed by Bobadillo as an affront to "heav'n, and nature, and thy Parents" (2.2.22)—i.e., divine, natural, and patriarchal law—actually involves positive civilized virtues. Lucio would, for example, willingly renounce the savage illogic whereby a bloody family feud is being perpetuated (2.2.44 ff.) and also the sword as instrument and symbol of male violence (2.4.84 ff.). And then his father, raging at Lucio's inability to become a "real" man, demands final proof of his masculinity: he must attack the very next man he sees and sexually assault the first woman (4.3.37 ff.). Though conceived as an absolute, uncompromising ethical stand ("Life's but a word, a shadow, a melting dreame, / Compar'd to essentiall, and eternall honour"—5.3.124–25), masculine honor is also represented as barbaric. Two of its basic characteristics are sexual prowess and violence, and they are inextricably related, as indicated for example by the conventional but still revealingly obsessive association of sword and phallus (e.g., at 2.2.86–90 and 5.3.194–96) and the ambiguity of "blood," at once sexual desire and what honor demands, literally, of the male opponent.

From such punning we see that masculine sexuality is confirmed not only by women, passively, but also actively by other men. Actively: it isn't so much that the culture of masculine honor is a sublimation of homosexuality; rather it repeatedly incites what heterosexually it cannot admit. The differential status of men and women in confirming masculine sexuality is neatly demonstrated at the climax of the play, the arranged duel between Alvarez and Vitelli (seconded, respectively, by the now masculine Lucio and Lamorall). As they square up to each other the spouses of the first three men "*Enter above*" and implore them not to fight. Plea after plea fails. "Are you men, or stone," cries the Governor; "Men, and we'l prove it with our swords" replies Alvarez (5.3.172–73). And what honor dictates must take place between men—alliance/violence—simply overrides honorable vows to women (162–64). In fact the women's pleas for peace only intensify the men's desire to fight. Within masculine sexuality the most significant other is the male—but it is a significance which still presupposes the female. Thus when the women threaten to kill themselves it's as if the currents of sexuality and violence, circulating between the men and sustaining sexual difference between male and female, are suddenly switched off; the threatened self-annihilation of the women is also a threatened breaking of the circuit. If they die the most necessary spectators and objects of masculine performance disappear. Also, in this *reductio ad absurdum* of masculine sexuality, men become redundant as the women threaten to perform phallic violence on themselves in order to forestall male violence (Genevora to the duelists: "The first blow given betwixt you, sheathes these swords / In one anothers bosomes" [177–78]).

Masculinity is rooted in a sexual violence performed inseparably against both men and women. Vitelli to Clara:

> When on this point, I have pearch'd thy father's soule.
> Ile tender thee this bloody reeking hand
> Drawne forth the bowels of that murtherer:
> If thou canst love me then, I'le marry thee.
> And for thy father lost, get thee a Sonne;
> On no condition else.
>
> (104–09)

In the reiterated pun, sword and phallus substitute for each other. But here we might read/see something more: Vitelli's violence against Clara's father is erotically identified with the sexual act performed "with" her. Vitelli will kill her father and replace him with a son born of her. It's the supreme narcissistic displacement of the rival male via the very woman whom each struggles to possess. Further, this promised birth will implicate Clara in Vitelli's violence without at all changing her status as its abject victim. And the violence against her father is as sexual as the proposed sexual intercourse "with" Clara is violent. Vitelli doubly substitutes himself for Clara's father: first as her husband, then as himself in her son.

This incident is not the first time that Vitelli has insisted to Clara that his sexual desire for her is conjoined with an equally strong desire to kill her father and brother:

> He, whose tongue thus gratifies the daughter,
> And sister of his enemy, weares a Sword
> To rip the father and the brother up.
> . . . .
> That my affections should promiscuously
> Dart love and hate at once, both worthily!
>
> (2.2.189–95)

Speaking of himself in the second person Vitelli presents masculine desire as spectacle, again narcissistically demanding confirmation of an audience even as he also conceives his masculinity as spontaneous, autonomous desire.

The opposite of honorable antagonism is honorable alliance, affirmed in the image and name of the brother. But what are in one sense
dramatically opposed kinds of relationships are in another simply alternative celebrations of masculinity. Elsewhere in Beaumont and
Fletcher's work valorous males similarly oscillate between honorable
antagonism and honorable alliance, in an almost erotic state of arou-
sal. In both kinds of relationship men recognize and reinforce each
other's sexuality in the triangle man-man-woman. But even as they enter into relations of honorable alliance it is with an unspoken understanding: "I don't desire you; I desire to be like you." This repeated
disavowal of direct desire in favor of imitative alliance is a crucial precondition of one kind of male bonding (what someone once called pe-
nises in parallel).

Frequently in this period the representation of the triangle suggests
that the desire which bonds men over women is as erotically invested
for the men in relation to each other as for each of them in relation to
the women. In *The Maid's Tragedy*, Melantius, approving his sister's
marriage to his best friend, tells her: "Sister, I joy to see you, and your
choice. / You look'd with my eyes when you took that man" (*The
Maid's Tragedy* 1.2.107–08). Another revealing recurrence in Jacobean plays is the way that male sexual jealousy, even as it is represented
as obsessively heterosexual in its demands, produces eroticized images of the rival male simultaneously with the denigration of the woman:

FERDINAND
                        my imagination will carry me
To see her in the shameful act of sin
. . . .
Happily, with some strong thigh'd bargeman;
Or one o'th' wood-yard, that can quoit the sledge
Or toss the bar, or else some lovely squire
That carries coals up to her privy lodgings.
. . . .
                                Go to, mistress!
'Tis not your whore's milk that shall quench my wildfire,
But your whore's blood.
                                (2.5.40–49)

In *The Maid's Tragedy*, when the King becomes sexually jealous of Amintor, he too evokes his rival in terms which eroticize him, showing again that the cult of masculine honor circulating in this court is ineradicably erotic (3.1).

Seemingly, masculine identity always requires masculine ratification, but in the process is potentially complicated by a homoerotic desire in the very situations in which heterosexuality is most ardently pursued. It's as if, with so much mutual admiration about, some of it just cannot help but transform into deviant desire for, rather than honorable imitation of, "man's" most significant other (i.e., man). But should we call this dynamic homoerotic? It certainly is erotic, but perhaps it is better described, following Eve Sedgwick,[17] as homosocial desire, if only to avoid erroneous assumptions about its origin and "nature." For example, it seems to me that this process does not necessarily involve the irruption of repressed homosexual desire as conceived by Freud;[18] rather it is the eroticizing of a bond, an eroticism largely preconditioned by the social intensity of that bond.

To shift in this analysis from the transvestite to the issue of masculine sexuality is only to follow one trajectory of transvestism itself during this period: in appropriating, inverting, and substituting for masculinity, the female transvestite inevitably put masculinity itself—and sexual difference more generally—under scrutiny. Further, in the attempted containment of transvestism (*Love's Cure*) masculinity and sexual difference are put in question in a different way; in the control of one hostile knowledge another is inadvertently produced; suppression of an (in)subordinate deviance discloses other, equally disturbing deviations at the heart of the dominant, homoerotic deviations whose repression is a condition of domination in one of its important forms: homosocial male bonding. Finally, the transvestite challenge to masculinity and sexual difference works in terms of transgressive inversion and reinscription, not of transcendence or the recovery of authentic selfhood. We are as free born as men, says the Hic Mulier figure, and she says it in drag. Not so much knowing thyself, then, as knowing thy discursive formations—knowing them in the process of living but also inverting them; reinscribing oneself within, succumbing to, dis-locating, demystifying them.

Notes

[1] For further analysis of custom in this respect see Dollimore, esp. 9–19.

[2] See also Crompton.

[3] Anthropological and historical studies of inversion in the Renaissance have stressed both its ubiquity and its cultural significance. But what and how it signified—in particular whether it disrupted or ratified those dominant forms being inverted—depended crucially on context and cannot be decided independently of it. See especially Davis, and Kunzle, both in Babcock; and Stallybrass and White.

[4] See Davis, and Kunzle.

[5] Cf. Freud: "defiance signifies dependence *as much as obedience does,* though with a 'minus' instead of a 'plus' sign before it" *(Introductory Lectures on Psychoanalysis* 495; emphasis added).

[6] Freud's noted instance of the return of the repressed also involves the Crucifixion. In an etching by Félicien Rops an ascetic monk looks to the Crucifixion to banish his own temptation, but in place of Christ he sees "the image of a voluptuous, naked woman, in the same crucified attitude. . . . Rops has placed Sin in the very place of the Saviour on the cross. He seems to have known that, when what has been repressed returns, it emerges from the repressing force itself." Freud, *Art and Literature* 60.

[7] Derrida 41–42. Derrida stresses the importance of inversion as a stage in the process of displacing the binary. Even with this formulation it is easy to overlook the extent to which, in actual practice, in historical reality, an inversion already achieves a degree of displacement.

[8] I explore this further in a related article, "The Dominant and the Deviant."

[9] This section is indebted to and was inspired by a number of recent studies of the transvestite controversy, especially the following: Dusinberre, esp. 231–305; Shepherd, esp. ch. 6; Jardine, esp. ch. 5; Woodbridge, esp. part 2; Rose, 367–91; Clark 157–83.

[10] See also Whigham 155–69.

[11] "A Common Player," 1615, quoted from Montrose 51 and 57.

[12] *Overthrow of Stage-Plays, 1599.* See also Binns 95–120; Jardine, ch. 1.

[13] See also Woodbridge 254–55.

[14] See Chamberlain 2: 286–89.

[15] Gomme, xiv; see also Shepherd 74–76.

[16] All quotations from *Love's Cure* are from the Williams edition. A much-needed single-volume edition of this text is in preparation by J. Marea Mitchell for the Nottingham Drama Texts Series, ed. George Parfitt et al. Mitchell also analyzes the play in her dissertation, "Gender and Identity in Philip Sidney's *Arcadia.*" See also Shepherd, and Clark.

[17] Sedgwick, esp. Introduction and ch. 1; see also Girard.

[18] See for example Freud's description of this in his account of the Schreber case in *Case Histories II*, esp. 199–200.

Works Cited

BABCOCK, BARBARA A. *The Reversible World: Symbolic Inversion in Art and Society*. Ithaca and London: Cornell UP, 1978.

BEAUMONT, F., and FLETCHER, J. *The Maid's Tragedy.* Ed. H. B. Norland. Regents Renaissance Drama Series. London: Arnold, 1968.

BINNS, J. W. "Women or Transvestites on the Elizabethan Stage?: An Oxford Controversy." *Sixteenth Century Journal* 5 (1974): 95–120.

BROWN, RITA MAE. *Rubyfruit Jungle*. London: Corgi, 1978.

CHAMBERLAIN, JOHN. *Letters*. Ed. Norman E. McClure. 2 vols. Philadelphia: American Philosophical Society, 1939.

CHAMBERS, E. K. *The Elizabethan Stage*. 4 vols. Oxford: Clarendon, 1923.

CLARK, SANDRA. "*Hic Mulier, Haec Vir*, and the Controversy over Masculine Women." *Studies in Philology* 82 (Spring 1985): 157–83.

CROMPTON, LOUIS. "The Myth of Lesbian Impunity: Capital Laws from 1270–1791." *Journal of Homosexuality* 6 (1980–81): 11–25.

DAVIES, SIR JOHN. *Nosce Teipsum. Poems*. Ed. Robert Krueger. Oxford: Clarendon, 1975.

DAVIS, NATALIE ZEMON. "Women on Top: Symbolic Sexual Inversion and Political Disorder in Early Modern Europe." *The Reversible World: Symbolic Inversion in Art and Society*. Ithaca and London: Cornell UP, 1978.

DERRIDA, JACQUES. *Positions*. London: Athlone, 1981.

DOLLIMORE, JONATHAN. *Radical Tragedy*. Brighton: Harvester, 1984; Chicago: U of Chicago P, 1984.

———. "The Dominant and the Deviant: A Violent Dialectic." *Critical Quarterly* 28 (1986).

DUSINBERRE, JULIET. *Shakespeare and the Nature of Women*. London: Macmillan, 1975.

FADERMAN, LILLIAN. *Surpassing the Love of Men: Romantic Friendship and Love between Women from the Renaissance to the Present*. London: Dent, 1981.

FLETCHER, JOHN. *The Dramatic Works in the Beaumont and Fletcher Canon*. Ed. George W. Williams. Gen. ed. Fredson Bowers. Vol. 3. Cambridge: Cambridge UP, 1976.

FOUCAULT, MICHAEL. *The History of Sexuality*. Vol. 1: *An Introduction*. New York: Vintage, 1980.

FREUD, SIGMUND. *Case Histories II*. The Pelican Freud Library 9. Harmondsworth: Pelican Books, 1979.

――――. *Introductory Lectures on Psychoanalysis*. The Pelican Freud Library 1. Harmondsworth: Pelican Books, 1976.

――――. *Art and Literature*. The Pelican Freud Library 14. Harmondsworth: Pelican Books, 1985.

GIDE, ANDRÉ. *The Immoralist*. Harmondsworth: Penguin, 1960.

GIRARD, RENÉ. *Deceit, Desire and the Novel: Self and Others in Literary Structure*. Baltimore: Johns Hopkins UP, 1965.

GOMME, ANDOR. Introduction. *The Roaring Girl*. By Middleton and Dekker. London: Benn, 1976.

GREENBLATT, STEPHEN. *Renaissance Self-Fashioning*. Chicago: U of Chicago P, 1980.

Hic Mulier: Or, the Man-Woman and *Haec-Vir: Or, the Womanish-Man*. 1620. The University of Essex: The Rota, 1973.

HOOKER, RICHARD. *Of the Laws of Ecclesiastical Polity*. 2 vols. London: Dent, 1969.

JARDINE, LISA. *Still Harping on Daughters: Women and Drama in the Age of Shakespeare*. Brighton: Harvester, 1983.

KUNZLE, DAVID. "World Turned Upside Down: The Iconography of a European Broadsheet Type." Babcock.

MIDDLETON, THOMAS, and THOMAS DEKKER, *The Roaring Girl*. The New Mermaid edition. Ed. A. Gomme. London: Benn, 1976.

MITCHELL, J. MAREA. "Gender and Identity in Philip Sidney's *Arcadia.*" Diss. U of Sussex, 1985.

MONTAIGNE, MICHEL. *Essays*. Trans. John Florio. 3 vols. London: Dent, 1965.

MONTROSE, LOUIS. 'The Purpose of Playing: Reflections on a Shakespearean Anthropology." *Helios* ns 7 (1980): 51–74.

NEWTON, ESTHER. "The Mythic Mannish Lesbian: Radclyffe Hall and the New Woman." *The Lesbian Issue: Essays from Signs*. Ed. Estelle B. Freeman et al. Chicago: U of Chicago P, 1985.

RAINOLDS, JOHN. *Overthrow of Stage-Plays.* 1599. Theatrum Redividium Series. New York, 1972.

ROSE, MARY BETH. "Women in Men's Clothing: Apparel and Social Stability in *The Roaring Girl.*" *English Literary Renaissance* 14 (1984): 367–91.

SALGÁDO, G., ed. *Cony-Catchers and Bawdy Baskets.* Penguin English Library. Harmondsworth, 1972.

SEDGWICK, EVE KOSOFSKY. *Between Men: English Literature and Male Homosocial Desire.* New York: Columbia UP, 1985.

SENNETT, RICHARD. *Authority.* London: Secker, 1980.

SHEPHERD, SIMON. *Amazons and Warrior Women: Varieties of Feminism in Seventeenth-Century Drama.* Brighton: Harvester, 1981.

SILVERMAN, KAJA. *The Subject of Semiotics.* New York: Oxford UP, 1983.

STALLYBRASS, PETER, and ALLON WHITE. *The Politics and Poetics of Transgression.* London: Methuen, 1986.

WEBSTER, JOHN. *The Duchess of Malfi. Selected Plays.* Ed. Jonathan Dollimore and Alan Sinfield. Cambridge: Cambridge UP, 1983.

WHIGHAM, FRANK. *Ambition and Privilege: The Social Tropes of Elizabethan Courtesy Theory.* Berkeley: U of California P, 1984.

WOODBRIDGE, LINDA. *Women and the English Renaissance: Literature and the Nature of Womankind,* 1540–1620. Brighton: Harvester, 1984; Urbana: U of Illinois P, 1984.

Class Conflict and
Social Mobility

Celebration and Insinuation: Sir Philip Sidney and the Motives of Elizabethan Courtship

LOUIS ADRIAN MONTROSE

RENAISSANCE LITERARY THEORISTS customarily note an analogy between the sacred psalm or hymn of praise ("the first forme of Poesie and the highest & the stateliest") and poetic celebrations of earthly rulers ("a second degree of laude: shewing their high estates, their Princely genealogies and pedigrees, mariages, aliances, and such noble exploites, as they have done in th'affaires of peace & of warre to the benefit of their people and countries").[1] This analogy of sacred and secular encomia is strengthened when the incarnation of temporal authority and power happens to be a virgin queen who is head of both state and church, and whose personal mythology is contrived to be a national and Protestant substitute for a cult of the Blessed Virgin.[2] An imperial mythology, infused with the conventions of Petrarchism and enhanced by metaphysical sanctions

---

1. *The Arte of English Poesie* [1589], ed. Gladys Doidge Willcock and Alice Walker (Cambridge, 1936), pp. 30, 35. I accept the editors' ascription of this work to George Puttenham. Further references will be to this edition, cited as "Puttenham, *Arte.*" I have modernized Elizabethan typographic conventions.

2. On the policy and iconography of the Elizabeth cult, see Frances A. Yates, *Astraea: The Imperial Theme in the Sixteenth Century* (London, 1974).

367

deriving from Neo-Platonism, gives to celebrations of Queen Elizabeth a unique richness of allusion. The relationship between courtier-poets and queen is idealized as a love purified of physical desire; its erotic energy has been transformed into art and service. Because authority is incarnated in a woman, the mythological projection of the prevailing ideology can merge the idealization of a power relationship with an idealized relationship of love. The public ritualizations of intimate relationship manifested in pageants, processions, masques, tilts, orations, and other royal entertainments affirm and celebrate a strong and beautiful union between the ruler and her subjects. Royal pageantry serves as an instrument of internal and international policy, as a romantic mystification of the motives of the queen and her privy council. But royal celebrations can also function as idealizations of the motives of the queen's poet-courtiers: the grace that the faithful worshiper hopes from his goddess is preferment.

I. Persuasion and Manipulation

Of the younger generation of Elizabethan men who came to maturity in the 1580s and 1590s, those within the ambience of the court—aristocrats, lesser gentry, common-born but university educated writers and servant-bureaucrats—have been characterized as a generation "of high aspiration, revealed most commonly in intense personal ambition."[3] The generations of Burghley and Elizabeth had experienced directly and intensely the rigors, crises, and chaos of the mid-Tudor period; in later life, they came to enshrine the virtues of moderation and increasingly to inveigh against the inherent evil and self-destructiveness of overweening ambition. Men of the younger generation were raised in the relative tranquility of Elizabethan compromise politics, stirred by the currents of the continental Renaissance and by widening geographic horizons, comparatively well-educated in preparation for public careers, and exposed early to the new opulence of the English court. This "generation of 1560" came to revalue aspiration in all its endeavors.

3. Anthony Esler, *The aspiring mind of the Elizabethan younger generation* (Durham, N.C., 1966). The following two paragraphs are directly indebted to Esler's analysis.

Aspiration was focused on courtship of the queen in a reciprocal relationship of service and reward. Honors, power, and wealth were the personal goals that the younger Elizabethan aristocracy most ardently pursued; the baseborn writers who were their contemporaries pursued analogous goals within an appropriately narrowed and lowered range. These ambitions encountered various impediments: the hostility of a politically cautious and socially conservative older generation of power brokers; the ever-present possibilities of personal failure, of ungracious and even fatal performances, in the topsy-turvy worlds of military, political, financial, and amorous affairs; and, most critically, the severely limited resources of the crown for the bestowal of preferments, the queen's conservative fiscal policies, and her parsimonious character.

In a masterful essay on Elizabethan patronage, Wallace MacCaffrey concludes that, although "the successful distribution of patronage" was one of the conditions upon which "the imposing stability of the Elizabethan regime depended," it nevertheless "lacked adequate safeguards against a free-for-all scramble for spoils."

Yet, in judging the regime as a whole, high praise must be given for the transformation of English political habits which was accomplished during these years. By the end of the reign Englishmen were turning away from their bad old habits of conspiracy and treason—the resort to force as the final arbiter in politics. Under the tutelage of Burghley and his royal mistress they had learned the peaceful, if sometimes corrupt, habits of a new political order. They had mastered the subtler arts of persuasion and manipulation.[4]

Life within the Elizabethan court and on its margins was characterized by intrigue, backbiting, and bribery; by intense competition for personal and political influence, office, prestige, and income. This strife was

4. Wallace T. MacCaffrey, "Place and Patronage in Elizabethan Politics," in *Elizabethan Government and Society*, ed. S. T. Bindoff, J. Hurstfield, and C. H. Williams (London, 1961), pp. 95–126; I quote from pp. 125–126. See also the chapter on "Office and the Court" in Lawrence Stone's magisterial work, *The Crisis of the Aristocracy 1558–1641* (Oxford, 1965), pp. 385–504. On matters of literary patronage, see: John Buxton, *Sir Philip Sidney and the English Renaissance*, 2d ed. (London, 1964); Edwin Haviland Miller, *The Professional Writer in Elizabethan England* (Cambridge, Mass., 1959), pp. 94–135; Eleanor Rosenberg, *Leicester, Patron of Letters* (New York, 1955); J. W. Saunders, *The Profession of English Letters* (London, 1964), pp. 31–92.

partially controlled by the imposition of collective aesthetic forms on unruly personal energies.

Courtly cultural forms functioned to impose some order upon the forces
of chaos within the court system at the same time that they facilitated
manipulation of the system to personal advantage. Puttenham provides
an unusually candid contemporary poetic and rhetorical analysis of these
forms and their functions. Consider his englishing of the figure *Allegoria*
as "the Courtier or figure of faire semblant."[5]

The courtly figure *Allegoria* . . . is when we speake one thing and thinke
another, and that our wordes and our meanings meete not. The use of this
figure is so large, and his vertue of so great efficacie as it is supposed no man
can pleasantly utter and perswade without it, but in effect is sure never or
very seldome to thrive and prosper in the world, that cannot skilfully put in
use, in so much as not onely every common Courtier, but also the gravest
Counsellour, yea and the most noble and wisest Prince of them all are many
times enforced to use it.

(p. 186)

In Puttenham's "figure of faire semblant," Castiglione's Courtier masks
Machiavelli's Fox. Puttenham's "Courtly figure *Allegoria*" operates as a
synecdoche for his own text: a treatise on poetics masks an exemplary
handbook on the conduct of relations among courtiers and between
courtier and prince. Puttenham teaches vital strategies of persuasion and
manipulation for survival and success in a complicated, dangerous, and
highly competitive social world.

Symbolic pageantry, poetry, drama, music, dance, and visual iconography enhance a ritualistic system of rules for decorum and deference.
They also proffer culturally refined media in which the queen's courtly
celebrants can variously express, explore, prosecute, obfuscate, and sub-
limate both their idealistic personal aspirations and their material ambitions. Both as *texts* and as *events,* Elizabethan entertainments encourage
us to explore the interaction of art with life, of cultural forms with social
forces, of celebration with manipulation and persuasion. In what follows,
I study how a uniquely gifted young gentleman-courtier-poet exploits the
occasions of royal entertainment less to praise than to oppose, instruct,

5. Puttenham, *Arte,* p. 299.

and petition his queen. The extant *texts* of Philip Sidney's royal entertainments are distillates of the literary, biographical, and sociopolitical processes in which they were originally conceived, presented, and experienced; as historical *events,* these performed entertainments were integral elements in the dialectic of Elizabethan social reality. By analyzing what and how Sidney's entertainments signify, we may better understand the Elizabethan uses of celebration.

II. Life and Art

The Renaissance courtly style endeavored to obliterate the distinction between life and art. To many in the late Elizabethan and Jacobean periods, Philip Sidney incarnated this ideal. Well before his early death, he had already been mythologized by his family, friends, and political allies, and by the beneficiaries of his generous patronage. Sidney's few public addresses and public acts are full of a resolute and uncompromising idealism that Queen Elizabeth undoubtedly found willful and potentially dangerous. His substantial literary work, however, is not an unreflective and naïve projection of idealism but rather an interplay of ideals and actualities, reason and the infirmity of will, personal aspiration and the circumstantial impediments to its full expression. Sidney was a literary "amateur," whose great expectation was not to decorate the court but to profess arms and statecraft; he had been trained for a brilliant and central role in the pageant of English, and, indeed, European, affairs. In his life, as well as in his art, Sidney was in a position to actualize rhetorical and poetic *topoi;* to live out the ubiquitous humanist debate about the relative merits of action and contemplation, the major literary dialectic of heroic and pastoral kinds. As a poet and defender of poetry, Sidney was concerned to use the imaginative act of fiction-making as an intellectual instrument to clarify motives and options on the world's stage, where he was—or, at least, hoped to be—an actor. Lesser-born patronage poets were, for the most part, mere spectators at the living theater of the Elizabethan court.

The unsuccessful pursuit of influence, office, and income that characterizes Philip Sidney's brief career is epitomized in the slight but

suggestive pastoral entertainment known as *The Lady of May*.[6] What we
have is the transcribed text of a show performed before Queen Elizabeth
in the garden of the earl of Leicester's estate at Wanstead (which had
been a gift from the queen) in May of 1578 or, possibly, 1579.[7] Sidney
created his royal show at a critical point in his own, his family's, and his

6. Like most Renaissance entertainments, *The Lady of May* (*LM*) is generically
hybrid. Stephen Orgel, *The Jonsonian Masque* (Cambridge, Mass., 1965), writes
that *LM* "is conceived in terms of the masque" (p. 45), and discusses it (pp. 44–
55) in the context of the evolution of the Stuart masque. Robert Kimbrough and
Philip Murphy, "The Helmingham Hall Manuscript of Sidney's *The Lady of
May*: A Commentary and Transcription" (*RenD*, N.S. 1 [1968], pp. 103–119)
identify *LM* as a mix of the "pseudo-dramatic pageants" Sidney probably witnessed
at Kenilworth during the celebrated Progress of 1575, and the *commedia rusticale*,
a "popular kind of farce" that he may have seen in Italy during his grand tour (p.
104). As Kimbrough and Murphy observe, this typology does not account for the
pervasive pastoral themes and conventions in *LM*. Sidney's slight pastoral must, in
fact, share primacy of place with Spenser's massive, contemporaneous effort (*The
Shepheardes Calender*, 1579) in the history of English pastoral literature. William
Ringler, Jr., in his edition of *The Poems of Sir Philip Sidney* (Oxford, 1962), calls
LM "the earliest example in English of conventionalized pastoral drama" (p. 361)
(to be cited as "Sidney, *Poems*"). I would add that we should credit Sidney with
having developed the dramaturgical possibilities latent in the eclogue, the poetic kind
that Puttenham classed with satire, comedy, and tragedy as morally reprehensible and
educative "*drammatick* poems" (*Arte*, p. 38). In its presentation of shepherds and
foresters, its rustic setting, its sophisticated treatment of the pastoral *topos* of contemplation and action (as well as in its structural exploitation of pastoral devices
of song, contest, and dialogue), *LM* demonstrates its generic affinity to the eclogue.
    7. *The Lady of May* received its title in the 1725 edition of Sidney's works.
There are two extant substantive texts: the version printed with the 1598 edition
of *Arcadia*, rpt. in *The Prose Works of Sir Philip Sidney*, ed. Albert Feuillerat,
4 vols. (1912; rpt. Cambridge, 1968), II, 208–217 (to be cited as "Sidney, *Prose
Works*"); and a manuscript recently published in Kimbrough and Murphy, "The
Helmingham Hall Manuscript," pp. 107–119. My citations of *LM* are from the
modernized text in *Miscellaneous Prose of Sir Philip Sidney*, ed. Katherine
Duncan-Jones and Jan van Dorsten (Oxford, 1973), pp. 21–32 (to be cited as
"Sidney, *Miscellaneous Prose*"). This edition uses the 1598 version as copy text but
incorporates readings from the Helmingham Hall manuscript, notably a final
speech by Rombus for which this manuscript is the sole authority.
    The queen visited Wanstead in May of both 1578 and 1579. Ringler (Sidney,
Poems, p. 362) favors "the spring of 1578 as the date of composition and presen-
tation" on stylistic grounds; Kimbrough and Murphy accept this dating. John
Nichols, *The Progresses and Public Processions of Queen Elizabeth*, new ed., 3

faction's fortunes; analysis of its meaning must proceed in a historical context.

In June 1577, a year before the performance of *The Lady of May*, Philip Sidney returned from an embassy to the leaders of continental Protestant forces. Still in his mid-twenties, Sidney seemed to have made a brilliant start on the diplomatic and military career for which he had been so carefully groomed. He was to wait eight years for his next important commission, one that would take him to his death. A recent biographer of Sidney's early maturity has speculated that the dislike and distrust Elizabeth henceforth would show toward him began in the wake of his personal triumph among the Dutch: she was concerned that the desire of William of Orange to have Sidney as his son-in-law and military commander would not only jeopardize her delicately balanced foreign policy but might eventuate in her subject becoming ruler of a united, independent Netherlands and the Dudley faction's candidate to be her own successor.[8] Whether or not we wholly assent to this hypothesis, it does justly convey the irony that pervades the rest of Sidney's life: a nearly universal recognition of his enormous promise, and a royal distrust sufficient to keep that promise from opportunities for fulfillment.

In the months following Sidney's return, royal enthusiasm for a Protestant League faded away; no further preferments were forthcoming to advance Sidney's career and to relieve his financial embarrassment; Count Casimir's request for money, troops, and Sidney's services in the

---

vols. (1823; rpt. New York, 1966), reprints *LM* (II, 94–103) and assigns it to 1578. Duncan-Jones and van Dorsten maintain that "the evidence on neither side seems strong enough for one to make a firm decision between the two years" (Sidney, *Miscellaneous Prose*, p. 13). I accept the conclusion that 1578 is more likely, but my argument does not depend upon its certainty.

8. See James M. Osborn, *Young Philip Sidney 1572–1577* (New Haven, Conn., 1972), pp. 496–498. Fulke Greville's *Life of the Renowned Sir Philip Sidney* (written ca. 1610–1614; printed, 1652; rpt., with an introduction by Nowell Smith, Oxford, 1907) is the incomparable primary source of information and commentary on Sidney and his milieu. (References will be to the 1907 reprint, cited in my text as "Greville, *Life*.") In addition to the work of Osborn, the following modern biographical studies have been valuable sources of fact and interpretation: Roger Howell, *Sir Philip Sidney: The Shepherd Knight* (Boston, 1968); Malcolm William Wallace, *The Life of Sir Philip Sidney* (1915; rpt. New York, 1967); Richard A. Lanham, "Sidney: The Ornament of his Age," *SoRA*, II (1967), 319–340; F. J. Levy, "Philip Sidney Reconsidered," *ELR*, II (1972), 5–18.

Netherlands campaign got no affirmative response from the queen; Sir Henry Sidney, Philip's father and one of Elizabeth's longest and hardest-working but poorest-rewarded administrators, was recalled from his thankless task in Ireland. In addition to all these private and public sources of frustration and concern, the project of Elizabeth's marriage to the duke of Alençon, brother to the French king, now began to loom as a serious possibility. Negotiations reached a climax between 1578 and 1580; these years saw a decline in the prestige and influence of the Leicester-Walsingham faction, who most bitterly opposed the match within the councils of state.

The critical year 1579 saw the anonymous publication of John Stubbs's stridently anti-Catholic and patriotic *Gaping Gulf*, for which he lost his right hand in the marketplace at Westminster; the anonymous publication of Spenser's *Shepheardes Calender*, whose religiopolitical allegories seem to have earned Spenser the enmity of Lord Burghley; and the manuscript circulation of "A Letter written by Sir Philip Sidney to Queen Elizabeth, touching Her Marriage with Monsieur," which angered the queen and provoked Sidney's retirement from court. It has sometimes been suggested that Sidney's *Lady of May*, like Spenser's *Shepheardes Calendar*, uses a pastoral mask to express strong but dangerous opinions on the burning issue of the royal marriage and its religious and political implications. Arguments that *The Lady of May* is a topical allegory about the Alençon affair lack substantiation and fail to convince; nevertheless, the relationship of the crisis to Sidney's personal convictions and aspirations forms part of the context of meanings for *The Lady of May*. Sidney's royal entertainment attempts to define and advance his place in the Elizabethan body politic, and his relationship to the queen, in the light of those recent and ongoing developments and disappointments that I have been enumerating. In his "Letter to Queen Elizabeth," Sidney is bold—too bold—in claiming the courtier's right and duty to offer counsel to his prince; in *The Lady of May*, he dons the mask of pastoral entertainer in order, "under the vaile of homely persons, and in rude speeches to insinuate and glaunce at greater matters, and such as perchance had not bene safe to have beene disclosed in any other sort." [9]

Between 1577 and 1580, Sidney spent much of his time away from the

9. Puttenham, *Arte*, p. 38.

court, living a life of what his Protestant humanist friend and mentor, Hubert Languet, delicately called "dignified ease." Sidney's persistent attempts to gain patronage and to influence government policy were wholly unsuccessful. He appears to have heeded Languet's advice, if only reluctantly and sporadically: "Persevere as long as you can do anything that may benefit your country, but when you find that your opposition only draws on you dislike and aversion . . . give way to necessity and reserve yourself for better times." [10] In his partly sought, partly enforced, pastoral retirement at his sister's estate at Wilton, Sidney wrote analytical pastorals—*The Lady of May* and the original *Arcadia*—to cope imaginatively with necessities and to prepare for better times. He also maintained a personal correspondence, of which the following letter to Languet, written in March 1578, may have been contemporaneous with the composition of *The Lady of May:*

My mind itself, if it was ever active in any thing, is now beginning, by reason of my indolent ease, imperceptibly to lose its strength, and to relax without any reluctance. For to what purpose should our thoughts be directed to various kinds of knowledge, unless room be afforded for putting it into practice, so that public advantage may be the result, which in a corrupt age we cannot hope for? Who would learn music except for the sake of giving pleasure? or architecture except with a view to building? But the mind itself, you will say, that particle of the divine mind, is cultivated in this manner. This indeed, if we allow it to be the case, is a very great advantage: but let us see whether we are not giving a beautiful but false appearance to our splendid errors. For while the mind is thus, as it were, drawn out of itself, it cannot turn its powers inward for thorough self-examination; to which employment no labour that men can undertake, is any way to be compared. Do you not see that I am cleverly playing the stoic? yea and I shall be a cynic too, unless you reclaim me.[11]

Sidney writes in the *serio ludere* tone of Renaissance humanists; it is the attitude which, in another letter to Languet, Sidney calls "that seemly play of humour that is so natural . . . in the characters of some of the wisest men." [12] Sidney starts from his central commitment to the fruition

10. *The Correspondence of Sir Philip Sidney and Hubert Languet,* ed. Steuart A. Pears (London, 1845), p. 170. In further references, this text will be cited as "Sidney, *Correspondence.*"

11. *Ibid.,* p. 143.

12. *Ibid.,* p. 65.

in action of study, training, and self-cultivation; then he asks, what is the use of right knowing which is prevented from eventuating in right doing? He rejects the answer that knowledge has intrinsic value, that the readiness is all—such would be mere self-deception. His own response to these frustrations, so he writes, is to lapse into an *otium* of moral and intellectual vitiation. This pose of self-debasement he then maneuvers into an ethically tenable pose of inward-turning contemplation. Despite the personal, ethical preoccupations of Sidney's wit in this passage, there is no mistaking the sociopolitical source of his predicament: the difficulty of achieving a union of *gnosis* and *praxis* "in a corrupt age." [13] Sidney's mind moves lightly over precisely those issues which, within two months, will be dramatized in Wanstead garden before the queen.

In its mode of presentation, *The Lady of May* fuses life and art: as the queen walks in Wanstead garden, she is confronted by a group of rustics who ask her to judge between the suitors of the country maiden who is the May Lady. The queen has descended into the pastoral province of her domains; the rustic world of Leicester's country estate has been transmuted into courtly art. The May Lady is a character engaged in playing an elevated and temporary role in a folk rite; though only the daughter of "an honest man's wife of the country" (p. 20), she is able to tell the queen that "no estate can be compared to be the Lady of the whole month of May, as I am" (p. 24). She abases herself before the queen, however, because she knows instinctively that "you excel me in that wherein I desire most to excel" (p. 24). This pastoral fiction contains within it a rustic world with its own ritual observances and ideals; the living queen is the fictional May Lady's transcendent Idea. The opening supplication to the queen is followed by the entrance of "six shepherds, with as many fosters, haling and pulling to whether side they should draw the Lady of May, who seemed to incline neither to the one nor other side" (p. 22). The queen is witnessing a dramatized debate which, like any serious Renaissance art, demands interpretation and application by its audience: "In judging me," the May Lady tells the queen, "you judge more than me in it" (p. 30). Sidney's entertainment thus an-

---

13. This letter is interpreted with a different emphasis, as a context for the Arcadian poems, in Neil L. Rudenstine, *Sidney's Poetic Development* (Cambridge, Mass., 1967), pp. 7–8, 289–290.

nounces itself as an embodiment of the pastoral formula that William Empson calls "putting the complex into the simple."[14] An allegorical equation is made between the dynamics of fictive pastoral courtship and those of actual royal courtship. The active role of the royal spectator is to comprehend the relationship between simple and complex. By rendering judgment in the simplified courtship of the May Lady, Queen Elizabeth is led by analogy to a particular judgment about the conduct of her own complex and conflict-ridden courtier system.

Therion, a lively forester, and Espilus, a rich shepherd, contend for the May Lady's hand in marriage:

Therion doth me many pleasures, as stealing me venison out of these forests, and many other such like pretty and prettier services; but withal he grows to such rages, that sometimes he strikes me, sometimes he rails at me. This shepherd, Espilus, of a mild disposition, as his fortune hath not been to do me great service, so hath he never done me any wrong; but feeding his sheep, sitting under some sweet bush, sometimes, they say, he records my name in doleful verses. Now the question I am to ask you, fair lady, is whether the many deserts and many faults of Therion, or the very small deserts and no faults of Espilus be to be preferred.

(p. 25)

In the tradition of the eclogue, Therion challenges Espilus to a singing contest in which they demonstrate their natures: the "dialogue" consists of Therion's challenge and his undercutting of each successive stanza that Espilus sings. Espilus (whose sheep farming is on the scale of a major Elizabethan landholder) compares the lady to the two thousand sheep he owns; he courts her acquisitively: "Let me possess thy grace." Therion contrasts her to the two thousand deer he hunts but does not own: "Them I can take, but you I cannot hold" (p. 26). *The Lady of May* associates the forester figure with a freely given, though boldly self-reliant, love of service, and insinuates that the shepherd's life of pastoral *otium* is merely self-serving and small-minded. Espilus is a voluptuary masking as a contemplative; the role of the contemplative who seeks to guide the actions of others by his wisdom is parodied in the figure of Rhombus, a pedantic country schoolmaster whose attempts to arbitrate the debate are rendered absurdly ineffectual by his own obscurantism.

14. *Some Versions of Pastoral* (1935; rpt. New York, 1968), p. 22.

The decision must ultimately reside with the queen, whose own humanist education has prepared her for the judicious exercise of power.

The pastoral entertainment is an allegorical microcosm of the Elizabethan court; in a sense, it temporarily becomes the court, by virtue of the queen's presence and participation. It is in this context that Sidney presents to his royal mistress a choice of exemplary courtiers. His intention is not merely to entertain and compliment the queen. True to his conception of literature as a moral rhetoric, he attempts to manipulate her responses in such a way as to persuade her to choose his kind of courtier for her own. Politic Elizabethan poets spend their wit in praising their royal mistress, not in trying to educate her; ingenuous Sidney is unusually restrained in his courtly compliments and in the business of idolatry but downright audacious in the giving of unsolicited advice. An aspiring statesman and a potentially brilliant poet and defender of poetry, Sidney is doomed to endure a royal aesthetic which prescribes that courtly makers should strive to please but never presume to instruct. Although both *The Lady of May* and the nearly contemporaneous "Letter . . . to Queen Elizabeth, touching her marriage with Monsieur" are written at the behest of the earl of Leicester, Sidney is not writing merely as his elders' tool but in service of his own ideological commitments and personal ambitions. In judging between the May Lady's alternatives, the queen has to judge what mode of courtship is truly in her own and her state's best interests. As in the court masque, here the royal personage is much more than the chief auditor and spectator of the work; she is the leading player, who must perfect the entertainment's open form. When the May Lady tells Elizabeth, "In judging me, you judge more than me in it," the implication is that the queen's judgment will be a judgment upon her own wisdom. From one perspective, the queen infolds the pageant; from another perspective, the pageant encompasses the queen.

The judgment asked of the queen requires a transformation of the traditional values inherent in the conventions that the entertainment employs. Elizabeth is being presented with a variant of the Judgment of Paris, a device often used to turn compliments to Tudor royalty. Goddesslike, the queen is an ultimate arbiter of the choice that the May Lady cannot make; at the conclusion of the judgment, Elizabeth will have proved herself (as Rhombus puts it), "Juno, Venus, Pallas *et profecto plus*" (p. 31). Thus, Sidney's entertainment utilizes the strategy of praise that will shortly become the *coup de théâtre* of George Peele's courtly pastoral, *The Araygnement of Paris* (performed at court, ca. 1582; printed, 1584). Sidney and Peele are of the same generation but of very different family background and social status. They make their literary debuts with courtly pastoral entertainments that employ the same mythological conceit, which is directed to the same audience of one. In Peele's play, Diana rejudges the contest between the three goddesses that Paris has mismanaged. Diana awards the prize to the nymph Eliza, whose kingdom is Elizium; play culminates in ritual as the goddess presents the golden apple to her incarnation, Queen Elizabeth herself. Because the queen infolds their separate perfections, the goddesses gladly resign to her; because her virtues are "more than may belong. / By natures lawe to any earthly wight," the Fates lay their instruments at her feet.[15] When compared to Peele's fulsome and spectacular exploitation of the device as a vehicle for flattery of the queen, the encomiastic restraint and the intellectualism of Sidney's treatment are all the more notable. Peele entertains and celebrates; Sidney instructs and tests.

It is my suggestion that Sidney's initial opposition of unbalanced and objectionable extremes—innocuous shepherd and savage forester—are allegorical caricatures of courtier types: roughly speaking, they caricature the pliable placeman and the impetuous free spirit. This confrontation is continued in the dialogue of Rixus, a bold young forester, and Dorcas, an old shepherd of the pastoral philosopher type that includes Spenser's Meliboe and Shakespeare's Corin. It is important to emphasize that the debate between Dorcas and Rixus does not merely repeat or elaborate the initial opposition of Espilus and Therion. (The May Lady has said that she likes them both and loves neither; the queen has little reason to like either of them.) Instead, it moves the debate to a higher level of analysis. Sidney's rhetorical strategy is to unfold the implications of the objectionable initial appearances.[16]

15. *The Araygnement of Paris,* ed. R. Mark Benbow, in *The Dramatic Works of George Peele,* C. T. Prouty, gen. ed. (New Haven, Conn., 1970); I quote lines 1221–1222. For the convention, see: J. D. Reeves, "The Judgment of Paris as a Device of Tudor Flattery," *N&Q,* N.S. II (1955), 7–11; I.-S. Ekeblad, "On the Background of Peele's *Araygnement,*" *N&Q,* N.S. III (1956), 246–249.

16. That the Espilus/Therion opposition reflects Sidney's support of the aggressive foreign policy advocates in the privy council has been suggested by Ringler

Dorcas's praise of the unaspiring, otiose pastoral life brings the work to the center of its concerns:

How many courtiers, think you, I have heard under our field in bushes make their woeful complaints, some of the greatness of their mistress' estate, which dazzled their eyes and yet burned their hearts; some of the extremity of her beauty mixed with extreme cruelty; some of her too much wit, which made all their loving labours folly? O how often have I heard one name sound in many mouths, making our vales witnesses of their doleful agonies!

(p. 28)

The conventions of pastoral provide an imaginary landscape into which to project the problems encountered in courting the great mistress whose name sounds in many mouths. The courtier suffers rejection and frustration in his struggle for advancement in the favors of a grudging and capricious monarch; this suffering provides a social referent for the impulse to flee, for the attraction of the mean degree, and for the ironic praise of a shepherd-courtier who is "as quiet as a lamb that new came from sucking" (p. 27).

As David Kalstone has pointed out, the explicit terms of Sidney's pastoral debate are the traditional ones of Contemplation and Action.[17] But poets as subtle as Sidney work complicating variations on these simplistic categories. Sidney harmonizes action and contemplation in the forester's life, while he transforms the traditionally contemplative shepherd into a personified conflation of the contemplative and voluptuary lives. At its worst, the shepherd's life is one of intellectual and moral sloth, of sly courting for material gain. At its best, the shepherd's life is merely an element in a life of active virtue that absorbs and transcends pastoral *otium*:

(Sidney, *Poems,* p. 362), and supported by Howell (*Sir Philip Sidney,* pp. 155–156). William Gray, Sidney's early nineteenth-century editor, suggested that Therion was an Aleçon figure; Kimbrough and Murphy assert that "the active Therion is clearly a Leicester-figure" ("The Helmingham Hall Manuscript," p. 105). Previous studies have paid insufficient attention to the shift from Espilus / Therion to Dorcus / Rixus, and to the interpenetration of politics and autobiography within the text.

17. *Sidney's Poetry: Contexts and Interpretations* (1965; rpt. New York, 1970), pp. 42–47. Kalstone finds the conventional active / contemplative, pastoral / heroic, duality; he stresses Sidney's synthesizing impulse. I find a triadic pattern, and stress Sidney's discriminating impulse.

The shepherd's life had some goodness in it, because it borrowed of the country quietness something like ours. But . . . ours, besides that quiet part, doth both strengthen the body, and raise up the mind with this gallant sort of activity. O sweet contentation, to see the long life of the hurtless trees; to see how in straight growing up, though never so high, they hinder not their fellows; they only enviously trouble, which are crookedly bent. What life is to be compared to ours, where the very growing things are ensamples of goodness?

(p. 29)

Rixus interprets the forester-courtier as a man of heroic action and virtuous aspiration; his impetuosity and occasional bluntness are the manifestations of his essential honesty and dedication to the best interests of his lady. Ideally, this relationship is one based on respect and love; it is a reciprocal relationship in which the courtier can expect to be justly rewarded for his devotion. Oppositions of young forester to old shepherd and of young trees that grow straight to those that are crookedly bent insinuate the intergenerational conflict of temperaments and policies that continues to keep Sidney, as well as Greville and other like-minded friends, from places of real power and sources of substantial income under the regime of Burghley and his queen.

Languet, Sidney's Protestant-humanist mentor, is in England from late 1578 to early 1579—about the time that *The Lady of May* is performed. Soon after, he writes to Sidney that,

To speak plainly, the habits of your court seemed to me somewhat less manly than I could have wished, and most of your noblemen appeared to me to seek for a reputation more by a kind of affected courtesy than by those virtues which are wholesome to the state, and which are most becoming to generous spirits and men of high birth. I was sorry . . . to see you wasting the flower of your life on such things, and I feared . . . lest from habit you should be brought to take pleasure in pursuits which only enervate the mind.[18]

Languet's observations and judgment help us to reconstruct the social basis of the shepherd and forester models, to put back the simple into the complex. Furthermore, Languet's letter suggests that, in *The Lady of May,* Sidney is as deeply engaged in clarifying issues for himself as in clarifying them for the queen. Sidney conducts a dialectical examination of the role of the courtier—Castiglione's theme—through the

18. Sidney, *Correspondence,* p. 167.

manipulation of pastoral *topoi*. Self-reflexively examining his own role as courtier-poet, Sidney simultaneously uses and judges both pastoral literary conventions and their analogous courtly social forms. He champions the legitimacy of virtuously directed personal aspiration which serves queen, country, and Protestant-humanist ideals while it satisfies the freeborn English gentleman's right to perfect his self. *The Lady of May* exemplifies, relatively simply but with considerable specificity, a mutual mirroring between art and life, between cultural form and historical moment; it gives substance and definition to Renaissance defenses of poetry's efficacy and to ideologies that claimed the courtier's self to be a work of art.

Sidney inclined to that mode of life which in the decorum of pastoral is exemplified by the forester type: his quick temper and ideological zeal are testified both by his actions and by the words of his friends.[19] Sidney's partiality is also clear from the internal structure of *The Lady of May*. Its debate structure is not a simple set of stated and restated oppositions but a dialectical unfolding and revision of oppositions; its rhetorical intention is to move the audience from a situation of indecision between two antithetical extremes to a realignment that shows one term to incorporate, revise, and transcend the other. That the mediation arrived at by Rixus was conceived by Sidney as the superior position is confirmed by the songs intended as an epilogue to the queen's judgment. In the songs, Silvanus the forest god wins his love, while Pan the shepherd god loses his love to Hercules. In Renaissance iconography, Hercules is preeminently a moral hero. The crucial decision in his life is to choose, on the threshold between youth and maturity, to follow the arduous path of virtue rather than the easy path of pleasure.[20] This sig-

19. Languet, for example, advises Sidney "to reflect that young men who rush into danger incautiously almost always meet an inglorious end. . . . Let not therefore an excessive desire for fame hurry you out of your course" (*ibid.*, p. 137).

20. Erwin Panofsky, *Hercules am Scheidewege* (Leipzig and Berlin, 1930) is the definitive iconographic study; Hallett Smith, *Elizabethan Poetry* (1952; rpt. Ann Arbor, Mich., 1968), pp. 291–303, discusses the theme's prevalence in English Renaissance literature. In September 1580, Languet writes to Sidney of European friends who "fear that those who do not so well know your constancy may suspect that you are tired of that toilsome path which leads to virtue, which you formerly pursued with so much earnestness. They are fearful too, that the sweetness of your lengthened retirements may somewhat relax the vigorous energy with which you

nificant variation on the judgment of Paris can be an iconological demonstration that virtuous life on earth is ideally a union of contemplation and action. No Renaissance humanist puts it better than Sidney himself, in his *Defence of Poetry:* "The highest end of the mistress-knowledge . . . stands . . . in the knowledge of a man's self, in the ethic and politic considerations, with the end of well-doing and not of well-knowing only."[21] In Greville's biography, Sidney becomes the fulfillment of an ideal that Rixus merely shadows. Greville consistently describes Sidney in terms that recall the forester ideal of *The Lady of May:*

> His very waies in the world, did generally adde reputation to his Prince, and Country, by restoring amongst us the ancient Majestie of noble, and true dealing: As a manly wisdome, that can no more be weighed down, by any effeminate craft, than *Hercules* could be overcome by that contemptible Army of Dwarfs. . . . His heart and tongue went both one way, and so with every one that went with the Truth.[22]

In Sidney's songs, the victory of Herculean hero over Panic shepherd and the successful courtship of the Sylvan forester leave no doubt as to his own inclinations. In Wanstead garden, however, the queen chose to smile upon Espilus. The extant texts invoke the limitations of pastoral decorum: they only note, with a certain cryptic brevity, that "it pleased her Majesty to judge that Espilus did the better deserve [the May Lady]; but what words, what reasons she used for it, this paper, which carrieth so base names, is not worthy to contain" (p. 30).

David Kalstone suggests that "perhaps Sidney's unorthodox treatment of pastoral convention went unnoticed, and the queen chose the shepherd as the usual representative of the contemplative life; royalty has been known to nod before and since."[23] If this were the case, the

---

used to rise to noble undertakings, and a love of ease . . . creep by degrees over your spirit" (Sidney, *Correspondence,* pp. 182–183). Here Hercules' Choice between Virtue and Pleasure is not cited as an exemplum; it occurs as an internalized conceptual category, through which a Renaissance humanist mind constructs and interprets experience.

21. Sidney, *Miscellaneous Prose,* pp. 82–83.

22. Greville, *Life,* pp. 34–35.

23. Kalstone, *Sidney's Poetry,* p. 46; Kalstone cites and seconds the opinion of Orgel, *Jonsonian Masque,* p. 54. My sense of Elizabeth's response is in basic agreement with that of Kimbrough and Murphy, "The Helmingham Hall Manuscript," p. 106.

entertainment's debacle would testify to the difficulty of communicating novel ideas in traditional literary forms; it would also preserve a rare moment of obtuseness in the public life of an exceptionally well-tutored and sharp-witted prince. But Sidney, like Dorcas's courtiers, might rather have had reason to complain of his mistress's too much wit. If we grant that the lady knew very well what she and Sidney were about, we are unlikely to suppose that her choice was merely a mistake. It was, surely, a conscious and pointed rejection of Sidney's pastoral paradigm for the just and temperate relationship that should obtain between freeborn English gentlemen and their sovereign; it was a repudiation of the relationship which Sidney wanted to establish between himself and his queen. Sidney, too, seems to have known what they were both about: in the texts that we have, Silvanus's song is given to Espilus, and Pan's song is given to Therion. Sidney must have been prepared for either choice. He can hardly have had much expectation that Elizabeth would be easily persuaded by his lively images. But it was characteristic of him to speak his mind (however obliquely) on an issue of obsessive personal concern which he believed to be of critical significance for the destiny of the English nation.

The *text* that we call *The Lady of May* is the surviving trace of one small constituent *event* in the dialectical process of Elizabethan history. An act of historical imagination, restoring *The Lady of May* to its living context, reveals that a slight pastoral entertainment can mediate a major distemperature of the body politic within its own symbolic form. When its immediate contexts in literary history and authorial biography are sufficiently enlarged, *The Lady of May* can be recognized as a crystallization in cultural form of an incipient social conflict. That conflict grows in intensity and complexity at the end of Elizabeth's reign and under the Stuarts; within seventy years, it culminates in open warfare and regicide.

III. Cultural Forms and Social Forces

Queen Elizabeth's conservatism in fiscal, social, and religious policy was the hard-won lesson of a youth that had witnessed the destructive effects of ambition, innovation, and faction at firsthand. The consensus of modern historians validates Elizabeth's cautious and temporizing foreign policy; it was the most realistic response to the European and intercontinental configuration of power, wealth, and resources. Had not the Elizabethan *via media* proved itself by keeping the Commonwealth of England relatively healthy and peaceful for two decades? Elizabeth's distrust of Sidney and his friends is understandable, but not above criticism.[24] Her choice of Espilus reflects a concern to promote the innocuous conventions of erotic pastoralism that helped to maintain a stable, elegant, and adoring courtly ethos. I am not suggesting that Elizabeth wanted to surround herself with advisers, administrators, and soldiers who were just so many silly sheep. For the most part, the men whom she entrusted with government were mature in years, in professional experience, and in the arts of political manipulation and accommodation. However, one of her most pressing domestic problems was effectively to check, control, and channel the talents and energies, the thirst for self-aggrandizement and the ideological zeal, of men in the upper strata of a mobile, disequilibrious, and intensely competitive society. It was a problem that began to intensify during the last two decades of the century and the reign, as the younger generation of gentlemen and university graduates grew to their majority in a socioeconomic order unable to supply the preferments and offices that they desired and had been led to expect.

By many means, ranging from the manipulation of sacred images to acts of physical mutilation and execution, the Crown sought to establish and maintain control over the various socioeconomic strata and religiopolitical factions of an unruly and changeful society. The institution of the court provided a resplendent aura of majesty and authority to the monarch; at the same time, it monitored and defused the independent

---

24. For a balanced assessment of Elizabethan foreign policy, see R. B. Wernham, "Elizabethan War Aims and Strategy," in *Elizabethan Government and Society,* pp. 340–368. Recently, in *The Causes of the English Revolution 1529–1642* (New York, 1972), Lawrence Stone has placed Elizabeth's achievements in a long and critical perspective. He concludes that, in matters of civil order, religion, parliamentary tactics, finance, and trade, "the very success of the Elizabethan policy of cautious compromise and artful procrastination was an important source of trouble for the Stuarts." " 'Love-tricks' were all very well in the short run, but they were no substitute for a consistent policy. . . . The tactical successes of Elizabeth, and her studied avoidance of dealing with underlying problems," are to be reckoned among the fundamental preconditions of the Revolution (see Stone, *Causes of the English Revolution,* pp. 115–116).

initiatives of the aristocracy and men from other socioeconomic statuses or occupational groups who bound their fortunes to the court system. Courtly poetry and pageantry were designed to create illusions of royal power; and the illusion of power helped to create the reality of power. Efficacious illusions would be well received by the Crown, and could advance their creators, performers, and promoters to a share in the fruits of the real power that they were helping to sustain. Sidney was as covetous of material advancement—and as desperately in need of it—as any prodigal young Elizabethan courtier committed to the code of ostentation and largesse.[25] But he was trapped within a patronage system that was reluctant to promote him despite—in part, because of—his accomplishments and promise. Puttenham reminded his courtly readers that it was the decorum of "a Courtly Gentleman to be loftie and curious in countenaunce, yet sometimes a creeper, and a curry favell with his superiours."[26] Sidney did not adjust himself to his situation by using his highly valued skills as a verbal maker to celebrate and energize the illusions of royal power. On the contrary, he went about to explore the foundations and limits of royal power, and to promote the rights and interests of men of his own status vis-à-vis the Crown and the peerage.

The commitments ineffectually insinuated through the pastoral mask of *The Lady of May* were more forcefully expressed in the following months. The second half of 1579 was a period of crisis for the political aims and personal fortunes of the Leicester-Walsingham-Sidney faction. The queen was intensifying her marriage negotiations with the duke of Alençon's representative, Simier, who revealed to her the secret marriage of Leicester to Lettice Knollys, the dowager countess of Essex. The queen's intense displeasure severely compromised the Dudley and Knollys families, and reached out to include Sidney's mother (Leicester's sister) and himself. During those tense weeks, there occurred Sidney's notorious public altercation with the earl of Oxford, Burghley's son-in-law. This flap drew from the queen a personal lecture to Sidney on "the difference in degree between Earls, and Gentlemen; the respect inferiors ought to their superiors; and the necessity in Princes to maintain their

25. See Wallace, *Life of Sir Philip Sidney*, pp. 169–173, 392–393. Estimates of the debts that Walsingham assumed after his son-in-law's death range from £6,000 to £17,000.

26. *Arte*, p. 293.

own creations, as degrees descending between the peoples licentiousness, and the anoynted Soveraignty of Crowns"; in response, Sidney "besought her Majesty to consider," among other things, "that although [the Earl of Oxford] were a great Lord by birth, alliance, and grace; yet hee was no Lord over him: and therefore the difference of degrees between free men, could not challenge any other homage than precedency." [27] When the loyal opposition mobilized against the royal marriage, Sidney was prevailed upon to act as spokesman. The active role taken by a private gentleman in this whole affair can hardly have endeared him to his anointed sovereign.

Sidney spent most of 1580 in retirement at Wilton, finishing the first version of his *Arcadia*. In August 1580, he wrote to Leicester: "For my selfe I assure yowr Lordeshippe upon my trothe, so full of the colde as one can not heere me speake: which is the cawse keepes me yet frome the cowrte since my only service is speeche and that is stopped." [28] Using "The Courtier, or figure of faire semblant," Sidney insinuates that he is sick with a politic illness caught of the queen's displeasure. [29] In writing poetry and prose fiction, and in writing a defense of such imaginative writing, Sidney is not merely utilizing enforced idleness; he is transforming it into the environment for mental action. Sidney's *Defence of Poetry* is a witty, impassioned, and eloquent defense of literary writing as a fit occupation for gentlemen, as an instigation to virtuous action, and as an intellectual form of virtuous action in and of itself. Sidney's *Defence* constructs a universal, systematic moral and rhetorical theory of poetry that precisely addresses his personal predicament: writing is almost the only avenue of action available to him. His *Defence of Poetry* is also a self-defense, and a self-consolation.

In May 1581, three years after the performance of *The Lady of May*,

27. Greville, *Life*, pp. 67–68.
28. Sidney, *Prose Works*, III, 129.
29. Compare Puttenham, *Arte*, pp. 299–300: "Is it not perchance more requisite our courtly Poet do dissemble not onely his countenances & conceits, but also all his ordinary actions of behaviour, or the most part of them, whereby the better to winne his purposes & good advantages, as . . . when a man is whole to faine himselfe sicke to shunne the businesse in Court . . . & when any publique affaire or other attempt & counsaile of theirs hath not received good successe, to avoid therby the Princes present reproofe, to coole their chollers by absence, to winne remorse by lamentable reports, and reconciliation by friends intreatie[?]"

a sumptuous pageant was performed before the queen in the tiltyard at
Whitehall; Sidney played a major role in its performance and, almost
certainly, in its creation. The French commissioners in the protracted
royal marriage negotiations were conspicuously present, and the pageant
must have been partially directed to them. In the only substantive analysis of this work, Norman Council writes that,

to the degree that the allegory of the tilt has a political purpose, it describes
the queen as being beyond the reach of Anjou's suit for marriage, and
thereby displays the queen's apparent decision against the match. But the tilters
also take this opportunity to add another hyperbolic chapter to the myth of
the Virgin Queen, distinguishing between her identity as the goddess of
merely natural beauty and her more proper and exalted identity as the goddess of heavenly beauty.[30]

These intentions are indeed conspicuously present. But I would suggest
that the political purpose—or, rather, the psychosocial function—of the
pageant involves much more than another factional slap at the French
and another Platonizing compliment to Elizabeth. Like *The Lady of
May*, the *Triumph of The Fortress of Perfect Beauty* is both an offering
of praise and a symbolic vehicle expressing the immediate personal and
collective concerns of its promoters and participants. Although it was
probably not yet clear that Elizabethan had decided against the French
marriage, it was already clear that any final decision would be hers
alone. Elizabethan courtiers and councilors had now to think of repair-
ing and ensuring the continuity of their personal ties to the queen, whatever shape the future might take.

The basic scenario of the entertainment consists of a challenge to the

30. Norman Council, "*O Dea Certe:* The Allegory of *The Fortress of Perfect
Beauty,*" HLQ, XXXIX (1976), 329–342; I quote from p. 330. The extant record
of the triumph is Henry Goldwell's composite text of songs, speeches, and descriptions, printed in 1581; I have used the reprint in Nichols, *Progresses and
Public Processions of Queen Elizabeth,* II, 312–329. (Parenthetical citations in my
text will be to vol. II of Nichols's work.) Although the authorship of the triumph
is uncertain, it has often and plausibly been maintained that Sidney had a large
share in its conception and its composition: Ringler (Sidney, *Poems,* pp. 518–519)
accepts the attribution to Sidney of the two sonnets in the triumph; the scenario
has been attributed to Sidney by Wallace (*Life of Sir Philip Sidney,* p. 264),
Howell (*Sir Philip Sidney,* p. 87), Council ("*O Dea Certe,*" p. 336), and Ronald
A. Rebholz (*The Life of Fulke Greville* [Oxford, 1971], p. 36).

queen by the Foster Children of Desire; an attack upon the Fortress of
Perfect Beauty, which allegorizes the queen's person and state; a defense
of the Fortress by a contingent of gentlemen-courtiers; and the final
capitulation of the challengers after two days of speeches, songs, heraldry,
and tilting. What is intriguing about this pageant is that two of the
"four Foster Children of Desire" whose challenge generated and governed the entire action were "Master Philip Sidney, and Master Fulke
Grevill." [31] Their challenge had been delivered to the queen some days
earlier: "A martial messenger of Desire's fostered children, without making any precise reverence at all, uttered these speeches of defiance, to the
Queen's Majestie":

Know ye . . . all onely Princesse, that hereby (for far of they are never)
there lyes encamped the foure long haples, now hopeful fostered children of
Desire; who having bin a great while nourished up with that infective milke,
and to too much care of their fiery fosterer, (though full oft that dry nurse
Dispaier indevered to wainne them from it) being nowe as strong in that
nurture, as they are weake in fortune, incouraged with the valiaunt counsaile
of never fainting Desire, and by the same assured, that by right of inheri-
taunce even from ever, the Fortresse of Beautie doth belong to her fostered
children. These foure I say . . . doe will you by me, even in the name of

31. Nichols, *Progresses and Public Processions of Queen Elizabeth,* II, 313. "The
Earl of Arundel" and "Lord Windsor" are named as the other two "Children."
With the help of *The Complete Peerage* (ed. G.E.C., rev. ed. Vicary Gibbs et al.,
13 vols. [London, 1910–1959]), I have identified these artistocratic companions of
Sidney and Greville as Philip Howard, Earl of Arundel, and Frederick Windsor,
Baron Windsor of Stanwell. All four were of the same generation, only four years
separating the oldest from the youngest. Windsor, like Sidney and Greville, was
in the elaborate train with which the Earl of Leicester escorted Alençon to the
Netherlands a few months before the tilt; he died in 1585, at twenty-six. (See
Complete Peerage, XII, pt. 2, 798–799.) Arundel, like Sidney, was the godson and
namesake of King Philip of Spain. Three years after the pageant, he was imprisoned in the Tower for converting to Catholicism and secretly attempting to
leave England. He was heavily fined and attainted for high treason; he died
(in 1595, at thirty-eight) in the Tower, after eleven years of imprisonment.
Among the family papers is a manuscript biography of the earl which describes him as wild, undutiful, profligate, and deeply in debt before his religious
conversion. (See *Complete Peerage,* I, 252–255.) Neither young aristocrat seems
to have had a literary bent. On the shape of Greville's life, see Rebholz, *The Life
of Fulke Greville*; and F. J. Levy, "Fulke Greville: The Courtier as Philosophical
Poet," *MLQ,* XXXIII (1972), 433–448.

Justice, that you will no longer exclude vertuous Desire from perfect Beautie.
. . . But if . . . Beautie be accompanied with disdainful pride, and pride
waighted on by refusing crueltie . . . they will beseige that fatal Fortresse,
vowing not to spare (if this obstinacie continue) the swoorde of faithfulnesse,
and the fire of affection.

(pp. 313–314)

This "plaine proclaimation of warre" (p. 314) will not be adequately
explained if interpreted merely in terms of the Neo-Platonic metaphysics
gracefully suggested by its erotic imagery. The allegory is transparently
political; the politics are internal as well as international, concerned with
the queen's relationship to her courtiers as well as with her relationship
to Alençon.

It is likely that much of the ubiquitous amorous literature of the period
enabled a transformed expression of desires for socioeconomic advancement. In an ideological system dominated by hostility to personal ambition and social change, desires for wealth, status, and power might be
intentionally disguised or unconsciously displaced in metaphors of erotic
and spiritual desire. Loss of specific historical and biographical contexts
for most of these works has left them with the illusory appearance of
being merely conventional, impersonally manipulated poetic ornaments.
Transformations of erotic imagery make possible a management of carnal-
spiritual tensions. The enactment by Sidney and Greville of the public,
ritual roles of Foster Children who desire to possess Elizabeth's Fortress
of Perfect Beauty suggests the possibility that these cultural conventions
can become vehicles for the sublimation of urgent *social* tensions, as well
as carnal-spiritual ones. This sort of amateur performance by vitally
interested social actors has the status of a *lived* topical allegory. It gives
added conviction to the hypothesis that Elizabethan courtly literature is
pervasively topical; at the same time, it suggests how much more affect
must have been generated by topical allegory in an actual performance
situation than by topical allegory occuring within the more heavily
mediated experiences of writing and reading.

Other knights come in to defend the Fortress; among them are the
"foure legitimate sonnes of Despaire, brethren to harde mishap . . .
long time fostered with favourable countenance, and fed with sweet
fansies, but now of late (alas) wholie given over to griefe and disgraced
by disdaine" (p. 325). These were, in fact, "the foure sonnes of Sir

Francis Knolles" (p. 324), a privy councilor squarely in the Leicester-Walsingham camp on the issue of the French marriage. Because of his policy positions and his daughter's marriage to Leicester, Knollys had been suffering the force of much of Elizabeth's irritation and spite of late. The quartet of young gentleman-courtiers who were Sir Francis's sons and Lettice's brothers had an urgent need to impress the queen with a romantic display of their own adoration, obedience, and utility. This they did by offering to defend her against the challengers, whom they explicitly associated with the Titans and with Phaeton, archetypes of illegitimate and doomed ambition.

At the end of the second day of tilting and pageantry,

> the foster children of Desire (but heires onelie to misfortune) . . . deliver . . . their most humble-hearted submission. They acknowledge this fortresse to be reserved for the eie of the whole world, farre lifted up from the compasse of their destinie. They acknowledge the blindnesse of their error, in that they did not know Desire (how strong soever it be) within itselfe to be stronger without itselfe than it pleased the desired. They acknowledge they have degenerated from their fosterer in making Violence accompanie Desire. They acknowledge that Desire received his beginning and nourishment of this fortresse, and therefore to commit ungratefulnesse in bearing armes (though desirous armes) against it. They acknowledge noble Desire should have desired nothing so much, as the flourishing of that fortresse, which was to be esteemed according to itselfes liking. . . . Therefore they doo acknowledge themselves overcome, as to be slaves to this Fortresse for ever.

(pp. 328–329)

Put among Sidney's other personal and literary performances, the *Triumph* assumes a significant position in the dialectic of his life and art. *The Lady of May* dramatizes the eclogue; *The Triumph of the Fortress of Perfect Beauty* dramatizes the chivalric romance. The two entertainments are generically interrelated as enacted versions of the pastoral and heroic kinds. Furthermore, the later, larger, and more spectacular work has as its predominant theme the opposition of the two fundamental modes of royal courtship upon which *The Lady of May* was constructed. Decorum of kinds demands a change in the allegorical vehicle: a singing contest and debate between shepherds and foresters becomes a series of armed encounters between opposed groups of knights. The fundamental difference between the two entertainments is that the outcome of the later contest is made to reflect the queen's choice in the earlier dispute.

Wild foresters have become attackers of the Lady; docile shepherds have become her defenders. In the audacious challenge, the repudiation, and the eventual submission of the Foster Children of Desire, we can see Sidney imaginatively identifying himself with the Therion-Rixus model, symbolically testing it, and finally abandoning the illusion that it can be effective within the constraining ideological system successfully manipulated by the queen. When we recall that "foster" is an Elizabethan variant of "forester" (one that occurs in both of the extant substantive texts of *The Lady of May*), the possibility begins to suggest itself that the conceit of "Foster Children of Desire" may contain a pun alluding to the strong-willed, impetuous, ambitious, even insolent stance toward the role of courtier that Sidney had so firmly associated with the forester type only three years before.

Among the "Juelles given to her Majestie at Newyer's tyde, 1580–81," is listed "a juell of goulde, being a whippe, garnished with small diamondes in foure rowes and cordes of small seede pearle. Geven by Mr. *Philippe Sydneye.*" [32] Like that recent gift, this current performance was Sidney's symbolic offering of submission to the great goddess who had blessed Espilus. But we can also detect Sidney's persistent audacity in his choice of New Year's gift: the gesture is sufficiently ambiguous to allow the symbol of Sidney's contrition and obedience to insinuate its own antithesis, an aesthetic sublimation of the giver's antipathy to the recipient. Puttenham writes suggestively that "devices" (a generic term including "liveries, cognizances, emblemes, enseigns and impreses"), "insinuat some secret, wittie, morall and brave purpose presented to the beholder, either to recreate his eye, or please his phantasie, or examine his judgment, or occupie his braine or to manage his will either by hope or by dread." [33] I would add that "devices" (and symbolic forms, generally) have emotive as well as conative and cognitive functions; their effect is to express the maker as well as to affect the beholder. Offerings of devoted submission may be functionally ambiguous. They may allow an oblique and limited expression of the aggression or independence that is being denied, and a purgation of the resentment that the submission en-

32. Nichols, *Progresses and Public Processions of Queen Elizabeth*, II, 300–301.
33. *Arte*, p. 108.

tails. The bejeweled icon that Sidney presents to the queen and the sumptuous pageant in which he performs before her are homologous cultural forms.

If we attend to the speech and action of the pageant, if we imaginatively experience it as a cultural event enmeshed in the process of Elizabethan social life, then its meaning emerges as something more complex than the sycophancy of its surface: it is a socially sanctioned cultural medium for the raising and casting out of discontent and hostility that would otherwise eventuate in overt dissent and civil disorder. *The Lady of May* is an aristocratic appropriation of May games; *The Pageant of the Fortress of Perfect Beauty* contains an aristocratic analogue of the Saturnalian rites of misrule. Men from within the ranks of the ruling elite are constrained by the highest levels of social and artistic decorum. Working through the allegorized oxymoron of erotic warfare, they can play out the flouting, threatening, and necessary reaffirmation of the royal personage who in fact has the power of life and death over them.[34] On the first day of the pageant, after the magnificent entry of the four challengers and their retinues, the bearer of their original challenge again addresses the queen on their behalf:

Your eies, which till now have beene onelie woont to discerne the bowed knees of kneeling hearts, and inwardlie turned, found alwaies the heavenlie peace of a sweet mind, should not now have their faire beames reflected with

34. The stifled and restless energy of the young, ambitious Protestant warhawks, and their resentments against the queen, are well testified in the actions and writings of Sidney and Greville. Sidney also had cause to resent the poor treatment of his dear parents at Elizabeth's hands: the lack of recompense or apparent gratitude for his father's long and devoted public service, and for his mother's selfless personal nursing of the queen. Council (*"O Dea Certe,"* p. 342) plausibly suggests that Arundel's presence in this anti-Alençon pageant was intended as a conspicuous display of loyalty to the Elizabethan Settlement and its incarnation by the heir of a family with noted Catholic sympathies. It is not unreasonable to surmise that this political necessity must have aroused ambivalent feelings in a young peer who had been made to wait unduly long for the Crown's confirmation of his title; whose father, Thomas Howard, duke of Norfolk, the greatest peer of the realm, had been beheaded in 1572 for continually conspiring against Elizabeth; who would himself, within three years, embrace Catholicism and, as a result, spend the rest of his life in the Tower.

the shining of armour, should not now be driven to see the furie of Desire, nor the fierie force of Furie. . . . You see them, readie in hart as you know, and able with hands as they hope, not onelie to assailing, but to prevailing.

(p. 317)

The erotic metaphor can accommodate the expression of desires for disinterested service and self-interested gain; and, at the same time, it can insinuate that stifled desire leads to hostility and aggression.[35] Performing in a ceremonial tilt and masking in a pageant are forms of action modified and controlled by their ludic context; their status is mediatory between the imaginative reality fictions and the tangible reality of overt political acts.

The sociopolitical circumstances of 1581 made possible the successful containment of potential violence in the play-forms of aristocratic culture. Exactly twenty years later, in the deep social discontent and political turmoil of Elizabeth's last years, her most brilliant courtier led a short-lived revolt of desperate losers in the deadly game of courtship:

The Essex rebellion derived from the impossible situation in which Essex found himself in the last years before 1601. Denied access to the source of patronage and influence, he must either see his power sterilized and his following shrink . . . or he must break through to gain access to—if necessary, control over—that source. . . . Essex in the end was caught in the ineluctable dilemma of power inherent in the existing political structure.[36]

That most observant of ornamental courtiers, Sir John Harington, wrote "that ambition thwarted in its career, dothe speedilie leade on to madnesse; herein I am strengthened by what I learned in my Lord of Essex, who shyftethe from sorrowe and repentaunce to rage and rebellion so suddenlie, as well provethe him devoide of goode reason or righte mynde."[37] Essex was, of course, the son of Lettice and grandson of Sir Francis Knollys; a protégé of Leicester, and his stepson; Sidney's companion-in-arms in the Netherlands; the second husband of Sidney's widow, Frances, daughter of Sir Francis Walsingham. Sidney, on his

35. Compare *LM:* "Therion doth me many pleasures . . . but withal he grows to such rages, that sometimes he strikes me, sometimes he rails at me" (Sidney, *Miscellaneous Prose,* p. 25).

36. Joel Hurstfield, "The Succession Struggle in Late Elizabethan England," in *Elizabethan Government and Society,* pp. 369–396; I quote from p. 390.

37. *Nugae Antiquae,* ed. Henry Harington (1779; rpt. 3 vols., 1968), II, 225.

deathbed, recorded in a codicil to his will: "Item, I give to my beloved and much honoured lord the Earl of Essex, my best sword." [38] It was a bequest of great symbolic significance for the impetuous young royal favorite, and for all those gentleman-courtiers who came to share in the idealization of Sidney and in Essex's discontent.

As a public incitement on the eve of their rebellion, Essex's supporters commissioned a performance of a play of Richard II—it was presumably Shakespeare's, and contained a deposition pageant and fictional enactment of regicide. They failed to raise the citizens of London. But that they even considered such a strategy remains an oblique testimonial to the potential power of the public theater. Another dimension is added to the complex dialectic between Elizabethan cultural forms and social forces by the awareness that play might be not only an effective way to contain violent action but might also effectively catalyze it. The Essex rebellion evidences a dysfunction in the process of cultural containment. [39] Harington's meditation on Essex closes with an image of frustration that has been twisted out of the amorous discourse of sonnet-courtships: "The Queene well knowethe how to humble the haughtie spirit, the haughtie spirit knoweth not how to yield, and the mans soule seemeth tossede to and fro, like the waves of a troubled sea." [40] The source of Sidney's relief was to play at aggression and submission—and to look in his heart, and write.

IV. Knight and Shepherd

I have sought to contextualize *The Lady of May* as a specific cultural mediation of a large and complex range of problems besetting Philip

38. Sidney, *Miscellaneous Prose*, p. 152.

39. Stone writes that "in the early and middle years of the reign of Elizabeth the Court successfully contained within a single political system of checks and balances the representatives of a series of conflicting ideas and interests. . . . After the rebellion and execution of the Earl of Essex . . . this central political switchboard broke down, and many of these diverse and increasingly hostile groups began to organize locally and to band together, independent of the national political process at Court and even in open opposition to it" (*Causes of the English Revolution*, pp. 85–86).

40. *Nugae Antiquae*, II, 226.

Sidney and other men of his social status, ideological persuasion, financial obligations, temperament, and generation in the late sixteenth century in England. Fulke Greville, Sidney's intimate friend, fellow ideologue, and brother in desire, wrote his justifying and idealizing *Life* of Sidney during the first decade of the new reign, when he himself was out of favor and out of office; his analysis of Sidney's situation by the mid-1580s harks back to the paradigmatic scenario of *The Lady of May:*

> Sir Philip found . . . his large, and sincere resolutions imprisoned within the pleights of their fortunes, that mixed good, and evill together unequally; and withall discerned, how the idle-censuring faction at home had won ground of the active adventures abroad. . . . [In] his Native Country, he found greatness of worth, and place, counterpoysed there by the arts of power, and favor. The stiring spirits sent abroad as fewell, to keep the flame far off: and the effeminate made judges of danger which they fear, and honor which they understand not.[41]

Frustrated in his attempts to unite knowledge and action in life, Sidney sublimated his predicament into the imaginative interplay of pastoral and heroic literary modes. "His active spirit . . . that had no delight to rest idle at home" (p. 78) had long been ready when his commission finally arrived. Sidney's life of frustrated action found an ironic consummation in the fatal, chance wound he received on his first military campaign.

The fusion of pastoral and heroic modes, contemplation and action, was only attainable through death and apotheosis: in pastoral elegies, Sidney could be venerated as a heroic shepherd; as *"Scipio, Cicero, and Petrarch* of our time"; as a blessed soul in that syncretic heaven where *"Venus* on thee smiles, *Apollo* gives thee place, / And *Mars* in reverent wise doth to thy vertue bow."[42] Elizabethan pastoral literature was largely created in the enforced idleness of a courtier who sought the role of an Elizabethan hero in his life; after his death, he was internalized within the pastoral literary tradition that he had shaped. Sidney himself became the subject of celebration. We can see this process of his trans-

---

41. Greville, *Life,* pp. 77–78.
42. See the pastoral elegies by Spenser and others, printed with Spenser's own pastoral court satire, *Colin Clouts Come Home Againe,* in 1595. I quote from the often reprinted *Oxford Standard Authors* edition of Spenser's *Poetical Works,* ed. J. C. Smith and E. de Selincourt, pp. 559, 553, respectively.

formation taking place before us in *Astrophel,* Spenser's pastoral elegy for Sidney. In narrating Astrophel's destruction and his transformation into a flower, Spenser's poem verbally enacts the metamorphosis it purports to recount:

> But thou where ever thou doest finde the same,
> From this day forth do call it *Astrophel.*
> And when so ever thou it up doest take,
> Do pluck it softly for that shepheards sake.
>
> (ll. 195–198)

Sidney is made perpetually available as a pastoral subject, enabling the inner tensions, contradictions, and ironies of courtship to be articulated, allowing the desires and ambitions frustrated in experience to be sublimated and gratified.

It remains dubious that Sidney's stifled career had really begun to flower just before his death. In a letter written to Walsingham from Utrecht only a few months before his death, Sidney complained of "how apt the Queen is to interpret every thing to my disadvantage. . . . I understand I am called very ambitious and prowd at home, but certainly if thei knew my ha[rt] thei woold not altogether so judg me." [43] In adversity, his self-resolve remained firm: "I think a wyse and constant man ought never to greev whyle he doth plai as a man mai sai his own part truly though others be out but if him self leav his hold becaws other marrin[ers] will be ydle he will hardli forgive him self his own fault" (p. 166). Wisdom, constancy, virtuous action, personal integrity—although the themes remain fundamentally unaltered from their first articulation by Rixus, they háve been deepened and confirmed by time; they are now reaffirmed directly and intimately, rather than through the mediations of a dramatic eclogue. What is fundamentally different is the openness with which Sidney expresses the distinction and priority of his allegiances: "Her Majesty . . . is but a means whom God useth and I am faithfully persuaded that if she shold withdraw her self other springes woold ryse to help this action. . . . I can not promis of my own cource . . . becaws I know there is a hyer power that must uphold me or els I shall fall, but certainly I trust, I shall not by other mens wantes be drawn from my self" (pp. 166–167). Sidney's role as Protestant hero is dissociated

---

43. Sidney, *Prose Works,* III, 167.

from his role as Renaissance courtier; the affirmation of the inviolability of personal conscience and personal faith is opposed to unconditional obedience to temporal authority. These trends are inseparable from the concern of Sidney and some of his friends and associates with relatively advanced political theories of limited monarchy and constitutional government.[44]

Sidney was no revolutionary. But he did play his part in the articulation of what Lawrence Stone calls "the preconditions" of the English Revolution:

Dissatisfaction with Elizabeth's refusal to modify her religious policy in a more Puritan direction, her refusal to marry or to settle the succession, her cautious and ambiguous foreign policy, and finally her obstinate defence of a morally untenable position about economic monoplies, slowly drove the more active members of the House of Commons to make wholly new constitutional claims. They moved from a position of asking to speak their minds on issues put before them without fear of punishment, to a position of demanding the right to initiate discussion and influence policy on any issue they chose.[45]

The sociopolitical transformations of the half-century following Sidney's death, fed by economic change and the incompetence of the reactionary Stuart monarchs, lead circuitously but surely from Sidney to Milton. Milton resonantly declared that "He who would not be frustrate of his hope to write well hereafter in laudable things, ought himself to be a true poem, that is, a composition and pattern of the best and honorablest things."[46] This was an apotheosis of the Renaissance courtly ideal, the moral dialectic of self and work that Sidney strove to exemplify. Critical and analytic functions of the kind that Sidney had attempted to insinuate into royal celebrations were purged as the romantically medieval pageants of the Elizabethan entertainment were transformed into the brilliant

44. See Howell, *Sir Philip Sidney*, pp. 212–218; Levy, "Philip Sidney Reconsidered"; James E. Phillips, "George Buchanan and the Sidney Circle," *HLQ*, XII (1948), 23–55; Ernest William Talbert, *The Problem of Order* (Chapel Hill, N.C., 1962), pp. 89–117.

45. *Causes of the English Revolution*, pp. 92–93. On Sidney's brief career in the House of Commons (which began in the Parliament of 1581), see Howell, *Sir Philip Sidney*, pp. 75–80.

46. "Apology for Smectymnuus" (1642), rpt. in John Milton, *Complete Poems and Major Prose*, ed. Merritt Y. Hughes (New York, 1957), p. 694.

High Renaissance illusions of the Stuart masque. For those outside the Stuart court system, the court masque came to epitomize the cultural isolation, political tyranny, and spiritual corruption of the monarch and the aristocracy.[47] For Milton, the task of the inspired Christian poet was to destroy the spurious Renaissance analogy of royal encomium and sacred hymn, to reveal that the celebration of kings was a demonic parody of the celebration of God.

47. See Stephen Orgel, *The Illusion of Power* (Berkeley and Los Angeles, 1975).

The Old and the New: The Spanish Comedia *and the Resistance to Historical Change*

ANTHONY J. CASCARDI

> Fear of the master is indeed the beginning of wisdom.
> —Hegel

> He who has more obedience than I, masters me.
> —Emerson

> The major enemy, the strategic adversary is . . . the fascism in us all, in our heads and in our everyday behavior, the fascism that causes us to love power, to desire the very thing that dominates and exploits us.
> —Foucault

IN A SERIES of articles which first appeared in print two and three decades ago, historians E. J. Hobsbawm, H. R. Trevor-Roper, Pierre Vilar, and J. H. Elliott advanced the claim that the "modernization" of Europe was precipitated by a variety of circumstances that coalesced in the form of a "general crisis" during the seventeenth century.[1] Despite substantial disagreements among them, their work confirmed the fact that a number of social, political, and economic transformations during this period led to the emergence of capitalist modes of production and exchange and also to the consolidation of the powers of the absolute state.[2] While there may have been manifestations of a nascent capitalism well before the seventeenth century, only at this time did social and economic pressures yield anything like a lasting revolution. Elaborating on Marx's view of the English Renaissance as a transitional stage between the dominance of the feudal aristocracy and that of the commercial bourgeoisie, Hobsbawm, for instance, rec-

401

ognizes that there may have been something at work to unsettle the feudal base of European society as early as the fourteenth century, but concedes that only in the seventeenth was there a full-scale recasting of the socioeconomic order.[3] The notion of "crisis" invoked both by Hobsbawm and by Trevor-Roper is already apparent among writers of the seventeenth century, as is the concept of "decline" which Elliott applies to the case of Spain. Yet if a crisis is thought to indicate "the passage from an ascending conjuncture to one of collapse" (Vilar 60), then it is important to note that the crisis tendencies of the feudal order are seen as being finally *overcome* in the seventeenth century. Thus whatever factors might have continued to resist the newly consolidated modes of production are regarded as in some way limiting or "immobilizing" them. In the case of Spain, for instance, Trevor-Roper points to the survival of the *ancien régime* "as a disastrous, immobile burden on an impoverished nation" (95). And Hobsbawm more generally observes that "Unless certain conditions are present . . . the scope of capitalist expansion will be limited by the prevalence of the feudal structure of society, that is of the predominant rural sector or perhaps by some other structure which 'immobilizes' both the potential labour-force, the potential surplus for productive investment, and the potential demand for capitalistically produced goods, such as the prevalence of tribalism or petty commodity production" (15).

The notion that certain political or social structures may have limited the expansion of capitalism may be useful in accounting for the unevenness of its pan-European development, especially in the seventeenth century, but this still leaves much to be explained about the social and political consequences that early capitalism did have. Why, for instance, did the expansion of the fifteenth and sixteenth centuries not lead directly into an industrial revolution? And why was the emergence of capitalism accompanied by a strengthening of absolutist forms of government? Some provisional answers to these questions have been suggested, respectively, by Maurice Dobb and Perry Anderson. In *Studies in the Development of Capitalism* and in the published debate surrounding that work (see Hilton) Dobb suggests that the embryo of bourgeois productive relations—the accumulation of small pockets of capital and the beginnings of class differentiation within an economy of petty producers—arose within a society that was essentially feudal in its socioeconomic relations. As we shall see in the case of the *comedia,* it is more the caste structure of medieval Spanish society than the economy of feudalism which forms the background of the modernist transformation, but still it is worth noting that the *comedia* appropriates these circumstances for strictly ideological ends, perpetuating premodern modes of awareness at a time when capitalism was elsewhere in Europe firmly afoot. Numerous economic historians have suggested that the Spanish conquests in the New World may have supplied the initial capital necessary for the economic transformation which did indeed take place elsewhere in Europe, but as Perry Anderson rightly notes in *Lineages of the Absolutist State* (61), no other Absolute State in Western Europe remained so resistant to bourgeois development. Thus if classical Marxism frequently comes to grief over the peculiar "lag" that occurs between any transformation in the modes of production and the (ultimately utopian) transformation of social relations, these factors may be seen in the case of Spain to be exaggerated to the degree where it would be more accurate to speak of a *resistance* to modernism than of the simple persistence of medieval values during early modern times.

   In reconsidering the phenomenon of modernism in light of the specific case of Spain and in advancing some general notions about the ideological function of the *comedia* during this period, one may begin with the observation that orthodox Marxism has itself been shown to conform to the shape of a literary "comedy" or romance, in which the various ends of secular and sacred narrative—familial harmony, the transcendence of the limiting consciousness of this world—are figured as some social version of the Utopian dream.[4] As we shall see, however, the Spanish *comedia* reinscribes this Utopian vision within the structure of a more complex comedy or romance, so that the Utopian telos serves to occlude an awareness of those same modernizing factors which precipitate the *agon* or "conflict" of each play, the purpose of which may be identified as the effacement of the historical conflict informing the genre as a whole. Thus if Marxism would envision the social changes at work in early modern Europe as in some way instrumental to the ultimate transformation of society, then it would not be unreasonable to read the *comedia* as one of the imaginary (which is to say, ideological) mechanisms through which Spanish soci-

ety was able simultaneously to confront and to resist that transformation. In this sense, the *comedia* may be regarded as a rigorously historical genre, even if that fact is made most evident in its resistance to
historical change: the *comedia* consistently admits a vision of the
"modern" or the "new," yet with equal consistency it sacrifices that
vision in favor of the stability to be achieved through the dominance
of the "old." The Utopian vision which it projects, such as in Lope de
Vega's *Fuenteovejuna,* is drawn explicitly from the past and consists
in the dream of the perpetuation of that past, and its pastoral society,
in the form of a changeless future. Thus a genre which Lope himself
described in the "Arte nuevo de hacer comedias" as exemplary of aesthetic modernism is in practice marshaled in support of the most traditional of value systems, that of honor as measured by *limpieza de
sangre;* the mobile forms of behavior most congenial to capitalism are
limited by rigidly hierarchical social arrangements, ones which leave
little room for the mobility of the self; and the motives which elsewhere in Europe were placed in the service of political, economic, and
philosophical individualism are made subservient to what Ortega y
Gasset described as the "psychology of the masses" and to their virtual
need for domination ("the masses, by definition, neither should nor
can direct their own personal existence, and still less rule society in
general" [11]).[5]

To say this much is already to suggest that the process of modernization in Spain as it passed through the crisis of the seventeenth century
was markedly different from that which occurred elsewhere in Europe. Although it is never legitimate to consider specific ideologies as
the invariable correlates of specific modes of production, one may
grant at least heuristic validity to the proposition that the aesthetic
modernism of the early seventeenth century was an ideological transformation of capitalism and of an emergent "consciousness of class."
Noël Salomon attempted to read the Lopean *comedia* and its glorifica-
tion of peasant existence in terms of the perpetuation of older, feudal
modes of production during such a period ("la société monarcho-
seigneurial de 1600–1640 perpétuait dans les temps modernes . . . un
système de production [placé historiquement entre le système esclava-
giste et le système capitaliste] et tout ce qui en derive" [744–54]). But
the play is for him an expression of genuine peasant insurgency, rather

than the locus of a historical conflict in which the new is met with fierce resistance by the old. While feudalism per se was never as firmly established in Spain as it was in England or France, a social axiology of caste was deeply entrenched. In part for this reason Spain could not easily consolidate a bourgeoisie or readily embrace bourgeois values. In 1600, Martín González de Cellorigo could complain that the middle classes of the fifteenth and early sixteenth centuries had all but vanished. He wrote that "Our Republic has come to be an extreme contrast of rich and poor, and there is no means of adjusting them to one another. Our condition is one in which there are rich who loll at ease or poor who beg, and *we lack people of the middle sort,* whom neither wealth nor poverty prevents from pursuing the rightful kind of business enjoined by natural law."[6] One consequence of this polarization of fortunes was the phenomenon which Pierre Vilar called the "irrationalism" of Spanish society, the paradoxical conjuncture of profligacy and miserliness, of consumption and waste, located within a single class or individual: "The rich man ate, was waited upon, entertained, gave, robbed, and allowed others to rob him. As a result of its situation and predicament . . . Spanish society of 1600, the antithesis of Puritan society, turned its back on saving and investment" (Vilar 60). Both Vilar and J. H. Elliott rightly abjure the notion of a Spanish "temperament" that may have been inhospitable to capitalism; "The Castilians, it is said, lacked that elusive quality known as the 'capitalist spirit.' This was a militant society, imbued with the crusading ideal, accustomed by the *reconquista* and the conquest of America to the quest for glory and booty, and dominated by those very ideals least propitious for the development of capitalism" (Elliott 184). Yet one must somehow account for the fact that Spain made relatively little capitalist use of the same American gold and silver which, in all likelihood, provided the nuclear mass for economic expansion in the rest of Europe during the fifteenth and sixteenth centuries. Elliott points to the steady diversion of capital in Spain toward *censos* (personal loans) and *juros* (government bonds), which carried guaranteed rates of return of between five and ten percent. González de Cellorigo saw in the attraction to these forms of investment debt the same "unproductiveness" that characterized the deployment of land and labor in Spain. Consider the following passage from the *Memorial de la política* (1600):

For when the merchant, lured by the certain profits which the bonds will yield, gives up his business, the artisan his craft, the laborer his field, and the shepherd his flock; when the nobleman sells his lands in order to exchange the amount they are worth for five times that sum in Government bonds, then the real income from their patrimonies will be exhausted, and all the silver will vanish into thin air, at the same time as for his own needs, for those of the lord of the estate, the rentier, the tithe-collector, the tax-farmer and so many others who have some claim to make on the land. Thus, from the bottom of the scale to the top, one may calculate that the ratio of those who work to those who do nothing is of the order of one to thirty. . . . Wealth has not taken root because it has remained, and still does remain, etherealized in the form of papers, contracts, bonds, letters of exchange and gold or silver coinage, and not in the form of goods able to bear fruit and to attract wealth from abroad by virtue of the wealth within.[7]

On the subject of *censos* and *juros* and the lethargic climate of capital investment in Spain, Cellorigo and others did not go completely unheard. In 1617 the Council of Finance complained that there was no chance of a Castilian economic revival as long as the bonds offered better rates of return than could be gained from investment in agriculture, industry, or trade.[8] Thus the apparent "failure" of capitalism in Spain might better be explained as the resistance to capitalism and to the more encompassing "modernization" of society that threatened to displace the fierce traditionalism of the Middle Ages and early Renaissance. While the contrast between Spain and the rest of Europe cannot be limited to these terms, still it is instructive to compare the most extreme manifestation of this traditionalism, the Spanish structure of social castes, with the class structure prevalent in the rest of Europe and North America. Because a caste society forms its evaluations primarily along racial lines and construes value in connection with lineage rather than personal wealth, there is little or no incentive to deploy economic capital toward the increase of value as a means to improve social standing; indeed, the very notions of profit or the increase of value are alien to the axiology of caste.[9] A caste society is overtly moral in its evaluations, but only covertly economic.[10] And because caste divisions are racially drawn, they produce a hierarchy that is relatively "closed," especially when compared with the mobility that is in principle open to members of a class society.[11] This fact remains true even where one takes the notion of "caste" in its weaker form, as José Antonio Maravall does, as indicating a structure of inherited offices and professions.[12] Still, the consequences of such an arrangement are a social sedimentation in which status and the value accorded to professional functions are rigidly circumscribed. The "traditional" order of society thus preserved, which Maravall perceives to be "medieval," is nearly identical to that which is put forward in neo-Scholastic terms by Calderón in his theological *comedias* and *autos sacramentales*. Consider especially the ways in which the apportionment of social roles into castelike divisions is seen as sanctioned either by nature or by God:

> Traditional society was founded on the idea that each person had a fixed and determined social function; that a definite social position corresponded to that function; that this carried with it a natural and proper mode of behavior for the possession and enjoyment of economic goods, whose limits were not to be transgressed; that all this was determined by known procedures, and that in accordance with such circumstances, unchangeable in themselves, there belonged to each one a certain education and cultural heritage. . . . As the external projection of this conjuncture of personal facts, identifiable with a place in the fixed social order [*un emplazamiento estamental*], each one was to use his resources and to present himself before others in such a way that his place in the social hierarchy could be recognized immediately. (Maravall, *Teatro y literatura* 41–42)

Ever since Américo Castro published his reinterpretation of the notion of "honor" in the Golden Age in *De la edad conflictiva,*[13] it has been apparent that the Spanish *comedia* was in some special way indebted to the axiology of caste. In the strongest formulation which Castro offered, the preoccupation over honor in view of potential threats to the bloodline provided the theater of Lope de Vega and his successors with its very reason for being ("La presencia del motivo de la honra en el teatro de Lope de Vega y la razón de existir aquel teatro son dos aspectos de una misma conciencia colectiva," *De la edad conflictiva* 49); as Lope himself remarked in the "Arte Nuevo," honor plots were able forcefully to move every member of the audience to enter into the sufferings of the stage heroes ("Los casos de la honra son mejores, / porque mueven con fuerza a toda gente" [327–28]). Yet Castro never considered the possibility that the axiology of caste might have served an ideological function, that this structure of social relations might have continued to emit "signals" (of which the *comedia* would have been one) long after the period of its historical efficacy was past. And yet this is precisely the possibility which must be considered in view of the fact that during the time of the *comedia*'s greatest prestige, in roughly the period from 1580 until Calderón's death a hundred years later, the three racial castes of Spain were reduced to one, thus placing in jeopardy the very structure on which the Spanish "traditionalism" of the Middle Ages was founded.

I have suggested that the axiology of caste may have taken on an ideological function in the *comedia,* but it is not so much Castro's extension of the idea of caste beyond its proper historical bounds which is the target of this critique as Maravall's simplistic analysis of the ideological structure of the genre. On his reading, the "traditional" order of society envisioned by the Spanish drama is one which was imposed on it in the interests of maintaining the status quo, in much the same way, and through many of the same techniques, that a theology was "imposed" by the preachers and moralists of the Baroque.[14] In Maravall's judgment, Spaniards made use of the *comedia* in order to legitimize a structure of social relations founded on the practical domination of one group by another and, in so doing, to avoid the ethical questions which such situations of domination are bound to raise ("Los españoles emplearon el teatro para, sirviéndose de instrumento popularmente tan eficaz, contribuir a socializar un sistema de convenciones, sobre las cuales en ese momento se estimó había de verse apoyado el orden social concreto vigente en el país, orden que había que conservar, en cualquier paso, sin plantear la cuestión de un posible contenido ético," *Teatro y literatura* 32–33). Yet nearly the reverse would seem to be closer to the truth. As we shall see exemplified in *Fuenteovejuna,* it is precisely an ethical opposition, that of absolute good and evil, which organizes the ideological "content" of the *comedia.* Ethics serves for the advancement of an ideology in such a way that the perfect closure offered by the binary oppositions of good and evil, right and wrong, self and other, function as what Fredric Jameson has called "strategies of containment,"[15] in this case as strategies for the containment of the modernizing threats to the traditional caste structure of Spanish society.

One may well be surprised to discover a strategic conservatism in the *comedia,* especially in light of the fact that the poetics of the genre, as conceived and articulated by Lope de Vega, are uniformly modernizing. Lope's "Arte nuevo de hacer comedias" seeks to locate the *comedia* in the very vanguard of artistic practice; even in the title, the emphasis falls on what Lope considers to be the "*new* way of writing plays." As is common among vanguard aesthetics, and notwithstanding the fact that the "Arte nuevo" was commissioned by a Madrid Academy, Lope's stance is explicitly anti-academic. In characteristically modernist fashion, Lope speaks of his as a practice which is not simply innovative but wholly discontinuous with the recognized traditions:

> cuando he de escribir una comedia,
> encierro los preceptos con seis llaves;
> saco a Terencio y Plauto de mi estudio,
> para que no me den voces.
>
> (40–43)

(when I must write a play, I lock up the rules with six keys; I throw Terence and Plautus out of my study so that they won't scold me.)

> Mas ninguno de todos llamar puedo
> más bárbaro que yo, pues contra el arte
> me atrevo a dar preceptos, y me dejo
> llevar de la vulgar corriente, adonde
> me llamen ignorante Italia y Francia.
>
> (362–66)

(But I can call none of these [writers] ruder than I, since I dare to give precepts that contravene the rules, and I allow myself to be carried by the common stream, where Italy and France may call me ignorant.)

In terms of aesthetic practice, however, the *comedia* roundly contradicts the modernizing claims made for it in the "Arte nuevo." Whereas Lope argues for the discontinuity of the *comedia* from known traditions, the configuration of the genre in fact depends on the formation of highly visible internal continuities. These are generated in part from its sources in the chronicle and ballad traditions and accordingly issue in structures which are more narrative than dramatic. Thus Lope can refer to the elements of the *comedia* as the parts of a generic narrative formula which, in theory at least, are capable of infi-

nite repetition (e.g., "divide the subject in two parts, establish the connection from the beginning"; "place the problem in Act One, tie the
events together in Act Two" [231–32, 298–99]). The regulation of subject matter and form similarly becomes a question of the interchange
of nearly preprogrammed units (e.g., "*Décimas* are good for complaints; / the sonnet works well for those who wait; / stories must be
told in ballad-verse," 307–09).[16] In practice, Lope's aesthetic of continuity requires a grace and an elegance which presuppose the natural
equivalence of style and form:

> Si hablare el rey, imite cuanto pueda
> la gravedad real; si el viejo hablare,
> procure una modestia sentenciosa.
>
> (269–71)

(If a king should speak, let him imitate insofar as possible the seriousness of a
king; if an old man should speak, strive for an unassuming pithiness.)

> Remátense las scenas con sentencia,
> con donaire, con versos elegantes,
> de suerte que, al entrarse el que recita,
> no deje con disgusto el auditorio
>
> (294–97)

(Finish off the scenes with wit and grace, with elegant verses, so that when
someone comes onstage to speak, he will not leave the audience displeased.)

In pleading for the autonomy of the *comedia* from any recognized
rules, Lope goes considerably beyond the notion of artistic convention that was characteristic of the European neoclassical traditions of
the sixteenth and seventeenth centuries.[17] He argues from a notion of
taste (*gusto*) which is revealingly indicative of the commodification of
the aesthetic object and of the ideological functions which any commodity may serve. Taste, as Lope understands it, refers principally to
the preferences of the paying public (Pierre Vilar remarked that the *comedia* was in fact the only literary genre which "paid its way" in
Golden Age Spain [70]); yet by virtue of its mass appeal the *comedia*
was able to create in the public the very desires which it was designed
to satisfy: "como las paga el vulgo, es justo / hablarle en necio para

darle gusto" (47–48), a passage which I would render in the following strong translation: "since the common people pay for these plays, it is right to speak to them like fools in order to please them." Thus if the *comedia* can be seen to enact a conflict between tradition and modernity, caste and class, old and new, this is accomplished in such a way that the pressures of the modern are consistently masked; the fundamental conservatism of the genre acquires all the force of an ideology which is welcomed by the masses and willingly taken on by them.

The dramatic energies thus generated may be made immediately apparent if one considers for a moment the case of Tirso de Molina's *El Burlador de Sevilla*. On one level, the figure of Don Juan would appear to be the very antithesis of the scheme that I have proposed thus far: if the *comedia* sustains a traditional and conservative ideology through the establishment of continuities, then Don Juan is both modern and subversive. His principal effort is to come into contact with a reserve of psychosexual energy which he discharges in the form of discontinuous flows. The fragmentary nature of his experience is marked by his rapid flight after each amorous conquest ("¡Ensilla, Catalinón!" ["Saddle up, Catalinón!"]), and since he makes no connection between one experience and the next the very structure of the play may be read as an attempt to subvert even the narrative continuities on which the *comedia*'s conservative ideology rests. As the inversion of the prototypical *comedia* hero—the hero who sustains his identity through an inflexible allegiance to the idealist principles of selfhood and honor ("Soy quien soy" ["I am who I am"])—Don Juan is able to join Shakespeare's Iago and those who subversively are able to fashion an identity from its near-demonic displacement through a series of disguises and feints (Iago: "I am not I"; Don Juan: "Soy un hombre sin nombre" ["I am a nameless man"]). Insofar as Don Juan thus attempts to free himself from the social structuration of power, he may fairly be described as the subversive or revolutionary characterized by Gilles Deleuze and Felix Guattari. The essential task of the revolutionary, as outlined in *L'Anti-Oedipe,* is "to learn from the psychic flow how to shake off the Oedipal yoke and the effects of power, in order to initiate a radical politics of *desire freed from all beliefs*. Such a politics dissolves the mystifications of power through the kindling, on all levels, of antioedipal forces—the schizzes-flows—forces that escape coding, scramble all the codes, and flee in all directions: orphans (no daddy-mommy-me), atheists (no beliefs), and nomads (no habits, no territories)."[18] As an anti-narrative, *El Burlador de Sevilla* threatens to dissolve into the simply repetitious and potentially gratuitous actions of Don Juan. And yet Tirso encloses this anti-narrative within a framework that, by virtue of the telos of divine justice and punishment, subsumes Don Juan within the most orthodox of theocentric paradigms. In this way, it may be said that the ideological consciousness most revealingly exposed in *El Burlador* corresponds not to that of Don Juan but to the women whom he conquers: theirs is a consciousness not of the colonizer but of the colonized, a consciousness not simply of desire but of the desire for conquest and domination.

Let us return, however, to the terms suggested by Lope de Vega in the "Arte nuevo." To view the *comedia* as one of the first truly commodified aesthetic objects is in the first instance to regard it as a practice fully located in history, where "history" is determined primarily as the relationship among those elements of a culture which Raymond Williams called "dominant," "residual," and "emergent" (121–27). A play like *Fuenteovejuna* takes as its subject the conflicts between the aristomilitary caste (the Comendador of the Order of Calatrava) and the peasants (the townspeople of Fuenteovejuna), which resulted in a civil uprising and the murder of the Comendador in 1476. Yet the historical dimension of the work is apparent only in view of the value which Lope de Vega, writing during the "critical" years of the seventeenth century, ascribes to these events. The historical "crisis" of the seventeenth century was produced by the clash of an emergent (modernist) culture with the culture of dominance, yet Lope "translates" this crisis into the late fifteenth century (a distinctly premodern period) and draws on the archaic resources of Platonic idealism and myth in order to contain that crisis within acceptable bounds.[19] To subsume the Utopian tendencies of *Fuenteovejuna* and similar works within a historical paradigm is thus to reverse the Platonizing interpretations which have been put forward in the leading formalist and stylistic interpretations of the genre (those of Leo Spitzer, Joaquín Casalduero, Karl Vossler, Alexander Parker, William McCrary, and Bruce Wardropper), all of which are to some degree totalizing in intent and all of which may be seen to repress their own historicity by framing their perspectives so as to preclude any engagement of the concept of ideology or the possibility of a political *non dit.* If one considers Spitzer's reading of *Fuenteovejuna* as a paradigmatic example of this type of criticism, it becomes apparent that such an approach not only de-historicizes the play but, in so doing, unwittingly absorbs the ideological conservatism which the work advances. Spitzer reads *Fuenteovejuna* as the fulfillment of a dream of universal harmony, "the naive dream of a Christian World Harmony, cherished by the Spanish poet of the Golden Age Lope de Vega." [20] His image of the village is of a place of beauty and innocence, outside of history, and his notion of Lope's accomplishment is that of having preserved an Arcadian or Utopian existence by the transcendence of history. Applauding Casalduero, who he says was the first to demonstrate that the play has "no political or revolutionary purpose . . . but treats a metaphysical or moral problem," [21] yet faced with the fact that *Fuenteovejuna* has a manifest political content, Spitzer ascribes politics to the forces of some demonic agency, to "transient and dark forces of disorder":

Lope worked, as it were, from the historical battle-cries, backward to their metaphysical source. By means of this projection he was able to lift the original village of Fuenteovejuna out of time and space as an island of metaphysical peace, the realization of the Golden Age in the midst of our age of iron, the locus of cosmic harmony in the midst of our world of chaos, at the same time an Arcadia and a Utopia. Thus the "political action" to which the villagers are forced to resort (and with which the drama is mainly concerned) is due only to a temporary and local invasion of that idyllic, timeless peace that is the principle of *any* "Fuenteovejuna," by transient and dark forces of disorder. (209)

In Spitzer's and Casalduero's approach, the concrete historical conflict between the Comendador and the town is seen as the defect or "lack" of perfect relations—where the standards of perfection are identical to those which Nature provides—rather than as structurally a part of the relationship between unequal groups, dividing those who defend and rule from those who work. Accordingly, the actions of the Comendador are abjured for the "irresponsibility" which they demonstrate toward the town, where the notion of responsibility is understood in strictly idealist terms. It is often said in this regard that as feudal lord of the town the Comendador should be responsible for the well-being of his vassals, and that he fails in his duty. What, then, is one to say of the fact that this "failure" takes the exceedingly violent form of sexual aggression? Similarly, as Comendador of Calatrava he is under obligation to protect the Crown, yet he enlists the support of the Master of the Order in a plot for the capture of Ciudad Real, the ultimate implication of which is political treason. Even where such a reading does acknowledge the historical conflicts which form the ostensible subject of the play, history is seen primarily as the object of moralizing critique. The Comendador's actions are taken as symptomatic of a certain malaise, the decadence of the Military Orders whose purpose was originally the defense of Christendom against Islam:

> la cruz roja obliga
> cuantos al pecho la tienen
> aunque sea de orden sacro;
> mas contra moros se entiende

(the red cross imposes an obligation on all who wear it on their chest, even though it is [the sign of] a holy order; but one means fighting against Moors.)

In spite of Spitzer's thoroughgoing Platonism—or perhaps *because* of it—his reading of *Fuenteovejuna* serves to make plain the fact that this *comedia* conforms to the shape of literary romance, which Arnold Reichenberger saw as characteristic of the *comedia* as a genre (307). The *comedia* moves, in Reichenberger's words, from "order disturbed to order restored," or in structural terms from *agon* to utopian resolution. The historical and political conflicts which comprise the *agon* of romance are characteristically set in what has been called the "mid-world," and also in the middle of the action, while there is at the same time a strongly teleological pull toward narrative and social closure: the telos is imagined in the form of a future which resists historical change. If Fuenteovejuna is an example of uncorrupted Nature, of the *locus amoenus,* then the Comendador may on one level be identified as the antagonist who disrupts that idyllic harmony, precipitating a nearly mythical "fall" from a state of innocence and grace, in whose wake there follows the rapid degeneration of all that may be called "natural": the labors of the peasants, ordered in accordance with the cycles of nature, are violently disrupted, and social relations begin a process of corruption by division; by the beginning of Act 3, the town has been split from its leader, the women are divided against the men, and the lovers Laurencia and Frondoso are separated from one another. Indeed, nature itself begins to show signs of decadence, and there are auguries of a poor harvest for the coming year ("el año apunta mal, y el tiempo crece, / y es mejor que el sustento esté en depósito" ["The harvest augurs badly and the year is wearing on; it is best that we have some food in storage"]).

Even if the notion of romance as described above is able to accommodate a vision of the Comendador as an agent of historical change, Spitzer's reading is nonetheless guided by the same principle that Fredric Jameson saw in Northrop Frye's archetypal approach to romance: "his identification of mythic patterns in modern texts aims at reinforcing our sense of the affinity between the cultural present of capitalism and the distinct mythical past of tribal societies, and at awakening a sense of the continuity between our psychic life and that of primitive peoples" (130). For Spitzer and those critics of the *comedia* who follow him, this principle of historical identity works by the machinery of transcendence: the decadence which mars the idyllic existence of *Fuenteovejuna* can reasonably be overcome, and the Utopia which Lope projects is in principle accessible to any historical community— including our own—if only it can sufficiently purify its collective life.

If romance lends itself to this style of moralizing critique, this is because the oppositions which organize it may be reduced to a pair that is itself essentially ethical in nature, the struggle of good and evil. As Nietzsche showed in *The Genealogy of Morals, Beyond Good and Evil,* and the fragments assembled as *The Will to Power,* however, the concepts of ethics of the kind we have seen to govern a romance like *Fuenteovejuna* are themselves the sedimented remains of the concrete praxis of situations of domination. Nietzsche demonstrated that what is meant by "good," for instance, is nothing more than my position as an unassailable center of power, in terms of which the position of anyone who is radically different from me (e.g., the weak) is marginalized as an "other" whose practices are then formalized in the concept of "evil." The Christian "reversal" of these circumstances, which we apparently witness in *Fuenteovejuna*, the revolt of the weak against the strong, and the generation of the repressive ideals of charity, care, and self-denial, are no less a function of the initial power structure than are the "ideals" of which they are supposedly the inversion.[22] Consider in this light the closing words of Esteban and the King in *Fuenteovejuna;* the laborers willfully submit themselves to the authority of an absolute monarch, while the King looks forward to the time when he can appoint a new feudal lord:

ESTEBAN
Señor, tuyos ser queremos.
Rey nuestro eres natural.
. . . .
REY
Y la villa es bien se quede
en mí, pues de mí se vale,
hasta ver si acaso sale
comendador que la herede.

(III. 2436–37, 2449–50)

(*Esteban.* Sir, we wish to become your own. You are our natural king. *King.* It is right for the village to remain as mine, since I am responsible for it, until such time as there may be a comendador to inherit it.)

Despite the strong tendency of the *comedia* to achieve narrative and social closure, moments such as these reveal the fact that such closure is achieved only by the erasure of power relations, or by what one recent critic has called the process of "euphemization." And yet what is effaced or repressed invariably returns, most often in the form of a repetition. Consider the prospect alluded to in the passage above, of Fuenteovejuna once again under the domination of a feudal lord; or consider the fact which has long puzzled critics about Calderón's ritualistically brutal *El médico de su honra,* namely, that Gutierre insists before the King that he may find his second wife unfaithful and that he may kill her as he killed the first. As if to remind us of the remainders of power which will not be erased, even in a genre which strives so hard to achieve perfect closure (e.g., the marriage of couples, the justice of God or of the King), there is at the end of *El médico* a bloody hand on Gutierre's door, and this blood will not wash off.

If Nietzsche's "deconstruction" of the ethical binary can be taken to apply to the *comedia* qua romance, then what remains is to ascribe specific values to the "concrete situations of ethical domination," in order to avoid reinscribing the *comedia* back into the idealizing structures from which we have been unable to clear free. A properly historicized reading of *Fuenteovejuna* would begin from the struggles represented in it—the mythical and historical conflicts between Fuenteovejuna and the Comendador, between the Order of Calatrava and Ciudad Real, and ultimately between the Catholic Monarchs of Spain and Alfonso V of Portugal—and proceed from there to an investigation of the motives at work behind the play's romantic and utopian passions. In this way, *Fuenteovejuna* as a structured whole can be seen as determined by the historical "crisis" outlined above, viz., the exhaustion of one socioeconomic order at a time when the newly emerging order is met with resistance and, perhaps, with fear. It is because of this resistance to change that *Fuenteovejuna* and the *comedias* it most resembles can project a future which is fundamentally identical with the past, one in which the tradition-oriented system of racial castes and inherited professions, of "natural" social and political relations, is protected from the reifying effects of the universalization of equivalent labor-power and from the free circulation of capital which the market system would abet. And insofar as the *comedia* may be seen as a strategy for the *containment* of these modernizing forms of existence and their ideological correlates, the genre may be described as the locus of a struggle between that traditional axiology which drew strength from the persistence in Spain of a system of racial castes, and the more modernizing ideology of social class.

If one historicizes romance in this way and views the narrative disposition of its elements in terms of the ideologies encoded by them, then the manifest structural and thematics of a play like *Fuenteovejuna* (e.g., of Comendador and town, of self-love and altruism, of *amour propre* and the general will) would have to be rewritten as the elemental constituents of a more essential romance, the principal condition of whose figuration is the historical one mentioned above, i.e., a moment of crisis or transition in which two competing modes of production, or stages of socioeconomic awareness, uneasily coexist as "dominant" and "emergent" portions of a cultural discourse. If this is so, then the Comendador would seem to function neither as the antagonist of romance, whose behavior is monstrously, and predictably, evil, nor as the demonic agent of history who disturbs Fuenteovejuna from the slumbers of its collective life and disrupts the idyll of its natural existence. Insofar as his relations with the town are determined according to a scale of quantitative pleasures and use-value, he is more accurately the decadent member of a caste society whose deeply historical resentment is manifested in the form of sexual and political acquisitiveness.[23] The crucial point of his opposition to the town would then lie in the fact that their relations with one another are determined according to qualitative standards, and their relationship to the products of their labor seen in strictly essentialist terms (cf. Edward M. Wilson's confirming judgment that in the relationship between Casilda and Peribáñez, "The husband [sees] in Casilda the fruits of the earth which he cultivates" [134]).

To the extent that the *comedia* may be seen as a struggle not simply of ethical or metaphysical forces but of different moments of socioeconomic awareness, it demonstrates marked affinities with the ideology of romance as described by Jameson in his essay on the dialectical use of genre criticism ("Magical Narratives"). Yet when one assigns specific values to the modes of socioeconomic consciousness which actually do come into conflict in it, then it becomes clear that the *comedia* significantly modifies the historical terms of Western romance as outlined in that essay. On Jameson's account, the binary oppositions which form the manifest content of romance are characteristic of those periods of history sometimes designated as "times of trouble," times more accurately associated with the degenerate phases of epic society such as one might see reflected in Guillén de Castro's *Las mocedades del Cid,* or with the archaic forms of social movement studied by Hobsbawm in *Primitive Rebels*—times when, in Jameson's words, "central authority disappears and marauding bands of robbers and brigands range geographical immensities with impunity" (118).[24] Romance of the "second-order" type he is discussing is seen as the historical engagement of that conflict which ensues when the rigidly binary mode of thinking characteristic of such times is confronted by the consciousness of a group which has overcome its social and geographical isolation and has developed an awareness of itself as a universal "subject" of history. Romance would provide a means of "solving" the problem of that group's need for (political) recognition and the legitimization of its power by subordinating the consciousness of another to its own. The result is a "new kind of narrative, the 'story' of something like a semic evaporation. The hostile knight, his identity unknown, exudes that insolence which marks a fundamental *refusal of recognition* and stamps him as the bearer of the category of evil, up to the moment when, defeated and unmasked, he asks for mercy by *telling his name*" (Hobsbawm 4; first italics mine). Yet insofar as *Fuenteovejuna,* and the Spanish *comedia* in general, resists the emergence of anything resembling a "consciousness of class," it seeks to dissolve these and similar power relationships into a neutral, not to say natural, hierarchy. The demonic agent in Fuenteovejuna is eliminated rather than reassimilated into the social order, as would be the case according to the paradigm Jameson proposes; in this way the King can call the people of the town his "proper" vassals and can place himself above them, but in a hierarchy which is neutralized insofar as he is seen as their natural ruler (e.g., "Y la villa es bien se quede en mí"; "Rey nuestro eres natural"). To say that the ideological content of romance turns on the problem of recognition (or the refusal thereof) is to imply that romance is deeply political, even if the politics which it advances depends, as in the case of the *comedia,* on the effacement of modern "subjectivity" or class consciousness. The action of *Fuenteovejuna* consists largely in the formation of a political consciousness out of passion and self-interest, yet the political is marked by a peculiarly utopian conjuncture. Similarly, the resolution of the plot may indeed depend on the pronouncement of a name, but this does not give the identity of a "bearer of evil" (i.e., one whose recognition is refused outright); rather, it names the group whose admission of collective responsibility ("Join the town together in one voice"; "Fuenteovejuna killed the Comendador," vv. 1801, 2107) is meant to negate the self-arrogating will of the Comendador, the proudly named Fernán Gómez de Guzmán.

Accordingly, one must seek a model for the political struggle for recognition in the *comedia* which would allow for the fact that independence and acknowledgment in it are granted not to those who defend and rule but to those who work and serve. To the extent that the *comedia* translates this struggle for political recognition into the Platonic terms that Spitzer and Casalduero saw in *Fuenteovejuna,* it asks to be read as analogous to the Hegelian text on which Marx was eventually to perform his materialist operation. The caveat which must be entered is that in the case of the *comedia* the struggle which most nearly prefigures the social transformation which Marx foresaw, the dialectic of Master and Slave, here takes the form of a *huis clos,* a dialectic with no exit. In Hegel's account of the conflict of bondsman and lord, these twin aspects of consciousness are seen as radically unequal and fiercely opposed: the one is independent consciousness, whose nature is to be "for itself" (the Comendadores of *Fuenteovejuna* or *Peribáñez* and, perhaps, the King as well), while the other is dependent consciousness (the villagers, Peribáñez) whose essence is to live "for another." As part of the embracing project of consciousness to achieve independence, each seeks the recognition of the other; and since each must be willing to stake his own life on this pursuit, the dialectic of their relationship naturally proceeds through a trial by death: "it is only through staking one's life that freedom is won. . . . The individual who has not risked his life may well be recognized as a *person,* but he has not attained the truth of this recognition as an independent self-consciousness. Similarly, just as each stakes his own life, so each must seek the other's death, for it values the other no more than itself" (*Phenomenology* 187). The outcome of the struggle of master and slave is recognition but, as Hegel says, "a recognition that is one-sided and unequal" (191). Both are, moreover, deeply unsatisfied: the slave remains dependent, and the lord achieves recognition from a consciousness that is dependent on, and not independent from, his own. Thus it may be said that "the truth of the independent consciousness is the servile consciousness of the bondsman" (193) or, in more strictly Marxist terms, that "the truth of ruling-class consciousness (that is, of hegemonic ideology and cultural production) is to be found in working-class consciousness" (Jameson 290).

The conflict of master and slave which takes place within consciousness is a mythical representation of the historical process by which the self seeks to achieve independence in its relations with others. Not least because of its radical instability, it is a conflict which brings us to the very edge of historical time and to the war and the work of self-consciousness contained within history, properly speaking. Thus the *comedia* as seen from the dialectic of master and slave may be regarded as the effort to educate the slave in the enjoyment of his servile condition, which is to say, in deriving pleasure from his work.[25] Thus while the powerful struggle for acknowledgment and independence of masters and slaves is reduplicated within history, the unhappiness generated therefrom is not entirely unmitigated; even the "unhappy consciousness" is not altogether unhappy: the *comedia* proceeds toward a nearly obligatory "happy ending"; the slave will know moments of enjoyment, despite his subservience to the master, and may indeed come to find satisfaction in the self-alienating nature of his work.

Consider *Peribáñez* in this light. The play has been seen as moving from a state of inauthentic or "false" consciousness on the part of *Peribáñez* to a state of self-awareness. In the judgment of one recent critic, this process begins in Peribáñez's "loss" of self-awareness, a loss signaled most notably by his acceptance from the Comendador of certain gifts, including a set of expensive wall-hangings embroidered with the Comendador's coat of arms (Larson 67–68). Yet the conclusion of the play may be seen to lie not in the recovery of an "authentic" self-consciousness, marked by Peribáñez's eventual rejection of those gifts, but simply in the transposition of his former relationship of subservience: Peribáñez and his wife, though freed from the personal domination of the Comendador, come willingly to accept for themselves the fact of their economic and social "humility." Casilda's initial profession of faith in the virtues of the peasant life,

> Más quiero yo a Peribáñez
> con su capa la pardilla
> que al Comendador de Ocaña
> con la suya guarnecida
>
> (771a)

(I love Peribáñez, with his humble brown cape, more than you, Comendador, with your embroidered one),

is internalized by Peribáñez as he is forced to repress his desire for the recognition bestowed upon him by the Comendador:

> Pienso que nos está bien
> que no estén en nuestra casa
> paños con armas ajenas:

> no murmuren en Ocaña
> que un villano labrador
> cerca su inocente cama
> de paños comendadores,
> llenos de blasones y armas.
> Timbre y plumas no están bien
> entre el arado y la pala,
> bieldo, trillo y azadón;
> que en nuestras paredes blancas
> no han de estar cruces de seda.
>
> (776a–b)

(I think it is wrong for us to have such cloths hanging in our house, with someone else's arms on them. I would not have Ocaña whisper that a peasant surrounds his humble bed with noble hangings, covered with symbols of knighthood. Crests and plumes go ill with plows and shovels, forks and hoes. Our whitewashed walls should not be decorated with silk crosses.)

For Hegel, the dialectic of Master and Slave finds stabilization, if at all, in the family; the state, we know from the *Philosophy of Right,* is an extension of the family and its ethical bonds. In the *comedia,* however, familial relations are conspicuously absent, or are reduced to the same terms of absolute authority and obedience, self and other, good and evil, which we have seen to be characteristic of *Fuenteovejuna* qua romance. The literary and ideological closure which the *comedia* is able to achieve thus depends, as in the final scenes of *Fuenteovejuna* and *Peribáñez,* on the possibility of legitimizing the power of those who wield it—the father, the feudal lord, or the perfected image of these, the king. Yet this is precisely where the *comedia* most radically transforms the dialectic which Hegel proposed, by effacing the fact of social contradiction and thus resisting the process of historical change wrought by the need of newly constituted centers of power to legitimize themselves: especially where power becomes subject to the process of effacement, where the unavoidably political dimension is "demonized" in an effort to make it appear as though the subversion of the dominant order could come only from without—especially in such cases, the superiority of the master comes to depend on the willing submissiveness of the bondsman.[26]

Seen in such a light, the *comedia* becomes illuminating of a mode of "resistance to subjectivity" which is all the more remarkable insofar as it proceeds in a direction diametrically opposed to that which Deleuze and Guattari outlined in *L'Anti-Oedipe*. If Deleuze and Guattari advocate a strategy which would recover the energies of the divided consciousness and its heterogeneous desires in order to resist the tyranny of the oedipal triangle over modern existence, then the *comedia* offers resistance to the modernizing functions of capitalism by the most reactionary of means, viz., by the cultivation of what Foucault described as the "fascism within," the desire of the individual to seek his own domination (the town of Fuenteovejuna is described as leaderless—"sin capitán" [1845], yet it looks to submit itself to the authority of the King): it is from the satisfaction of this desire that the *comedia* derives the rhetorical force with which Lope credits it in the "Arte nuevo," its ability to please the masses, to "mover con fuerza a toda gente." By elaborating only slightly on Lope's terms, one might describe the *comedia* as a practice designed to provide pleasure in the repression of the very desires which it summons up: if the resistance to historical change implies the self-domination of the masses, then Lope's most important discovery was the fact that the psychology of the masses is to some extent always a fascist phenomenon, and that the resistance to historical change could best be achieved by making their domination a pleasurable experience.

Notes

[1]An earlier analysis of the seventeenth-century crisis is that of Roland Mousnier in the *Histoire générale des civilisations*. See also his contribution to "Trevor-Roper's 'General Crisís': A Symposium." Elliott's study of "decline" is anticipated by E. J. Hamilton ("The Decline of Spain").

[2]On absolutism in Spain, see Perry Anderson.

[3]See the essays and critical discussion of Maurice Dobb in Rodney Hilton. Lawrence Stone is useful for the case of England. In connection with Shakespeare in particular, see Rosalie Colie and Paul Delany.

[4]Hayden White qualifies this in relation to the Comic structure of Hegel's vision, which Marx sets out to rewrite:

Hegel's Comic conception of history was based ultimately on his belief in the right of life over death; "life" guaranteed to Hegel the possibility of an ever more adequate form of social life throughout the historical future. Marx carried this Comic conception even further; he envisioned nothing less than the dissolution of that "society" in which the contradiction between consciousness and being had to be entertained as a fatality for all men in all times. It would not, then, be unjust to characterize the final version of history which inspired Marx in his historical and social theorizing as a Romantic one. But his conception did not envisage humanity's redemption as a deliverance from time itself. Rather, his redemption took the form of a reconciliation of man with a nature denuded of its fantastic and terrifying powers, submitted to the rules of technics, and turned to the creation of a genuine community. (281–82)

The notion of romance as deliverance, and specifically as "deliverance from time," has been amply discussed in connection with Shakespearean drama by Northrop Frye.

[5]For two attempts to read the *comedia* as a means for the "direction" of the masses, see José Antonio Maravall, *Teatro y literatura,* and José María Díez Borque.

[6]González de Cellorigo, as cited in Elliott 184–85.

[7]González de Cellorigo, as cited in Vilar 66–67.

[8]Archivo General de Simancas, Hacienda leg. 395–547, Consulta of 3 September, 1617; cited in Elliott 186.

[9]The word "caste," which is Spanish in origin, did not carry the Hindu meaning, even though the Portuguese did later apply it to Indian society. See Américo Castro, *The Spaniards* 51.

[10]See Martin Green for this formulation.

[11]The late-fifteenth-century Spanish humanist Antonio de Nebrija defined caste as "good lineage." In the seventeenth century, Covarrubias explained that "caste means noble and pure lineage; he who comes from good family and descent, despite the fact that we say 'he is of good caste' or 'he is of bad caste.' . . . Those who are of good lineage and caste we call 'castizos.' " See Castro, *The Spaniards* 51.

[12]See Maravall's description of the "sociedad estamental" in connection with the *comedia* in *Teatro y literatura.*

[13]Castro is here radically revising his more conventional account of honor in the Golden Age published in "Algunas observaciones." See *De la edad conflictiva* 49ff.

[14]See Maravall's *Teatro y literatura* and also *La cultura del Barroco.*

[15]This notion is developed throughout Jameson's *The Political Unconscious.*

[16]On the generic repeatability of the *comedia,* see Díez Borque 357ff. ("Una estructura fija para unas funciones repetidas").

[17]Cf. Lawrence Manley.

[18]From the "Introduction" by Mark Seem xxi.

[19]The process is akin to that which Jonathan Dollimore has described as "containment," adopting Williams's rather than Jameson's sense: "Three aspects of historical and cultural process figure prominently in materialist criticism: consolidation, subversion, and containment. The first refers, typically, to the ideological means whereby a dominant order seeks to perpetuate itself; the second to the subversion of that order, the third to the containment of ostensibly subversive pressures" (10).

[20]Spitzer, "A Central Theme," 192. See also *Classical and Christian Ideas.*

[21]Casalduero's study was conceived as a reaction against Menéndez y Pelayo's nineteenth-century aesthetic, and marks the beginning of a Platonizing approach to the play from which Spanish criticism has been unable to clear free. Javier Herrero seeks to save the strictly political dimension of the play, but remains within the field of political theory rather than political praxis.

[22]See Jameson's discussion of Nietzsche's "deconstruction" of ethics, 114–17.

[23]That *Fuenteovejuna* is not written against the nobility as a class is evident from the fact that Lope provides for the regeneration of the young Master of the Order of Calatrava, Rodrigo Téllez Girón. There is some possibility that Lope may have favored the Master because of political connections between the Girones and the Osunas, Lope's patrons.

[24]Hobsbawm (*Primitive Rebels*) makes the following observation on the role of banditry, which helps shed light on its place in in early modern Spain:

The coming of the modern economy (whether or not it is combined with foreign conquest) may, and indeed probably will, disrupt the social balance of the kinship society, by turning some kins into "rich" families and others into "poor," or by disrupting the kin itself. The traditional system of blood-vengeance and outlawry may—and indeed probably will—"get out of hand" and produce a multiplicity of unusually murderous feuds and embittered outlaws, into which an element of class struggle begins to enter. (4)

Lope's *Pedro Carbonero* would repay further investigation in this light. See Avalle-Arce on this subject.

[25]For an illuminating discussion of this point, see Rosen 67–68.

[26]On effacement and legitimization in connection with Renaissance drama, see Dollimore:

Legitimization further works to efface the fact of social contradiction, dissent and struggle. Where these things present themselves unavoidably they are often demonised as attempts to subvert the social order. Therefore, if the very conflicts which the existing order generates from within itself are construed as attempts to subvert it from without (by the "alien"), that order strengthens itself by simultaneously repressing dissenting elements and eliciting consent for this action: the protection of society from subversion. (7)

Works Cited

ANDERSON, PERRY. *Lineages of the Absolutist State.* London: Verso, 1979.

ASTON, TREVOR, ed. *The Crisis in Europe 1560–1660*. New York: Basic, 1965.

AVALLE-ARCE, JUAN BAUTISTA. "Pedro Carbonero y Lope de Vega: Tradición y comedia." *Dintorno de una epoca dorada*. Madrid: José Porrúa Turanzas, 1979. 353–69.

CASALDUERO, JOAQUÍN. "*Fuenteovejuna*." *Revista de filología hispánica* 5 (1943): 21–44.

CASTRO, AMÉRICO. "Algunas observaciones acerca del concepto del honor en los siglos XVI y XVII." *Revista de filología española* 3 (1916): 1–50, 357–86.

———. *De la edad conflictiva*. Madrid: Taurus, 1972.

———. *The Spaniards*. Trans. Willard King and Selma Margaretten. Berkeley and Los Angeles: U of California P, 1971.

COLIE, ROSALIE. "Reason and Need: *King Lear* and the 'Crisis' of the Aristocracy." *Some Facets of King Lear*. Ed. R. Colie and F. T. Flahiff. Toronto and Buffalo: U of Toronto P, 1974. 185–219.

DELANY, PAUL. "*King Lear* and the Decline of Feudalism." *PMLA* 91 (1977): 429–40.

DELEUZE, GILLES, and FELIX GUATTARI. *Anti-Oedipus: Capitalism and Schizophrenia*. Trans. Robert Hurley, Mark Seem, and Helen R. Lane. Minneapolis: U of Minnesota P, 1983.

DÍEZ BORQUE, JOSÉ MARÍA. *Sociología de la comedia del siglo XVII*. Madrid: Cátedra, 1976.

DOBB, MAURICE. *Studies in the Development of Capitalism*. London: George Routledge, 1946.

DOLLIMORE, JONATHAN. "Shakespeare, Cultural Materialism and the New Historicism." *Political Shakespeare: New Essays in Cultural Materialism*. Ed. Jonathan Dollimore and Alan Sinfield. Ithaca: Cornell UP, 1985. 2–17.

ELLIOTT, J. H. "The Decline of Spain." In *The Crisis in Europe,* ed. Trevor Aston. 167–73.

FRYE, NORTHROP. *The Myth of Deliverance*. Toronto: U of Toronto P, 1983.

GONZÁLEZ DE CELLORIGO, MARTÍN. *Memorial de la política necesaria y útil restauración de la república en España*. Valladolid, 1600.

GREEN, MARTIN. *Dreams of Adventure, Deeds of Empire*. New York: Basic, 1979.

HAMILTON, EARL J. "The Decline of Spain." *Economic History Review* 8 (1938): 168–79.

HEGEL, GEORG WILHELM FRIEDRICH. *The Phenomenology of Spirit.* Trans. A. V. Miller. New York: Oxford UP, 1977.

HERRERO, JAVIER. "The New Monarchy: A Structural Reinterpretation of *Fuenteovejuna.*" *Revista hispánica moderna* 36 (1970–71): 173–85.

HILTON, RODNEY, et al. *The Transition from Feudalism to Capitalism.* London: NLB, 1976.

HOBSBAWM, E. J. "The Crisis of the Seventeenth Century." In *The Crisis in Europe,* ed. Trevor Aston. 5–58.

———. *Primitive Rebels: Studies of Archaic Forms of Social Movement in the 19th and 20th Centuries.* New York: Norton, 1965.

JAMESON, FREDRIC. *The Political Unconscious.* Ithaca: Cornell UP, 1982.

LARSON, DONALD R. *The Honor Plays of Lope de Vega.* Cambridge: Harvard UP, 1977.

MANLEY, LAWRENCE. *Convention, 1500–1750.* Cambridge: Harvard UP, 1980.

MARAVALL, JOSÉ ANTONIO. *La cultura del Barroco.* Barcelona: Ariel, 1975.

———. *Teatro y literatura en la sociedad barroca.* Madrid: Seminarios y ediciones, 1972.

MCCRARY, WILLIAM C. "*Fuenteovejuna:* Its Platonic Vision and Execution." *Studies in Philology* 58 (1961): 179–92.

MOUSNIER, ROLAND, et al. *Histoire générale des civilisations.* Vol. 4. Paris: PUF, 1961.

———. "Trevor-Roper's 'General Crisis': A Symposium." In *The Crisis in Europe,* ed. Trevor Aston. 97–104.

ORTEGA Y GASSET, JOSÉ. *The Revolt of the Masses.* New York: Norton, 1960.

REICHENBERGER, ARNOLD. "The Uniqueness of the *Comedia.*" *Hispanic Review* 27 (1959): 303–16.

ROSEN, STANLEY. *G.W.F. Hegel: An Introduction to the Science of Wisdom.* New Haven: Yale UP, 1974.

SALOMON, NOËL. *Recherches sur le thème paysan dans la "comedia" au temps de Lope de Vega.* Bordeaux: Féret & Fils, 1965.

SEEM, MARK. Introduction. Deleuze and Guattari. xv–xxiv.

SPITZER, LEO. "A Central Theme and its Structural Equivalent in Lope's *Fuenteovejuna.*" *Hispanic Review* 23 (1955): 274–92.

_____. *Classical and Christian Ideas of World Harmony.* Baltimore: Johns Hopkins UP, 1963.

STONE, LAWRENCE. *The Crisis of the Aristocracy 1558–1641.* Oxford: Clarendon, 1965.

TÉLLEZ, FRAY GABRIEL [Tirso de Molina]. *El Burlador de Sevilla y convidado de piedra.* Ed. Joaquín Casalduero. Madrid: Cátedra, 1977.

TREVOR-ROPER, H. R. "The General Crisis of the Seventeenth Century." In *The Crisis in Europe,* ed. Trevor Aston. 59–95.

VEGA CARPIO, LOPE FELIX DE. "Arte nuevo de hacer comedias en este tiempo." Ed. Juan Manuel Rozas. *Significado y doctrina del "Arte nuevo" de Lope de Vega.* Madrid: Sociedad general española de librería, 1976. 181–94.

_____. *Fuenteovejuna.* Ed. Francisco López Estrada. Madrid: Castalia, 1969.

_____. *Peribáñez y el Comendador de Ocaña.* Ed. Federico Carlos Sainz de Robles. *Obras escogidas de Lope de Vega.* Vol. 1, Teatro. Madrid: Aguilar, 1969.

VILAR, PIERRE. "The Age of Don Quixote." *New Left Review* 68 (July–August 1971): 59–71.

VOSSLER, KARL. *Lope de Vega y su tiempo.* Trans. R. de la Serna. Madrid: Revista de Occidente, 1933.

WARDROPPER, BRUCE. "*Fuente Ovejuna: el gusto* and *lo justo.*" *Studies in Philology* 53 (1956): 159–71.

WHITE, HAYDEN. *Metahistory: The Historical Imagination in Nineteenth-Century Europe.* Baltimore: Johns Hopkins UP, 1973.

WILLIAMS, RAYMOND. *Marxism and Literature.* Oxford: Oxford UP, 1977.

WILSON, EDWARD. "Images et structures dans *Peribáñez.*" *Bulletin Hispanique* 51 (1949): 125–59.

Intrigue Tragedy in Renaissance England and Spain

WALTER COHEN

COMPARISONS BETWEEN English and Spanish drama of the late sixteenth and early seventeenth centuries characteristically evoke the magical names of Shakespeare and Lope de Vega. Each playwright combined extraordinary verbal and stylistic range with a violation of neoclassical norms; each displayed a profound interest in the fate of the nation, manifest not only in the symptomatic mingling of kings and commoners but also in the recurrent recourse to the genre of the national history play itself; each wrote for the commercial public theaters that emerged in the late sixteenth century and soon focused theatrical activity on the capital cities of London and Madrid; each thrived under the sway of a partially centralized monarchy. These parallels might be considerably extended, and they might be, and indeed often have been, generalized to suggest the unique similarities between the Spanish and English theaters in the age of the Renaissance. Yet the resemblances can be overstated, not only because the two countries differed from one another, but also because what they had in common they also shared as well with the rest of Europe.

Such is the case with intrigue tragedy, a genre that came into its own in England between 1609 and 1614 and in Spain between 1622 and

1643. In these transitional years, English drama and Spanish drama began to lose their collective uniqueness, a movement coincident with and in part conditioned by changes in the theatrical context and the social and political milieu. It is against this larger background that I hope to explain the origin, nature, and significance of intrigue tragedy.

I

In the early seventeenth century, both England and Spain entered a period of crisis that culminated, during the 1640s, in aristocratic rebellion against the crown, civil war, and, consequently, the virtual destruction of absolutism. These developments constituted less a radical break with the past than an elevation to preeminence of those subversive tendencies that were present all along, beneath the superficial calm of the absolutist state. Profound economic problems lay behind the political eruptions of mid-century. The complex chain of causality differed in the two nations, but in both it led to aristocratic revolt against the state—the defining feature of the general crisis of the seventeenth century. [1]

The early Stuart monarchs inherited from the Tudor line both irreducible feudal premises and profound conflict with a capitalist nation. The commercialization of agriculture, the growth of manufacturing, and the increase of domestic and foreign trade all accelerated after 1600, as England embarked on its great colonialist adventure. So, too, did the corresponding social changes—the rise of the gentry, the merchants, and the common lawyers, and the simultaneous decline of the crown, the peerage, and the clergy. [2] The Stuart monarchy, in the absence of an adequate fiscal base from which to remedy its traditional lack of an integrated nationwide administrative apparatus, a sizable armed forces, and a homogeneous institutionalized religion, generally had recourse to a combination of budget-cutting and extraparliamen-

1. Perry Anderson, *Lineages of the Absolutist State* (London, 1974), pp. 53–55.

2. Christopher Hill, *The Century of Revolution, 1603–1714* (New York, 1966), pp. 15–42; and Lawrence Stone, *The Crisis of the Aristocracy, 1558–1641* (Oxford, 1965), pp. 139, 162–164, 269, and *The Causes of the English Revolution, 1529–1642* (New York, 1972), pp. 68, 71–72.

tary fund raising. The latter method also served the more general conservative purpose of strengthening absolutism by stabilizing the social structure, building up the aristocracy, and aligning the crown with the peerage and urban patriciates, while excluding the gentry and newer mercantile interests, centralizing the economy, and restricting the growth of capitalism. [3]

But absolutist dynamism generated an increasingly vocal, organized, and united opposition. Conflict arose from the first year of James's reign and soon ranged over such issues as economic policy, international trade, finance, court extravagance and corruption, diplomacy, religious ritual, and the legal system. The period from 1610 to 1614 represents something of a turning point. The first of these years saw the failure of the Great Contract, a compromise that would have abolished the monarchy's feudal economic prerogatives in return for an annual grant from Parliament of a fixed sum. By then, whatever slim chance there remained for a national church had also disappeared. In both 1610 and 1614, the king dissolved Parliament without receiving the supplies he wanted. And in the later year, the monarchy's disastrous intervention in the economy via the Cokayne Project helped end a decade of prosperity and inaugurate a prolonged depression that lasted until mid-century. When Commons, by then the central institution in the struggle against the crown, met again in the 1620s, it tended to view specific local issues in broader, constitutional terms. Well before 1640, a crown that combined High Church Anglicanism or even Catholicism with prerogative courts, restrictive economic regulation, and arbitrary exercise of power found itself dangerously isolated against a coalition of Puritan ministers, common lawyers, free traders, and, most important of all, the gentry both in Commons and in the country. [4]

In Spain, too, the seventeenth-century monarchs inherited the basic problems from their predecessors, only to exacerbate them. After the turn of the century, imperial overextension in Europe forced the

---

3. Anderson, pp. 138, 140–141; Hill, pp. 29, 47, 52–53, 69–73; and Stone, *Causes,* pp. 62, 86, 117–135, and *Crisis,* pp. 65–128.

4. Stone, *Causes,* pp. 83, 92–95; Hill, pp. 10, 35–37, 49–51, 80, 321 (Appendix D); and Anderson, p. 138.

crown to attempt a belated centralist solution to its problems, with the not surpri⌄ing result that the aristocracies of the periphery threw off the Castilian yoke. At the same time, the flow of American bullion into the royal treasury began to slow down: the volume during the 1620s was less than half what it had been in the 1590s. The chronic fiscal crisis of the state, unsolved by the widespread sale of offices, is evident in the backruptcies of 1607 and 1627, as well as in the alternating inflation and deflation of the currency—a recurrent pattern throughout the century.[5]

The political turning point for Habsburg absolutism probably came in the two decades following 1618 or 1621, with the revival of imperialism. As late as 1628 Spain could have extricated itself from its European involvements, serious military reverses began only after 1635, and genuine collapse was a phenomenon of the second half of the century. But the logic of the Spanish state was always to sacrifice domestic economics and politics—capitalism and absolutism—to imperial needs. The onset of the Thirty Years' War in 1618 therefore evoked a predictably aggressive response in Madrid. The opening of Philip IV's reign in 1621, coincident with the expiration of the Dutch peace treaty, then determined the course of the monarchy. Under the new *privado,* or favorite, the Count-Duke of Olivares, Philip IV's government, like that of Charles I in England, pursued a more active program than had its predecessor. On the one hand, Olivares's grandiose European strategy led inexorably to conflict with France's refurbished military apparatus and hence to the defeat of Spain.[6] On the other, the *privado* realized that the success of his foreign policy depended on the absolutist integration of the Habsburg empire, and especially of the two main peripheral regions of the peninsula, Portugal and the Crown of Aragon. But his attempt to implement this program failed disastrously in the 1640s, as a series of regional rebellions came close to dis-

5. J. H. Elliott, *Imperial Spain, 1469–1716* (New York, 1964), pp. 175, 297–299, 320–321; Antonio Domínguez Ortiz, *The Golden Age of Spain, 1516–1659,* trans. James Casey (London, 1971), pp. 144–145; Jaime Vicens Vives, *An Economic History of Spain,* collab. Jorge Nadal Oller, trans. Frances M. López-Morillas (Princeton, N.J., 1969), pp. 446–450, 463; Fernand Braudel, *The Mediterranean and the Mediterranean World in the Age of Philip II,* trans. Siân Reynolds (London, 1973), II, 755–756; and Anderson, pp. 76–77.

6. Elliott, pp. 330, 375; Domínguez Ortiz, pp. 90–97; and Anderson, pp. 78–79.

membering not only Spain's European empire, but its territorial homeland as well. [7]

Increasingly, as the century progressed, all open ideological roads led backward into the past. As in politics, 1620 represents a point of demarcation, after which reformism gave way to escapism. Feudal separatism on the periphery triggered off in the center not a capitalist revolution, as in England, but just more feudal separatism. For those unwilling to abandon monarchical consolidation for aristocratic particularism, the options were even narrower. In the words of Pierre Vilar, "around 1600, on its own soil in Castile, *feudalism entered upon its death struggle without there being anything to replace it.*" [8]

II

The consequences for the stage were relatively straightforward. During the first half of the seventeenth century, absolutist centralization, combined with deepening social conflict, gradually led to the decline of the public theater. Despite some striking chronological coincidences between England and Spain, the pace of theatrical events differed in the two countries. A tentative periodization might stress the following analogies: England 1597–1608 and Spain 1598–1621, England 1609–1614 and Spain 1622–1643, England 1615–1619 and Spain 1644–1650, and England 1620–1642 and Spain 1651–1700.

As noted earlier, our primary concern is with the second of these subperiods, 1609–1614 in England and 1622–1643 in Spain. These were the last ages of major public theater in each country. Although it is customary to date the decline of the London public stage from this era, by 1609 it was the private, children's companies that were in trouble. [9] The real threat to the public theaters came from within, specifi-

7. Elliott, pp. 339–373; Domínguez Ortiz, pp. 98–111; Vicens Vives, pp. 465–466; and Anderson, pp. 80–82.

8. Pierre Vilar, "The Age of Don Quixote," *New Left Review*, no. 68 (July-August 1971), pp. 59–71, esp. pp. 60, 67–68. The quotation appears on p. 66.

9. Leo G. Salingar, Gerald Harrison, and Bruce Cochrane, "Les Comédiens et leur public en Angleterre de 1520 à 1640," in *Dramaturgie et société: Rapports entre l'oeuvre théâtrale, son interprétation et son public aux xvie et xviie siècles*, ed. Jean Jacquot, with Elie Konigson and Marcel Oddon (Paris, 1968), II, 556, and E. K. Chambers, *The Elizabethan Stage* (Oxford, 1923), II, 7, 22–23, 54–55, 60–61, 67.

cally in the form of the decision of the King's Men in 1608 to spend their winter season at the private theater known as Blackfriars. The long-run theatrical significance of the children's companies, in other words, was to reveal to the professional actors a means of raising their profits by concentrating primarily on an upper-class clientele.

After Shakespeare's death, Blackfriars was the main theater of the King's Men, and by the 1630s they seem to have spent almost two-thirds of the year at it, with the summer reserved for the Globe. Average daily receipts at this time were more than twice as high at the indoor as at the outdoor playhouse, and the discrepancy in prestige was comparably great.[10] This may not have been the case between 1609 and 1614, however. Certainly, the Globe was still considered London's leading theater. And even if the King's Men and their theaters are excluded as atypical, the position of the public theaters during this period appears quite strong. Both the number of professional companies and the number of active public theaters in London increased.[11] There seems little doubt, moreover, that the total audience at the public playhouses continued to grow throughout the first fifteen years of the seventeenth century.[12] Finally, the public-theater plays themselves scarcely reveal signs of decline. Dekker was active until 1611 or 1612 at the Fortune and the Red Bull, and Heywood continued writing through 1612 for the latter theater. In the same year, the Red Bull was also the site for the initial performance of Webster's *White Devil*. Middleton's *Chaste Maid in Cheapside* probably opened at the Swan in 1613, and Jonson's *Bartholomew Fair* inaugurated the Hope in 1614. In a manner partly reminiscent of Shakespeare's final plays, these works do not entirely belong to the popular dramatic tradition. But they are strong evidence that through 1614 the public theaters continued to produce some of the most distinguished plays on the English stage. In short, the period from 1609 to 1614 was that unique transitional moment when the public and private theaters were of almost

10. Gerald Eades Bentley, *The Jacobean and Caroline Stage* (Oxford, 1941–1968), I, 3, 23–24; VI, 12–17, 192–194.

11. Chambers, II, 236–240, 242–243, 246–247, 404, 413–414, 464–469; and Bentley, I, 158–160; VI, 124, 130–131, 134, 200–201, 206–207.

12. Bentley, VI, 219; Chambers, II, 189, 371, 465; and Alfred Harbage, *Shakespeare's Audience* (New York, 1941), p. 33, and *Shakespeare and the Rival Traditions* (New York, 1952), pp. 24, 45, 124 n. 56.

equal importance, before the latter achieved the dominant position in English drama they have never subsequently relinquished.

The overall pattern was much the same in Madrid from 1622 to 1643. It has been necessary to counter the tendency in English scholarship to pronounce a premature death for the public theater. Owing to the recent, and justified, revaluation of Calderón and his school, it is equally essential to stress the early symptoms of decline in Spain not of the stage in general, but of the public stage in particular. The first two decades in the reign of Philip IV saw an extension and intensification of the centralizing trends of the early seventeenth century. The machine play, meanwhile, began to pose a still more serious challenge to the traditional *comedia*. The opening in 1633 of Buen Retiro, the new royal palace, provided another impetus to stage pageantry, and in subsequent years the physical reproduction of the *corral* at court inevitably entailed a loss of spontaneity and authenticity. What is often claimed of the *comedia* in the public theater was undoubtedly true of the court play, whether open to a popular audience or not: it was a conscious instrument of royal propaganda. [13]

Crown patronage of the drama also had the effect of turning players and playwrights from the *corrales* to the court. Beginning in the 1630s, spectacle plays in particular earned them far more than they could hope to receive in the public theater. Calderón began writing as much for the palace theaters as for the *corrales* from about 1635 on, and he was hardly alone in this respect. Finally, the tastes of a more aristocratic audience than attended the public theaters partly account for the elevation of style and tone in the *comedia* after 1620, even though most plays, whatever their premiere, ultimately found their way to the *corrrales*.

After this ambiguous era, in which the open-air, commercial stages of London and Madrid continued to thrive despite the encroachments of more aristocratic drama, there came a period of collapse from

13. Hugo Albert Rennert, *The Spanish Stage in the Time of Lope de Vega* (New York, 1909), pp. 233–237; Ruth Lee Kennedy, *Studies in Tirso,* I: *The Dramatist and His Competitors, 1620–26,* North Carolina Studies in the Romance Languages and Literatures, Essays, no. 3 (Chapel Hill, N.C., 1974), pp. 65, 194–195; N. D. Shergold, *A History of the Spanish Stage from Medieval Times until the End of the Seventeenth Century* (Oxford, 1967), pp. 275, 278, 284, 293, 295, 300, 329, 549; and Charles V. Aubrun, *La comedia espanōla (1600–1680),* trans. Julio Lago Alonso (Madrid, 1968), p. 81.

which the public theaters never fully recovered. We need only follow these developments in England where, between 1615 and 1619, there was a crisis of overexpansion, exacerbated by the overall slump of the British economy.[14] The consequences were predictable. The number of professional companies fell from five to four, the number of active public theaters from five to three. Most of the leading playwrights abandoned the stage, and it is in this period that one can first detect a decline in the quality of the drama performed in the public theater.[15] By the beginning of the recovery of 1620, the public theater was in clear decline and had lost the lead to the private playhouses and the court. This was particularly true after 1629, with the opening of still another private theater, the Salisbury Court, and the much increased involvement of Charles and Henrietta Maria's court with the stage. While the public theater seems to have undergone a weakening that was more qualitative than quantitative, the private stages catered to an increasingly aristocratic, even courtly, coterie. The plays designed for these theaters were far superior to those at the Caroline public playhouses and often scarcely inferior to the private-theater drama composed earlier in the century.[16] Finally, it must be noted that these changes occurred not, as most critics have argued, because the audience abandoned the actors, but because the actors abandoned their audience. But their decision was merely consistent with the growing divisions in all areas of English life.

III

Intrigue tragedy is one of the characteristic dramatic responses to this social and theatrical conjuncture. Its defining features are a loss of a national perspective combined with a sense of the problematic na-

14. Andrew Gurr, *The Shakespearean Stage, 1574–1642* (Cambridge, Eng., 1970), p. 142; Hill, pp. 317–318 (Appendix C); and Salingar, Harrison, and Cochrane, pp. 550, 555–558.

15. Bentley, I, 158–164, 177, 201; III, 243, IV, 556, 609–610, 754, 857; and VI, 208–209.

16. Salingar, Harrison, and Cochrane, p. 560; Bentley, I, 47 n. 3; and VI, 32–36, 146–149, 166, 194, 238–247.

ture of moral action. Compared to Shakespeare's tragedies of the previous decade, the British plays reveal a narrowing of range and a deeper pessimism. Though the constriction was not so extreme in Spain, the break was if anything sharper, involving as it did the elevation of tragedy to generic preeminence for the first time since the 1580s. In both countries, the new form dramatizes not so much the failure of the nobility to adapt to political change as the irrelevance of politics altogether. As history relinquishes its dynamic significance, the dominant temporal perception is of decay, entrapment, or stasis. In the absence of alternative modes of coherence, the characters and their deeds acquire a kind of opacity that defies clear judgment[17] and that consequently has resulted, as we shall see, in substantial interpretive controversy over a number of plays.

It may prove more illuminating than reductive to establish an internal subclassification of a major form, in this instance positing three main kinds of intrigue tragedy—heroic, satiric, and romantic—according to the relative influence of prior drama. Thus the satiric strain is stronger in England, the heroic and romantic in Spain. On the London stage, it is possible to discern a chronological progression from heroic to satiric to romantic that corresponds to the reduction of scope mentioned above and that usually constitutes a defensive reaction to rising social opposition and growing isolation. This is not the case in Spain, but within each type the tragedies of the 1630s generally present a darker vision than those of the previous decade. The peninsular theater dramatizes a class disoriented not, as in England, by a threat to its hegemony, but by a loss of self-confidence, by an awareness of an inability to function effectively or to prevent collapse.

Heroic intrigue, though sharing many of the assumptions of prior national drama, portrays the values that underlay traditional aristocratic power in such a way as to drain them of political significance. Chapman's *Bussy D'Ambois* (1604) and *The Revenge of Bussy D'Ambois* (1610), composed for the private theaters, focus from the start on the court, rather than the nation. As different as the two works are, the

---

17. For a roughly similar description, see Jean Alexander, "Parallel Tendencies in English and Spanish Tragedy in the Renaissance," in *Studies in Comparative Literature,* ed. Waldo F. McNeir (Baton Rouge, La., 1962), pp. 84–101.

protagonists, both of whom display only the most casual and intermittent interest in politics, are victims of state power at court: the heroic temper is ineffective and, more often than not, irrelevant. The earlier and more complex play dramatizes the gap between Bussy's assertion of virtue, freedom, and natural law, on the one hand, and the sordid, increasingly private conduct that defines him as a neofeudal aristocrat out of place at an absolutist court, on the other. *The Revenge of Bussy* culminates in the main character's suicide, which is justified as Stoic individualism and constitutes a conscious withdrawal that condemns the monarchy. In both plays, then, the protagonist's ideology serves a classic rationalizing function. Whatever Chapman's awareness of this process may have been, in both plays a reactionary perspective, typically indebted in part to bourgeois values, produces a simultaneously critical and positive vision that, while damning the present, looks to both past and future. [18]

Philip Massinger's *Unnatural Combat* (1624–1625) re-creates the contradictory outlook particularly of *Bussy D'Ambois,* perhaps because it is probably a late public-theater play composed by a primarily private-theater dramatist not entirely comfortable with the task. [19] Its hybrid nature is a consequence of this temporal, institutional, and authorial conjuncture. Frequently criticized for structural disunity, [20] the play begins as a heroic drama, but increasingly turns into an intrigue tragedy. Similarly, although Theocrine, the protagonist's daughter, is as innocent and virtuous as the young female victims of Shakespearean tragedy, she is raped and, it seems, "deform'd" before she dies. [21] The bluff Captain Belgarde also is at home in the public theater, where he was apparently meant to appeal to patriotic enthusiasm and lower-class pride. [22] Bursting in on an aristocratic state dinner, he rebukes the Governour for not granting him his back pay:

18. For similar descriptions, but symptomatically opposed evaluations of the plays, see Leonard Goldstein, "George Chapman and the Decadence in Early Seventeenth-Century Drama," *Science and Society,* XXVII (1963), 23–48, and J. W. Lever, *The Tragedy of State* (London, 1971), pp. 37–58.

19. For attribution to the Globe, see Bentley, IV, 824.

20. E.g., by T. S. Eliot, *Selected Essays* (New York, 1950), p. 187.

21. *The Unnatural Combat,* in *The Plays and Poems of Philip Massinger,* ed. Philip Edwards and Colin Gibson (Oxford, 1976), vol. II, V.ii.190. Subsequent references are noted in the text.

22. Edwards and Gibson, II, 183–184.

and yet remember
Tis we that bring you in the meanes of feasts,
Banquets, and revels, which when you possesse,
With barbarous ingratitude you deny us
To be made sharers in the harvest, which
Our sweat and industrie reap'd, and sow'd for you.
The silks you weare, we with our bloud spin for you.
(III. iii.84–90)

This extraordinary passage is the ideological key to the play. It is, of course, an expression of popular assertiveness and in particular an insistence on the reality and fundamental significance of surplus extraction, viewed from the perspective of the exploited class. The imagery suggests that Massinger has in mind the position of the peasant in the feudal mode of production. As the context reveals, however, Belgarde is really talking about the booty won for the ruling class by the common sailors. In the zero-sum game of feudal economics, the quickest path to accumulation is not technological innovation but outright expropriation. Although the metaphor of the harvest is in one sense mystified, in another it accurately reveals the dramatist's precapitalist premises.

For, despite the attack on the court here and elsewhere from a popular point of view, *The Unnatural Combat* is resolutely aristocratic in outlook. It largely lacks the critical perspective of Chapman's works or, for that matter, of almost all the other Jacobean intrigue tragedies, public or private, that we will be considering. It is not only a matter of the passing jibes at wealthy city merchants, remarks that seem to be unnaturalized immigrants from Massinger's satiric comedy. It is mainly the fate of Belgarde himself. The Governour and his aides generously respond to the pleas of the Captain, who learns as a result, and to his chagrin, what we have already been told in the previous scene: that to be a poor servant is preferable to being a wealthy lord. Belgarde likewise discovers that it is advisable to know one's place. At the end of the play, he is given an appropriate soldier's reward—not money, but responsibility for a fort.

Massinger's ambivalence is also evident in the portrayal of his protagonist. Essential knowledge about Malefort is withheld until almost the end of the play. We are always being surprised by the revelation of another of his former crimes, a method that is totally alien to earlier technique in the tragedies of the public theater. More damaging, in the first scene the Governour refers to him as "Our late great Admirall," praising "his faire actions, / Loyall, and true demeanour" (I.i.203, 208–209). Only much later, however, does the same man reveal his true, far more negative, opinion (III.ii.34–39). Thus we are never sure what purpose our ignorance, and that of the other characters, is meant to serve. Is Massinger incompetent, opportunistic, or original? Whatever the answer, the play suggests the dilemma of tragedy in the public theater after 1620.

The Spanish heroic tragedy, precisely because neither its competence nor its integrity is in doubt, raises theoretical issues of interpretation even more clearly. The anonymous *La Estrella de Sevilla* (1623–1624) and Calderón's *El médico de su honra* (1635) consider the painful consequences of applying the traditional and rigid standards of the feudal code of honor to complex social relations. In *La Estrella de Sevilla* the code is unquestioned. Indeed, unless the audience accepts it as a premise, the play becomes literally incomprehensible. The second, and related, assumption on which the plot is based is the inviolability of the monarch, rooted in the medieval notion of the king's two bodies. The tragedy is generated by the lecherous and murderous conduct of the young ruler, abetted by his amoral *privado*. If these two characters are modeled on Philip IV and Olivares, respectively, the uncommonly harsh portrayal of the king in particular acquires an additional critical edge.[23] In any case, the consistently honorable response of the Sevillians is exemplary in intent and effect. The erring monarch is educated against his will and virtually forced to take public responsibility for his crimes. Insofar as his moral conversion is permanent, the honor code, though here confined to a private affair, has demonstrated its ultimate efficacy in a manner that has potential political relevance. Just as important, however, the play reveals the costs of honor when the crown fails to act according to its principles: two people are murdered, and two others have their lives ruined.

Midway through Act II, Busto tells his sister Estrella of his fear that she had engaged in dishonorable conduct the night before when the king sneaked into their house to visit her. Here is a significant moment in the exchange:

23. For the identifications, see Kennedy, pp. 53–54, 340–341.

> BUSTO
> Esta noche fué epiciclo
> del Sol; que en entrando en ella
> se trocó de Estrella el signo.
> ESTRELLA
> Las llanezas del honor
> no con astrólogo estilo
> se han de decir: habla claro,
> y deja en sus zonas cinco
> el Sol. [24]

Estrella's stylistic critique seems to be to the point, but then we recall that the entire play is about "las llanezas del honor" and that both before and after this scene the noble characters, Estrella included, consistently employ precisely the rhetorical elaboration that she here reproves. Elevated conduct apparently requires elevated diction, from which there can be only brief escape. So it is with the conduct itself. At the end of the play, Estrella and Sancho's culminating feat of honor—mutual rejection, despite mutual love—elicits this sequence of comments from the *privado,* the *gracioso* (or clown), and the king:

> DON ARIAS
> !Brava constancia!
> CLARINDO
> Más me parece locura. [*Aparte*]
> REY
> Toda esta gente me espanta.
>
> (III.xviii, p. 221)

Clarindo and the king speak for at least part of the audience, evoking the absurdity and the terror of the extravagant behavior that has dominated the action. But these qualifications do not suggest a positive alternative: in the end there is no ethically defensible choice but the code of honor, with its attendant tragic price.

El médico de su honra presents a more extreme version of the same dilemma. *La Estrella de Sevilla* concerns the violation of the code at the apex of the feudal pyramid—a serious matter. In Calderón's play,

24. *La Estrella de Sevilla,* in *Peribáñez y el Comendador de Ocaña; La Estrella de Sevilla,* by Lope de Vega (Madrid, 1938), II.ix, p. 165. The subsequent reference is noted in the text.

however, the problem is the code itself, which leads a husband to murder his innocent and beloved wife, only to be rewarded for his pains by the king. For whom is the plot problematic, however, for Calderón or for us? Nineteenth-century scholars, assuming that the playwright approved of his protagonist's conduct, were understandably appalled. Only in the last thirty years have critics consistently argued that Calderón was attacking the honor code, at least in this its most extreme form. [25]

It seems fair to conclude that a critical polarization of this sort could arise only because the bases of Calderón's own judgment are unclear. In the greatest peasant plays—Lope de Vega's *Peribáñez* (1604–1614) and *Fuenteovejuna* (probably 1612–1614), and Calderón's *El alcalde de Zalamea* (1630–1644)—or in *La Estrella de Sevilla,* once the audience understands the principle of honor, it experiences no difficulty in appropriately allocating its sympathies to the various characters. Here, the same understanding produces no such result. Although Calderón's exact intention may thus be irretrievable, this very obscurity can be explained. Wife-murder over a point of sexual honor was more common in the Middle Ages than in the seventeenth century, when it was almost always condemned and usually punished quite severely. [26] Calderón's return to the sources of Spanish national character is accompanied by a fourteenth-century setting, in the reign of Pedro I of Castile, known to history as both *el Cruel* and *el Justiciero.* It is this duality that is built into the code of honor in *El médico de su honra.* But cruelty is not the mere excess of justice: it is equally inherent in the code. The play reveals that Spain cannot have it both ways. *El médico de su honra* is a critique from within, launched by a great dramatist against the only ideology available. Calderón's play simultaneously affirms and decries the essence of aristocratic culture. It is at once a moving and horrific sign of the impasse of Spanish society.

In both countries, then, the ideological ambivalence that accompanies the potent critique of the present is traceable to the dramatists' reactionary perspectives. By and large, this is also the case in those in-

25. A relatively moderate statement of the currently dominant position is C. A. Jones, Introd. to his edition of *El médico de su honra* (Oxford, 1961), pp. ix–xxv.

26. Melveena McKendrick, *Woman and Society in the Spanish Drama of the Golden Age: A Study of the "mujer varonil"* (London, 1974), pp. 35–39.

trigue tragedies indebted to satire, with its ironic view of lust, greed, and social conflict. The seemingly irresolvable critical disputes that many such plays have inspired may be understood, though of course not adjudicated, from this point of view. The tragedies of Marston, Tourneur, Webster, and Middleton are satiric intrigues. Marston, Middleton, and to a lesser extent Webster composed satiric comedies, and Middleton's *Women Beware Women* (1621) almost seems like his *Chaste Maid in Cheapside* (1613) rewritten with a generic surprise at the end.[27] That this wholesale appropriation of social satire, to the exclusion of politics, risked undermining the recipient form altogether is suggested by Middleton's recourse to an unsatisfying melodramatic finale for the later play, in order to give the illusion of tragic doom to decidedly untragic characters and events. Something of the same might also be said, though with reservations, of the leading tragedies by all four dramatists. The similarities should not be overstated, however. The extremism of Middleton may be a sign of both his atypicality and the special properties of satiric intrigue tragedy. The detached, morally rigorous, and consistent perspective of *Women Beware Women* and *The Changeling* (1622, with the comic subplot by William Rowley) probably derives from Middleton's adherence to the parliamentary Puritan cause, a decidedly progressive, rather than reactionary, position.[28] Webster, moreover, does not seem unquestionably backward-looking either. Precisely because of the predominant negativity produced by satire, playwrights of opposing outlooks could employ the same form—just as opposition to Stuart policy at least temporarily united groups and classes that had little else in common. This generic linkage had an institutional basis as well. Like satiric comedy, satiric intrigue tragedy, though owing much to the private theater, was usually most successful when it had some contact with the public stage. Middleton again constitutes the major exception, but the form generally seems to have reached its apogee in the transitional era from 1609 or a little earlier to 1614.

27. T. B. Tomlinson, *A Study of Elizabethan and Jacobean Tragedy* (Cambridge, Eng., 1964), p. 158.

28. The ending of *Women Beware Women*: Robert Ornstein, *The Moral Vision of Jacobean Tragedy* (Madison, Wis., 1960), p. 179; Middleton and the Puritans: Margot Heinemann, *Puritanism and Theatre: Thomas Middleton and Opposition Drama under the Early Stuarts* (Cambridge, Eng., 1980), esp. p. 173.

In Spanish intrigue tragedy, the nearest approach to a satiric vision occurs in Tirso's ultimately unclassifiable *El burlador de Sevilla* (probably 1616–1620) and Lope's *El castigo sin venganza* (1631). The final title of Tirso's play conceals a double meaning: "de Sevilla" can refer to Don Juan's hometown, but it can also designate the victim of his "burlas." [29] In the latter sense, it points to a function of the protagonist that links him to important characters in the English tragedies. Like Webster's malcontents, for example, "el burlador" combines witty insouciance with an at times murderous immorality in such a way as to reveal the sordid reality lurking just beneath the surface of society. More generally, Tirso treats Don Juan's activities, as well as the sexual immorality and social climbing of many of the other characters, with an ironic, but scarcely tragic, detachment that may recall Middleton's technique in *Women Beware Women*. [30] Although in his concluding damnation Don Juan becomes something of a lightning rod for the sins of society, the play does not leave us with a sense that moral order has been fully restored, despite the best efforts of a good king. [31]

El castigo sin venganza is even darker in tone. Like the English tragedies, it ultimately draws on Italian sources and re-creates an Italian setting centered on the sexual corruption of the court. [32] Lope condemns his unpleasant protagonists to a claustrophobic world of passion from which they can find no escape. The sense of entrapment is in turn compounded by a pattern of self-deception. But though deeply ironic, the play is not satiric. The characters are developed with unusual psychological depth, and hence with some sympathy, and the whole is pervaded by a tragic sense. Guilty at once of incest and adultery, the doomed young lovers are aware of their wrongdoing and its inevitable consequence, but can do nothing about it.

29. Henry W. Sullivan, *Tirso de Molina and the Drama of the Counter Reformation* (Amsterdam, 1976), pp. 152–153.

30. Raymond R. MacCurdy, Introd. to *"El burlador de Sevilla y convidado de piedra" and "La prudencia en la mujer,"* by Tirso de Molina (New York, 1965), p. 19. The reference to *El burlador de Sevilla* below is to this edition and is noted in the text.

31. Edward M. Wilson and Duncan Moir, *The Golden Age: Drama 1492–1700,* vol. III of *A Literary History of Spain,* gen. ed. R. O. Jones (London, 1971), p. 90.

32. Amado Alonso, "Lope de Vega y sus fuentes," in *El teatro de Lope de Vega: Artículos y estudios,* ed. José Francisco Gatti (Buenos Aires, 1962), pp. 200–212, discusses Lope's reworking of his sources here.

In both countries, the satiric tragedies were also influenced by earlier efforts in the Italian Senecan revenge tradition. For the English playwrights, the seminal works were Kyd's *Spanish Tragedy* (1587) and, later on, Shakespeare's *Hamlet* (1601). The fullest anticipation of the characteristic Jacobean combination of satire and revenge, however, is probably to be found in *The Jew of Malta* (1589).[33] But sixteenth-century Elizabethan revenge tragedy, despite its significant popular dimension, did not completely succeed in striking roots in British soil. The final nationalization of Seneca was carried out partly by Shakespeare, of course, but also by Marston and the author of *The Revenger's Tragedy*, who accomplished this end, paradoxically enough, by setting their tales in Italy.[34] The increasing replacement of a personal by a social perspective in seventeenth-century tragedy did not usually allow for detailed scrutiny of the psychology and morality of the avenger in the manner of Kyd and Shakespeare. But revenge motifs and at times even characteristic revenge structures continued to appear, in the drama of Chapman, Webster, Middleton, and others.

Particularly in the satiric intrigues, the revenge tradition gave a specificity to social criticism by centering it on the well-established Renaissance opposition of court and country. A Senecan concern with the tyranny of the former soon gave way to a primarily social, rather than political, attack. What is repeatedly portrayed is the treacherous surrender of the feudal aristocracy, supposed guardian of medieval morality, to the forces of capitalism. As in Shakespeare's late tragedies, the absolutist state is betrayed from within—an important, if not wholly accurate, perception. But it is somewhat misleading to speak of the state at all in these plays. As the social status of the protagonists becomes increasingly incidental to their deeds, the scene shifts at least in part to the country or the city, where gentry and merchants, respectively, take the leading roles: *Women Beware Women* and Tourneur's *Atheist's Tragedy* (1609) exemplify the trend. But this democratization reflects not an ideological allegiance to capitalism, but a grim rec-

33. The most extended treatment of the subject remains Fredson Bowers, *Elizabethan Revenge Tragedy 1587–1642*, rev. ed. (Gloucester, Mass., 1959).
34. G. K. Hunter, "English Folly and Italian Vice: The Moral Landscape of John Marston," in *Jacobean Theatre*, ed. John Russell Brown and Bernard Harris, Stratford-upon-Avon Studies, no. 1 (London, 1960), pp. 91–106.

ognition of its presence. The metaphysical optimism of Tourneur's play is thus balanced by a social pessimism. Moreover, the change in social setting entails a diminution of scope: the lives of members of the capitalist classes were not yet able to typify the fate of the nation.

Usually, however, the country retains its standard connotation as the innocent antithesis of the court. *Bussy D'Ambois* opens with its main character in a green world and proceeds to assess the impact of the court on a natural man. *The Revenge of Bussy* and Marston's *Antonio's Revenge* (1600) conclude with Stoical retreats from court to monastery, the efficacy of which, however, is called into question, at least in Marston's play. In Webster's *Duchess of Malfi* (1614), even a flight from court to country cannot protect private, family experience, based on interclass marriage (III.v.18–21). *The Revenger's Tragedy* (1606), by Tourneur or Middleton, is perhaps the most interesting case. Vendice is a country gentleman come to cleanse a court whose corruption he instead succumbs to. Speaking for the gentry, he complains of the court's impoverishment of the land. His morally dubious, but ultimately successful, testing of his family thus generates a fundamental contrast between the lust and greed of the court and the chastity and poverty of the country. Given the class background of Vendice and his family, and the dynamic, if unequal, relationship established between the two social poles of the action, the reactionary ideological assumptions of *The Revenger's Tragedy*, ironically, contribute to the historically progressive formation of precisely the gentry-dominated country party that was later to overthrow the monarchy.

In Spain, of course, the revenge tradition was far weaker. But *El burlador de Sevilla* is partly indebted to Juan de la Cueva's Senecan tragicomedy, *El infamador* (1581),[35] and in the concluding act the references to "venganza" become increasingly insistent and ominous (e.g., III.2260–2267). For this very reason, the play reveals a symptomatic incongruity between human and divine justice. The benevolent monarch remains consistently in the dark about Don Juan's true conduct, busying himself with futile efforts to marry the powerful aristocrat off and thus, he hopes, maintain social stability. Only after the actual execution of divine vengeance does he call for the protagonist's death.

35. MacCurdy, pp. 14–15.

All of this is orthodox enough theologically, but it inevitably raises doubts about even the best of human institutions. Conversely, the difficulty most critics have had in finding in Don Juan's deeds sufficient cause for his damnation raises questions about divine justice. In general, the vitality of "el burlador" and the at once alarmingly and attractively anarchical challenge he represents to human and metaphysical order perhaps inadvertently transform a superficially didactic work into a tragedy that is both personal and social, one that moves, moreover, on two related but different planes.[36]

The title of *El castigo sin venganza* reveals a similar concern, although in this instance the morality of revenge is given a deeply ironic treatment. The Duke sees his concluding murder of his wife and son as "el castigo sin venganza." But his own considerable responsibility for their sins, his near-lifelong commission of the very same ones, and the covert and underhanded method by which he executes his sentence produce the opposite result, vengeance without punishment or, it may be added, justice. To preserve social appearances, to give the illusion of "el castigo sin venganza," the Duke's son "is punished for a crime he did not commit in revenge for a crime which he did." From the perspective of divine justice, however, the resolution of the plot does produce "el castigo sin venganza," not only for the Duke's wife and son, but also for the Duke himself, who must live on with the knowledge of having been responsible for the deaths of the two people about whom he most cared and thus of having deprived himself in addition of a much-desired heir to the throne.[37] In the intractable dilemma of the belatedly reformed Duke, in the slippery, often antithetical relationship between human and divine justice, in the discrepancy between intention and consequence, Lope's drama offers a critique of the state that seems to reflect as well the country's growing inability to control its own destiny.

Both Spanish plays, then, investigate the ironic interplay of revenge and justice far more deeply than do the comparable English tragedies, where the very notion of justice dispensed at court is all but unimaginable. Complementarily, the contrast between country and court does

---

36. *Ibid.,* pp. 19–21

37. R. D. F. Pring-Mill, Introd. to *Lope de Vega (Five Plays)*, trans. Jill Booty (New York, 1961), pp. xxxi–xxxv. The quoted passage appears on p. xxxiii.

not figure prominently in *El burlador de Sevilla* and *El castigo sin venganza*. In a way, Tirso's play effaces the distinction. Don Juan sexually deceives four women—first an aristocrat, then a peasant, then another aristocrat, and finally another peasant. The pattern seems more iterative than developmental. Although the two classes are not conflated, Tirso's main purpose is to emphasize the range both of Don Juan's subversiveness and of society's failings. To do so, however, it was necessary to take seriously not just the honor of the nobility, but that of the peasantry as well. The flawed conduct of the latter class could not acquire its full force unless it was seen as a deviation from that class's own ideals. Tirso's prior experience with peasant drama probably served him well. Finally, the concentration on court intrigue in *El castigo sin venganza* precludes extended concern with the country, but here, too, the antithesis is denied. The illicit passion between Federico and Casandra has its origins not in the back rooms of the palace, but in a pastoral *locus amoenus*. By 1631, it would seem both pastoral and peasantry had lost their redemptive powers, at least for Tirso and Lope.

The distance between these two plays and the comparable English works may be suggested by saying that where the Spanish characters are defective, the British ones are repellent. This is so because the satiric intrigue tragedy had a different historical function in each country. In England, its effect was mainly destructive; despite an anticapitalist outlook that even today retains a contemporary appeal, it fundamentally served to remove the remaining ideological justifications of absolutism, to clear away the detritus, as it were, of a disintegrating social system, so that another might be constructed in its place. The mission of the Spanish tragedies was in a sense more modest. With fundamental change out of the question, they could only draw attention to the crisis confronted by their nation and clarify its nature. Theirs is a more normal world, governed more firmly by traditional morality, than the one portrayed in the English plays. Hence, on the one hand, Tirso and Lope do not approach the cynicism or nihilism of the Jacobean satiric tragedians but, on the other, they are also largely denied the moments of not-quite-conscious re-creation that we have observed in Chapman and *The Revenger's Tragedy,* and that is also present in the latter part of *The Duchess of Malfi.*

Even sharper contrasts emerge from a review of romantic intrigue tragedy. In a sense, however, the comparison is inappropriate. Although the relevant plays in both countries fall mainly in the 1620s and 1630s, it will be recalled that this was in effect an earlier historical and theatrical period in Spain than in England. There is accordingly a qualitative difference between the pathetic tragedies composed for the private stage in London and the love tragedies designed for the *corrales* of Madrid.

Pathetic tragedy is an extreme version of English intrigue tragedy, recapitulating and intensifying selected features of the form. In its pure state, pathetic tragedy has no other purpose than to elicit a pitying response from its audience. Although incompatible with ideas and out of touch with serious moral and political issues, it skillfully plays with them so that they will heighten the emotional effect without acquiring any significance in the process. Beaumont and Fletcher's *Maid's Tragedy* (1610) is both the founder and most perfect representative of the form.[38] The heyday of pathetic tragedy did not come until the Caroline era, however: Ford's *Broken Heart* (1629) and Shirley's *Traitor* (1631) are leading examples. The dominant moods of such plays include aristocratic quiescence, withdrawal, indifference to life, and attraction to death.

Slightly to one side stand two other works by Ford, *'Tis Pity She's a Whore* (1632) and *Perkin Warbeck* (1633). The former, like *Women Beware Women,* sets its scene among the merchant patriciate, a class whose sordid social life provides a contrast and impediment to the protagonists' idealistic, incestuous, and doomed love. The latter is still more unusual. An English history play, it conscientiously investigates national issues, particularly through the character of Henry VII. But the protagonist of the piece is not Henry but the titular figure, a fraudulent pretender whose persistent self-delusion finally becomes a tribute to his nobility. Politically defined and damned by his lower-class following, and easily defeated by Henry, he nonetheless triumphs in the private sphere, where the pattern of devotion he engenders, cen-

38. A corroborating description may be found in John F. Danby, *Poets on Fortune's Hill: Studies in Sidney, Shakespeare, Beaumont and Fletcher* (1952; rpt. Port Washington, N.Y., 1966), pp. 152–183.

tered on his loyal wife, evokes Ford's characteristic heroic pity. Shakespearean tragedy, despite its repeated depiction of aristocratic failure,
almost always leaves open a path to the future, if not for the protagonist then at least for his society. This is hardly so in intrigue tragedy,
where the conclusion of the play signifies the end of history, the closing off of opportunities. But as *Perkin Warbeck* shows, in pathetic
tragedy not merely the future has been lost: for the protagonist, for
several of the supporting characters, and at least in part for the author
himself, the past has disappeared as well.

  Pathetic tragedy is also the form in which women came into their
own. The feminization of tragedy is discernible in Shakespeare's final
efforts with the genre, is given special impetus by *The Maid's Tragedy*,
and is unmistakable in Webster and Middleton. There is thus no absolute distinction to be made in this respect among the various kinds of
intrigue tragedy or even of tragedy in general. Behind the growing
prominence of women lay a broader emerging concern with the sex's
social position. To this extent, intrigue tragedy helped extend the
range of the genre, and its frequent depiction of the oppression of
women may be considered a humane and progressive perception. At
the same time, such an orientation was inseparable from the abandonment of politics and a consequent reduction of scope. But women became uniquely functional even in intrigue tragedy only with the full
exploitation of the helpless victimization and sentimental appeal that
are characteristic of pathetic tragedy.

  With these contradictory implications in mind, it may be possible to
evaluate the ongoing concern with the decadence of Jacobean and
Caroline tragedy. The charge is often extended back to Marston and
sweepingly made to include virtually all of his successors. Here, we
may limit the investigation to the more restricted compass where the
case is strongest, to the plays of the pathetic tragedians. Although
Caroline tragedy at times displays a hostility to both the court and the
bourgeoisie, it lacks the aggressive destructiveness that is one of the
most distinctive and distinguished qualities of the generally earlier satiric intrigue tragedies. It is aimed not at another class, but at its own,
the nobility. Pathetic tragedy enables us to imagine how a class feels
when it senses that it no longer has a social function, that history has
passed it by. The substitution of nobility of sentiment for a larger coherence of meaning that is no longer available is not an expression of

universal truth, but an act of accommodation by a class that has lost its hegemony. Ironically, however, in this fashion pathetic tragedy unwittingly serves the progressive purpose of reconciling one sector of the aristocracy to its own supersession. The special prominence it accords to women likewise undermines the ostensible intention of the form. Even female characters of the highest social birth rarely have available to them the ordinary power and freedom of their class: their sex systematically reduces their status. The women of pathetic tragedy thus mark an initial break with a class-based conception of tragedy. In these ways, then, the form contradictorily retains not just a historical and theoretical interest, but a human plausibility and social significance as well.

Spanish love tragedies such as Lope's *El caballero de Olmedo* (1620?) and Luis Vélez de Guevara's *Reinar después de morir* (by 1644) share with pathetic tragedy, and especially with Ford's plays, a sense of fated defeat, of doom combined with a preoccupation with private life scarcely obscured by a superficial interest in affairs of state. But these two works, and especially Lope's, are really much closer in spirit to *Romeo and Juliet* (1595) and Lope's own *El marqués de Mantua* (1596), and thus to a tradition of tragedy with deep affinities to romantic comedy: *El caballero de Olmedo* has even been faulted for the excessively comic tone of its first two acts.[39] To the extent that either drama is not understood in these terms, both its emotional force and its ideological significance are lost. The relatively recent tendency to view Lope's play as a tragedy of moral failing and deserved retribution seems to have given way to a far more defensible and traditional insistence on the innocence of the protagonist in a just and divinely ordered, but nonetheless inscrutable, universe.[40] Inés de Castro, the heroine of *Reinar después de morir,* has remained free of any comparable suspicions of misconduct, but the play may seem at least as concerned to attack *Realpolitik* as it is to celebrate love. In fact, the political issue is suppressed. Only the king even feels a conflict between

39. See Wilson and Moir, p. 67, who reject the charge.

40. The claim that the hero is justly punished is made by A. A. Parker, "The Approach to the Spanish Drama of the Golden Age," *TDR*, IV (1959), 46–48. The counterposition is argued by Willard F. King, Introd. to her edition and translation of *The Knight of Olmedo (El caballero de Olmedo),* by Lope de Vega (Lincoln, Neb., 1972), pp. xi–xxvii.

private morality and reasons of state. His son and heir, who is also
Inés's lover, must not, or else the purity of his love would be compromised. In general, moreover, national problems cannot be too strongly developed; otherwise, the audience would share the king's dilemma. Vélez makes certain that we respond exclusively to the lovers'
predicament, however.

What assumptions underlie the dramatization of a tragic destiny?
Like much other Renaissance drama, both plays appropriate bourgeois
values to serve aristocratic ends. Here, the crucial borrowing is marriage for love, with all its attendant idealism. In the name of this principle, *Reinar después de morir* rejects the class-conscious condescension of Inés's more nobly born rival. Vélez would appear to be on
more traditional aristocratic terrain in his attack on the king and his
privados, and in his antithetical praise of the country. Yet the pattern
is complicated by linking the country to domesticity and family life.
Finally, as in *El caballero de Olmedo,* the central love relationship is
expressed in courtly, Petrarchan terms.

The feudal dimension of Lope's play is much less ambiguous and the
tragic irony of its crisis correspondingly more social in resonance. The
chivalric valor that brings Don Alonso fame also leads him to his
death. Although he is frightened by a supernatural warning in the form
of a popular refrain, his feudal code forces him to press on. A matchless swordsman like Bussy D'Ambois, he, too, is murdered by gunshot,
military symbol of the supersession of medieval aristocratic warfare.[41]
The repetition of the portentous refrain earlier in the play develops a
feudal perspective in another way as well, by producing a double vision. On the one hand, most of the time the audience is emotionally involved in the sequence of events unfolding before it in the present; on
the other, the refrain invites it to distance itself from the action, to
view with at least historical detachment a tragedy set in the romantic,
glamorous, but irrecoverably past early fifteenth century. In this way,
El caballero de Olmedo simultaneously celebrates feudalism and intuits its inevitable demise, conceiving of the latter as part of a divine plan
whose meaning remains hidden from seventeenth-century Spaniards.
In common with *Reinar después de morir,* its dominant mood is one
of loss, although the later tragedy, its title notwithstanding, does not

41. Stone, *Crisis,* p. 243.

offer even enigmatic metaphysical consolation. Finally, despite the far more peripheral role of politics in Lope's play than in Vélez's, *El caballero de Olmedo* reveals a surer grasp of historical process, and one, it may be added, that is not really equaled in pathetic tragedy, even by *Perkin Warbeck.*

IV

Golden Age drama is often denied the status of tragedy, although recent decades have seen something of a reversal of this attitude.[42] Certainly there was less tragedy than in England, largely, it would seem, because the relative absence of a conflict between modes of production reduced the ideological space for the genre. On the other hand, if Shakespeare is excluded from consideration, it is possible to argue seriously that during the seventeenth century the *corrales* of Madrid surpassed the London theaters, public and private, not only in serious drama in general—which could include heroic, peasant, and religious plays—but in the narrower field of tragedy as well.

The comparison between England and Spain may also serve a simultaneously broader and narrower purpose. Throughout Western Europe during the sixteenth and seventeenth centuries, intrigue tragedy's characteristic combination of depoliticization and moral uncertainty represented a response to a crisis in the state. The predominance of a relatively unsuccessful form of intrigue tragedy in most of sixteenth-century Italy ultimately testifies to the absence of an indigenous absolutism, to the lack of a political organization that could be the object of serious dramatic reflection.[43] In France, the movement from Cor-

42. Defenses of Spanish tragedy include Edwin S. Morby, "Some Observations on 'Tragedia' and 'Tragicomedia' in Lope," *Hispanic Review,* XI (1943), 185–209; Parker, "Towards a Definition of Calderonian Tragedy," *Bulletin of Hispanic Studies,* xxxix (1962), 227–237; and A. Irvine Watson, "*El pintor de su deshonra* and the Neo-Aristotelian Theory of Tragedy," in *Critical Essays on the Theatre of Calderón,* ed. Bruce W. Wardropper (New York, 1965), pp. 203–223.

43. Hunter, "Italian Tragicomedy on the English Stage," *RenD,* N. S. VI (1973), 130–131, suggests that Italian tragedy failed to interest the Elizabethans because its protagonists, however exalted, are involved with personal passions that lack political and social resonance.

neille's heroic drama to Racine's tragedies of private experience, pessimism, and moral relativism can be connected to the changing relations between nobility and monarchy, and in particular to the latter's definitive suppression of the Fronde and with it of centuries of aristocratic political independence.[44] Similarly, the late-seventeenth-century pathetic tragedies of Dryden, Lee, Otway, and their successors, following hard upon more than a decade of heroic drama, constitute a belated, disillusioned realization that the Restoration of the monarchy in 1660, with the attendant return of the Cavaliers, did not involve a true restoration of an absolutist state or a neofeudal nobility.[45] In all three instances, the audience for intrigue tragedy was dominated culturally, if not always numerically, by the crown and aristocracy. Unlike the tragedies of Shakespeare or the peasant plays of Lope de Vega, then, English and Spanish intrigue tragedy of the early seventeenth century belonged to a broadly international generic movement. The triumph of the form in London and Madrid accordingly signaled the end of the unique theatrical development that served as our point of departure.

44. See especially Lucien Goldmann, *The Hidden God: A Study of Tragic Vision in the "Pensées" of Pascal and the Tragedies of Racine,* trans. Philip Thody (London; 1964), pp. 103–141.

45. Laura Brown, *English Dramatic Form, 1660–1760: An Essay in Generic History* (New Haven, Conn., 1981), chap. 3.

Massinger's The City Madam and the Caroline Audience

MARTIN BUTLER

I N HIS SEMINAL STUDY *Drama and Society in the Age of Jonson* (1937), L. C. Knights represented Jacobean and Caroline "city comedy" as the reaction of a society with a deeply rooted conservative world-view to the changes and new economic forces that threatened to overturn all its old hierarchies of social degree and moral value, a pattern which would seem to be epitomized by Massinger's *The City Madam*. The downfall of Massinger's avaricious citizen Luke Frugal and the humiliation of Luke's proud sister-in-law and her daughters provoke the quasi-authorial moral that there should be "In their habits, manners, and their highest port, / A distance 'twixt the city and the court" (V.iii.154–55),[1] and most critics agree to find in Luke and Lady Frugal "representatives of the early Stuart trading class whose hunger for financial power and social prestige is, Massinger feels, endangering the social integrity of the upper class—the aristocracy and minor gentry which form the basis of traditional society."[2] Massinger shows this traditional society avenging itself on those who defy

I am grateful to the British Academy for a "Thank-Offering to Britain" Research Fellowship that has enabled me to research and write this paper.

1. All references are to the text edited by Colin Gibson in *The Selected Plays of Philip Massinger* (Cambridge, Eng., 1978).

2. A. G. Gross, "Social Change and Philip Massinger," *SEL*, VII (1967), 330.

its norms, and at the close "the framework of the hereditary class system is reasserted" while Luke Frugal "is rendered ineffectual and Sir John and his wife repent."[3] *The City Madam* is the anti-acquisitive play *par excellence*.

However, there is also a widely held feeling that city comedy's inherent conservatism represents a *failure* to come to terms with social change, that Massinger was on the wrong side of a historical process which within a decade would render any attempt to keep the city in its place absurdly irrelevant, and that the quality of his insight was unequal to his situation. One writer, noting a split in the play between the "characters of the trading class whose ambitions were very much part of the social world to which they belong" and Massinger's "traditional, Christian analysis of the difficulties these ambitions create," describes his "fear and hatred" of these developments as "definite impediments to his understanding."[4] Another, more crudely, describes this as merely "the distaste of the son of an old retainer family for the vulgar bourgeois."[5] To put it another way, Massinger wrote as the servant of the fashionable and exclusive Caroline audience, and could only be horrified by the forces that would eventually destroy the court's social and political hegemony, but his arguments exerted no authority in the intractable "real" world outside the playhouse from which the conditions that enabled both court and theater to exist would soon disappear. As M. C. Bradbrook says, in the heady Blackfriars milieu of 1632—one "increasingly alienated from the city"—Massinger would "find no audience among citizens."[6] The play's narrowness was dictated by the environment for which it was written.

If *The City Madam* really was as "decadent" as this, a "rearguard action on behalf of . . . a decaying or collapsing culture,"[7] it would be an interesting social document but no more. I wish to defend Massinger's intelligence and show that his play is much more "open" than the simplified formula "court versus city" suggests. We may begin by questioning this

    3. *Ibid.*, pp. 338, 340.
    4. *Ibid.*, pp. 330, 331–332.
    5. R. A. Fothergill, "The Dramatic Experience of Massinger's *The City Madam* and *A New Way to Pay Old Debts*," *UTQ*, XLIII (1973), 74.
    6. *The Living Monument* (Cambridge, Eng., 1976), p. 102.
    7. Terms borrowed from J. P. Danby, *Elizabethan and Jacobean Poets*, 2d ed. (London, 1965), pp. 181–182.

traditional picture of the play's audience as inherently prejudiced, by its
elitist social composition, against the city and toward the court.

I

Colin Gibson[8] has paralleled Sir John Frugal's career with that of Sir
William Cokayne, an erstwhile apprentice of the Skinners' Company who
rose to become alderman, sheriff and Lord Mayor of London (1619), the
governor of the London companies' Ulster colony (1612), and, through
trading ventures with the Eastland Company and the East India Company,
one of the richest citizens of his day. He was a prominent example of
citizen stock moving into the nobility, earning a knighthood, and gaining
aristocratic promotion for his son, Viscount Cullen (1642), and daughters.
What Gibson overlooks is that Cokayne was related to at least one well-
known theatergoer. Sir Aston Cokayne, author of three plays and friend of
many dramatists, including Massinger (for whom he supplied commenda-
tory verses), belonged to a Derbyshire gentry family representing the elder
branch of the stock from which Sir William descended.[9] The connection
was fairly remote; nevertheless, Sir Aston's *Chain of Golden Poems* (London,
1658) includes an epigram to *"the Lady* Mary Cokaine, *Viscountess* Cullen,"
Sir William's daughter-in-law (p. 186). Moreover, Sir William's widow,
herself the daughter of a Master of the Ironmongers' Company, remarried
Henry, Earl of Dover, for whom Thomas Heywood wrote private theatrical pieces in the 1630s. Dover's son, Viscount Rochford, who in 1630
married his own stepsister, Abigail Cokayne, was the dedicatee of
Nathaniel Richards's tragedy *Messallina* (1640).[10]

Such links between wealthy citizenry and theatergoing circles were by
no means exceptional, as may be illustrated in the city connections which
would be taken for granted by the Essex gentleman and diarist Sir

8. "Massinger's London Merchant and the Date of *The City Madam*," *MLR*, LXV
(1970), 737–749.

9. "Pedigrees Contained in the Visitations of Derbyshire 1569 and 1611," *The
Genealogist*, N.S. VII (1891), 70–72; G. E. Bentley, *The Jacobean and Caroline Stage*, 7 vols.
(Oxford, 1941–1968), III, 166–167.

10. G. E. Cokayne, *Some Account of the Lord Mayors and Sheriffs of the City of London
During the First Quarter of the Seventeenth Century* (London, 1897), pp. 83–89; T. Heywood,
Pleasant Dialogues and Dramas (London, 1637; dedicated to Dover), pp. 242–247.

Humphrey Mildmay, who in several ways was a representative Caroline playgoer.[11]One companion Mildmay took to the theater was his brother-in-law Sir Christopher Abdy, the son of a lawyer, but also a member of a leading London merchant family governing the Clothworkers' Company. Sir Christopher's uncle Anthony was Master of the Clothworkers (1632), an alderman and sheriff, and held high office in the East India Company, Levant Company, and Virginia Company.[12] The Abdys were rising to county importance in Essex, and had commercial and blood ties with other powerful city dynasties. Sir Christopher's aunt came of the wealthy Cambell family. Her father and brother were both lord mayors; the former founded a charity school, and the latter, Sir James Cambell, was colonel of the trained bands and president of St. Thomas's Hospital (1629–1642). An ironmonger, he had interests in the East India Company, the French Company, and the Merchants of the Staple, and left £50,000 in charitable bequests in his will. Another brother was sheriff (1630) and father of a baronet.[13] A cousin of Sir Christopher matched into another distinguished city family, the Soames. His wife's grandfather, an Elizabethan lord mayor, died worth £46,000; her father, Thomas Soames, traded with India, Russia, the Adriatic, and the Levant, was sheriff (1635) and colonel of the trained bands. In 1640 he was elected MP for the city on the radical platform.[14] He has particular interest for us since it was to him that the playwright Nathaniel Richards dedicated his *Poems Sacred and Satirical* (1641).

Another brother-in-law of Humphrey Mildmay was John Bennet, himself the father of Henry Bennet who wrote verses for Killigrew's *Prisoners and Claracilla* (1640). John Bennet was the son of a diplomat, but also an offshoot of citizen stock. His great-uncle, Sir Thomas, a mercer, was an alderman until his death (1627), and had been lord mayor (1603). He was governor of the Irish Society, and as president of Bridewell and

11. See Bentley, *Jacobean and Caroline Stage*, II, 673–681, for Mildmay's diary.

12. *Publications of the Harleian Society*, XIV, 627; V. Pearl, *London and the Outbreak of the Puritan Revolution* (Oxford, 1961), pp. 288–289; G. E. Cokayne, *Complete Baronetage*, 5 vols. (Exeter, 1900–1906), II, 98; III, 34, 55.

13. Pearl, *London and . . . Revolution*, pp. 294–295; Cokayne, *Some Account of the Lord Mayors*, pp. 41–45.

14. Pearl, *London and . . . Revolution*, pp. 191–192; Cokayne, *Complete Baronetage*, II, 98.

Bethlem Hospital he controlled two of the best-known city institutions; his son was raised to a baronetcy.[15] His second son, an alderman and mercer, died in 1626 leaving a widow reputedly worth £20,000; her suitors in 1628–1629 included Sir Edward Dering, a regular visitor to the London theaters.[16] Bulstrode Whitelocke, a face so familiar in the Black-friars that the coranto he composed for Shirley's *Triumph of Peace* (1634) was played whenever he "came to that house (as I did sometimes in those dayes)," married the daughter of another Thomas Bennet, Mildmay's brother-in-law's uncle, also an alderman and sheriff (1619). A second daughter married Sir Gamaliell Capell, cousin to Mildmay on his mother's side.[17] Finally, another Bennet widow married Sir Thomas Shirley, father of Henry Shirley the dramatist (d. 1627); the same match made her aunt to Jane Crofts, newly the wife of Sir Humphrey Mildmay.[18]

Mildmay had connections with two other city families. In 1635 he accompanied to a masque Joan, wife of Sir John Coke, secretary of state. Her father was Sir Robert Lee, merchant tailor and former mayor (1602), who had interests in the Levant company; her first husband, William Gore, had been sheriff (1615) and died in 1624 on the point of becoming mayor.[19] Finally, Mildmay's brother Sir Henry Mildmay, a courtier and Master of the Jewel House, married in 1619 a daughter of Alderman Halliday, mercer, sheriff (1617), and chairman of the East India Company. On his marriage King James gave Mildmay "as they say, two manors worth £12,000, to make his estate somewhat proportionate to his wife's." Her mother, also the daughter of a mayor, married after the alderman's death Robert Rich, the puritan Earl of Warwick.[20]

15. V. Barbour, *Henry Bennet, Earl of Arlington* (London, 1914), pp. 1–4 (this confuses Sir Thomas with his nephew, Thomas); Cokayne, *Some Account of the Lord Mayors*, pp. 16–18, 65–67.

16. L. B. Larking, *Proceedings, Principally in the County of Kent* (London, 1862), pp. xiv-xxxiii; M.A.E. Green (ed.), *The Diary of John Rous* (London, 1866), p. 34; T.N.S. Lennam, "Sir Edward Dering's Collection of Playbooks," *SQ*, XVI (1965), 145–153.

17. Bentley, *Jacobean and Caroline Stage*, I, 40; Cokayne, *Some Account of the Lord Mayors*, pp. 65–67; *Publications of the Harleian Society*, XIII (1878), 32, 171.

18. E. P. Shirley, *Stemmata Shirleiana*, 2d ed. (London, 1873), pp. 235, 271.

19. Cokayne, *Some Account of the Lord Mayors*, pp. 12–15, 73–74.

20. T. Birch, *The Court and Times of James I* (London, 1849), II, 152; Cokayne, *Some Account of the Lord Mayors*, pp. 78–80.

These families were among the city's elite, immensely powerful, and influential dynasties that controlled the livery companies, constituted the aldermanic bench, and, as the people most extensively engaged in commerce, dominated the great trading organizations. Often they were men of deep Puritan conviction; Thomas Soames, for example, entered parliament as a fierce court opponent, and Sir James Cambell held "earnest and zealous prayer with his family all the dayes of the weeke."[21] With the Abdys, Cambells, Soameses, and Bennets, we are in the heart of London's big business world.

II

It has long been recognized that the small citizen was a minor quantity in the audience of the Caroline "private" theaters. Jonson's *Magnetic Lady* (Blackfriars, 1632) scorns "the [faeces], or grounds of your people, that sit in the oblique caves and wedges of your house, your sinfull sixe-penny Mechanicks";[22] in the praeludium to Goffe's *Careless Shepherdess* (Salisbury Court, 1638) the citizen, Thrift, leaves for a less fashionable theater; Henry Peacham's *Art of Living in London* (1642) includes a cautionary fable about gallants taking advantage of a citizen's wife who sat in a playhouse box.[23] But it is clear from my evidence that the theaters' fashionable tone did not mean that they had lost contact with the city and that the greater citizenry, the "acquisitive" classes whose families were rising to supply the ranks of the aristocracy, were excluded from the audience. Massinger would have expected a not insubstantial proportion of his Blackfriars audience of 1632 to have had close links with, or even to have been, people who would consider themselves more "city" than "court." Indeed, one of his own patrons had married the daughter of a lord mayor.[24]

21. E. Browne, *A Rare Pattern of Justice and Mercy* (London, 1642), p. 38; cf. Pearl, *London and . . . Revolution*, pp. 191–192.

22. In *The Works of Benjamin Jonson, The Second Volume* (London, 1640), pp. 5–6.

23. The presence of small citizens is suggested by the prologue to Davenant's *Platonic Lovers* (Blackfriars, 1635), which says that "'Bove half our City audience would be lost, / That knew not how to spell [the play's title] on the post." *The Works of Sir William Davenant* (London, 1673), p. 384; the Blackfriars prologue to Habington's *The Queen of Aragon* (London, 1640), which mentions the presence of "wife of Citizen" in the audience (sig. A2ᵛ); and the epilogue to Brome's *Court Beggar* (Phoenix, 1640), which addresses ladies, knights, citizens, and country gentry in turn.

We must not read the real feeling of class antagonism between gentleman and Cheapside shopkeeper that we find in the lower-class Jacobean comedies of (say) Middleton onto the world of Massinger, but allow for the greater ease with which interaction occurred between the gentry and the more established commercial families in the Caroline period. These aldermanic families were respected businessmen whose affairs involved continual contact with the theatergoing gentry class and drew them into dependence on the crown rather than into opposition to it. They needed commercial privileges and protection which only the king could grant; conversely, the government needed their specialist business expertise, and many magnates became trusted intermediaries between Whitehall and the city. [25] Their interests harmonized with those of the gentry; as city fathers, they held positions carrying great trust and prestige. Their life-style was gentlemanly. One merchant family in the 1630s visited the court at Greenwich, played bowls, viewed the king's flagship, feasted daily "with thir relations and acquentance, which were then many in London," and made an entertainment on their Hertfordshire estate for

the Earl of Salisbury and his Countesse, the Lord Cranborne his son, with the rest of his sons and daughters, and the Lord Norris, and several other persons of honor, where thir was all varieties that England could afford, for viands and severall sorts of wines, and cost, as I was informed, one hundreth and fortie pounds. [26]

Before one could become an alderman, a property qualification of £10,000 was required; a sheriff or mayor might disburse £4,000 in expenses of office. [27]

Moreover, it was quite normal for younger sons of gentry families to be apprenticed into trade. In a mock petition of 1641 the London apprentices claimed their "blouds are mingled with the Nobility, although it were our fortune to be younger brothers." [28] Sons of gentlemen constituted 15 percent of those apprenticed in London in the years 1630–1660; the

24. See D. S. Lawless, "Sir Warham St. Leger," *N&Q*, CCXXIV (1979), 411–412.

25. For example, Anthony Abdy (Pearl, *London and . . . Revolution*, p. 288). See also R. Ashton, *The City and the Court 1603–1643* (Cambridge, Eng., 1979), pp. 2, 12, 28.

26. R. Davies (ed.), *The Life of Marmaduke Rawdon* (London, 1863), pp. 24–25.

27. R. G. Lang, "Social Origins and Aspirations of Jacobean London Merchants," *Economic History Review*, XXVII (1974), 44–45.

28. *The Petition of the Women of Middlesex* (London, 1641), sig. A4^r.

Oxindens, a Kent family of similar status to that of Sir Edward Dering, had two sons apprenticed in the 1620s and 1630s.[29] Sir John Frugal's apprentices are explicitly described as gentlemen's sons ("Are you gentlemen-born, yet have no gallant tincture of gentry in you?" [II.i.51]). Critics have treated them simply as citizens[30] or as evidence of the gentry's decline at the hands of citizen affluence,[31] but they reflect a quite ordinary form of interaction between the two classes.

So the interpretation of the play as consistently anti-citizen is tricky, and we must carefully distinguish the sort of citizen the Frugals represent. Firstly, to discriminate between Jacobean and Caroline city comedy, Sir John Frugal is not the small Cheapside tradesman of Middleton's plays (for example), but offers huge dowries for his daughters (II.ii.1), and his business is all on the Exchange (I.iii.114). His apprentices "are no mechanics, / Nor serve some needy shopkeeper, who surveys / His everyday takings" (II.i.52–54), but clerks and factors. Sir John has indeed risen, but the details are deliberately left vague, and curiously little sense of the actual *acquisition* of status surrounds him. He rose through his "industry" (I.iii.50, IV.iv.71), necessitated because his inheritance was passed over in favor of Luke, who dissipated it (I.iii.138)—it is as though he has, so to speak, regained his status. This is in striking contrast with, for example, Dekker's *Shoemaker's Holiday*, in which Simon Eyre is a fellow of shoemakers even when lord mayor. There is a real dynamic emphasis on Eyre's achievement of new rank, emphasized by a strong feeling of social (and moral) dislocation when he semi-legally "borrows" an aldermanic robe to clinch the business deal that makes his fortune. Whereas Simon Eyre climbs to high status, Sir John seems to be entitled to it.

Secondly, to adopt Robert Ashton's distinction between those businessmen "whose interests were confined to orthodox commodity trade, and those who dabbled extensively in domestic concessions, such as customs farms, licenses and patents of monopoly,"[32] Sir John has no domestic

29. S. R. Smith, "The Social and Geographical Origins of the London Apprentices," *The Guildhall Miscellany*, IV (1973), 199. D. Gardiner (ed.), *The Oxinden Letters 1607–1642* (London, 1933), pp. 39–42, 189–190.

30. See, e.g., Gibson's note on V.ii.6.

31. See, e.g., Gross, "Social Change and Philip Massinger," p. 333.

32. *The City and the Court*, p. 28; cf. pp. 16–28.

concessionary interests. Concessionaires established intimate—occasionally spectacular—relationships with the court by acting, usually in association with favored courtiers, as the operators of the crown's economic controls, implementing government economic policy while exploiting to their private profit fiscal devices or privileges which the crown rented or granted as rewards to them. It is just this distinction that separates Sir William Cokayne from the other citizens I have mentioned, for he held a large variety of concessions from the crown. He was purveyor to the English forces in Ireland, belonged to a syndicate renting (for £150,000 a year) the Great Farm of Customs, held a monopoly for the transportation of tin, and had money out on loan to the king. He also promoted the infamous King's Merchant Adventurers' Company (1614), a scheme to profit the king and stimulate the dyeing industry, but also designed to enable Cokayne and his fellow racketeers to take over the privileges of the cloth trade. This collapsed disastrously, plunging the cloth industry into a huge depression, and earning Cokayne great opprobrium.[33] Cokayne was wholly a creature of the crown, and it is this sort of courtly monopolist, capitalizing for a huge personal return on government favors, that Massinger attacked violently in *A New Way to Pay Old Debts*.[34] *A New Way* and *The City Madam* are often treated as if they made the same points, but Sir John Frugal's activities are delineated as wholly regular and carefully distinguished from such notorious preferential enterprises.

Sir John is presented primarily as a merchant trading to India and the East; the Red Indians also link him with ventures to America.[35] Secondarily, he is a usurer dealing with the nobility and smaller citizens. These were operations characteristic of men like the Abdys, Bennets, and Cambells, large magnates with considerable reserves of capital to manipulate, who were engaged in commerce, in the widest sense, rather than in

---

33. Gibson, "Massinger's London merchant," pp. 740–742; F. C. Dietz, *English Public Finance 1559–1641*, 2d ed. (London, 1964), pp. 159, 334; J. F. Wadmore, *Some Account of the Worshipful Company of Skinners* (London, 1902), p. 173; Ashton, *The City and the Court*, pp. 105–106; M. Prestwich, *Cranfield: Politics and Profits under the Early Stuarts* (Oxford, 1976), pp. 113, 163–170.

34. Based on the activities of Buckingham's client, Sir Giles Mompesson.

35. Cf. I.i.20, II.i.70–72.

manufacture.[36] Less is said of Sir John's participation in the administrative side of civic life. However, the question of the serious commitment of the city fathers to the maintenance of social and moral discipline is raised fairly explicitly in the scene in which the rebel apprentices so to speak re-enroll in the service of Luke, the anti-type of the good master ("We'll break my master to make you," one says [II.i.139]), and in the brothel scene (III.i) in which representatives of municipal coercion, the magistrate and constable, are ironically transformed into a libertine and musicians. Similarly, the list of "services and duties" (II.ii.99) that Frugal's daughters make for their suitors, usually regarded as an anticipation of Restoration "bargain scenes," is perhaps more appropriately interpreted as a mock indenture, another inversion of civic authority (Sir Maurice refers to Anne's conditions as "my apprenticeship" [II.ii.102]). In general, the context of *The City Madam* is aldermanic. Sir John is expected to "wear scarlet" (I.ii.143) and when Luke comes into wealth his debtors

> see Lord Mayor written on his forehead;
> The cap of maintenance, and city sword
> Borne up in state before him.
>
> (IV.i.70–72)

III

In view of the usual opinions about *The City Madam*, it cannot be emphasized enough that this picture of the world of a great citizen is painted in considerable detail and is largely sympathetic. It is difficult to maintain the view that this is an anti-citizen play when we consider the dignity in which Massinger invests Sir John Frugal. Tradewell's first description of him strikes the dominant note:

> 'Tis great pity
> Such a gentlemen as my master (*for that title*
> *His being a citizen cannot take from him*)
> Hath no male heir to inherit his estate,
> And keep his name alive.
>
> (I.i.11–15; emphasis mine)

36. Cf. Ashton, *The City and the Court*, p. 39.

So it is stressed at the outset that being in trade makes Sir John no less a gentleman, and two acts later Lord Lacy calls him "noble" in a eulogy of his character:

> 　　　　　　　　　The noble merchant
> Who living was for his integrity
> And upright dealing (a rare miracle
> In a rich citizen) London's best honour . . .
>
> 　　　　　　　　　　　　　　　(III.ii.39–42)

Sir John's first appearance, issuing from his house to intervene in the brawl between the suitors, is calculated to reinforce this impression:

> Beat down their weapons! My gate Ruffians' Hall?
> What insolence is this? . . .
> 　　　　　　　　　　If you proceed thus
> I must make use of the next justice's power,
> And leave persuasion, and in plain terms tell you
> *Enter LADY {FRUGAL}, ANNE, MARY, and MILLISCENT*
> Neither your birth, Sir Maurice, nor your wealth,
> Shall privilege this riot. See whom you have drawn
> To be spectators of it! Can you imagine
> It can stand with the credit of my daughters
> To be the argument of your swords? I'th'street too?
>
> 　　　　　　　　　　　　　　(I.ii.76–93)

The distant echo of *Othello* ("Look if my gentle love be not rais'd up!") is appropriate. Sir John, restoring civil order and admonishing the suitors to preserve self-respect, has here an authority which stays with him throughout the play. He is the peacemaker, the responsible citizen, commanding courtier and country gentleman alike, and consorting on equal terms with Lord Lacy. Although his household is disordered, the play charts his personal[37] plan to regulate it, and the final scene endorses his precedence utterly.

　　Similarly, his business procedures establish him as a prototype for imitation. Luke, admitting that Sir John, as "a citizen . . . would increase his heap, and will not lose / What the law gives him" (I.ii.140–

---

37. Cf. II.iii.1–6.

142), still denies reports that in "the acquistion of his wealth he weighs not / Whose ruin he builds upon" (I.ii.138–139). The following scene shows Sir John collecting his debts with a conscience. He is severe but just toward his debtors, having nothing but contempt for "drones" like Hoist who game and "keep ordinaries, / And a livery punk, or so" (I.iii.13, 7), for an "infidel" like Penury who neglects his family's welfare (I.iii.19), and for the prodigal speculation of Fortune. Nevertheless, at Luke's entreaty, he forbears with them, even though if publicly known it would harm his business prospects. Luke sums up the character of his dealing:

> the distinction
> And noble difference by which you are
> Divided from 'em [other traders], is that you are styl'd
> Gentle in your abundance, good in plenty,
> And that you feel compassion in your bowels
> Of others' miseries (I have found it, sir,
> Heaven keep me thankful for't), while they are curs'd
> As rigid and inexorable . . .
>
> (I.iii.55–62)

Sir John's "affability and mildness" will gain him his debtors' thanks and providential reward (I.iii.64–68, 101–106). Related to mercy in usury is the depiction of Luke as the profligate redeemed from prison:

> I am a freeman, all my debts discharg'd,
> Nor does one creditor undone by me
> Curse my loose riots. I have meat and clothes,
> Time to ask heaven remission for what's past.
> Cares of the world by me are laid aside,
> My present poverty's a blessing to me;
> And though I have been long, I dare not say
> I ever liv'd till now.
>
> (I.ii.127–134)

Although this action was the natural duty of brother to brother, Luke's pious tone (making it a spiritual, as much as an economic redemption) invites us to connect it with the wide range of charitable and religious activities to which puritan businessmen were known to be deeply committed. This can be illustrated from a contemporary eulogy on Sir James Cambell which presents him as "a rare example of Justice moderated by

Mercy."[38] Cambell's business and administrative acumen went hand in hand with his zeal for practical godliness. Though reputed, like Frugal, "a neere, austere and hard man," he was directed by human tenderness:

He was so farre from oppressing any with tedious suits in law, that to my knowledge during the time that I lived with him, he was very unwilling that any should bee cast into prison at his suit, and would rather agree upon a small composition, then take the rigour of the Law against any, though he lost thereby. For I doe not remember that he caused above one or two to be arrested, though he hath had many bad debtors, as his Executors shall find.[39]

Cambell's upright dealing, severe yet humane, followed God's way, for he too is a hard master who expects a just account. At his death the fruits of a just life were reaped, for he was blessed with profits to husband "for the glory of God, and good of others."[40] There follows a long list of his vast bequests, for the sick, the poor, the enslaved, the imprisoned (like Luke), and for public works, cheap loans, and city institutions.[41] It is in relation to such a nexus of thrift and conscience that I believe we are intended to read Sir John Frugal's character.

The first act, then, establishes a strong positive, the representative of which is the citizen and gentleman, Sir John Frugal. Equally, its antithesis is stated in citizen terms. Luke Frugal's behavior—swindling his master and encouraging his apprentices to debauchery and falsification of the accounts (II.i.45–56, 66–67)—is wholly abhorrent from the perspective of the merchant and of the sheriff who shuts down the brothel. Furthermore, although the play principally attacks proud city dames, it by no means refrains from criticizing the court. The scene that establishes Sir John's authority also shows Sir Maurice Lacy, the lord's son, put down by Plenty, the country gentleman, with a satire on the penury of the aristocracy and their neglect of their social responsibilities for the sake of following fashions:

38. Browne, *A Rare Pattern of Justice and Mercy*, p. 37.
39. *Ibid.*, pp. 42–43.
40. *Ibid.*, pp. 44, 66.
41. The whole will is printed in J. Nicholl, *Some Account of the Worshipful Company of Ironmongers*, 2d ed. (London, 1866), pp. 539–542. As well as sums for members of the Abdy family, it includes typically Puritan bequests to lecturers and silenced clergy.

> Though I keep men, I fight not with their fingers,
> Nor make it my religion to follow
> The gallant's fashion, to have my family
> Consisting in a footman, and a page,
> And those two sometimes hungry. I can feed these,
> And clothe 'em too, my gay sir . . .
>   . . . my clothes are paid for
> As soon as put on, a sin your man of title
> Is seldom guilty of, but heaven forgive it.
> I have other faults, too, very incident
> To a plain gentleman. I eat my venison
> With my neighbours in the country, and present not
> My pheasants, partridges, and grouse to the usurer . . .
> I can make my wife a jointure of such lands, too,
> As are not encumber'd, no annuity
> Or statute lying on 'em.
>
>   (I.ii.38–60)

Sir Maurice can only reply with a stale jest about country upstarts, and after their abortive duel, Plenty remains on the offensive against courtly complimenting:

> SIR MAURICE [to ANNE]
>   May I have the honour
> To support you, lady?
>   PLENTY [to MARY]
>   I know not what's supporting,
> But by this fair hand, glove and all, I love you.
>   (I.ii.101–103)

Lord Lacy comes off no better. He is principally a foil to Sir John with whom he disagrees concerning Luke's true nature, and, of course, he is proved spectacularly wrong. There is fine comedy in the scene in which he gives Luke the countinghouse keys, admonishing him to "make good the opinion I held of you, / Of which I am most confident," and exclaiming, "Honest soul, / With what feeling he receives it" (III.ii.105, 121). His disabusal is swift and hilarious, leaving him incredulous as the hitherto deferential Luke makes promises of unparalleled pomp to the women.[42] It

42. In this the audience is superior to Lacy, having been alerted to Luke's true nature in II.ii, and possibly as early as I.i.135.

is notable that the formula about keeping decorum between court and city first occurs in Lacy's mouth in this wholly ironic context (III.ii.152); such easy moralizing is speedily deflated. The rest of the play sees Lacy apologizing for his error (even in his final line), and in the penultimate scene he is totally speechless as his erstwhile protégé suddenly turns on him for the recovery of overdue debts:

> I find in my counting house a manor pawn'd;
> Pawn'd my good lord, Lacy Manor, and that manor
> From which you have the title of a lord,
> And it please your good lordship . . .
> I would be loath your name should sink, or that
> Your hopeful son, when he returns from travel,
> Should find you my lord-without-land. You are angry
> For my good counsel. Look you to your bonds. Had I known
> Of your coming, believe it, I would have had sergeants ready.
> Lord, how you fret!
>
> (V.ii.64–80)

The comedy of this clever speech is surely at Lacy's expense, rather than Luke's.

The diatribes aimed at the Frugal women also have a double edge. This is the household Anne Frugal wants:

> my page, my gentleman-usher,
> My woman sworn to my secrets, my caroch
> Drawn by six Flanders mares, my coachman, grooms,
> Postillion, and footmen . . .
>   . . . mine own doctor;
> French, and Italian cooks; musicians, songsters,
> And a chaplain that must preach to please my fancy;
> A friend at court to place me at a masque;
> The private box took up at a new play
> For me, and my retinue; a fresh habit,
> (Of a fashion never seen before) to draw
> The gallants' eyes that sit on the stage upon me . . .
>
> (II.ii.113–124)

This satirizes not just city ambition, but fashionable society in general; its references out of the illusion to those actually watching the play would ensure its significance was felt not only by citizens. Similiarly, Holdfast's lament at citizen extravagance expands into a description of *court* gluttony ("Their pheasants drench'd with ambergris, the carcasses / Of three fat wethers bruis'd for gravy to / Make sauce for a single peacock," etc. (II.i.4–6), the fashionable lasciviousness of the Frugal girls (I.i.133) involves a comparable judgment on bona fide society ladies, and Luke's lengthy rebuke to the women takes full cognizance of the court's "superfluous bravery," "pomp and bravery," and "prodigality" (IV.iv.46, 91,95). In laughing at city pride, the audience also, to a considerable degree, laughs at itself.

Massinger's distinction between court and city cannot, then, be interpreted as a nostalgic, simpleminded defense of the sanctity of rank. The principal point of attack on the women is their violation of rank, but the whole attack is not only made in social terms. The women's first appearance establishes they are guilty of more personal forms of *superbia*. They are vain, easily flattered (I.i.83), and lascivious (I.i.133); they love rare fashions (a characteristically Puritan charge), extravagance, and excessively sumptuous food. They are especially tyrannous toward their menfolk, the enslaved dependent Luke, and those who would normally command them, their husbands and suitors. Later the sins of hypocrisy, ostentation, and impiety are added (IV.iv.110, 113, 116). Clearly, not only social status is at stake. The women offend against a moral and domestic order, too, their actions travestying as much the city's values of thrift, piety, and wifeliness as they do the court's. Holdfast laments that their extravagance "would break an alderman, / And make him give up his cloak," and the point of his description of their vast banquets is not that they challenge a privilege due only to the court, but that they go far beyond that too and outdo *all* example (II.i.16–27). It is the citizens, Sir John and "the cater Holdfast" (II.i.131), who discipline the women, not the courtiers.

All critics accept without qualm the scene in which Luke humiliates the women (IV.iv) as though it expresses unequivocally Massinger's own views. It seems to me much more ambiguous; Luke is, to say the least, not a disinterested party. He does issue a public disclaimer, that he acts "not in revenge / Of your base usage of me" (IV.iv.133–134) but "with judgement" (IV.iv.48; at II.i.92 he expressed admiration for a world where "judgement" had "nought to do"), but alone with Holdfast he admits his tyrannous intentions: "He's cruel to himself, that dares not be / Severe to those that us'd him cruelly" (IV.iv.159–160). We have already *twice* seen the reality behind Luke's pretenses of moral probity. He arrests in IV.iii the very debtors for whom in I.iii he pleaded, announcing that his talk of charity "when I was in poverty . . show'd well; / But I inherit with [Sir John's] state, his mind, / And rougher nature" (IV.iii.37–39); and in IV.ii he arrests the prentices whom he himself encouraged to bad courses ("Will you prove yourself a devil? Tempt us to mischief, / And then discover it?" [IV.ii.82–83]). Massinger puts his condemnation of the women into the mouth of the man whose moral credibility is most thoroughly bankrupt.

Rather than IV.iv representing Massinger's norm, it is a fast after a feast, Lent after carnival (IV.iv.4). Luke, a "rough physician" (IV.iv.150), pretty clearly overdoes his retribution. Although he promises the women their "natural forms and habits" (IV.iv.133), they appear in *"coarse habit"* (IV.iv.23 s.d.) more suited to "Exchange wenches" or "some chandler's daughters / Bleaching linen in Moorfields" (IV.iv.36–37). The true valuation of the city is much higher. Even Luke admits that his sister is a lady and entitled to considerable privileges:

> It being for the city's honour, that
> There should be distinction between
> The wife of a patrician, and plebeian.
>
> (IV.iv.79–81)

This is not just another distinction between court and city,[43] but a discrimination within the city itself. In 1640, Alderman Soames refused to assist the court in a forced loan, saying "his reputation as an honest man, won while a commoner, was as dear to him now that he was an Alderman,"[44] and it is this distinction the women are conceded. As Soames's language indicates, it is a considerable claim. It places the women firmly among the governing classes, and when the suitors complain of the women's scorn, Sir John insists that

> Though they are mine, I must tell you, the perverseness
> Of their manners (which they did not take from me,

43. As Gibson has it, in his note on IV.iv.81.
44. Pearl, *London and . . . Revolution*, p. 192.

> But from their mother) qualified, they deserve
> Your equals.
>
> (II.iii.33–36)

This indeed they do get, for Massinger does *not*, in fact, maintain a distance between city and court, but concludes with intermarriage between them, the two cooperating under conditions of mutual respect and benefit, and this state of harmony and reciprocity between the estates in a well-ordered society is what I believe he intends the point of his moral to be. It is a more attractive interpretation than the usual one for it emphasizes the range of his tolerance equally with his intolerance, and widens the scope of his moral beyond mere respect for rank to imply a broader ideal of dignified, responsible, and rational social and moral behavior conducive to the interests of all. In the courteous relationships that exist between Lord Lacy and Sir John (II.iii.46–51) and between Lacy and Old Goldwire and Tradewell (V.ii.1–8), Massinger illustrates the mutual deference at the level of manners which is the exterior manifestation of a society cooperating healthily and harmoniously at a more fundamental substratum. The play is not opposed to social advancement as such, but is committed to ensuring that modifications in the shape of society occur smoothly and without undermining the survival and good order of the whole.

IV

Luke Frugal obviously typifies behavior that obstructs such smooth adjustments, but he must be considered in his own right as the second prong of Massinger's attack, on *avaricia*. He has been taken to symbolize the "financial ambitions of the trading classes";[45] however, his crime is personal and moral, not social. Earlier citizen cheaters, such as Middleton's Hoard and Quomodo, exhibited an overwhelming desire to eject the gentry and translate themselves into their place. Luke has nothing of this. He completely lacks social ambition, but preys like a "wolf" (V.iii.116) on all humanity without distinction, undoing the small tradesman, whore, and gamester as readily as the lord and gentleman. He is

45. Gross, "Social Change and Philip Massinger," p. 335.

motivated by a numbing devotion to his own selfish benefit, made more horrific by a malicious delight in "the fatal curses / Of widows, undone orphans" (V.iii.33). His ambition is to sit

> Alone, and surfeit in my store, while others
> With envy pine at it—my genius pamper'd
> With the thought of what I am, and what they suffer
> I have mark'd out to misery.
>
> (V.i.146–149)

It is a form of self-worship; he agrees with the first Indian that "Temples rais'd to ourselves in the increase / Of wealth, and reputation, speak a wise man" (III.iii.109). He threatens not just the stability of rank, but the survival of human society itself.

Hence it is not the acquisition of wealth that makes Luke what he is; wealth only facilitates his inhumanity. He sees human relationships as power relations; the greatest good is to dominate others, and there is only approbation for success and scorn for failure. This he holds *before* he comes into wealth. In the important soliloquy opening III.ii he discloses he has no pity, only self-contempt, for his own poverty:

> I deserve much more
> Than their scorn can load me with, and 'tis but justice
> That I should live the family's drudge, design'd
> To all the sordid offices their pride
> Imposes on me; since if now I sat
> A judge in mine own cause, I should conclude
> I am not worth their pity.
>
> (III.ii.3–9)

In fact, he *admires* Lady Frugal's tyranny over him for its spirit (II.i.33), and he despises conventional Christian pieties as self-deceiving consolations for weak men. Of Holdfast's "honest care," he says, "With the fortunes / Of a slave, he has a mind like one" (II.i.32–33), an idea of virtue he repeats to the Indians:

> LORD LACY
> Continue
> As in your poverty you were, a pious
> And honest man.   *Exit.*

LUKE
That is, interpreted,
A slave and beggar.

(III.iii. 102–104)

The women, having used him as their "slave" (I.i. 102), are amazed to find
"he that was your slave, by fate appointed / To be your governor"
(III.ii.93–94), and the play culminates with the parade of those he has
enthralled:

'Tis my glory
That they are wretched, and by me made so;
It sets my happiness off. I could not triumph
If these were not my captives.

(V.iii.67–70).

The climax of Luke's career is not his entry into wealth, but the display of
the power it has enabled him to gain over others.

It seems to me unlikely that Massinger would have expected any citizen
element in his audience to have been offended by Luke. Like the women's
pride, Luke's cruelty is as abhorrent from a civic as from a courtly perspective. Indeed, since Luke "can brook / No rival in this happiness"
(V.iii. 14–15), he especially wishes to overreach other London merchants,
hoping his "private house in cramm'd abundance / [May] prove the chamber of the City poor" (IV.ii. 126–127), and he scorns Sir John's citizenly
quality of "thriving industry," boasting that his own riches have come by
"dissimulation" (V.iii.22). Massinger carefully establishes that he misuses
his fortune; he is wealth without conscience:

Religion, conscience, charity, farewell!
To me you are words only, and no more;
All human happiness consists in store.

(IV.ii. 131–133)

The deliberateness of this rejection of conscience is driven home by its
repetition to the apprentices (II.i.44; cf. l. 76), their fathers (V.ii.37), and
the Indians:

I fear you will make
Some scruple in your conscience to grant [our requests].

LUKE
Conscience! No, no; so it may be done with safety,
And without danger of the law.

(V.i.17–20)

So in clear contrast with Sir John's humane usury, Luke is the malignant, pitiless usurer. He denies "mercy" to his apprentices (IV.ii.104) and debtors (whose pleas move even the sergeants to pity [IV.iii.70]), and repudiates it conclusively in the final scene:

Ha, ha, ha!
This move me to compassion, or raise
One sign of seeming pity in my face?
You are deceiv'd. It rather renders me
More flinty, and obdurate. A south wind
Shall sooner soften marble . . .
                    than knees, or tears, or groans
Shall wrest compunction from me.

(V.iii.59–67)

Only Sir John's return restores "Mercy" (V.iii.125), but Luke is excluded from the general reconciliation. The man who has abjured pity gets no pity wasted on him in return (cf. V.iii.58).

In Luke, then, Massinger attacks not the acquisition of wealth but its abuse, condemning his neglect of humanity, honesty, and pity, values that are respected by the citizen of conscience, Sir John Frugal, who is returned to wealth at the end. The full extent of Massinger's respect for the values of the godly citizen, though, can only be properly appreciated in relation to the fake Indians who belong entirely to Luke's part of the play.

V

New World visitors were first brought to England by Elizabethan explorers, but excited greatest comment in the early seventeenth century, culminating in 1616 with the arrival of a dozen or so including Pocahontas, the Indian wife of an Englishman, who was presented at court. Indians appeared in two masques of 1613. In 1635 the governor of the Saybrook colony was still being urged "to send over some of your Indian Creatures alive," and as late as 1645 Hollar drew a Virginian from life in London.[46] T. S. Eliot ridiculed Massinger's Indians as "extravagant hocus-pocus,"[47] but they are quite at home in Sir John's mercantile household and their function must be taken seriously. They are connected with another of Frugal's charitable activities, a pious project to convert to Christianity some unfortunate heathen (III.iii.71–86), and they bring to bear on the Luke plot a consciousness of the godly citizen ideals underlying the North American trade as a framework within which Luke's actions may be judged.

The travel literature that included descriptions of Indian life was suffused with religious feeling. Samuel Purchas's monumental compilation *Purchas his Pilgrims* (4 vols., London, 1625) opens with Solomon's "Ophirian *Nauigation*" (I, 2) interpreted as a type of man's pursuit of Grace; the companion volume, *Purchas his Pilgrimage*, describes all the religions of the world, beginning at Creation. Purchas saw exploration as part of the laborious process of overcoming the Fall; God gave man navigation that he might carry the Gospel to all nations, and regain in return that dominion over the earth lost by Adam. Colonization would recover "the right to which the true Children of the Church haue in Christ and by him in all things" (I, 16). North America, in particular, had been set aside by Providence as another Eden awaiting English exploitation, and would bring wealth to the country, new subjects to the king, and further the political and religious struggle with Spain. If the English sought "the Kingdome of God" in Virginia, they would have "an earthly Kingdome in recompence, as the earnest, and the heauenly Kingdome for our full paiement" (IV, 1816). The Virginia Company attracted investment and leadership from political and religious puritans, and its propaganda was written and coordinated by clergymen (Like Purchas); their religious zeal was inseparable from their zeal for empire.[48]

46. J. O. Halliwell (ed.), *The Works of William Shakespeare* (London, 1853), I, 325; F. Mossiker, *Pocahontas: The Life and the Legend* (London, 1977), pp. 220–221; P. L. Barbour, *Pocahontas and Her World* (London, 1971), plate facing p. 140; G. Chalmers, *An Apology for the Believers in the Shakespeare Papers* (London, 1797), pp. 93–95.

47. *Elizabethan Dramatists* (London, 1963), p. 151.

48. See L. B. Wright, *Religion and Empire*, 2d ed. (New York, 1965), p. 100 and *passim*; and P. Miller, "Religion and Society in the Early Literature of Virginia," in *Errand Into the Wilderness* (Cambridge, Mass., 1956), pp. 99–140.

So Purchas encouraged colonists to "plant Christianity, to produce and multiply Christians, by our words and works to further the knowledge of God in his Word and Workes" (IV, 1813), and the Virginia Company declared in 1610 that the first of its *"Principal* and *Maine Endes"* was to "preach and baptize into the *Christian Religion* and by propagation of the *Gospell*, to recover out of the armes of the Divell, a number of poore and miserable soules, wrapt up unto death, in almost *invincible ignorance."*⁴⁹ Pocahontas was welcomed as the first Indian convert in England; the Bishop of London entertained her, and her husband defended their marriage as advancing God's glory, "the converting [of] an irregenerate to a regeneration."⁵⁰ The idea underlies Chapman's *Memorable Mask* (London, [1613?]) in which Virginian masquers renounce "superstitious worship" in favor of the "heauens true light" of "our *Britan Phoebus"* (Sig. D4ᵛ). The Indians, though, were not meek spiritual innocents, for all authorities agreed that they had already been seduced by the devil. Captain John Smith, who greatly emphasized the "yelling and howling" of Indian religious rites, said, "their chiefe God they worship is the Devill. Him they call *Okee*, and serue him more of feare then loue."⁵¹ Purchas believed the Virginians were enslaved "to Satans tyranny in foolish pieties, mad impieties, wicked idlenesse, busie and bloudy wickednesse; hence haue we fit obiects of zeale and pietie, to *deliver from the power of darknesse"* (IV, 1814), but he was frustrated by his own inability to convert Pocahontas's servant, "a blasphemer of what he knew not, and preferring his God to ours" (IV, 1774), and concluded, "Let vs obserue these things with pitty and compassion, and endeuor to bring these silly soules out of the snare of the Deuill, by our prayers, our purses, and all our best endeuors."⁵² Comparable statements can be multiplied almost indefinitely.⁵³

49. K. Glenn, "Captain John Smith and the Indians," *The Virginia Magazine of History and Biography*, LII (1944), 229.
50. P. L. Barbour, *The Three Worlds of Captain John Smith* (London, 1964), p. 329.
51. J. Smith, *The General History of Virginia* (London, 1624), p. 35; Massinger echoes this idea at V.i.3–4.
52. *Purchas his Pilgrimage*, 4th ed. (London, 1626), pp. 843–844.
53. E.g., *Purchas his Pilgrims*, IV. 1662, 1774, 1867; W. Wood, *New England's Prospect*, ed. A. T. Vaughan (Amherst, Mass., 1977), p. 101; H. Spelman, "Relation of Virginia," in J. Smith, *Works*, ed. E. Arber (Birmingham, 1884), cv; Wright, *Religion and Empire*, p. 103. Cf. the description of Caliban as a "devil" in *The Tempest*, II.ii.

Moreover, the Indians believed themselves to be in direct contact with the devil, who "appeareth to them out of the Aire . . . in form of a personable Virginian, with a long blacke locke on the left side," and would make their children "hardy and acceptable to the Deuill, that in time he may appeare vnto them."[54] On these occasions, they take counsel from him, but also (as do Massinger's Indians, V.i.26–41) receive instructions for human sacrifice. Henry Spelman said that their "coniurers who are ther preests, can make [him] apeare unto them at ther pleasuer," and that annually the tribes go into the woods

wher ther preests make a great cirkell of fier in ye which after many obseruances in ther coniurations they make offer of 2 or 3 children to be giuen to ther god if he will apeare unto them and shew his mind whome he will desier. Vppon which offringe they heare a noyse out of ye Cirkell Nominatinge such as he will haue, whome presently they take bindinge them hand and footte and cast them into ye circle of the fier, for be it the Kinges sonne he must be giuen if [once] named by ther god . . .[55]

Purchas's American chapters have many allusions to human sacrifice, but the best-known instance was probably John Smith's account of the Huskanaw, a Virginian rite of passage which he mistook for an annual sacrifice of children. Smith described this as a violent ritual which some of the boys survived, but the others "the *Okee* or *Divell* did sucke the bloud from their left breast, who chanced to be his by lot, till they were dead." Smith himself was captured by Indians in 1607 and expected to be sacrificed "to the *Quiyoughquosicke*, which is a superior power they worship, a more uglier thing cannot be described." Few theatergoers could have been ignorant of his celebrated description of the "strange and fearefull Coniurations" practised over him, and of Pocahontas's intervention to prevent his execution.[56]

Luke's dealings with the devil, *via* the "Indians," and his plans for human sacrifice, would thus have been entirely serious for Massinger's

54. *Purchas his Pilgrimage*, p. 843; *Purchas his Pilgrims*, IV, 1868.
55. "Relation of Virginia," pp. cv-cvi. Wood, *New England's Prospect*, p. 101, said the devil, to keep the Indians in fear, "was wont to carry away their wives and children."
56. Smith, *The General History*, pp. 36, 48; *A True Relation of Such Occurrences* (London, 1608), sig. C3^r.

audience. In Virginia, the colonists were actively waging Christ's struggle with Antichrist; "the very prosperity and pregnant hopes of that Plantation made the Deuil and his lims to enuy, feare, and hate it."[57] The great massacre of colonists by Indians was only a decade past, and renewed Indian troubles were coming to be seen as God's war.[58] The arrival of the Indians in *The City Madam*, therefore, is not gratuitous melodrama, for they, devotees of the devil fighting against the true Word, are the negative to Sir John's positive, and introduce this holy war into the design of the play. Against Sir John's pious project, Luke's assertion to the Indians that "You are learn'd Europeans, and we worse / Than ignorant Americans" (III.iii.127–128) would have seemed a horrific and blasphemous inversion. Once again, Massinger evaluates the action with a citizenly eye.

VI

From Sir John's compassionate usury to the women's final "sacrifice of sighs" (V.iii.84), *The City Madam* is pervasively shaped to suggest a religious scheme. The problem of usury is first raised as a choice between angelic and diabolic uses of money:

SIR JOHN
When I lent my moneys I appear'd an angel;
But now I would call in mine own, a devil.
HOIST
Were you the devil's dam, you must stay till I have it.

(I.iii.2–4)

Luke's oration specifically exhorts Sir John to "moral honesty" and "religion," an argument which will "damn him / If he be not converted" (I.iii.95, 80), and his mercy makes his debtors, like Luke, his "beadsmen" (I.iii.101; III.ii.1). Lacy admires Luke as a man "of a clear soul, / Religious, good, and honest" and concludes that "our divines / Cannot speak more effectually" (I.iii.151, 96), whereas he suspects Sir John "an atheist"

57. *Purchas his Pilgrims*, IV, 1819.
58. R. H. Pearce, *Savagism and Civilization*, 2d ed. (Baltimore, 1967), p. 24; cf. J. Underhill, *News from America* (London, 1638), pp. 22, 29–30, 33–35, 40. Some tribes were said to be "cruell bloodie Caniballs"; see P. Vincent, *A True Relation of the Late Battle* (London, 1637), and Wood, *New England's Prospect*, p. 76.

toward his brother (I.iii. 123). Later, he presses Luke to use his new wealth
with equal piety:

> . . . use it with due reverence. I once heard you
> Speak most divinely in the opposition
> Of a revengeful humour. To these show it
> And such who then depended on the mercy
> Of your brother, now wholly at your devotion.
>
> (III.ii. 100–104)

Watching Luke accept his fortune as "A curse I cannot thank you for," he
exclaims, unctuously, "Honest soul, / With what feeling he receives it"
(III.ii. 115, 121).

This angel, however, proves a devil (again, *Othello* comes to mind).
Luke's celebrated soliloquy (III.iii), spoken as if awakening into a higher
reality, a mystery which "weak credulity could have no faith in" (l. 34),
travesties a religious vision. The countinghouse is "Heaven's abstract, or
epitome" (l. 31), and the gold, a god whose body may be touched with
reverence, parodies the Incarnation:

> It did endure the touch;
> I saw and felt it. Yet what I beheld
> And handl'd oft, did so transcend belief
> (My wonder and astonishment pass'd o'er)
> I faintly could give credit to my senses.
>
> (III.iii.4–7)

The arrival of the Indians to initiate Luke into the "sacred principles" that
there is "no religion, nor virtue, / But in abundance, and no vice but
want" (III.iii. 106, 126) renders his conversion to false pieties apparent
after the manner of a morality play. Their presence is a visual sign of his
membership of the devil's party; he is to be "confident your better angel is
/ Enter'd your house" (III.iii. 115–116).[59]

Usury was of course traditionally associated with the devil,[60] but the
inclusion of the Indians raises this association to the status of a system of

---

59. Tradewell, at II.i. 131, was "converted" to riots by Luke.

60. See, e.g., Middleton's Dampit (*A Trick to Catch the Old One*, 1605) and Brome's
Vermin (*The Damoiselle*, 1638).

belief rivaling Sir John's Christian profession. Luke's pursuit of riches for their own sake leads him naturally into devil worship, for if "you / Desire to wallow in wealth and worldly honours, / You must make haste to be familiar with him" (V.i.26–28). Allusions to his devilishness accumulate overwhelmingly in Acts IV and V. His actions in IV.ii "prove [him] a devil" (l. 82); in IV.iii the "tongues of angels" will not alter him, and he is left to "the devil thy tutor" (ll. 46, 65). His plan for disposing of a "distress'd widow, or poor maids" to the devil is a hideous parody of Sir John's charitable works (V.i.47). Lacy now regrets having thought "This devil a saint" and, describing him as "Such a devil" commends him "To thy damnation"; one is forgiven, he believes, for speaking "unchristianly" of Luke (V.ii.5, 54, 83, 85). In the final scene, Luke glories in his impiety:

> this felicity, not gain'd
> By vows to saints above, and much less purchas'd
> By thriving industry; nor fall'n upon me
> As a reward to piety, and religion,
> Or service for my country.

> (V.iii.20–24)

His entertainers, he believes, are the devil's spirits, and the masque— Orpheus descending to hell—powerfully restates his own situation. Luke is indeed *becoming* a devil, for it proves his fiendish nature that music does not soften him (V.iii.44–47), and he delights to watch his victims suffer in the personal hell he has created. Moments later Sir John, condemning him as a "Revengeful, avaricious atheist," consigns him to Virginia where the other devil-worshipers live (V.iii.134, 144).

This pattern of rival pieties is anticipated earlier in the presentation of the Frugal women, themselves left "in hell" by their suitors for a pride "saints and angels" cannot cure (II.ii.110, II.iii.37). The presence of Stargaze makes this more explicit. Keith Thomas has shown that in the Jacobean-Caroline period, astrology came under Puritan attack as the devil's device to draw men from God's worship.[61] For example, the Calvinist bishop George Carleton argued that astrologers predicted "not

---

61. *Religion and the Decline of Magic*, 2d ed. (London, 1973), pp. 435–439.

by that faith by which God taught his Church: therefore by that faith by which the Divell teacheth." They operate "by plain compact, or else by a secret illusion of Satan" whose spirits "make shew of obedience, to catch the soule of man in these snares; requiring strong Credulity and excessive desire of the Soule: and so drawing the service of the Soule to themselves, from God and from godliness."[62] Such devilish irreligion has seduced the Frugal women. Lady Frugal calls Stargaze's prophecies "oracle" and "The angels' language" (II.ii.72, 64), and in an act of great blasphemy she and her daughters kneel to the astrologer. Luke, too, having agreed that "sacrifice to an imagin'd power" shows man only "A superstitious fool" (III.iii.108), praises the divinity of his stars:

> Brightness to the star
> That govern'd at my birth! Shoot down thy influence
> And with a perpetuity of being
> Continue this felicity . . .

(V.iii.17–20)

He is defeated by the lawful "sacrifice" and "magic art" of Sir John Frugal (V.iii.106, 99).

Massinger, then, is closely dependent on a godly, citizen perspective to articulate his criticism of Luke, for he has deeply embedded the Virginian struggle between earthly saint and monstrous devil into the structure of the Luke plot. It accounts for the special intensity of Luke's presentation and condemnation. He is no ordinary sinner who has fallen into error and may be recovered to virtue by penitence. Rather, he is frightening because his malice is entirely deliberate and the depravity of his behavior gratifying to him. He has consciously and wholeheartedly turned away from piety and devoted himself to its opposite, a religion of mercilessness that puts him beyond mercy and makes him more anti-Christian than un-Christian. Luke is doomed to his damnation, both by his predestined nature and his own conscious choice, and Sir John's gesture toward reconciliation (V.iii.150) is empty after Luke's conclusion that "what's" done, with words / Cannot be undone" (V.iii.146–147).[63] *The City Madam*, in the

---

62. *Astrologamania*, 2d ed. (London, 1651), pp. 16, 38, 132 (first published in 1624). Compare T. Cooper, *The Mystery of Witchcraft* (London, 1617), p. 142, and James I, *Daemonologie*, ed. G. B. Harrison (London, 1924), pp. 10, 14.

63. Compare *Othello*, V.ii.303; *Macbeth*, III.ii.12, V.i.68 (Riverside ed.).

absolute, unpassable divide it makes between the just and the unjust man, is a powerfully puritanical, Calvinist play. The unregenerate being, utterly lost to Grace and actively fighting against it, ends the play more a devil than a man.

Another religious frame of reference also underlies the defeat of Luke. In relation to the other characters, Luke is essentially a bringer of retribution. He imposes a vengefully strict justice on them, vowing that "what I felt [when poor], you all shall feel, and with rigour" (IV.iii.42) and using all the forces of authority from the lord chief justice (IV.ii.74–75) to marshal, sheriff, and sergeants. He flings his victims' own words back into their teeth, ironically condemning or overreaching them out of their own mouths (IV.ii.84–89, 94–96; IV.iii.51–59). Like other usurers he is a "Jew" (IV.iii.60, V.iii.32), and these actions mirror the unredeemed strictness of the rule of the Law, under which all men stand condemned. Sir John's return, though, makes the day "sacred" to mercy (V.iii.126) bringing hope of a new order of forgiveness and freedom to transform the rigors of Law. This moment has the quality of an epiphany: the women's repentance is answered by a miracle—Sir John's metamorphosis from red man to white, and the magical infusion of life into the statues—which overcomes Luke at a stroke. Beneath the concluding reconciliations are suggestions of a wider, sacramental pattern; the supercession of the Jewish rule of loveless Law by the Christian rule of loving Grace.

VII

The City Madam, then, while attacking the excessive or immoral behavior of citizens, adopts a basically sympathetic and enlightened attitude toward the great citizenry, endorsing entirely the values of Sir John Frugal, the godly citizen. It is not, though, an isolated instance of the positive presentation of mercantilism on the early Stuart stage. In 1623, a tragedy of "*The Plantation of Virginia*," presumably alluding to the Indian massacre of 1622, was produced at the Curtain; in 1625 the officials of the East India Company (some of whom this paper has discussed) tried to stage a play on the massacre of their agents at Amboyna by the Dutch, but were prevented by the Privy Council.[64] Eight years later, the governor, deputy-

64. Bentley, *Jacobean and Caroline Stage*, V, 1395–1396; M. C. Heinemann, *Puritanism and Theatre* (Cambridge, Eng., 1980), pp. 209–210.

governor, and "committees" of the EIC were actually animated on stage in *The Launching of the Mary*, a propaganda play by a minor EIC official. This alternates the story of the puritanical wife of a seaman who, in her husband's absence, heroically defends her chastity from lascivious courtiers and suchlike, with a long vindication of English trade in the East, including several references to England's potential greatness at sea and the Amboyna massacre (expunged by the censor). The EIC spokesmen argue that their trade brings profits to Christendom that would otherwise go to the Infidel Turk, and publicize the Company's charitable works ("Th'East India gates stand open, open wide / to entertayne the needie & the poore, / with good accommodation") which the listening admiral enthusiastically admires ("Heauns blesse theyr store for relligious deeds / such pious actes of Boundles Charitie").[65] England's commercial opponents were again ridiculed in Henry Glapthorne's *The Hollander* (Phoenix, 1635) and Davenant's *News from Plymouth* (Globe, 1635), the latter a popular comedy set among seamen windbound in harbor.[66]

Moreover, whereas earlier criticism has taken Sir John's retirement to Louvain to indicate Massinger's Roman Catholic sympathies, I have suggested that the play's religious coloring is of a much more thoroughly puritan type. The private theaters are normally conceived to have been violently and traditionally aggressive toward citizens and puritans, but Massinger's attack on vanity and unchristian selfishness clearly draws profoundly on their spiritual and moral convictions. In the perspective of our modern historical understanding of puritanism as a powerful social and political movement, there is a level of deep significant contact between the two plots. In just such colonial projects as the Luke plot alludes to, yoking commercial investment and spiritual intention, were foundations laid on which the success of the parliamentary-puritan front of the 1640s was built. In the 1620s and 1630s, many leading "puritan" noblemen, including Massinger's patron Pembroke, engaged in overseas enterprises that established and consolidated their connections with the godly trading class; from these and similar associations would emerge the broad "opposi-

---

65. W. Mountfort, *The Launching of the Mary*, ed. J. H. Walter (Oxford, 1933), ll. 377, 1713; cf. Heinemann, *Puritanism and Theatre*, pp. 210–213.

66. These two, though, have courtly overtones. *News from Plymouth*, for example, is about privateering rather than commerce.

tion" synthesis of a wide spectrum of moderate puritan feeling which agitated effectively for a return to parliamentary government.[67] Massinger concludes with the establishment—on the understanding that the citizens know their place—of an alliance between aristocracy and citizen, a social development mirroring the evolving political alignments of the 1630s. Insofar as one wishes to extract a crudely political moral from the play, and given that Massinger would never have formulated it this way himself, *The City Madam*, contrary to the usual assumptions about the courtly elitism of the Caroline stage and the traditionalism of city comedy in general, is on the side of progress, rather than of conservatism.

Massinger is here responding to, and helping to shape, the attitudes of an audience which, though not "popular," was still no "Cavalier" coterie. The play is most notable for its distinctively *bourgeois* qualities—its strenuousness and moral severity. There is no temptation toward sentiment or flippancy; rather, the play achieves perfectly that balance between tragedy and comedy which the Caroline drama is most often criticized for lacking. For example, in the tragicomedies of a more courtly dramatist, such as Fletcher, the characters are placed in a dilemma of warring opposites which the playwright does not take seriously and which is resolved when one of the obstacles simply collapses. *The City Madam*, by contrast, is tragicomic in a chaste, non-Fletcherean manner. That is to say, the play is successful as a comedy directly in proportion to the extent to which the conception of Luke is allowed to approach a truly tragic status. Luke is not reintegrated at the end but remains outside, a threatening and, above all, a wholly convincing figure (the echoes of Shakespearean tragedy which I have noted in passing are not gratuitous but contribute to this total effect). Massinger takes the tragic aspect of his plot entirely seriously; being quite in earnest about his conflict of values, he is willing to push it to its limits, and the play's peculiar imaginative vigor is a product and a measure of this seriousness. *The City Madam* exhibits a consistent, coherent, and comprehensive attitude toward life. It cannot be interpreted as evidence of the narrowing of the drama into subservience to the private interests of a single, declining class; it is rooted in a world that is altogether wider, more public, and more complete.

67. See J. H. Hexter, *The Reign of King Pym* (Cambridge, Mass., 1941), pp. 77–88; C. Hill, *Intellectual Origins of the English Revolution* (Oxford, 1965), pp. 161–164; Heinemann, *Puritanism and Theatre*, p. 269.

Ideology and Class Conduct in The Merchant of Venice

FRANK WHIGHAM

O NE OF THE MOST SIGNIFICANT ISSUES in *The Merchant of Venice* is the rhetorical assertion of social status. Shakespeare locates this activity in a context of social mobility and class conflict, where language and other modes of self-projection serve as both enabling and repressive forces. The styles of the Christians and of Shylock are calculated: each aims to manipulate its audience, to secure access to the society's resources of power and privilege. In each case the movements of wooing and assault constitute ideological assertion. Insofar as the play presents an examination of political or class interaction, the normative aristocratic style is not simply the medium of presentation, nor even the harmonious sign of authorial approval; it is itself a subject for scrutiny. To accept these words and actions "in the rainbow hues of romance," as some interpreters suggest,[1] is to accept without question a mode presented for questioning, to surrender to the imperatives of the style itself.

Contemporary records attest to a widespread fascination with the uses of stylized identity as a social tool. Queen Elizabeth and Prince Hal carefully

---

1. A. R. Humphreys, *The Merchant of Venice (Shakespeare)*, Notes on English Literature, No. 50 (Oxford, 1973), pp. 62–63.

constructed public images of magnificence in order to defuse their inheritance from problematic forebears. Othello and Sir Henry Sidney artfully purchased elite status, the former with exotic tales, the latter with a false pedigree.[2] Tamburlaine and Coriolanus declaimed their transcendent excellence. Sir Christopher Hatton, eventual lord chancellor, was accused of dancing his way to office and his queen's heart.[3] Sir Fridericke Frigoso proposed to define the ideal courtier in order "to disgrace therfore many untowardly Asseheades, that through malapartnesse thinke to purchase them the name of a good courtier."[4] The analyst might thus focus on the individual action, or on its representative status, or on its audience. Praise and blame for achievement or imposture, fiction or perception, were distributed according to the ideological stance of the viewer.

The Merchant of Venice anatomizes this social rhetoric through parallel focuses of inclusion and exclusion. As style reveals relation with one's equals and discrimination from one's inferiors, so the plot enacts these concepts in linear fashion. The marriage plot chronicles Bassanio's courtship of and assimilation into the elite; the trial plot depicts Shylock's critical invasion of their preserve of power. These actions are parallel, because each focuses on the promulgation of instrumental style, culminates in an interpretive trial, and results in the clarification of social identity.

I

The marriage plot takes place in a context where insecurity is held at bay by reassuring assertions of class solidity and value. In the choric dialogue of the first scene Salerio and Solanio respond to Antonio's sadness with a practiced flattery supportive of his social value, and, by reflection, their own. References to the magnificence of his tonnage overcome any sense of anxiety and vulnerability through the force of weighty dignity. Commercial and social superiority are fused:

    2. Roger Howell, *Sir Philip Sidney: The Shepherd Knight* (Boston, 1968), p. 18.
    3. Neville Williams, *Elizabeth I, Queen of England* (1967; rpt. London, 1971), pp. 185–186.
    4. Baldassare Castiglione, *The Book of the Courtier* (1528), trans. Sir Thomas Hoby (1561; rpt. New York, 1928), p. 29.

There [on the sea] where your argosies with portly sail,
Like signiors and rich burghers on the flood,
Or as it were the pageants of the sea,
Do overpeer the petty traffickers
That cur'sy to them (do them reverence)
As they fly by them with their woven wings.[5]

The social imagery embodying the values of the life of commerce expresses their ideological status: material and aesthetic distinctions take on almost moral force. This accretion owes something to the Marlovian excess of Barabas's world-girdling trade empire in *The Jew of Malta*. However, the emphasis here is not on a heroic imperialism of the sea, with implications of self-determining social mobility and disrespect for established boundaries, but on the solid value of those who are impregnably dignified within those bounds. These first lines go far to suggest the world of the play, where appearances govern reality, money governs appearances, and class expectations and mystifications govern the use of money.

However, the threats of the sea question the security Salerio has invoked. He describes them in terms of social degradation (to "see my wealthy Andrew dock'd in sand / Vailing her high top lower than her ribs / To kiss her burial" [I.i.27–29]) and apocalyptic misdirection and usurpation of Antonio's luxury imports ("rocks, / Which touching but my gentle vessel's side / Would scatter all her spices on the stream, / Enrobe the roaring waters with my silks" [I.i.31–34]). For Salerio thoughts of pleasurable security inescapably arouse fears for its loss; he thus voices the other of the play's twin subjects—the invasion, usurpation, or loss of security and privilege. The safety of position and wealth is continually embattled, not given but achieved, and always requiring vigilant defense. The complexity of the play's treatment of these issues is latent in the fact that the tools of assault and defense are the same—stylized assertion and its enabling force, money.

When Bassanio makes his request for funds to Antonio, his ornate style belies the humility of its content. The comparison of his "project" of

5. *The Merchant of Venice*, ed. J. R. Brown, The Arden Shakespeare (London, 1955), I.i.9–14. All quotations are taken from this edition, and are identified by parenthetical references in the text.
Regarding the social moralization of the sea we may also note Morocco's reference to "the watery kingdom, whose ambitious head/Spets in the face of heaven" (II.vii.44–45).

obtaining Portia's hand to Jason's search for the Golden Fleece makes his plan a quest, magnificent and dangerous (and more deserving of underwriting). The parallel with Jason has a shady side, however, since Jason and Medea were both associated with untruth and deception, and since the Golden Fleece image was frequently used to signify the goal of commercial enterprise, monetary profit.[6] Bassanio's language also has a specifically commercial vocabulary: he frequently uses such terms as "rate," "owe," "hazard," "richly," "undervalu'd," "worth," "means," and "thrift." The intermixture of heroic and mercantile language emphasizes their relation to each other; the tonal disjunction suggests an ironic reading, since in romantic heroics financial foundations are usually suppressed as tawdry. Bassanio's request is for the "means to hold a rival place" with the other suitors; this turns out to consist of "rare new liveries," "gifts of rich value," and followers with "courteous breath." Bassanio romanticizes in heroic terms the pragmatic web of technique, effort, and self-interest which baser men work with more openly.

Antonio makes it clear that Bassanio shall have the money for friendship's sake rather than for the art of his appeal. That he should feel the need to make the appeal, and insist on delivering it in full despite clear signs from Antonio that it is superfluous, suggests his insecurity in the friendship. Such covert alienation informs many relationships in this play. The purest expression of this occurs in Act III, where Solanio tells Salerio the rumor of the loss of Antonio's shipping. The brief conversation is mired in rhetorical cleverness:

I would she [Report] were as lying a gossip in that, as ever knapp'd ginger, or made her neighbours believe she wept for the death of a third husband: but it is true, without any slips of prolixity, or crossing the plain highway of talk, that the good Antonio, the honest Antonio;—O that I had a title good enough to keep his name company!—

(III.i.8–14)

The disjunction of style and content in the obtrusively witty conveyance of fearful rumor for their friend and patron suggests the tenuous nature of attachment and regard in this society, where tragic news is an occasion for gratuitous self-display.

6. See Elizabeth S. Sklar, "Bassanio's Golden Fleece," *TSLL*, XVIII (1976), 502–503.

In scene ii Shakespeare presents aristocratic life from another angle, the boredom of country-house life, where the only activity of interest for a daughter is speculation regarding marriage. Portia's stylized and petulant world-weariness is put in perspective by Nerissa's observation of its origin in surfeit and idleness. Her rebuke does not really register with Portia, who chafes under the curb of a dead father's will. Nerissa soothingly assigns the government of the suitors to heaven, the casket device being sacramental, the inspiration of a holy man. However, the casket device in fact functions with quite secular effectiveness to select, by stylistic tests, a man of just the right sort of awareness, ultimately reaffirming and supporting a particular class-oriented definition of value. Lawrence Stone provides an equation for the relation between money and status:

Money was the means of acquiring and retaining status, but it was not the essence of it: the acid test was the mode of life, a concept that involved many factors. Living on a private income was one, but more important was spending liberally, dressing elegantly, and entertaining lavishly. Another was having sufficient education to display a reasonable knowledge of public affairs, and to be able to perform gracefully on the dance-floor, and on horseback, in the tennis-court and the fencing-school.[7]

Shakespeare presents such items in emblematic moments and small touches, placing at the center of his plot the crucial element implicit in Stone's catalogue: the ability to judge as well as to manifest style. Castiglione had stressed the import of this in general; Shakespeare creates an emblematic test conceived specifically on stylistic lines.

The emphasis on such criteria is central from the first mention of the casket device. All the suitors who are unwilling to risk their futures on such a test are shown to be, in Portia's eye, defective in style. Her mockery of them allows her to demonstrate her own impeccable credentials. Their weaknesses range from innocence of proper styling to obsessive concern with it. The Neapolitan prince seems to have been persuaded to wish himself a horse. The County Palatine is never merry, and Monsieur le Bon is infirm of image ("every man in no man"). Falconbridge, the English baron, is ill-educated (having neither Latin, French, nor Italian) and ill-clothed, with a hodgepodge of fashions from around the world. The German, out of regard for tradition, is a drunkard. The Scottish lord

7. Lawrence Stone, *The Crisis of the Aristocracy* (Oxford, 1965), p. 50.

fares most poorly of all, being only a mark for Portia to shoot wit-cracks at. Portia's mockeries deal primarily with external manifestations of style; as she judges others, she reveals herself.

Shakespeare's comic observation of Portia deepens into irony at the end of the scene, where the two most important suitors, Morocco and Bassanio, are brought together. Of the latter there is a bare mention, revealing at least a visual impression made on his last visit. (Here, presumably, were given the "speechless messages" which led Bassanio's mind to "presage thrift" [I.i.175] in his venture.) Morocco too is considered (and condemned) in visual terms, as having "the complexion of a devil." Throughout the scenes with Morocco the element of complexion provides a measure of the exclusive implications of courtesy in Portia's society.

The remainder of the casket action is divided into three segments: the failures of Morocco and Arragon and the success of Bassanio. The failures provide criteria by which to examine Bassanio's success. The action of Morocco opens with his statement of defiant insecurity regarding his skin color. He dresses in white, and declares that his blood is as red as that of any blond's, asserting inner virtue over outward defect. He converts his color to a virtue by assimilating it to fierceness: "I tell thee lady this aspect of mine / Hath fear'd the valiant" (II.i.8–9). In this, as in many other ways, he reminds one of Tamburlaine.[8] His imagery of martial exploit and confrontation is in the style of early Elizabethan rant, which is ineffective with this young sophisticate. The world of physical action and martial valor, the natural violence of the she-bear and the lion, are all unwelcome in Belmont, legitimate only as figurative language. Morocco finds that what he sees as his "own good parts" gain scant credit with Portia. Unlike Desdemona, she does not love the Moor for the dangers he has passed, but seems to find him something of a barbarian. (Portia is not a rebel against her culture; she is its judgmental representative.) She alludes to his color when she remarks that he stands "as fair / As any comer [she has] look'd on yet" (II.i.20–21). He seems, in sum, to be handicapped by his race, his lack of sophistication, and his outmoded style. The attribute of his style most relevant here is his lavish claims made for his own desert. In the early days of Elizabethan drama the non-European setting and character, presented with extensive rhetorical ornament, gave the exotic an incanta-

8. See M. C. Bradbrook, *Shakespeare and Elizabethan Poetry* (London, 1951), p. 175.

tory power over Elizabethan audiences. In the courtly context, however, the imperialistic titanism of Tamburlaine is ill-adapted to purposes of wooing. In *The Merchant of Venice* the requirements for success have moved into a lower key, more civilized and guileful. A polished Bassanio may succeed where a Morocco weighted with golden attributes will fail. The conqueror no longer spins Fortune's Wheel with his hand, but plays the odds and wins with a "system."

Shakespeare further exposes these patterns in the scene of Morocco's choice, which sets up a major irony for the casket action. Morocco is governed by two assumptions, of his own worth and of the validity of appearance in displaying value. Like Tamburlaine he insists on correct ranking for himself: "A golden mind stoops not to shows of dross" (II.vii.20). He also assumes, like Tamburlaine, that the world dare not deceive him; shows of dross must contain only dross: "Is't like that lead contains her?—'twere damnation / To think so base a thought, it were too gross / To rib her cerecloth in the obscure grave" (II.vii.49–51). So, of course, he chooses the best exterior, and loses. His judgment is rooted in a simpler world, with a more linear scale of value, less obscure and demanding less of one in the way of training and education. It is a world in which men are still intoxicated with the thrill of power attendant upon might, and less concerned to exercise that power within society's complexities. A more discriminating member of a more differentiated society, Portia rejoices because she is not to be allied to an image so primitive and out of place. The displacement of typical Elizabethan ethnocentrism to Italy, where one of the victims is an Englishman, emphasizes the focus on the exclusive motive itself. Portia requires one of her own sort, with whom she can share assumptions and jokes, and her father's device skillfully excludes the unfit. Virtue without appropriate external appeal has no traction in this world.

Unlike Morocco, Arragon recognizes the possible falsity of externals, yet he ignores lead. Gold he condemns as the choice of the many:

> The fool multitude that choose by show,
> Not learning more than the fond eye doth teach,
> Which pries not to th' interior, but like the martlet
> Builds in the weather on the outward wall,
> Even in the force and road of casualty.
>
> (II.ix.26–30)

Here is the sense that judging by externals is risky, and that the wise man
will look inward to avoid hazard. The hazard Arragon fears is to be ranked
with the barbarous multitude (a class-oriented objection that never occurs
to Morocco). He laments the corrupt derivation of place:

> O that . .
> > clear honor
> Were purchas'd by the merit of the wearer!—
> How many then should cover that stand bare! . . .
> How much low peasantry would then be gleaned
> From the true seed of honor!
>
> > > > (II.ix.42–47)

The primary impact of Arragon's speculations is a stress on the disjunction
between surface and inner value, and on the frequent misreadings of
externals. This complication of Morocco's interpretive approach serves to
heighten our awareness of the stylistic character of Bassanio's entry, which
follows at once. His gifts of rich value, his retinue with courteous breath,
and his resemblance to costly summer manifestly impress Portia and
Nerissa, but we should be aware of the reflection of Arragon's words on
this flashy entry.

Bassanio's choice of the leaden casket is the culmination of all the
motifs suggested so far: by the demonstration of stylistic class affinities
Bassanio wins marital bliss, a splendid fortune, and a solid class grounding. The scene is set with a series of allusions to artistic signs of harmony.
They conduct a witty duet, cleverly playing variations on the Petrarchan
theme of love torture, creating an effect not dissimilar to the sonnet
spoken by Romeo and Juliet. As they test and reveal their verbal affinity,
they establish social congruence and foreshadow a decorous love match.
Each builds on the other's remarks in a fashion reminiscent of the witty
games of repartee depicted in *The Book of the Courtier* or Guazzo's *The Civile
Conversation*, with the same effect of mutual reinforcement.

Bassanio's meditation on his choice concerns the deceptiveness of appearance, especially ornamental appearance. He finds it in law, in religion, in assertions of valor and beauty. Of all these elements he says that
"ornament is but the guiled shore / To a most dangerous sea: the beaute-
ous scarf / Veiling an Indian beauty (III.ii.97–99).[9] There is no reason to

9. The verbal parallel with Salerio's earlier description of the threats to Antonio's
luxury trade invites us to note the suggestions of danger and falsehood specifically.

question these familiar perceptions (though the racial stereotype is a revealing term for evil: he casts it as dark and non-European). However,
when he concludes sententiously, "Therefore, thou gaudy gold, Hard food
for Midas, I will none of thee, / Nor none of thee thou pale and common
drudge / 'Tween man and man" (III.ii. 101–104), one may wonder how to
take his reflections. For we can hardly forget Bassanio's borrowing from
Shylock through Antonio, his rare new liveries and costly gifts, all of
which, bred from Shylock's gold (as Sigurd Burckhardt notes),[10] were
meant to nurture his chances for success in Belmont. Maybe Bassanio is so
unreflective as to be unaware of the irony of his words; even his medita-
tions may be so rhetorically ordered as to preclude self-consciousness.
Insofar as he may be imagined to conceive the self as a configuration of
public gestures, the perception of irony may be somewhat anachronistic.
He may be unconcerned with the tension between the artful form of his
meditation and its moral content; aesthetic and moral perspectives often
seem askew from one another in this play. Perhaps some such com-
partmentalization, and the instrumental utility it implies, are part of
Shakespeare's point here.

Indeed, in *The Book of the Courtier* troublesome moral matters regarding
deception are often suppressed or obscured by the proponents of the
aestheticized personality. When Lord Gasper Pallavicino, the book's chief
devil's advocate, labels a certain rhetorical stratagem "a very deceite," Sir
Fridericke Frigoso replies in defense that it is "rather an ornament . . .
than a deceite: and though it be a deceite, yet it is not to be disalowed."[11]
One might suggest here that Bassanio speaks against falsehood to disguise
his own operations, but this would assume an unlikely degree of intellectual self-consciousness on the courtier's part. Perhaps we can only say that
an excessive concern for the rhetorical projection of self somehow works
against self-knowledge. The irony in *The Merchant of Venice* seems most
explicable if placed in the gray area between deception and self-deception,
rhetorical conspiracy and illusion.[12]

The actual choice of the leaden casket results logically from this meditation on the implications of appearance. Bassanio seems to act on the basis

10. Sigurd Burckhardt, *"The Merchant of Venice*: The Gentle Bond," *Shakespearean Meanings* (Princeton, N.J., 1968), p. 215.
11. Castiglione, p. 132 (variations in spelling follow the original).
12. For this distinction see Kenneth Burke, *A Rhetoric of Motives* (1950; rpt. Berkeley,
Calif., 1969), p. 114.

of stylistic *sententiae* derived from Castiglione. The interlocutors of *The Book of the Courtier* repeatedly enjoin us to hide art with art, to underplay our attributes in order to generate greater impact when the truth is revealed. When Bassanio decides to trust the least prepossessing casket, he assumes it promises reward by the principle of *ars celare artem*. He imputes this paradigm to the test itself; it is the intuition that constitutes passage, into marriage and membership.

Portia, chosen rightly, proceeds to wish herself, her beauty, and her money arithmetically multiplied, that "only to stand high in [his] account, / [she] might in virtues, beauties, livings, friends / Exceed account" (III.ii.155–157). The elaboration of this quantitative imagery belies the "unlesson'd . . . unschool'd, unpractised" girl, whose modesty is an art of ostentation. Her surrender of self emphasizes her own value and its accompanying material benefits almost as strongly as Bassanio did in seeking her:

> Myself, and what is mine, to you and yours
> Is now converted. But now I was the lord
> Of this fair mansion, master of my servants,
> Queen o'er myself: and even now, but now,
> This house, these servants, and this same myself
> Are yours.
>
> (III.ii.166–171)

At this, Bassanio is bereft of words. He would seem to agree with Francis Osborne, who advised his son that "as the fertilitie of the ensuing year is guessed at the height of the river Nilus, so by the greatness of a wive's portion may much of the future conjugall happiness be calculated." [13] Bassanio becomes solvent, Portia is married to a fit mate, and Antonio is to be repaid, after which all are to live happily ever after.

To many this is an adequate reading of the entire play. The hero meets the test and wins the rich and beautiful lady who is the prize. As often happens in fairy tales, beauty, goodness, and right-feeling intelligence have been assimilated to one another; the achievement of the lady is the achievement of the comedy. However, Shakespeare has written a more complex play than this model suggests. Several matters remain to be integrated with what has gone before; some are quite critical, even subver-

13. Quoted in Stone, p. 613.

sive, of the dominant ideology articulated in the marriage plot. But criticisms are tucked safely out of sight, and we are left with what appears to be an entertaining play. (The Elizabethan political climate was hostile to playwrights who meddled with matters beyond their proper sphere. Obtrusive neatness is thus often legalistic camouflage, a sign of prohibited criticism underneath.)

When one reads *The Merchant of Venice* as a study of courteous ideology, a different sort of coherence is revealed: the trial plot, far from simply providing an antagonistic movement, *mirrors* the marriage plot. The collective rituals of language and style reaffirm the dominant ideology not only by the induction of consonant suitors, but also by the expulsion of "malapart asseheades." Both actions rest upon assumptions of the revelation of natural hierarchy.

II

The narrative structure of the trial plot parallels that of the casket plot in that they are both organized by the social rituals surrounding a bid for power. Bassanio and Shylock both seek power in a social context where the old feudal hierarchy is being reordered by the pressures of capitalism. Bassanio's procedure was perceived as reaffirming the model of sanctified natural hierarchy, and thus the bulwarks between the elite and its inferiors. As we have seen, however, his assertion of the natural distinction of the elite is itself positive, in the sense that it is in fact posited, created by the human powers of imagination and money. He therein implicitly represents one major version of disruptive social mobility.

Shylock represents another. Unlike Bassanio, he does not seek membership in the power-wielding class. (Indeed, his contempt for their ways matches theirs for his; both sides endorse the structure of exclusion and the self-righteous perception of elitism.) Shylock does aim at the achievement and exercise of power, and like Bassanio denies the natural status of class distinction. Shylock's overt version of positivism leads him to a disruption of the courtly ideology apparently quite unlike Bassanio's affirmations of it, but the implicit positivist threat to social rigidity is the same. Shylock is also subjected to trial, and is finally punished for his heterodox self-assertion. And just as Bassanio's reward (marriage and enrichment) is fitting to his courtly mode, Shylock's punishment and reduction to insignificance grow out of his legal and commercial mode of self-definition. This portion of the play then reveals the alternative to Bassanio's successful quest: the exclusion and baffling of the unsuccessful impostor or poacher.

The mode of Shylock's bid for power is first registered stylistically. In dealing with Bassanio and Antonio, he strives to demystify their power and prestige, to strip to essences what is romantically obscured. He takes the incantatory terms with which Solanio and Salerio sang Antonio's reputation and stands them on their feet.

. . . His means are in supposition: he hath an argosy bound to Tripolis, another to the Indies, I understand moreover on the Rialto, he hath a third at Mexico, a fourth for England, and other ventures he hath squand'red abroad,—but ships are but boards, sailors but men, there be land-rats and water-rats, water-thieves and land-thieves, (I mean pirates), and then there is the peril of waters, winds, and rocks.

(I.iii.15–23)

Shylock's epistemology threatens their heroic self-concept (and the supremacy it implies), revealing adventure as risk, dangerously akin to weakness. The Christians prefer to control the frame of their public image, needing to be witnessed rather than inspected. Their right to power and privilege will not bear Shylock's demystifying examination.

Similarly, they are unwilling or unable to use Shylock's observations to reexamine themselves from a new perspective. This is revealed as Antonio, with the force of public morality behind him, humiliates Shylock in the marketplace for his "Jewish" business practices: "he rails / . . . On me, my bargains, and my well-won thrift / Which he calls interest" (I.iii.43–46). The divergent vocabularies suggest a gap in communication, combining in Antonio's case an inability to perceive the object with a readiness to judge it. Shakespeare reveals the social impact of this communication gap in the reception of Shylock's tale of the "scientific" manipulation of Laban's sheep.

Shylock tells the tale to justify his taking of interest. The precedent is obscure, and Antonio's overready interpretation emphasizes the rigidity of his conceptual vocabulary, under which Shylock stands condemned. Before he can even complete the tale of Jacob, Antonio demands to know "And what of him? did he take interest?" (I.iii.70), moving instantly to interpret in the terms of his predetermined code. Shylock responds that his example works in other terms: "No, not take interest, not as you would say / Directly int'rest,—mark what Jacob did" (I.iii.71–72). Antonio's reductive stock response to the obscure story makes clear that he perceives only in his own derivative vocabulary:

> This was a venture sir that Jacob serv'd for,
> A thing not in his power to bring to pass,
> But sway'd and fashion'd by the hand of heaven.
> Was this inserted to make interest good?
> Or is your gold and silver ewes and rams?

Shylock's response, "I cannot tell, I make it breed as fast" (I.iii.86–91), attempts to cut across the arbitrary terms of Christian philosophy to a pragmatic standard that reveals Antonio's response as predetermined and conventional. The latter is unwilling or unable to make the venture of thought required by Shylock's irony; he blatantly ignores Shylock's "But note me signior," turning to Bassanio with a series of complacent *sententiae*:

> Mark you this Bassanio,
> The devil can cite Scripture for his purpose,—
> An evil soul producing holy witness
> Is like a villain with a smiling cheek,
> A goodly apple rotten at the heart.
> O what a goodly outside falsehood hath!
>
> (I.iii.92–97)

These lines demonstrate Antonio's dismissive prejudgment of Shylock's Mosaic tale, which Antonio sees as an attempt to use a Christian argument. Shylock's explanation in biblical terms is seen as *prima facie* proof of falsehood, an illegitimate assumption of (Christian) image: the book is their book, and can only legitimately reveal their truths. His attempt to enlist their language in order to be taken seriously is doomed to confusion.

It is significant that Shylock is condemned in terms of having a false outside: a double attitude toward assumed surfaces is revealed here. The creation of an attractive image can be regarded as a deception when one dislikes the perpetrator, while the same sort of performance by an ally is regarded either as laudable decoration or revelation of consonance of inner and outer value. The flexibility of this attitude allows for any convenient labeling of artificial surface, from moral falsehood to aesthetic accomplishment.

The rest of the third scene, and indeed of the entire bond story, revolves around the assumption that those excluded from the elite circle of community strength are powerless to change their state or affect those within. Shylock speaks bitterly of the contradiction between their normal debasement of him and their suit to him for money, with its implicit trivialization of any resentment he might feel. When he complains of a previous humiliation, Antonio says, "I am as like to call thee [dog] again, / To spet on thee again, to spurn thee too" (I.iii.125–126), inviting all the ruin he believes Shylock can offer. Shylock, more responsively aware of the ambiguity of language and experience than Antonio, conceives a revenge that is primarily a gesture that will evidence his existence as a figure of significance to those who feel safe inside the circle. The plan for revenge is couched in language whose threat is unreal to Antonio. It is more apparent to Bassanio, whose experience on the periphery has perhaps taught him more of life's unfunny jokes. Shylock's "merry sport," like Morocco's she-bear, is so violently and barbarically alien to Antonio's world that he regards it as absurd, and therefore trivial. Shylock has clearly counted on this, and to silence Bassanio, he shows how profitless the pound of flesh is from a mercantile point of view.

> If he should break his day what should I gain
> By the exaction of the forfeiture?
> A pound of man's flesh taken from a man,
> Is not so estimable, profitable neither
> As flesh of muttons, beefs, or goats,—I say
> To buy his favour, I extend this friendship.
>
> (I.iii.159–64)

By trivializing the bond in commercial terms and casting himself in the role of suitor, of "petty trafficker," Shylock suggests his comparative insignificance and the accuracy of the flattering social model earlier proposed for Antonio. Remaining orderly and insignificant in Antonio's eyes will enable Shylock to reduce him to the status of powerless and trivial tool, to be the definer instead of the defined.

In using the law for his own purposes of dominance and self-expression, Shylock performs an act of invasion formally parallel to Bassanio's—both attempt to engineer a change in status through the use of an ideologically weighted language. Bassanio's goal is participation in the group conferring identity, and in the attendant social and financial privileges. He compels desert by the manipulation of the systems of courtesy. Shylock desires not community with but dominance over his social superiors. He wants to invert the hierarchy, using the powers of authentication himself to spite the principles of reciprocity falsely asserted by the aristocratic ideology. This he aims to accomplish by precipitating out another ideologically affiliated system—the law—from its particular social and historical context, and positing it to be objective and available for use by all. In other words, he insists, in his literalist fashion, on taking the law at its face value. He insists on accepting as authentic and natural the law's claim to universality. He sees that his hope of power and parity rests on the separation of the law from single factional affiliation. He fails in the end precisely because the law is itself an ideological expression of the imperatives of the elite. In a most literal way, the ruling ideas here are the ideas of the ruling class; the law remains finally in the sole employ of its owners. The duke (a partial judge) has striven to recall Shylock to subordination through his own positive powers, "generously" attributing to him the "Christian" qualities of mercy and gentleness, contrasting him with "stubborn Turks, and Tartars never train'd / To offices of tender courtesy" (IV.i.32–33).[14] Shylock refuses these proffered signs of social inclusion because they would return him to hierarchical submission.

14. The function of the duke's intervention may be unfolded by reference to an analytic statement by Max Weber regarding the residual presence of such behavior in the legal context in the nineteenth century, when Shylock's perception of the law (though not his use of it in *The Merchant of Venice*) had become normative.

The modern capitalist concern is based inwardly above all on *Calculation*. It requires for its survival a system of justice and an administration whose workings can be *rationally calculated*, at least in principle, according to fixed general laws, just as the probable performance of a *machine* can be calculated. It is as little able to tolerate the dispensing of justice according to the judge's sense of fair play *in individual cases* or any other irrational means of principles of administering the law . . . as it is able to endure a patriarchal administration that obeys the dictates of its own caprice, or sense of mercy and, for the rest, proceeds in accordance with an inviolable and sacrosanct, but irrational tradition. . . . What is specific to modern capitalism as distinct from the age-old capitalist forms of acquisition is that the strictly rational *organisation of work* on the basis of *rational technology* did not come into being *anywhere* within such irrationally constituted political systems nor could it have done so. For these modern businesses with their fixed capital and their exact calculations are much too sensitive to legal and administrative irrationalities. They could only come into being in the bureau-

His power rests on his assertion of the law's absoluteness; admission of the possibility of interpretation or compromise would return him to the realm of the contingent, and place his status in the determination of others. He insists on staying beyond their reach, refusing to justify his acts in their terms. He replies instead in language which to them is irrational, beyond the pale of intelligibility, a language of other inexplicable acts, of cats and pigs and hatred which, long denied entrance to the system of civilization, now refuses to be domesticated. Shylock is no longer bound to communicate at all, for he now sees himself as not bound to the hierarchical social body, but to the law. He is therefore not bound to confer upon them the commensurate status that conversation implies.

Shylock has engineered a figure-and-ground reversal by forcing the elite to accept the sort of diminution of identity and social stature which grows directly from their own systematic oppression. In this way he universalizes his own plight as dehumanized tool and disposable slave of order.

> You have among you many a purchas'd slave,
> Which (like your asses, and your dogs and mules)
> You use in abject and in slavish parts,
> Because you bought them,—shall I say to you,
> Let them be free, marry them to your heirs?
> Why sweat they under burthens? let their beds
> Be made as soft as yours, and let their palates
> Be season'd with such viands? you will answer
> "The slaves are ours,"—so do I answer you:
> The pound of flesh which I demand of him
> Is dearly bought, 'tis mine and I will have it:
> If you deny me, fie upon your law!
> There is no force in the decrees of Venice:
> I stand for judgment,—answer, shall I have it?
>
>   (IV.i.90–103)

At the moment of his greatest power, Shylock presses his audience to recognize the implications of the ideology of universal harmony by redi-

---

cratic state with its rational laws where . . . the judge is more or less an automatic statute-dispensing machine in which you insert the files together with the necessary costs and dues at the top, whereupon he will eject the judgment together with the more or less cogent reasons for it at the bottom: that is to say, where the judge's behaviour is on the whole *predictable*.

(Quoted in Georg Lukacs, "Reification and the Consciousness of the Proletariat," in *History and Class Consciousness*, trans. Rodney Livingstone [Cambridge, Mass., 1971], p. 96).

recting its oppressive faculties onto one of their own, thereby forcing them to confront an example they cannot ignore. In demonstrating its oppression of one, he reveals its oppression of many, demystifies the universal harmony of the dominant ideology, and stops the dance. It is an arresting moment in Elizabethan literature.

It is also very brief, for the play shifts its tone from tragicomic insight to saturnine *deus ex machina*: ironically named Portia, the voice of inequity[15] enters to restore the imbalance after Shylock's profound demystification. Her famous "quality of mercy" speech is specifically presented as a *compulsion* ("on what compulsion must I be mercifull," he has asked); mercy itself is presented as an attribute of power. Portia also offers Shylock apparent membership in the class establishment in return for his assent to a vocabulary that would wash away the foundation of his power. She argues that they are governed by a Christian rule of mercy, and that Shylock is one of them:

> Though justice be thy plea, consider this,
> That in the course of justice, none of us
> Should see salvation: we do pray for mercy,
> And that same prayer, doth teach us all to render
> The deeds of mercy.
>
> (IV.i.194–198)

Therefore, she reasons, "must the Jew be merciful." Shylock scoffs at her concern for his salvation ("my deeds upon my head!") and insists on the solidity of his claim at written law, rather than trust in the law his opponents call divine. He knows they are not bound by this law, and he cannot bind them with it either. His power is contingent upon the escape from the positive into the putatively natural.

Bassanio sees this, and seeks to have the duke take this weapon from Shylock by setting aside the law. But this, of course, would involve setting aside its claim to be natural rather than positive. Shylock, as Burckhardt notes, would be forcing them to espouse publicly the mode of

15. Regarding the discussion of equity in relation to *The Merchant of Venice*, see Mark Edwin Andrews, *Law versus Equity in 'The Merchant of Venice'* (Boulder, Colo., 1965); W. Moelwyn Merchant's introduction to his New Penguin edition of the play (Harmondsworth, 1967); W. Nicholas Knight, "Equity, *The Merchant of Venice*, and William Lambarde," *ShS*, XXVII (1974), 93–104.

positivism which he shares with them, but which they deny.[16] To admit the law's flexibility would call the fictive ground of their power into question; they dare not do so, and Shylock knows it.

Portia has, of course, a prepared solution to the problem, and the way she implements it shows, as A. D. Moody observes, that her goal is not just saving Antonio, but "putting Shylock at the mercy of his enemies."[17] By repeated ironic demonstration of the irreducible nature of the stated law she leads Shylock to be utterly confident in it, and to reveal his murderous urge to destruction and revenge; in so doing she creates an emotional setting ideal for his destruction.

This she accomplishes with great economy by means of two graceful strokes of positive power. First, she reveals that the objective certainty of the law, by means of which Shylock thought to bind its makers, is still subject, despite all his efforts, to creative interpretation. When she finds no mention of a jot of blood, she reveals the language of the law as infinitely interpretable, as the ongoing creation of its native speakers, who maintain their power precisely by "ad libbing" with it. Portia discovers the necessary escape clause in the white spaces between the lines, where no strict construction is possible.

Though the reading regarding the blood is sufficient for Shylock's destruction (loss of lands and goods and—according to line 328—life), Portia adduces a second legal weapon (Shakespeare's own creation, not in the sources) which not only renders Shylock's defeat irrevocable, but places it in an explicitly ideological perspective. It seems that any *alien* who plots against the life of a citizen loses his goods and places his life at the mercy of the duke. As W. H. Auden observes, the effect of this is to show that factional bias is built in even in law, that Shylock was excluded by definition as alien to begin with.[18]

The ideology is redeemed, and the aristocratic identity reaffirmed, through Shylock's destruction. Portia's speech on mercy functions precisely as an ideological weapon. The final driving-home of this irony is Shylock's forced conversion. Blatantly a mockery and punishment (here an

16. Burckhardt, pp. 229–230.

17. A. D. Moody, *Shakespeare: The Merchant of Venice*, Studies in English Literature, No. 21 (London, 1964), p. 43.

18. W. H. Auden, "Brothers and Others," in *The Dyer's Hand* (1963; rpt. New York, 1968), p. 229.

alternative only to death), compulsory conversion is associated historically with confiscation of goods by the state.[19] Shylock is denied his wealth, his original means to power, which excludes him thoroughly from creative activity in the world of significance.[20] In this light the brilliance of the solution to the Shylock problem is evident even now: it still has such power to bend the perception of observers to its will as to lead some readers to say, with Nevill Coghill, that "Shylock [has] at least been given the chance of eternal joy"![21] This issue of generosity is a phantom, however; Shylock has simply been rendered totally powerless in the secular world of the play (the only world there presented—real Christian transcendent options are completely absent). He equates his impoverishment with death: "you take my life / When you do take the means whereby I live" (IV.i.372–373). Spiritual generosity to Shylock is in fact a guise for material generosity to Antonio, the state, and Lorenzo and Jessica. The dissonance of this ironic windfall of goods with the traditional schematic access of joy and riches in comic resolution suggests that Shakespeare began earlier than is usually thought to test the implications of genre (and the awareness of his audiences) as he later did in the "problem comedies." The resolution fits in letter but not in spirit, as is appropriate for its legalistic content.

Shylock's defeat concludes with one last reminder of positive power. If Shylock refuses to submit to the proposed conversion, the duke says he will withdraw the pardon just offered. The immutably natural law of Venice is shown again to be open to interpretation and revision whenever it is advantageous to its own. The trial finally crushes Shylock between the law's immutability and its fluid capacity to redefine itself at will. Shylock cannot maintain his heterodox identity; he is stamped into the mold designed for him.

19. See Wilbur Sanders, "Appendix A: Barabas and the Historical Jew of Europe," in *The Dramatist and the Received Idea* (Cambridge, Eng., 1968), p. 349.

20. It is interesting to note a sexual parallel here with the unsuccessful suitors for Portia's hand, who are forbidden to wive, to build a family. Shylock, whose loss of his bags and stones has already been mocked in implicitly sexual terms, and whose "gentle" daughter has (been) stolen away, is here financially castrated, rendered impotent. In yet another way Bassanio and Shylock ventured for similar rewards, and ran similar risks.

21. Nevill Coghill, "The Basis of Shakespearean Comedy," *Essays and Studies*, N.S. III (1950), quoted in Moody, p. 18.

III

The deflation of Shylock is the enabling event for the fifth act's generically typical articulation of harmony. The denseness of Shakespeare's resolution of the play's issues goes beyond the concerns of this essay, but
certain of his uses of traditional symbols for harmony infold and bring to
summation the problem of class invasion and the ideological hedges which
render it so difficult. The obtrusive references to art and the folk motif of
the ring are the two chief such tools.

Lorenzo and Jessica effect a counterpoint to the actions of Bassanio and
Portia which provides a context for the allusions to artful harmony. In
each case an outsider enters the privileged group by means of manipulated
appearance. Jessica's entry recasts Bassanio's in such a way as to reveal
much more openly the strategic nature of the venture and the rewards at
its end.

> She hath directed [says Lorenzo]
> How I shall take her from her father's house,
> What gold and jewels she is furnish'd with,
> What page's suit she hath in readiness.
>
> (II.iv.29–32)

Jessica has prepared to direct and act in her own drama, the fictional status
of which is appropriately offensive to her father on various grounds. His
mode of dealing with Christian assertions of status has been shown to be
that of demystification. He objects repeatedly to the public legitimation
of licensed display and disguise ("varnish'd faces") embodied in Lorenzo's
masque; the creative and interpretive mode which governs the wooing
plot is contemptible to him. He condemns this prominence of style as
merely superficial, as "shallow fopp'ry," under which hide the same selfish
motivations belied by the elite's abstract claims to law and honor. These
motivations are made quite clear during the actual "theft" of Jessica:
"Here catch this casket, it is worth the pains," she says; "I will make fast
the doors and gild myself / With some moe ducats, and be with you
straight"; "Now, by my hood, a gentle, and no Jew," Gratiano observes;
Lorenzo judges that "true she is, as she hath prov'd herself"
(II.vi.33,49–51,55). Jessica proves her truth by falsehood to her father,
and she is finally a more faithless Jew than he. She is true, however, to the
canons of truth of the class she has joined, both in her acquisition of her

financial inheritance and in her celebration with Lorenzo in Genoa, where they display their credentials by lavish spending and revelry, trading Leah's ring for a monkey. True love, exploitation, and the demonstration of identity here coalesce.

They continue this demonstration in Belmont, trading classical allusions and reflexively apostrophizing the music of the spheres, praising its reduction to order of the "wild and wanton herd." "The man that hath no music in himself," Lorenzo says, "nor is not moved with concord of sweet sounds, / Is fit for treasons, stratagems, and spoils" (V.i.83–85). Given the ideological connotations of art already established in earlier acts, Lorenzo's assimilation of himself and Jessica to the celestial harmony is suggestive. While his lines do assert Shylock's unmusical discontinuity with the romantic world of Belmont, as has often been noted, their underlying reference here is to the "treasons, stratagems, and spoils" of the elopement of Lorenzo and his bride. The familiar redemptive force of the harmonious consciousness is questioned here. The imagination is turned to competitive uses, the "concord of sweet sounds" is chiefly a stratagem, and the spoils accrue to those who artfully elevate private urges to the status of universal harmony. The comic decorum of Act V is achieved with many of the same tools of poetic assertion which make the endings of happier plays glow with warmth and love, but their earlier use for gain, and to maim Shylock, render their full credibility suspect in this play. The mythic glow of the final circle's inclusiveness is founded upon the suppressed factional benefit of its exclusions.

The ring motif with which the play ends makes this concrete. In the first place, it presents the resolution of the trial (in the destruction of Shylock) as a comic matter for the Christians, in the risible as well as beneficent sense. Portia had always found it so, laughing from the start in Act III about the fun she and Nerissa should have at their play-acting. During the trial there are repeated comic asides and ironies, and after Shylock is expelled Portia institutes the practical joke of taking the rings as payment. Auden has noted in his analysis of Iago, another Venetian, how the practical joke depends on the contemptuous objectification of its victim.[22] This principle underlies Iago's destruction of Othello, and Portia's defeat of Shylock in this play. Her game with the ring echoes the trial

22. "The Joker in the Pack," in *The Dyer's Hand* (1963; rpt. New York, 1968), pp. 246–272.

in a comic key, judging Bassanio's transgression to be insignificant and including the victim in the final mutuality. The risk of the loss of community emphasizes its value: the social fabric is intentionally torn and then reestablished by the revelation of the threat's ludic status. The strategy is similar to the use made of Shylock: the threat is made ludicrous (as Gratiano's graceless laughter shows), and the shared joke again confirms the group's identity.

The play closes on a final note of joking anxiety combining the major themes of sharing and exclusion: "Well, while I live, I'll fear no other thing / So sore, as keeping safe Nerissa's ring" (V.i.306–307). The comedy ends not with the departure for a wedding, since that has already taken place, but with an anticipation of future anxiety. The obsessive Elizabethan cuckoldry joke was founded on both fear of and delight in the burglar. Here its application to the play's themes of inclusion and exclusion, invitation and invasion, wooing and assault, allows Shakespeare to synthesize the erotic and class-oriented aspects of his purposes in one image. The fascination with cuckoldry seems to have arisen from the conjunction not primarily of sexes, but of classes: the typical cuckold is bourgeois, his burglar a socially elevated or pretentious rake. If in this play the lover enters through the front door, and gains rank and status as well as sex, he still partakes of the scheming trickster. He must still pick Portia's locks with the keys of courtesy, while Lorenzo, his masked alter ego, steals daughter, stones, and ducats alike. Both circumvent the safeguards of possessive old men. Gratiano, Bassanio's most figural alternate, is most given to blunt signals; his itch and his fear, on the way to the marriage bed, close the play with a carefully infolded emblem of these major themes of class interaction. For, as Kenneth Burke suggests, "the relations between classes are like the ways of courtship, rape, seduction, jilting, prostitution, promiscuity, with variants of sadistic torture or masochistic invitation to mistreatment."[23] If the audience delights in the cuckoldry joke, if the climber, the social second-story man, cannot think of enjoying his bride without crossing himself with the talismanic invocation of the housebound husband, *The Merchant of Venice* must simply be seen to end with, and arouse in its audience, the contradictions of the socially mobile culture it reflects.

23. Burke, p. 115.

IV

Lawrence Stone provides a convenient summary of the nature and function of the dominant ideological patterns of late-sixteenth-century England. They

present a picture of a fully integrated society in which stratification by title, power, wealth, talent, and culture are all in absolute harmony, and in which social mobility is consequently both undesirable and unthinkable. Reality, however, is always somewhat different.

This ideological pattern and . . . measures designed to freeze the social structure and emphasize the cleavages between one class and another were introduced or reinforced at a time when in fact families were moving up and down in the social and economic scale at a faster rate than at any time before the nineteenth and twentieth centuries. Indeed it was just this mobility which stimulated such intensive propaganda efforts.[24]

Carefully restricted social and sexual intercourse played major roles in this ideology of harmony, which presented itself as a natural model of reciprocal interaction while exploiting the less artful. Despite his investment in the discriminations of hierarchy, Castiglione provided "conventions of enrichment and fantasy"[25] both to those who would freeze the class structure and to those who would invade its upper reaches from below. At the same time Elizabethan jurists were energetically elaborating a legal system which came increasingly to be used as a major weapon in the war between those who sought and those who denied. The outcry against law-mongering from all sides reveals its universal employment. These pursuits of power through stylistic nuance and verbal complexity had by the century's end generated profound disorder among the supposedly mutual and well-beseeming ranks of the Elizabethan polity. Yet the pursuit of status and privilege was always coated with the necessary legitimating colors—for which the justification of another charming Shakespearean thief may stand: "Why, Hal, 'tis my vocation, Hal, 'tis no sin for a man to labour in his vocation."[26]

24. Stone, p. 36.
25. See note 1 above.
26. *The First Part of King Henry IV*, The Arden Shakespeare (London, 1960), I.ii.101–102.

Notes on Contributors

DON E. WAYNE teaches English literature and critical theory at the University of California, San Diego. He is the author of *Penshurst: The Semiotics of Place and The Poetics of History* (1984). In addition to his work on Jonson, he has published essays on the new historicism and on cultural history and theory.

RONALD L. MARTINEZ is associate professor of Italian at the University of Minnesota, Minneapolis. He has lectured and published on Dante, Boccaccio, and Machiavelli. He is the author, with Robert M. Durling, of *Of Time and the Crystal: Studies in Dante's "Rime Petrose"* (1990) and is currently working on a book on Virgil and Statius in Dante's *Purgatorio*.

JAMES SHAPIRO is assistant professor of English and comparative literature at Columbia University and assistant editor of *Shakespeare Studies*. He has recently completed a study of the literary relations of Marlowe, Shakespeare, and Jonson, and is currently working on a book called *1559: The Drama of Shakespeare's London*.

RUTH EL SAFFAR is research professor of Spanish literature at the University of Illinois-Chicago. She is the author of four books, and editor of a collection of essays, on Cervantes. She has published over sixty-five articles and reviews on various aspects of Spanish literature and is

511

especially interested in psychoanalysis and cultural history in their relation to literary works.

KATHARINE EISAMAN MAUS, associate professor of English at the University of Virginia, is the author of *Ben Jonson and the Roman Frame of Mind* (1985) and editor of *Soliciting Interpretation: Literary Theory and English Seventeenth-Century Poetry* (1990); she has published essays on Renaissance and Restoration literature in *ELH, English Literary Renaissance, Representations, Shakespeare Quarterly,* and *Renaissance Drama.*

GORDON KIPLING is professor of English literature at the University of California, Los Angeles. He has written *The Triumph of Honour: Burgundian Origins of the Elizabethan Renaissance* (1977) and has edited *The Receyt of the Ladie Kateryne* (1990). In addition to "Triumphal Drama," he has published a number of articles on medieval and Renaissance spectacles and is presently completing a book-length study of drama and ritual in the medieval royal entry.

TIMOTHY J. REISS is professor and chair of comparative literature at New York University. His most recent book is *The Uncertainty of Analysis* (1988). He is presently completing *The Meaning of Literature.* His essay in this collection is a version of a chapter in that volume.

GAIL KERN PASTER is professor of English at George Washington University. She is the author of several essays on Elizabethan-Jacobean drama and of *The Idea of the City in the Age of Shakespeare* (1985). Her current work in progress, provisionally entitled *The Body Embarrassed: Drama and the Disciplines of Shame,* concerns dramatic representation of bodily function in the context of changing canons of bodily propriety in early modern England.

MARY BETH ROSE is director of the Center for Renaissance Studies at the Newberry Library and adjunct associate professor of English at Northwestern University. She is the author of *The Expense of Spirit: Love and Sexuality in English Renaissance Drama* (1988) and the editor of *Women in the Middle Ages and the Renaissance: Literary and Historical Perspectives* (1986).

CATHERINE BELSEY is professor of English at the University of Wales College of Cardiff, where she chairs the graduate Centre for Critical and Cultural Theory. Her books include *Critical Practice* (1980), *The Subject of Tragedy: Identity and Difference in Renaissance Drama* (1985), and *John Milton: Language, Gender, Power* (1988).

G. K. HUNTER is the Emily Sanford Professor of English at Yale and chairman of the Program in Renaissance Studies. He has written on Elizabethan drama, modern drama, and Renaissance literature. For the last five years he has been working on volume 4 (Drama 1584–1642) of the *Oxford History of English Literature*.

ANGUS MACKAY is professor of medieval history at the University of Edinburgh. He is the author of *Spain in the Middle Ages: From Frontier to Empire* (1977); *Money, Prices and Politics in Fifteenth-Century Castile* (1981); and *Society, Economy and Religion in Late Medieval Castile* (1987).

GERALDINE MCKENDRICK is a lecturer in King's College, the University of London. She is the author of a study of Franciscan spirituality in late medieval and early modern Castile (forthcoming in the Cambridge History of Early Modern Europe Series).

JONATHAN DOLLIMORE teaches in the School of English and American Studies at the University of Sussex. He is the author of *Radical Tragedy: Religion, Ideology, and Power in the Drama of Shakespeare and His Contemporaries* (1984) and the coeditor with Alan Sinfield of *Political Shakespeare: New Essays in Cultural Materialism* (1985). He is currently completing a book called *Sexuality, Transgression and Sub-cultures*.

LOUIS ADRIAN MONTROSE is professor of English literature at the University of California, San Diego. He has published extensively on the sociopolitical dimensions of Elizabethan literature, drama, and culture, and on literary and cultural theory.

ANTHONY J. CASCARDI is associate professor of comparative literature and Spanish at the University of California, Berkeley. He is the author, most recently, of *The Bounds of Reason: Cervantes, Dostoevsky, Flaubert*, as well as of a study of Calderón entitled *The Limits of Illusion*. He is currently at work on a project that examines the origins of the modern age in the seventeenth century.

WALTER COHEN teaches comparative literature at Cornell University and has published *Drama of a Nation: Public Theater in Renaissance England and Spain* (1985).

MARTIN BUTLER is a lecturer at the School of English, University of Leeds. He is the author of *Theatre and Crisis 1632–1642* (1984) and of numerous essays on early Stuart drama, and he has edited *The Selected Plays of Ben Jonson*, volume 2 (1989).

FRANK WHIGHAM teaches English at the University of Texas at Austin. He has written various studies of early modern English literature and culture, including *Ambition and Privilege: The Social Tropes of Elizabethan Courtesy Theory* (1984). He is now completing a book on the tensions inherent in status and family structures in Renaissance drama from Kyd to Middleton.

15 34
   71